GELDENHUYS

GENEALOGY

12 Generations
Volume One

PRELLER MATT GELDENHUYS

Copyright © 2015 by Preller Geldenhuys

The rights of the author of the Work have been asserted by him,
Copyright in the text rests with the author Preller Geldenhuys

To Order: http://www.lulu.com/spotlight/Peysoftpublishing
Peysoft Publishing
International: http://www.Lulu.com/JustDone

Cover design by Shirene Dovey and Just Done Productions
Contact Prop Geldenhuys oupey@editek.co.nz or www.pey.co.za

Other books by the author:
- Rhodesian Air Force Operations with Air Strike Log *
- Nickel Cross – biography *
- Operation Miracle – A Tribute to three bold Airmen *
- Rhodesian War Casualties *
- Rhodesian Memorials *
- The Anglo-Boer War Diaries of Jan Geldenhuys *
- Rhodesia - Zimbabwe Roll of Honour
- Beulah - A place where Memories are Made

*Published by Just Done Productions

ISBN: 978-1-920315-71-9

Paeroa

2015

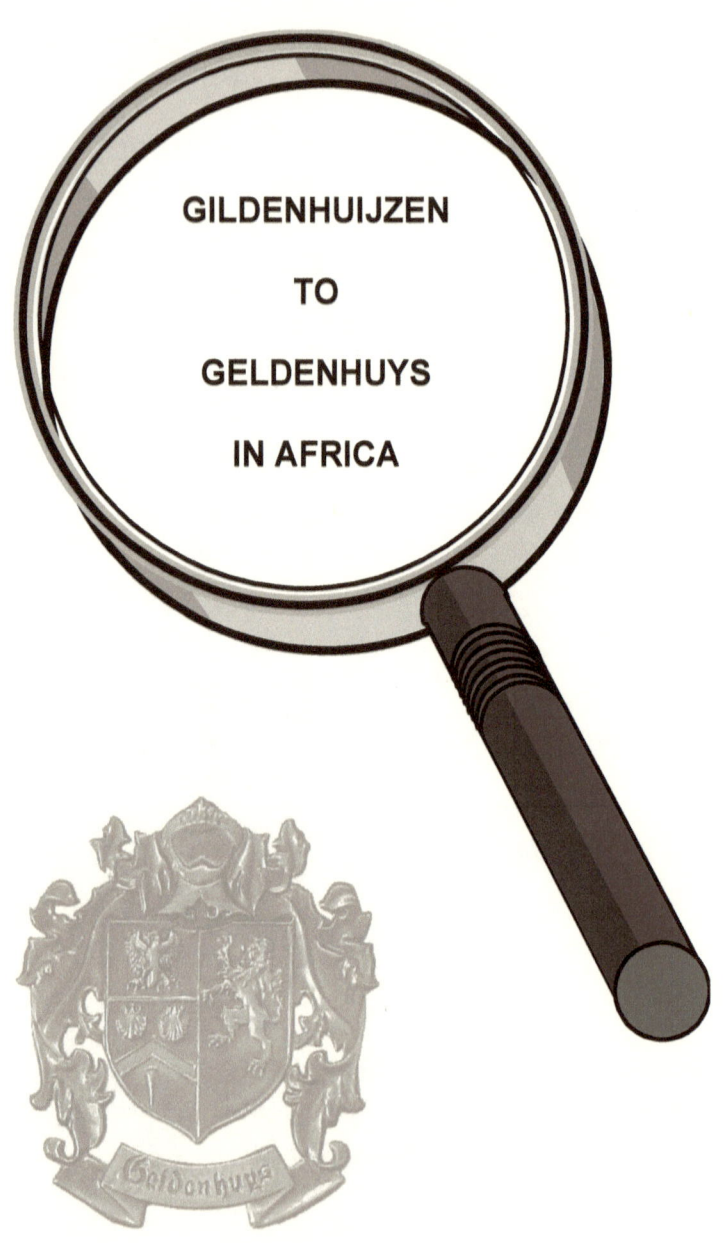

GILDENHUIJZEN TO GELDENHUYS IN AFRICA

By PRELLER M GELDENHUYS
Year 2014

For

Jake

DEDICATION

To Courtney and Brendan Jelley

Chanel and Craig Geldenhuys

Matthew Dylan

Lucy Hope

Mia Faith Geldenhuys

And to the Memory of Baby Jake Geldenhuys

This sixth edition, in two volumes, is intended to replace all the earlier editions of the Geldenhuys genealogy books previously published or printed. As oft stated, this story is not complete – it will never be complete, it is but a brand new beginning. Our heraldry has been traced for twelve generations, which is something really special. Future generations will take much pleasure in reading about the many colourful characters in our past and that is what this family genealogy is all about. Enjoy this journey of discovery – of our cousins, nephews and nieces, second cousins, Aunts and Uncles and even Grandparents who you will find that you never knew existed.

The MyHeritage website is highly recommended; and well worth getting familiar with all its interesting features such as:

- Family Tree
- Photographs
- Family Statistics
- Smart Matching

Find the MyHeritage website at:

http://www.myheritage.com/site-72814171/preller-geldenhuys

Ou Pey

First edition Christmas 1999
Second edition April 2007
Third edition December 2009
Fourth edition September 2011
Fifth edition – two volumes – December 2011
<u>Sixth edition – November 2012</u>
<u>Seventh edition - 2014</u>

GELDENHUYS GENEALOGY 1650 to 2010+

Contents

STAMREGISTER / FAMILY REGISTER	9
RELATIONSHIP WITH DISTANT RELATIVES	14
NAME CHANGES	15
SOUTH AFRICAN SURNAMES and THEIR MEANINGS	18
PERSONALITIES AND PLACES OF INTEREST	23
BLOOD RIVER and THE VOW	36
THE BOER-BASOTHO WARS	38
KROONSTAD & BOTHAVILLE HISTORY	39
FIRST ANGLO-BOER WAR	41
ANGLO-BOER WAR of 1899-1902	45
WORLD WAR II 1939-1945	63
RHODESIA – ZIMBABWE WAR 1967 –1980	68
MASONITE (AFRICA) LIMITED	73
THE KIWIS – NEW ZEALANDERS	78
MALAN REUNION	81
ADIO AFRICA – FAREWELL	92
DICTIONARY OF FAMILY BIOGRAPHY	100
VOLUME 2	**323**
GEDCOM INSERT	338
ABBREVIATED GENEALOGIES	396
GELDENHUYS, MALAN and PRELLER GENEALOGY	396
JELLEY	449
MALAN	452
PRELLER	461
RELATIONSHIP CHART	469
RELATIONSHIP WITH DISTANT RELATIVES	469
RELATIONSHIP TO PRELLER GELDENHUYS	469
GELDENHUYS INTERMARRIAGES	504

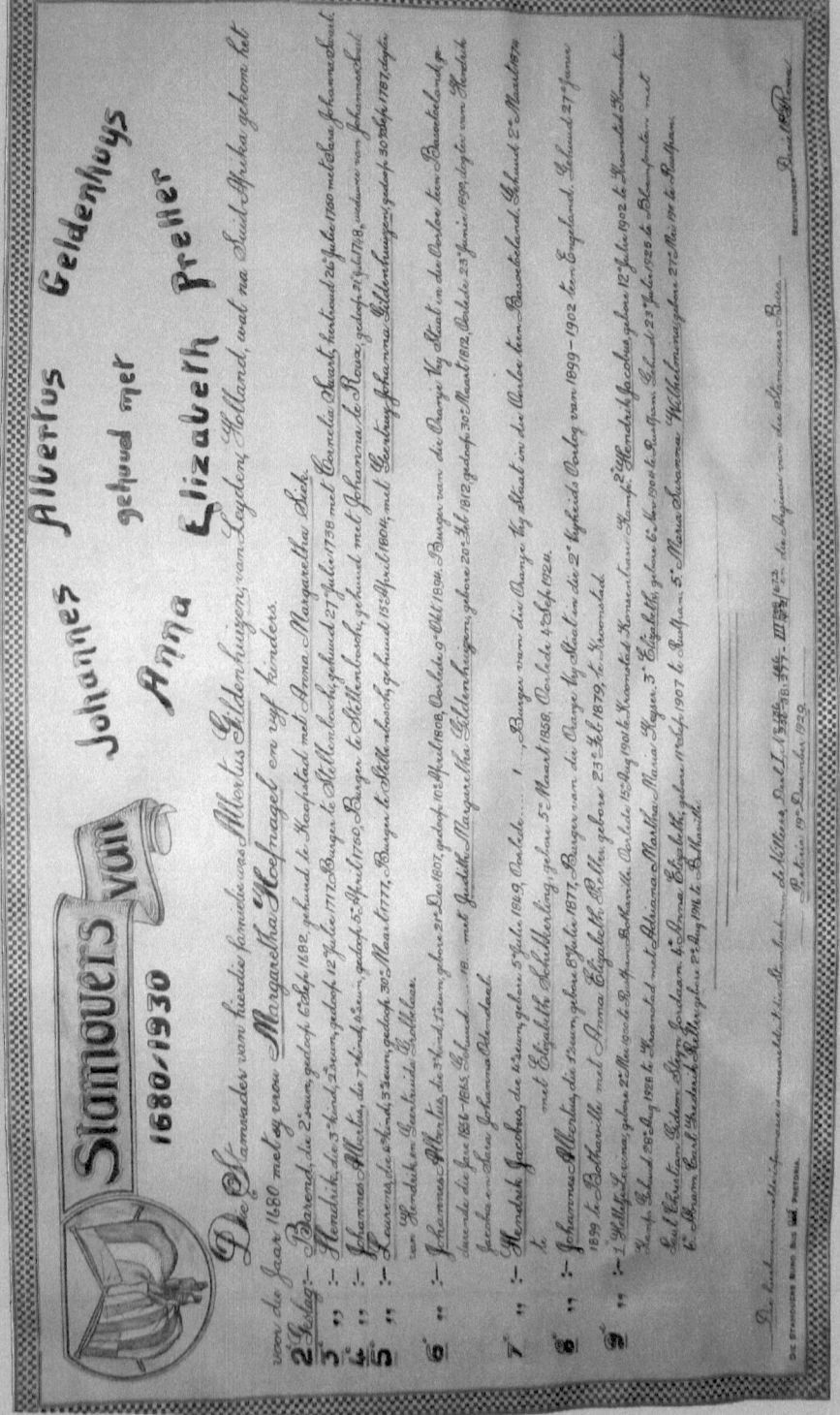

The preceding family heirloom reads as follows:

STAMOUERS van Johannes Albertus Geldenhuys
Gehuud met Anna Elizabeth Preller
1680 – 1930

Die Stamvader van hierdie familie was Albertus Gildenhuizen, van Leyden, Holland, wat na Suid Afrika gekom het voor die Jaar 1680 met sy vrou Margaretha Hoefnagels en vyf kinders.

2de Geslag:-	Barend, die 2de seun, gedoop 6de Sep 1682, gehuudte Kaapstad met Anna Margaretha Siek
3de Geslag: -	Hendrik, die 3de kind, 2de seun, gedoop 12de Julie 1717. Burger te Stellenbosch, gehuud 27ste Julie 1738 met Cornelia Swart, hertroud 26ste Julie met Sara Johanna Swart.
4de Geslag: -	Johannes Albertus, die 7de kind, 4de seun, gedoop 5de April 1750, Burger te Stellenbosch, gehuud met Johanna le Roux, gedoop 21ste Julie 1748, widow of Johannes Swart.
5de Geslag:-	Lourens, die 4de kind, 3de seun, baptised 30ste Maart 1777, Burger te Stellenbosch, gehuud 15de April 1804, with Geertruy Johanna Gildenhuizen, gedoop 30ste Sep 1787, dogter van Hendrik en Geertruida Grobbelaar
6de Geslag: -	Johannes Albertus, die 3de kind, 1st seun, gebore 21ste Dec 1807, gedoop 10de April 1808, Oorlede 9de Okt 1894. Burger van die Oranje Vry Staat in die Oorloe teen Basoetoeland, gedurende die Jare 1856 -1865. Gehuud ..18.. met Judith Margaretha Gildenhuizen, gebore 20th Feb 1812, gedoop 30ste Maart 1812, Oorlede 23ste Junie 1890, dogter van Hendrik Jacobus en Sara Johanna Odendaal.
7de Geslag: -	Hendrik Jacobus, die 4de seun, gebore 5de Julie 1849, Oorlede ..19.., Burger van die Oranje Vry Staat in die Oorloe teen Basoetoe Maart 1874 te. . met Elizabeth Schikkerling, gebore 5de Maart 1858, Oorlede 4de Sep 1924.
8ste Geslag:-	Johannes Albertus, die 1ste seun, gebore 8ste Julie 1877, Burger van die Oranje Vry Staatin die 2de Vryheids Oorlog van 1899 – 1902 teen Engeland. Gehuud 27th Junie 1899 te Bothaville met Anna Elizabeth Preller, gebore 23ste Feb 1879, te Kroonstad.
9de Geslag: -	Helletje Levina, gebore 2de Mei 1900 te Rustpan, Bothaville, Oorlede 15de Aug 1901 te Kroonstad Konsentrasie Kamp, 2de Hendrik Jacobus, gebore 12de Julie 1902 te Kroonstad Konsentrasie Kamp, Gehuud 28th August 1928 te Kroonstad met Adriana Martha Maria Keyser. 3rd Elizabeth gebore 6 Nov 1904 te Rustpan. Gehuud 23ste Julie 1925 te Bloemfontein met Paul Christiaan Gideon Steyn Jordaan. 4de Anna Elizabeth, gebore 11de Sep 1907 te Rustpan. 5th Maria Susanna Wilhelmina gebore 27ste Mei 1911 te Ruspan. 6de Abram Carl Frederik Preller gebore 2de Aug 1916 te Bothaville

Die - - - informasie versamel uit die Stamboek van de Villiers, Deel 1 No 136/286-98, 186/277. III 808/1402/672 in die Argriewe van die Stamouers Bura - - - Pretoria 19de Desember 1929 - - - - Bestuurder: Daniel P. Re?

STAMREGISTER / FAMILY REGISTER

STAMVADERS / ANCESTORS

Geldenhuys, Albert Barend Gildenhuizen arrived at the Cape in 1661 from Burgsteinfurt, Wesfale, Holland, as a sailor on board the ship 'Princesse Royale'. He became a "vryburger" on 23rd September 1661, the year before Cape founder Jan van Riebeeck returned to the Netherlands. He is the Stamvader to Pey Malan, Lucy Hope, Craig Jannie and Chanel (South Africans), Brendan Vaughan and Courtney Sacha Jelley (Zimbabweans), Tal, Nea, Deu and Gem Brink (New Zealanders), and Ian and Louise (Swazis). His descendant son, Barend Gildenhausen, was the first purchaser of Vergelegen – the Hottentots Holland wine farm established by Willem Adriaan van der Stel (now Somerset West).

Geldenhuys, Casper Heinrich Gildenhuysen or Gildehausen, from Osnabrück (Germany), born 1748, was the second Geldenhuys to arrive from overseas. He arrived circa 1771 and was a blacksmith in the Cape between 1791 and 1793. He married Johanna Dorothea Bam on the 21st July 1793. She was the widow of Johann Philipp Fuchs. Casper and Johanna had one child. No direct relationships have been established with Casper – his name is added purely for historical correctness.

Bouwer, Johann Ludwig (Bauer), arrived in 1724 from Kassel, Germany; and is the ancestor of New Zealanders Tal, Nea, Deu and Gem Brink.

Brink, Andries, from Waarden, Zeeland circa 1718. Tal will be pleased to discover that his ancestors possibly hailed from his country of birth – and will no doubt one-day still remain very proud of his South African connections.

de Waal, Jan, arrived in 1715 from Amsterdam, Netherlands. Interestingly, Jan was a seventh generation descendant of a landowner Rozenburg, near Haarlem, in 1473. The German de Waal can be traced back to 1410 at Emmerich. The 'OerStamvader' apparently came from Wale in Belgium. Craig Jannie and Chanel Geldenhuys are challenged to trace their ancestors back for 600 years!

Dippenaar, Johan Marthinus Depner (or Dipner) arrived in 1735 from Wehlau, East Prussia. He became a burger in 1746. He owned and died on the farm "Groene Valley", along the Olifantsrivier, in 1790. He is the Stamvader of Craig and Chanel Geldenhuys.

Jelley, William Jelly was a mariner in Creetown in 1798 (a 'rondloper'?). A Thomas Jelle held a tenement in Ayr, Scotland 1518. The earliest 'form' of Jelley was a Thomas Jely in 1472. The earliest South African Jelley was Godfrey, circa 1875, grandfather to William Paterson Jelley, and great-great-grandfather to Courtney and Brendan Jelley.

Lotter, Matthias, arrived in 1734 from Augsburg Germany. Matthia Martha Lotter, who married Abram Carl Frederik Preller Geldenhuys, is the great-grandmother to Craig Jannie, Chanel and Lucy Hope Geldenhuys and Courtney and Brendan Jelley.

Malan, Jacques, arrived in 1688, through Netherlands, from Merindol, near Avignon, Provence, France. Jacques established the farm La Motte, Franschoek. Rina – Susanna Catharina is a ninth generation Malan, which makes Courtney Sacha and Brendan Vaughan Jelley and Lucy Hope eleventh generation descendants. Pey Malan can also be proud of his second name relationship to his ancestors through his mother, Rina.

Preller, Johann Friedrich arrived in 1786 as a soldier, from Halle a.d. Saale, Germany. He became a hunter and cattle buyer for a butcher. Preller Matt and Paul Preller Geldenhuys inherited this Stamvader's name as a Christian name. In 1813 he was a burger of Graaff-Reinet. Courtney, Brendan, Chanel and Craig Jannie are seventh generation descendants.

STAM-MOEDERS / ANCESTOR MOTHERS

Hoefnagels, Margaretha, married Albert Barend Gildenhuizen in Legden and accompanied the Stamvader when he returned to the Cape in 1672. She gave birth to Barend on 6th September 1682 as Stam-Moeder of the Geldenhuys's.

de Beer, Zacharia Christina, born 9th November 1777, married stamvader Johan Frederik or Johann Friedrich Preller (from Halle on the Saale, Germany, who arrived in 1786) on 23rd November 1794. She had seven children and died on 6th March 1845. Both she and her mother-in-law, Johanna Dorothea Philemann can be considered as the Preller "stammoeder".

Geldenhuys, Annette, married Curly Kluyts. They had three children, Theo, Annalise and Seun, 14th July 1960. Annette became the stammoeder of Kluyts.

Geldenhuys, daughter of D.H.J. Geldenhuys, married John Watson Jonson (born 31st December 1910, Wikowmore) on 4th March 1939. She became the stammoeder of Jonson, and had two sons and a daughter.

Gildenhuysen, Johanna Margaretha, married Johann Jürgen Hamman on 12th January 1738. Johann Hamman arrived from Dresden, Germany, and she became the stammoeder of Hamman.

Gildenhuizen, Elsje, born May 1674, married Jacobus van der Heiden of Haarlem, Netherlands in 1691 and became the van der Heiden stammoeder with the birth of their first son Jacobus. Please note: - Barend, and Jacobus, were brothers-in-law ... who both bought "quarter allotments" of the farm "Vergelegen" in present day Somerset West.

Gildenhuizen, Margaretha, married Heinrich du Plooy, who arrived in 1701 from Soest, Westfale, Germany, on 5th July 1704. Margaretha became the du Plooy stammoeder with the birth of their first son Hendrik Willem on 13th October 1707. Margaretha also re-married, on 10th June 1725, to Philipus Richter. She was thus the stammoeder of Richter as well.

le Long, Elizabeth (Isabeau), arrived from France, married Jean Jourdan and then re-married to Jacques Malan. Became the stammoeder of the Jordaans and Malans. Jacques bought the fourth quarter of the Willem Adriaan van der Stel farm "*Vergelegen*" in the present day Somerset West.

Philemann, Johanna Dorothea (wife of Johann Friedrich Preller) was the mother of Johan Frederik who arrived at the Cape in 1786. She together with her daughter-in-law, Zacharia Christina de Beer, is considered the stammoeder of the Prellers.

Siek, Anna Margaretha, born 13th March 1695, daughter of Johann and Geertruyd Helm from Bremen, married Barend Gildenhuysen on 31st August 1710. They had 7 children and as such were the Stam-Moeder of our branch of the Geldenhuys family tree. In 1722 she also married German seaman Michael Otto and had 7 children with him.

Geldenhuys

Geldenhuys

PRELLER   GELDENHUYS

RELATIONSHIP WITH DISTANT RELATIVES

The family tree below may assist to clarify relationships with distant relatives - especially where "removed" cousins occur. Note the diagonal relationship for easier understanding.

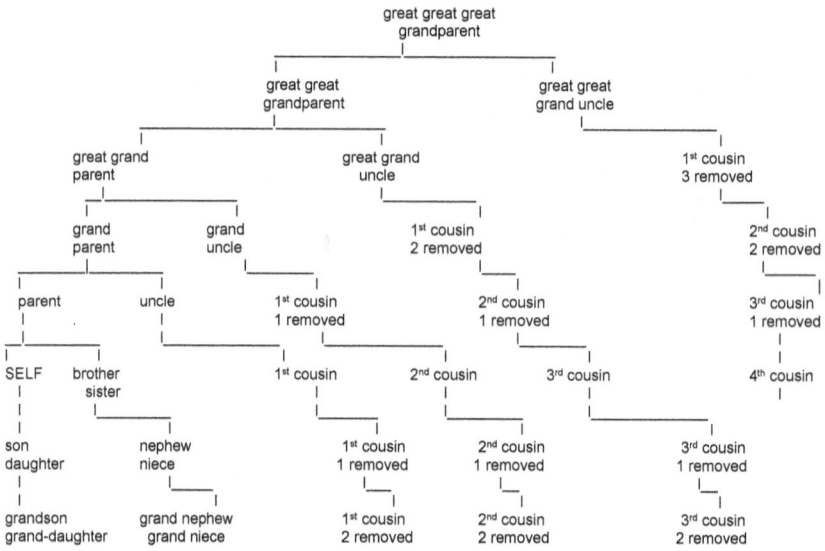

Tracing family, or working out your relationship with distant relatives can be difficult. The above chart will simplify the relationship for you.

THE GELDENHUYS INTERNATIONAL REGISTRY

Country	Total Estimated Households	Total Households in Registry	Total Estimated Population	No of Provinces	Most Populous Province
South Africa	4,928	3,520	13,798	4	Cape
Britain	1	1	3	1	Herts
Canada	1	1	2	1	Ontario
France	1	1	3	1	Dordogne
U.S.A.	6	4	13	2	Florida
TOTAL	4,937	3,527	13,819	9	

The Geldenhuys International Registry provides genealogical research of which the 3,527 Geldenhuys families related to the Geldenhuys' that settled in the Free State areas of Kroonstad and Bothaville at the turn of the previous century. The Registry prompted visits to various libraries in order to document the summaries that follow. It is perhaps of little factual significance when inaccuracy or discrepancies in dates or events were found – even in more learned literature the authors claimed their versions corrected previous inaccuracies. The same was found – suffice to say that the time and effort spent to resolve the issues were not warranted. The fact of the matter is that a story needs to be told and this is what this 'record' is all about.

NAME CHANGES

Sooner or later, the question will be posed "How does Gildenhuizen or Gildenhuyzs, or for that matter how Geldenhuis or Gildenhuys become Geldenhuys?" The answer is quite simple, really – especially when reference is made to the research conducted by Professor du T. Malherbe. He found that even the "experts" tended to spell names differently - depending from which their so-called original reference was taken. He also found that Dippenaar was in fact previously called Depner and Dipner! The bottom line is that it really does not matter - feel free to "adopt" whichever name you wish!

Malherbe's findings include the following name changes: -
Andreas – became Andries; Berndt – Barend; Becker – Bekker; Both or Bode – Botha; Bourchier – Bowker: Brodtruck – Brodryk; Burcherdt – Burger; Bruckheiser – Broekhuysen; Bruére – Bruwer; Cellier – Cillie or Cilliers; Coetse – Coetzee; Crosnier – Cronjé; Kluthe Kloete – Cloete; Kraukhamer – Croukamp; De la Port(e) – Delport; Depner – Dippenaar; Eckstein – Eksteen; Esterhuyse – Esterhuysen; Flock – Vlok; Geldenhuis, Gildenhuys, Gildehausen, Gildenhuyzen, Geldenhuyzs – Geldenhuys; Gauche – Gous; Germershausen – Germishuysen; Grunwald – Groenewald; Jehle, Jelle, Jellie, Jelly, Jely – Jelley; John White – Jan de Wit; Johann – Jan; Jourdan – Jordaan; Köth – Keet; Kretschmar – Krytsman; Le Roex - le Roux; Matzdorf – Maasdorp; Matthias – Mattys; Mesnard – Minnaar; Niel – Nel; Peter – Pieter; Pierre – Petrus; Pinard – Pienaar; Potter – Putter; Hoppringill – Pringle(1270); Rasch – Ras; Retif – Retief; Rieckeherr - Rykheer; Villion – Viljoen; Von Eschwede – Van Aswegen; Von Eitzen – Van Eyssen; Wilhelm – Willem; Wohlegemuth - Welgemoed

Malherbe found that name changes occurred over time; was influenced by the various nationalities that settled in South Africa, interbreeding between races, the birth of Afrikanerdom, registration of heraldic crests and various other factors such as places of origin e.g. Juli van die Kaap – see or look up Matthys Johannes Gildenhuyzs, born 22nd April 1822 as recorded in the writers Dictionary of Biographies later on!

I was very fascinated when studying the *Stellenbosse* and *Drakenstein Doopregister* (Baptism Registers). For example, our stamvader's eldest son Arend and his wife Judith names are entered in the registers thus:-

arent gijldenhus / ijudick smijdt — with baptising Margrijet 11th April 1700
Arent Gildenhuis / Judith Smit - with baptising Margareta 10th December 1702
Arent Gildenhuyse / Judith Smit – as witnesses on 13th May 1703
Arend Gildenhuys / Judith Smith – baptising Henrikus 16th August 1705
Arent Gildenhuys / Judith Smit - baptising Elsje 15th July 1708
Arent Gildenhuys / Judith Smit - baptising Albert Barentse – 22 September 1709

And, just as fascinating, is the spelling of Arent's (or is it Arend with a 'd') brother-in-law Jacobus van der Heyden's (who the writer also changed it to 'Heiden') name:-

Jacobis van der Heijde, with Elsie gildehuijsen – 1697 with the baptism of their son Albert
Jacobis van der Heijde, with Elsie Gildenhuijse - 1697 as witnesses.
ijacop van der heijde, with machtelt van dieden - July 1699 (as witness for Pijetter van der bijl)
ijacop van der heijde en sijn vrou - April 1700 (as witness for Arend)
Jacobus Vander Heiden, with Geertruyt Elbers - December 1701
Jacobus Vander Heiden, with Margareta Gildenhuijsen – December 1702
Jacobus Vander Heiden, with Abigail Vroom - August 1705

Please note – Arend, Elsie (or Elsje) and Margaretha were brothers and sisters, and all three have their Geldenhuys surnames spelt differently. So which is the correct spelling? Is it Arend or Arent, or is it Smit, Smith or Smijdt, or is it Ijacop, Jocobis or Jacobus, and finally, is it Gildenhuisen, Gildenhuijse, Gijldenhus? It does not matter!

Another interesting discovery is the number of different ladies who accompanied Jacobus for the various birth registrations. Dare I venture and say he was maybe a *rondloper*? I also found that his "accomplices" in the downfall of the Cape Governor (look up Vergelegen wine farm) also appears in the Doopregister. It makes for interesting reading, because it confirms that they not only knew each other intimately and also attended the same churches, but also schemed together. I refer particularly to Messrs Adam Tas and the other ringleaders Henning Husing, Jacobus van der Heiden, Pieter van der Bijl, Ferdinandus Appel (and Jan Meerland – who died at sea). Take particular note of the name spellings as it appears in the Stellenbosse Doopregister:-

Datum	Naam	Ouers	Getuies
14 April, 1695	Joghem	Matijs greef Zusanna Klaas	Henningh Huijsing Fintie Cloeten
(Geen datum), 1697	Albert	Jacobis van der Heijde Elsie gildehuijsen	Pietter van der Byl Sofia boss
12 July, 1699	Soffija	Pijetter van der bijl soffia bos	ijacop van der heijde machtelt van dieden
25 December 1701	Adrianus	Ferdinandus appelFijtie Kloeten	Jacobus Vander Heiden Geertruyt Elbers
11 May, 1704	Joan	Adam Tas Elisabeth van Brakel	Henning Husing Helena Gulih
25 March, 1708	Helena	Francois Vander Stel Johanna Wessels	d'Oud Heer Simon Vander Stel Katryna Vander Stel
7 December, 1710	Abigael	Ferdinandus appel Fijtie Kloeten	Adam Tas Abigail Vroom

Note: apparent lower case anomalies are intentional – as actually recorded

It would appear that the spelling of Geldenhuys, where the 'e' replaced the 'i' (as in G*e*ld) started to become popular from 1850 onwards.

Also, I wonder whether 'Jelley' did not originate from "Jehle"? Probably not. Name changes for Jelley is parallel to the colloquial *jest* for *just* and *jedge* for *judge* which is found in the variation between *Justice* and *Jestice*. The earliest forms are Thomas Jely 1472 and mariner William Jelly of 1798. See also the Dictionary of Biographies that follows later on. What is important, however, is to realise that the name you have is <u>your</u> personal possession and identification, and it tells the world who you are. One's surname is indeed a matter of pride. The intriguing story of surnames dates back thousands of years. How and where they began, what they originally meant and their <u>various</u> spellings, is called the study of onomastics.

Perhaps of interest is the fact that the Chinese were the first known people to acquire surnames about 2853 BC. They customarily have three names, with the surname placed first. The early Romans had only one name, but later changed to using three names. The modern hereditary use of surnames originated among the Venetian aristocracy in Italy about the 10th or 11th centuries. By 1370s the word "surnames" was found in documents.

Most surnames evolved from four general sources; Occupation; Location; Patronymic (father's name), and Characteristic. It is not uncommon to find names spelt differently hundreds of years ago. Language changes, carelessness and a high degree of illiteracy (sometimes the man himself did not know how to spell his own name) compounded the number of ways a name might be spelled. Often the Town Clerk spelled the name the way it sounded to him.

The Dutch tended to use hereditary names. The English used a variety of sources – biblical in origin, saints and martyrs of the early Christian Church, Nordic origin or Anglo-Saxon survivals or revivals. Most German surnames are derived from occupations, colours or locations. The French system of names closely resembles that of the English.

My message thus is: your surname identifies the family, it provides a link with the family's past, and we need to preserve its identity in the future. Preservation is essential to perpetuate family pride.

SOUTH AFRICAN SURNAMES and THEIR MEANINGS

GELDENHUIS	-	Place name in Holland.
PRELLER	-	From Old German Bruhl, a marshy meadow. Similar origin to English word "Imbroglio". Also derived from Preller (Bruller), one who shouts or roars. i.e. a Town Crier.
MALAN	-	"Sick Person" or "Heretic" in Old French. Used originally as a term of abuse because of the family's traditional disobedience to the Catholic Church, it became a title of honour in Huguenot times.
BOUWER	-	"Peasant" in Old Dutch. Compare "Boer"
BRINK	-	(1) "Village Green in Dutch (2) Also ground surrounding homestead (3) "Small Grassy Hill" Old Dutch name.
COURTNEY	-	"Short Nose" in Old French.
CRAIG	-	"Rock" in Scots (Cragg in England)
DE WAAL	-	French-speaking person from Belgium (Walloon)
DIPPENAAR	-	"Tub-Maker" In Old Dutch. (Compare Cooper in English)
LE ROUX	-	"The Red One" in French. Applied to hair and complexion.
LOTTER	-	Corruption of Old German name Lothar.
MOODIE	-	"Bold, Impetuous" in Old English.
RADYN	-	Place name in Russia (Radin)
SCHIKKERLING	-	"One who arranges things" From Old Dutch Schikker.
SWART	-	"Black" in Dutch. Not to be confused with Zwaard (q.v.).

Reference: South African Names by ERIC ROSENTHAL, 1965 Howard Timmins, Cape Town

COMMON GELDENHUYS CHRISTIAN/NICKNAMES

MALE:
Pey; Preller–Prop; Pey
Abram–Braam
Abram Carl Frederik Preller
Adrian Izak
Albert Barends
Albertus
Barend
Carl
Craig Jannie
Fredrick or Frederick
Gelly
Hendrik–Henry
Hendrik Jacobus
Jacobus–Jaco
Jake
Jan - Jannie
Johannes–Jantjie; Jannie
Johannes Albertus
Johannes Albertus Bernardus
Lourens
Lourens Pieter Arnoldus
Machiel
Oompie; Oubaas
Oudad
Paul Preller
Pey Malan
Pieter

FEMALE:
Anna
Chanel
Cornelia Margaretha
Margaretha
Dawn–Dawnie
Delene Elizabeth
Elizabeth
Elizabeth Maria

Elsie
Ernastina Helena (Este)
Geertry Anna Johanna
Helletjie-Hettie
Johanna
Johanna Cornelia; or Elizabeth
Johanna Susanna Maria
Joey
Judith Cornelia Margaretha
Levina
Lucy

Lulu
Margaretha
Maria; Mariana
Renene Delene
Sannie
Sara Johanna
Sara Johanna Elizabeth Elsabe
Susanna Maria
Susanna
Wilhelmina
Zacharya Geertruy

GELDENHUYS – PLACES OF BIRTH

Amanzimtoti, Natal
Bothaville (Rustpan), OFS
Cape Town, Cape
Durban, Natal
Gwelo, Rhodesia
Johannesburg, Transvaal

Kroonstad, OFS
Malgasrivier
Oudshoorn, Cape
Stellenbosch, Cape
Swellendam, Cape

FAMILY FARMS

BELMONT, Kroonstad	Adriaan Izaac Geldenhuys – 1870 - 1872
	BESTERKRAAL, Bothaville Carel Friedrich (Charley – brother to Oumam) Preller – 1881-1918
BLESBOKFONTEIN, Cape	Hendrik Albertus Geldenhuys 1897
BOTHARNIA – Bothaville	Theunis Louis Botha 1893
BRAAMFONTEIN, Jhb	Frans and Lou, two sons of Lourens Geldenhuys of Elandsfontein
DANSFONTEIN, Kroonstad	Barend Petrus (Ben) and Anna (father of Gen Geldenhuys) 1935
DE BANK, Bothaville:	Oupa Abram Preller 1890
DEELKRAAL, Tvl	Petrus Johannes Geldenhuys 1866
DOORNBULT, Kroonstad	JA and Judith M Geldenhuys 1894
DOORNDRAAI, Kroonstad	Theunis Louis Botha - 1885
DOORNKOP-WES, Kroonstad	Hendrik Philippus Malan 1870-1872
DOORNSPRUIT, Kroonstad	Adriaan Izak Geldenhuys – 1875
DOORNSPRUIT, Kroonstad	Hendrik Jacobus Geldenhuys - 1875
ELANDSFONTEIN, Barberton	Lourens Geldenhuys 1853+
GLADDEDRIFT – Bothaville	Theunis Louis Botha – 1873 - 1885
HOLFONTEIN, Kroonstad	Barend Petrus Geldenhuys 1868 (see also Dansfontein)
KATBOS VIEW, Bothaville	Oudad Jan & Oumam Lizzie Geldenhuys 1899
KLIPDRIFT, Pretoria	Robert C.L. Preller 1846-1916 (father of Gustav)
KLIPRIVIER (now Jacksondrif)	Lourens Geldenhuys 1853
KROMKUIL, Willowmore	Abraham Jacobus 1848
KROMSPRUIT, Ventersburg	Hendrik Jacobus (Hennie) Geldenhuys - 1997
KWAGGASDRIFT, Bothaville	Abraham Christoffel Naudé Preller – 1895-1963
LANGDEEL, Kroonstad	Theunis Louis - 1874
LEKKERLEWE	Oom Henry & Max Geldenhuys
MALGASRIVIER, Cape Town	Lourens Geldenhuys 1777
MODDERRIVIER, OFS	Hendrik Jacobus Geldenhuys 1858
NORMANDY, Bothaville:	Oom Henry & Jacomina Geldenhuys 1956 – 1967
PALMIETFONTEIN	Abram Preller (* 1960) & Christine Visagie
RIETGAT, Kroonstad	Hendrik Jacobus Geldenhuys, died there 4 September 1924
RUSTFONTEIN, Swellendam	Petrus Arnoldus Geldenhuys 1846
RUSTPAN, Bothaville	Johannes Albertus Geldenhuys 1903 - 1944
RUSTVERSTOORING, K-stad	Hendrik Jacobus Geldenhuys - 1879

ROODEPOORT, Winburg	Hendrik Jacobus Geldenhuys 1857
SIDESTEP, Bothaville	Ernastina (Este) Helena Geldenhuys (1966) x Riaan Steyn
SNEEUBERG, Graaff-Reinet	Johannes Hendrik Geldenhuys 1852
STANFORD, Caledon/Bredasdorp.	Petrus Arnoldus Geldenhuys 1887
STANMORE, Fort Victoria:	Oudad ACFP Geldenhuys 1958
VERGELEGEN, Somerset-Wes	Barend Geldenhuys 1712 of Hottentots-Holland
VOGELVALLEI, Caledon	Petrus Arnoldus Geldenhuys 1815-1846
VRUGBAAR, Bothaville	Mariana Geldenhuys (1968) x Johan Rautenbach.
WELGELEGEN, Bothaville	Neef Johannes Albertus (1937-1985) & seun Hendrik Jacobus (1964-1997)
WILGESPRUIT	Lourens Geldenhuys 1853+
WONDERHEUVEL, Kroonstad	Carel F Preller 1870
ZOUTEKLOOF, Cape	Albert Barend Geldenhuys 1748-1784

Note: NORMANDY was previously also called DRIEKOPPIES and BESTERSKRAAL. GLADDEDRIFT, RUSTPAN, BRAAMFONTEIN and VERGELEGEN (see page 15) are of particular interest – the latter two are of historic significance.

MALAN PLASE

La MOTTE, Franschhoek - Cape	Jacques Malan 1688 – 1719
RHONE, Groot Drakenstein	Jacques Malan 1702
WELGELEGEN, Cape	Jacques Malan 1709
MORGENSTER, Somerset-West	Jacques Malan 1709 – 1726, then his son Daniel to 1770
MORGENSTER, Somerset-West	Jacobus Malan 1770-1778
LAND-EN-ZEESICHT, Somerset-West	Jacques Malan 1709
PALMIET VALLEIJ, Drakenstein	Jacobus Johannes Malan (c3), 1796 - 1806
NAVARRE (Nooitgedacht), Cape	Daniel Josias Malan 1796, then his son Johannes Jacobus And grandson Hermanus Johannes 1858
LIBERTAS, Stellenbosch	Jacobus Hermanus Malan 1760 – 1768
STRYDFONTEIN, Kroonstad	David Daniel Malan 1816
HAPPY VALE (Verdruk-my-Niet), Cape	Daniel Wouter Malan 1824
DE HOOP OP CONSTANTIA, Cape	Daniel Gerhardus Malan 1856 +
DAL JOSAFAT and	
DOORNKOP-WES, Kroonstad	Hendrik Philippus Malan 1870 - 1872
LEEUWENVALLEI, Wellington	Daniel Malan (c4)1763 – 1828
BUFFELSHOEK, and	} David Malan 1771 - 1824
ZWAGERSHOEK, Somerset-East	} - ditto -
LEEUWENJACHT, Paarl	DG Malan (c5)1848-1926.
KUIPERSKRAAL, Durbanville	Stephanus Malan (c7)1794 – 1836
KNORHOEK, Hottentots-Holland	Jacob Malan (c9) 1784 – 1843 (later lived in Cape Town)
VERREKIJKER, Tulbagh	David Malan (d2) 1791 -1851, then his son Daniel Stephanus Malan (e5) 1827 – 1869 and grand-son David Jacobus (f2) 1854 – 1885, and his son Francois Daniel (f9) till 1915
EIKEBOOM, Wellington	Daniel Johannes Malan (d6) 1794 – 1828
GROENFONTEIN, Bovlei, Wellington	Jacobus Francois Malan (d9) 1802 – 1863
TWEELINGSPRUIT, Lichtenburg	Hendrik Francois Malan (h1) 1903 – 1959
DOORNHOEK, Lichtenburg	Frederik Jakobus Malan (h2) 1933 – 1943
WATERKLOOF, Rustenburg	Daniel Stephanus (h3) 1931 - 1982
RIETGAT, Lichtenburg	Birthplace of Francois Daniel Malan, 1st October 1907
RUSTHOF, 1941,	farmed by Francois Daniel Malan
BEGA, 1951,	farmed by Francois Daniel Malan
CHINDITU, Gutu 1954,	farmed by Francois Daniel Malan
BLACKWOOD, Beatrice	farmed by Francois Daniel Malan
KOMBISA, Chatsworth.	farmed by Francois Daniel Malan
TRICKLING WATERS, Fort Victoria/Masvingo, Rhodesia-Zimbabwe,	

BLACKSTONE, Beatrice 1972, KNUTSFORD for Louis Ferreira, Chipinga

farmed by Francois Daniel Malan Francois Daniel Malan.

OTHER FARMS

ANKER	Johannes Jurgens 'Hansie' Bezuidenhout
LOURENSFORD	Jacobus van der Heiden
ERINVALE	Jacobus van der Heiden
GROENE VALLEY, along the Olifantsrivier	Johannes Marthinus Dippenaar 1790.
GROOTVADERS BOSCH and	Benjamin Moodie 1817
MELKHOUTBOOM, Swellendam	Benjamin Moodie 1817
DOORN KOP, Klip River district	Donald Moodie 1857
WATERFALL MOODIES REST, Chipinga	Groot Tom(as) Moodie 1893
KENILWORTH,	Dunbar Moodie 1893
SKOORSTEENBERG, Smithfield district:	Jan de Waal 1884

PLACE NAMES

Botharnia = Bothaville. *Botha* as in Theunis *Botha*, *r* as in Ha*r*tley, *n* as in *N*aude, second name of Abram Preller and *nia* as in Le*vina*, the second name of Abram Preller's wife. Botharnia was a subdivision of the 8000 morgen farm Gladdedrift – subdivided on 7th April 1891 – two years before the founding of the town Bothaville on 1st June 1893.

Braamfontein. Farm bought on 9th December 1886 by Lourens Geldenhuys and his eldest brother Frans Eduard.

Emmarentia. Johannesburg suburb, named after Rand pioneer Lourens Geldenhuys' wife.

Frans Geldenhuys Park. The park is situated on the south-east corner of West Park Cemetery, and south of Emmarentia Dam (between Preller Street and Louw Geldenhuys View).

Geldenhuys Bowling Club. Situated in Malvern East – in Geldenhuys Road, north-west of the Geldenhuys railway siding in Germiston.

Geldenhuys Deep Mine, developed (it is believed), by Dirk Cornelis Geldenhuys - Rand pioneer.
In 1895 the deepest shaft intersection of the reef was the Main Incline of the Geldenhuys Deep mine which had been extended to 473 feet beyond the No 1 Vertical Shaft, some 2 200 feet from the outcrop measured on the dip. The "deep level" mines were only deep in the sense that they were not on the outcrop of the reef. None of them, at that stage, held ground under which the reef laid more than 1 000 feet below the surface and so they were followed by later mines which were deep level in the accepted sense of the term and have followed the reef down to depths of 11,000 feet below the surface in 1970.

Just before the fall of Johannesburg and the end of the Second Anglo-Boer War, news had been received of an imminent British attack on the Geldenhuys Deep mine, on Braamfontein (the farm had been purchased by Dirk Cornelis Geldenhuys). Commandant General Louis Botha had instructed Dr. F.E.T. Krause, the State prosecutor as the Special Commandant, on 29th May, 1902, to abandon the defence of Johannesburg and to save the gold mines at all costs. (Hot heads, like Judge Kock whose father, a Boer General, had been killed at Elandslaagte, tried to defy Louis Botha's order to save the mines – intent to destroy and deny the British the gold wealth). Judge Krause handed over Johannesburg intact to Lord Roberts and Lord Kitchener on 31st May 1902.

Geldenhuys House and Old Oak Tree – Historical place, in Emmarentia, west of Park View golf course.

Geldenhuys Inter-change – the big N3 freeway inter-change situated to the south-east of Johannesburg. Named after the Rand Pioneer Lourens Geldenhuys on whose property the national road was built.

Geldenhuys Station. Railway station in Germiston to honour Lourens, born in Heidelberg in 1864, the Rand pioneer and politician who with his three sons contributed to the development of gold mining and the establishment of Johannesburg in the early 1890's. The Siding is situated between Cleveland and Driehoek sidings – and was established to service Elandsfontein and Simmer & Jack Gold Mines. See also Dirk Cornelis, Lourens and the Geldenhuys Deep mine.

Geldenhuys Road – Bonaero Park. East of Jan Smuts Airport. Near the apex of the Great North Road and Atlas roads. It runs opposite the Blaaupan and Pamula Park Nature Reserve, and serves the Kempton Park Conference Centre. It is the second longest of all the Geldenhuys streets in Johannesburg.

Geldenhuys Straat - Strubensvallei. Situated north-west of Johannesburg Central, between Kloofendal Nature Reserve and Randpark Ridge (halfway between Roodeport and Randburg – west of the N1 Western bypass). Interestingly, it is close to D.F. Malan and Christiaan de Wet roads.

Geldenhuys Street – Putfontein. This is a main road and is the longest of all the Geldenhuys roads.

Geldenhuis Road – Elandsfontein. With a "uis". Leads off the Main Reef Road to Geldenhuis railway Siding - - north-west of the Geldenhuys Interchange on the N3 / Eastern by-pass.

Geldenhuis Road – Malvern East. Leads to the Geldenhuis Deep Bowling Club, and become the Jules to the west, and the Cydonia road to the east. This Geldenhuis road is just west of the N3 Eastern by-pass road, and just north of the Geldenhuis Railway siding in Germiston.

Geldenhuis Street – Protea North – situated south–west of Johannesburg Central. It is one of the shortest streets, west of Soweto, between Oosthuizen and Pelotonia roads (north of the N12, which runs to Potchefstroom).

Geldenhuis Street – Kroonstad. Named after Jan J. Geldenhuis, Station Master (retired in May 1947 as head of Goods and Passenger Services) and successful businessman. Father of Johan and Francois.

Gustav Preller Laer Skool – Selwyn, north of Florida Lake and halfway between Krugersdorp and Johannesburg Central.

Louw Geldenhuys Street – Emmarentia – runs along the Emmarentia Dam, and leads into 3rd Avenue Linden and to the Louw Geldenhuys Laer Skool

Louw Geldenhuys Primary School. Afrikaans medium school in Linden, Johannesburg, named after Lourens Geldenhuys 1864-1929

Malanskraal, small dorp, turnoff between Heidelberg and Villiers on the N3 freeway, near the Eskom Grootvlei Power Station. Origins unknown but noted for further research.

Malanspruit, small farming village near Estcourt, Natal, turn-off at Willowgrange on the old national road between Estcourt and Mooi River. Origins unknown.

Melville Kopies – north-west of Johannesburg, approx 5km, the home of Frans Geldenhuys.

Preller Place – Sharon Park, north of Dunnottar / Nigel

Preller Sentrum – Shopping Centre in Bloemfontein. Origins unknown, but most likely Gustav Preller.

Preller Street – Bothaville. Named after Abraham Christoffel Naudé Preller (1895-1963). He served as the Mayor of the town from 1934 to 1937, then for the term 1938/39, and from 1961 to 1963.

Preller Street – Dan Pienaarville, west of Johannesburg Central, towards Krugersdorp.

Preller Street – Georgetown, just east of Geldenhuys Interchange N3 / Geldenhuys railway siding.

Preller Drive – Franklin Roosevelt suburb, Johannesburg. (NW of city centre) Suspect named after Gustav Schoeman Preller – the historian.

West Park Cemetery. Subdivision of Emmarentia estate

PERSONALITIES AND PLACES OF INTEREST

Theunis Louis Botha	- Founder of Bothaville, grandfather to Lizzie Preller
Cornelis Brink	- Large family of 20, similar to the Hans Jacob
Camphor trees	- 300 year old, page 23.
Abram Carl Frederik Preller Geldenhuys	- SAAF pilot, copper miner
Albert Barends Geldenhuys / Gildenhuizen	- Stamvader and name changes
Dirk Cornelis Geldenhuys	- Braamfontein and Rand pioneer
Hans Jacob Geldenhuys	- Large family of 20, see page 80.
Johannes Albertus Geldenhuys	- Afrikaner Boer
Matthys Johannes Gildenhuyzs	- Uncertain parentage and Cape slavery, see Index
Kroonstad and Bothaville history	- Early settlers and founders
Magersfontein	- Boer War battle
David Malan	- Eloped with Zara)
Francois Daniel Malan	- Farmer
Phil Malan	- Twin brother to Rina, poet, musician
Thomas Moodie	- Rhodesian settler
Anna Elizabeth "Lizzie" Preller	- Boere meisie
Gustav Schoeman Preller	- Historian
Gerhard Geldenhuys	- Applied Mathematician
Rustpan	- Familie plaas / farm – various.
Dot Serfontein	- Author and Geldenhuys inter-marriage finding
Vergelegen	- Willem Adriaan van der Stel's wine estate

SOUTH AFRICAN ORIGINS

ALBERT BARENDS – Onboard "PRINCESSE ROYALE"

Geldenhuys' originated in the Cape from "Stamvader" Albert Barends Gildenhuizen (or Gildenhuisz or Gildenhausen), from Burgsteinfurt in Westfale. He arrived in the Cape as a sailor on the ship *"Princesse Royale"* in 1661.

A brief South African history would read as follows. In 1488 Portuguese Bartolomeu Dias rounded the Cape and landed his three ships at Fish Bay, near the mouth of the Gouritz River. In 1498 Vasco Da Gama stopped on the south-eastern coast in Pondoland which he dubbed Natal (in observance of the day of Nativity). In 1579 Englishman Thomas Stevens rounded the "Cape Das Agulias" followed a year later by Sir Frances Drake who described the Cape as the "fairest Cape". In 1615 Sir Thomas Smythe sent eight condemned men to Table Bay but after the death of their leader Captain Cross the remainder fled to Robben Island – the surviving three being transported back to England.

In the mid 1600's English sea captains Fitzherbert and Shillinge (who incidentally, could be related to Elizabeth Schikkerling) arrived at the Cape from Britain. In April 1652 Dutchman Jan van Riebeek (note: Jan has ever since been a very popular Geldenhuys Christian name) settled in Table Bay with 90 men contracted by the Dutch East India Trading Company in Amsterdam. Cape history records that during Jan van Riebeek's time, on 23rd September 1661, Albert Barends Gildenhuisz was declared a "Vryburger" or free Burgher. It is a historical fact that in 1660, there were only forty-six free adults and fourteen children. In fact, the first group of only twelve men were granted "their papers of freedom as freemen" – by visiting Councillor Extraordinary Rijkloff van Groen. The Geldenhuys Stamvader was employed as a farm labourer from 1662 to 1665, and were known as *knechts* (– hired hands released from the Garrison), working on various farms, among others with farmer Jacob Cloete.

Jacob Cloete was a personality of note. He was one of the oldest emigrant farmers, having arrived in 1652 from Keulen, Germany, with his wife Fytje (Sophia) Raderotjes. He became a corporal in the VOC and had four children (his son Gerhard or Gerrit was born in Cape Town in 1655, his daughter Christina Catharina in April 1660 and son Coenraad in April 1663). In February 1657 he signed the document releasing him from Company service and registering him as one of the first nine "free burghers" – and granted 11.5 hectares of land along the Liesbeek River. They were exempt from tax for a period of 12 years, and they were allowed to trade with the Khoikhoi for sheep and cattle, so long as they did not pay more than the Company did. They were supplied with the necessary implements at cost price, with the Company holding a mortgage over their lands. They were permitted to grow only those crops not already grown in the Company's own garden, the cultivation of cereals being encouraged. Since they were now landowners, these first 'vryburghers' naturally required labour; and with strict instructions from the Company not to enslave the local Khoikhoi, they had to look elsewhere. Jacob Cloete's son Coenraad, had a grandson Hendrik, born 1725, who became the largest landowner, including Constantia – he married Hester Anna Lourens and they had eleven children). Jacob Cloete was murdered on 23rd May 1693.

Fortuitously, the ship *Amersfoort* put in early 1658 with a cargo that included 170 slaves, the survivors of 250 taken from a Portuguese vessel off Angola. The free burghers were allowed to purchase two or more slaves on credit, the remainder being reserved for the use of the Company – van Riebeeck himself eventually acquiring 23 slaves. (It is an interesting and noteworthy fact, that in 1656 the first slave, Catharina Anthonis, was freed in order to marry Dutchman Jan Woutersz. The second intermarriage was between Jan Stael from Amsterdam and Maria van "Bengalen" – from Bengal, India). In 1656 no fewer than 44 vessels called at the Cape.

In August 1658 there were only four married and six single vryburghers. In 1662, by the time German Zacharias Wagner (became Wagenaar) replaced Jan van Riebeeck, there were 31 freemen all told - - 42 knechts or hired men, 11 wives, and infamous Herwerden's widow who was running the "Inn". There were also 20 children and 39 slaves – already outnumbering the freemen who bought them. By 1672, now ten years later, the freemen's numbers had increased to only sixty-four – hence the

Geldenhuys stamvader was but one of very few that had been granted vryburger status, i.e. one of 64 free burghers. A.B. Gildenhuysz then returned to Duitsland to get married and came back to the Cape with his wife and newly born son in 1672. Very few freemen were given their papers between 1662 and 1666.

Albert married Margaretha Hoefnagels, born 28th March 1649, in Legden, a Holland town near Burgsteinfurt. She was previously married to Hendrik Schakelmann and was the daughter of Arend Hoefnagels and Grietje Cornelis. Their first-born was Arend, in Legden. Their first daughter, christened in Cape Town on 11 April 1700 possibly died shortly thereafter, because their third child also christened in Cape Town – on 10 December 1702 – is recorded as having married a Jan Louw in October 1725.

Margaretha, who was born in 1864, the younger sister to our ancestor Barend born 6th September 1682, also led a somewhat historically noteworthy life. She grew up in the Cape and married a German to become the 'stammoeder' of the Du Plooy's!

Governor Simon van der Stel arrived in October 1679. The number of freemen now amounted to 87, of whom 55 had found wives, and there were 114 children. It is an uncontested historical fact that the Vryburghers / freemen who took out freeman papers became the founders of Cape families. Simon was a competent Commander of the Cape – a position he held for over nineteen years. He established his vineyards at Constantia, introduced forestry, and lent his name to the naval base at Simonstown, Simons Berg and Simons Bay.

In 1685 disenchanted farmers were released from their obligations and could sell their produce on the free market. In the 1690's, the free Burghers, as these released farmers became known, were given additional farmland in the Liesbeeck Valley. Others became millers, hunters, tailors and tavern keepers. More colonists came to the Cape to promote agriculture, grow mielies and raise livestock. By now there were 260 free burghers and the cattle farming burghers required more land, expanding eastwards. Dutch, French, German, Swiss, Flemish and Scandinavians relocated to the colony in the newly founded town of Stellenbosch. The 156 French Huguenots of 1688 was the first sizeable migration to the Cape, settling mainly in the Berg River Valley. Stamvader Jacques Malan arrived on board the *Berg China* (1688) and on the 18th October 1694 he became the owner of a farm in Franschhoek, which he named *"La Motte"* – having emigrated from Merindol nearby Abignon in the Province of La Motte-d'Aigues in the southeast of France.

In 1693, Jacob Cloete, the oldest pioneer and one of the oldest farmers, was murdered. His great-grandson, Hendrik, became the largest landowner at the Cape (including Constantia).

In 1699, Jacques Malan married Elisabeth le Long, widow of Jean Jourdan (Jordaan) – they had 7 children. Meanwhile, between 1700 and 1714, an average of 67 ships per year called at the Cape - somewhat considerably up on the 44 of 1656. Settlers were mainly male, and very few woman folk arrived in the late 1600's early 1700's.

Also in 1699, on 11th February, Simon handed over the reins of office to his eldest son, Willem Adriaan van der Stel, and retired to his Constantia farm to live out the rest of his life – another twelve years – as a freeman.

Barend, son of Albert Barends Gildenhuizen and Margaretha Hoefnagels, was christened in Cape Town on 6th September 1682. He married Anna Margaretha Siek on 31st August 1710 - she was also christened in Cape Town, on 13th March 1685, and was the daughter of Johann Siek and Geertruy Helms. In 1712 Barend acquired *Vergelegen*, the 'model' farm in Hottentots-Holland which had been developed, at Company expense, by corrupt and disgraced Governor Willem Adriaan van der Stel – son of Simon – in February 1707, and sold off in four lots during 1707. *Vergelegen* was situated thirty miles east of Cape Town and due south of Stellenbosch; in what is now Somerset-West. Co-incidentally, Jacques Malan bought "Morgenster", one of the four Vergelegen sub-divisions in 1709 – and sold his Franschhoek farm La Motte in 1719 – to his step-son Pierre Jourdan. And very interestingly, Barends younger sister Elsje married Jacobus van der Heiden, who bought the third sub-division. This substantial acquisition of the prestigious Vergelegen warrants a special insert at this juncture. . . .

Vergelegen was established by Willem Adriaan van der Stel in Hottentots Holland, in 1700 – in what is now Somerset West. Dutch East India Company Commissioner Wouter Valkier, during his annual inspection, granted Governor Willem Adriaan van der Stel the 400 morgen property in the Hottentots Holland area. van der Stel then added a further 200 morgen. 600 morgen = 515 hectares, about ten times larger than what the average burger got.

Re-enter our first Cape born Geldenhuys! Elsje was born to Stamvader Albert Barends and Margaretha in May 1674. She married Jacobus van der Heiden, Heyden from Haarlem, Netherlands, in 1691 and they settled on Vergelegen after her husband had successfully vindicated his grievances against Willem Adriaan van der Stel – and was obviously one of the first allotment purchasers. They had seven children – and became the stam-moeder of the van der Heiden's with the birth of their first son Jacobus. Jacobus married Aletta Nobel in September 1717 and also had seven children. Their second son, Andries, married Maria Odendaal on 11th January 1728, had 5 children and produced 11 grandchildren. Large families in those early days were very necessary for the survival of the family unit – and more so as a source of manpower needed for farming, especially in remote locations.

Jacobus was a signatory to the grievances that were notarised by Adam Tas and his nephew-in-law Henning Husing against the Governor Willem Adriaan – about February 1706. It was resolved that the ringleaders of the rising should be sent to the Netherlands to be dealt with there. The ringleaders were Henning Husing, Jacobus van der Heiden, Pieter van der Bijl, Ferdinandus Appel and Jan Meerland. They were ordered to be ready for sail within three days – while Tas remained in gaol. Further

THE JELLEY CLAN AT VERGELEGEN

arrests and interrogations took place before the departure of the fleet. Tas, not formed of heroic mould, had recanted and apologised. One man stood out boldly and maintained the justice and truth of everything he had put his name to. That man was Elsje Geldenhuys' husband Jacobus. The document that the four deportees (Jan Meerland had died on the way) smuggled over to Holland contained thirty-eight clauses of monstrous charges against the Governor. These included: -

- The first charge accused the Governor of having built a palatial residence upon a vast property large enough to set up fifty burghers.

- The Governor was said to run this place (Vergelegen) with the labour of sixty men of the garrison at the Company's charge; with a hundred slaves, and with runaway slaves of the freeman, whom he encouraged to take sanctuary with them.

- Other issues also related to the loss of the meat supply monopoly that Husing had enjoyed.

To these charges the governor replied that his house was a modest dwelling of six rooms, with storage closets under the slope

Rina Geldenhuys – in front of the rear gable – Vergelegen

windows. Outbuildings numbered a labourer's cottage; slave-quarters; a building to hold the winepress; work- and tool-rooms; a mill and sheep- and cattle-pens.

Jacobus van der Heiden (Heyden), Appel and van der Bijl returned to the Cape as soon as they had satisfactorily concluded their business. Husing remained in Holland for another year and succeeded in persuading the Directorate to give him half of the meat contract for three years till December 1710. The burghers believed themselves to be completely successful in their mission to Holland - - The Directorate determined to recall the Governor (as well as his younger brother, freeman Frans van der Stel – who was required to "remove himself from the territories of the Company'). The Directorate ruled that "the homestead and farm buildings are to be bought from van der Stel by the Company at a valuation. Should this arrangement fail he may break down the homestead or dispose of it, as he likes. The Company will not buy it, but only the farm buildings, because such buildings as the homestead 'which are ostentation and pomp rather than for use have been built by Company's servants at the Cape and elsewhere, greatly to our annoyance'. They have not found guilty the four freemen charged with mutiny."

Ex-Governor van der Stel's property Vergelegen was not sold until 31st October 1709 when it was put up for auction in four lots. The homestead was not broken up. According to the official Journal appraisers went out by order of the Council to value the place. They advised that the homestead, surrounded by other buildings, would be useful to whoever bought the plot on which they stood. Buildings other than on the homestead plot the Company was to purchase from van der Stel, at the Company's valuation. Excess in price over and above the Company's payment to van der Stel, gained at the resale at public auction would accrue to the Company. It was therefore in the Company's interest to place the lowest possible value upon what they had to pay for. This the appraisers did. Van der Stel's agents were offered 3,000 rixdollars for the whole of the farm buildings exclusive of the homestead. However the Directorate refused to pay and were then advised that the property should be split up. "Eventually" the agents accepted this price.

Three plots were sold without difficulty; the fourth – the homestead plot – was withdrawn from the sale. This plot measured about 380 acres, rather over 200 of which were arable land, and rather over 40 acres under vines. The highest bid was Rds 9,000 (Rands 3,750). After the sale "the burgher Barend Geldenhuijs made a private offer of Rds 9,500, and a deposit of Rds280.33. The Governor advised that Geldenhuijs should be allowed to have the plot 'on condition that he produces satisfactory security, and as long as Van der Heiden is alive, who is already in possession of a large quantity of land and immovable property, he will not directly or indirectly sell or alienate it, so that the orders of the Directorate [on the subject of equality among the burghers] may be explicitly obeyed.' Van der Heiden as Geldenhuys's brother-in-law was suspected of collusion between them (bearing in mind that Jacobus had purchased one of the plots at the auction). The four lots were thus sold as follows: -

Lot 1 South – to Catharina Cloete (later became Cloetenburg / Somerset West).

Lot 2 South West – to Jacques Malan (later Morgenster and Land-en-Zeesicht).

Lot 3 North West – to Jacobus van der Heiden (later Lourensford / Erinvale and part of Vergelegen)

Lot 4 South East – to Barend Gildenhuys (later Vergelegen).

Barend Gildenhausen thus became the first purchaser of the Vergelegen homestead allotment. The house was built on the double "H" plan, but Barend could not comply with Company directives and was forced for practical reasons to demolish the back portion of the homestead – which included three gables. Unfortunately, Barend died within a few years of the sale.

Albert Barend, second generation Geldenhuys grandson to the Stamvader, was born in February 1712. Then the following year, 24th March 1713, Geertruy Geldenhuys was born on Vergelegen – first daughter to Barend and Anna Margaretha. Hendrik Barend and Johanna Margaretha were the next children to follow. Barend must have died shortly before 1722.

Barend's widow Anna married Michael Otto, a German from Stettin. Otto was a sailor, having arrived in the country in 1714. He became "Superintendent of the wood cutters behind the Steenbergen", later he acquired burgher papers and on his marriage in 1722 to the widow Gildenhausen, the farm Vergelegen. Otto was noted for viticulture, but will be remembered for his savage and tyrannical behaviour towards his slaves. He soon became notorious for his cruelty and consequently lost through desertion many of his slaves who fell into the hands of the Fiscal and the law. He was commonly known as 'Baas Otto' or Michael Os (Ox). O.F. Menzel in his *A Geographical – Topographical Description of the Cape of Good Hope* gives some details of his inhuman conduct. Generally in summer he used to bind slaves who had committed some offence naked to a tree or pole in the sun, had their entire bodies smeared with honey and thus they were tortured unbearably for hours by flies, wasps, bumble-bees and other pests, especially by the African flies, called mosquitoes in India. Public censure for his brutality did little to deter him and at least one slave died at his hands. For most farmers this was senseless behaviour as slaves were costly at the Cape. Instead they used threats of selling their slaves to Otto, to keep them in order.

In 1740 when the roof required its first re-thatching, Vergelegen got all its side gables. The current front gable, originally at the back, was added 40 years later.

Anna Gildenhuys then had a daughter by Michael Otto. They named her Dorothea. After Otto had suffered great loss of slaves and also severely punished several times by the Government on account of his inhuman conduct, he became bored, left his wife to farm alone on the estate and bought himself a house in the city. There he sold his own wine at retail what he could not sell he drank himself being never quite sober.

Then in 1751, Dorothea Otto and Jurgen Radyn became the third owners of Vergelegen. I have not yet found out whether they married (they did – authors note in 2007), or just became joint owners – for a rather short six years.

Then in 1757, ownership passed to Arnoldus Maasdorp. He also bought Section 3 with the remaining buildings, (which were originally sold to Jacobus van der Heiden). In 1763 Vergelegen passed to Nicolas Vlok – and then in 1775 to Johannes de Waal. In

1778 Vergelegen was bought by Jacobus Malan of 'Morgenster' – the other sub-division of the original Van der Stel farm.

Now for the juicy bit! A brother-in-law of Jacobus Malan, who was living on Vergelegen, caused a scandal that same year, 1788, by eloping with a slave woman: he was David Malan and she Zara, a slave belonging to Jurgen Radyn! They disappeared into the interior and after a time David was declared dead. However, he reappeared many years later, to be reunited with his wife and settled on the eastern frontier. Riaan Malan refers to this episode in his book, *My Traitors Heart*.

After Jacobus died his widow, Catharina Morkels married in 1780 and they became joint owners of the two farms. They undertook major renovations to the wine cellar, slave lodge, mill and homestead at Vergelegen. The homestead took its present H-shape with 'voorhuis' and 'agterkamer', and four side rooms. The west facing gable with its curvilinear outline dates from this period. Twice widowed, Catharina Morkels sold Vergelegen and Morgenster to Wouter de Vos in 1796, but Vergelegen reverted to the family when son-in-law Martinus Wilhelmus Theunissen bought it two years later. Marthinus Theunissen later became famous as "Die Held van Blaauwberg" – The Hero against the British invasion of 1806. In 1816 he added the T-section wine cellar. After his death his son and grandson inherited the farm and it became more popularly known as "Theunissen se Plaas".

In 1917 Sir Lionel Phillips and Lady Florence were responsible for restoring Vergelegen to its former glory. After they both died, the farm passed to Mrs Cynthia Barlow, whose son Tom is the current owner. Up until 1987 the farm was not open to the public – but now features as one of the most sought after wine farm tours in the whole of the Western Cape.

Another interesting fable relates to buried treasure! In November 1722 a ship, the *Schonenburg* was wrecked off Cape Agulhas. Legend has it that the ship's treasure was buried in an orchard at Vergelegen and that the people involved in the plot died mysteriously. Some believe it was their bones that were found beneath the kitchen floor almost two centuries later. Perhaps this just adds to the intrigue that draws tourists to this magnificent wine farm in the Cape.

Before leaving Vergelegen, I would like to touch on the other lots that were sold. As we now know, Cloetenburg has been wholly swallowed up by the rapid development of Somerset-West as a sought after retirement option. The Malan stamvader, Jacques, named his lot Morgenster, and passed it on fourteen years later to his son Daniel. Daniel was the father to 13 children (so a substantial, "H" Cape Dutch homestead was built), with his son Jacobus inheriting the farm in 1778. But he died young at age 26 – two years after his marriage to Catharina Morkel. Catharina Malan sold the farm to her younger brother, Philip Morkel – with the farm remaining in that family till 1885. By then, Daniel Morkel sold out to his brother-in-law Alexander van der Byl (probably spelt van der Bijl – like the fellow who accompanied van der Heiden to Holland to partition The Seventeen!). After van der Byl's death, Morgenster passed to his cousin Major William Barnett, and in turn to his daughter. Mrs Leonard Hawkins started the extensive restoration of the original homestead in 1958. The property then passed on to her daughter, Mrs Shirley Bainsfather-Cloete. Her son Pieter, a descendent of the Cloete's of Alphen, is now the current owner.

In concluding this short story, the re-visit carried out to Vergelegen by the writer, with his grandchildren Courtney and Brendan Jelley (in December 2003), was a life experience not to be missed. Just appreciating the 300-year old landmark Camphor trees alongside the Cape Dutch styled original homestead was an unforgettable experience – see photograph. Although I doubt whether the enormity of the occasion dawned on the 'youth of to-day', I trust this record will suffice. Successive owners of this original Cape Dutch homestead have truly made us proud of our heritage.

The farm Land-en-Zeesicht has an interesting history. When Somerset-West was still a small dorpie, this farm as the name implies, afforded views from the Helderberg to the breakers on False Bay. It was part of Morgenster that was subdivided from Vergelegen. The farm was purchased by Hendrik Hendriksz, in whose family the farm remained till 1971 (except for a short period from 1941 to 1951). A noteworthy event was Hendrik's granddaughter Alida's wedding to J.H. (Onze Jan) Hofmeyr in 1880 – small world, I trust the average reader will conclude – Onze Jan and Gustav Preller are credited with promoting Afrikaans as a spoken and written language. Anyway, by the time W. Marais bought Land-en-Zeesicht in the late 1970's, it has shrunk and is now not much more than a suburb of Somerset-West. Ownership then passed to Graaf Zamoyski, whose widow currently occupies the homestead.

Whilst mentioning significant properties, permit me to add Libertas. *"Libre est Tas"* – Tas is free – are the words spoken by our friend Adam Tas after his release from the prison cells in the Castle, after his 14 months imprisonment in 1707. And so legend has it that Adam Tas named his farm in the Stellenbosch district *Libertas*, in memory of the times against his archenemy, Willem Adriaan van der Stel. Interesting? But not so – the plot thickens. The name Libertas was in use at least 10 years before Adam Tas became the owner in 1703 - - and then he only got it because he courted the rich Germans' widow – Elisabeth van Braken, the widow of Hans Jurgen Grimpe. Another interesting fact is that after a few changes of ownership, Libertas in 1760 became the property of Jacobus Hermanus Malan – the son of David Malan of Morgenster. Six months after his death in 1768, his widow Anna Elizabeth Louw, the mother of three young children, married a widower Hoffman with his 12 children. She then had another six children by him – 21 children in the household! They sure didn't have TV in those days.

In 1709 our friend the well-to-do Ferdinandus Appel, who had also been active in the Willem Adriaan van der Stel commotion, became the first burgher to be granted land eastwards of the Hottentots-Holland range. His grant lay at the foot of the southern slope of the Zwartbergen where the hot spring rose - - and where a century later a village to be named Caledon. I presume Jacobus van der Heiden, his travel mate to Holland, and Jacobus's in-law Barend Geldenhuys, must have frequented the Caledon hot springs – seeing that Appel still lived on his farm near Henning Husing - - and where it is reported that Appel entertained the Cape Governor.

Barend and Anna had five children between 1712 and 1721, with our ancestor being the Hendrik, the third born and second son. Hendrik, christened on 12th July 1717 had two marriages – possibly sisters. He married Cornelia Swart on 27th July 1738 and then Sara Johanna Swart exactly twelve years later on 26th July 1750. The record shows that she died 20 years later – on 6th August 1770. Anyway, it is speculated that Cornelia died with childbirth with Johannes Albertus who was christened on 5th April 1750 because Hendrik married the second Swart three months later! We are descendants of Johannes Albertus Gildenhuisz (born 1750) and who married Johanna le Roux (who was the widow of Johannes Swart).

A smallpox pandemic in 1713 resulted in the death of 963 whites. This epidemic is mentioned because of its devastating effect on the Cape population at that time.

Heinrich du Plooy arrived at the Cape in 1701, from Soest, Westfale, Germany. He married Barend's younger sister Margaretha on 5th July 1704. They had six children; including Hendrik Willem in 1707 and Albert Barend (named after the Geldenhuys 'stamvader'), thereby becoming the stam-moeder of the Du Plooy's. However, according to the stamregister, Margaretha also married Philippus Richter on 10th June 1725. According to the "Family Register of the South African Nation" by Dr. D.F.Du T. Malherbe, the first Richter arrived in 1786 – so it was not confirmed whether Margaretha also became the stam-moeder of the Richter's as well?

Matthias Lotter was born in Augsburg, Germany, († 1752), and arrived as a naval cadet midshipman in South Africa in 1734 as the "Stamvader" with his wife Susanna Roge. They had three children. His descendant Matt Lotter would be destined to marry Abram Carl Frederik Preller Geldenhuys.

Johannes Marthinus Dippenaar, originally Depner, from Wehlau in Oos-Pruise (Duitsland) arrived in 1735. He became a burger in 1746 and two years later, on 10th November 1748, married Maria Magdalena Schmidt. She was the daughter of Christian Schmidt, from Halle Germany. They had ten children. Johannes possessed the farm "Groene Valley" on the Olifantsrivier – where he died in 1790.

Hendrik was born in December 1744 to Hendrik Gildenhuisz (born 1717) and Cornelia Swart. He was the fifth child. In August 1773 Hendrik married Geertruyda Grobbelaar and their marriage lasted for twenty-eight years because Hendrik took a second wife, Margaretha Maria Wessels whom he married in January 1801. Hendrik junior, in this case, is significant in that intermarriages occurred between his descendants, and his younger brother Johannes Albertus born six years later in 1750.

Although the Huguenots and Germans outnumbered the Dutch, Dutch was kept as the official language. These early settlers became known as Afrikaners and those who farmed were called "Boer" in Dutch. The boere became restless with restrictive trade practices and the resultant "trekboers" penetrated the interior up the Hex River pass into the Great Karoo, into the Little Karoo down the Lang Kloof, and along the south-eastern coast to Mossel Bay.

Simon van der Stel founded Stellenbosch soon after his arrival at the Cape – and the third town in the Cape, Swellendam was named after Governor Hendrik Swellengrebel in 1745. It is noteworthy that Swellendam had only four houses thirty years after it had become the seat of a landdrost – there were few specialised artisans around, and every trekboer was a jack-of-all-trades. In 1777, Hendrik Swellengrebel described trekboer living condition thus: -

"One finds quite respectable houses with a large room partitioned into 2 or 3, and with good doors and windows, though mostly without ceilings. For the rest, however, and especially those at a greater distance, they are only tumble-down barns, 40 feet by 14 or 15 feet, with clay walls four feet high, and a thatched roof. These are mostly undivided; the doors are reed mats; a square hole serves as a window. The fireplace is a hole in the floor, which is usually made of clay and cow dung. There is no chimney; merely a hole in the roof to let the smoke out. A Hottentots reed mat separates the beds. The furniture is in keeping. I have found up to three households – children included – living in such a dwelling."

"The majority, by far, of the farmers from the Overberg (beyond the mountain escarpment) come to Cape Town only once a year, because of the great distance – I have discovered that some are reckoned to live 40 "schoften" or days' journey away – and because of the difficulty of getting through the kloofs (passes) between the mountains. To cross them they need at least 24 oxen; two teams of 10 to be changed at every halt and at least 4 spare to replace animals that are crippled or fall prey to lions. Two Hottentots are necessary as well as the farmer himself. The load usually consists of 2 vats of butter (1000lb. In all) and 400 to 500 lbs soap."

On reflection by modern-day standards, one can only marvel at the hardships that our ancestors endured. A second smallpox epidemic in 1767 claimed another 179 lives.

The Cape slaves require special mention. Jan van Riebeeck was reluctant to recruit local Khoikhoi labour and at an early stage requisitioned slaves for manual Company works. By the end of the seventeenth century, it was an accepted prerequisite of manumission that a slave should be baptised, speak good Dutch, and have a guarantor who would pay the Poor Fund, which might provide relief if the freed slave became destitute. Throughout the Company period, there were a few marriages between European men and freed slave women. There was also a great deal of extramarital sexual activity across the status and colour lines nearly all of it between white men and slave women. Visiting sailors fathered numerous children by Cape slaves, especially in the Company's Quarters. Male slaves outnumbered their masters. Much debauchery took place in the Company's slave-lodge.

Burghers also patronised the urban slaves and had extramarital affairs with slave and Khoikhoi or Hottentot women on the farms, where men always exceeded women in the burgher population. The children of free fathers and slave mothers were slaves, but many of the female children became the mistresses and, in some cases, the manumitted legal wives of burghers. Early examples were Catharina Anthonis and Maria van Bengalen. Also, a Jan Andreas Bam who arrived in 1725 as a soldier from Schwerin, Germany, had four children from Ragel van die Kaap. A descendant of Jan, Johanna Dorothea married blacksmith Casper Heinrich Gildenhaus from Osnabruck, on 21st July 1793. As a result of these relationships, the "black" population of the colony became considerably lightened, while the "white" population of the colony became somewhat darkened. As will be seen later, the abolition of slavery in 1834 was an intolerable blow to the trekboers.

The writer was not surprised to find that the Geldenhuyse contributed to creating *Hotnots* – Coloureds. In fact I am rather proud of the fact that my research revealed fascinating findings – which I may venture to add that that great academic (and a family relative I might hastily add) Dr Malherbe of Stellenbosch, would not find amiss. Without sounding derogatory, terms like Hotnot, Baster – and even Bastard and Kaffir – were considered common, acceptable speech in its day. Stories concerning several personalities of note is worthy of repeating, and include Matthys Johannes Gildenhuyzs, born Swellendam 22nd April 1822, the son of Johanna Susanna Elizabeth Gildenhuizen (christened Stellenbosch 28th September 1785), is one, if not more, from uncertain parentage as well as an ancestor. His father is unknown, and his mother's father, also unknown, was given as "Juli v.d. K." – in those days taken to mean "male, from the Cape". It is known that his grandmother, Geertruy Anna was christened on the 28.9.1785, no record of "husband" found, but was the mother of Johanna Susanna! (The reader is referred to the Dictionary of Family Biography Section of this book). Refer also to all the Geldenhuys intermarriages. And remember that Albert Barends 'Geldenhuys' was made a Vryburgher in 1661, and was permitted to own two or more slaves originating off the *Amersfoort*. He surely must also have serviced a lot of Madam/widow Herwerden's clients who ran an Inn, as well as the Malay quarters and hostels built by Van Riebeeck for the pleasure of all those seamen who called. He had spent ten years as a bachelor in the Cape before he fetched Margaretha Hoefnagels. Take note our direct descendant Hendrik had two wives both named "Swart" – dare I take authors licence and speculate? The bottom line is our family lived with slavery for 173 years.

On the other end of the scale is the unforgivable cruelty meted out by Barends widows' second husband Michael Otto – Baas Ox to his slaves on Vergelegen.

Hendrik died in August 1770 – aged 53 – very much par for the course for a Geldenhuys. I presume his two wives, possibly Swart sisters, hastened his end. M. Whiting Spilhaus, the writer of *"South Africa in the Making"* aptly described the early Afrikaners as ". . . it was not surprising that it (SA) bred a race of men extraordinarily independent, self-confident, and wilful".

By mid 1750's there were 1000 free burgers – in Swellendam, Graaff-Reinet, Tulbagh and Uitenhage (Geldenhuyse settled initially mainly in Stellenbosch and later in the Swellendam areas in 1806, in Caledon in 1814, in Colesberg in 1827 and Graaff-Rienet by 1835). The reader should distinguish the differences between the VOC ("**V**ereenigde **O**ost **I**ndische **C**ompagnie") Company employee, and the free burgher, followed by the trekboer; and finally the "Groot Trek" Voortrekker and pioneer people. It is believed that by and large, the Geldenhuyses were vryburgers, but the odd one may well have fallen into the trekboer category because of their early movements into newly established settlements like Stellenbosch, Swellendam, Caledon, and Graaff-Reinet. By 1770 the trekboers had penetrated the Fish and Gamtoos rivers. British troops and a Boer commando built military posts at Craddock and Grahamstown to resist Xhosa skirmishes. Scotsman Colonel John Graham established Grahamstown in 1812 (he married Jacob Cloete's descendant Johanna Catharina). The Cape was ceded to the British in 1814.

In 1786 Johan Frederik Preller arrived at the Cape as a soldier, from Halle on the Saale, Germany. He was born in 1764 and was the son of Johann Friedrich Preller and Johanna Dorothea Philemann. He became a hunter after the service of the VOC. In 1794 he secured employment with a butcher named Frederik van Reenen, apparently as a cattle buyer. That same year he married Zacharia Christina de Beer. In 1813 Preller became a burger of Graaff-Reinet. They had seven children - two sons and five daughters.

In 1817 the first British immigrants to come to South Africa in a body arrived in Table Bay. They numbered two hundred tradesmen who had been sent out by Benjamin Moodie to whom they were indentured for three years, but so great was the demand for their labour here that Moodie had little difficulty in disposing their indentures at a handsome profit. Before long the men's wives and families came out to join them. John Wedderburn Dunbar Moodie arrived at the Cape on 12th September 1819 Between March 1820 and May 1821, 5 000 applicants, out of 90 000, arrived at the Cape (i.e. the 1820 Settlers) including younger brother Donald. More about the Moodies will be told later.

The Albany Settlement followed in 1820, in 21 emigrant ships, and each new immigrant was granted a 100-acre plot in the Zuurveld, on the West Side of the Fish River. Owing to a quarrel which had developed among them on the voyage out, a handful of Settlers were landed at Saldanha Bay and established themselves at Clanwilliam; a few took work in Cape Town, but the great majority were disembarked at Algoa Bay where, by 25th June there were one thousand and twenty men, six hundred and seven women and one thousand and thirty-two children encamped in tents in the vicinity of Fort Frederick.

Anyway – back to the 1750's. The first Johannes Albertus in our family line was born on 5th April 1750 and became a burger of Stellenbosch. He married Johanna le Roux who was the widow of Johannes Swart. Their fourth child, and third son, Lourens, a character of note was born in early 1777. Christened 30th March at Malgasrivier, a burger of Stellenbosch, married his first cousin twice removed, Geertruy Johanna Gildenhuizen, the daughter of Hendrik and Geertruyda Grobbelaar (who remained in Cape Town but later relocated to Swellendam). Lourens's heirs also established the Geldenhuys Estate, which later led to the Geldenhuys Interchange on the N3 as well as the Emmarentia suburb – but more about Lourens offspring later.

The second Johannes Albertus was born on 21st December 1807 and christened at Swellendam on 10th April 1808 (he was the third child and first son of Lourens and Geertruy Gildenhuizen). He also married a Gildenhuizen! – His cousin – a Judith Margaretha who was the daughter of Hendrik Gildenhuizen and Sara Johanna Odendaal – the elder brother Geertruy Johanna who had married Lourens!! Dit is nou 'n kak spul!! In other words; Johannes Albertus (I'll call him the 2nd) parents *and* grandparents married relatives – daughter and granddaughter of Hendrik (born 13.12.1744) and who was the elder brother of Johannes Albertus, the 1st (born 5.4.1750).

Anyway Johannes Albertus (the 2nd - 1807), became a burger of the Free State, fought in the Basoetuland war and subsequently died at Doornbult, Kroonstad on 9th October 1894, aged 86 years 9 months and 19 days!

It will be recalled that very few "Vryburgers" had the capital or means to break away from the Dutch East India Company's contractual hold over the early farmers until 1685. The Geldenhuyse were traditionally boere and latterly storekeepers, militiamen, and with the odd sprinkling of industrialists, historians, doctors and urban dwellers. Oumam Anna Elizabeth Preller often referred to the Vryburgers and the Kaap Kolonie – or KK, burgers, boere, Oom Hennie or Hendrik Schikkerling (a distant relative of sea captain Schillinge?) who was Pey's great-great-great-grandfather's cousin in the late 1890's. Hennie Schikkerling farmed on Schikspruit between "Lace-later Kroon Myn" and Kroonstad. Oudad Jannie Geldenhuys was a Veldkornet in the burgerkommando during the Anglo-Boer War. His father and mother were Hendrik Jacobus and Elizabeth Schikkerling – married 2 March 1874.

In 1830 Carel Friedrich Preller (the only son of Stamvader Johan Frederik Preller, who had children, albeit fifteen of them!) married the first of three wives. One of his sons, Johan Carel, born 1838, was destined to become a member of the ZAR *Volksraad* and became the *Prokureer-Generaal*.

In 1834 the abolition of slavery at the Cape alienated the Boers. So for 173 years the Geldenhuys boere had slaves – and no wonder they got *"gatvol"* with the Establishment interfering in their domestic affairs. Two years later, in 1836 the Great Trek of Boers from the Cape Colony north across the Oranje and Vaal rivers commenced. The Voortrekkers also settled in Natal after defeating the Zulus (1838).

It is noteworthy that in the 1850's the spelling of the "familienaam" changed to Geldenhuys. Another noteworthy event in the early 1850's in the Preller household was the birth of Abraham Christoffel Naudé, the twelfth of fifteen children - who was the grandfather to Abram Carl Frederik Preller Geldenhuys. A.C.N. Preller also took three wives (not all at once, but successively!).

Anyway, relations between the Albany settlers and the Boers were friendly because of a common desire to defend the Cape Colony's eastern border and remain autonomous from both the Cape and England. By 1850 the Dutch community was enlarged by a small stream of newcomers from Holland but relied mainly on natural increase for its expanding population. Boers trekked further inland to escape Anglicisation – to form the foundation stone of Afrikaner nationalism. The Voortrekkers were not the same as the trekboers who had been migrating out of the Cape since the 1820's, searching for seasonal grazing areas only to return to the Colony during the winter months.

The Voortrekkers were long established settlers, hailing mostly from the eastern-Cape districts of Albany, Beauford West, Craddock, Graaff-Reinet, Somerset East, Swellendam and Uitenhage, with a strong desire to escape and follow Piet Retief to migrate beyond the border of the Cape Colony. In 1834 Piet Uys went to Port Natal, Louis Trichardt towards Delagoa Bay and onto Lorenco Marques (later renamed Maputo) and Johannes van Rensburg towards the Soutpansberg – where Van Rensburg's party was massacred by a Shaka tribe.

Andries Potgieter of Tarka, with 30 families, headed north, defeated the Mzilikazi's Ndebele at the Battle of Vegkop near the Vaal River, forcing them north into

Matebeleland. Gerrit Maritz, who had left Graaf-Reinet with 100 wagons, proved himself a valuable ally during the battle. Dutch Reformed Church deacon Sarel Celliers and his party arrived on the scene and together continued on into the northern part of what is now the Orange Free State. Piet Retief, whose 100 wagons made them about 1000 strong, joined them in 1837. Retief was elected Governor and The Free Province of New Holland in Southeast Africa was established. However, bickering resulted in Potgieter opening up the Transvaal while Uys, Retief and Maritz headed towards Natal.

Retief lost 66 trekkers by Dingane's trickery on 6th February 1838, including Hercules Philip Malan (born 1792). Piet Retief had just concluded an agreement with Dingane, ceding Natal from the Umzimvubu River to the Tugela, from the Drakensberg Mountains to the sea, and including Durban. The Boers had been invited to a farewell dance, with massed regiments stamping and chanting, rattling their assegais against their great ox hide shields, and swirling through the intricate drill manoeuvres. When the dance was at its height, Dingane suddenly leapt to his feet and screamed, "*Bambani abaThakathi!* (Kill the Wizards!)". The unarmed Boers were dragged out of the kraal to the neighbouring hill of execution, impaled and had their skulls smashed by knobkerries, and their bodies tossed out on the hillside.

A further 281 trekkers – including 41 men, 56 women and 185 children, plus 200 Hottentot Coloured retainers were massacred at Blaauwkrantz River and Moordspruit, together with 25,000 cattle driven off. When a Boer village eventually arose in the area, it was simply called Weenen – Weeping. Dingane had stirred up a hornet's nest and signed the eventual death warrant of his nation.

Gerrit Maritz died and Piet Uys was fatally wounded in the battle at eThaleni that followed. Piet Uys died when whilst going to the rescue of his eldest son. He rode back to the foot of the pass when a Zulu speared him in the back. Three Malans' also died with Piet and Dirkie Uys on 9th April 1838 – they were father Jacobus (born 1787) and son David Malan born 1826. The third was a youth; Johannes Augustinus Malan aged 14 years, whose father Hercules Philip Malan (1792 – 1837) was murdered with Piet Retief. Andries Pretorius arrived on the scene, and joined by Sarel Celliers at Danskraal, planned a reprisal against Dingane and the Zulus. The 600 Voortrekkers laagered on the banks of the Ncome River and faced the 12,000 Zulus at the Battle of Blood River – killing some 3000 to avenge the Afrikaners – and declaring the Day of the Vow in honour of the covenant made with God.

No Boer history will be complete without reference to the Battle of Blood River – 16th December 1838. From a Zulu perspective, The Washing of the Spears, by Donald R. Morris, makes excellent reading (Thanks to Stu McColl).

Meanwhile, British soldiers occupied Port Natal and built Fort Victoria. But the trekkers established themselves at Pietermaritzburg (so named after their heroic co-leaders), forced Dingane to flee to Swazi territory – where he was later murdered – and confronted the British in Durban. The alarmed Cape Governor dispatched Captain Thomas Smith to tear down the Boer Republican flag and hoist a British one. Pretorius masterminded a counter-attack, trapping Smith in a small encampment in the stockade. This resulted in Dick King – whose statue is on Victoria Embankment, to the east of Pey's the Grand Gables – riding in record time to seek help at Grahamstown. The arrival of the warship Mazeppa, with cannons blazing, forced the trekkers to retreat to Pietermaritzburg, and subsequently over the Drakensberg to Potgieter's self proclaimed independent Republic of Transorange. Potgieter moved farther north to establish the village of Andries-Ohrigstad.

Andries Hendrik Potgieter was an ambitious leader who quarrelled bitterly with the other trekkers in many places. He and his followers had settled at Potchefstroom (Chief Potgieter's Stroom) and in the Magaliesberg area (Rustenburg). After more conflict with fellow trekkers, Potgieter moved eastwards and founded the settlement of Andries-Ohrigstad.

Feuding between the Natal trekkers and Potgieter led him to move his party even further north to Soutpansbergdorp, where he lived until his death in 1852. In 1848, Sir Harry Smith annexed the territory between the Orange and Vaal Rivers declaring the Orange River Sovereignty. Those inhabitants south of the Vaal River became British citizens. The Boers under Andries Pretorius led a commando to fend off the British but were defeated at the Battle of Boomplaats. The Free Staters weren't too happy under British rule and the Afrikaner was once again faced with a choice; and so the great trek resumed further north beyond the Vaal River to establish the South African Republic or Transvaal in 1853 at the Sand River Convention.

This Sand River Convention is in fact so significant that the writer went out of his way to locate the site - - the Sand River runs across the Bloemfontein to Kroonstad road - - and was used extensively by the Boer Commandos during the *Tweede Vryheidsoorlog* (namely my grandfather who was fighting against the British). The plaque at Sand River reads:-

"On this site Commandant General AM Pretorius and other delegates of the Boer emigrants north of the Vaal River and the British Assistant Commissioner W.S. Hogge and C.M. Owen met and signed the Sand River Convention on the 16th January, 1853. By the Convention Great Britain formally recognised the independence of the South African Republic north of the Vaal River."

A worthy digression is the "*God Save the Queen*" declaration by Ian Douglas Smith of UDI fame on November 1965. My other hero had the foresight to end his "Winds of Destruction" autobiography with the cutting remark "*Please God, Save the Queen*"!!! The relevancy to my (hi)story is that Rhodesian Premier Ian Smith made the salutary in all humility, but history proves that he was *Betrayed* by the British. Now considering the reasons for the Anglo-Boer wars, have the British not once again *Betrayed* the undertaking given at the Sand River Convention! That is why I state that my flying instructor Peter Petter-Bowyer aptly concluded the plea to God, to Save the Queen.

The neighbouring Republics of Lydenberg, Ohrigstad and Utrecht were incorporated and Pretoria chosen as capital. Pretoria was named on land donated by MW Pretorius. By 1852, there were 15,000 inhabitants of European descent. Two years later at the Bloemfontein Convention the Orange Free State was created with Bloemfontein as capital. By 1856 the OFS contained 12,000 inhabitants of European descent – no doubt several named Geldenhuys who chose to farm in the Bloemfontein and Bothaville/Kroonstad areas. The Geldenhuys's considered themselves free burgers or boere, aligned them with President Marthinus Steyn and were very wary of the Engelse – or Khaki's as the Brits became known during the latter Boere Oorloë.

Johannes Albertus Geldenhuys (born 21st December 1807) was an early "*burger van die Oranje Vrystaat wat in die Oorloë teen Basoetuland gedurende die jare 1856 tot 1865 geveg het*". It is noteworthy that he married Judith Margaretha Gildenhuizen, in 1827, who was the daughter of Hendrik Jacobus Geldenhuys and Sara Johanna Odendaal. Their son, and Pey's great-great-grandfather Hendrik – born 1849 – was also a burgher of the Orange Free State during the Basoetuland war. Our direct ancestors were thus involved with the Basutoland – now Lesotho – wars during the time when Britain attempted to establish a confederation.

BLOOD RIVER and THE VOW

The Vow

"My brothers and fellow countrymen
We stand here now
For a moment before a Holy God
Of Heaven and earth to make
A promise to Him.
If He would give our enemy into our hands
So that we may defeat them,
We shall pass the day and date
Each year as an anniversary and
A day of thanksgiving in His honour
Like a Sabbath
And we promise that we shall
Build a temple to His Honour
As it shall please Him, and that
we shall tell this to our children
So that they may share in this with us
To remember also for
Our rising generations
So that the Glory of His name
May be sanctified thereby
And the Glory and Honour of victory
Shall be given unto Him."

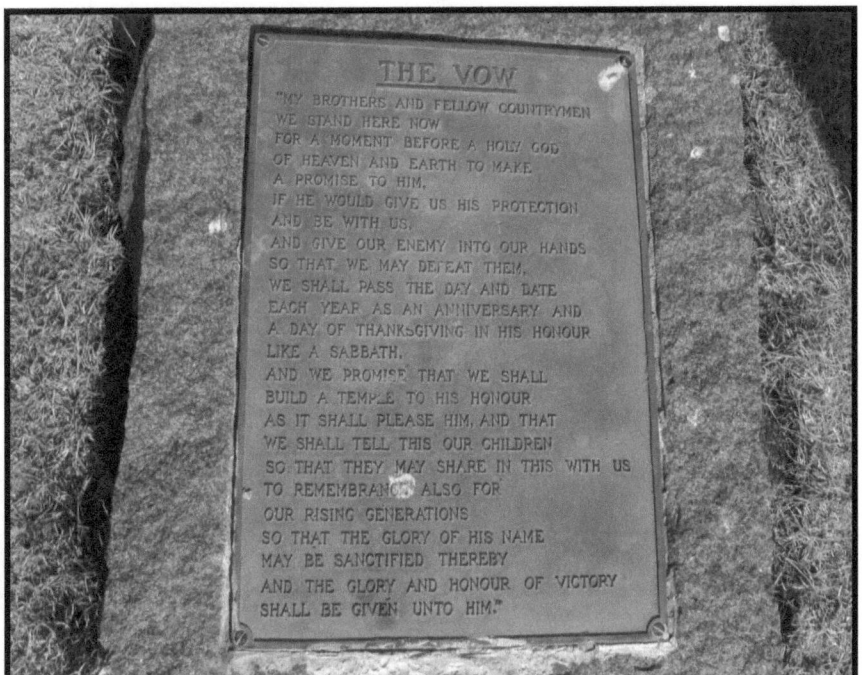

Ben (Barend Petrus) Geldenhuys wrote the author in to say that while on holiday in the Drakensberg, at Kerkenberg, Ben came across an inscription on a rock by Piet Retief's daughter. Immediately below Retief's name there is also a BP Geldenhuys name inscribed – Ben has been unable to obtain further information – he researched the names of the people that died with Retief, but Geldenhuys does not appear amongst them. Neither does it appear amongst the names of the Voortrekkers at Blood River [the author is not surprised, since the Geldenhuys were 'Trek-Boers' and not 'Voortrekkers']. Voortekkers were the early settlers whereas the Trekboers were the followers – they followed the Voortrekkers into the interior of 'Darkest Africa'.

Some modern historians still take humbrage that the Trekboers 'colonized Africa' whereas others quite rightly point out to 'civilizing savages' and bringing Christianity to the continent. The heated debate will continue for decades to come.

Acknowledging ones heritage is important – and visits to historical sites can only bring about better understanding of the past, like for instance, the Afrikaner's biblical belief in the acceptability of slavery.

THE BOER-BASOTHO WARS

The first Free State-Basoetuland war (also called the BaSotho War) broke out in March 1858 – 1500 burghers against some 20,000 BaSotho over continuing land disputes – the Afrikaners and the Sotho jostled one another for control of the land and raided each other's cattle. Open warfare broke out in 1858, when the Boers invaded BaSotholand from two points, from both north and south, capturing cattle and ravaging villages. Chief Moshoeshoe (born 1786) harried them with constant skirmishing as he fell back on his flat-topped mountain retreat, Thaba Bosiu.

Although the BaSotho scored a number of successes – at Hell Kloof, on 3rd April, BaSotho warriors trapped and killed 16 Boers – they were, for the most part, out-gunned and unable to press home attacks in the open. On 6th May the Boers reached the outskirts of Thaba Bosiu and formed a defensive laager but, as would happen time and again over the next 50 years, the BaSotho then proved reluctant to risk the necessary casualties that would result from an assault in the open. Outlying BaSotho responded by raiding into Free State territory, unsettling Boers at the front by threatening their families and farms at home. Eventually the war ground to a halt, with British arbitration on the question of disputed boundaries.

Moshoeshoe/Moshesh was given an ultimatum to retire behind the Warden Line by February 28, 1865 – but they failed to heed the warning.

The second Free State-BaSotho War (Basoetuland war) was thus declared by OFS President Sir John Henry (Jan) Brand on May 29, 1865 and started in June 1865, with a number of clashes bitterer than the first. Four BaSotho impi's fanned out and ravaged the Free State. One laid waste to the Smithfield district; another got as far as Brandfort; a third reached the Geldenhuys stronghold of Kroonstad and the fourth attacked Natal. H. Pretorius, a brother of Andries, his three sons and a man named Smit was murdered on 27th June 1965

The Boers were reinforced by a large number of volunteers from across white South Africa, who converged on Thabo Bosiu, attacking and reducing local strongholds along the way. President Jan Brand arrived on 14th August and held a council of war. It was decided to mount an assault on the mountain, bombarding the summit and then to storm the main pass to the top, albeit with the resultant loss of Boer leader Louw Wepener, 11 killed and 9 Boers seriously wounded. A William Samuel Wood is also known as a casualty of the Basutos war.

Robbie Preller (Robert Clunie Logie - my great-granduncle, on my grandmother's side) fought in the Basoeto War at Noupoort, Thaba Bosigo and Korannaberg from 1865 to 1868. He was an Assistant-Veldkornet during the war against Sekhukhune, but reverted to an ordinary burger in the war against Mapocho. From 1893 to 1895 he served in the Soutpansberge-occupation Commission.

Moshoeshoe, who was nearly eighty years old, was losing control over his sons. They were intriguing for the succession and indulging in uncoordinated raids. In January 1866 the Basutos attacked Bethlehem and Winburg, but the attacks were easily beaten off. Some of Moehesh's sons were killed and the Basutos were beginning to feel the pinch of war. Moshesh treated for peace, which was signed in April 1866. The peace was a mere truce and war broke out again. Guerrilla warfare continued well into July 1867.

The Free State commandos destroyed Sotho property so relentlessly that Molopo, Moshoeshoe's second son, whom Moshoeshoe had placed as his chief in the northern part of the kingdom, surrendered, and Moshoeshoe himself signed a treaty ceding much of the kingdom. But hostilities continued.

Further research is needed to establish what role Johannes Albertus Geldenhuys and his son played. Recovering stolen cattle and reciprocating action for attacks in the Kroonstad areas would most likely be very safe bets.

The fighting spluttered on until early 1868 when Moshoeshoe persuaded the British to intervene. The Free State was on the verge of achieving a complete victory over a demoralised and famished enemy when, dramatically, Sir Philip Wodehouse, Governor of the Cape Colony and British high commissioner for South Africa, annexed Lesotho, resulting in the control of the BaSotho kingdom passing to the British. Moshoeshoe died on Thaba Bosiu on March 11, 1870, aged 84.

Lesotho continued to experience internal political turmoil. They suffered from intense rivalries among the chiefs, notably among Moshoeshoe's sons and grandsons. Moreover, Great Britain, who had annexed "Basutoland" in 1868, incorporated it in the Cape Colony in 1871. Resentment by the chiefs led to a popular uprising in 1880. Using guerrilla tactics honed in their wars against the Orange Free State, some 23,000 armed and mounted Sotho warriors outmanoeuvred the government's poorly led amalgam of white, Coloured, and African police, volunteers, and conscripts. Eventually, the colonial government suspended the disarmament legislation and implored Britain to reassume responsibility for Basutoland, which Britain did in 1884.

KROONSTAD & BOTHAVILLE HISTORY

Kroonstad or Cronstad originally, was established on 20th April 1855 when the Winburg magistrate Joseph N Orpen auctioned the first 21 plots for a total of £331:10:0. Johannes Albertus Geldenhuys bought the premium Plot No 10 for the above average price £16:2:6. His immediate neighbour to his left (Plot No 9) was Theuns Louw Botha. Unbeknown to them at the time, little did they realise that their grandchildren would one day marry (Oudad and Oumam). In fact, their other close neighbours would also influence their lives. On plot number 8 was Johannes Gerhardus Dreyer, and further down Murray Street was the Voortrekker Charles Cilliers at No 12 – of Sarel Celliers fame. On No 6 was David Daniel Malan. Is it thus small wonder that the Geldenhuyse, Botha's, Dreyers and Malans would intermarry? The Preller's would arrive later and also became large landowners in the district.

Winburg deserves a brief mention. It was situated on the major Voortrekker route from the Cape to the "interior". Just outside the town was the birthplace of highly popular Free State President Steyn. The Voortrekker Monument is now erected in close proximity – to pay tribute to such great men like Potgieter, Pretorius – and Celliers.

Johannes Albertus and Hendrik Jacobus Geldenhuys bought farms in the district – Doornspruit and Doornbult. The latter is on the road to Bothaville.

A further read of Dot Serfontein's *Keurskrif vir Kroonstad* is highly commended. It documents Kroonstad's history completely. It also contains valuable Geldenhuys historical facts.

Bothaville, in the north-west Orange Free State, owes its founding to Lizzie Preller's father-in-law – Theunis Louis Botha – on her mothers side of the family, and also latterly to her father, Abraham Christoffel Naudé Preller. Theunis Louis Botha bought the eight thousand morgen farm Gladdedrift in 1873 from the estate of the Voortrekker "Lang Piet"

Theunis Louis Botha - owner of Botharnia

– Jacob Pieter van Wyk. The Voortrekker had acquired Gladdedrift for a song – *"vir 'n appel en 'n ei"* – on 31st June 1852, from Lukas Ignatius Dreyer. Not much is known of Dreyer, except that he was granted the property on 7th December 1849 (Authors note: See also the Dreyer's of Kroonstad). The farm derived its name from the well-known ford through the Vals River, which bisected the farm. The neighbouring, downstream sub-division, De Bank, features prominently in the Preller generation.

Gladdedrift was situated in the ward or district "Onder-Valsrivier of Kroonstad". Around 1870, other families other than the Botha's, had lived and inter-married, who would also feature in the establishment of the town Bothaville. The whole community was blood related in one form or another. It was thus that Oom "Kil" Dreyer, whose daughter, Elizabeth, was married to Theunis Botha. That is where Oumam Lizzie got her name! Incidentally, Lourens Petrus Greyling lived on the western adjoining farm "Balkfontein". His daughter was married to his neighbour Lang Piet van Wyk's (the Voortrekker) son, Christiaan Johannes – who farmed on his fathers farm across the river until it was sold to Theunis Botha. At about that time, Abraham Christoffel Naudé Preller, was chief clerk in the commercial trading firm in Kroonstad. He was married to Heiltjie Levina, a daughter of Theunis Botha. This connection only became evident to the writer many years later when I researched the first batch of property owners in Kroonstad. Even then the Botha's and Prellers' were neighbours – no wonder their children inter-married.

Theunis Botha divided Gladdedrift into four lots on 7th April 1891 – Gladdedrift, Botharnia, Grootdraai, and De Bank. The first three were transferred in his name and he ceded the fourth sub-division to his son-in-law ACN Preller. Preller persuaded Botha to cede the farm with the fountain, north of the Valsrivier, Botharnia, for the purpose of building a church and starting a town. However, another community group favoured establishing the new town at Bothadrift, also known as Onze Rust and then Johannesrust. Turmoil reigned for three years, while each group pleaded their case to Bloemfontein, and tabled memoranda to the Volksraad and President Reitz. Botha jumped the gun though and employed the government land surveyor Theo Thesen to lay out the town and measure off 100 plots, which were sold for prices ranging from R30 to R80. Large areas were set aside for the Dutch Reformed church. On 28th July 1891 the new N.G. church community of Bothaville was founded on Botharnia. In view of the advantage enjoyed by Botha, the Volksraad decided thus *"De Raad erkent het dorp op de plaats Botharnia, onder den naam Bothaville"* – and so the town was officially established on 1st June 1983.

Bothaville has grown into a thriving maize and agricultural producing granary for South Africa – if not for Africa as a whole. The Prellers and Geldenhuys'e were a part of this fine heritage. May our offspring be proud of their forefathers.

FIRST ANGLO-BOER WAR

The decided attempt to keep the Boers landlocked, and the British move to acquire the Transvaal, sparked off a rebellion and the outbreak of the First Anglo-Boer War (or "Eerste Vryheids Oorlog " as named by the Afrikaners), which lasted from 1880-81. A point of historical interest is that a Hercules Philip Malan served as a Kommandant in the 1st Vryheidsoorlog in 1880. His father was murdered with Piet Retief in 1837; his elder brother Johannes Augustinus died aged 14 with Piet and Dirk Uys at Italeni in 1838; and his younger brother was known as Jacob "Kaffer" Jacobus Malan, born 16th January 1820. (Incidentally, Piet Uys junior, a younger brother to Dirk, was massacred with his eldest son 40 years later at the Zulu battle of Hlobane, in support of British Evelyn Wood and Redvers Buller left flank column during Lt General Chelmsford's invasion of Zululand). In any event, the Boers rebelled and regained their independence with a victory at Majuba Hill on 27th February 1881.

The war was sparked off when a Transvaal Boer, Petrus Bezuidenhout in late 1880, refused to pay his taxes. The landdrost ordered the seizure of his wagon. This action precipitated a general meeting on the Geldenhuys farm Paardekraal (near where Krugersdorp stands today – the farm was co-owned by a S.J. Kaltwasser), and which resulted in the armed rising by the Boers. Commandos quickly cut off the imperial garrisons in the Transvaal and invaded Natal, where they inflicted a series of defeats on ineptly led British forces, at Laing's Nek and Majuba Hill in 1881. The brief war culminated when a commando stormed Majuba Mountain in broad daylight and virtually annihilated the 280 British soldiers on the summit.

The popular clamour for a British revenge was resisted, and in August 1881 British commissioners signed a convention giving the Transvaal "complete self-government, subject to the Suzerainty of Her Majesty" – a reservation with no precise meaning. In any event, the boers had won their 'vryheids oorlog'.

By 1887 the British annexed Zululand into Natal: and within the last two decades of the century, the British incorporated Basutoland, Griqualand West, and Pondoland – the final frontier on the eastern coast – into the Cape Colony. The British attempt to incorporate the Transvaal into the proposed confederation failed and never came about. A second outbreak of the Anglo-Boer War 1899-1902 followed – but more about the Tweede Vryheids Oorlog later!

Meanwhile, the British annexed Bechuanaland or modern day Botswana, and had access to the interior as secured by Cecil John Rhodes whose British South Africa Company had been granted mining concessions from Ndebele Chief Lobengula. The Ndebele territory covered almost the entire eastern half of Southern Rhodesia, or modern day Zimbabwe. The BSA Company forces defeated the chief in 1893.

John Robert Dunn (1833-1895) was a character of note during the early history of Natal. Legend has it that he and G.C. Cato shot the last elephant in Natal in 1850. He was also a white chief among the Zulus – having had forty-eight mainly Zulu wives (his first was of Malay descent) and fathered a whole tribe of children - more than 100 hundred coloureds! He became the most powerful and wealthy man along the Natal border in the southern part of Cetshwayo's kingdom. There he accumulated ten thousand followers, and vast herds of cattle. (Thanks for the story, Stu McColl - and especially for recommending *The Washing of the Spears* by Donald R. Morris; the story of *The Rise and Fall of the Zulu Nation*).

In 1879, Anna Elisabeth ("Lizzie") was born to Abraham Christoffel Naudé Preller and his first wife, Helletta Lephina Botha. Her mother died when she was ten years old. When she was twenty, Lizzie Preller married Johannes Albertus Geldenhuys, on 27th June 1899 – a mere four months before the outbreak of the second Anglo-Boer War.

However, short of jumping the gun, it may interest some readers for us to go back a little into 'history'.

It is perhaps appropriate, at this juncture, to mention [1] Rhodesian pioneers but more specifically [2] the Thomas Moodie trek to Chipinga / Melsetter in Rhodesia in 1892-3 - and to trace his descendants to Courtney and Brendan Jelley. Courtney and Brendan's grandmother, Margaret Mary Elaine Jelley (maiden name Whiteley) was a great-granddaughter of Margery Hester Coleman (maiden name Moodie) who was the granddaughter of "stamvader" Benjamin Moodie.

Take a minute to look up the ***Abbreviated*** Moodie genealogy, as listed in the last chapter of this book – specifically from Benjamin Moodie to Courtney and Brendan Jelley:-

--------------------------------O--------------------------------

RHODESIAN PIONEERS

A great-great-grandfather to Courtney and Brendan Jelley, Trooper Sydney Nathaniel Arnott was a member of the Pioneer Corps that raised the Union Jack at Fort Salisbury on the 13th September 1890. Arnott was grandfather to Margaret Elaine Whiteley, married to William Patterson Jelley. Then during the 1896 Rebellion, Arnott again features in Rhodesian history when the heroic rescue of the stranded Alice Mine and Mazoe settlement were carried out by the now well-known Mazoe Patrol of a mere 13 Volunteers – on the 21st June 1896. A month later Sydney Arnott was wounded near Hartley. Sydney's other exploits are also mentioned in slightly more detail in the Dictionary section of this genealogy record. The photographs were scanned from the excellent library of books maintained by Grahame and Renene Jelley.

Rhodesian Pioneer Column camp

Fort Salisbury - Flag raising - 13 September 1890 by Major Frank Johnson of the Pioneer Corp

Actual photograph taken to record the raising of the flag – no apology is made for the poor reproduction. What is important, is the event, 13th September 1890.

Raising the Union Jack - Fort Salisbury
13 September 1890

See caption above – on what appears to be a drawing or painting illustrating the raising of the flag when the Pioneer Corps reached their objective, and thereby established the siteing of Salisbury

HOISTING THE FLAG, SEPTEMBER 13TH, 1890

Nesbitt and Arnott

In the picture on the left, Trooper Sydney Arnott is standing next to, and slightly behing the expedition leader, Captain Richard Nesbitt – with the full photograph reproduced below.

Nesbitt was decorated with the Victoria Cross and everyone else earned the Mashonaland Medal.

MAZOE PATROL and ALICE MINE SURVIVORS - June 1896
Top Row: Berry, Zimmermann, Pascoe (on roof), and George (driver)
Standing; Capt R Nesbitt, Sydney Arnott, A Nesbitt, Harbord, O Zimmerman, Ogilvie, Salthouse, Fairbairn, Spreckley, Niebuhr, Darling, Carton-Coward, Hendrikz, Henfrik and Honey
Front Row: Edmonds, McGregor, Mrs Cass, Mrs Salthouse, Mrs Dickinson Judson and Pollett

---------------------------------------0---------------------------------------

MOODIE TREK

Benjamin Moodie is reckoned to be the Moodie "Stamvader" in South Africa. Benjamin was a trader and coloniser. He was born in Melsetter, Orkney Islands (Scotland) on New Year's day 1789. In February 1817 his father James transferred to him as tenth Laird the already heavily mortgaged property, Melsetter. About this time he and a partner, a Cape Town merchant decided to subsidise the passage to the Cape of some displaced, skilled Scottish labourers. On 5th May 1817 he sailed with the first fifty of them. Subsequently his partner left him in the lurch and he was forced to sell Melsetter. This, however, did not yield the money necessary and he could not continue his scheme; but he himself immigrated with his family to the Cape Colony.

In 1817 he bought the farm Melkhoutboom near Swellendam and by subsequent purchases developed this property into a large family farm called Grootvaders Bosch. He was, however, essentially a coloniser and in 1840 he was entrusted with the execution of a new emigration scheme which, however, also failed owing to a lack of financial support. Benjamin's youngest brother, John Wedderburn Dunbar Moodie arrived at Cape Town on 12th September 1819, followed by younger brother Donald's arrived with the 1820 Settler emigration to the Cape colony. The three of them visited the George and Swellendam districts – with John and Donald given land in the abortive settlement at Fredericksburg, beyond the Fish River.

Family interest in the Melsetter and Chipinga areas was rekindled when Grahame Jelley and Renene Geldenhuys build their home in Chipinga (Doc Grahame established and expanded the Chipinga Clinic – before immigrating to New Zealand. However, back to the good old gold-rush days - - - and diamond diggings for the Malan brothers.

Meanwhile, the gold rush was on. Several Geldenhuys' were in, on the ground floor so to speak. The most noteworthy, Dirk Cornelis Geldenhuys, and the most unfortunate, had stakes in portions of the Witwatersrand farms of Langlaagte, Braamfontein, Elandsfontein and Paadekraal.

The others were F.D., F.E., L.D. and R. Geldenhuis.

Dirk Cornelis directed most of his efforts on Braamfontein and was basically out-manoeuvred by J.B. Robertson. Anyway, by 1895, the deepest shaft intersection of the reef was the Main Incline of the Geldenhuys Deep mine which had been extended to 473 feet beyond the No 1 Vertical Shaft, some 2 200 feet from the outcrop measured on the dip. The "deep level" mines were only deep in the sense that they were not on the outcrop of the reef. None of them, at that stage, held ground under which the reef lay more than 1 000 feet below the surface. And so later mines that were deep level in the accepted sense of the term and have followed the reef down to depths of 11,000 feet below the surface in 1970 followed them.

The story of Dirk Cornelis, his brother Lourens and third brother Frans Eduard (or Edward) are far from being told. As Rand pioneers they have deep roots in the founding of Johannesburg, the development of the Rand Gold Mines and their humanitarian efforts in the founding of schools and cemeteries! They concerned themselves literally from the cradle to the grave.

Melville Koppies, Emmarentia, Lourens Geldenhuys, Judith, West Park – all make for fascinating personal history.

Lourens and Emmarentia Geldenhuys. They had fifteen children of whom the eight shown survived. Deaths were mainly due to diphtheria. The children, in roughly by age, include Emma, Frank, Marie, Frans, Elsa, Louw, Jurie, Eunice and 'Timo' Timotheus.

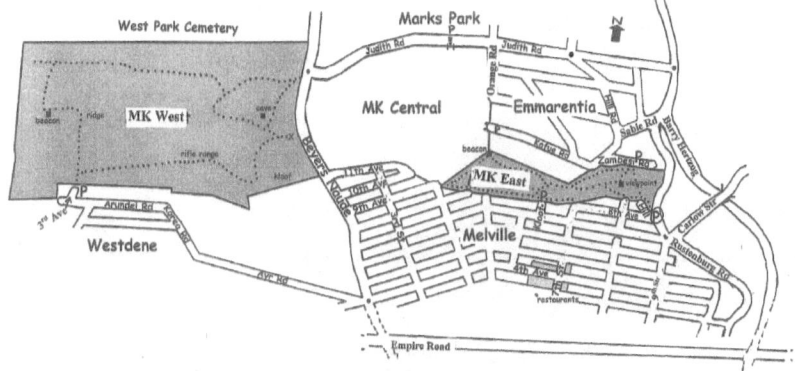

MK = Melville Koppies

This dramatic statue stands at the entrance to the Womens Museum and Monument, in Bloemfontein, commemorating the Anglo-Boer War 1899 – 1902.

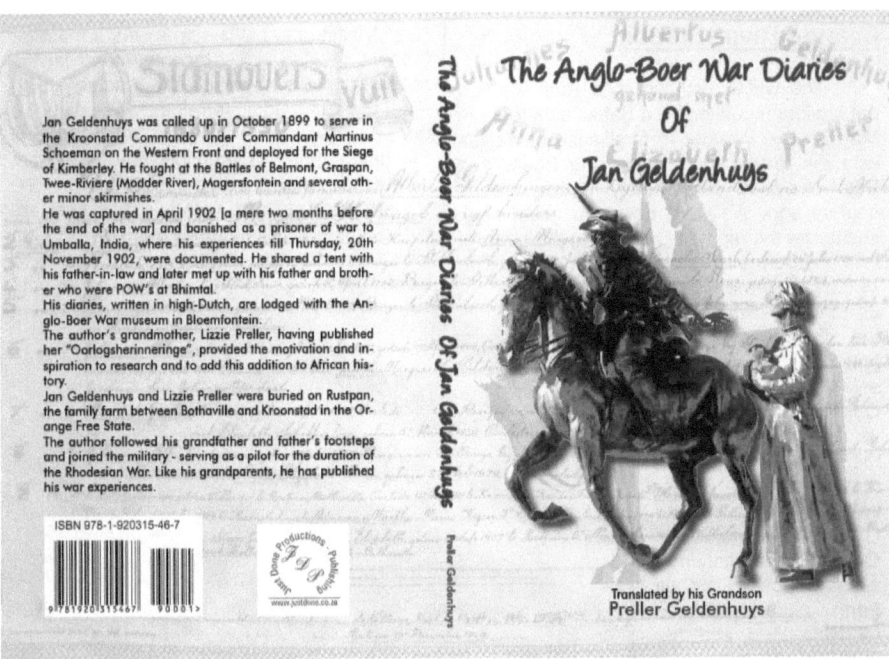

Jan Geldenhuys was called up in October 1899 to serve in the Kroonstad Commando under Commandant Martinus Schoeman on the Western Front and deployed for the Siege of Kimberley. He fought at the Battles of Belmont, Graspan, Twee-Riviere (Modder River), Magersfontein and several other minor skirmishes.

He was captured in April 1902 (a mere two months before the end of the war) and banished as a prisoner of war to Umballa, India, where his experiences till Thursday, 20th November 1902, were documented. He shared a tent with his father-in-law and later met up with his father and brother who were POW's at Bhimtal.

His diaries, written in high-Dutch, are lodged with the Anglo-Boer War museum in Bloemfontein.

The author's grandmother, Lizzie Preller, having published her "Oorlogsherinneringe", provided the motivation and inspiration to research and to add this addition to African history.

Jan Geldenhuys and Lizzie Preller were buried on Rustpan, the family farm between Bothaville and Kroonstad in the Orange Free State.

The author followed his grandfather and father's footsteps and joined the military - serving as a pilot for the duration of the Rhodesian War. Like his grandparents, he has published his war experiences.

ISBN 978-1-920315-46-7

The Anglo-Boer War Diaries Of Jan Geldenhuys

Translated by his Grandson
Preller Geldenhuys

The 'Afskeid' statue also formed the cover of the writers book which records the war experience and capture of Johannes Albertus Geldenhuys, set against the watercolour of the Geldenhuys Genealogy chart that was drawn up for the writers grand-father.

The clever design of the book cover was done by John Dovey of Just Done Productions Publishing. Immediately behind the Afskeid / farewell statue, is the faint water-colour print of the "Bittereinde" or bitter-end statue – essentially representing the beginning, and the end of the three-year Anglo Boer War of 1988 to 1902. When the cover of the book is opened fully, one can still recognise the "Stamouers van Johannes Albertus Geldenhuys gehuud met Anna Elizabeth Preller" – the forefathers of my grandparents.

Visitors to the Anglo-Boer War museum in Bloemfontein will need to climb the hill behind the museum, to get to the Bittereinde statue which is erected, very appropriately and albeit out of sight, for the average visitor to realise its significance.

ANGLO-BOER WAR of 1899-1902

The Boer and Briton dispute in South Africa is known by several names: the War of Independence (*Vryheidsoorlog*), the Second War of Independence, the Great Boer War, the South African War and the Engelse Oorlog. To re-cap, the second Anglo-Boer War occurred over another British attempt to annex the Transvaal. This time the Boers were defeated.

Oudad Jannie Geldenhuys was involved in the British victories at the Battle of Belmont on 23rd November 1899, Graspan and Enslin two days later, despite the British taking heavier casualties. Oudad Jannie had a very narrow escape from death during the Belmont battle, when his horse was fatally wounded and with Oudad cutting his saddle loose and only then making good his escape from the battlefield.

The Anglo-Boer War Diaries of Jan Geldenhuys was published by the writer during November 2009. This tells the story as he told it. It also compliments the book that printed by the writers grandmother, Anna Elizabeth 'Lizzie' Geldenhuys, born Preller.

Orange River Station

The writer, with his wife Rina, carried out a pilgrimage along the Battlefields route in May 2005 – in order to familiarise ourselves with the terrain, over which the Boers and Brits came to such heavy blows over a century ago. We were bold enough to seek shelter for the night at Oranje – in the heart of Afrikanerdom in the "New" South Africa. The owners of Herberg Oranje kindly arranged for us to be shown around the British stronghold that had been established at what Oumam had described as "the Groot River" – the Orange River, forming the border between the Cape and Orange Free State. The Orange River Station is situated on Dornbult Farm, currently owned by Rina Wiid and her husband. Its location is now easily recognisable by the subsequent erection of huge grain silos visible for miles around.

Battle of Belmont
– 23 November 1899

The first action, recorded in Rina Wiid's "Die Oranjerivierkampe" occurred on 9th November when Kommandant van der Merwe's commando had a skirmish with Colonel Gough's two squadrons of the 9th Lancers – losing Lt Col Keith Falconer killed and Lt Wood fatally wounded. Lord Methuen arrived on the 12th to take over command of the British forces.

Minor clashes occurred on the 21st and 22nd while Lt-General Methuen moved his forces 19 km from the Orange River Station. At Belmont the Free Staters had less than a hundred casualties, whereas the British suffered over 300 dead, wounded and missing – which included General Featherstonhaugh. Boer General Prinsloo withdrew his commandos the 21 kilometres east to Ramdam, across the Free State border.

Visiting the battle scene was a must for the writer – and highly recommended for the reader. There is not much at the actual siding – but the surrounding terrain is fascinating. To the south-west of the rail and road is Finchams' Farm, surrounded by hills, with plenty of water - a green oasis in the wilderness of an arid Karoo. To the east are two prominent hill features – Vernier and Gun Hills – the obvious choice for the Boers who would have commanding views over the

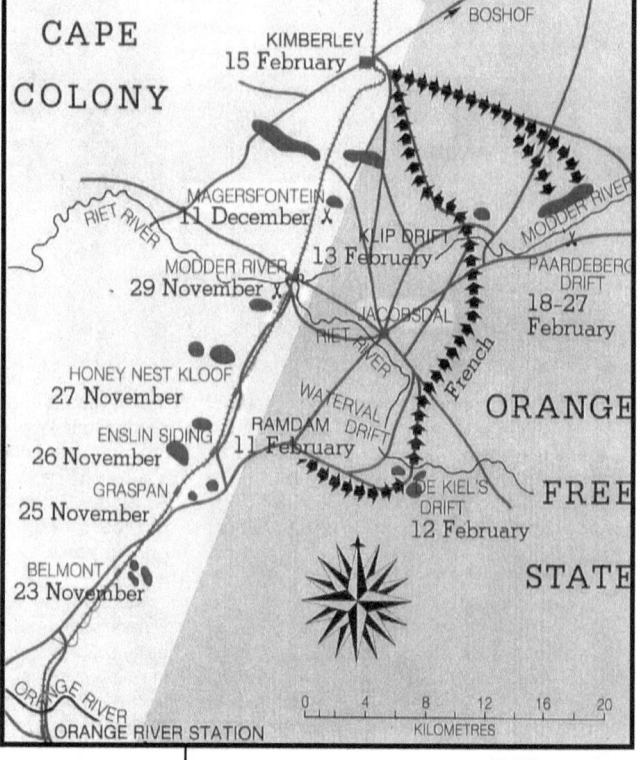

valley floor leading to the Orange River Station. And from where the British movements would be spotted while maintaining their own invisibility – and thus element of surprise – so essential from a principle of war is concerned. It was this action that my Grandfather Ou Dad Johannes Albertus Geldenhuys took part in – together with his younger brother Pieter and father-in-law Braam Preller.

Addendum: During a subsequent visit to the battlefield with my sister Delene and her husband Stu McColl, and after having collected my grandfather's diaries from the Bloemfontein Boer Museum, this second visit prompted me to translate the high Dutch and published 'The Anglo-Boer War Diaries of Jan Geldenhuys' in November 2009, as already mentioned. It was here that Ou Dad had the narrowest of escapes. He had his horse shot from under him, and with bullets lodging in his saddle pack immediately behind him.

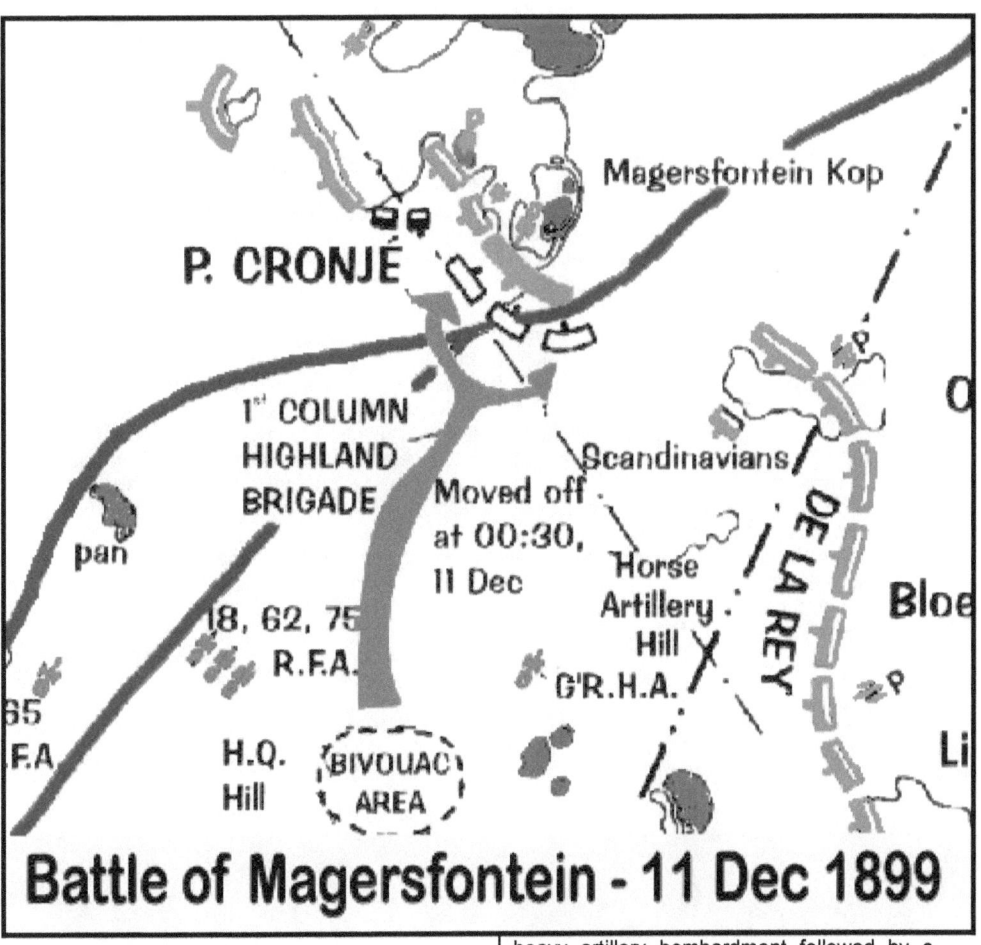

Battle of Magersfontein - 11 Dec 1899

Battle of Graspan –
25 November 1899

Gen. Koos de la Rey had arrived to command the Battle of Graspan two days later on the 25th, and after some fierce fighting, withdrawing the Boers just in time – but for the loss of pro-Boer millionaire Uitlander Jeppe. Once again the Boers suffered fewer casualties than the British.

Battle of Enslin

At the Battle of Enslin the British continued to follow the same tactics of a heavy artillery bombardment followed by a frontal infantry attack, and again it resulted in a Boer retreat at the cost of heavy British casualties. The action lasted some six hours, with the Boers making good their escape during the hours of darkness. The Brits were thus able to advance on to Klokfontein – being within striking distance of Modder River, as well as having the advantage of an adequate supply of water for men and beast.

It should have been clear to Methuen by this time (Belmont, Graspan and Enslin), that the mobility of the Burghers enabled them to fight delaying battles, inflicting heavy casualties on the attacking force with minimum losses to themselves and then beat a hasty retreat, safe in the knowledge that, ideal though the terrain was for cavalry, the British force was quite unbalanced in this direction and that what it did have was hopelessly outshone by the tough veld-bred ponies used by the Boers. The road to Kimberley was to be no walkover and that the Boers would be found defending every ridge and group of hills.

Battle of the Modder River –
28 November 1899

At the Battle of Modder River (also sometimes referred to as the Battle of Tweeriviere – Riet and Modder) on 28th November 1899, General Methuen suffered a reversal with the loss of over 500 men, mainly due to the brilliant tactic employed by Gen. Koos de la Rey – of digging in the Boers along the top edges of the riverbanks. The shallow trajectory of the Boer rifle fire resulted in the British falling like ninepins. The Boers withdrew during the night to take up defensive positions at Magersfontein. It was a hollow victory for the British, despite, de la Reys' son being killed at Modder River (he was wounded at Modder river, died at Jacobsdal, and buried at the Burgher Monument – some five kilometres north-east of Magersfontein).

Battle at Magersfontein –
11 December 1899

The Battle at Magersfontein – near Jacobsdal – on 11th December 1899 was a major victory for the Boers. de la Rey, with remarkable military acumen, had the Boers dug in a narrow trench stretching across some 19 kilometres in a crescent at the foot of the hills. Cronje would not accept de la Rey's plan, but was overruled by President Steyn who had just arrived to bolster the Free Stater's morale. In a driving thunderstorm and in the dead of night, 4000 British Highlanders commanded by Major General 'Andy' Wauchope (pronounced War-cup) that led the attack on Magersfontein. The men, at first in close formation, were about 500 meters from the hills when ordered to deploy. Suddenly a terrifying barrage of fire opened at point blank range. Thousands of Boer rifles, almost at ground level, were directed at the British with such intensity that they had the effect of machine guns.

Methuen's artillery onslaught against Magersfontein koppie the day before proved a wasted effort for most of the Boers were not on the hills as he had believed, but safely in the trenches below (Trench warfare was certainly a very novel one at the end of the 19th century).

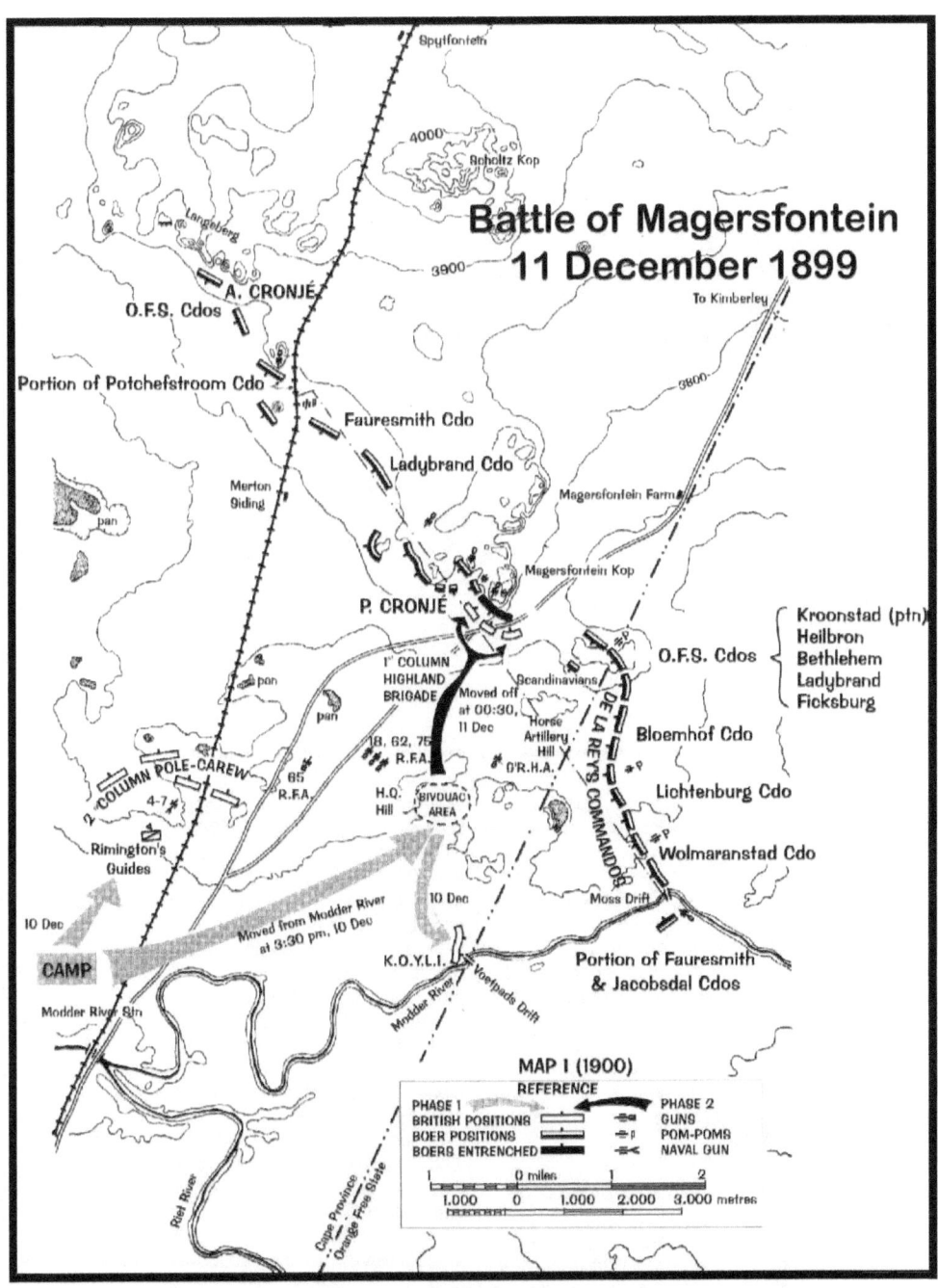

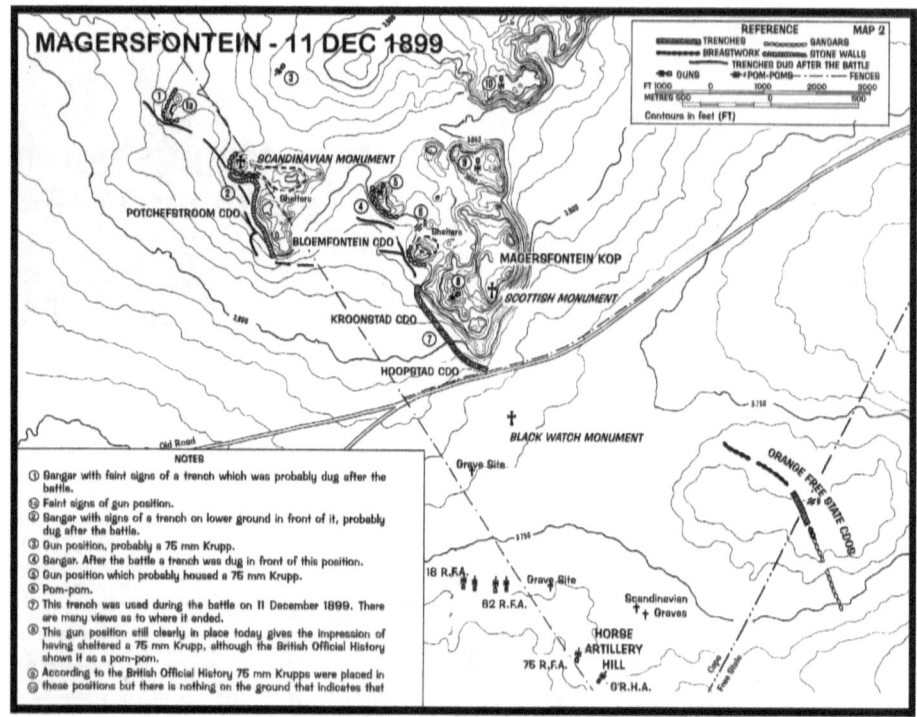

Andy Wauchope was struck down within the opening moments – and Oumam records that the Major General fell a mere 14 paces from Ou Dad's Kroonstad Commando – mortally wounded and destined to die moments later. The British casualties numbered over 1000; the Boers had lost 250. The mighty British army was stopped in its tracks by a brilliantly fought battle by the Boers. Every Afrikaner needs to do a pilgrimage to this battle ground, at least once, during their lifetimes. It was a very profound, awe inspiring time, to stand at the well preserved viewing platform and to cast one's gaze towards Modder River.

Scholtz Neck and Armoedskopie

Scholtz Neck and Armoedskopie warrant special mention. Whilst neither played any significant role during this phase of the War, the writer went to great lengths to establish the relationship of the locations, since mention had been made in Oumam's *Oorlogsherinnige*. The Battle of Langeberg is well signposted to the west, and slightly beyond, Magersfontein. Spytfontein siding is situated in the saddle between Langeberg and Scholtz kop – about 6 kilometres north of Magersfontein. The writer's research has concluded that General Cronje had intended to set up his main defences around Spytfontein as decided at a council of war held on 29th November, rather than Magersfontein as recommended by General de la Rey. It is a known fact that the British advance to Kimberley tended to follow rigidly along the line of rail – for maintaining his extending lines of supply and communications. It thus makes sense that the writer's grandfather would have spent much time and energy in constructing his scanses and embattlements there (the following day after retreating from the Boer victory at Modder River). At the subsequent Krygsraad held on 4th December, at which President Steyn intervened and sided with de la Rey, the move from Spytfontein (or Scholtz Kop, in the case of my grandfather) to Magerfontein commenced. The Kroonstad Commando was split into three sections – with one section being on the Boers extreme right flank below Langeberg under Andries Cronje; the second section under Piet Cronje immediately below Magerfontein Kop; and with the third platoon part of the O.F.S. Commando's just east of Magerfontein Kop and along the left flank (near the Bloemhof and Lichtenburg commandos commanded by de la Rey).

However, as mentioned earlier, the rapid British advance had been halted at Magerfontein. Cecil John Rhodes, who was under Boer siege in Kimberley, was hopping mad at the slow British progress. His frustration had to endure well over a week – till General French by-passed the Boer defences and managed his breakthrough to Kimberley. This, then, resulted in most of the Free State burghers assembling in the Paardeberg area – which was the most direct route to their Capital, Bloemfontein.

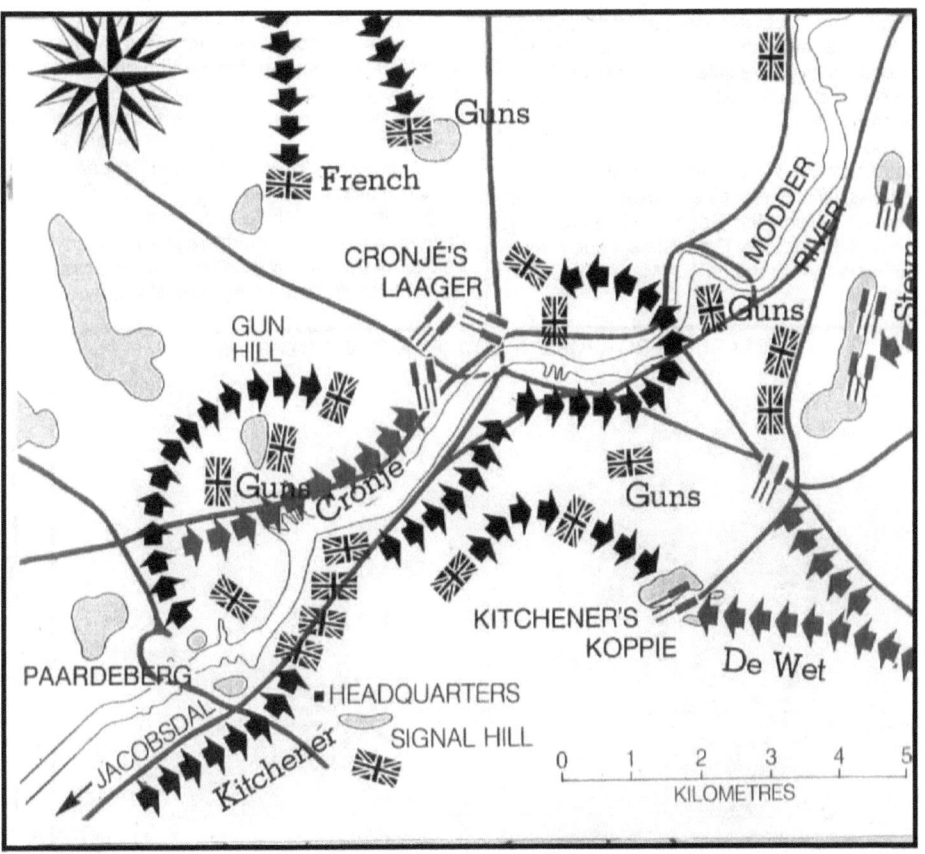

Paardeberg Tragedy – 20 to 27th February 1900

After Gen French relieved Kimberley, he successfully intercepted General Cronje, who had laagered some distance upstream along the Modder River, at Wolveskraal. Lord Roberts had taken ill and Kitchener assumed control of the British forces. With Cronje being quickly surrounded, he fought delaying tactics and withstood terrific artillery pounding for nearly ten days. General de Wet came to Cronje's rescue, and offered an opportunity to escape south across the river. Danie Theron had managed to crawl through the British cordon – and repeated his heroic performance by returning unscathed to de Wet – with the message that the bulk of Cronje's Kommandante had voted not to abandon the women and children – and then surrendered to Roberts.

51

The loss of some four thousand Boers was a terrible blow to Boer morale – in fact it was the turning point in the Boer War.

Poplar Grove and Abraamskraal.

President's Paul Kruger and Martinus Steyn had a narrow escape when they were caught unawares at Poplar Grove, and beat a hasty retreat to Abraamskraal. Rina and I were fortunate to study this last ditch stand against the British onslaught. The magnificent rock skanse are still standing 105 years after the event – and requires binoculars to appreciate how well the Boers were in fact camouflaged amongst the rocky outcrops. It is rumoured that Kruger was forced to use his shambok to exhort the Boers not to surrender so easily to Lord Roberts' killing machine. However, despite this last bastion the Boers gave hardly any resistance and the Free State capital thus fell easily to Roberts on 13th March 1900.

Rhodesians under Lt.-Col. H.C.O. Plumer to secure the railway initially up to Gaberone and subsequently to Ramathlabama (just north of Mafeking). Plumer was reinforced by Canadians and New Zealanders (via Beira, Zeedeberg stagecoach, and Bulawayo line of rail – as originally feared by the Boer High Command). Plumer joined up with Colonel Bryan T. Mahon – Lord Robert's specially appointed Flying Column, and they both successfully relieved General Robert S.S. Baden-Powell in Mafeking on 17th May 1900.

A Lotter also featured during the declaration of hostilities during the Anglo-Boer War. It is known that he, together with Scheepers, Kritzinger and Malan operated south of the Orange River, in the Colesberg – Noupoort district. (As opposed to de Wet in the Free State; Botha, Beyers and Viljoen in ZAR/Transvaal, de le Rey / Kemp in Klerksdorp – Mafeking area; and Maritz / Jannie Smuts in north-western Cape). Further research will be needed to establish his contribution to the outcomes of history.

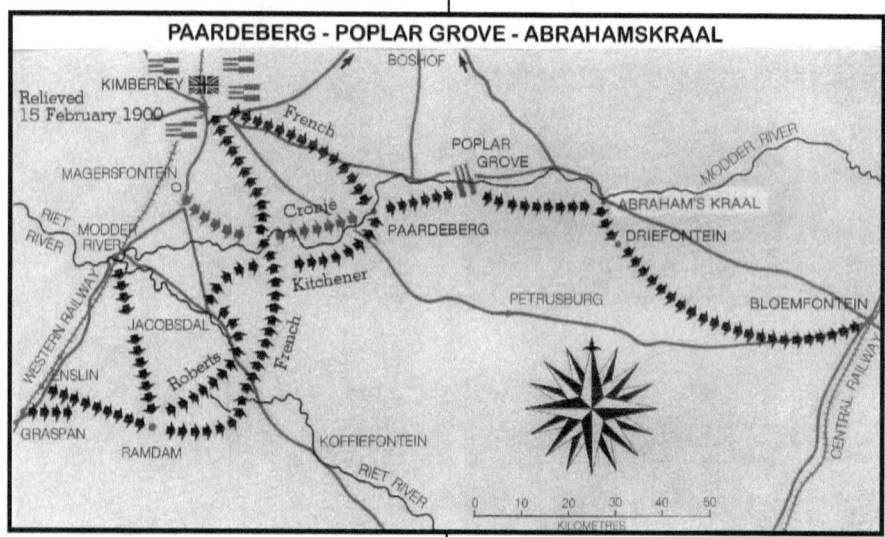

Waterberg - - - -
General Frederik Albertus Grobler, who commanded the Waterberg and Zoutpansberg commandos, was ordered to attack Fort Tuli and then destroy the railway right up to Bulawayo. Pretoria was concerned in the "probability that the English would come via Beira", rail down to relieve Mafeking and march onto the Boer capital (lessons learnt from the ill-fated January 1896 Dr. L.S. Jameson raid). This Gen. Grobler failed to do – and permitted the

According to the *Malan-gedenkboek*, page 53, a Komdt Hercules Philip Malan, born 2nd November 1836, died on 2nd December 1899 during the war. General Wynand Charl Malan, born 16th August 1872, from Beyersfontein, Murraysburg, was also a famous Boer general, who went to Tanganyika in 1907. Komdt Abram Hugo Malan, 14th child of Carel Wynand and Magdalena Hugo, married Hendrina Joubert, daughter of Boer General Piet Joubert.

Robert Clunie Logie Preller (born 5th May 1846, the fourth son and seventh child of Carel Frederik) had married Stephanie Maria Aletta Schoeman – daughter of Kommandant-General Stephanus Schoeman. During the war he fought the Brits on the Colesberg, southern front. I should mention that he served with distinction in the Colesberg and Philippolis areas and is quoted extensively by Professor Fransjohan Pretorius, historian at the University of Pretoria, in his "*Kommandolewe Tydens die Anglo-Boereoorlog 1899-1902*", which was published by Human and Rousseau in 1991. In fact, it is believed that Kmdt Preller also served as the "Landdros of Philippolis" and Chairman of the "Krygsraad" during November 1899 / January 1900, when he sentenced a burger to fourteen days imprisonment or the payment of a £5 fine for drunkenness! As already mentioned, Robbie Preller had fought in the Basoeto War at Noupoort, Thaba Bosigo and Korannaberg from 1865 to 1868. From 1893 to 1895 he served in the Soutpansberge-occupation Commission.

Their son Gustav Schoeman Preller served in the State artillery and took part in major battles in Natal: Dundee, Modderspruit, Colenso and Platrand (Wagon hill), Ladysmith (6.1.1900). By May 1900 Gustav was back in Pretoria to help the State Attorney, J.C. Smuts, move the Government's gold bars from Pretoria to safety. He continued to serve in the artillery and became the War Correspondent. Four months before the war ended, he was taken prisoner near Ermelo and sent to India (his father, Robbie Preller, was also captured later on during the War– after having been wounded – on the 7 September 1901, and sent to India as a POW)..

Bloemfontein, the Free State capital fell on 13th March, Kroonstad on 12th May 1900.

My grandfather Jannie Geldenhuys took leave of absence on the 30 March 1900, to be with my grandmother who was expecting her first baby. A month's leave was granted, but on finding a substitute, this was extended to two months, in order for my grandfather to be present with the birth of his daughter. It was during this time that the Free State fortunes changed dramatically – with regard to the rapid inroads made by the British. De Wet had given the Boers permission to return to their homes after Bloemfontein fell – which I am sure significant influence on the majority of demoralised burgers. Ou Dad Jannie Geldenhuys took full advantage to witness the birth of his daughter Hettie on the 2nd

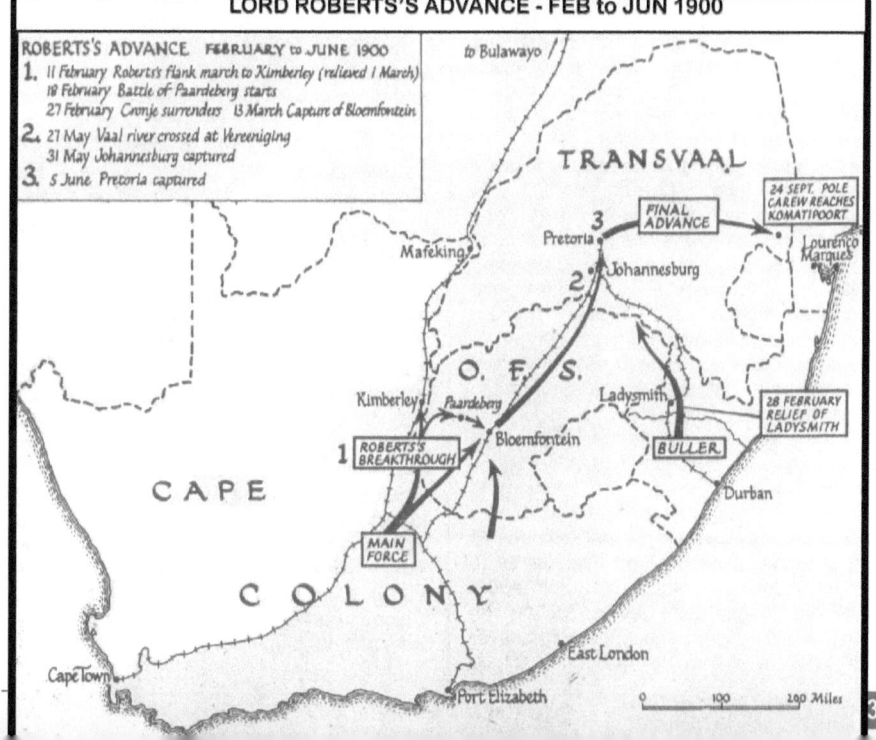

May 1900 – and a month later summoned to re-join his Commando and proceed to Waterberg (that would be the last time that he saw his daughter alive).

General CR de Wet wrote in his "*Three Years War*" about Thring as follows: . . . At Kroonstad there was not a single burgher left. Only the inhabitants of the township remained, and they were too ready to "hands-up." One of these, however, was of a different mould. I refer to Veldcornet Thring, who had arrived with me at Kroonstad that morning, but who had suddenly fallen ill. On the day following he was a prisoner in the hands of the English. Thring was an honourable man in every way. Although an Englishman by birth, he was at heart an Afrikaner, for he had accepted the Orange Free State as his second fatherland. Like many other Englishman, he had become a fellow-citizen of ours, and had enjoyed the fat of the land. But now, trusty burgher that he was, he had drawn his sword to defend the burgher's rights. His earliest experiences were with the Kroonstad burgers, who went down into Natal (fought at Ladysmith); later on he fought under me at Sanna's Post (sabotaging the Bloemfontein water works and supply), and Mostertshoek, and took part in the siege of Colonel Dalgety at Jammersbergsdrift. He had stood at my side at Thaba'Nchu and on the banks of the Zand River (Sand River). I had always found him the most willing and reliable of officers, and he had won the respect and trust of every man who knew him." Now that was quite a praiseworthy commendation coming from the famous General!

A. Lester Thring wrote an unpublished manuscript titled "*Seven Months on commando under Commandant Prinsloo and General De Wet*". He is mentioned briefly in Pretoria University historian Prof. Fransjohan Pretorius' "*Kommandolewe tydens die Anglo-Boereoorlog 1899-1902*". Oumam Lizzie Geldenhuys also mentions him in her "*Oorlogsherinneringe*" where the Vredefort, Kroonstad and Bothaville burgers numbered about two thousand men.

As already mentioned, Ou Dad Geldenhuys was dispatched to Waterberg – and very little has so far been found as to exactly what their whereabouts had been – and where they operated. What is known is that after Johannesburg and Pretoria fell to the British, the Commandos split up into very small groups and were tasked to 'Veg en Vlug' – to 'fight and flee' whenever confronted by overwhelming odds – and to sabotage enemy supply lines – railways and telegraph infrastructures in particular.

Generals Beyers and Kemp make mention of a Geldenhuys in their book titled *Veg en Vlug* – but whether this reference is of my Grandfather, I do not know. All I know is that Oumam writes that he went to Waterberg for several months. Their separation was to last thirteen months – and quite a lot happened during that time. Note: Beyers and Kemp feature as marriage partners to Geldenhuys'se.

Battle of Bothaville –
27 October 1900

General de Wet crossed the Vaal on 27th October while being pursued by General Charles Knox and De Lisle – making good his escape during a violent thunderstorm. Knox and De Lisle headed north, but Colonel Le Gallais's mounted men headed in the opposite direction. De Wet halted near Bothaville to refit, and was caught by surprise by Major Lean with forty men of the 5th Mounted Infantry who stumbled on three weary Boers sleeping upon the veldt. Just beyond the rise was De Wet's laager – over a thousand men sleeping, horses grazing and wagons out spanned. Without a moment to lose, Lean called for reinforcements while opening fire upon the Boer camp. In an instant there was a hive of activity as De Wet rushed for their horses and made good their escape from the killing ground. Meanwhile a rearguard action that occupied an enclosed kraal and a farmhouse kept Lean at bay. This allowed the Boers to make a flanking counter-attack. By this time the reinforcements from Le Gallais had arrived on the scene, but were still outnumbered by the Boers.

The British took shelter in a small stone shed – but it was here that a Ross of the Durhams was wounded, and Colonel Le Gallais got himself killed. A Major Taylor of U gun Battery assumed command and gallantly kept up the barrage of the Boer stronghold. The battle raged on till well past eight-thirty, while several companies of Australians reinforcements also arrived. Just before the British and Australians were about to storm the farmhouse, a white flag was hoisted and 114 Boers surrendered. Nine Boers died, including Veldcornets Jan Viljoen of Heilbron and Van Zijl of the Cape Colony. Between twenty and thirty Boers were wounded that day – including the Stads

Procureur Jacob or Japie de Villiers and Jan Rechter (also spelt Richter - the latter subsequently died as a result of his wounds). De Wet lost six Krupp field guns, a pompom, 20 supply wagons and 1000 head of cattle. The British lost twelve killed (including four officers, one of which was Major Welch) and thirty-three wounded. Thomas Pakenham, in his *The Boer War*, published 1979, claims that 25 Boers were killed and 130 captured, of which 30 were wounded. Surprisingly, he also quotes De Wet's *Three Years War*!

From a Boer perspective, written by Hilogarfste Piet S Lombard, in his "*Uit Die Dagboek van 'n Wildeboer*", De Wets commando had trekked through Bothaville at four o'clock and found the town nearly totally burnt down by the English. They were en route to Hoopstad and arrived at Rooibult where the battle took place, where they were caught by surprise and President Steyn who had a rude awakening just managed to escape on his horse named Boetie. The Boer spies had just returned to the camp to report no danger, and while Lombard was fetching his horse, the surprise attack was sprung. The Presidents buggy, as well as his overcoat and rifle, fell to the Brits as spoils of war. In addition to the casualties already mentioned, Lombard reports that General Froneman, Komdt. Jan Theron and Tom Brain also escaped wounded. He says 120 burgers were captured by the British (Parkenham claims 130, albeit including 30 wounded).

Coen Groenewald writes in "*Bannelinge oor die Oseaan*" that his father, who manned the artillery guns, was captured. The prisoners were robbed of all their valuables – like rings off their fingers, watches, pocket-knives, money and anything else of value. When the Burghers protested that this was blatant robbery, they were bluntly told to "Shut up, you Dutch bastards!" Even bundles of clothing that were taken from the Boers and sold at ridiculous prices to the Blacks who were the trackers for the British. Amongst those captured were two "Kolonialers" who were duly separated from the rest, and never to be seen or heard of since. The rest of the spoils that could not be carried away or disposed of were set alight and burnt to ashes. The prisoners were then force-marched to Kimberley and railed in cattle trucks to Cape Town Groenpuntkamp, where they boarded the troopship Catalonia for Ceylon and the Diyatalawa camp.

Not one, but many Burghers became critically seasick, and died at sea. Doctor Gustav Preller, a prisoner on the Tagus, describes in his book "*Ons Parool*" the burial at sea of Vrystaatse burger C.P. Venter of Wepener, en route to India. Dominee Liebenberg of Bethal conducted the service.

De Wet also reported that . . . "according to English reports, Doctor de Landsheer, a Belgian, was killed in this engagement. The English newspaper asserted that the doctor was found dead with a bandoleer around his body. I can vouch for the fact that the doctor possessed neither rifle nor bandoleer, and I am unable to believe that he armed himself on the battlefield." I would tend to believe De Wet's side of the story.

And so, Bothaville fell to the Brits on 6th November 1900, while the much loved and highly respected Free State President Marthinus Theunis Steyn was conferring with General Christian De Wet. Steyn and De Wet went south, then south-east to Thaba'Nchu and on to attack the British garrison of Dewetsdorp (named after his Voortrekker father) – a town some forty miles to the south-east of Bloemfontein.

Just before the fall of Johannesburg and the end of the war, news had been received of an imminent British attack on the Geldenhuys Deep mine, on Braamfontein (the farm had been purchased by Dirk Cornelis Geldenhuys).

Commandant General Louis Botha had instructed Dr. F.E.T. Krause, the State prosecutor as the Special Commandant, on 29th May, 1902, to abandon the defence of Johannesburg and to save the gold mines at all costs. (Hotheads like Judge Kock whose father, a Boer general, had been killed at Elandslaagte, tried to defy Louis Botha's order to save the mines - intent to destroy and deny the British the gold wealth). Krause met with Roberts to arrange terms for the burghers to vacate Johannesburg and then on 31st May 1902 escorted Lord Roberts and Lord Kitchener for the handover of the main reef gold mining town.

Ou Dad Jannie and Oupa (Abram) Preller were taken prisoner on 23rd February 1902 by Colonel Colleton, and sent to Umballa, India. They were not the only ones – as the list further on testifies. They were captured on the van Rensburg Farm, on the Vaal River. The other three men folk taken into custody included brothers Ernst and Martiens van Biljon; and Frank Brewis. Fortunately, the womenfolk were not molested – but were abandoned and left alone to fend for themselves. These women were Kitty and Lettie van Biljon, Frikkie Brewis and Lizzie Geldenhuys. Then there were also the four van Biljon children – Mara, Millicent, Ivon and Aubry (this was the last time that their father saw them alive!)

Commandant Robert (Robbie) C. Preller was wounded in the Colesberg area on 7th September 1901, taken prisoner and sent to Shajahanpur, India.

Many of them were placed in concentration camps during the war and often reduced to utter poverty. Many of our own direct relatives were taken prisoner and interned in India and Ceylon. In order to secure their release from the Boer Camps, all interns were required to "Declare their Allegiance" to King Edward the VII - which Ou Dad Johannes Albertus Geldenhuys duly signed under duress on 25th August 1902 - nearly three months after the peace declaration of Vereeniging! (This delayed signing is a very interesting story in itself – which is expanded upon elsewhere). The following family (all Geldenhuys, unless otherwise indicated) was all sent overseas: -

- Johannes Albertus – my grandfather – Umballa, India.
- Hendrik Jacobus – My great-grandfather affectionately known as Oubaas, also incarcerated at Umballa, India.
- Pieter – Ou Dad's brother.
- Lourens Geldenhuys – of Braamfontein / Emmarentia fame, surrendered after the fall of Pretoria.
- Lourens Pieter Arnoldus – my great-granduncle – elder brother of Hendrik – who died in Ceylon on 22nd January 1902.
- Hendrik Petrus (Oom Hein) – interned and died on 21st May 1904 at Batticaloa, Ceylon – for refusing to sign the Oath of Allegiance after the war ended.
- Uncle Aap – Umballa – Oupa to the two Attie grandsons (Attie Bok and Attie of Randfontein).
- Dirk C. Geldenhuys – at Green Point. (either Dirk Cornelis or Dirk Christoffel).
- Abram Christoffel Naude Preller – my other great-grandfather – Bhimtal, Himalayas.
- Gustav Schoeman Preller - our grandmother's cousin – India.
- Robert Clunie Logie Preller – my great-granduncle (Gustav's father) – Shajahanpur, India.
- Hennie Schikkerling – Umballa – my Ou Dad's uncle (his sister Elisabeth was married to Hendrik Jacobus Geldenhuys – Ou Dad's father Oubaas).

Gideon Scheepers is one of the 'martyrs' of the Boer War. Like Jacobus Francois Geldenhuijs, he was shamefully executed for fighting a guerrilla type war - - was labelled, accused and convicted of being a rebel. Jacobus Francois Geldenhuys (also spelt Geldenhuijs on some headstones) was a Boer burgher who was executed by firing squad by the British on St. Valentine's Day, 14th February 1902, towards the end of the 1899-1902 Anglo-Boer War. He was the last one shot, after the shameful assassination of Boer martyrs Komdt Gideon Scheepers (less than a month earlier on January 1902).

A monument has been erected in Graaff-Reinet for those Boers who were likewise shot by firing squad to Scheepers and Geldenhuys. They were PJ Fourie, J van Rensburg and LFS Pfeiffer who were executed on 19th August, 1901; Daniel Olewagen and Ignatius Nel on 26th August, 1901; Johannes Hermanus Roux on 7th October, 1901. Permission was granted to the Botha Commission for the exhumation of the Boer soldiers that were executed. It was discovered that the un-slaked lime which had been thrown over the corpses and then watered had formed a hard crust around the bodies instead of destroying them, and had preserved them so well that even the bullet holes were still discernible.

1920's inquiries. A trained historian, he collected letters, interviewed men like Wilfred Harrison, visited Mr and Mrs Scheepers in 1924, studied the original diary and the translations, and sounded out all kinds of people on the matter of Scheepers execution. Talking to the parents in the sitting room at Roodepoort, Preller's eyes kept wandering to the portraits of Gideon Scheepers on the walls. The most haunting was the one taken before his execution, the tragic figure with drooping moustache and famous hat. The parents told Preller that the photograph was taken in the Graaff-Reinet prison at a time when Gideon's temperature was rarely under 100°F.

Two years later Dr Preller wrote to the High Commissioner in London and received a reply in December 1926. The War Office had not recorded the locality of the grave,

Scheepers's first grave was established beyond doubt by the discovery of lumps of lime, pieces of chair and, particularly of his hat, but there was nothing else. So the search continued for the second grave, but this proved fruitless. (Johannes Meintjies – *Sword in the Sand* – Tafelberg-Uitgewers 1969).

My Oumam Lizzie Geldenhuys had written about Scheepers in her *Oorlogs Herinneringe* – and I am also pleased to discover that my Great Uncle Dr Gustav Schoeman Preller also became interested in the Scheepers story. My own interest in Scheepers stems from the fact that because my grandmother fed him and his commando, she had her house burnt down as retaliation by the spiteful British. That is why I just had to carry out a detour to Graaff-Rienet to visit his assassination site (because he was shot for exactly the same thing he was doing to the Cape 'enemy rebels' as Roberts and Kitchener had done to my Oumam!!). Shame!

Whereas most Afrikaners have forgiven the British for destroying their homes, very few have, or ever will, forget these shameful deeds. While the picture on the right is neither Katbos View, De Bank nor Rustpan, it truly depicts what happened widespread in the Free State.

For whatever reason, Gustav Preller became interested in the Scheepers story and began his own

Blowing up and burning farm houses

Before

The explosion

After

but it was presumed to be in the vicinity of Graaff-Reinet. And so, in the absence of finding the second burial site, gallant Gideon became an Afrikaner Martyrdom at the young age of twenty-three. Preller had Nasionale Pers publish his *Scheepers se Daagboek en die Stryd in Kaapland* in 1940.

According to Oumam Geldenhuys, her father (my great-great grandfather), Abraham Christoffel Naude Preller also served as a Kommandant during the Boer War. During the very interesting facts and figures that I came across, what disturbed me most was to discover just how many Geldenhuys casualties there were during the war. I found it rather shocking.

The casualties of the war were: -

Helletje Levina Geldenhuys
Born 2nd May 1900 at Rustpan Bothaville and died 15th August 1901 in the Kroonstad Concentration Camp.
Lourens Pieter Arnoldus Geldenhuys
Born 10 October 1835 in Swellendam and died in captivity in Ceylon, in the Colombo hospital on the 22 January 1902 (Aged 66 years and 3 months).
Dorothea M Geldenhuys
Died 15 February 1902 in Orange River Station concentration camp. She was 4 years old, from Fauresmith – and was buried in grave number 152.
Jacobus Francois Geldenhuijs
Executed 14 February 1902 at Graaff-Reinet. See Scheepers Monument – shamefully shot a month after Komdt Gideon Jacobus Scheepers.
Jacobus Viljoen Geldenhuys
Born 1857 and died in captivity in Ceylon on the 6 January 1901 (aged 44.8)
J.V. Geldenhuis – died in captivity – Diyatalawa.
P.J. Geldenhuis – died en route to Bermuda.
Hendrik Petrus Geldenhuys – died Colombo (Batticaloa), Ceylon (with L.P.A. – Lourens Pieter Arnoldus, above).
J.N. Geldenhuys – at Paardeberg, with the Wolmaranstad Kommando, under General S.P. du Toit.
Komdt. Hercules Philip Malan
Born 2 November 1836, from Rustenburg area, died 2 December 1899
Maria Magdalena (Maraai) Preller
Born 13 December 1899 and died on 5 April 1901 in the Kroonstad Concentration Camp
Johanna Catharina Geldenhuys died 18th January 1902 in the Standerton Refugee camp. She was born in Swellendam during 1862
Johanna Catharina Steyn died 10th September 1901 in the Pietermaritzburg camp. She was born in 1840, and was the wife of Hendrik Petrus who was held in captivity in Ceylon and buried at Batticaloa.

31,000 Boers - 4000 killed in action and 27,927 died in concentration camps, mainly from disease.
15,423 Black people died in concentration camps.
21,000 Anglo - fatalities, plus 52,000 other casualties, including some 62% from disease, out of just fewer than 450,000 troops (357,500 British, 16,715 Australians, 6,400 New Zealanders, 6,000 Canadians and 52,000 of South African descent).

POW and Concentration Camps Conclusions

Diamond Diggings, Lichtenburg.

Shame on you, Britishers and Lord Kitchener in particular! The statistics speak for themselves. How Great the Betrayals – Sand River Convention, the inhumane treatment of defenceless women, children and elderly folk, scandalous incarceration and starvation of all 'so-called' prisoners, and even the reneging of countless undertakings. Ian Smith didn't nearly say it all in his "*Great Betrayal*" following the appeasement of Black Terrorism in 1997. Is it that history was just repeating itself? Despite the British might, vastly superior infrastructure, and having all the wherewithal, they failed to defeat the Boers on the battlefields. Presidents Kruger and Steyn, and Generals like de Wet, de la Rey, Louis Botha, Jannie Smuts, Beyers, Kemp, Hertzog and so many others evaded the British might. At the going down of the sun, and in the morning – let Britain hang its head in shame.

Coen Groenewald, whose father was interned at Diyatalawakamp, published his most enlightening *Bannelinge oor die Oseaan – Boerekrysgevangenes 1899 – 1902*, in 1992. He frequently quoted Dr Gustav Preller, who also came up with very interesting aspects of POW life and personalities. It appears Preller was an intern, or very familiar with the Trichinopolykamp in India. Camps were established in such far-flung countries as Ceylon, Bermuda, St. Helena, Portugal and India – that interned over 32,500 Boere. Groenewald mentions some very interesting escapes. Umballa is strangely omitted from the 28 camps that he mentioned in his book – they were, for the record:-

Abrantes, Alcobaça, Caldas da Rainha, Fort Peniche, Fort de São Juliao da Barra and Tomar – all in Portugal

Bellevue (Simonstown), Groenpunt

Broadbottom, Deadwood (also part 'Blikkiesdorp') – at St Helena

Burtseiland, Darrelseiland, Hawkinseiland, Hinsoneiland, Longeiland, Morganseiland, Nellyeiland, Porseiland, Tuckerseiland – Burmuda

Diyatalawa, Hambantota, Mount Lavinia, Ragama, Urugas and Welikada – Ceylon.

Trichinopoly, Wellington and Umballa – India.

Boer camps totalled a staggering 43 – 17 in India, 8 on the Burmuda Islands, 5 in St. Helena, 5 in Ceylon, plus the 6 refugee camps in Portugal and the two holding camps in the Cape. The Bloemfontein Museum fortunately shows all the POW camps – including Umballa.

As mentioned elsewhere, I luckily, together with my sister Delene, managed to retrieve a copy of Ou Dad Jannie Geldenhuys's Umballa camp experiences!

To say conditions were dreadful would be an understatement. Lizzie Geldenhuys' stories in her '*Oorlogsherinneringe*' are a masterpiece. I must have read it a dozen times, and every time I just marvel at the fortitude and all the hardships that the burghers endured.

The British arrested Jan Christoffel de Waal on 13th May 1901. During the war his farmhouse on Skoorsteenberg, in the Smithfield district, was destroyed and he virtually lost all his stock. Although arrested, he was allowed to live in his house in Bethulie until the end of the war. Thereafter, he sold his farm and continued to live in the Bethulie house until 1912.

The repatriation and re-establishing farming enterprises makes for fascinating reading. On the 10th October 1902 the first lot of Burghers returned from India on board the troop-ship Urania – including 'Oubaas' Jan Geldenhuys (Ou Dad's father), his son Pieter Geldenhuys and Uncle Hennie Schikkerling – who had been interned in the Bhimtal – and who had signed the Oath of Allegiance. My grandfather, Ou Dad Jannie Geldenhuys arrived over a month later, on

Jan A. and A.C.F. Preller GELDENHUYS
05 September 1931

the 12th November 1902 on board the ship Ionian – together with my grandmother's father Braam Preller and Ernst van Biljon. They were quarantined in the Umbilo Camp for eight days before being permitted to continue their journey to Kroonstad. Ou Dad and Oumam thus had their re-union on the 20th November 1902. This was the first time he saw his eldest son Hennie, who was now already four months old!

In 1904, two years after the Anglo-Boer War ended, the widow of Lourens Pieter Geldenhuys applied, and was granted permission, to rebury her husband on his Free State farm – at his descendant's expense.

Abram Carl Frederik Preller was born on 2nd August 1916 on Rustpan, Bothaville OFS – the sixth child of Johannes Albertus and Anna Elizabeth Preller. It will be recalled that the eldest was born and died during the Boer War, 2nd May 1900 to 15th August 1901. The eldest brother, Hendrik Jacobus was born in the Kroonstad Concentration Camp on 12th July 1902. He farmed on Normandy (adjoining Rustpan), married Adrianna Marta Maria Keyser on 28th August 1928 and had two children – Carine and Johannes Albertus. Next came Elizabeth, born 6th November 1904 at Rustpan, married Paul Christiaan Gideon Steyn Jordaan in Bloemfontein on 23rd July 1925 and then continued to farm Rustpan: they had three children – Lulu, Paul and Johannes Albertus. Next born was Anna Elizabeth, also at Rustpan, on 11th September 1907. She married Gideon Malherbe, settled in Stellenbosch and had three sons – Willem who married Louna, Jan (another Johannes Albertus) who married a Peggy, and 'Deon' Gideon. Then Maria Susanna Wilhelmina was born 27th May 1911, also on Rustpan. She married Theo van Rensen and had Elizabeth, Johan and Adrian – she was murdered in her home in Rietondale, Pretoria. Then laat-lammertjie ACFP Geldenhuys was born.

Preller Geldenhuys (senior) was encouraged at an early age to pursue a military career. His father was a veteran of the Boer War, he had served in the capacity of Veldcornet, and as seen in this old photograph taken in September 1941, where Preller proudly poses in uniform as father and son. In fact, his elder brother Henry was also encouraged to join the Commandos.

Gustav Preller, the co-founder of the Afrikaans language and renowned historian, wrote Johannes Albertus Geldenhuys to warn him of war clouds looming in Europe, and the likelihood of Italy siding with Germany. The photograph on the previous page shows father and two sons in uniform during World War II that followed shortly after Gustav Preller's predictions. My Dad is in the uniform of the South African Air Force – my Ou Dad and Uncle Henry in the Army and wearing the ranks of Captain and Lieutenant respectively.

After qualifying as a pilot, Preller was deployed up north – to Abyssinia. That is another chapter.

The Bitter-einde statue - revisited

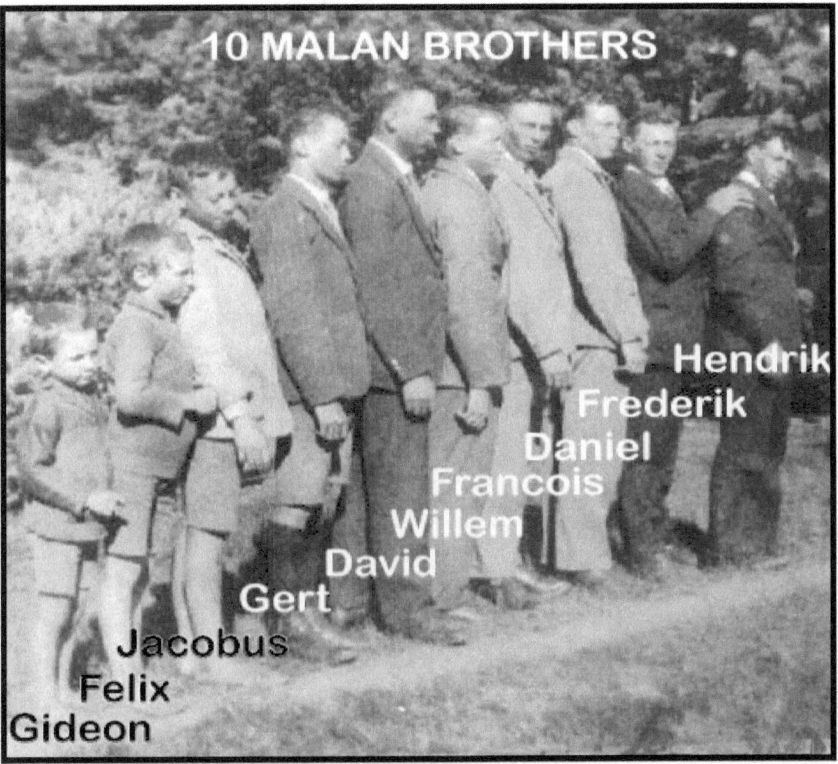

THE MALANS

Meanwhile, a word or two about the diamond fields and diamond digging in the Lichtenburg area by the Malan brothers deserves a mention. Rina's father was one of ten brothers but only one sister who died in infancy. The photo on page 53 shows the diamond fields – the Malan brothers had a good reputation for pegging claims.

The next photo is the Malan family standing around the graveside of Heila, the only daughter in the family, who only lived 27 days.

Pegging diamond claims, and playing in a wind-instrument band was a means of supplementing incomes. The Malans were generally farmers – especially in view of the need to feed twelve mouths. I also presume having so many sons helped was a great help with farming operations. The Malan boys were surprisingly well dressed in all the photos that we have of them. For that matter even the Boer prisoners-of-war were more than often seen wearing neck-ties. Even town folk were always well dressed. The same can't be said of the 21st Century folk. The following picture of the ten brothers is taken in order of age.

Their longevity were as follows:-

Hendrik Francois	- lived 81 years	- 14 Dec 1878 to 29 May 1959.
Gertruida Johanna	- lived 68 years	– 5 Feb 1883 to 6 Aug 1951.
Hendrik Francois	- lived 56 years	- 16 Apr 1904 to 6 Aug 1960.
Frederik Jakobus	- lived 38 years	– 27 Jul 1905 to 20 Aug 1943.
Daniel Stefanus	- lived 76 years	- 13 Aug 1906 to 4 Sep 1982.
Francois Daniel	- lived 81 years	- 2 Oct 1907 to Apr 1988.
Willem Stefanus	- lived 67 years	- 13 Oct 1908 to 9 Mar 1975.
David Jakob	- lived 74 years	- 28 Oct 1910 to 9 Apr 1984.

Gert Johannes	- lived u/k	-16 Apr 1912
Jacobus Bernardus	- lived 65years	- 15 Aug 1916 to 20 Mar 1981.
Heila Magdalena	- lived 27 days	- 11 Jul 1918 to 7 Aug 1918.
Felix Festus	- lived u/k	- 29 Mar 1920
Gideon van Eeden	- lived u/k	- 26 Oct 1924.

HEILA MAGDLENA MALAN 11/7/1918 - 7/8/1918

(CLOCKWISE FROM CROSS)
GIDEON, FELIX, JACOBUS, GETRUIDA JOHANNA (Mother), HENDRIK FRANCOIS (Father)
HENDRIK, FREDERIK, FRANCOIS, DANIEL, WILLEM, DAVID and GERT

Writers note: Several discrepancies on names and dates will be discovered between my list above and that of my father-in-law at page 123. My list has been taken from *The Malan van Suid-Afrika*.

WORLD WAR II 1939-1945

Abram Carl Frederik Preller courted and married Johannesburg born Matthia Martha Lotter shortly after the outbreak of World War II, producing Johannes Albertus the IV, born in Johannesburg on 15th August 1940. But the war story must be told first. ACFP was dispatched to Addis Ababa. Warrant Officer Class II A C F Preller Geldenhuys had arrived in East Africa to make his contribution to the SAAF war effort in World War II.

The detailed historical record is fully documented in the authors *Nickel Cross* book that was published in 2006 – refer to pages 22 through to page 52 of Nickel Cross.

However, since then, a few maps were updated and several photographs came to light. These are now included for the record, for those who wish to take the time to cross refer the newer additions to earlier published accounts.

Duplications in this book, where they occur, have thus been intentionally deleted – despite the picture of Johannes Albertus Geldenhuys (Ou Dad), Hendrik Jacobus (Oom Henry) and Abram Carl Frederik Preller Geldenhuys (OuPey) being lost in cyberspace!

Gazing At The Wild Blue Yonder

Tenth generation Johannes Albertus was born in Johannesburg on 15th August 1940. He was later schooled on the Northern Rhodesian (now Zambia) Copperbelt, qualified as an artisan – boiler making and diesel mechanics – at Chingola Copper Mine. After a short farming spell in the Free State, he returned to Zambia to manage several Garages and marry Julia Lillian Dippenaar – on 27th March 1964. They had three children:-

Stuart William, born Bulawayo 8th September 1957, married Joy Goldsworthy in Manzini, Swaziland on 10th July 1980 and had Ian Jannie, born Johannesburg 22nd February 1985 and Louise born Johannesburg 5th May 1987.

Charmaine, born Salisbury 7th January 1959, gave birth to Jason born Midrand 4th January 1996.

Paul Preller, born Ndola 15th December 1966, married Karen de Waal (born Vanderbylpark 29th May 1966) in Edenvale

Johannesburg and had Chanel born Durban 18th April 1990 and Craig Jannie born Durban 15th March 1993.

After a short spell in Abyssinia, North Africa, Oudad Preller returned to produce a second war baby, Preller Matt was born on Rustpan, the family farm at Bothaville, Free State on 20th February 1943. It seems Dad took leave of absence from 12th February to 9th March 1943. Preller completed his schooling in Gwelo Southern Rhodesia and enlisted in the Royal Rhodesian Air Force. He married his school sweetheart Susanna Catharina Malan in Fort Victoria on 5th March 1966. They had two children: -

Renene Delene, born Gwelo 8th August 1968, married Grahame David Jelley on 6th June 1992 in the Drakensberg and had Courtney Sacha born Triangle 13th September 1993 and Brendan Vaughan born Chipinge 15th November 1996

Pey Malan, born Gwelo 22nd December 1970 and married Marion Muller in Welkom 2nd April 1994. After an unfortunate miscarriage, they divorced. Pey then teamed up with Marcelle Gilson for about seven years, before settling down with a delightful lady Eloise Howard. They married in Durban on 27th April 2007 and had Jake born and died in December 2007, and Lucy Hope born 29th March 2009.

Delene Elizabeth was born in Oudtshoorn on 27th February 1945 and married Johannes Jacobus Francois Bouwer at Pretoria on 2nd June 1966. They had two girls, Chanli G (born 12th October 1970) who married Charles Roy Brink (born 1 January 1960, Pretoria) on 6th February 1993, and Rensha (born 15th February 1972) who married Craig Brown.

Dawn was born in 1949 but died 1954 at Musenga Plots outside Chingola on the Northern Rhodesia Copperbelt – when a Swahili set fire to the thatched homestead.

By the end of 1943, South Africa had suffered 30,000 casualties in World War Two, of whom some 5,400 had been killed or died on service and about 14,000 were languishing in prisoner-of-war camps. The number of ships sunk, damaged or captured by enemy raiders and submarines in South African coastal waters rose from only 16 between the outbreak of war and the end 1941, to 85 during 1942. During 1943 the number was 54.

Lieutenant Preller Geldenhuys remained Officer Commanding Battle Flight until the end of November 1943.

Adolf Hitler had committed suicide on 30th April 1945, with Germany forces in Italy surrendering on 2nd May. The War in Europe ended on 8th May 1945. On August 6th, the first atomic bomb was dropped on Hiroshima, on the 8th, Russia declared war on Japan, on the 9th the second atomic bomb was dropped on Nagasaki and on 14th August 1945, Emperor Hirohito announced Japan's surrender. World War II ended on 15th August 1945.

On 9th October 1945, Lieutenant Preller Geldenhuys was posted to Lyttelton for a month and released from the SAAF at Hector Norris Park on 7th November 1945. Shortly after his de-mobilisation, Dad packed his bags and immigrated with his young family to Northern Rhodesia – to become a miner on the Copperbelt. The pioneer spirit of Abram Carl Fredrik Preller Geldenhuys, to trek north, will be continued shortly. In the interim, it is evident that other 'distant relatives' also contributed to the war effort.

The following members of the Geldenhuys family served in, and gave their lives, during World War II. Captain M Geldenhuys was a pilot serving on No 3 Squadron, South African Air Force, on 10th November 1943. The squadron was based at Savoia, Eastern Mediterranean, and tasked with convoy protection and shipping standby as 25 ships and five escorts were passing en route to Bengasi. He was one of six Hurricane II Cs pilots scrambled to intercept six Junker 88s and five Dornier 217s escorted by five fighters about to attack the ship convoy. A Captain R Yeats attacked two Ju 88s and sent one down, but after attacking another his screen frosted up and he lost contact with the enemy in the gathering darkness. A second Hurricane pilot fired at a Ju88 and saw it crash into the sea but did not claim a share. Captain M Geldenhuys led his section into an attack during which the pilots individually fired bursts at four Ju 88s, one of which went into the sea. Another lost height, with port engine smoking and a Do 217 was also destroyed. The enemy single-engined aircraft made no attempt to intervene before the engagement had to be broken off because of darkness.

Much later, during October 1944, No 3 Squadron SAAF, as part of No 8 Wing, was based at Borghetto (Near Ancona and Florence, Italy), and by now equipped with Spitfire aircraft. Captain M Geldenhuys is again mentioned as playing his full part in 8 Wing activities, in leading missions either against designated targets or on cab-rank patrol.

Petty Officer J C M Geldenhuys served in the South Africa Naval Service at the outbreak of World War II. South Africa possessed no real naval vessels on the outbreak of war, but their strength consisted of three officers and three ratings. Geldenhuys was subordinate to Lieutenant Commanders J Dalgleish and F J Dean. More research is needed to establish his relationship.

For interest, Geldenhuys combatants that did not survive World War II were: -

Warrant Officer Class II G J Geldenhuys, of No 15 Squadron, Royal Air Force, was posted missing, presumed dead (drowned at sea). Geldenhuys was the third crew member of a Baltimore bomber, piloted by Lieutenant DB Dick. On 30th January 1945, No 15 Squadron's Baltimore with a crew of four disappeared on a night cross-country flight. A Boston aircraft reported seeing a fire at sea, and eventually a rescue launch off Bellaria picked up three Mae Wests, two of which belonged to No 15 Squadron. The missing aircrews were Lieutenants D B Dick and W E Ellis, Warrant Officer G J Geldenhuys and Sergeant Slaughter of the RAF, reported lost.

By a strange twist of fate, 15 Squadrons first loss since February 1944 was suffered during the Baltimore's final operation before standing down on 19th January. OC Lieutenant Colonel Shuttleworth led the mission of nine aircraft to attack a stores dump at Massa Lombarda, where they met with intense heavy anti-aircraft fire. His port engine was set on fire. The Baltimore was crash-landed about 16 km from base - at Casenatico. WO II G J Geldenhuys was thus lost at sea, after the squadron had stood down eleven days earlier.

Warrant Officer Class II, J N Geldenhuys, was killed in action during the closing stages of World War II. It is speculated that his initials stood for Johannes Norval. J N Geldenhuys was a crew member on a Liberator of No 34 Squadron, South African Air Force, piloted by Captain L J de Jager that was hit by flak during their bombing run on Villach. Villach was a key point on the railway line into Austria, which was attacked twice within four days. 50 heavies were very successful on the night of 25/26 March 1945, when the goods and transhipment depots were almost totally destroyed. Unfortunately, the flak was accurate. The Liberator was manned by pilot plus a crew of eight. The members of the crew killed in action were Lieutenants R L Chegwyn, P M Tylden-Wright, I J Doble, Flying Officer R Warrington, WOs J N Geldenhuys, J Robbertse and W A J Venter, and Sergeant A C Phillips.

G J and J N Geldenhuys relationships still need to be established. Genealogy research is still incomplete and I trust their connections will be determined in due course.

Courtney and Brendan Jelley also need to know that their maternal great-grandfather, Alan Whiteley, served with the Royal Flying Corps during World War I and with the Southern Rhodesia Air Force during World War II.

Alan Whiteley enlisted into the British Army when he was 17 years old, then transferred to the RFC two years later in 1917. He trained at Spittlegate on BE 2C and Avro aircraft and flew to France on his 20th Birthday (11th October 1917) to join No 82 Squadron, equipped with Armstrong Whitworth MK 8 aircraft. His operational flying was mainly Army Observation with some bombing. Alan was discharged as a Flying Officer in mid-June 1919. He then arrived in Rhodesia in January 1928, and joined the Municipality of Salisbury on 5th March 1928. Alan Whiteley met and married Stella Nesta Arnott born in Queenstown on 27th May 1902. They got married on 12th August 1928. They married in Rhodesia. During World War II he was a Link Trainer instructor with the Rhodesian Air Training Group, serving for two years and was stationed at Mount Hampden and Induna, both of which were Elementary Flying Training Schools, and then at Cranborne Service Flying Training School. These were RATG Units, Nos 28, 27 and 20, respectively. Unfortunately, this fact is not recorded in the excellent *Pride of Eagles*, by Beryl Salt, published in March 2001. It is thus with a sense of pride that I am able document our family history in this biography.

He retired from the Municipality at the end of October 1957 and worked for a while at Cream Line Taxis (Pvt) Ltd until 1980. He died on 14th March 1989, at the ripe old age of 92 years.

Ou Dad Jannie Geldenhuys had meanwhile died during World War II on 28th May 1942. The extensive land holdings along the Vals Rivier between Bothaville and Kroonstad was divided up and allocated to the five children. The three girls obtained equal portions of land and the two boys / men were allocated the homesteads. The eldest son, Hendrik Jacobus Geldenhuys was allocated the larger portion and continued farming. The youngest, Abram Carl Frederik

Preller inherited the "familie plaas" – Rustpan. However Oudad Preller had other ideas – he had flown over the Jewel of Africa and had decided that he would venture north after the cessation of hostilities. He then ceded Rustpan to his eldest sister Bess, who had married Steyn Jordaan, and who was an astute farmer. With the Rustpan homestead, together with her portion of inherited land, made the family plaas the envy of everybody.

And so it came to pass that after being de-mobbed from the South African Air Force in November 1945, Preller Geldenhuys (Senior) immigrated to Northern Rhodesia and joined the Roan Antelope Copper Mine in Luanshya. In those days, Central Africa was a long way into "darkest Africa" – tar roads non-existent, wild animals in abundance with lions roaming around, elephant and giraffe everywhere and more often than not the low-level bridges would be in flood during the rainy season. After about four years mining at Luanshya, Oudad took a transfer to Nchanga Copper Mine at Chingola

Favourite past-times were fishing trips to the Central African Lake districts – Lake Nyasa (now Malawi), Lake Mrewa and Lake Bangwelo. Every now and then we would return to the Rustpan familieplaas at Bothaville, invariably detouring to all the hot mineral springs en route – the favourites being Warmbaths, Tshipise and Hot Springs (between Umtali and Birchenough Bridge).

Our youngest sister Dawn was born in 1949 in Luanshya, but she tragically died in 1954 at Musenga Plots outside Chingola on the Northern Rhodesia Copperbelt – when a Swahili set fire to the thatched homestead. This tragic sequence of events is documented elsewhere (see the biographical section), but suffice to say that led my mother to a drinking problem and, luckily, an unsuccessful suicide attempt.

It was during one of our visits to Hot Springs that Oudad befriended Hester Vermaak and Daan le Roux, which resulted in my parents taking up farming in the Fort Victoria (now called Masvingo) area of Southern Rhodesia (Zimbabwe). Daan introduced Oudad to Hester Vermaak who gladly offered Stanmore farm for crop and cattle farming. The Jewel of Africa had been found, albeit a financial disaster by the Mugabe Government.

Rhodesia – The Jewel of Africa

Preller Matt completed his schooling at Thornhill High School in Gwelo Southern Rhodesia and enlisted in the Royal Rhodesian Air Force as a pilot. He married his school sweetheart Susanna Catharina Malan in Fort Victoria on 5th March 1966. They had two children:-
- Renene Delene – was born in Gwelo on 8th August 1968, and
- Pey Malan – was also born in Gwelo, on 22nd December 1970.

As mentioned, Delene Elizabeth was born in Oudtshoorn on 27th February 1945 and married Johannes Jacobus Francois Bouwer at Pretoria on the 2nd June 1966. They had two girls, Chanli G (born 12th October 1970) who married Charles J Brink (born 1st January 1960) and Rensha (born 15th February 1972) who married Craig Brown.

Johannes Albertus Geldenhuys had meanwhile been indentured as an apprentice on the Copper Belt, and remained behind when my parents took up farming on Stanmore. The farming venture was a disaster, forcing Oudad Preller to utilise his blasting licence to build the tar road to the Kyle Dam site. After a short spell he took a job selling life insurance, immigrated back to the Free State, and then rejoined the South African Air Force at 10 Air Depot, Voortrekkerhoogte. After several years in uniform, he died in service from the narrowing of the arteries on 13th February 1972 and was fittingly accorded a military funeral in Pretoria.

- o – O – o -

The picture overleaf, is of Rustpan, the family farm in the Bothaville / Kroonstad district. It was the place of so many happy and noteworthy events, but it was found in ruins during a 2006 visit to the graveyard of the writer's grandparents.

However, Libby Beukes (Elizabeth van Rensen) gave Jan Geldenhuys and I a letter written 8th April 1920, which was buried in the in the walling of the farmhouse, during extentions carried out at that time.

The letter read:-

To whom it may Concern

We, the undersigned, hereby leave a few statements so those surviving ourselves and who

may in coming generations recover this paper.

This document was plastered in its nitch of the house of Jan A. Geldenhuys on his farm Rustpan on the 8th of April, 1920 a.d.

The weather is very promising:- in the west a heavy thunderstorm is brewing. The mealies are growing beautifully. The sheep have started lambing.

There is a school on this farm.

With kindest wishes to the world at large, we remain

Your ancestors:-
J.A Geldenhuys
(wife) Lissie Prellar
Family:- Henry Geldenhuys
Bessie Geldenhuys
Lilla Geldenhuys
Minnie "
Kleinbaas Prellar
H. Douwes (Teacher)

Rustpan
Dist. Bothaville
8th April, 1920

Writers note: The document was most likely written by the school teacher H. Douwes, who spelt Preller with an 'a' instead of the correct 'e' – and it also illustrates how and why the spelling of names changed over times

RHODESIA – ZIMBABWE WAR 1967 –1980

The above heading is perhaps misleading, because the Rhodesian War story is also the subject of another biography titled *Nickel Cross*. It is a story of the writer's experience in the Anglo-Rhodesian conflict, but also basically covers 100 years from 1900 to the year 2000. Only 50 copies of the book were distributed to family and friends. Then in 2005 it was decided to write a second book titled *Rhodesian Air Force Operations, with Air Strike Log* – a book which may well appeal to the military strategist than would a book with too much of a personal touch. Both books are dedicated to my soul mate and are available from Rina whoever wishes to read more about the Rhodesia – Zimbabwe War 1967 – 1980. Suffice it therefore that this chapter mentions the relationships between the Geldenhuys'se and the Bezuidenhout's, Malan's and the Jelley's.

Hansie Bezuidenhout was the husband of Gerta Malan (and elder sister of Rina Geldenhuys) and the father of Johan "Bez" Bezuidenhout (of special forces SAS fame). Hansie owned Anker in the Tengwe Block between Karoi and Sinoia and was a very active tobacco forefront farmer as well as a PATU – BSA Police Anti-Terrorist Unit combatant. Farmers were invariably in the front line of the cowardly and murderous terrorist attacks. Farms were also a source of food for the infiltrating gangs. Strained labour relations did not take much to accelerate specific farmers as prime targets. Despite Hansie being an active PATU member, his Anker Farm escaped the ravages of the Rhodesian War. However, it was subsequently found that terrorist gangs had in fact criss-crossed his farm, but his labour had convinced the infiltrators to leave Anker unharmed.

On retirement from active farming, Hansie and Gerta had a magnificent home built at Mica Point, on the shores of Lake Kariba. When all their children left Rhodesia / Zimbabwe, they sold up and moved into a retirement complex in Bulawayo.

Johan Bez served under Brian Robinson and Grahame Wilson's command of the Special Air Service battalion – and was involved in numerous battles during the war – most operations being documented in *"The Elite"* - the story of the Special Air Service by Barbara Cole, and Ron Reid-Daly's book about the war. Barbara made several references to Sergeant *Small Bez* and her own husband – Peter Cole. At least half a dozen exploits, mostly external in Zambia and Mozambique I might add, by *Small Bez* is documented.

Frans Malan, younger brother to Rina Geldenhuys, was a territorial Force Company Commander who spent a commendable time on Army call-up during the whole of the bush-war. Rina's twin brother Philip also served in the TF – and had the dubious pleasure of spreading second-hand carrots all over yours truly during some high gravity aerobatics manoeuvres in a piston engined Provost aircraft! Hendrik Malan, Rina's eldest brother, was a mercenary in the early 1960 Congo disturbances.

Bill Jelley, Renene Geldenhuys's father-in-law, joined the Rhodesian Air Force on No 6 Short Service Unit flying training course. In the early 1960's he flew twin engined Canberra's. By December 1966 he took command of No 4 (Provost) Squadron, Thornhill. On 19th January 1967 he flew for the first time with 'Prop' Preller Geldenhuys, in a Provost, to Bulawayo. On 26th May 1967 he rated Prop Master Green on an Instrument flying test. During July of the same year he stood in for Wing Commander Mick McLaren as OC Flying Wing Thornhill. The following month Squadron Leader Bill Jelley handed over command of the Provost squadron to Peter Cooke, in order to assume command of the Vampire squadron – No 2 Squadron. Prop carried out the first Provost air strike in the country – at the Battle of Inyantue in August 1967 when the whole of the infiltrating Lupani Detachment was annihilated.

Prop Geldenhuys was then posted to No 2 Squadron in October 1967 and flew his first Vampire sortie with Boss Jel on a border reconnaissance sortie on October 23rd. Vampire drop tank trials were carried out the following month. During early January 1968, 60x20 millimetre cannon air-to-ground trials were carried out by Prop.

Operation Cauldron, from 18 to 23rd March 1968 was one of those highly successful counter insurgency operations that accounted for a major terrorist incursion from the Zambia / Mozambique border. The group was intercepted on the Angwa River and 3x60lb squash-head rockets, plus 151x20mm high explosive incendiary cannon airstrikes were carried out. Both Vampires were dead on target, as confirmed by cine camera recordings. This was the first time that Vampires were used to carry out air strikes in the country. In the ensuing ground contact, 1 RLI Trooper E. Ridge and one RAR Corporal Erisha was killed in action from gunshot wounds (RLI = Rhodesia Light Infantry; RAR = Rhodesian African Rifles). The School of Infantry situated in Gwelo, named one of their auditorium lecture room 'Cauldron'.

Squadron Leader Bill Jelley also commanded the successful *Operations Griffin* and *Mansion* in July. *Operation Knuckle*, from August 26 to September 11th 1968 was carried out at Bulawayo airfield. The city was treated to 55 minutes of spectacular formation flying by eight Vampire aircraft on the 8th. Boss Jell led the formation, with Prop, as No 5, led the 'box' of four Vampires.

On 3rd March 1969, Bill Jelley carried out 8x20lb bombing trials, with the writer. He handed over command of No 2 Squadron to Sqn Ldr Tol Janeke. By October 1972 he had been promoted to Wing Commander and appointed Officer Commanding Flying Wing,

Air Force Base New Sarum. Bill, by the way, was one of the two pilots on completing No 6 SSU, remained on Medium Service and retired as Wing Commanders (the other being Peter Cooke).

On retiring, he moved to South Africa where he did a couple of flying jobs. He returned to Zimbabwe doing Freelance flying, and settled at Christon Bank, where he renewed old friendships with Peter and Anne Cooke. Both Bill and Margaret have been staunch supporters of the Air Forces Association of Zimbabwe functions. Bill and Margaret have also hosted several Christmas family gatherings at which the Jelley's and Geldenhuys' cemented highly valued bonds.

Bill's eldest son Grahame David qualified as a medical General Practitioner and subsequently married Renene Delene, elder child of Preller Matt Geldenhuys and Susanna Catharina (Rina) Malan on 6th June 1992 in the Drakensberg. They had Courtney Sacha born Triangle 13th September 1993

and Brendan Vaughan born Chipinge 15th November 1996.

English Electric Canberra B2 Bombers

Prop then enjoyed a Hunter posting in 1970 and was appointed Flight Commander on No 1 Squadron. This was a plum posting because it meant having the opportunity to fly faster and higher than any of the other Squadrons in the Rhodesian Air Force. On one memorable sortie the writer climbed to the oxygen deficient altitude of 55 000 feet above sea level, and then flying through the sound barrier. The Mach Meter was clocked at Mach 1.05. An innovative step taken in 1970 was to allocate the Hunter aircraft to individual pilots, with their names painted on the canopy rails. The photograph on the previous page shows the proud writer alongside "his" Hawker Hunter FGA 9 (Fighter Ground Attack – Mark 9) aircraft.

1970 was a momentous year for more reasons than just a plum posting. It was the year that Rina made our family unit complete - Pey Malan Geldenhuys, born Gwelo 22 December 1970.

Pey married Marion Mueller in Welkom on 2nd April 1994. After an unfortunate miscarriage, they divorced on 17th January 1997. He then met a lovely lady, Marcelle Gilson and they settled down for seven years, having built up successful businesses like Annotech, Webdynamix, and Peysoft software development. They separated in April 2006 and the following month Pey met and teamed up with another beautiful lady, Eloise Howard. They married a year later – 27th April 2007 – and moved into a lovely home in Durban North, which they altered extensively. Eloise already had a six year old son, Matthew Dylan. Pey and Matthew bonded beautifully.

Tragedy befell the family with the loss of their second son Jake, born 18th December 2007 but died 12 days later on 30th December 2007. They were blessed with the birth of their daughter, Lucy Hope, on 29th March 2009 – and immigrated to Auckland, New Zealand, in July 2009.

The picture above is a "filler" (to fill up the page before the next Dictionary Section). It is a picture of the Graceful Canberra, which both Bill and the writer flew. Bill flew them in the 1960's and I in the early 1970's.

Rhodesia----In Memory of those who fell | *It was 1964*

We were young with plans, most of them barmy,
I was called up for training in the Rhodesian Army.
Some arrived heads shaved, like chicks without feathers,
But I rocked up on a bike with long hair and leathers.

I parked the bike and was directed to a hanger,
My first mistake, arriving on that Banger.
I was greeted by a soldier, a sadistic sob.
Who was feared by all recruits, meet CPL BOK.

He wore his cap like a Nazi, with dark glasses,
Derived great pleasure when he was kicking arses.
"Am I hurting you soldier?" he asked with a stare.
"No CPL." "I should be. I am standing on your hair!"

Within minutes my long black hair disappeared,
Cut by a huge brute with a thick red beard.
"From now on my darling you are going to be alone"
"So you can hand me that long black comb"

Next we were issued our complete combat dress,
Nothing fitted properly, I looked a sorry mess.
"Don't worry son, in over a week and a bit."
"All these nice clothes and shoes will begin to fit"

All that army issue, including boots and belt.
Had to be polished using brass and velt.
There were black fellows who did it for a price.
You got it back quickly looking real nice.

Cleaning the barrack walls, windows and floor.
Took all night and by morning my bloody hands were sore.
You would finish just in time for the inspection.
If something was wrong, it did not miss detection.

You slept on the floor to keep your bed neat and straight.
A really good night's sleep would have to wait.
They worked us day and night with little to eat.
By the 3rd week we were all but out on our feet.

That Friday afternoon we were asked to line up.
Really pissed-off, we were on our way to the pub.
"Any musicians amongst you please raise your hand."
This is nice I thought, we're going to start a band!

Tree idiots raised their hands, including me.
We had to move a huge piano from hanger A to hanger C.
I vowed there and then never again to volunteer.
And went to the pub to drown our sorrows with beer.

Next Friday we were lined up by the same bugger.
"Any one amongst you who enjoys a game of rugger?"
Four soldiers stepped forward, boy they never learn!
I laughed at them and said "Now it's your turn!"

That bastard then did something you cannot believe.
Something only a sadistic mind could conceive.
He gave them 4 tickets without a hint of shame.
"There's a great match on to-morrow, enjoy the game."

He turned to me and with that Nazi smile.
He said "The rest kit up, we're going to drill a while!"
I laughed because I knew we had been had.
It later turned out the CPL wasn't all that bad.

We had to run, march, shoot and train.

But by this time, thank heavens, there was less pain.
We became professionals, proud of one another.
The stranger you started with, was now a brother.
I made a point of it to have lots of fun.
But never lost respect for my best friend, my gun.
We were trained in our skills, sometimes a bore.
We all knew we would soon be fighting a Rhodesian War.

Things slowly got worse as the war escalated.
All the fighting forces were drastically inflated.
Reserve Force call-ups were dramatically increased.
And the merciless hunt for gooks never ceased.

I was proud to serve in the 10th Bat T. Force.
Sanctions limited resources, but we stayed on course.
We spent most of our time far away from home.
Worried about our wives and kid who were alone.

We all fought bravely as the war got older.
But often we grieved at the loss of a soldier.
Whole families' lives were messed up forever,
Whoever starts a war is just not very clever.

There were times when situations got really tight
Then we welcomed the BLUE JOBS in thunderous flight.
Many a time they gave us needed air support.
And those spineless floppies were forced to abort.

As the war waged on my kids got older.
With more foreign support the insurgents got bolder.
With heads held high we tried to stand tall.
But we all soon realised, the writing is on the wall.

Now 26 years later we look back in sorrow.
All those sacrifices made, now what about tomorrow?
They discarded prosperity; they chose to thrive on hate.
Will things return to normal, or is it too late???

40148 Malan P.J. Sir!!

Words of Wisdom
In the midst of the 1960's Congo trouble, Dr Albert Schweitzer said;
"I have given my life to try to alleviate the sufferings of Africa. There is something that all white men must learn and know, as I have, that these individuals are sub-races. They have neither intellectual, mental or emotional abilities to equate or share equally with the white men in any of the functions of our civilisation. I have given them my life to try and bring unto them the advantages which our civilisation must offer, but I have become aware that we must retain this status – white the superior and they the inferior. For whenever a white man seeks to live among them as their equal, they will either destroy him or devour him, and they will destroy all his work. And so for any existing relationship or for any benefit of these people, let white men from anywhere in the world who would come to help Africa remember that they must continually maintain this status – you the master and they the inferior – like children you would help or teach. Never fraternise with them as equals. Never accept them as your equal socially or they will devour you. They will destroy you."

No wonder they had not invented the wheel yet when the white men set foot in Africa.

This brings to mind the story of the Ant and the grasshopper.

THE ORIGINAL LEGEND.
An ant and a grasshopper both live in the same field. During the summer, the ant works hard all day and all night bringing in supplies for the winter and he prepares his home to keep him warm during the cold months ahead. Meanwhile the grasshopper hops and sings, eats all the grass he wants and pancreases. Come winter, the grass dies and it is bitterly cold. The ant is well fed and warm in his house, but the grasshopper has not prepared for the winter, so he dies, leaving a whole hoard of little grasshoppers without food or

shelter. The moral of this story is that one should work hard to ensure that you can take care of yourself.

THE AFRICAN VERSION:

The first part is the same but because it happens in Africa there are a few complications. The starving, shivering offspring of the grasshopper demand to know why the ant should be allowed to be warm and fed, while next door they are living in terrible conditions without food or proper clothing. A TV crew shows up and broadcasts footage of the poor grasshoppers, contrasting this with footage of the ant, snug and warm in his comfortable home with a pantry full of food. The public is stunned: how can it be, in this beautiful field, that the poor grasshoppers are allowed to suffer so, while the ant lives in the lap of luxury. In the blink of an eye AGU (African Grasshopper Union) is formed. They charge the ant with "species bias" and claim that grasshoppers are the victims of 30 million years of green oppression. They stage a protest in front of the ant's house and trash the street. The TV crew interviews them, and they all state that if their demands are not met they will be forced into a life of crime. Just for practice, they loot the TV's crews luggage and hi-jack their van. The TRC (Take and Redistribute Commission) justifies their behaviour by saying this is the legacy of the ant's discrimination towards the oppression of grasshoppers. They demand that the ant apologies to the grasshopper for what he has done, and that he makes amends for all the other ants in history who have done the same thing to the grasshoppers. The PAGAD (People Against Grasshopper Abuse and Distress) state that they are starting a holy war against ants. The President appears on the eight o'clock news and says that he will do everything he can for the grasshoppers, who have been denied the prosperity they deserve by those who have benefited unfairly during the summer. The government drafts the EEGAD (Economic Equity for Greens and Disadvantaged) Act retrospective to the beginning of the summer. The ant is fined for failing to employ a proportionate number of green insects and having nothing left to pay his back-taxes, his home is confiscated for government redistribution.

The story ends as we see the grasshopper finishing off the last of the ant's food while the government house he is in (which so just happens to be the ant's old house) crumbles around him because he does not know how to maintain it. Showing on the TV (which he stole from another ant) the President is standing before a group of wildly singing and dancing grasshoppers announcing that a new era of "equality" has dawned on the field. The ant, meanwhile, is not allowed to work because he has historically benefited from the field. In his place, ten grasshoppers only work two hours a day, and steal half of what they actually harvest. When winter comes again and not enough has been harvested, they strike and demand a 180% increase in their wages so they can buy more food, which now has to be imported because the grasshoppers are not productive enough to produce adequate food legally.

As for the ant: Well, the ant packs his things and emigrates to another field, where he starts a highly successful food company and becomes a millionaire by selling food to the field from where he came.

So the Geldenhuys family emigrated to New Zealand in 2011.

MASONITE (AFRICA) LIMITED

I joined the Masonite brand hardboard manufacturing company in Estcourt, Natal on the 5th January 1982 as their Personnel Superintendent. After about a year at the Estcourt Mill, an opportunity arose to move with the Forestry Division to Pietermaritzburg – in order to be more central to the seven forestry plantations that supplies the Mill with its raw material.

The Forestry employed more people than the manufacturing plant. Labour totalled some 1161 employees, with a two million Rand payroll.

Rina and I soon found a very comfortable house at 27 Christie Road, equidistant from the University, Girls High, Maritzburg College and Alexandra High Schools. Unfortunately, we couldn't find places at Girls High or Maritzburg College, so enrolled Renene at Russell and Pey at Alexandra. The Forestry Office rented offices in Longmarket Street and I commenced my transfer officially on 1st February 1983. The nature of the job was such that a company car was a requirement and I took delivery of a brand new Toyota Cressida sedan – the first of many brand new cars during the course of my 20-year career with the Company.

My stay with the Forestry Division lasted some seven years – with just as many changes in job title. From Personnel Superintendent-Forestry, I became Personnel and Administration Superintendent on 1st May 1984, then reverted to plain Personnel Supt. on 1st February 1985 following rationalisation. Further restructuring occurred on the 1st August 1986, assuming responsibility for the Safety portfolio, as Personnel Safety Superintendent. It was during this time that Forestry was outsourcing a lot of their silviculture and harvesting operations, with retrenchments reducing the staff compliment to some 700 odd people. The retrenchment exercise was quite a major challenge for me, and taking over the Safety function as well added to greater responsibility.

FINALLY GROUNDED

Fire Season, from July to the first rains in November, is a particularly stressful period for the Forestry Industry with ones crop going up in smoke that has taken anything from ten to fifteen years to grow. Saw logs can take an additional ten years. It makes sense that the industry spares no effort to protect themselves from the ravages that forest fires can inflict on producers. When the opportunity arose to fly on forest fire spotting missions, I jumped at the prospect to exchange my Masonite bomber for the controls of a light aircraft. The spotter flights were co-ordinated from the Natal Midlands Forest Protection Association Offices at Oribi airfield, Pietermaritzburg.

I was indeed fortunate to have flown on several such missions. These covered plantations in the Kranskop area north of Greytown, to afforested areas in the Harding and Kokstad towns on the Transkei border. Popular turning points also included Bulwer, Creighton, Ixopo, Eston, Crammond and Howick. My first sortie with Johann van Niekerk, in Cessna 182, ZS-RMC was on the 21st August 1988. It took us sixty-five minutes to fly the northern round route to Kranskop and Howick. After a breather at Oribi, we took off again for an eighty-minute fire patrol of the Southern plantations.

I need to mention that Renene had befriended the Stott's from Port Shepstone, who also owned a Cessna hangared at Margate. Jo Stott was an honorary civilian pilot in the Air Force - and I was thus also able to get my bum in the air on at least three occasions. One in particular that I recall was with Pey as a passenger - I believe Pey was not all that keen on my steep turns over Albert Falls dam. I have often wondered whether Pey recalls that particular sortie. Anyway, the Stott's son was a privileged scholar at the upper crust Hilton College - he had eyes for Renene, or was it the other way round? Who was I to complain, as long as I could enjoy "The wild blue yonder" once again. Renene no doubt has her own story to tell, concerning her affair - and it is perhaps best to leave that side up to her.

On 9th September I had another memorable sortie which lasted three hours, spotting eleven fires, and giving a good olde Air Force beat-up at Masonite Rockvale plantation situated between Ixopo and Highflats. Unbeknown to me at the time, Area Manager Richard Guy was on the telephone to my Boss, Jack Hubble, in Maritzburg. The aircraft noise on the very low flypast drowned any coherent discussion between the foresters. When my Boss enquired what all the racket was about, Richard casually replied that it was only "Prop's normal antics on Fire Patrol". Needless to say, the message was received on the other end of the phone went down like a lead balloon. Accordingly, my sorties on the following day were regrettably my last. I was duly grounded, because the Company was not prepared to take the risk of having to notify next of kin of misadventure in the line of duty.

For the record, I had managed to get my bum off the ground at least nine times before my final 'wheels-up'. The last ten odd hours did not feature in my logbook - I was truly *grounded* once for all.

During this time, Renene completed her high schooling and commenced a nursing career at respectable Greys Hospital. Pey, meanwhile, also did well at Alex, and enrolled at Technikon Natal to pursue a National Diploma in Computer Data Processing. I might add that Masonite generously subsidised their higher education. With our offspring vacating the coup, we sold the Christie house and bought a two bedrooms duplex right in town – Murrayfield in Burger Street. The Forestry Office also relocated to Church Street, and the office was thus within walking distance from home.

In 1990 I transferred from the Forestry Division, in Pietermaritzburg, to the Manufacturing Division in Estcourt. Masonite MD's, Alan Wilson and his successor, Mike Slater humbled me with the Excellence Award. The company also has an Honours Board in their Head Office reception, displaying the names of the recipients. I was also nominated and awarded the NOSA 'Safety Practitioner of the Year' for two years, the awards being made at the Annual Banquets – once in Pietermaritzburg and the second in Durban. They also count as career highlights - - but not as highly treasured as my first trip overseas to America. To say that Masonite was good to me is an understatement. Rina and I were truly blessed with having two complete careers – first in the Air Force, followed by a second twenty years with Masonite. Seems everything happens in two's? We will need to break the cycle, because we have also had two trips to New Zealand – and that definitely won't be our last (at the time of going to press, this has now led to us planning our fourth, and permanent visit to New Zealand).

USA TRIP

My trip to the States was the highlight of my twenty years service with Masonite. 1999 was our best safety year ever when we broke our previous record of 3,3 million hours without a disabling injury. We had also celebrated our 50th Anniversary earlier in the year. For my 57th birthday present I was given a fortnight's notice to attend a safety conference to be held at Disney World - and to include a visit to two of Masonite Corporation mills in the States. I chose the Towanda Mill situated close to the Canadian border, and Laurel mill in Mississippi, in the south.

Rina opted to spend the fortnight with her sister Lettie at Tweeling in the Free State. After dropping Rina off, I motored to Atlasville where the Beaver's kindly took me to Johannesburg International.

My flight schedule took me to Atlanta, Pittsburgh and Elmira in order to reach Towanda. I flew SAA to Atlanta, routed via Cape Town, Fort Lauderdale, Philadelphia arriving at Elmira six and a half hours later than scheduled. From Towanda I flew to New Orleans, routing via Pittsburgh as planned, to reach Laurel. Then it was on to Orlando and a twenty-minute shuttle-bus ride to Disney World. I returned to Johannesburg via Orlando and Atlanta.

The highlight of this USA trip was visits to the National Warplane Museum in New York State, and the Kennedy Space Centre in Florida.

NATIONAL WARPLANE MUSEUM

What do you know - the Museum displayed a Canberra - called a B 57 in the States. Or Martin RB-57A to be exact. The Canberra was one of 26 aircraft included in the Museum's collection.

The National Warplane Museum, established in 1983, is dedicated to preserving the history and heritage of military aviation, from 1914 to today. The exhibits honour the development and sacrifices made in military flight from pre-World War II years through to the present day. One of its primary aims is the preservation of vintage aircraft in flying condition and is also host to the annual *Wings of Eagles*® Air Show - which has been described in the Air Classics magazine as one of the best all-military shows in the States. The Museum maintains a fleet of several flying 'planes', including of course, the Canberra.

They also had a Piper Cub in their restoration hanger - the same type of aircraft that my father had given my brother Jan his first air experience way back in September 1957.

MASONITE USA MILLS

I visited Towanda Mill in picturesque Pennsylvania where the rivers were iced up and the hills were covered in snow. Road signs read "Speed Limit 55 mph" and "Ice on Bridges in Cold Weather". The golf courses were spectacular, with the 'pin' flags on the greens protruding through the snow blankets along the fairways. I considered the houses 'cute', invariably double-storied and of wood construction. There were no frontage walling or hedges, and one erf seemed to merge with the property next door without any visible intervening separation. Shovelling snow away from the driveways leading from the road to the garages seemed to be the only popular outdoor activity. The mainly white population was estimated at about 6,000 souls. The countryside was slightly hilly, with undulating high points only rising to about 500 feet high. All the people were rather large and thick set in stature - possibly as insulation against the wintry cold. Although pretty to the eye, it was not the sort of environment that I would like to live in. I spent two nights and three days in Towanda, and then took a US Air flight to Pittsburgh (by DC-9), and then on to New Orleans by B737-300. Captain Feltcott flew the latter leg - and he had a true 'greaser' on landing at New Orleans.

The Mississippi River estuary enters the sea at New Orleans - and the area along the river is steeped in American history. I was met at the Airport by DJ Shuttle services from

Hattiesburg and driven the 120 odd miles to Laurel. En route we crossed over the impressive Lake Ponchetrain on a bridge 5½ miles long. Dan, my driver, mentioned that the road bridge that was to our left was 7½ miles long and a third bridge across the Lake was in fact 26 miles long. I must say it felt quite unusual driving a motor car in the middle of a lake where the shores could hardly be seen. The countryside was very flat and marshy - with the marshy areas called creeks. The one that caught my fancy was named Hobolochitty Creek. For the first time I saw racoons - but they were all dead - struck by oversized American cars and trucks travelling on the Interstate freeways - at 70 mph - which is the speed limit on the Louisiana roads. Another New Orleans observation was that all the tombstones were massive above ground structures - apparently because of water seepage in the low-lying area on which New Orleans was established.

Laurel was somewhat larger than Towanda. The Mill is a massive place, the home of Masonite, and where Masonite was first manufactured in the 1925s. The Mill itself is sited on 600 acres, with 64 acres under roof. The factory is so large that the staff drive battery powered golf-cart type buggies. Within the factory, select employees get around riding tricycles. I spent three days and two nights at Laurel and was fascinated to see timber-chip lorries raised bodily to about 40° from the horizontal, in order to discharge their load of wood chips in a matter of seconds. The press floors were also fully automated and the factory as a whole was exceptionally clean. Laurel fully justified itself as the flagship of Masonite Corporation.

I returned to New Orleans via Hattiesburg, and booked into the Holiday Inn situated close to the airport. After dumping my kit in the room, I caught a lift with DJ Shuttle into the city centre. Dan, my driver, dropped me off in Bourbon street - because no visit to Louisiana would be complete without visiting the Hillbrow type highlights of the city. A Mardi Gras was in progress, so I seated myself at a pavement café to witness the spectacle of an odd procession winding their way through the narrow streets. I then went on a shopping trip to the Mississippi River Walk where paddle steamers were plying the river. I had no joy locating the specific computer software that Pey wanted, and settled on buying a scanner for myself in order to digitise the selection of pictures for my autobiography.

Early the next morning I boarded a Delta Airlines flight to Orlando in Florida. We took off, flew past nice sounding Tallahassee, and landed at Orlando, Florida. The co-pilot put down an absolute greaser and I complimented him on his landing. The Captain mentioned to me that the CL68, being a low wing airliner, was generally easy to land. I familiarised myself with the airport layout and established that I needed to get to the 'B' Concourse for my return flight for Atlanta. Having done that, I then boarded Mears Shuttle for the 26-minute minibus ride to the Double Tree Guest Suite hotel at Disney World. It seemed to me that everybody in the States not only expected to be tipped, but actually demanded some form of gratuity. The hotel room was also quite pricey, but then it had a separate lounge, with microwave oven, fridge, coffee maker, - and three televisions - including one in the bathroom. Everything in the States was big, real big. The king-size bed, the motor cars, the people, the shopping centres, the factories - just about everything.

DISNEY WORLD

Talking of big - Disney World was spread over something like half a dozen sites over ten to fifteen square miles. Downtown Disney and Pleasure Island at about two miles was within walking distance. Epcot Centre was about ten miles away, Magic Kingdom about fifteen miles, Sea World, MGM Studios and Animal Kingdom like distances. Buses ran frequently between all the pleasure resorts. Although I spent one week at Disney World, the time waster was queuing up at the various popular shows - some taking as long as an hour to gain admission. While I wish not to list all the various attractions, I intend only to elaborate on those that were memorable. But before doing so, permit me to summarise some of the attractions at the many Disney resorts:

Planet Hollywood – a landmark at Downtown Disney. The structure is global shaped with the inner spiral staircase lined with portraits of current and past 'stars'. The exhibits glamorised the world of film and television, with its celebrity-style dining amid Hollywood's greatest memories. Unfortunately the pictures I took inside the building did not come out and I was unable to show Rina some of the suspended cars, sailing ships and aircraft.

Rainforest Café – with its animations and column aquariums. The volcano erupted periodically, spewing clouds of steam and thundering waterfalls. The restaurant was always full, with the diners being able to marvel at the tropical fish swimming up the glass pillars and along inter-linking tubular aquariums. There were also a large variety of animated tropical robotic reptiles and animals suspended amongst artificial foliage.

World of Disney – Smoking is prohibited in most restaurants, all merchandise shops, waiting areas and rest rooms. I pitied all like habitude oxygen poisoning Homo sapiens.

The visit to the Space Centre was the highlight of my USA trip. I joined a bus shuttle tour to travel the sixty odd miles from Orlando to the east coast of Florida. We travelled on the Bee Line Inter-State (USA terminology for Freeway), so called because of the Bee and Honey industries as a result of all the pine trees growing in the flat lands which Florida is renowned for. As the bus approached the Kennedy Space Centre, we spotted the odd alligator lazing in the water courses along the freeway. Nearer our destination a couple of real monsters were around – like about three to nearly four metres in length, with girths that I wouldn't be able to put my arms around.

After going through the turnstiles I made a beeline to the Space Shuttle Explorer that had been pensioned off and now stands on sturdy frames to permit tourists access to the cockpit. It was awesome to think that here I was, in a space ship that had actually been in space and landed successfully back on earth. Other space shuttles included Discovery, Endeavour and Atlantis.

I walked around the static display of the various rockets that were the forerunners of landing man on the moon. Seeing the Mercury and Gemini rockets just blew one's mind. Right at the back was a Saturn 1 rocket, which launched man around the moon. It made the other displays pale into insignificance. From there, visitors could board busses to visit other areas of interest.

From there, I visited Launch Control LC-39, from where the shuttles are propelled into space. After clambering all over the gantry, I jumped the long queues that was a feature of my visit to the States. I was pleased that I did so, in order to inspect the Saturn V hangar. Well, if one thought that the Model 1 was enormous, there was just no comparison to Saturn V. I stopped to ponder the achievements of Apollo 11 – from 16th to 24th July 1969, when Commander Neil Armstrong broadcast his historical words "Tranquillity Base here. The Eagle has landed." The headlines flashed throughout the world – "Man Walks On The Moon – A small step for man, a leap for mankind". The space crew on Apollo 11 were Commander: Neil Armstrong, aged 38, a veteran of Gemini 8. Command Module 'Columbia' Pilot: Michael Collins, also aged 38, and flew on Gemini 10. The Lunar Module 'Eagle' pilot was Edwin Buzz Aldrin, aged 39, and commander of Gemini 12.

Apollo 11 achieved President Kennedy's goal of landing on the Moon with only 30 seconds of fuel remaining, astronauts Armstrong and Aldrin planted the American flag and collected the first samples of lunar soil. A sample of lunar rock was appropriately mounted on display, and visitors were able to touch the surface of a foreign planet.

There is a memorial for all the astronauts that died in space. Most people will recall the horrific visuals when the Space shuttle Challenger exploded whilst launching in February 1986. During my walkabout I was also able to sit in one of the Lunar Buggies on which the astronauts practised their routines on the moon.

x – 0 – x

The year 2000 was eventful for the family. Apart from my good lady Rina, we all did some Globetrotting. Shortly after I returned from America, Grahame, Renene, Courtney and Brendan went to New Zealand, and Pey had an envious trip to Israel. Dr Grahame Jelley landed a locum position at Westport, South Island. Having time to enjoy some of the sights and sounds such as the Frans Josef and Fox Glaciers, skiing in the Alps, visiting the hot springs, doing crazy things like bungee jumping, the KiwiJells soon found job offers in Hokitika and Westport. Zimbabwe land invasions by the so-called war veterans, with its breakdown in law and order, enticed the KiwiJells to seek their fortunes elsewhere. Then Pey and his lady friend Marcelle joined a tour group to the Holy Land. They visited Cairo, went to the biggest under-water observatory in Eilat, toured Tel-Aviv, Bethlehem, Nazareth, Jerusalem, the Dead Sea, Galilee and all the Mounts that are so popular in the Bible. Rina was green with envy, but relived the stories and pictures via the Internet.

My dear sister Delene went on an extended holiday to North Island, New Zealand in late 1999, ostensibly to be with daughter Chanli who was expecting their third Kiwi, and stayed there, waiting for her husband Stuart McColl to sell up shop in Kloof, to join her in their new homeland. That left my brother Jan and I to make the most of the last British outpost – on the Natal south coast.

THE KIWIS – NEW ZEALANDERS

The writers daughter Renene, with husband Grahame and children Courtney Sacha and Brendan Vaughan, immigrated to Westport, South Island, New Zealand in 2000. Grahame joined a medical practice on the West Coast – and stayed a number of years. Then in November 2002 they arranged a Geldenhuys Family re-union at 'Gentle Annie' – to which my son Pey, my sister Delene and niece Chanli Brink gathered. New Zealand had become a popular destination for disenchanted Africans - - Chanli was the first to emigrate with her husband Charles – settling initially in the Tauranga area, where their first child, Tal was born; Nea was born in Waitakere and the last two girls Deu and Gem in Auckland.

My sister Delene relocated to New Zealand after being brutally attacked in their Kloof home. Her husband Stu McColl followed as soon as the family affairs were wrapped up – settling initially on the large plot that Chanli and Charles had bought.

GENTLE ANNIE – NEW ZEALAND

A really special reunion was arranged and organised by my daughter Renene, for the Geldenhuys "clan", for Christmas 2002. I had just retired from Masonite, relocated to Durban, and boarded the Qantas flight to Christchurch towards the latter part of November. We were met by Doug and Yvonne Pasea and had a good old chinwag to the wee hours. Doug took some leave for a couple of days and showed us around all the highlights. Then after taking the Trans-Alpine express to Greymouth, we spent awhile on the West Coast, plus a week-end retreat to the popular north coast – also spent with my son Pey – who had flown in from South Africa, via Kuala Lumpur – for the reunion. My sister Delene, living in Whangaparoa, Auckland, joined us at Mokihunui, Gentle Annie holiday resort. Interestingly, her entire family, like mine, were able to make the reunion (of a lifetime – six relatives having flown out from South Africa). All credit goes to my dear daughter Renene who had organised every detail to the tenth degree – from sleeping arrangements, all meals to feed an army, entertainment for the hordes of children, sight-seeing excusions and seeing that everybodies needs were met. Thank you, Askoek!

Rina and I spend three months getting to know and see all in Kiwiland. The memories that linger are Sandflies and needing jackets during summer to keep the chill out. After all is said and done, we remain content that our grandchildren are raised in a beautiful, and peaceful, part of God's creation.

The highlight of 2003 was a trip to the volcanic active White Island, approx 50 miles off-shore from the Bay of Plenty, as a 60th birthday gift by my daughter Renene - - and her bidding me farewell from Auckland in the morning, and my son meeting us at Durban airport in the evening - - the 20 February 2003 was thus a 36-hour day - - certainly the longest day / longest 60th-birthday for me.

2007 was noteworthy for the very short life that my youngest grandson Jake only lived a mere 12 days. I need not tell any parent or grandparent who has lost a child the torment and sorrow that one experiences. We think of Baby Jake every day and pray that this bitter cup be taken away. As a grandfather, I had extremely high hopes and expectations of a worthy successor to carry on the family tradition of documenting our Geldenhuys heritage - - but God must have other plans.

The year was also marked by the launch of two books, Rhodesian Air Force Operations with Air Strike Log, and Nickel Cross. Operation Miracle was launched with the Unveiling of the Miracle Memorial on the 3rd October 2008. It was particularly satisfying to having flown Rene Strydom out from London to Durban to witness the tribute paid to her father who was killed in action in the Canberra that was shot down in the Manica Province of Mozambique.

In November 2008 my son Pey flew to Auckland to see whether he could find employment and thus get his family to join him. Whilst there, Bill Jelley died very unexpectedly – on the 15th January 2009. Bill's younger son Keith and his wife Jean, flew in from Australia to attend the memorial service and cremation. The last flight of WPJ

– William Paterson Jelley was flown five days later – with the scattering of his ashes over the sea at Ohope Beach.

A service was held in the chapel of Brent Willetts Funeral Services Ltd, 21 King Street, Whakatane followed by a private cremation.

Bill was born in Durban South Africa and moved with his family to Rhodesia as an infant.

He grew up drawing aeroplanes and all he dreamed of was flying. He trained as an air force officer and served his country with distinction. Later he flew as a commercial pilot for many years gaining respect wherever he travelled.

A loving husband, a father figure beyond reproach, a caring brother, an attentive Grandfather and a good friend to all.

Bill was an Officer and a Gentleman always and this is how he will be remembered for ever

The Family wish to thank you all for your love and support with your presence here today and extend a warm invitation to you all to join with them for refreshments at the Ohope Bowling Club, Harbour Road, Ohope at the conclusion of the service

William Paterson Jelley

✈ ✈ ✈ At 9am on Monday 19th January 2009 ✈ ✈ ✈

MALAN REUNION

Francois Daniel Malan turned 60 on 7th February 2009. To celebrate this event, the Malan family gathered at Amanda and Charles Stopforth's Game Farm in the Polokwane (called Pietersburg during White Rule) area.

Being a strong believer in there is a right time for everything, the appropriate time arose to hand over Frans' Oupa Malan's manuscript, complete with original photographs, to its rightful owner. This valuable family history has been 'preserved' for the past 22 years.

I might add writing family history can be 'terminal'! Within a year of Oupa Frans Malan completing his manuscript, he passed away! Bill Jelley is another – who was writing articles for ORAFs (Old Rhodesian Air Force Sods) – and I suspect, having put the finishing touches to his own Jelley family history. So any budding authors out there – beware, your days may well be numbered when you sit back and say my story is done. Thank goodness I concluded that this Geldenhuys Genealogy will never end, because the family just continues growing, and it thus requires frequent and regular updates.

Having said that, lets get back to Uitkyk Game Farm - -

The first photograph shows all the Malan sisters and brothers together, according to age: from left to right they are:

- Lettie van Aardt [nee Malan] – all the way from Bredasdorp, southern Cape. Spouse is Nic van Aardt.
- Gerta Bezuidenhout [nee Malan] – from Bulawayo, Zimbabwe. Spouse is 'Hansie' Johannes Jurgens Bezuidenhout.
- Hendrik Malan – from Pretoria, Gauteng. Spouse is Rina [nee Gerber].
- Rina Geldenhuys [nee Malan] – from Durban, Kwa-Zulu Natal. Spouse is Pey (or Preller – as known by most of the Malan family).
- Phil Malan – from Pretoria, Gauteng. Spouse is Elcora [nee Bouwer].
- Frans Malan – from Vereeniging, Gauteng. Spouse is Helena Alberta [nee Lock].

Other family, friends and relatives present included:

- Charles Stopforth and Amanda [nee Malan], with their three children, Dominique, Michael and Andrew – from Polokwane.
- Martie Stopforth – Charlies mother.
- Pieter and Charmaine Stopforth, with their daughter Rochelle.
- Johan Bezuidenhout and Adele [nee van der Walt], with Jared –from Roodepoort, Johannesburg.
- Roux Malan and Leslie, with Monique and Dillan – from Pretoria.
- Francois Malan and Adele, with their children Damien and Cloe – from Vereeniging.
- Phillip Malan and Maritza (nee Lourens) – from Pretoria.

- Nicolene Olivier [nee van Aardt], with her son Jaco – from Johannesburg.
- Hugo Lock, with Willem, Tom, Shelley and Jacquelene – from Binga.
  - Ian Currin and Ina [nee Lock] – from Mooi River.
  - Graham Currin and Margie, with their children Ian, Taylor and Sarah Kate- also from Mooi River.
  - Shaun Palmer and Gail [nee Currin], with their children Brandon and Nicky.
- Gideon and Winnie van Zyl, from Vereeniging.
- Jakkie Jacobs, a family friend – also from Vereeniging.
- Esme Rautenbach and friend Piet Uys – from Nelspruit.
- Albert de Beer – from Pietersburg / Polokwane.

The next couple of photographs shows a variety of chalets and self-contained cottages.

The Malan family, starting with Lettie, Gerta, Boet, Rina, Phil and Frans – otherwise known as Aletta Magdalena Susanna van Aard, Getruida Johanna Bezuidenhout, Hendrik Malan, Susanna Catharina Geldenhuys, Phillipus Johannes Malan and Francois Daniel Malan

Some of the developments on the Stopforth's Uitkyk game farm in the Polokwane (Pietersburg) area, including a watch-tower, adorned with a beautiful African rainbow.

The Malan and Lock family gathering at Uitkyk Game Farm

The Malan family – with their spouses – Phil with Elcora, Lettie with out Nic, Gerta with Hansie, Rina with Preller, Frans with Helena and Hendrik with Rina (who passed away suddenly a few months later)

Another milestone in 2009 was the birth of our second granddaughter, Lucy Hope Geldenhuys on the 29th March, with the whole family immigrating to New Zealand, where Pey took up a position with Abel Software Solutions. Later on in the year, a further three books were added to the family library – *Rhodesian War Casualties and Air Force Memorials*, *Rhodesian Memorials* and *The Anglo-Boer War Diaries of Jan Geldenhuys*.

The end-of-year highlight was a sponsored flight by our daughter Renene to join the New Zealand family for Christmas. What a joyful Christmas present for ageing grandparents to spend some quality time with our precious grandchildren. Courtney had achieved the highest award that Saint Johns can bestow – The Grand Prior Award. Brendan did particularly well with his speech and drama presentations – which all told makes for very proud and appreciative grandparents. These life skills will stand the youngsters in good stead later in life.

The Geldenhuys Reunion – Waihi Log Cabin

Renene Jelley again arranged a memorable Geldenhuys reunion in New Zealand. The first gathering was Christmas 2009 at Pey and Eloise's recently occupied home in Auckland, followed by another reunion at a delightful log cabin in Waihi – which coincided with Rina's 65th Birthday – and her 44th wedding anniversary. For the first gathering, the Brink family joined the festivities, with everyone dressed in traditional African dresses. However, the gathering at the Log Cabin was particularly special, with Rina being joined with all her grandchildren in the hot-tub!

Africans in New Zealand – another major cross-road in life

Back Row: Stu and Delene McColl, Courtney Jelley, Matthew Geldenhuys and Brendan Jelley
Front Row: Eloise and Pey Geldenhuys with baby Lucy, Rina and Preller Geldenhuys, Renene and Grahame Jelley

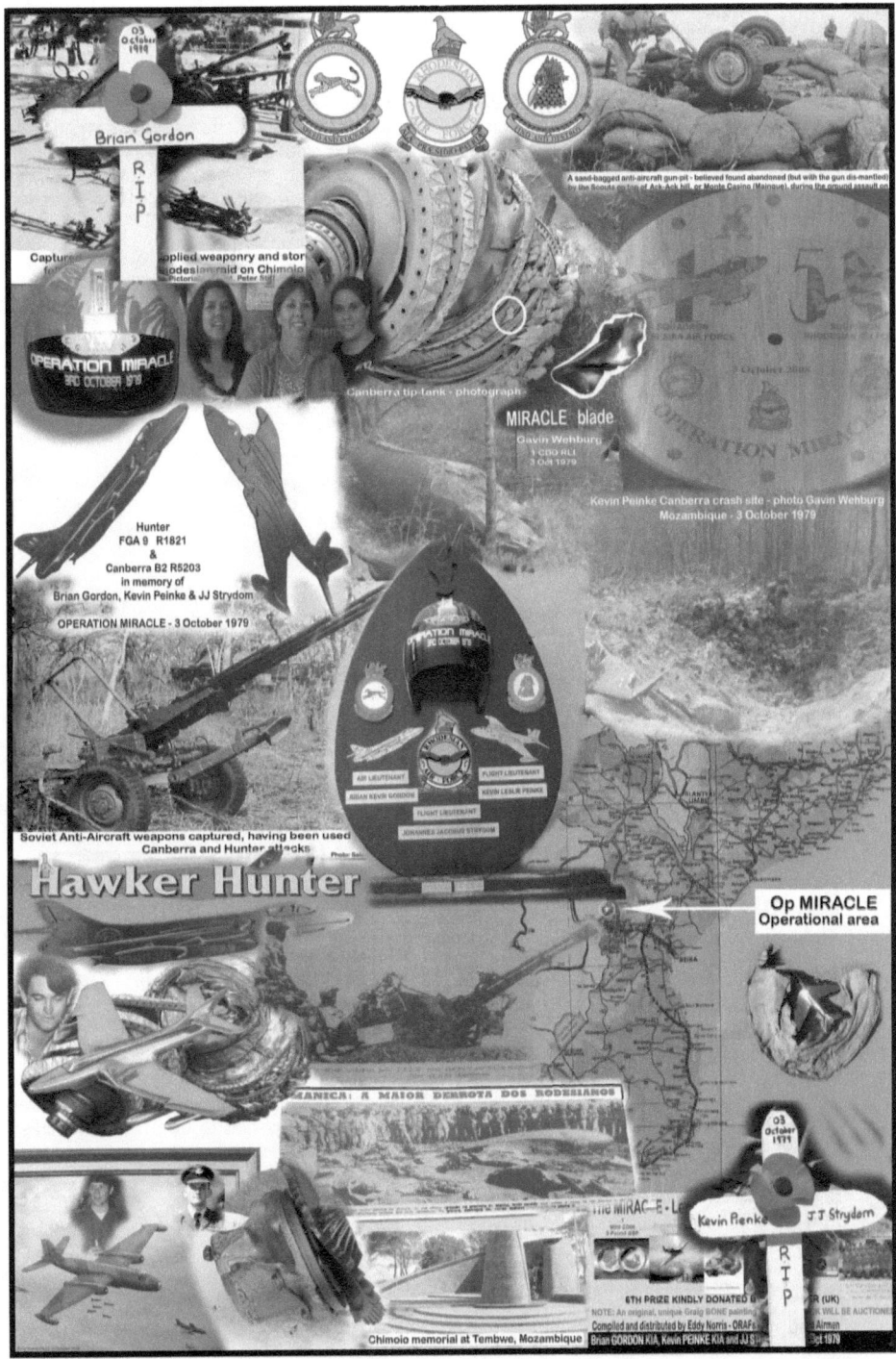

KiwiJell Sea Cruise - May 2011

The Jelleys boarded the Pacific Pearl luxury liner for a cruise to the Great Barrier Reef, off the Australian east coast. This was followed nearly three months later when Courtney joined her class mates on a week's marine-studies trip to Heron Island which boasts of being one of Australia's top dive destinations on the Great Barrier Reef. The students were privileged to visit the University of Queenland's Heron Island Research Station, as well as carrying out some spectacular Scuba dives, capturing all sorts of coral and colourful tropical fish, as well as giant turtles. These experiences will last a life time.

Brendan and Courtney Jelley – on a cruise to the Great Barrier Reef

Exodus to Kiwiland

While enjoying a family reunion in a 'hot-tub', in a log-cabin setting in Waihu in New Zealand, we were persuaded to consider relocating to New Zealand, sponsored by the generous KiwiJels. This was a tough decision – but the right one to get Rina established near her children. At first I was reluctant to sell our 10-year 'holiday home' overlooking the Durban harbour. In socialist South Africa, ramifications would be ending up with defaulting tenants who would be difficult to evict.

Rina's twin brother Philip Malan had taken the decision to emigrate to Scotland. Two or three sales of their Pretoria / Tswane home collapsed for various reasons, but they did manage to secure a successful sale in June 2011. Frans Francois Malan, the youngest brother, also had the sale of their Vereeniging home fall through – intending to move to Polokwane (previously Voortrekker named Pietersburg) to join their daughter and son-in-law Amanda and Charles Stopforth on their Game-farm. We had better luck – our Durban flat was sold within three weeks! It happened to be a buyers market, but considering the economic climate prevailing in South Africa, we are satisfied with the deal that was concluded. Jan and Julia was having financial difficulties with their Amanzimtoti property development – mainly due to the building slump. Meanwhile, our residence permit applications, submitted to London, was taking a lot longer than anticipated. A hastener sent was turned down. However, a Grandparent / parent multiple entry visa was considered the best short term interim arrangement and this course was duly explored – timings would be crucial – since we still wished to bid farewell to our South African / Zimbabwean relatives before departing African shores.

The Guys and Dolls on board the Pacific Pearl Cruise ship

ADIO AFRICA – FAREWELL

We left Durban on the 22nd September 2011, for Gauteng, to lodge our 'multiple entry visas' at the New Zealand Immigration office in Pretoria. First stop, however, were the Beavers, living in Goud Street. With the aid of Nelson (our friendly Mandela Tom-Tom GPS) we duly arrived alongside the Joe Slovo street adjoining Goud Street, in the Joberg city centre – instead of Goud Street Goedeberg – where our lifelong friends the Beavers live! This meant we were faced with jockeying for road space with thousands of road hogs in the 5 o'clock rush hour traffic. Got to Richard and Caroline's posy for a slap up lamb gourmet dish, leaving at sparrows for Pretoria in the early morning traffic rush to the capital city.

Rina and Preller with Libby Beukes and Christopher and his girlfriend Karla van der Waal

Pey and Rina with Jule and Jan Geldenhuys, prior to departing on our Adio Africa journey

Nelson [Mandela] took us straight to the New Zealand Immigration, on the Friday, only to discover that the Kiwi were having their Heritage Day public holiday – and the offices would only open on the Monday for business again. Well – that put paid to our carefully planned 'Adios' journey – but we made up for it to venture into Faerie Glen where Boet (Hendrik Malan) lives with his youngest son, Eddie. After some revealing revelations of Hendrik's youthful escapades. This took us to the Pretoria rush hour traffic for a Friday; if we thought Johannesburg was bad, Pretoria – or Tshwane as the ANC Government prefers to call their high jacked Capital City – proved worse than eGoli

A selection of wild flowers in the arid Cape, en-route to Bredasdorp

Our detour into Matjiesfontein was well worth the time – a place my grandmother Lizzie Preller spoke often about. She said that OuDad Jannie Geldenhuys and she would take a break en route to Cape Town to reflect on the Anglo-Boer War where the British had erected a monument to General Andy Waucup – who was killed in action during the battle of Magersfontein (the British did not distinguish Magersfontein in the Northern Cape with Matjiesfontein in the Southern Cape.

During the War, a vast Remount Camp, with 10,000 troops and 20,000 horses, was established on the village outskirts. The veld southwest of the station is still littered with camp remnants including rusty old bully beef and biscuit tins. Part of the recently finished Hotel Milner served as a convalescent hospital for British officers and its central turret serving as armed look-out post. Matjiesfontein was also the site of the Old

Courthouse where the trial of Boer hero Gideon Scheepers was held. Readers may recall my earlier report of how and why Scheepers was shot by the British as a Cape rebel – and the burning down of my grandmother's homes in Bothaville, because she had fed his commando when he passed briefly by their De Bank / Katbos View homes.

This bit of unfinished business convinced me to once again route via Graaff Reinet – to see whether I could find any untold history of the Scheepers assassination by the British.

Van Aardt family (with maiden names): Hendrik van Aardt, Joleen Geldenhuys, Preller Geldenhuys, Rina and Lettie Malan, Nic van Aardt

Our detour via Graaff-Reinet was indeed fruitful – finding a special Scheepers dispay corner in the Military Museum section, as well as the Ivory serviette rings that Jan Petrus Geldenhuys brought back from the Ceylon prisoner–of-war camp. I also concluded that it was his son – Jacobus Francois Geldenhuys who was executed by Firing Squad on that fateful St Valentines day in 1902 – 14th February - - with his name appearing immediately after that of G.J. Scheepers – Gideon. The charge sheets also attracted my attention.

Gideon was tried on the 18th December 1901 and shot a month later on the 18th January 1902. The day Gideon was shot is the same day that Jacobus Francois Geldenhuys was tried - - and he was shot on the 14th February 1902.

Geldenhuys's charges were for being active while armed, attempted murder and plundering. Scheepers' charges were 7 counts of murder, attempted murder, cruel behaviour, mistreating of prisoners, three counts of corporal punishment, destroying the railway line, destroying trains and sixteen charges of arson.

Gideon Scheepers look-a-like corner

Additionally, my interest in genealogy was further enriched when I came across the death notice of Jan Petrus Geldenhuys's wife – Martha van Heerden – who died at the residence of M.Dippenaar (Graaff-Reinet), aged 49-years and 10-months, on the 22nd June 1896, having borne seven children to Jan Petrus Geldenhuys. They were Martha Geldenhuys (named after her grandmother, Martha Burger), Jacobus Francois Geldenhuys (listed as a minor – the son who was assassinated by the British Firing squad short of six years later), Margaretha thye third child, then a son Jan Petrus named after his father, then another son Andries, then Burgert Christian and the last named Hendrik Jacobus.

A trip to the Cape is not complete without visiting the most-southern tip of Africa – at Cape L'Agulhas – as witnessed by the next two photographs.

Cape L'Agulhas – Southern-most tip of Africa

Preller Geldenhuys with Lettie van Aardt and sister Rina Geldenhuys (nee Malan)

Adrian and Libby van Rensen
The next stop was a very pleasant hot-spring swim at Tshipise – spoit somewhat with a power failure from early evening till the very early hours of the following morning.

Elcora and Phil Malan, with twin-sister Rina

Hot spring swim at Tshipise
After a harrowing couple of hours getting through the Beit-Bridge border post into Zimbabwe, we were graciously received by Hansie and Gerta Bezuidenhout at their retirement village home, 71 Qalisa, in Bulawayo.

Johan and Jared Bezuidenhout

Back in Pretoria, Libby Beukes took us to lunch at a Chinese Kung-Fu restaurant, and then met up with my other cousin, Adriaan van Rensen – who is the family expert on palms and things botanical.

Rina with her sister Gerta, and Hansie Bezuidenhout

On impulse I motored up to Gweru / Gwelo in order to revisit the aircraft that featured so prominately in a very satisfying career with the Rhodesian Air Force.

Percival Provost – at the Aviation Museum

Vampire T11 – originating from South Africa, during the height of the Rhodesian War 1965 – 1980

This particular Hunter had my name on the Canopy rail during 1970 – as Flight Commander on No 1 Squadron

R1188 showing evidence of the 1982 sabotage at Thornhill base

Flew this Canberra many times

Thornhill High School – where our courtship began

Cranwell Head of House - 1981

Gweru Dutch reformed church

Bogies clock – Gweru centre

Brother and sister – Hendrik and Rina

Keith Nell presenting his-story – Viscount Down – the true story

With Danny Hartman (Hamilton, New Zealand), Johan and Brent Bezuidenhouit

Last official function – laying the Air Force wreath at the SAS Memorial Sevice, Flame Lily Park, Durban – 5 November 2011
Good bye, Africa

Remembering – 11 November 2011
Layed the Air Force wreath at the memorial service

The Geldenhuys Reunification

Christmas 2011 marks the uniting of the Preller Geldenhuys family in New Zealand. Thanks to the Jelley's, who two years earlier at the Waihi Log Cabin re-union, convinced the parents / grandparents to join them permanently. It was a very difficult decision, bearing in mind that tracing the family heritage for twelve generations, meant that African blood truely flowed in our veins. Grahame and Renene very generously sponsored our residence applications and made short shrift of the necessary medical examinations and x-ray requirements.

Residence applications is a lengthy process that requires a good three months to get the police clearance certificates and unabridged birth certificates timeously. Then a processing qeue starts with referrals from Hamilton, to London, to Pretoria – and now most probably back to New Zealand to complete the circle. Air fares to get to Auckland on Christmas day 2011 came up out of the blue; we accepted this good fortune as a twist of fate which hastened our efforts to wrap up all our affairs in time, including getting this Geldenhuys Genealogy published in time, as our gift to family and friends – to remember our African heritage.

Adios Africa – welcome the Frontier of Dreams, a new beginning in a new land, in New Zealand

ALL BLACK IN TRAINING

Mini-All Black in Training

Is this Zimbabwean an All Black in training? In earlier days Oudad recalls a "Doctor in Taining". Perhaps Brendan Vaughan Jelley will join his other sporting relatives – like Pey Malan Geldenhuys at World Championship Waveskiing; Jason Froneman at Golf and Craig Jannie Geldenhuys at Blue Bulls rugby? Watch this space, because time will tell.

2011 was World Rugby Cup fever in New Zealand – but more importantly, it is the Geldenhuys reunification, as Kiwis.

DICTIONARY OF FAMILY BIOGRAPHY

During 1999 the writer came across the academic reference book DSAB – Dictionary of South African Biography – by Professor W.J. de Kock -- which gave rise to creating our own Dictionary of Geldenhuys family biography! I make no apology for obvious plagiarism, for reasons to retain historical accuracy, albeit much of the research conducted is entirely the compilers' responsibility. Hopefully, this attempt may facilitate easier cross-referencing as the "plot thickens"!

Geldenhuys, Albert Barends (Gildenhuisz or Gildenhuyzen – born Burgsteinfurt in Wesfale and died Cape Town 1693), sailor, settler, farmer, Vryburger, deacon of the Cape Community. He was the "Stamvader" of the Geldenhuys family in Southern Africa. He arrived at the Cape of Good Hope on board the Dutch ship *Princesse Royale* during the time of Jan van Riebeeck and became a *Vryburger* on 23rd September 1661, one of 46 (very few freemen were given their papers between 1662 and 1666). Between 1662 and 1665 he was employed as a farm labourer on various farms. First he helped a Hermann Fer Schekhoven; then in 1663 he farmed with Coenelis Claas; and then from 1664 to 1665 for a Jacob Cloete who had arrived at the Cape with Jan van Riebeeck. (Cloete died 1693 - was murdered - but his grandson, was the first Hendrik Cloete, of Stellenbosch, who acquired the famous Constantia estate in 1778). By 1672, six years after temporary Commander Wagenaar left, the freemen's numbers had increased to only 64.

In 1666 Albert Barends returned to Duitzland and married Margaretha Hoefnagels, born 28th March 1649 in Legden, a town near Burgsteinfurt (she was previously married to Hendrik Schakelmann), and was the daughter of Arend Hoefnagels and Grietje Cornelis. Albertus, Cornelis and Hendrik were subsequently very popular names for their descendants.

Albert Barends came back to the Cape in 1672 with his wife and first child, on board the *Vrye Lieden*, Their next seven children were all born in the Cape. He became a Deacon in the Cape Community in 1689 and died ca 1693.

Geldenhuys is derived from the Dutch form of a dorp near the Holland border in Germany. The family crest came into being in 1945.

Albert Barends Geldenhuys is a direct ancestor (9 generations; great-great-great-great-great-great-great-grandfather to the author).

Anthonis, Catharina, born in Bengal, India, was the first slave to gain freedom, and married Jan Woutersz from Middelburg, Woutersz in 1656. He was promoted to the position of supervisor on Robben Island soon after his wedding – not based on merit, but because he was found 'unsatisfactory' and later sent back to Batavia. A few years later, Jan Stael from Amsterdam married Maria van Bengalen (note: - Bengal), a union found more acceptable as Maria could speak Dutch and had some knowledge of Christianity. See also the write-up on Matthys Johannes Gildenhuyzs.

Most slaves carried names given by slave-dealers or their owners. Slaves owned by the VOC Company ("**V**ereenigde **O**ost **I**ndische **C**ompagnie", also known as the Dutch East India Company) often retained versions of their real names, usually miss spelt by the Company's clerks, such as Sao Balla, Revotes Kehang or Indebet Chemehaijre. Privately owned slaves were generally called Anthony, Jan, Pieter, Anna and Catrijn. They also received classical and biblical names, such as Titus or Rachel, or named after the months of the year as in April, Juli, September and October. Their 'surname' usually referred to their places of origin, as in Paulus van Malabar or Lisbeth van Bengalen (Elizabeth of Bengal – India), while those born at the Cape were known as 'Van de Kaap' (of the Cape) as in Juli v.d.K., who fathered Matthys Johannes.

It is speculated that Catharina could well be considered a "Stam-Moeder" of the coloureds!

Armstrong, Patrick married relative Mary Walls, the daughter of Lieutenant General Peter Walls. The picture of Pat was taken in Mozambique, when the author accompanied the Rick van Malsen led team into the *Search for Puma 164* (published in 2011).

Arnott, Sydney Nathaniel (born St Marks, Queenstown, Cape Colony, 28th November 1867, died Salisbury Hospital, 14th December 1924). Rhodesian Pioneer and survivor of the Mazoe Patrol. Great-great grandfather to Courtney Sacha and Brendan Vaughan Jelley.

He attested into the Pioneer Corps on 18th April 1890 and was appointed a Trooper in 'B' Troop under the Pioneer Column commanding officer Major Frank Johnson, when the Union Jack was hoisted in Cecil Square at 10a.m. on the 13th September 1890. He prospected on the Mazoe River after the disbandment of the Pioneer Corps. Later did contracting work in Umtali. Entered into partnership with E Finucane in brick-building venture. Built first brick building in Salisbury – at the corner of Pioneer Street and Manica Road. Became a Forwarding agent in Salisbury in 1895. Farmed at Komani and Gletwin Farms. Member of first Committee, Agricultural and Horticultural Society in 1896. Was one of thirteen Volunteers to relieve the Alice Mine / Mazoe garrison – in which their leader Captain R Nesbitt was awarded the Victoria Cross – June 21, 1896 during the 1896 Rebellion. Was wounded a month later when serving under Beal's Column near Hartley on the 27th July 1896.

He also served with the Rhodesian Forces during the Anglo-Boer War. Thereafter, farmed at Thabanchu (near Pretoria), but returned to Rhodesia in 1903. Settled on Good Hope Farm, near Salisbury. Arrested after a farmers protest meeting outside the Drill Hall. Sometime Chairman of Pioneer Society, and Secretary to Farmer's Co-op.

He died in Salisbury Hospital, 14th December 1924, after taking a dose of corrosive sublimate in mistake for quinine.

Sydney Arnott married Lucretia Maria Coleman (descendant of Benjamin Moodie) in Salisbury on 3rd March 1896 and had 3 sons and 2 daughters.

DICTIONARY OF FAMILY BIOGRAPHY

Badenhorst, Marile (born Gansbaai, Western Cape, 30th January 1981), married Regardt Geldenhuys. Went to Hoërskool Overberg, is a Pharmacist assistant and owner of the Gansbaai Boekwinkel.

Belfour-Cunningham, Bianca married Chad Porter. Daughter of Vivian Carr, who is Jounita Dippenaar's daughter.

Bester, Wilna (born Vanderbijlpark, Gauteng), went to Transvalia Hoërskool, class of 1978, then studied at the University of Orange Free State, class of 1984. Lives in Pretoria where she is a Anaethetist. She married Izak George Geldenhuys and is the mother of Cabous and Lena.

Bester crest

Beukes crest

DICTIONARY OF FAMILY BIOGRAPHY

Beukes, Christopher, son of 'Libby' Elizabeth van Rensen

Bezuidenhout crest

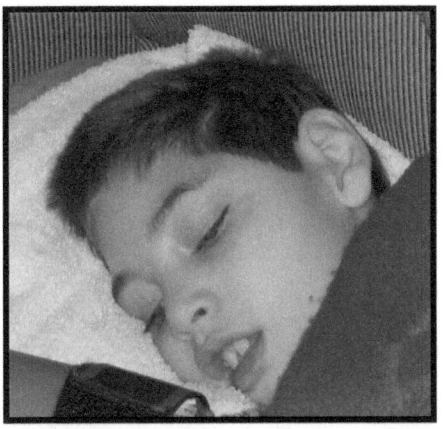

Bezuidenhout, Aiden Kyle, (born 2nd October 1998, died 13th March 2008). Eldest son of Johan Bezuidenhout and Adele van der Walt. Died 13th March 2008.

Bezuidenhout, Brent, Johan's son, married to Vicky Kleynhans; they have two children and live in Amanzimtoti. The writer met up with Brent at the SAS annual meeting in Durban in November 2011 (his picture above was taken at the Natal Mounted Rifles Officers' Mess).

Bezuidenhout, Bronwyn, daughter of Johan Bezuidenhout, married Dan Thompson. They have one child.

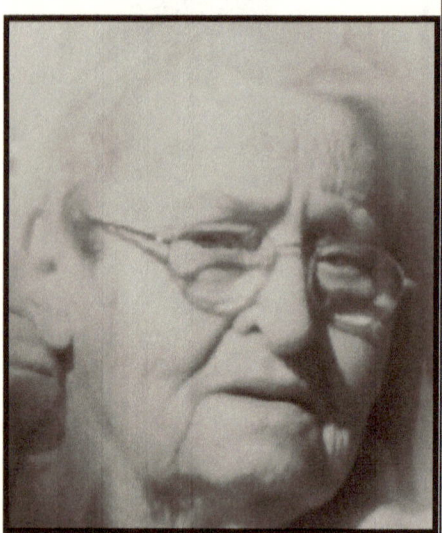

Strangely enough, Betty wrote a letter the day before she died, with Hansie receiving it a week after her funeral.

Bezuidenhout, Francois (born Salisbury Rhodesia 16th June 1962), a pilot flying for a Sheik in Saudi Arabia but currently living in Australia. Francois married Valerie Linda Wigston at the Jameson Hotel Chapel in Harare Zimbabwe in January 1994. Valerie is the daughter of Doug and Jessie Wigston from Northern Rhodesia, born in Wales, England. Francois and Valerie have two children, Jaydene born 1st August 1994 in Harare and Tane Jurgens born 29th September 1997 in Harare, Zimbabwe. 'Bez' is a keen musician, playing the guitar and keyboard. Sporting prowess includes the art of Kiyokushin self defence.

Bezuidenhout, Elizabeth 'Betty' Susanna (born Enkeldoorn 12th March 1924 and died Pietersburg 4th September 2011), sister to 'Hansie' Johannes Jurgens Bezuidenhout, married Benjamin James Bezuidenhout [son of Thomas]. They had three children, a son Tom and two daughters Elisabeth Susanna 'Elise' who married a van Rensberg and Matilda 'Hilda' who married a Long.

Bezuidenhout, Gerda (born 6th November), not to be confused with 'Gerta' Gertruida Johanna Bezuidenhout [nee Malan], has a son Jacques born 3rd November 1987, and a daughter Jacky.

Bezuidenhout, Johannes Jurgens 'Hansie' (born, Enkeldoorn, Rhodesia 17th July 1932), son of Johannes Wilhelmus Bezuidenhout and Elizabeth Susanna Hamman, schooled at Bothashof, Salisbury, married Gertruida Johanna "Gerta" Malan, tobacco farmer in the Tengwe district of Karoi, retired to Mica Point in Kariba and subsequently relocated to Qalisa retirement home, Bulawayo.They have three children – Johan, Letitia and Francois. His elder brother Wynand, gets his name from great-grandfather Wynand Allen. His great-grandmother Mary Ann Dorothy Berry was also Irish, born in County Cork, Ireland. Hansie has Scottish blood from his mothers side – Ouma van Niekerk was a McDermott, with Isobel, Agnes and Elsie coming from his Grandfather's sister side of the family.

The Bezuidenhouts arrived in Rhodesia prior to 1900; settling in the Lionsdale, Silverdale and Rockydale areas all in the Enkeldoorn, Gutu and Felixburg areas. His fathers cousin, Fred Bezuidenhout, settled in the Odzi area (west of Umtali, on the eastern border with Mozambique).

Hansie has a passion for woodworking, having obtained a distinction whilst still at school.

"Hansie" Johannes Jurgens Bezuidenhout is the brother-in-law to the authors wife

Bezuidenhout, Johan, son of Hansie and Gerta Malan.Small Bez, as Johan was known in the Rhodesian Special Air Service, served his country of birth with distinction during the Rhodesian War.Johan had two children from his first wife, Bronwyn, and two boys from his second wife, Adele van der Walt.

Johan Bezuidenhout is a nephew of the authors wife.

Bezuidenhout, Johannes Wilhelmus (born Enkeldoorn, Rhodesia, 6th October 1900), is the great-great-grandson of

Johannes Jurgens Hamman born Mooifontein in the Free State 18th October 1814 - - - and in turn is the father of 'Hansie' Johannes Jurgens Bezuidenhout, also born Enkeldoorn 17th July 1931 (who married Gerta Malan, and is the brother-in-law to the authors wife).

Bezuidenhout, Jared, son of Johan and Adele van der Walt; and is the grandson of a sister to the authors wife.

Bezuidenhout, Letitia (born Fort Victoria 10th November 1958) daughter of Hansie and Gerta Malan. Went to Sinoia High School. Married Ronald Mark Gooding at the Tengwe Community Church, Karoi on 11th November 1978. They have five children – Adam Daniel born 5 February 1979, Cherie Jane born 6th February 1982, Dean Mark born 18 June 1984, Benjaman Luke born 25th February 1987 and Braydon Lee born 12 August 2004. Facebook friend in 2011.

Letitia Gooding [Bezuidenhout] is the neice of the authors wife.

Bezuidenhout, Jaydene (born Harare, Zimbabwe 1st August 1994) to Francois and Valerie Wigston.

Jaydene is the grandson of a sister to the authors wife.

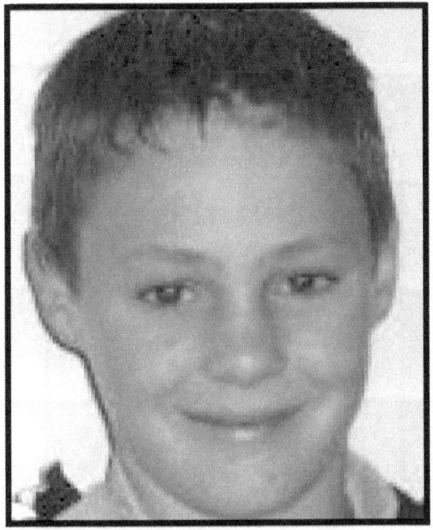

Bezuidenhout, Tane Jurgens (born Harare, Zimbabwe 29th September 1997), son of Bez Bezuidenhout and Valerie Wigston. Tane inherited his middle name from his grandfather. Tane is a budding Australian rugby player, joining his cousin Craig Geldenhuys, who has been signed up with the Blue Bulls rugby team.

Tane Jurgens Bezuidenhout is a grandson of a sister to the authors wife.

Bezuidenhout, Wynand (born 1927), married Dorothea 'Dot' Johanna Kruger, brother to Johannes Jurgens Bezuidenhout [who is a brother-in-law to the authors wife].

Wynand was also an early farmer in the Karoi area of Rhodesia, who later build a house on Mica Point, Kariba.

Borruso, Charmaine, born 7 January 1960, to Peter Borruso and Julia Lillian Dippenaar – see Charmaine Geldenhuys (name changed).

Borruso, Stuart, born 18 September 1957 to Peter Borruso and Julia Lillian Dippenaar – see Stuart William Geldenhuys (name changed).

Botha crest

Emmarentia Margaretha Geldenhuys (born Botha)

Thanks to the writers 4th Cousin, Marita Brodie (nee Geldenhuys), who lives in Fiji, the gavestone of Lourens and Emmarentia above, is gratefully reproduced.

Botha, Emmarentia Margaretha (born 16th November 1866 and died 15th November 1938), married Rand Pioneer Lourens Geldenhuys (1864 – 1929), in 1887, the year after her fiancé named a portion of his farm 'Emmarentia', which later became a prestigious suburb of Johannesburg. Emmarentia and Lourens had 15 children, but only eight survived. The others died mainly due to diphtheria.

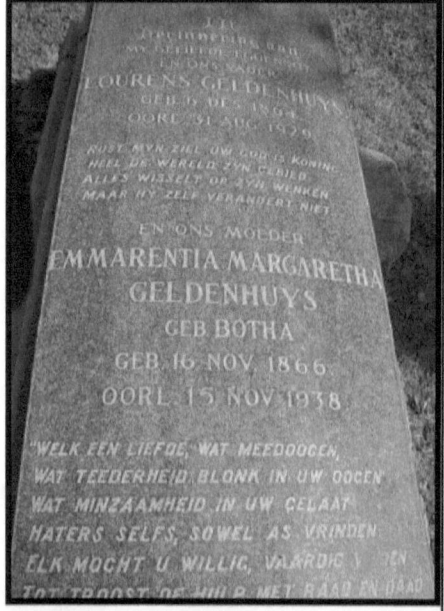

Botha, Theunis Louis was the founder of Bothaville and one of the earlier settlers of Kroonstad. He was the grandfather to Lizzie Geldenhuys, nee Preller. He purchased Gladdedrift farm in 1873 and sub-divided it into four lots – Gladdedrift, Botharnia, Grootdraai and De Bank. Botha ceded De Bank, which was part of Gladdedrift, to his son-in-law Abraham Christoffel Naudé Preller.

His wife was Anna Elizabeth Dreyer (from whom Lizzie Preller got her names) and his parents were Lourens (Louw) Rasmus Botha and Helletje Levina Bester. They had 15 children, with Theunis being the eldest. Theunis' twelfth sibling and his daughter were named Helletje Levina. The daughter married ACN Preller who obviously was Oumam Lizzie's parents. Oumam and Ou Dad Jannie's first daughter was born during the Boer War but died in the Kroonstad Concentration Camp. She was named 'Moeder se liefling Helletje Levina'. The writer derived much pleasure in discovering the origins of names – so one can rest assured that Delene owes her middle name to Ouma Groetjie Anna Elizabeth Dreyer (and incidentally also to Elizabeth Johanna Erasmus, our Theunis Louis Botha's grandmother).

Theunis Louis Botha is a direct ancestor (4 generations; great-great-great-grandfather to the author).

DICTIONARY OF FAMILY BIOGRAPHY

Bothma, Rita (born 2nd May 1950), married her husband Ulrich Geldenhuys on her birthday. She has a daughter, Louise Maritz.

Bouwer crest

Bouwer, Chanli G. (born Vereeniging 12 October 1970). Chanli is the eldest daughter Dr Johannes Jacobus Francois Bouwer and Delene Elizabeth Geldenhuys. Married Charles J Brink on 6th February 1993 and emigrated to Tauranga, New Zealand where they had their son Tal J in August 1995. Chanli then had three beautiful daughters – Nea in Waitakere on Delene's birthday 1998, Deu and Gem in Auckland in November 1999 and October 2001 respectively.

Bouwer, Debra (born 26th December 1966), Her maiden name is Simpkins. Honours degree at the University of South Africa, in Ancient Egyptian Studies. Married Johannes

Jacobus Francois Bouwer. Owner of Nomadic Adventures and has climbed Mount Kilamanjaro seven times.

Debra Bouwer [Simpkins] is the wife of an ex-husband of a sister to the author).

Bouwer, Elcora (born Groblersdal, Transvaal 26th October 1951), married Philip Malan who is the twin brother to the authors wife.

Elcora and Phil have two children. A son Roux Daniel Malan and Elsa-Lou Cornelia. Roux married Lesley Ann Reeve and Elsa-Lou married Willem Petrus Nel.

Elcora and Phil are about to emigrate to Scotland, to join their daughter Elsa-Lou and son-in-law WP Nel.

Bouwer, Johannes Jacobus Francois (born 1942), who featured in the earlier editions, married Delene Elizabeth Geldenhuys. Qualified as a doctor at the University of Pretoria. They had two daughters, Chanli and Rensha. Johan had his practice in Hartley, and then relocated to Hillcrest in Natal, where he married Debra Simpkins.

Bouwer, Johann Ludwig, arrived in 1724 from Kassel, Germany. Married Cornelia Burger on 19thFebruary 1736 and had 14 children, including their fourth child Jeremias (born 1743) who married Susanna Vermaak in 1765 (5 children). Their eleventh child Willem Christiaan (born 1758) married Aletta Catharina Nel in 1784 (also 5 children) and Petrus Frederik (1760) who had 11 children with Regina Dorothea van der Bank.

Dr J.J.F. Bouwer married Delene Elizabeth Geldenhuys in Pretoria – and they had Chanli and Rensha. Descendants are Tai, Nea Deu and Gem Brink

DICTIONARY OF FAMILY BIOGRAPHY

Brink crest

Bouwer, Rensha (born Salisbury 15 February 1972 and married Craig Brown in Durban). Rensha is the younger daughter of Dr Johannes Jacobus Francois Bouwer and Delene Elizabeth Geldenhuys. She married Craig Brown in Durban but the relationship did not last very long. Her artistic talents came to the fore at an early age and she was able to make a full time living from it.

Rhensha got on very well with her cousins Pey and Paul Geldenhuys. She also enjoyed scuba diving and joined Paul on several sea trips to the Aliwal Shaul off the KwaZulu Natal coast.

Rhensha moved to Auckland and enrolled in a Catering / Cooking course – much to the delight of close family and friends.

Brink, Andries (born circa 1700), from Waarden, Zeeland, married Sophia Grove on 13th July 1738 (born 1722, daughter of Andries, from Viborg, Juutland) and then married Alida de Waal on 30th March 1749. Andries had 13 children, 4 by Sophia and 9 from Alida. All his children had large families; - his first son Andries had 8; the second, Jan Godlieb had 10, the 7th Johannes had 14, the 11th Daniel had 11; the 12th Cornelis a whopping 18 children and 13th Arend had a round dozen 12!

A descendant, Charles Brink, born on New Year's Day 1st January 1961.

Brink, Anje – sibling to Jana Geldenhuis. Facebook friend.

Brink, Charles Roy (was born on New Year's Day 1st January 1961). Charlie is an Accountant by profession. He married Chanli G Bouwer on the 27th August 1995, eldest daughter of Johann Bouwer and Delene Elizabeth Geldenhuys. Charles fathered four children, Tal J, Nea D, Deu G and Gem, all born in New Zealand. Charles settled initially in the Bay of Plenty Tauranga area, then Waitakere, and finally at Arkles Bay in the Whangaparoa peninsular north of Auckland.

Brink, Carol (born Ballito, Natal north coast, South Africa 16th June 1970, youngest sister to Charles Roy. Partnered Stephen James Murray and is mother to Jordan Elizabeth Murray, born Sandton Clinic, Randburg, South Africa.

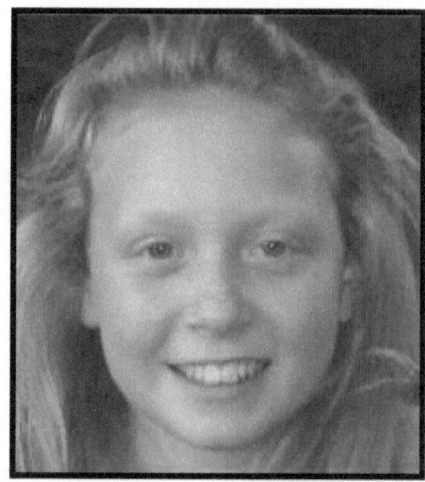

Brink, Deu G (was born in Auckland 7th November 1999). She is the second daughter born to Charles Brink and Chanli Bouwer.

Deu is particularly athletic and an excellent role model for her sibling sisters. They all live in Whangaparoa, New Zealand.

Brink, Gem (was born in Auckland 17th October 2001). She is the youngest daughter and a real gem born to Charles Brink and Chanli Bouwer.

Gem shared a most memorable 10th birthday celebration with her older cousin, Bevan Muirhead. Christmas 2011 will also hold a special surprise for OuPey's favourite relative – she was just so cute at Pey's wedding to Eloise Howard.

Brink, Jana, sister to Anje Brink. Married Mellie Geldenhuis 10th December 2005

Brink, Jenny (born Pretoria 7th October 1967), went to Stangar High School, married Rory Terence Culhane on the 7th May 1993, in Alberton,Johannesburg and they have two boys, Liam Connor and Glenn Cameron. They live in Sydney, or is it Quakers Hill, NSW, Australia.

Jenny is the webmaster of her excellent MyHeritage site – a passion she shares with the author.

Brink, John Robert (born Pretoria, South Africa 28th August 1963), brother to Charles Roy, married in Krugersdorp 18th October 1998 to Yolande Prinsloo, who was born on 15th November 1974. They have a son, Joshua Dean, born 18th December 2002 in the Sandton Clinic, Randburg, South Africa.

Brink, Joshua Dean (born Sandton Clinic, Randburg, South Africa 18th December 2002), son of John Robert Brink and Yolande Prinsloo.

Brink, Nea D (was born in Waitakere, New Zealand on 27th February 1998). She is the second child but first born daughter to Charles Brink and Chanli Bouwer. Tap, Jazz and Ballet comes naturally to Nea, who also performed as a dancer in the Intermediate School production of "*Joseph and his Technicolor Dreamcoat*". Nea also landed the role of *Tootles*, one of the lost boys in the musical production "*Peter Pan*". Nea has also auditioned for local amateur theatre production Centre stage of the musical "*The Railway Children*" which is staged in early 2010.

Brink, Richard (born Johannesburg, South Africa, 21st January 1957), married Brenda Joan Matheson on 27th December 1980. They have two daughters, Kellie Marie born 23rd October 1981 and Christie born 11th February 1988, both born in the Sandton Clinic, Randburg, South Africa.

Brink, Schalk Reginald (born 8th November 1933), married Mona Daphne van Rooyen. Schalk is the grandfather to the Brink, Culhane and Muirhead children. He died on the 23rd February 1988, on the south coast of Kwa-Zulu Natal, South Africa.

Brink, Schalk Richard (born 1864, died 11th December 1918), married Jane Sarah Glenn, born 9th February 1866 and died in Johannesburg 12th November 1933.

Brink, Schalk Richard 'Ben' (born 10th August 1891). He married Maud Nellie Liversage, and died 13th May 1972. He was the father of Schalk Reginald, and grandfather to Charles Brink.

Brink, Tal J (was born in Tauranga, New Zealand on 27th August 1995[and nota day earlier as previously published – his mother pointed out that Tal's grandmother and the writers sister Delene McColl nee Geldenhuysalso get the date wrong because New Zealand is 10 to 11 hours ahead of South Africa, and as Tal was born at 3:04 hours on the 27th August, it was still the 26th in South Africa when the good news was phoned to grandmother Delene. I trust Tal will forgive the writer for tis indescretion]). As the first born son of Charles Brink and Chanli Bouwer, Tal has become responsible to always look after the welfare of his three younger sisters. He is answerable to OuPey to discharge this duty! Tal enjoys reading anything and everything, which in turn has equipped him to speak his mind on a very wide range of topics. He also enjoys playing the guitar and is a band member in three bands at College. Drama and dancing also featured as an activity that was performed for ten years – culminating in the Dance School's "Sole Movement" annual show in 2009 – where Tal performed Ballet numbers – and giving up Ballet mainly because taking strain on his knees – and did achieve his Intermediate level grade. Tal also performed in a musical where he landed the minor lead role of "*Zeke*" in the North Shore Musical Theatre's "*High School Musical*".

At the time of writing, a 'Bouwer' family reunion is New Zealand is being planned for March / April 2012. This open secret will be more widely publicised when this Two Volume family history is published and distributed.

Brody, Donald Ross (born Christchurch 27th January 1922 and died Timaru, New Zealand 29th September 1982), father of Donald Ross born 1947 and father in law to fouth-cousin Marita Geldenhuys.

Brodie crest

Brodie, Donald 'Ross' (born Gerldine, New Zealand 29 January 1947) married fouth-cousin Margaretha Helene 'Marita' Geldenhuys born Ermelo December 1946. They have two children, and are currently separated.

John Ross Brodie

Burns crest

Brodie, John Ross (born in Greenock, Renfrewshire 1848, and died Timaru, New Zealand 23rd October 1923), father of Ross and great-grandfather of Marita Geldenhuys.

Ross Brodie

Brodie, Ross (born Dunedin 26th September 1892 and died Rangitata River 16th April 1953), father of Donald Ross and grandfather of Marita Geldenhuys. Uniform indicates that he fought in the Second World War (and possibly the First as well).

Burns, Deirdre (5th March 1967), went to Lewisam Primary School in Salisbury, Rhodesia, class of 1979. Married Hermann Erwin Rudibert 'Rudi' Geldenhuys (born Pretoria 8th September 1964) and they have two children – Adriaan born April 1993 and Andrea 'Annie'. They live in Faerie Glen, Pretoria and Deirdre is the co-creator of the Infobracelet and now Infoaides. Facebook and MyHeritage friends in 2011.

Deirdre is the wife of the writer's third cousin. It may be that Burns is the adopted surname from Tapson, and that Deirdre had also been married to Dougie Stylianou and a third marriage to Jan Bezuidenhout. Time did not present itself to resolve the mystery fully.

Carr, Vivian, married Belfour-Cunningham. They had Bianca, who married Chad Porter.

Cloete crest

Cloete crest

Cloete, Jacob (born Cologne - died Kaapkolonie 23rd May 1693), oldest settler farmer, arrived from Keulen, Germany, with his wife Fytje (Sophia) Raderotjes.

He came to the Cape with Jan van Riebeeck in 1652 and employed Albert Barends Gildenhuysz as a farm labourer. Jacob Cloete will go down in history as one of the first nine men released by the Dutch East India Company, in February 1657 to become a 'free burgher' and granted 11,5 hectares of land along the Liesbeek River. Albert Barends Gildenhuysz also became one of the select free burghers on 23rd September 1661.

Jacob became a Corporal in the VOC. He had four children. His son Gerhard or Gerrit was born in Cape Town in 1655, his daughter Christina Catharina on 4th April 1660 and son Coenraad on 23rd April 1663. Coenraad's grandson Hendrik, born 1725, was the largest landowner, including Constantia (he married Hester Anna Lourens and they had eleven children).

Jacob Cloete's fifth generation granddaughter, Johanna Catharina, married Colonel John Graham (born 24th April 1778 in Linlathen, Scotland) - who established Grahamstown in 1812.

Jacob Cloete was murdered on 23rd May 1693.

Culhane crest

Cloete, Johanna Elizabeth, married Jan Gerhardus de Waal. Affectionately known as 'Anna'. She is the mother to Karen and grandmother to Chanel and Craig Jannie Geldenhuys. Her husband Jan Gehardus who died in Vanderbylpark in December 1972

It would not be amiss to speculate distant relationships to Jacob Cloete who employed Albert Barends Gildenhuisz 1662-1665, Cape wine farmer, as well as World War 1 fighter pilot hero 2nd Lieutenant Dirk Cloete, and the same Major Dirk Cloete who was responsible for the formative years of the Rhodesian Air Force.

Culhane, Caitlin Sinead (born Roodepoort, South Africa, 20th August 2004), is the daughter of Sean Kevin Culhane born in Johannesburg on 27th February 1964 and Carol-Ann du Preez.

Culhane, James Joseph Michael (born Melbourne, Australia 14th October 1869), married Jessie Oats, in Sea Point, Cape, South Africa. He died on 5th March 1949, in Sea Point.

Culhane, James Michael Sheenan (born in the Sandton Clinic, Randburg on 18th June 2000), son of Michael William Culhane born Johannesburg 13th November 1965; and Marilyn Rosemary Jury, born 8th February 1968, in South Africa.

Culhane, Rory Terence and Jenny (born). Jenny is a Facebook and MyHeritage relative who regularly keeps in touch. She went to Stangar High School and lives in Sydney, Australia. Jen is the expert on the Brink, Culhane and Muirhead families.

Culhane, William Joseph Michael (born Krugersdorp, South Africa, 23rd December 1936), got married in Johannesburg on the 27th May 1961 to Alison Glastonbury.

Culhane, Joseph Aloysius (born 12th March 1905), married Annie Alida Schulze, and died in Natal, South Africa on 17th May 1987.

de Oliveira, Carlos Alberto Lopes, married Salome Malan, daughter of Philip Johannes Malan and Ria Venter

DICTIONARY OF FAMILY BIOGRAPHY

de Oliveira, Michael, grandson of Philip Johannes Malan

Delport crest

de Oliveira, Michelle, grand daughter of Ria Venter. Lives in Bothas Hill, Hillcrest, Kwa-Zulu Natal.

Delport, Danita "Dee-Dee" (born 1st November 1990), daughter of Hennie Delport and Sonja Geldenhuys. Sonja's father was Danie Geldenhuys born 15th November 1938, grandfather was Barend Petrus Lodewyk Geldenhuys, of the Strand.

de Villiers, Cobus (born 23rd September 1974), married Liesl Adriana Oosthuisen – daughter of Alta van Aardt, and live in the Paarl, Cape Province. They have three sons, Jacques born 23rd April 2003, Adriaan born 28th January 2005 and Ben born 19th April 2008.

de Waal crest

de Waal, Jan (born Holland, 3rd January 1692), Stamvader, arrived in 1715, from Amsterdam. He fathered 17 children; married Elisabeth van Eck on 3rd May 1716 – they had 13 offspring, then married Anna Elisabeth on 24th March 1748 and had the remaining 4 children.

Jan's ancestors could be traced back to 1410/1473. He was a seventh generation descendent of Jan De Waal who became the landowner of Rozenburg, near Haalem in Holland. The "oerstamvader" apparently originated from Wale in Belgium (also 'De Wael' in Vlaams). The German branch, or 'tak', of de Waal, since 1410 hailed from Emmerich, Germany as well as Arthur de Waal from Koblenz.

Jan and Elisabeth had four noteworthy children. - b1 Jacoba, born 1717, who married Cornelis de Leeuw on 21st March 1756 and thus became the 'stammoeder and stamvader' respectively; secondly – b2 Arend, born 15th October 1719, with, who married Maria van Breda on 21st August 1740 (they had nine children); - b3 Cornelis, born 1721, married Hilletje Mostert on 13th May 1742 (they had 13 children), and – b8 Hendrik, born 1732, married Elisabeth Judith Louw on 23rd May 1756, 4 children and then married his second wife, Catharina Maria Hoppe on 1st December 1771. They had 3 children.

Karen's father, grandfather and great-grandfather were all named Jan Gerhardus. It is thus most probable that Karen is a descendent of Arend (born 1719). She married Paul Preller Geldenhuys. One day, when Craig Jannie becomes curious, he will find the de Waal genealogy most fascinating!

de Waal, Jan Christoffel (born Stellenbosch, 8th April 1844 - died Paarl, 16th October 1936), farmer and member of the Orange Free State Volksraad, was the son of Pieter de Waal (of Langverwacht, near Kuilsrivier) and Susanna Gertruida Louw. He was the tenth of fourteen children. All of his six brothers became prominent farmers

He spent three years at Moddergat School, then one year at Uiterwyk and then continued his education through private study. He left in 1866 to become a sheep farmer in the Free State. For the first few years he hired farms Kroonpos and Constantia in the Bethulie district. Selling produce on the diamond-fields, he farmed successfully. In 1873 he bought a house in Bethulie and in 1888 he went to live on the farm Skoorsteenberg in the Smithfield district, which he had bought in 1884. Here he built a spacious house and made the property a model farm

He served his community with regard to religion, education, local government and farming. From 1881 to 1889 he represented the Grootrivier ward, and from 1893 to 1900 the Slikspruit ward in the Volksraad. He was among those who, in 1899, opposed war with Britain. His farmhouse on Skoorsteenberg was destroyed during the war; he was however, arrested on 13th May 1901 but was allowed to live in his Bethulie house until the end of the war.

He went to Australia in 1906, to buy 7000 stud sheep for shipment to the Free State. On 14th January 1870 he married Martha Elizabeth Bosman (she died 12th January 1890). They had four children. On 2nd July 1891 he married Christina Beyers and in 1912 he settled in Paarl, where he lived until his death.

de Waal, Jan Gerhardus. Great-great-grandfather to Chanel and Craig Jannie Geldenhuys

de Waal, Jan Gerhardus. He married Christina Johanna. He is the Great-grandfather to Chanel and Craig Jannie Geldenhuys.

de Waal, Jan Gerhardus (died Vanderbylpark 19th December 1972). He married Johanna Elizabeth Cloete. They are Grandparents to Chanel and Craig Jannie Geldenhuys.

de Waal, Jan Hendrik Hofmeyr (Jannie) (born Bakkerskloof, Somerset West, 30th December 1871 - died Cape Town, 30th October 1937), champion of Afrikaans, author, journalist and politician, was the second eldest of the seven children of David Christiaan de Waal and Hester Sophia Hofmeyr, the eldest sister of Jan Hendrik Hofmeyr. de Waal was named after his grandfather, Jan Hendrik Hofmeyr.

He married Emmarentia de Kock, 22nd December 1898, and they had six children. From his fifth year, the family lived on a wine farm, Bellevue, in the Gardens, Cape Town.

de Waal, Karen (born Vanderbylpark 29th May 1966) melktert-bakker, cook, party organiser and proud mother. Met Julia Geldenhuys whilst working at Avis Rent-A-Car at Edenvale and married her son, Paul Preller. Relocated to Bengu drive, Amanzimtoti and was instrumental in establishing the family SAFA Juice distribution business with her father-in-law, then helped to manage the tourist facility of Ferry and Bay Services in the Durban harbour, and then managed the office of Bush Babies Lodge, Amanzimtoti. She has two children, Chanel and Craig Jannie, both born in Durban. Karen is extremely protective of her children and always speaks very highly of them. She supports Chanel's ambition to become a Zoologist and is looking forward to her daughter studying horticulture, landscaping and design at Nong Nooch Tropical Gardens in Thailand in 2008. This, however, did not happen. Chenel got her Bachelors degree at Port Elizabeth University instead, and at the time of going to press, was studying for her Honours degree at the University of Natal in Durban.

Karen often also speaks with pride that her son Craig managed to gain admission to Glenwood School on a sports bursary, playing first class rugby and being offered a handsome contract with the Blue Bulls to play rugby professionally for them.

de Waal, Sir Nicolaas Frederic (born Netherlands 1873 - died Cape Town 1932), 1st Administrator of the Cape Province in 1910, arrived in 1880, married the daughter of A.F. du Toit from Graaff-Rienet, in 1885. They had one son and one daughter.

The de Waal's produced numerous people of nobility – in addition to the above Knighthood, a study of the family reveals the following: -

    1 Kommissaris – Arend (1719)
2 Doctors – Dr. Gideon Daniel (1871), Dr. Daniel Malherbe (25.4.1914)
    1 Judge – Justice Daniel (1873)
1 Advocate – Adv. Jan H.H. (30.12.1871)
    1 Dominee – Ds Pieter (19.10.1875)
1 Professor – Prof. dr. Hermanus Lambertus (27.2.1848)

Once again, I would challenge Craig Jannie Geldenhuys to research family relationships, should his curiosity ever be roused!

Dippenaar, Alwyn Jacobus, (born 23rd July 1924), brother to Julia, affectionately known as 'Dippy'. Son of Johannes Petrus Dippenaar born 24th October 1898 and Louzya Christina de Bryn born 30th November 1898.

Dippenaar, Anna Johanna Sophia (born 20th February 1920), eldest sister to Julia Lillian.

Dippenaar, Johanna Maria Barendina (born 12 January 1918), first child of eight, born to Johannes Petrus Dippenaar born 24th

DICTIONARY OF FAMILY BIOGRAPHY

October 1898 and Louzya Christina de Bruyn born 30th November 1898. Known as 'Joey'.

Dippenaar, Johannes Marthinus, (born c. 1720 - 1790), Stamvader, originally Depner, from Wehlau in Oos-Pruise (Duitsland) arrived in 1735. He became a burger in 1746 and two years later, on 10th November 1848, married Maria Magdalena Schmidt. She was the daughter of Christian Schmidt, from Halle, Germany. They had ten children. Johannes possessed the farm "Groene Valley" on the Olifantsrivier – where he died in 1790.

Descendant Julia Dippenaar married Johannes Albertus Geldenhuys, who are the grandparents to Craig and Chanel Geldenhuys.

Dippenaar, Johannes Petrus (born 24th October 1898), married Louzya Christina de Bruyn (born 30th November 1898), parents of Julia Lillian Dippenaar.

Dippenaar, Julia Lillian, (was born Ficksburg, Orange Free State 12th July 1936), businesswoman, sewer and homemaker. She is the eighth child born to Louzya Christina de Bryn and Johannes Petrus Dippenaar. Her schooling was carried out at Warner Beach on the South Coast, and married an Italian, Peter Borruso. They had two children. When Stuart was five, and Charmaine three, Julia divorced her husband. Peter Borruso then immigrated to Australia where he later died.

Julia married Johannes Albertus Geldenhuys in Luanshya, Northern Rhodesia, on 27th March 1964, and they produced a son Paul Preller on 15th December 1966. The family immigrated first to Swaziland, then to Edenvale and then to Natal where Julia established her "Bits and Pieces" haberdashery business. Having settled initially in Amanzimtoti, they bought a flat at Illovo Beach. With husband Jan expanding the SAFA fresh juice business, they moved to Bengu place, and commenced property development.

Main social activities centred on playing lawn bowls where Julia aspired to Vice-Captain of the Winkelspruit Bowling Club.

By 2005, her son had built up Bush Babies Lodge, and Julia then managed the Butterfly restaurant. By 2007 she took over management of the complex single-handedly, while daughter-in-law found full-time employment and husband Jannie continued to spend their money on Wave Master! The Butterfly restaurant was eventually closed down and converted to a house for Jan and Jule amongst the Taurico Gardens property development – with Julia focusing on the 'Gardens' beautification and managing the sub-letting of all her cottages on the property.

Dippenaar, Jouanita (born 16th January 1931), sixth child of Johannes Petrus Dippenaar born 24th October 1898 and Louzya Christina de Bruyn born 30th November 1898, married Jack Carr.

DICTIONARY OF FAMILY BIOGRAPHY

Dippenaar, Louis Hosea, (born 15th February 1929), brother to Julia, who married Johannes Albertus Geldenhuys.

Dippenaar, Lousya Christina (born 30th August 1922), another family member of the Dippenaars that originated in the Warner Beach, Amanzimtoti area, south of Durban.

Dippenaar, Schalk Willem (born 14th January 1933, seventh child of Johannes Petrus Dippenaar born 24th October 1898 and Louzya Christina de Bruyn born 30th November 1898. Schalk is the elder brother of Julia Lillian.

Dreyer crest

Dreyer, Anna Elizabeth – Daughter of Jan Dreyer, married Bothaville founder Theunis Louis Botha, and grandmother to Lizzie Geldenhuys (nee Preller).

Dreyer, Johannes Gerhardus (born 18th March 1812, died 28th March 1888, aged 76) – Cattle farmer, and next door neighbour to Louw Botha and Johannes Albertus Geldenhuys when the first Kroonstad plots were sold by public auction. He became the great-grandfather to my grandfather, Jannie Geldenhuys. His daughter Anna Elizabeth, married Louw Botha's son Theunis Louis, who bought Gladdedrift and on whose farm Botharnia the town of Bothaville was established.

His parents were Christiaan Lourens Dreyer and Christina Steyn. His first marriage to Johanna Maria Malan produced ten children, and his second marriage to Martha Magdalena Borman produced two children. The first born was Anna Elizabeth, the fourth Herculaas Philip and the ninth Christiaan Lourens "Kil" – more about the forenamed later on.

du Plessis, Adele married Francois Daniel Malan (junior) in Vereeniging on the 8th May 1999, the wife of the nephew of the authors wife.

du Plooy, Andre married Nicolene Olivier, nee van Aardt, in Bredasdorp, in December 2012.

du Plessis, Jan married to Eugene Geldenhuys.

Dunckers crest

DICTIONARY OF FAMILY BIOGRAPHY

Dunckers, Arné (born Pretoria 4th March 1986), grand-daughter to the writers cousin, 'Libby' Elizabeth van Rensen. Daughter of Libby's son Brandon Dunckers (born 20th July 1965 and Karen Botha. Arné studied at the University of South Africa, lives in Cape Town and works for MediaVision Interactive. Facebook friend in 2011.

Engelbrecht, André (born 4th February 1967), married Julanda Geldenhuys, born 15th July 1969. They married on 3rd October 1992, have two children, a son Adriaan and a daughter Suzanne. They live in Swellendam.

Engelbrecht crest

Estment crest

Estment, Ingrid Stella (born Johannesburg 1st September 1950). Ingrid is the mother-in-law to Pey Geldenhuys and grandmother to Matthew Dylan. She is the eldest child of William Henry Estment, born 1929/30 and Martha Petronelle (Floss) Coetzer, born 1931 and died at age 67 on 16th December 1999. Ingrid has a younger sister June, and a younger brother Norman Bruce. Ingrid married Kenneth Steve Howard (born 4TH October 1947) in Durban on 6th June 1970. They have two children, Eloise and Dylan. Ingrid and Steve liked the song "Eloise" so much that they named their daughter after the song. When Ingrid gave birth to their son, they named him after the singer Bob Dylan. The Howard's and Geldenhuys' met early 2006 as a result of their children Eloise and Pey getting together. The parents, like their children, got on very well – like a house on fire – and being doubly blessed with Matthew Dylan (who is an expert on Dinosaurs).

The writer believes that young Matthew owes much of his formative development to his Granny.

Froneman, Jason, born 4 January 1996 in Johannesburg to Lance Froneman and Charmaine Geldenhuys. At age 14, Jason was already playing amateur golf and intends taking the sport up professionally.

Froneman, Lance, partner to Charmaine Geldenhuys, fathered Jason. His grandmother, Mien Lotter, was the writers aunt – sister to Matt Lotter. Mien married Beljon – whose daughter Madel, was Lance's mother – married Froneman. The Lotter family tree still needs researching. It is significant that the Biljons were Anglo-Boer War captives of Abram Carl Frederik Preller Geldenhuys (the writers father) and Bram Preller – writers grandfather's father-in-law – who shared a tent in the Umballa prisoner-of-war camp in India. During the Anglo-Boer War, a Commandant Froneman features prominently with General de Wet. Much research is needed to document Froneman's war experiences.

Geldenhuijs, J.F – see Geldenhuys, Jacobus Francois – shamefully shot by firing squad at Graaff-Reinet 14th February 1902, shortly before the end of the Anglo-Boer War 1899 - 1902.

Geldenhuis, Albertus Hendrik, son of Martinus, married Maria Catherine Susana 'Modi' Naude. He is the grandfather of Gilbert Jacobus born 1st November 1975, who is the webmaster of the Geldenhuis My Heritage website.

Geldenhuis, Albertus Hendrik 'Bert', (born 1st October 1935 and died Graaff-Reinet 21st May 2000), married Maria Elizabeth 'Elbe' Hayward. Elbe was born in Richmond on 15 May 1941. They had three children, a daughter Arina and two sons, Albertus Hendrik and Gilbert Jacobus (named after the grandfather, who was an 'Ouderling' in the church).

Geldenhuis, Albertus Hendrik (born 26th November 1969), married Anneen Botha born 21ST September 1969. They have three children, Hendru, Johaaeke, and Marli.

Geldenhuis, Albertus Hendrik Stephanus (born 10th October 1822, died Colesberg, Northern Cape, 18th May 1894), married Getruida Petronella Swart born Jasfontein, Colesberg, 1st November 1904. Their two sons were Stephanus Johannes Jacobus born 9 th July 1863, and Marthinus Johannes Geldenhuis born Caledon 28th February 1867.

Geldenhuis, Christo (born Pretoria 30th May), studied at Technikon Pretoria, self-employed. Currently in a relationship.

Geldenhuis, Dawie (born Kimberley, Northern Cape 9th April 1954), widowed, farmer. With grandson Daniel, called Danny Geldenhuis.

Geldenhuis, Dawie (born Louis Trichardt 16th August 1969), lives in Benoni, Gauteng.

Geldenhuis, Christo – brother to Eban, and facebook friend of the author.

Geldenhuis, Eben (born 4th July, 1978), married Nerissa Gurney and lives in Hamilton, New Zealand. They have two daughters, Cleopatra and Joanna. Pieter Geldenhuis, from Australia, attended their wedding (was best man to Eben, his brother?). Eben studied at the University of Waikato.

Geldenhuis, Dewald (born 17th October 1983) is the son of Jacobus Stefanus 'Cobus', from Kempton Park.

DICTIONARY OF FAMILY BIOGRAPHY

Geldenhuis, Eddie, father of Trevor, who lives in Sydney, Australia

Geldenhuis, Elsie (born), married to Koos Geldenhuis, both Facebook friends in 2011. No further details (joined the Geldenhuys group on Facebook).

Geldenhuis, Gilbert Jacobus (born 1st November 1975), third child and second son of Albertus Hendrik 'Bert' Geldenhuis. He married Debbie-Anne Pretorius on the 15th March 2009. She was born 9th December 1980. Gilbert is the father of Jaun-Pierre born Cape Town 1st April 2002 and Chrisna born Mosselbay 28th May 2005.

Gilbert manages the Geldenhuis MyHeritage website / Geldenhuis family tree – which is still very much in the development stage.

Geldenhuys, Jana – sibling to Anje Brink. Possibly born 'Brink and married a Geldenhuis? Facebook friend and relationship still to be researched.

Geldenhuis, Jacobus Stefanus 'Cobus' (born 31st March1960), from Kempton Park, son of Christian Andrew Geldenhuis and Maria Magdalena Pretorius. He is the father of Werner born 28th July 1981 (and died 5th May 2006); and Dewald born 17th October 1983. His much older brother, Dirk Jacobus Petrus Rocco, was born 25th September 1949. Cobus is the proud grandfather of Louw born 19th May 2003.

Geldenhuis, Jacobus Viljoen (born 1854 – died 1900). - Boer war POW casualty, who died in captivity at Diyatalawa, Ceylon. He was 46 years old when he died of Typhoid fever on the 5th January 1901. He was descendant from Brandfort, and was captured at Fouriesmith on the 30th July 1900. His name is inscribed on the Banneling monument, Boer War Museum, Bloemfontein.

Geldenhuis, Ken. Has two daughters, Outstanding relationship. Facebook friend.

Geldenhuis, Marthinus Johannes (born Caledon 28th February 1867 and died Cypherwater, Richmond, Cape 15th October 1930), married Johanna Magrieta Willemina Viljoen born Richmond 16th February 1874.

DICTIONARY OF FAMILY BIOGRAPHY

Geldenhuis, Maureen (born Vanderbijlpark, Gauteng 5th December 1970), went to Hoerskool Langenhoven, class of 1987. Married, lives in Kathu, northern Cape. Facebook friend in 2011.

Geldenhuis, Melda married Renaldo Nortje. Facebook friends.

Geldenhuis, Melchoir J, Active facebook friend.

Geldenhuis, Mellie with his bride, Jana Brink, 10th December 2005.

Geldenhuis, Monja (born) daughter of Trevor Geldenhuis and Monja Harding (named after her mother), lives in Sydney, Australia. Has a sibling, Faith Dabin, and nephew / cousins Kuean and Ticara.

Geldenhuis, Pieter (born), brother to Eben, lives in Australia

Geldenhuis, Pieter Jacobus. (born 1837 – died 1901) - Boer war POW casualty, who died in captivity at sea on board the Montrose ship en route for Bermuda. He was aged 64 and died of debilitation ('Verswaking' – weakening). He was descendant from Boschhoek, Potchefstroom – and was captured at Naaupoort, Transvaal on the 30th June 1901. His name is inscribed on the Banneling monument, Boer War Museum, Bloemfontein.

Geldenhuis, Rhodean – very interesting Christian name! And not only a pretty face too.

Geldenhuis, Tionette Kritzinger (born Kempton Park, Gauteng 19th December 1979), Studied in Lichtenburg, went to Kempton Hoër in 1993 and Nordelig Hoër in 1994. Lives in Rustenburg. Facebook acquaintance 2011. Friends with Lena Geldenhuys.

Geldenhuis, Trevor (born 6th January 1974) went to Princess High School, married to

Monja, Facebook and Farmville friend in 2011. Lives in Sydney, Australia.

Geldenhuys crest

Geldenhuis, Tyger (born Cape Town 25th February 1971), went to West Ridge High School, lives in Cape Town and is the Director of African Spirit Trading. Facebook friend in 2011.

Geldenhuys crest

Geldenhuys crest

Geldenhuys crest

Geldenhuys, Aap (born in the mid 1850's), is the grandfather of Attie Geldenhuys Randfontein, and Attie (Bok) Geldenhuys. Aap was taken as a prisoner of war during the Anglo-Boer War 1899 – 1902, and was interned at the Umballa camp in India. His close family members who were interned with him included Oubaas Geldenhuys and Ou Dad's younger brother Piet(er). Dot Serfontein has a picture of him in her *Keurskrif vir Kroonstad*, with him posing with Renier Botha (father of Renier and Hendrik Botha of Cyferfontein), Boet van der Linde – who was the son-in-law of Oom Aap, and Hennie Schikkerling. Hennie was Ou Dad's uncle.

Geldenhuys, Abram Carl Frederik Preller (born Rustpan, Bothaville 2nd August 1916 - died Pretoria 13th February 1972). Air Force pilot, miner, farmer, Insurance salesman, was the son of Johannes Albertus Geldenhuys (1877 – 1943), of Rustpan, a farm in the district of Bothaville, and his wife Anna Elizabeth Preller, daughter of Abraham Christoffel Naude Preller and his first wife Helletta Lephina Botha.

ACFP married Mattia Martha Lotter in 1940 in Johannesburg, the daughter of Jan Lotter and his wife Van Biljon. Two sons and two daughters were born.

ACFP went to a farm school and matriculated at Bothaville. He returned to the family farm but enlisted in the South African Air Force as a pilot when World War II was declared. He soloed in a Tiger Moth on 23rd September 1940 at No 1 Elementary Flying raining. School, Baragwanath – Transvaal, posted to Kimberley in December and qualified for *wings* in March 1941. After a short conversion spell at Zwartkop and Cranborne, Salisbury Rhodesia, he was dispatched for active service with No 3 Squadron in the North African Abyssinia Campaign. On 27th June 1941, flying Gladiator 2283 from Addis Ababa to Gimma, he crashed, landing on the canopy but was very fortunate to survive. After a spell in Eritrea, he returned to Dabat for the end of the Abyssinian Campaign in November 1941. ACFP excelled in the battle for Gondar, and was scrambled with his training instructor who shot down the last Fiat fighter aircraft of the Italian Air Force in East Africa. By February 1942 ACFP was back at Zwartkop and then joined No 10 Fighter Squadron in Durban;

then posted to 45 Air School Oudshoorn October 1942, flying mainly twin-engined Anson's and later Oxfords.

ACFP did the family proud with his World War II exploits. His detailed experience is more fully covered in the novel titled Nickel Cross. However, to do justice to this Dictionary of Geldenhuys biography, and also to avoid unnecessary duplication, please page back to the section headed "World War II", page 34. Oudad Preller and Mum Matt had four children – two boys and two girls. The first born inherited the traditional Christian names of our grandfather, Johannes Albertus. The second, yours truly, was named Preller from my father and grandmothers' surname, and Matt from my mother's plus Lotter Stamvader's Matthias cum Matt(hew). The third was Delene Elizabeth, from my fathers' mother side (see also "Lizzie" Geldenhuys nee Preller). The fourth was Dawn, who died tragically when the thatched cottage was set alight whilst my parents were away.

Abram Carl Frederik Preller Geldenhuys remustered into the South African Air Force and died in service from the narrowing of the arteries on 13th February 1972, aged 55½ years.

Geldenhuys. They live in Gaansbaai. They have two children, Michael Conrad and Karli-Mari. Adéle lists Philip Geldenhuys as her brother!?

Geldenhuys, Alta (born Heidelberg 9 May 1989), daughter of Hannes and Magda Geldenhuys, studied Theology at the University of Pretoria.

Geldenhuys, Adri, married to Alta and parents of Charne, Simeon and Zane. Facebook friend in 2011.

Geldenhuys, Adéle (born Gansbaai, Western Cape, 10th May), studied at Tygerberg College and is the General Manager at Taurus Chemicals (Cape Kelp)(Pty) Ltd. Married to Michael Petrus

DICTIONARY OF FAMILY BIOGRAPHY

Geldenhuys, Adriaan (born George, Western Cape 18th April 1989, son of Hermann Erwin Rudibert 'Rudi' and Deirdre Geldenhuys of Boksburg, Gauteng. Adriaan lives in Hansmorskraal, George.

Geldenhuys, Adriaan Johannes b6c3d10e5f2 (christened 22nd April1810), died Heidelberg, Cape Colony 26th October 1867. He got married in Swellendam on the 18th January 1835 to Elsabe Dina Lourens, genealogy number b3c5d2e?. Adriaan headed up a large branch of the Geldenhuys family that moved from Swellendam to settle in Heidelberg in the Cape. The writer was contacted by a descendant, Gerhard, who was born in Worcester on 19th November 1937, and a great deal of Geldenhuys genealogy was exchanged.

Geldenhuys, Albie (born Hennenman 1st April 1973), went to Hennenman High School and is the branch manager at Freestate Piling.

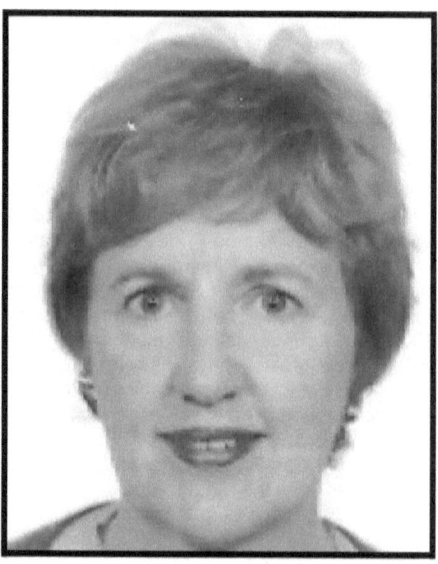

Geldenhuys, Aletta (born 16th September), studied at RAU – Randse Afrikaanse Universiteit, class of 1981 – MSc; and UNISA – University of South Africa – Class of 1993 – PhD. Lives in Auckland, New Zealand.

DICTIONARY OF FAMILY BIOGRAPHY

Geldenhuys, Aletta (born Pretoria 16th December 1983), in a relationship with Roberts Robin; and works as a florist.

Geldenhuys, Alfred, (born Bloemfontein 29th January 1982), went to Grey College Secondary School, class of 2000. Studied BCom Human Resource Management at the Universiteit van die Vrystaat. Employed as the Human Resource Manager at Bras Trucking in Pretoria.

Geldenhuys, Allan (born 27th January 1989), brother to Willie. In a relationship with Leandi Basson. Facebook friend in 2011. Face is familiar om MyHeritage site, were lineage is easier to follow.

Geldenhuys, Almaré (born 12th March 1986). Siblings are Wessel and Martelize Geldenhuys. Lounette Geldenhuys is a cousin. Facebook friend in 2011.

Geldenhuys, Alwyn (born Hermanus, Western Cape 30th January), went to Hoërskool Labori Paarl. In a relationship with Maryna Vermeulen.

Geldenhuys, Amor (born Secunda 17th December 1991), went to Hoërskool Oostland. Is an Admin Clerk at Sasol, in a relationship with Eduard Bruwer. Facebook friend in 2011.

Geldenhuys, Andre – from Johannesburg

Geldenhuys, André (born 6th May 1963), went to Hoër Tegnies Benoni, married to Vanessa and lives in Rustenburg. They have a daughter, Charné.

André works as the Production and Quality manager at Smith's Dairy in Rustenburg. Facebook friend in 2011.

Geldenhuys, Andre (born Louwna, North-West, South Africa 1st June 1982). Married to Ellen Geldenhuys. Sibling is photographer Lucille Geldenhuys who lives in Bloemfontein and is in a relationship with Victor Fincham.

DICTIONARY OF FAMILY BIOGRAPHY

Geldenhuys, Andrea (born Centurion, Gauteng 12th April 1988), went to Strand High School, class of 2006 and studied at CPUT, class of 2010, and lives in Hopefield, Western Cape.

Geldenhuys, Anel (born Westonaria, Gauteng 8th June 1979), went to Hoërskool Westonaria, class of 1997. Anel has a daughter, Bernadette, 10-year old, and is engaged to marry.

Geldenhuys, Andries (born 27th December 1984), brother to Lue-Ann Geldenhuys and cousin to Renier Geldenhuys and Lou-Mare Geldenhuys. Facebook friend in 2011.

Geldenhuys, Angelique (born Germiston, Gauteng 13th June 1986), went to Hoërskool Alberton, works as Admin and Sales Clerk at NewGenn Solutions in Germiston. In a relationship with Etienne van Staden.

Geldenhuys, Annette Gallianos (born). Lives in Greece, wrote: This is wonderful news! I have been trying for many years to do the Geldenhuys genealogy chart and have been struggling with my fathers immediate family - uncles, aunts etc. My email is: ibaqu@yahoo.co.uk Please contact me because doing it through facebook is difficult. Just to start off, my father was Johannes Joachim Geldenhuys son of Jurie Johannes Geldenhuys that was shot and killed by a sharpshooter during the minerstrike of 1921 in Brixton, Johannesburg. As far as I know but I am not sure is that he had 5 brothers. I don't know any of them or where to find any information. I really hope you are going to be able to help me!

Geldenhuys, Anthony, SAAF pilot and author of Canaan North. Attended the SAAF College course 'Senior Joint Warfare Course with the author – and also exchanged novels. Tony lives with his wife Joan in Centurion.

Geldenhuys, Anthonina (born Cape Town 21st March 1989), went to OVSS (Oranje Vry Staat School, and worked as a cosmetics consultant at TFG. Is in a relationship with Antonia Carelse. Facebook friend in 2011.

Geldenhuys, Anzelle (Worcester, Western Cape 19th August 1988), went to Worcester Gymnasium class of 2007, studied at Northlink class of 2009. In a relationship with Daniel Rossouw. Sister to Hilda?

DICTIONARY OF FAMILY BIOGRAPHY

Geldenhuys, Barend – 1675 (born Capetown 23rd December 1675), second son of 'stamvader' Albert Barend Gildenhuisz and Margaretha Hoefnagels, believed died as an infant because two other subsequent brothers were also named Barend.

Geldenhuys, Barend – 1678 (born Cape Town 27 October 1678), third son of 'stamvader' Albert Barend Gildenhuisz and Margaretha Hoefnagels, also believed to have died in infancy.

Geldenhuys, Barend - 1682 (born Cape Town 6th September 1682 died Somerset-West), farmer and sixth child of 'stamvader' Albert Barend Gildenhuisz and Margaretha Hoefnagels, who arrived in the Cape in the mid-1650's.

Little is known of his early childhood. Barend had two elder brothers, by the same Christian name, who had been christened on 23rd December 1675 and 27th October 1678 respectively (it is presumed they died at an early age). He married Anna Margaretha Siek, who was christened in Cape Town on 13th March 1685, on 31st August 1710, and who was the daughter of Johan Siek and Geertruy Helms.

In 1712, two years after he married Anna, he moved to Hottentots-Holland (Somerset-West), to the farm *Vergelegen*. Vergelegen was established by Willem Adriaan van der Stel, successor to his father Simon of Stellenbosch fame, in February 1700. Master gardener Jan Hertog laid out the grounds, garrison personnel used to develop the property, including the building of a handsome residence and erection of a flour mill, a tannery, wine and grain stores, an overseer's cottage, a slave lodge and other extensive out-buildings which included a workshop for the manufacture of wooden pipes. At the time of Willem Adriaan's downfall, *Vergelegen* measured over six hundred morgen and more than a quarter of vines in the entire Colony flourished there.

Barend and Anna had five children – Albert Barend christened 21st February 1712; Geertruy christened 24th March 1713; then our forefather Hendrik, christened 12th July 1717 (married Cornelia Swart and possibly her sister, Sara Johanna Swart); Barend christened 22nd January 1719 (married Christina Magdalena Radyn) and lastly Johanna Margaretha christened 22nd March .1721 (married Jan Jurgen Hamman).

He befriended Jacobus van der Heiden, who became his brother-in law, and acquired the second allotment of Vergelegen (Erinvale and Lourensford). Also befriended were Adam Kok, the arch-enemy of, and instigator of the downfall of Cape Governor Willem Adriaan van der Stel.

Barend was thus the second generation South African Geldenhuys! – see also 'Gildenhuisz'.

Geldenhuys, Barend Johannes Hermanus (born 1837), married Elizabeth Martha Muller. Father of Barend Hermanus and grandfather of Mauritz Herman Otto (6th cousin once removed to the writer).

Geldenhuys, Barend Nicolas Daniel, Is the son of Johannes Wilhelmus Geldenhuys, who is the son of Barend Nicolas Daniel Geldenhuys and "Pollie" Wandrag. Lives at Hoekwis, Wilderness.

Geldenhuys, Barend Petrus (Ben) (died circa 1946), Initially served in a South African mounted regiment and later in the South African Instructional Corps. Married to Anna, and was father to General Jannie Geldenhuys, who was born on 5th February 1935 on the farm Dansfontein in the Kroonstad district. He was transferred from one place to another until he eventually went "up North". The family moved to Piet Retief, and then to Ladysmith, where the mounted regiment was converted to an armoured car regiment. After the war, Ben was stationed at the Demobilisation Depot in Pretoria – as a Captain. After a short while he suffered a stroke and died.

DICTIONARY OF FAMILY BIOGRAPHY

Geldenhuys, Barend Petrus (Ben) (born 13th April 1974), son of Antonie Michael Geldenhuys born 17th December 1949 and Elsa Vermeulen born 18th April 1953. Barend – Ben – went to Hoërskool Bekker, class of 1990. He married Anneke Stoltz born Krugersdorp 24th October 1969 and they have two sons, little Barend Petrus born 27th December 1993 and Izak Jacobus born 3rd March 2000. Ben's father, Antonie, was the middle brother – the elder Barend Petrus dying while still young and the third son Coenraad Johannes being born 12 years after Antonie. Ben's Grandfather was also named Barend Petrus who died in 1976, and his great-grandfather also named Barend Petrus who died in 1941. Ben wrote the author to say that while on holiday in the Drakensberg, at Kerkenberg, Bem came across an inscription on a rock with Piet Retief's daughter. Immediately below Retief's name is there also BP Geldenhuys – Ben has been unable to obtain further information – he researched the names of the people that died with Retief, but Geldenhuys does not appear there. Neither does it appear amongst the names of the Voortrekkers at Blood River [the author is not surprised, since the Geldenhuys were 'Trek-Boers' and not 'Voortrekkers']. Ben works for Huis van Oranje.

Geldenhuys, Barend Petrus Lodewyk (born 26th May 1866 and died 8th May 1950), married Henrietta Wilhelmina Cornelia Fritz who was born 18th May 1880 and died 2nd May 1960. They had 17 children which included two miscarriages. Their sons included Hendrik Andreas born 4th November 1900, Joseph born 13 January 1902, Barend born 11th July 1903, Jan born 6th January 1907, Koos born 17th June 1908, James Henry born 9th February 1910, George born 22 November 1912 and Nicolaas.

Geldenhuys, Barend Petrus Lodewyk (born 11th July 1903 and died 11th January 1964)), son of Barend Petrus Lodewyk and Henrietta Fritz, and father to Danie born 15th November 1938 who married Rita Conradie. Settled in the Strand. Some missing links still need to be researched. His father, same name, fathered 17 children – hense a very large family which popularised the Barend Petrus family names.

Geldenhuys, Beukes (born ?). Manages the Old Mondoro Bush Camp with his wife - married Jacomine Pretorius on 13th December 2008. They live in Centurion, Gauteng, South Africa. Facebook friend in 2011.

Geldenhuys, Barend Petrus (Ben) (born Krugersdorp 27th December 1993). Son of Barend Petrus and Anneke Stoltz. Brought up in Randfontein. Went to CVO Pretoria (and lives in Pretoria).

DICTIONARY OF FAMILY BIOGRAPHY

Geldenhuys, Bruce le Roux (born Cape Town 29th September 1986), Worked at Shell Oil. In a relationship with Lauren van der Merwe. Facebook friend in 2011.

Geldenhuys, Bruwer (born 6th April 1968). Bruwer is the second son of Gen Jannie Geldenhuys. Bruwer did his national service plus eighteen months voluntary duty, and served in 32 Battalion. His elder brother Harper Martin also served in the same Battalion, but was killed in August 1991 at his unit at Pomfret. Bruwer got his name from General Jannie Geldenhuys's mothers' maiden name – that lived in the Bethlehem area.

Geldenhuys, Burger, Springbok rugby player and cattle farmer. Burger played provincial rugby for his preferred team Northern Transvaal, and represented his province a record twenty-six times. His position in the national side was also played at flank, and his speed on the ball, combined with the ability to 'take the gap' resulted in many a try scored that had the spectators on their feet. When Burger retired from competitive rugby, he returned to the family Free State farm, owned by his father, Jan Geldenhuys, to specialise in Afrikaner Cattle breeding. His business acumen led him to operate a series of successful bakeries in the surrounding towns.

Geldenhuys, Byron (born Benoni 2nd June), went to Benoni High School. In a relationship with Tremayne Calitz.

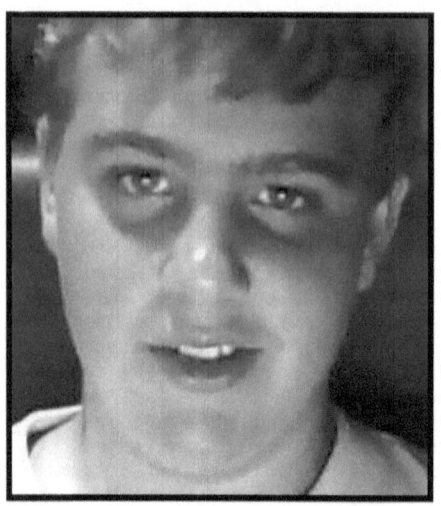

Geldenhuys, Cabous (more likely Jacobus – born 2nd February 1998) to Izak George and his second wife Wilna Bester. Sibling is Lena, and three half-sisters Suzanne, Marianne and Liezel.

Geldenhuys, Carienie, (born 1st October 1931) cousin, daughter to 'Henry' Hendrik Jacobus Geldenhuys and Adianna Marta Maria (Max), married Alphonso 'Phonnie' Macrae, born 6th April 1931. They had three children and live in California, USA. Her brother, Johannes Albertus born 1937 died 1985.

Geldenhuys, Carin, related to Jurie, who added her photo to the MyHeritage website.

Geldenhuys, Chanel (born Durban 18th April 1990), is a very talented young lady of Paul Preller and Karen de Waal. Chanel owes her beautiful looks to her mother. She is a gifted scholar who has disciplined herself to put her school career above all other interests. Her father, it is predicted, will have his hands full in the years ahead to ensure that Chanel's escorts are decent gentlemen. The first fellows were lectured by a caring Dad who warned the suitors that their courting behaviour was honourable, or else!

On completing her schooling, Chanel intends specialising in Zoology and is hoping to gain practical horticulture, botanical studies, landscaping and design experience at the world famous Nong Nooch Tropical Gardens in Thailand. Whilst this still remains a wish, Chanel wasted no time to qualify for her Bachelor of Science degree in Environmental Science at the Nelson Mandela Metropolitan University in Port Elizabeth, and continuing her Honours studies in Biology at the University of KwaZulu Natal in Durban (and hopefully her Masters degree in Botany at Rhodes University in Grahamstown). Sy is die slimkop in die familie! The studies will stand her in good stead for overseas travel later in life.

Geldenhuys, Charné went to Suid Natal High School and Hoërskool Bergsig. Daughter of André and Vanessa Geldenhuys, lives in Rustenburg and studies at the North West University (class of 2014).

Geldenhuys, Charl. Is a Zimbabwe farmer, victim of so-called war veteran invasions. Charl and his wife Tertia was forced to abandon their Two Treehill Farm, twenty miles north of Chinhoyi in 2001. They were woken up in the early morning by a bob of about seventy Zanu-PF supporters who arrived in stolen vehicles and began loading up fertiliser, seed, and equipment. When Charl Geldenhuys confronted them, they shot his dog and then opened fire on him, missing narrowly. He retreated to the homestead, remaining besieged there with his wife, young daughter, and six-month-old infant for nine hours. In mid-afternoon a team of Zanu-PF politicians arrived – Chombo, Chiyangwa, and Peter Chanetza, the provincial governor – accompanied by a police escort. While a state television crew filmed the proceedings, they began to interrogate the Geldenhuys couple, claiming they had provoked the violence. Chiyangwa pointed menacingly at Charl, accusing him of shooting his own dog. The couple painstakingly denied doing so. Clutching her infant, Tertia pleaded with Chombo, "Minister, we are God-fearing people." Chombo told them to pack their belongings and leave. They left that night.

In a subsequent incident in the same area, Chiyanga was unwittingly filmed by a television crew giving instructions in ChiShona to a group of Zanu-PF youths. "If you get hold of MDC (Movement for Democratic Change) supporters, beat them until they are dead. Burn their farms and workers' houses, then run away fast and we will blame the burning of the workers' houses on the whites. Report it to the police, because they are ours."

Across the Chinhoyi district, Zanu-PF mobs went on the rampage, burning own and looting farmhouses; stealing tractors, vehicles, equipment, and fertiliser; slaughtering cattle and driving off entire herds of livestock. Police officers participated in the raids, using police vehicles to ferry groups of attackers to farms and to take away the loot. Scores of white families fled the area, abandoning their homes.

This Geldenhuys tragedy was documented by Martin Meredith in his *Our Votes, Our Guns* in 2003. Catherine Buckle also abandoned their Stow Farm – in her story *African Tears*, about the Zimbabwe land invasions.

Geldenhuys, Charles, brother of Joleen, and son of Okkie and Baby Geldenhuys (born Anna Josephene Olivier). As a 11-year old, Charles was shot in his left eye.

Geldenhuys, Charmaine, born 7 January 1960 to Peter Borruso and Julia Lillian Dippenaar, changed her name when adopted by Johannes Albertus Geldenhuys. Her biological father divorced her mother when she was three years old, emigrated to Australia where he later died. Charmaine grew up in Luanshya and then Swaziland before settling in Johannesburg, where she partnered Lance Froneman and had a baby son by him – Jason.

Jason has been coached as a golfer, by his father, and this natural talent will soon develop for Jason to earn him professional status.

His grandmother, Julia Geldenhuys, is mighty proud of his amateur achievements.

Geldenhuys, Charne (born Port Elizabeth, 15th April 1986), daughter-in-law of Adri and Alta Geldenhuys, and married to Simeon. Studied at Varsity College, and Hotel Management at Jean Pierre. Lives in Dijon, France.

Geldenhuys, Chris, father of Renier who was born in 1983. No other information at time of going to press.

DICTIONARY OF FAMILY BIOGRAPHY

Geldenhuys, Chris (born Gansbaai, Western Cape 11th August 1957). Married to Joan Human – their daughter is Estie Geldenhuys. Facebook friend in 2011.

Geldenhuys, Christiaan (born Worcester, Western Cape 31st March), went to Higher Technical School Drostdy and Stellenbosch. In a relationship with Lauren Hunt.

Geldenhuys, Christelle (born George 29th April 1987), named after her father, Christoffel Geldenhuys. Sister to Alicia. Studied at the Nelson Mandela Metropolitan University, lives in George and worked as a trainee accountant at JE Odendaal and Associates. Christelle is a neice to Adri and Alta Geldenhuys and close cousins to Charlne, Simeon and Zane Geldenhuys.

Geldenhuys, Christo (born Pretoria 31st August 1989), went to Hoërskool Kempton Park.

Geldenhuys, Christina. Born , lives in Gordon's Bay and engaged to Johan Seegers. Facebook friend since 2012.

Polokwane and studied Human Resource Management at the North-West University (Hons B Com). Facebook FarmVille friend in 2011.

Geldenhuys, Christoffel – father of Christelle (born April 1987) and Alicia – and brother of facebook friends Adri and Alta Geldenhuys.

Geldenhuys, Cornelius (born Wellington, Western Cape, 10th September 1959), went to Adamantia, class of 1977. Facebook friend in 2011. Also friends with de Kock, Janine, Marna and Wimpie Geldenhuys – as well as Adam Tas [not *the* Adam Tas that was imprisoned in the Cape Castle in Cape Town]!

Geldenhuys, Coenraad (born Pietersburg 21st March 1977). Went to Hoërskool Vereeniging – class of 1995. Lives in

DICTIONARY OF FAMILY BIOGRAPHY

Geldenhuys, Craig Jannie (born Durban 15th March 1993 ab6c3d7e8f7g9h1i6j1k3l2), is the son of Paul Preller and Karen de Waal. Craig is currently the furthest direct descendant of Albert Barends Gildenhuisz who arrived at the Cape as a sailor onboard the *'Princesse Royale'* three hundred and fifty years ago.

Craig excelled at sport whilst at school. He swam like a fish and displayed natural ball skills in rugby, soccer and hockey. He is also not short on stamina in that he runs effortlessly and is already accumulating an impressive array of athletic certificates and medallions. His admission to Glenwood School in Durban North with a sports bursary is a noteworthy achievement, selected for 1st Team rugby, KZN rugby, KZN Sevens and landing a contract with Blue Bulls U19 rugby.

I trust Craig will now keep on passing on this initial research document for the benefit of our future generations.

For ease of reference, ancestors are as follows:-

GELDENHUYS	DIPPENAAR	DE WAAL
Albert Barends c1640-1693	Johann Martin Depner 1735/90	Jan 1692-
Barend 1682-	Alwyn Johannes 1780-	Arend 1719
Hendrik 1717-1770		Pieter 1753
Johannes Albertus 1750-		Arend 1775
Lourens 1777-		Jan Christoffel 1812
Johannes Albertus 1807-1894		Jan Christoffel 1859
Hendrik Jacobus 1849-1924		Missing Link
Johannes Albertus 1877-1944	Alwyn Jacobus	Jan Gerhardus
Abram Carl Frederik Preller 1916-1972	Johannes Petrus 1898	Jan Gerhardus
Johannes Albertus 1940-	Julia Lillian 1936	Jan Gerhardus † 1972
Paul Preller 1966-	Paul Preller 1966-	Karen
Craig Jannie 1993-	Craig Jannie 1993-	Craig Jannie 1993-

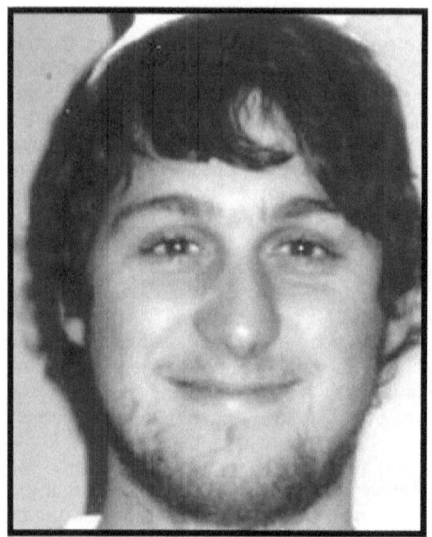

Geldenhuys, Dane (born Strand, Western Cape 9th June 1987), lives in the Strand.

Geldenhuys, Daniel (born Somerset West, Western Cape 13th February 1988), son of Riaan and Elnarette Geldenhuys. Sibling sister is Riandi. Went to Hoërskool Strand and studied at Boland College, class of 2010. In a relationship with Elizma Oosthuizen.

Geldenhuys, Danie (born 15th November 1938), son of Barend Petrus Lodewyk Geldehuys from the Strand, Western Cape. Married Rita Conradie and has three children – Sonja married to Hennie Delport, Ryno and Riaan.

Geldenhuys, Darryn (born 26th March

1984), engaged to Roxanne Krause – from Pinetown, lives in Durban.

Geldenhuys, Dawn (born Luanshya 1949, died Chingola 13th August 1954) the first Rhodesian born Geldenhuys, to Abram Carl Frederik Preller and Matthia Martha Lotter. She was our youngest sister, was born at Luanshya, and had just grown out of babyhood when my father was transferred from the Roan Antelope Copper Mine in Luanshya to Chingola and bought a ten-acre plot at Musenga Plots, some ten miles out of town.

On one Friday evening, August 13th, a Swahili set fire to our thatched cottage which was occupied at that time only by eldest brother Jan, and sister Delene and six year old Dawnie. Jan and Delene survived the inferno - Dawnie didn't. Our parents were visiting Preller at that time, having been hospitalised with Malaria. They had gone to catch a movie before Dad went on night shift, while Mom returned to the plot - only to be confronted by the tragic events of that unlucky Friday the 13th.

The Swahili, who had been recruited as a domestic following our frequent fishing trips to the lakes -Tanganyika, Bangwelo and Mrewa -, was never brought to justice for his arson. Even despite setting our caravan and several thatched rondavels alight, invariably at weekly or fortnightly intervals.

The loss of Dawnie caused our mother to have several bouts of severe depression - the worst being when she put a revolver under her chin and pulled the trigger - and was fortunately saved by her false teeth. The round deflected off the bottom set, shattered the top plate and exited via the mouth. Apart from having her broken jaw wired up, Mum was indeed lucky to survive the suicide attempt. It is pleasing to record that Mom survived untold "All Things Bright and Beautiful, All Things Great and Small" thereafter, (the tune was Dawn's favourite) - and even outlived our late father.

Geldenhuys, Deirdre (born Pretoria, 5th March), married to Rudi and is the mother of Adriaan Geldenhuys who is in George; and his much younger sister Andrea. She is from Pretoria, while her husband is in Boksburg. Worked as CEO of Brela Procurement Solutions.

Facebook friend in 2011. See also Deirdre Burns – her maiden name.

Geldenhuys, Delene Elizabeth, (born Oudtshoorn 27th February 1945) is the younger sister to Preller Matt. She is the third child of Abram Carl Frederik Preller Geldenhuys and Matthia Martha Lotter. Delene completed her junior schooling at Andrew Louw farm school in the Fort Victoria area of Rhodesia, and went on to complete her high schooling at Chaplin in Gwelo. She became a hairdresser in Pretoria and married Johann Jacobus Bouwer. Johann qualified as a medical doctor at the Pretoria University and established his practice at Hartley.

Married Johannes Jacobus Francois Bouwer and had two daughters, Chanli – who married Charles Brink, and Rensha, who married Craig Brown. Her second marriage was to Stuart John McColl on 26th September 1991. Stu had one child, Dayvd John Charles (with noticeable unusual spelling). Stu and Dee immigrated to New Zealand in October 1999 – when her third grandchild was born to Charlie and Chanli. Just before her departure, Delene and her husband Stu had these messages for OuPey and Rina:

OuPey – "You have run the good race – stay strong to the finish, for: Psalm 121:7&8 'The Lord will keep you from harm; He will watch over your life;
The Lord will watch over your coming and going, both now and for evermore."

Rina – Psalm 23: "Yea though you walk in the shadow of death – you need fear no evil" (Thank you Delene, for those treasured memories).

The McColl's and Brink's settled in Whangaparaoa just north of Auckland. Rensha's relationship with Craig Brown ended in divorce. Delene and Stu then moved to a quaint house before buying a large property in Beach Haven, North Shore City, Auckland (and big enough to accommodate the African Geldenhuys'se!)

Delene would like to be remembered for "I tried". She did!

Geldenhuys, Deon (born Humansdorp 8th August 1971), went to Robertson High School class of 1991 and Oxford High School in 1998, and studied at Nelson Mandela Metropolytan University and lives in Port Elizabeth, Eastern Cape. Has a sister named Zena Mulder. Shares the same birthday and month as Renene Delene Geldenhuys. Facebook friend in 2011.

DICTIONARY OF FAMILY BIOGRAPHY

Geldenhuys, Derek (born 4th November), Studied MBA at the University of Cape Town, works as CEO of Consol Capital Management and lives in Bellevue, Washington.

Geldenhuys, Dina and Dirk, grave headstone – Dina was born 26th February 1912 and died 6th October 1985.

Geldenhuys, Dirk Cornelis (born 6th March 1907), as per gravestone above, died 23rd September 1985.

Geldenhuys, Dirk Cornelis (born 18?), miner, Rand Pioneer.

On 17th of May 1885, the owner of Langlaagte farm on the Witwatersrand (white waters shed) Mrs GC Oosthuisen granted Dirk Cornelis a lease to search for minerals. He also acquired lease interests on the nearby Braamfontein farm. The latter was his main interest. The following year, in February 1886, the Main Reef was discovered by George Harrison when, with George Walker, he "stumbled over a projecting", gold bearing rock. Later on 12th August 1886, Dirk was still a lessee of a portion of Langlaagte - in partnership with Steenkamp, de Jager and Smit. He was then granted "special mining leases" as official recognition of the pioneering work done

Johannesburg was founded by a Proclamation made by Paul Kruger on 8th September 1886.

See also Lourens, Frans Eduard and Geldenhuys Deep mine.

Geldenhuys, Dirk. Son of Dirk senior, the Rand pioneer pictured earlier. Dirk, together with his elder brother Lourens, were interned as prisoners-of-war at Groenpunt in the Cape during the Anglo-Boer war. He appears in a photograph in Dot Serfontein's *Keurskrif vir Kroonstad,* with his father Dirk, Uncle Hendrik Geldenhuys and two other elderly brothers – Messrs Piet van Coller and Stoffel van Coller.

Geldenhuys, Dirk Cornelius, (died 1965), married Maatje Catharina Jacoba Steenkamp born 17th June 1887 and died 27th October 1918 from the great flu epidemic. Dirk is a great-grand uncle of the writer - - his granddaughter Myrl Maureen Geldenhuys born 11th October 1938 is a 4 th cousin. He settled in the Ermelo district of Mpumalanga – Eastern Transvaal.

Geldenhuys, Dirk Cornelius (born 6th March 1907 and died 23rd September 1985), married Dina Maria, born 26th June 1912 and died 6th October 1985.

Geldenhuys, Dorothea, (born Fauresmith 1898, died Oranjerivier Concentration Camp 15th February 1902). Dorothea is of unknown parentage. The writer came across her name in a register maintained by the owner of Doornbult farm, Rina Wiid, who maintains the notorious Boer War Oranjerivier Concentration Camp site and immediate surrounds. The register reflected an unknown grave number, but despite this a search of the cemetery was made and it seems pretty certain that 4 year old Dorothea was buried with another in Grave Number 152.

DICTIONARY OF FAMILY BIOGRAPHY

Geldenhuys, Douw (born Port Elizabeth 4th February 1980), went to DF Malherbe, class of 1998 and works for PwC.

Geldenhuys, Elnarette (born 20th October 1965), went to Hoër Handelskool Tygerberg. Married to Riaan and mother of Daniel born Somerset West on 13th February 1988 and Riandi.

Geldenhuys, Elsabe. Is a Radio Pulpit broadcaster who brought priceless pleasure to Rina Geldenhuys, for spiritual upliftment. Radio Kansel / Elsabe broadcasts every Friday morning on SABC at 07h00. Her inclusion in this novel is an aide-memoire to facilitate tracing her lineage as and when time permits.

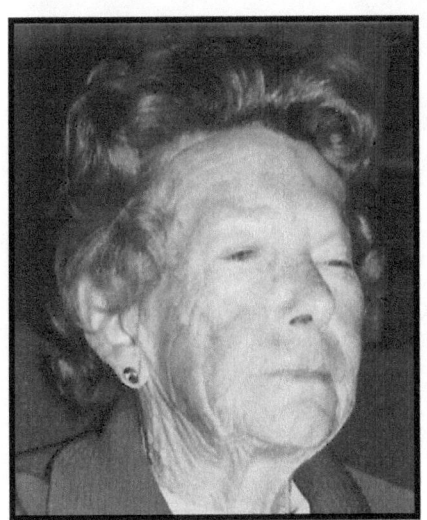

Geldenhuys, Maria Susanna Wilhelmina (born on Rustpan farm, Bothaville on the 27th May 1911). 'Mienie', married Theo van Rensen. Mother to Libby Beukes (nee van Rensen). Aunt 'Mienie' was brutally murdered in her home in Rietondale, Pretoria, on 15th March 1995.

Geldenhuys, Ernastina Helena (Esté) (Born Bothaville 1966), is the eldest daughter to Johannes Albertus and Johanna Elizabeth (Linette) Kotzé of Welgelegen, Bothaville. Married Riaan Steyn in Welkom on 19th December 1987, farmed at Sidestep, but currently farming Aandster, Bothaville. They have two children, Henriëtte born 15th April 1987 and Adriaan Willem born 23rd January 1992.

Geldenhuys, Elisabeth 'Bess' (born Rustpan, Bothaville 6th November 1904) married Paul Christiaan Gideon Steyn Jordaan in Bloemfontein on the 23rd July 1925. They had three children, Lulu who married a Ferreira, Paul Jordaan who married Theresa Theron and Johannes 'Jannie' Albertus who married Sue Bam.

Geldenhuys, Elsje (born Kaapstad unknown date but christened on the 1th May 1674). She was the second child of 'stamvader' Albert Barend Gildenhuisz and Margaretha Hoefnagels, but the first Geldenhuys born in South Africa – herelder brother Arend was born in Netherlands / Holland. Elsje married Jacobus van der Heiden , from Haarlem (Netherlands), who was instrumental in getting Cape Governor Willem Adriaan van der Stel removed from office owing to enrinching himself at VOC expense. When van der Stel's Vergelegen estate was autioned, Jacobus van der Heiden purchased Lot 3, the North West section and named his farms Lourensford and Erindale. Erindale is now a prestigious suburb of Somerset-West.
Elsje's husband becme firm friends as her younger brother Barend who acquired the Vergelegen homestead – currently owned by the Anglo-American Group. Elsje is thus a second generation Geldenhuys / South African and allocated the genealogy number of ab2.

Geldenhuys, Eugene (born 3rd October 1978), went to Hoerskool Die Burger, married to Jan du Plessis and lives in Johannesburg, Gauteng.

Geldenhuys, Eugene (born George, Western Cape 21 August 1990), son of Jeanne Geldenhuys; schooled at Outeniqua High School, class of 2008, studied at Nelson Mandela Metropolitan University. Lives in George. Facebook friend.

Geldenhuys, Finette (born Mpumalanga, 20 March 1996). Daughter of Michael Francis and Susan Geldenhuys of Middleburg. Went to Gekombineerde Skool, Hendrina and lives in Blinkpan, Mpumalanga, South Africa. Facebook friend since May 2011.

Geldenhuys, Francois. Is the Managing Director of Azisa (Pty) Ltd in 1998.

Geldenhuys, Frans (born George, 21st August 1990). Son of Jeanne Geldenhuys and sibling to Cathy and Eugene. Like his brother, also studied at the Nelson Mandela Metropolitan University.

Geldenhuys, Frans D. (born?) Frans? D. was a lessee of a portion of Elandsfontein as at 12th August 1886, as well as lessee of a portion of Braamfontein. See also Lourens Geldenhuys.

Geldenhuys, Frans Eduard (born 9th May 1856 and died 26th August 1934), married Judith Fredrika Salomina Grobler. Her gravestone was found by Marita Brodie nee Geldenhuys – who has traced the family history on her MyHeritage website.

Geldenhuys, Frans Eduard (born Johannesburg 24th September 1889 - died Pretoria, 28th July 1961) agriculturist, journalist and diplomat, was the son of Frans Edward Geldenhuys, circa 1860. His grandfather, Lourens Dirk Cornelis Geldenhuys (1836 – 1891) settled in the Transvaal Republiek. Frans Eduard presumably had his early education in Johannesburg, where his father lived. His schooling was interrupted by the Second Anglo-Boer War (1899 - 1902), but when peace was declared he continued his studies at the Hoër Jongenschool, Stellenbosch and at the Victoria College where he was awarded a B.A. degree. Although his original intention had been to enter the teaching profession he decided instead to study agriculture, agricultural economics and agricultural education in North America, and attended universities of Cornell, Wisconsin, Illinois, California and Washington, D.C. After obtaining his Ph.D. degree in agriculture he went on to research at Cornell until 1917.

He then returned to South Africa and occupied, from 1918 to 1934, various positions in the agricultural sector. He was successively a teacher in Agriculture at Greys College, Bloemfontein (1918 - 19), the first editor of *Die Landbouweekblad* (1919-24), first head of the Division of Agricultural Economics and Marketing in the Department of Agriculture (1925-26), deputy secretary of the same department (1927-31) and Director of Forestry (1931-34).

In 1934 he was transferred as economics advisor for Southern Europe to the diplomatic service at the South African legation in Rome, and served as Councillor Commercial for Europe. He occupied this position until June 1940 when Italy entered the Second World War (1939-45). During his term of office he undertook extensive tours in Europe and was in close liaison with the South African Minister Plenipotentiary in Berlin, Dr. S.F.N. Gie.

In 1940 he returned to South Africa and took up farming near Stellenbosch, but gave it up in 1945 and moved to Pretoria, where he lived for the next few years, serving on the Council for the Development of Natural Resources, the Immigrant Selection Council and the Council of the University of Pretoria.

In January 1957 he returned to the diplomatic service when appointed South African Ambassador in the Netherlands in succession to Col. P. Imker Hoogenhout. In 1961, Frans Eduard was succeeded by Mr. A. Rust and returned to South Africa where he died approximately twelve months later.

Frans Eduard was not only an expert in his own field but also had a sound knowledge of philosophy, theology, and psychology. During his lifetime he built up an extensive library, a large section of which was donated to the University of Pretoria. In 1925 he published *Landbouonderwys deur die skool* (Bloemfontein) which gave a survey of the history of agricultural teaching in South Africa. A versatile scholar, he did pioneering work in many fields in the Union. Of special importance were his persistent attempts when he was editor of Die Landbouweekblad to establish the Division of Agricultural Economics and Marketing.

In 1921 he married Eunice Elizabeth Jordaan; they had two children, one of whom Frans Gert, later became professor of Gynaecology at the University of Pretoria.

F.E. GELDENHUYS, *Landbouonderwys vir die skool*, Bloemfontein, 1925 - *Die Landbouweekblad*, 6.5.1969; - S.E.S.A. v. 5 C.T., 1972; - Private information: Mrs. F.E. Geldenhuys.

Geldenhuys, Frans Edward (born1860 -.) Frans Edward, together with his brother, Dirk Cornelius, obtained the rights over C.W. Bezuidenhoud's part of Braamfontein in August 1885. He was the father of Frans Eduard, born September 1889.

Geldenhuys, Geertruy Johanna (christened 30th March 1787) married Lourens Geldenhuys in Cape Town on 15th April 1804. Lourens was the son of Johannes Albertus Geldenhuys and Johanna le Roux. She was the fifth child of Hendrik Geldenhuys and his first wife Geertruyda Grobbelaar. Lourens is also a direct relative.

Geldenhuys, Frans Johannes (born 28th November 1853 and died 14th May 1929. He was the son of Hendrik Petrus born 1816 and Sara Johanna Uys. He married Anna Margaretha Degenaar.

Frans Johannes Geldenhuys

Geldenhuys, Frans Johannes (born 19th June 1880 and died 1st September 1956), married Francina Catharina Hendrika Paulina Prinsloo who was born 9th March 1886 and died 12th October 1969.

Geldenhuys, Frans Johannes (born 10th April 1893 in Vrede and died in Newcastle 30th December 1958). He married Margareha Elizabeth and later married Maria Catharina Elizabeth – who was born 14th December 1913 and died 26th November 1992. He was the son od Frans Johannes 1853-1929 and Anna Margaretha Degenaar.

Geldenhuys, Gerda (born 6th November) – see Gerda Bezuidenhout.

Geldenhuys, Gerhard (born Worcester 19th November 1937) eldest son of Gert Bernardus and Hendrika Francina Cloete, married Annaline Odendaal. They have three children, Lisa born 31st December 1964, Henriëtte born 18 October 1966 and Gerhard born 10th March 1970.

Gerhard was a lecturer in Applied Mathematics at the University of Stellenbosch from 1960 until 1998, the last 24 years of these as professor. He received an M.Sc in Applied Mathematics from the University of Stellenbosch in 1961 and a Ph.D in Mathematics from the Rand Afrikaans University in 1971.

Geldenhuys, Gerhard (born 10th March 1970) is the son of Gerhard and Annaline Odendaal. He is in the television and film industry, where he does free-lance work in the photography sections. He has done work on commercials, TV programs and a number of films, including Blood Diamond and Disgrace. He married Vanessa Clark and they have two children, Gerhard Robyn and Mila Cecilia. Both Robyn and Cecelia were baptised on the same date – 6th July 2008 at Stellenbosch-Sentraal.

DICTIONARY OF FAMILY BIOGRAPHY

Geldenhuys, Gertuida Johanna born 1813, daughter of Lourens Geldenhuys who was born 1777, and Margaretha Geldenhuys 1787 - 1878. A kwaai looking vrou – probably lived as long as her mother?.

Geldenhuys, Geruan (born Johannesburg 4th August 1989), went to Helpmekaar College, class of 2007 then studied at the University of the Free State. Lives in Bloemfontein. He has a younger sister, Caroli Geldenhuys

Geldenhuys, Glen Llewellyn (born Port Elizabeth 17th April 1956). Business executive. He is the son of Frederick Jacobus Wagenaar and Susanna Magdalena Joubert. Glenn married Lisa Grobbelaar on 15th December 1979. He obtained his B.Eng. (Hons) (Pta), MBL (Unisa) and Pr. Eng. He is the Managing Director of DPI Holdings, established in 1998 through a merger of AECI owned Durapenta Plastics and Everite owned Paxit Pipekor, which is currently a subsidiary company of Polifin & Group 5. He was ex-MD of T&E Engine Cooling Systems, Silverton Engines (Pty) Ltd 1997 – 98, and Feroda Heat Exchanges.

Geldenhuys, Gysbert Jacobus (born c.1926 died 30th January 1945, aged 19), Warrant Officer Class 11, of No 15 Squadron, South African Air Force, posted missing, presumed dead (drowned at sea). Geldenhuys was the third crewmember of a Baltimore bomber, piloted by Lt. David Buntine Dick. On 30th January 1945, No 15 Squadron's Baltimore, V FW 830, with a crew of four, disappeared on a night cross-country flight. A Boston aircraft reported seeing a fire at sea, and eventually a rescue launch off Bellaria picked up three Mae Wests, two of which belonged to No 15 Squadron. The missing aircrew were the pilot Lieutenants David Buntine Dick and observer William Ewart Ellis, wireless operator/air gunner Warrant Officer Gysbert Jacobus Geldenhuys and Sergeant Slaughter of the RAF, reported lost.

No 15 Squadron's first loss since February 1944 was suffered during the Baltimore's final operation before standing down on 19th January. OC Lt.-Col Shuttleworth led the mission of nine aircraft to attack a stores dump at Massa Lombarda, where they met with intense heavy anti-aircraft fire. His port engine was set on fire. The Baltimore was crash-landed about 16 km from base - at Casenatico. WO 11 Gysbert J. Geldenhuys was thus lost at sea, after the squadron had stood down eleven days earlier.

By a strange twist of fate, I had my son Pey with me at the SAAF Association lunch at AFB Durban when No 15 Squadrons history book "Agean Pirates" was launched – at which ex-OC 15 Sqn Laurie Shuttleworth was present. In fact, Laurie had also flown with my father, Abram Carl Frederick Preller Geldenhuys.

DICTIONARY OF FAMILY BIOGRAPHY

Geldenhuys, Hanna (born Kimberley, 24th June 1955), worked at SAPS (Captain, in Loss Control). Married and lives in Kimberley, Northern Cape.

Geldenhuys, Hans Jacob (born 1st September 1842 – Swellendam, died Marquard 10th August 1899, fathered eighteen children. He married his first wife Gesina Catharina de Jager at Heidelberg on 10th February 1862. She was the daughter of Carel Pieter de Jager who died in 1876. He married his second wife, Maria Elizabeth Susanna Luwes who was born on 9th June 1851 (and died 18th October 1920), a widow of Jacobus Johannes Wentzel. His 18 children were named Jurie Johannes, Carel Pieter, Gesina Catharina, Elizabeth Catharina Christina, Jacoba Catharina, Hans Jacob Blom, Hendrik Petrus, Andries Johannes, Hester Johanna, Wybrand Hebershausen, Johanna Elizabeth Catharina, Jacobus Petrus Cornelis, Maria Elizabeth Susanna, Adriana Alberta, Elsabe Johanna Jacomina, Anna Margaretha Magdalena, Adriaan Hendrik, and Andries Lodewikus Stephanus!

Phew – that was quite an achievement caring for a family of twenty!!! Just imagine his wife Maria having to prepare 60 meals a day (or perhaps they did not eat three meals a day?).

Very large families in the early days were not uncommon. In most cases the family unit was totally involved in farming operations. Many of the children did not enjoy formal school education – the Bible was invariably the only text book available in the household – and sometimes a travelling school teacher would make his rounds between farms and settlements. I trust the reader will imagine the likely "hand me downs", in spanning probably two or even three ox-wagons to attend church, holding a roll-call to ensure nobody was left behind after outings, and feeding 20 mouths every day – never mind all the food consumed at each mealtime! Or cross border travel arrangements, passports, or filling in all the names at the Customs / Immigration border posts!!!

I can speak from personal experience. I recall how my own father dreaded the forms every time we passed through the Beit Bridge, Chirundu or Livingstone / Victoria Falls, and Vila de Manica border posts to fill in just his names – Abram Carl Frederik Preller Geldenhuys. Imagine having to do that for a family of 20!!! (But then, I suppose, they did not have full of nonsense border control in those days?).

On a positive note, I presume family ties must have been very close – nobody in their right minds would dare pick a fight with a family member lest one dared being on the receiving end of a feud. However, imagine having such large families' now-a-days – how would you cope?

Geldenhuys, Harper Martin (born ?, died 17th August 1991). Major, serving in the S.A. Defence Force – 32 Battalion, killed in an aircraft incident at his unit at Pomfret. Eldest son of General Jannie Geldenhuys.

Geldenhuys, Heinrich Facebook friend in 2011

Geldenhuys, Helletta Levina (Born De Bank 2nd May 1900, died Kroonstad 15 August 1901). Helletta was the first-born to Johannes Albertus Geldenhuys and Anna Elizabeth (Lizzie) Preller. She was born shortly after the commencement of the Anglo-Boer War and died whilst interned in the Kroonstad Womens Concentration Camp, by the British.

Geldenhuys, Hendriëtte (born Stellenbosch 18th October 1966) is the second daughter of Gerhard Geldenhuys and Annaline Odendaal. She is a journalist and has worked for the *Cape Times*, *Cape Argus*, *Fair Lady* and the *Sunday Times*, and is currently employed by a media firm *Oryx Media Production* in Cape Town.

Geldenhuys, Hendrik (born Cape Town 2nd February 1687), son of Stamvader Albert Barends and Margaretha Hoefnagels

Geldenhuys, Hendrik (born July 1717, died 1770, son of Barend of Vergelegen, married Cornelia Swart in 1938 and then married Sara Johanna Swart in 1750. Direct ancestor, C3, seven generations: great-great-great-great-great-grandfather!

Geldenhuys, Hendrik (christened 30th July 1775, married Sophia Margaretha Matthee in Caledon on the 6th February 1814. His elder brother, Johannes Albertus, also married a Matthee, Johanna.

Geldenhuys, Hendrik Jacobus (born 10th October 1816), christened in Swellendam on 24th December 1816, married Cornelia Margaretha Swart in Swellendam on 27th December 1835. He married a second time, to Johanna Margaretha Geertruyda Rossouw. He died in Kroonstad, on the 4th May 1879, aged 62 years and six months.

Geldenhuys, Hendrik Jacobus (born November 1837, died Rietgat 4th September 1924), farmer and Boer War fighter. More commonly known as Oubaas and Bessie Geldenhuys (Elizabeth Schikkerling), whose eldest son, Johannes Albertus (born 1877), was the writers grandfather – Ou Dad Geldenhuys – who married Elizabeth Preller. Oubaas was the son of Johannes Albertus and Judith Margaretha Geldenhuys. He was captured, together with Aap Geldenhuys and his second son Pieter, and interned in the Umballa prisoner-of-war camp in India.

Geldenhuys, Hendrik Jacobus (born 5th July 1849, died 12th December 1930), aged 81years – and buried on Rustpan, Bothaville. There appears to be a certain mystery to the writer, because "Oubaas" with identical names (born November 1837 and died September 1924) is believed buried on Rietgat – which belonged to Johannes Albertus Geldenhuys.

DICTIONARY OF FAMILY BIOGRAPHY

Geldenhuys, Hendrik Jacobus (born 1902, died 1967). Boer, and uncle to the author. He was born in captivity during the Anglo-Boer war to Jannie and Lizzie Geldenhuys. Henry married Adriana Martha Maria (Max) Keyser in 1928 and they had 2 children. Max died 1955 and Hendry then married Widow Jacomina Margaretha Bukes (nee Badenhorst) in 1956.

Henry grew up on Rustpan and after his marriage to Max they then farmed on a subdivision called Lekkerlewe, where and Jannie were born. After Max's death, he met his second wife and moved in with her on her farm Normandy. He then sold Lekkerlewe and bought another farm, Welgelegen – about 10 kilometres from Normandy, on which his son Jannie then farmed.

Geldenhuys, Hendrik Jacobus (Hennie) (born Bothaville 31st August 1964). Hennie farmed on Welgelegen – the farm bought by his grandfather when Lekkerlewe, a subdivision of Rustpan, was sold.

Hennie married Johanna Elizabeth (Linette) Kotzé from Theunisen, in Welkom, and they have two children, Johannes (Jannie) Albertus born Bothaville hospital 6th February 1989 – a twelfth generation Geldenhuys, and Johanna Elizabeth (Joané), also born in the Bothaville hospital on 3rd May 1991. Hennie made a surprise e-mail contact with Pey Malan, at the end of January 2007 – in tracing the family history. His father, Johannes Albertus born 1937, died at a young age of 48 in the Universitas Hospital. Hennie sold Welgelegen in 1997 and currently lives on the farm Kromspruit (Ventersburg) that previously belonged to his father-in-law. He kindly sent the writer a photograph of the family tree that was prepared by *Die Stamouers Buro, Pretoria* on 19th December 1929. This was treasure indeed – as it reconfirmed much history as researched by the writer.

Hennie matriculated at Bothaville High School in 1982. He completed his training with 1 Parachute Battalion and then posted to 1 Inligtingskool Kimberley. In January 1985 he studied Agriculture at the Landbou College, Potchefstroom (but did not complete the course due to his father's death). His father flew model aircraft but Hennie qualified for his PPL (Private Pilot's License) in February 1986. However, flying for pleasure became prohibitively expensive and his flying currency expired in 1997. Because Linette Kotzé is originally from Theunisen, they decided to get married in Welkom.

Kromspruit was bought by Linette's grandfather Eddie Pienaar in 1945. After his death, Linette's father bought the farm from the Estate. Mr Kotzé stopped active farming in 2005 and retired. That is when Hennie decided to sell Welgelegen, and bought Kromspruit, where Hennie and Linette currently farm. Both their children are doing exceptionally well – see Jannie and Joané.

After his father's death, his mother remarried – to Coen Wessels in May 1998. They are now retired and live on the farm Uitkyk which now belongs to Johan Rautenbach. Very interestingly, Uitkyk used to belong to Kil Dreyer.

Geldenhuys, Hendrik Petrus (born between 1838 and 1842 – died 21st May 1904) Boer war POW casualty, who died in captivity at Colombo, in Ceylon, and was buried in the Batticaloa cemetery, Colombo. He refused to sign the Oath of Allegiance and was thus prohibited from returning to South Africa. His wife, Johanna Catharina Steyn 1840-1901, had died in the Pietermaritzburg Camp on the 10th September 1901.

Geldenhuys, Hendrik 'Hennie' (born 26th February 1988), studied Mechanical Engineering at the University of Technology, Free State. Lives in Bloemfontein. Facebook friend in 2011.

Geldenhuys, Herman. Born 13 July 1977, son of Petrus Johannes and grandson of Louis Geldenhuys. Married Leonie Scott and they have two daughters, the younger Bianca started school in 2011. Herman has been a Facebook friend since January 2011.

Geldenhuys, Herman (born Pretoria, 7th March), speaks Spanish and Japanese in addition to Afrikaans and English. He is the Web and Mobile engineer at Qsens and lives in Waterkloof, Pretoria, Gauteng.

Geldenhuys, Hermann Erwin Rudibert 'Rudi' (born Brakpan, Pretoria, Gauteng 8th September 1964) – lives in Brakpan, married to Deirdre Burns and is the father of Adriaan who was born on 18th April 1989 and who lives in George, Western Cape. [Rudi is his Facebook name]. Rudi and the writer are third cousins.

Geldenhuys, Hermanus Christoffel (born Bellville, Cape, April 1954), son of Jockie and Patsy of Langebaan, attended the Belville North Primary School and Vredenburg High School. 'Manie' joined the South African Air Force straight from school and qualified with a B Mil(BA) degree from the Military Academy, before gaining his wings in October 1975.

His total of 3 150 flying hours consisted initially of Impala jet flying. He served on 4 and 8 Squadron at Air Force Base Bloemfontein. He qualified as a flying instructor at CFS Dunnottarbefore moving to FTS Langebaan. From mid 1983 he converted to Alouette and Pumas on 16,17 and 19 Squadrons and has commanded both 30 and 22 Squadrons.

Manie retired as

Geldenhuys, Hilda. Born 30 August 1990. Studied at the Cape Peninsula University of Technology and lives in Worcester, Western Cape. Class of 2008 at Worcester Gymnasium. Facebook friend since 2011.

Geldenhuys, Ian Jannie (was born Johannesburg 22nd February 1985) scholar, son of Stuart William Geldenhuys and Joy Goldsworthy. Ian displayed natural ball skills and attended Maritzburg College where he represented the school at squash and cricket.

Geldenhuys, Izak George, married Debra Viljoen, parents of Jacobus 'Kotie' Strydom born Kroonstad 1st November 1929; and Izak George 'Sakkie' of Sonneskyn.

Geldenhuys, Izak George of Sonneskyn – younger son of Izak George and Debra Viljoen, and father of Izak; Jurie, Adriaan 'Attie' and Sebastiaan 'Basie' of Nelspruit (who married Veronica Engelbrecht).

Wife of Izak George "Sakkie" Geldenhuys, (born 21st October 1939)(NN – on MyHeritage site, and thus also Gedcom section towards the end of Volume 2). Aged 72 in 2011 – has four sons.

Geldenhuys, Izak George (born Kroonstad 10th July 1958, married Hannelie Booysen and had three children: Susanne, Mariaane and Liesel. Izak George then married a second wife, Wilna Bester, and they had Cabous and Lena.

DICTIONARY OF FAMILY BIOGRAPHY

Geldenhuys, Izak Jacobus (born Krugersdorp 3rd March 2000). Son of Barend Petrus and Anneke Stoltz. Brought up in Randfontein.

Geldenhuys, Jaco - 1982 (born 6th November 1982, Bredasdorp, Western Cape). Jaco is a sergeant with the South African Police Service, having studied at the SAPS Training College, Graaff-Reinett. Currently lives in the Strand, Western Cape and is married to Evelyn

Geldenhuys, Jaco – 1986 (born 25th May 1986), from Heidelberg, Western Cape, engaged to Monique Russell. Facebook friend in 2011.

Geldenhuys, Jacobus 'Jaco' (born 28th March 1971, Bellville)

Ahnentafel Report for Geldenhuys, Jacobus

Generation 1
1. Geldenhuys, Jacobus. Jacobus was born on 1971-03-28 in Bellville.

Generation 2
2. Geldenhuys, Lukas Marthinus. Lukas Marthinus was born on 1941-04-01 in Caledon.

3. Obbes, Alta. Alta was born on 1946-07-09 in Malmesbury.

Generation 3
4. Geldenhuys, Jacobus. Jacobus was born on 1908-12-02 in Kleinmond. He died on 1990-01-05 in Kleinmond.
5. Niemand, Maria Magdalena Susanna. Maria Magdalena Susanna was born on 1914-02-21 in Hawston. She died in 2002 in Bellville.
6. & 7.

Generation 4
8. Geldenhuys, Lukas Marthinus. Lukas Marthinus was born on 1872-07-29. He died on 1960-05-12.
9. Cooper, Susanna Maria Margaretha. Susanna Maria Margaretha was born on 1870-09-09. She died on 1947-06-25.
10. Niemand, Jacobus Magiel. Jacobus Magiel was born on 1885-02-21. He died on 1976-01-04.
11. West, Maria Magdalena Susanna. Maria Magdalena Susanna was born on 1883-12-04. She died on 1919-03-28.

Jaco manages an interesting website - which details his Systems Software Verification at the University of Stellenbosch department of Mathematical Sciences since April 2005. Prior to that, he was a post graduate student / researcher at the Finland University of Technology at Tampere..

His research focuses on Software engineering, model checking and process algebra, static analysis, testing, and open source software. Jaco is also interested in automata & language theory and data structures and algorithms.
For information:

DICTIONARY OF FAMILY BIOGRAPHY

(1) http://www.genlias.nl/nl/page0.jsp is a great site for finding records of Dutch ancestors. (Click on "Zoeken in Genlias").

(2) Since the original Albert Barend Geldenhuys came from Burgsteinfurt, Jaco looked at a German map and found a small town named Gildehaus near Bad Bentheim. It is about 32 kms away and wondered if this is the origin of Albert Barend. It might just be a coincidence: It is often thought "Geldenhuys" ultimately came from "golden house", but of course it could also be "guild house". Jaco and his father plan to take a trip there some time 2012. E-mail: jaco@cs.sun.ac.za or jacogeld@gmail.com

martyrs Komdt Gideon Scheepers (less than a month earlier on January 1902). A monument has been erected in Graaff-Reinet for those Boers who were likewise shot by firing squad to Scheepers and Geldenhuys. They were PJ Fourie, J van Rensburg and LFS Pfeiffer who were executed on 19th August, 1901; Daniel Olewagen and Ignatius Nel on 26th August, 1901; Johannes Hermanus Roux on 7th October, 1901. My Oumam Lizzie Geldenhuys had written about Scheepers in her *Oorlogs Herinneringe* – and I am also pleased to discover that my Great Uncle Dr Gustav Schoeman Preller became interested in the Scheepers story and began his own inquiries in the 1920's.

Geldenhuys, Jacobus Adriaan 'Kotie' Jr (born 4th May 1973), fouth child of Jacobus Strydom (Kotie Sr) and Enrnestine Marlene Steinbach – is the great-grandson of Adriaan Izak 'Aap' Geldenhuys. Lives in Melville, Pretoria and married Marriët Kloppers on 25 October 2008. See also Izak George and Hermann Erwin Rudibert 'Rudi' Geldenhuys.

Geldenhuys, Jacobus Francois (died Graaff-Reinet 14th February 1902). Boer burgher – executed by firing squad by the British on St. Valentine's Day, 14th February 1902, towards the end of the 1899-1902 Anglo-Boer War. He was the last one shot, after the shameful assassination of Boer

Geldenhuys, Jacobus Jacob 'Kobus' (born Bredasdorp, Western Cape 30th October 1954), the son of Johannes Wessel, married Danah and they have two children, Johannes Jacobus (Jaco), married to Evelyn, and Madiah married to Jaco van Dam. Facebook friend since 2011.

Geldenhuys, Jacobus Viljoen. Born 1857 and died in captivity in Ceylon on 6th January 1901 (aged 44.8). Jacobus is believed to be the same person who Coen Groenewald wrote about in his *"Bannelinge Oor Die Oseaan"* – and also mentioned as being from Brandfort, the best friend of Free Stater Schalk Johannes Burger who came across his friend's grave at the Diyatalawakamp cemetery on 11th May 1901. Burger writes in his *"Die Oorlogsjoernaal van S.J. Burger"* that he was shocked when he came across the grave of his young best friend.

Geldenhuys, Jacques (born 3rd November 1987), son of Gerda Bezuidenhout, studied Website Design and Development at Intec College, and employed as IT Support / Projects at Otomys Software Solutions.

Geldenhuys, Jake, on Facebook, relationship not yet established.

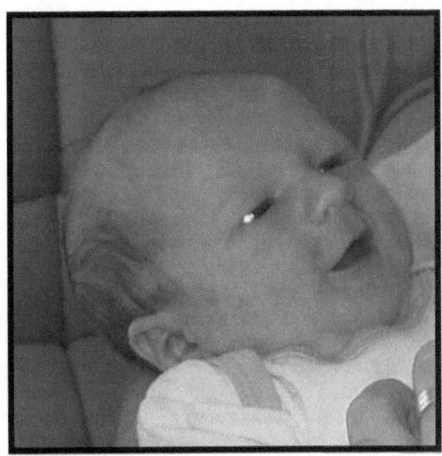

Geldenhuys, Jake (born Durban 18th December 2007, died Estcourt 30th December 2007). This family history is dedicated to the writers' only grandson who lived a mere 12 days. Jake was the first son of Pey Malan Geldenhuys, and second son of Eloise Howard. He died of heart failure.

Geldenhuys, James Henry (born 9th February 1910 and died 13th June 1992), Married Louisa Frederick Botes who was born on the 8th November 1918. They had seven children, the second boen being Louis Frederick Botes Geldenhuys, who married Louisa Regina Knoop from Pretoia.

Geldenhuys, Jannie (born Kroonstad 5th February 1935). Professional soldier,

General, commanded the South African Defence Force. Jannie was born on the farm Dansfontein in the Kroonstad district, the second son of Barend Petrus (Ben) and Anna Geldenhuys. Spent most of his early childhood in the Bethlehem area, and matriculated in 1952. The following year voluntarily trained at the Military Gymnasium at Roberts' Heights – of Boer War fame – and which was already then known as Voortrekkerhoogte. Married Marié Martins on 6th February 1960, and had one daughter Annamarié and two sons, Harper Martin in November 1964 and Bruwer in April 1968. Was promoted to major general in 1976 and appointed General Officer Commanding (GOC), SWA Command. He experienced firsthand the war in Angola and South West Africa.

He is the author of "*A General's Story*", Jonathan Ball Publishers, Johannesburg, 1995. It is a story of war and peace in Southern Africa – 'Angolans, Boers and Cubans – Aldana, Botha, Crocker!'

Geldenhuys, Jason, born 4 January 1996 in Midrand to Lance Froneman and Charmaine Geldenhuys. At age 14, Jason was already playing amateur golf and intends taking the sport up professionally.

Geldenhuys, Joleen (born Ladismith, Cape 27th October 1957), daughter of Hendrik Willem van Eeden Geldenhuys and Anna Josephene Olivier, married Hendrik Jacobus van Aardt and lives in Bredasdorp. They have two children, Nicolaas Daniel born Bredasdorp 25th August 1988 and Leane born Alberton 29th May 1987.

Geldenhuys, Johan (Ouboet) (was born circa 1932). Brother to General Jannie Geldenhuys and eldest son of Barend Petrus (Ben) and Anna Geldenhuys. He Schooled at Frankfort and Bethlehem. Johan served in the Citizen Force in the Regiment Louw Wepener.

Geldenhuys, Johanna Elizabeth (Joané) (Born Bothaville 3rd May 1991). She was a Grade 10 scholar in 2007 at the Oranje Meisies Skool, Bloemfontein. Joané is the only daughter but younger child to Hennie Hendrik Jacobus and Linette Kotzé; named after her mother (Johanna Elizabeth). Joané is also a talented swimmer, and swam the Midmar Mile in 2007.

Joané studied at the North West University and currently lives in Potchefstroom.

Geldenhuys, Johannes Albertus (born 25th August 1743) – elder brother of like named (see next), and who is believed died in infancy. The significance, however, is the name Johannes Albertus. Possibly, all the JA's in the family owe their Christian names to this ancestor.

Geldenhuys, Johannes Albertus (baptised 5th April 1750) – Fourth Generation Geldenhuys, and the first survivor of the name Johannes Albertus. He was the seventh child of Hendrik, who was twice married (both Swart – presumed sisters). I suspect his mother Cornelia Swart must have died with his birth, because Hendrik's second wife Sara Johanna, who he married in 1750, gave birth to a daughter, also named Sara Johanna the following year – born 31st October 1751.

JA had an elder brother also christened Johannes Albertus – on 25th August 1743, but it is speculated that he died in infancy, otherwise why would he be christened with the same names (other than his father having had two wives?). The name Johannes is significant in that Johannes appears for the first (or second only to the presumed earlier brother) time. Albertus obviously originates from Stamvader Albert.

JA married Johanna le Roux, who was a widow of Johannes Swart (hopefully not his uncle's wife – note the Swart surname!). JA became a burgher of Stellenbosch, and they had eight children.

It is apparent from research conducted by the writer that our branch of the family left Stellenbosch to settle in the Swellendam and Malgasrivier districts.

Geldenhuys, Johannes Albertus (christened 5th April 1772), First born to Johannes Albertus (1750) and Johanna le Roux. He married Johanna Magdalena Matthee on 20th September 1801, and they had ten children – his first born, on 20th February 1803, also christened Johannes Albertus (who in turn also christened his first born JA – thus the fourth in succession!). This branch of the family settled in the Caledon district.

Geldenhuys, Johannes Albertus (born 21st December 1807), christened 10th April 1808, got married on 6th May 1827, in Swellendam, to his cousin Judith Margaretha Gildenhuizen (who was born 20th February 1812). He fought in the Basotho war 1856 – 1865. He died on the family farm Doornbult, in the Kroonstad district, aged 86 years and nine months, on the 9th October 1894. His genealogy number or reference is ab6c3d7e4f3.

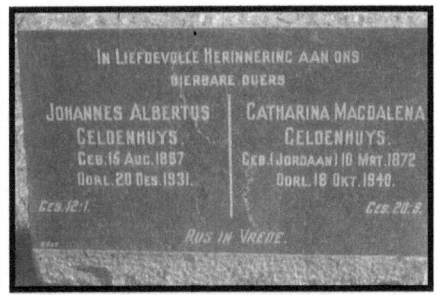

Geldenhuys, Johannes Albertus (born 15th August 1867 and died 20th December 1931) son of Barend Petrus Geldenhuys (1815-1879) and his second wife, Catharina Helena Oosthuizen), married Catharina Magdalena Jordaan 1872-1940. He was also a grandson to Lourens (Louw) Geldenhuys who was born in 1777 at Malgasrivier.

Geldenhuys, Johannes Albertus (born 5th April 1772) married Johanna Mathee on the 20th September 1801. His youger brother, Hendrik, married the other Mathee sister, Sophia Margaretha Mathee.

Geldenhuys, Johannes Albertus (born 8th July 1877 died 28th May 1944), farmer, burger fighter in the Boer War and World War II, son of Hendrik Jacobus and Elizabeth Schikkerling (more affectionately known as "Oubaas and Bessie Geldenhuys". He married Anna Elizabeth (Oumam Lizzie) Preller on 27th June 1899 just prior to the declaration of war with Britain. They had six children, with their first born being a casualty of the Boer-War.

Thanks to granddaughter Delene, valuable war documents were handed over in 1999 which records the cessation of hostilities and repatriation from the Boer camp in Umballa, India around 25th August 1902. Also, during the early stages of World War II, a Pass was issued to Burger J.A. Geldenhuys on 22nd November 1914 to enable him to proceed to Rustpan and return to No. 10 District, Union of South Africa Citizen Force (presumed Kroonstad).

Yes, Lizzie and Jannie Geldenhuys had a distinctly spectacular wedding but perhaps the Geldenhuys's were not so impressed. That would have been Oubaas and Bessie Geldenhuys, Jannie's parents, Aap and Meraai Geldenhuys, Hendrik and Nelie Geldenhuys, his uncles, and his cousins Jurie, Lang Jan, Jan Staar, Dik Willem and Tol and others. Although the Geldenhuyse in those years could not compete one on one with the Botha's as far as property were concerned, or compared with the legal beaver Preller's, they did consider themselves a step above the average. Their farms were between the fertile Renoster and Vals rivers towards Kroonstad, and although they also had sand-veldt farms, they wouldn't dream to brag about it.

The following extract was taken From Dot Serfontein's book "*Amper Onse Mense*" and translated from Afrikaans, by the writer:-

He was twenty-two years old and only married for four months when the Anglo-Boer War of 1899 broke out. He, his father-in-law Abraham Preller, his brother Pieter, his friends Ernst and Martiens van Biljon set off for the Western front at Kimberley. They certainly were not too concerned, nor struggled with the trip – they had horses, packhorses, an ox-wagon half-tented and eight oxen. In his diary that he kept as a prisoner-of-war in India he wrote "We had our cook who drove the ox-wagon, one kaffir to take care of our horses, and De Vc who joined us later. We had cake, rusks and tinned meat, and slept on feathered beds. We lived like 'Lords' ".

He fought here and there – at Armoedskoppie, Belmont and Magersfontein and describes his first major battle that he fought in. "We stood and fought until about 7 p.m., when Pieter's horse was shot. We defended our position, when I saw the burghers withdrawing. I signalled Pieter to make good his escape and waited till the last minute to make a dash for it on my horse. I mounted my horse and galloped amidst heavy small arms and cannon fire. After I had covered about 800 yards my horse received a flesh wound to his foreleg. I met up with the Commandant and a couple of others in another defensive position. I joined them to continue the fight. My horse bolted and received bullet wounds to its hip and another in the saddle flap. The horse gave a jolt and I found myself in dire straits – and thought it best to make another for my own safety. I cut the saddle loose from the horse, removed the bridle and retrieved my belongings – I only possessed one good saddle and no ways was I going to leave them behind in the battle as spoils of war . . . "

Years later my grandmother Lizzie also wrote her war memoirs, for her grandchildren, and recalls this particular incident, describing what the young burgher of that time had to endure. "Now another small incident" says she, "to relate Ou Dad's predicament. While Ou Dad together with other burghers from Magersfontein was returning from the battle, his horse was fatally shot. The horse collapsed but Ou Dad remained calm, dismounted, loosened the saddle, took his raincoat and inspected it – but the good new saddle, bridle and stirrups were not being left behind. After folding the coat he placed it on his head and placed his saddle on top of it. And there he strolled, amongst the English salvos. Dear old Ou Dad, ever nonchalantly, but the new saddle and nickel silver stirrups he definitely was not leaving behind!"

"Daar de officieren niet vlink met schrijven was, was ik hung root te pos geweest als secretaries - - - Like those officers who were proficient writers so was it that I appointed to the post of Secretary" relates Jannie when he was appointed as secretary to Veldcornet Karel Coetzee. After three months at the front line he is "ziet en vol" – sick and tired of everything and was highly relieved when his wife had sent him a 'substitute' named Christiaan Grobbelaar who was willing to fight in his stead till the end of the war at a cost of one and a half cattle per month.

No time was wasted to bring the journey home to an end for him and his brother Pieter, relates Jannie "in een groot geest - - in great haste". In their rush they manage to overturn their cart several times. As far as Jannie Geldenhuys was concerned, his war involvement was at an end, and he devoted him to his farming, his young wife and recently born daughter. When the British troops arrived several months later in

Bothaville, he buried one rifle in a gully and with the other he surrendered. But five months later we find him, his father-in-law, his brother and his friends at Schoemansdrift on the Vaal River. They were part of a group of two hundred "hensoppers" as he calls them that had decided to take up their guns again. They were with the commando awaiting the arrival of De Wet

Their clothing, tidy and without any patches, groomed hair and beards and fresh horses differentiated them from the rest of the other burghers. The most recognisable feature was their anxious, expectant appearance as compared to the relaxed, some lounging while others are scattered asleep under the shade of trees. I can imagine how the veteran fighters were grooming each others beards, how some was opportunistically cutting up strips of the meat ration dished out, into thin strips and hung out to dry on thorn bushes; and how some sitting just with their underpants while stitching sheep hide to the seat pants of the captured trousers. There would be others patching their shoes, still others baking mieliemeel cakes over coals – their discussions very subdued and relaxed, and movements unconcerned. Although the English columns could surprise them any moment at their camp site, a very calm atmosphere prevailed – like they were hundreds of miles away from the fighting front.

Then a couple of horse riders arrived. They dismounted together and entered a small round tent. The two-hundred burghers stood up and found themselves surrounded by hundreds of other burghers. There is immediate tension in the hollow. Even the horses stop their grazing. The mooing of the plentiful oxen is heard for the first time, and the out-riders and oxen guides move to their allotted stations. The tent flap opens and two men emerge and strolled to the outspanned ox wagons; Martinus Theunis Steyn and Christiaan de Wet (Free State President and Commando General).

This was Jannie Geldenhuys' first experience of something that he would get quite used to; how you trekked around with De Wet. You don't know where you are going, the one moment you in flight and the next fighting. At night you lay down for a couple of hours sleep on a grassy patch, with your arm around the reins while your head rests against the saddle. Long before daybreak you have already gulped a couple of pieces cold pap (mieliemeel porridge), and trek miles from the resting place. This pattern repeats itself for days on end till eventually you find after such a night that the sun has already risen. The birds are singing, the horses are grazing, the burghers are braaing meat on open fires, and there is no sign of an Englishman. Then you know: De Wet departed during the night; the war has followed him - - until you meet up with him again after two or three days.

Jannie Geldenhuys related how Gen de Wet stood on a wagon and addressed them. A person visualised how he stood with one hand behind his back, the other around the lapel of his jacket while talking to the two-hundred "*hensoppers*" (hands – uppers) who broke their oath of neutrality to take up arms again in support of the Boer forces. Are you still honourable after breaking your oath? But, he asks, who broke the oath first? The hensoppers or the English opponent who in exchange for the oath of neutrality undertook security of tenure of person and property then forcibly confiscated their cattle and sheep, and forced them to reveal information of Boer spies and informers? So an opponent had already broken their side of the neutrality oath. They had in any case sworn an oath they were not at liberty to do because they still had their freedom and their own government. They could thus not swear to another oath . . . .

If someone had the foresight to record this "speech" of Gen de Wet it would have counted amongst one of the greats in SA history, because within the hour he had received word from a few couriers from the secretary of Gen Martinus Prinsloo that his commandos had surrendered unconditionally to the English. A few weeks previously De Wet was the Free State commandant that fought under Gen Paul Roux behind the Red mountains of Bethlehem.

When Gen de Wet spoke of the Free State Boer forces, then he meant the two thousand five hundred haggard, starving men with their skinny horses and run-down carts surrounding him. And when he spoke of the Government, he meant the small round tent and the man with red-brown beard standing next to him. His country was the burnt down and plundered farm houses, his folk, those who by their thousands were interned in concentration camps. When he spoke of freedom, he saw forty-thousand English troops who moved from north to south along the river to corner him here at Schoemansdrift.

Or would he like a Moses secure a freedom for a latter generation? Would he see his country under a new constitution during harvest time? I don't think so. Christiaan de Wet was never known as a dreamer or a fortune teller like Niklaas van Rensburg. He was just big – big of thought, courage and love. He lived and fought until he found his final resting place in the land of his birth. That is why he could purposefully and calmly stand there and inspire and light the fire of belief in a young man like Jannie Geldenhuys.

That same night the de Wet commando encumbered and delayed by hundreds of carts and wagons escaped under the noses of the English columns to the Waterberge in the Transvaal.

When Jannie Geldenhuys returned to Bothaville months later was he just as ragged as the rest of the commando – and the war lust was in his blood. He discovers his house burnt down, and his wife removed to Kroonstad, but gives no thought to surrendering.

Then on a particular day he is awakened by a burgher who informs him that there is someone who wants to see him. When he went outside it is his wife, Lizzie. She and her mother-in-law had got a pass from the chief provost de Bertodano to go out specifically to get their husbands to give themselves up. They had a set of men's clothing on under their dresses – so bulky that they needed to be lifted up on to the small mule and dead-beat horse-drawn cart. Lizzie and Jannie's baby daughter had died of sleeping sickness or fever (slapende koors). Lizzie had been working for months in a Kroonstad café to keep body and soul going: the war was also in her blood.

Thereafter she stayed, together with a few other women, with the commando, to make good her escape in a horse-drawn cart while the squirmiest is on the go – to meet up with the commando at a pre-arranged rendezvous'. After a while, having endured English columns, block-house fences and kafferspies they were cornered in an abandoned farm house in the bend of the Vaal River. War activities centred on the need to acquire food.

Lizzie Geldenhuys tells her grandchildren of this thus: "Our bunch then peacefully, as the saying went, safely and at ease, spent quite a while at Tweefontein, extremely busy milling mielies, burning "mielie-coffee", and drying ribbed meat for the days when we need to take flight. It is already December 1901 and fruit is plentiful on farms and thus a big item where vegetables are unobtainable.

It is often steamed when the fruit is still raw, and then honey is added, which the men folk had found during their travels, frequently in the crevasse between rocks or in holes in the ground.

They also made soap from sheep fat and buck ashes. Haricot-plants are pulled out of the ground, as it and other weeds are plentiful. The stew is then dried and burnt to get the ash. Thorn tree ash is also used and soaked in a bucket of water, and the water is then used with fifteen pounds of sheep fat. Fortunately there was an old soap pot hidden amongst the thorn bushes. The whole process could take days before the soap is ready.

"There is naturally a lot more to be done while waiting to prepare the lixivium before the soap is ready. The women folk constantly have other chores to do – under very primitive and trying conditions. Around midday the unfinished soap is ladled out into a larger bucket in order to cool it down and placed in a few sacks in readiness, so that in case the enemy attack at night we don't have to leave anything behind, not even our half-cooked soap. Then there was our own washing that had to be done".

"A couple of men would also be sent to the salt pans near Brandfort – those times still safe – to fetch salt. Two or three carts together with six to eight horse riders are sent along . . . the salt is naturally raw, and must be shovelled into sacks and returned to the camp for further refinement. Oh, we are only too happy to get some salt, albeit filthy and dirty, which we then dissolve in water so that the impurities can sink to the bottom, which we then call First Class."

Lizzie's younger brother is a Heliograph operator with Gideon Scheepers and one day he and a group of Vredefortse recces surprised the band there in their dongas. They stayed for ten days, repairing clothes, and established a choir! Lizzie never went anywhere without her old Globe song fascicle which she kept in the box in the seat of the cart. In the afternoons each group practices in the embankments, and at night the choir sings without (piano) accompaniment arranged four voices and with the young men setting up debate points – and late at night in the moonlight argue their case the night away.

Unbelievable! Cornered and thoroughly searched, through the barbed wire fencing and the enemy search patrols, they sing the enemies own songs without the benefit of musical instruments, and while the ruins of the house silhouettes against the horizon, debated over the legal aspects of the war and a free commonwealth. Is it a wonder that history turned out as it did?

That Christmas they could still spend safely and anxiously together, but on 22nd February 1902 they were caught unawares by the British. Lizzie describes it as follows:

"After we had been alone for about three weeks our small troop visited us again, namely Pa Preller, ou Dad, Ernst and Martiens van Biljon, Frank Brewis with their two carts and horses, together with the two loyal servants Aaron and Jonas. Their arrival was essentially to bring us a bag of mielies with the Scotch cart, and also came to fetch for themselves a little salt and mielie-coffee.

"Well, early before dawn Pa Preller had himself ridden off on horseback, far away up to the ridge to scout for any signs of the enemy. Oh, I can still see Pa in my mind how he had returned after two hours, dismounted in front of the house, off-saddle and knee-halter the beautiful dapple-grey horse – I co-incidentally on the veranda busy dishing up our breakfast of pap and milk.

"I offered him a cup of fresh milk. While he was drinking the milk, Martiens van Biljon looked up from working on his children's shoes and said 'Who is that who is approaching? (The house is in a hollow, with high ridges encircling the Vaal River on one side, and on the western side on the bank of the river a high cliff with a deep ravine).

As Martiens said so, it was as if a thunderstorm broke out around us. We just heard horses' hooves and here they were, hardly fifty metres from our front door. Alas the powerlessness and awfulness gripped everybody. Poor Pa ran through the house, out the back door, towards the ravine, with the purpose of taking shelter there – but alas before he covered forty yards a couple of soldiers charged at him, shouting "*Hands Up!*" – and as he raised his hands, one of the soldiers fired and the gunpowder burnt Pa on his left hand... Meanwhile other soldiers dismounted their horses and stormed into the house. Some of them plunder – and we see how they stuff forks, knives and spoons into their 'putties'. But as fast as they stuff the cutlery down the side of their legs, Kitty extracts it just as quickly – with the women folk hanging on to it in their hands. The men are herded into the room off the veranda, with guards placed in the doorway."

In the medley Lizzie manages to smuggle her father's case containing all his incriminating documents from the horse carriage and succeeds to conceal the papers in an old mattress, in order that the soldiers would not get wind of that Preller was an officer.

The soldiers searched the house, and Lizzie says: "In Kitty and her children's room, the floor was loose and sandy. With her four children in the room she always said the children caused the floor to break up; and nearly every day needed to smear the floor with dung and soil in order to keep it neat and tidy since all the bedding is laid on the floor – no beds. The soldiers started prying everywhere with their bayonets and soon thereafter arrived with small shovels which were attached to their saddles, and started to remove the soil. And what do we see? It is a large, long Kist – a wagon box – full of sheets, pillow cases and towels. And another one, both covered in and sewed with sacking – but the second kist you wouldn't guess – a coffin. It contained all the requisites for a burial – black material to line the coffin, a long white night gown, a few yards of white linen, nails and pins. Naturally the Colonel had to decide what is to be done with the entire linen etc. He decides that we may purchase some of the stuff. I remember well – we could buy the pillowcases for one and six each, the double bed sheets for four shillings and the towels also for one and six. We were only too pleased regarding the prices and Pa Preller gave me two pounds and said 'Child, buy some of the stuff because you are going to need it later'. I bought sheets, pillow cases and some of the towels, and saved the rest of the money, knowing that I would need it later. Kitty bought some of the black material, night gown and the remainder of the bedding. You may well ask what happened to the coffin? Well, this and the other kist were chopped up into small pieces and tired to the soldiers saddles.

When the column departed with their husbands, Kitty said "*Come, let us sing in English 'God be with you till we meet again*"!

"Dear children, that is where the good Lord gives you the strength to raise your voices and sing with gusto. Colonel Colleton halted his men, removed their helmets till the song was sung, saluted and then set forth. When the last pair of soldiers slowly passed us, said one '*Thank you ladies, but such a pathetic scene I've never experienced.*'"

The women folk are abandoned, but Lizzie ends this story "While we are sitting forlornly, Kitty started laughing, saying 'You did not see the humorous side this morning. While the troops were snooping around the house, and we were removing the knives and forks from their putties, I was watching another scene unfolding. The poor old Frank Brewis has a pair of black trousers which he considers his most treasured possession, and it was fastened on his saddle with a piece of canvas. In the initial hyper activity he quickly went to his horse and recovered the package, and busied himself in the corner of the lounge to pull the pants on over his existing pants so as not to lose it. The more he tries pulling the pants on, the more his foot got caught in the crutch, and the more his bundle of nerves. After a long struggle he managed to get the pants on, but as he stood erect he noticed that he was circled by soldiers who burst out laughing . . . "

The men were taken to Bothaville and thereafter by open trolleys to Kroonstad. Their so-called friends mocked them as they were paraded through the streets, but "een ding weet ik, God slap niet. Zoodanige stukken word ook in Zyn dagboek opgeteken - - - but if there is one thing that I know it is that God never sleeps. Everything is written up in His diary [for judgement day]", Jannie consoles himself. They are placed in goal, up to 52 persons in one room. The place was infested with lice and the short time spent there (Kroonstad) was taken up hunting down all the lice. From Kroonstad they were sent to Bloemfontein, then back to Kroonstad and then on to Durban – all in open rail coal trucks.

They are given the choice of accepting parole at each of these stopovers, in which case they would be sent to Greenpoint Camp, and there set free on condition that they would not return to the war front. Jannie sees the sea and ships for the first time in his life. They do not sign the declaration and are sent to India. At sea they sail into a storm and two burghers die in the cramped and squashed holds of the ship. He experiences the trauma of a sea burial.

They are again offered parole on arrival in India. Those who sign are sent to the cooler mountainous regions at Bhimtal. Those who decline remain in the stuffier low-lying area of Umballa, to "Sweat for your fatherland" say the prison wardens sarcastically.

Jannie, his father-in-law and friends, as well as hundreds of others, stayed behind together. To his utter dismay Jannie discovers that his own father and his younger brother could not endure the harsher treatment – and had signed for the cooler mountain camp at Bhimtal.

Jannie Geldenhuys became a teacher at Umballa. He took some of the exercise books that had been given him, and using a blunt pencil started to write "*On 3rd October 1899 in the avond kwam the commandeer man and commandeered myself and my father-in-law A.M. Preller . . .* " This part of the War that fell within his own grasp he committed to writing. He does so regularly, accurate and without remorse, hatred or sentimentally. He could not realise at that moment what significance it would take in the history of his people. He could not gather how his own life would be influenced by it.

One day after the other passes by, and what account can one give thereof? He writes about the poverty and dreadfulness of the local populace, about the English who unholy the Sabbath by plastering barracks, about the food that they have to prepare, sickness, and the odd letter received from the fatherland, the scriptures and sermons at prayer meetings and church services, funerals, photographic sessions, xxx that are made and the everyday heat, sandstorms, homesickness and longing for beloveds.

He writes in the eenvoudige Dutch language of the day, a particularly clean, versogte style and long forgotten grammatical sayings and mannerisms, comes across like the smell of the good earth, to the reader of today. A person relives the besonder/ particular power of the strong vergoeding of the verb in sentences like "wy vroeg om water" "wy ging van daar de ander dag se morgen" (translated literally "he xx for water", "he longs for the other days day morgen")

When he was captured, the English officer ordered the removal of his trousers and shoes and marched him along the main street of Bothaville. "I complied in humiliation of the Afrikaner" he said.

There are good old sayings that were lost in the adoption of Afrikaans " half after nine o'clock" for half-ten, a aanspraak for a talk, "prepare for" for get ready, "it happens to be my turn" for it's my turn, vortgaan (advance).

If the author writes about things with in his experience – using the K if it is foreign or deftig, or uses the c. Everything concerning the railways which was a new development for the Afrikaner gets a c such as in compartement, and concerning the military as in commandant, escort, veldcornet. He speaks of circus, ceremonies and courante (newspapers), and it is amusing that he applies 'medicyne' medicine. English words are inserted in brackets, because he feels it does not belong in his language.

The exercise books in which Jannie writes his diary are attractive. There are full-page drawings of her majesty Queen Victoria "the Queen of England and Empress of India" on the front pages, artistic designs with flower and leaf patterns. The fact that despite the books being published in the East proves 'it' that the mighty British Empire had its limitations during those glorious times.

Weeks before the conclusion of the peace, is the terms thereof already known to the prisoners of war, and they are absolutely sure that no Boer 'officer' would sign it. When peace finally arrived, the Umballa inmates decided not to sign. They anticipate being approached but nobody ask them to sign. Days and weeks go by, and still nobody asks them to sign. Dejected and bitter they have to eventually go and beg to sign in order to return home. Boere with money pay their own way to return home, thereafter follow those who signed parole, and thereafter the rest have to wait their turn. Boere who had shops sold all their stock and everybody tries to exchange possessions into cash.

Jannie Geldenhuys's journal undergoes a noticeable change: he writes circumstantial, jovially, especially when the letter he receives in which he finds out that his wife in the Kroonstad concentration camp gave birth to their second child, a boy – small Oubasie.

They are now permitted to move around freely in Umballa, and attend a Hindu funeral, an Eastern circus and befriend the widow manageress of the hotel, "*Ik kryg een cab van de stasie naar die kamp, het was nog donker, ik kwam voor de kamp hek en een van die wachten riep hard uit 'Holt. Who is there? Een ogenblik wis ik niet te antwoord, maar het hom my te binnen en ik zei: "Vriend" en hy zei "Pass Friend, all's well."* - translated broadly as "I took a cab from the station to near the camp gate. It is already quite dark, and one of the guards called quite loudly; 'Halt! Who is there?'. In the blink of an eye I do not know how to answer, but replied "Friend". He in turn said "Pass Friend – all's well".

Unbelievable. It is already October, and still they're in Umballa. Up to four times they advanced up to the camp gate with their bundles and four times the arrangements are cancelled. The rains arrive, it pours in the tropical heat, they get sick and tired, fighting breaks out, the Peace becomes a joke, and the fatherland a dream world.

There is Jannie's father-in-law Abraham Preller, one of the founders of Bothaville, justice of the peace, church member and town councillor. His imposing homestead on his farm has been burnt to the ground; he owns neither any cattle, or sheep, or a wagon nor a cart. His young wife was from an early stage of the war in the Kroonstad Concentration camp. Their youngest daughter died there, just like Jannie's eldest. She has already been released a long time ago, and there are hundreds of young men repatriated from the battles. She writes how they help to care and clothe the orphans. The dampness permeates his whole being, he gets rheumatism, water on the knee, and he pines to a shadow of his former self. He struggles in prayer, holds prayer meetings, and pines . . . .

Ernst van Biljon, Jannie's friend, that big, well-built man with the moustache, is hospitalised for weeks. The English doctor could not extract a problematic tooth after five painful attempts, and the infection spreads to his ear. At night he tosses and turns with pain on his iron bed, in the lantern-light. He is the only one left over from his whole family. His wife and two of his children died in the Brandfort camp. He received the tragic news in a note from his only surviving twelve-year old son. His brother Martiens died in the Umballa camp. Ernst had to carry him from an English gun carriage to a sand grave. Martiens wife, the jovial Kitty who had scrounged the burial gown retrieved from the coffin, died of pneumonia a couple of days before the Peace – when she wanted to bake rusks for her children in the Klerksdorp concentration camp. Her children have been placed somewhere with people in Pretoria . . .

Jannie Geldenhuys writes long letters to his "*Dearest Meidje*," and his recently born son, but they are thousands of miles from him. Helplessness manifests in his diary. He no longer devotes careful study to which scriptures are read and which psalms are sung. He no longer becomes outspoken concerning the English Sabbath day sinning, he does not become sarcastic about Afrikaners who overindulge in drinking. He stumbles through the streets in the town, on horseback, on foot, by train and riding elephants. He gets lost, attends English dance parties, he visits the widow on Sundays for lunch. He receives presents from her, his language becomes muddled with English words and his writings no longer place them in brackets.

He eventually arrives in Kroonstad six months after Peace was signed, to claim his wife and baby son from friends. He does not have a sheep or a cow to his name; he is twenty-five years old but has aged double that.

He starts a farm shop with his father-in-law and later continues alone. They have another three children who know nothing of the tragedy and misery and prosper with their farming. Jannie Geldenhuys becomes a blessed farmer, a man of substance in the church and state and never again leaves his farm. He keeps his diary that as a priceless possession, a photo album and news cuttings about India which is not in his handwriting. Here and there annotations are made that are more than purely factual. Perhaps he got it as a parting gift from someone who was more than a casual acquaintance, because who would ever know how deep and wide the war affected Jannie.

Ou Dad Jannie is buried at Rustpan. Oumam had the following inscribed on his gravestone *"In die tyd van liefde sterf die blom van soete herinneringe nooit – Ges.106:7"*

Die Oorlogsherinneringe van Lizzie Geldenhuys Limited edition published 20.4.1954. *Amper Onse Mense* - Dot Serfontein. *Keurskrif vir Kroonstad* – Dot Serfontein. *Bothaville en sy Mense* – v.d. Schyff and Van Eeden

mothers farm Welgelegen. They had three children, 1961 she married Hendrik Jacobus (Hennie) born 31st August 1964 Bothaville, Ernastina Helena (Esté) born 1966 Bothaville and Mariana born 1968 Klerksdorp.

Jannie suffered a stroke at a very young age. He was admitted to the Universitas Hospital but died two days later on 3rd May 1985. His widow then married Coen Wessels in May 1998 and they retired to Uitkyk farm, owned by her son-in-law Johan Rautenbach. Very interestingly, Uitkyk used to belong to Kil Dreyer. They currently farm Kromspruit, Ventersburg.

Geldenhuys, Johannes (Jan) Albertus (born Johannesburg 15th August 1940), taxidermist, miner, boiler-maker, diesel mechanic, farmer, garage-owner, road haulier, builder, storekeeper, property-developer, naturalist and businessman, was the eldest son of Abram Carl Frederik Preller Geldenhuys of Bothaville, and his wife Matthia Martha Lotter of Johannesburg, daughter of Jan Lotter.

In 1964 Jan married Julia Lillian Dippenaar. Paul was born in December 1966 (Julia had a son and a daughter by a previous marriage; both children were adopted and changed their surnames to Geldenhuys).

In 1946 Jan's parents emigrated to Luanshya in Northern Rhodesia to commence a mining career on the Copperbelt. Jan started his junior schooling in Luanshya and completed his Schooling at Chingola. At an early age he displayed a marked aptitude for things mechanical – and by the tender age of

Geldenhuys, Johannes (Jannie) Albertus (born 15.3.1937, died Bothaville 3rd May 1985). Farmer. JA is the second child of Hendrik Jacobus Geldenhuys and Adrianna Marta Maria (Max) of Lekkerlewe, Bothaville. Married Helena Frederika Steyn of Kroonstad on 11th March 1961 and settled on step-

19 he had already owned and fixed no fewer than 17 motorcars! In those days, cars were big: like Buick, Studebaker, and Ford V8; whilst quick money was to be had with smaller Morris Coupe and VW Carmen-Ghia cars. The writer recalls with fond memories the mission of towing the Buick from Luanshya to Chingola – with no brakes and no lights – at night! At home Jan would not bother with block and tackle, preferring to build up his Herculean muscle strength by bodily removing V8 blocks from the engine compartments!

In 1954 Jan heroically saved the life of our younger sister when the family thatched cottage on Musenga plots were set alight by a disenchanted Swahili. The family was re-housed by Nchanga Copper mine and our parents then sold the property. At about this time, Jan took up taxidermy and delighted in sucking out the grey matter from the skulls of his experiments. A particularly distasteful experience is recalled which entailed preparing a partridge, which had been skinned for stuffing. The carcass was wrapped in newspaper, then entombed in mud (as per Boy Scout fashion) and anthill oven baked – whist yours truly and Jan set off to the nearby river steam for a spot of fishing - no doubt to lay our hands on additional taxidermy experiments. Upon returning to enjoy the oven baked pheasant, to our horror, the whole plot was once again ablaze! Needless to say, the pheasant tasted like newspaper and to add insult to injury, our bottoms glowed red from the subsequent spanking!

Jan and I took up boxing and wrestling - but were forced to give it up when we "lost" our annual subscriptions (We had gone swimming at the local pool, and left the cash in our clothes to be stolen). A certain opponent named Lightfoot is recalled - except that he was no lightweight! If anything, he was a mean heavy-weight. The punishment our parents inflicted on us did not warrant continuing with the sport. We took up the cheaper fishing option.

Jan was no mean fisherman either. He soon fabricated sophisticated bicycle-drawn trailers to load fishing and camping gear for week-end trips to the Kafue and other like sized rivers/gorges to catch Spike and Tiger fish. Family camping trips to Lakes Tanganyika, Bangwela and Mwera invariably produced childhood memories of 19 Tigers per hour, or 600 pounds of can-fruit bottled curried fish, rowing the mile wide Lampula River in dugouts and catching leguaan by the tail!

By the late 1950's, Jan became a miner, completed his Blacksmith apprenticeship, as well as mechanic – stripped semi-naked and covered in black slippery grease and all! His natural ability to make all things mechanical to work provided the life skills to lead a very productive life. After a short spell of farming in the Free State – in the Bothaville, Kroonstad (of "*al in die ronte*" toast habit) and Viljoenskroon areas, Jan returned to the Copperbelt by the mid-1960. A spell of managing garage workshops followed, together with farming with rabbits and guinea pigs as a meat supplement.

Having met and married Julia Lillian Dippenaar in 1964, in Luanshya, Jan embarked on operating long-distance "Hell – Run" heavy duty trucks from the Copperbelt to Mbeya on the Tanzania border. Shortly thereafter they immigrated to Swaziland to harvest and haul timber to Usutu pulp mills. The fancy Ford Ghia was used to lug chainsaws, as well as their operators, more often than not in the boot of the car. Timber haulage is an expensive business and a few mishaps down treacherous mountain passes led to another career change. This time to the Transvaal to pursue building houses, affecting insurance claim repairs and ending up producing the household SAFA juice brand name. The business needed expanding and Natal was selected as a growth opportunity.

The relocation to the coast provided opportunities for deep-sea sailing, fishing and boating. This ranged from rubber duckies to ocean going vessels. Lance Froneman's "Waikiki" sank 5 kilometres off the harbour mouth in May 1999. The boat sank within seven minutes when taking on sea water was first noted – and settled some 65 to 70 metres below sea level. However, Lance Froneman subsequently purchased a replacement ocean-going catamaran, and did not need to twist Jan's arm to help sail the new acquisition from Langebaan on the Cape west coast to Durban. Hakuna Matata became a household word at the yacht mole, where Jan and Jule managed Ferry and Bay Services.

Having previously produced beer in KwaMakuta, that site was selected to establish a SAFA juice outlet. Shortly thereafter, the whole of the Umdoni shopping complex was purchased – and expanded with the purchasing of liquor licence to operate a bottle store and erection of the Trek service station which is still active on the Umdoni forecourt. Purchase of the present Bhengu site followed – where property development is expanding. One of Jan's many hobbies was protecting fauna and flora - from transplanting fully grown mature trees to collecting all variety of birds. He was particularly partial to guinea fowl and peacocks, and whenever losses occurred for whatever reason, went to great lengths to replace and safeguard his stock.

Jan and his son Paul not only maintained their interest at the 'Bay' and soon converted Wave Dancer into a triple-deck pleasure craft, for cruising around the Durban Harbour. This boat is the largest pleasure craft at the Bay. Paul was the skipper and the business ran profitably. However, a disagreement arose with the majority shareholder and Paul resigned.

Then together with Paul, Jan established and expanded a new venture – Bush Babies Lodge – all built in log cabin style. The long term objectives were very sound – to continue providing income for both of their retirement in due course.

In 2007, Jan acquired 100% of Wave Master, which the boat had been re-named. This was just about the time that Jan had decided to build twenty-four duplexes on their plot. Whilst waiting for the plans to be approved by the Council, Jan purchased a non-runner Bobcat, dumper, industrial cement mixer and a TLB tractor unit. These they overhauled in short sift. As and when their estate development materialises, their retirement incomes will be assured.

Bothaville en sy Mense – v.d. Schyff and Van Eeden. *Nickel Cross* – "Prop" Preller Geldenhuys

Geldenhuys, Johannes Albertus (born Bothaville 6th February 1989). He is a Matriculant at Grey College, Bloemfontein (in 1997). He is the eldest son of Hennie – Hendrik Jacobus Geldenhuys and Linette Kotzé. Jannie is a dashing rugby player and was selected for Grey College First IV in 2007.

Jannie, or Janna-man as he is sometimes called, studied at the University of the Free State and currently lives in Bloemfontein, working for the Junior Rugby Academy.

His younger sister Joané is also a talented swimmer, and swam the Midmar Mile in 2007.

Geldenhuys, Johannes 'Hannes' (born Brakpan, Gauteng 23 August 1963), went to Stofberg and is a farmer in Heidelberg, Gauteng. Hannes married Magda and they have three children, Martin Lourens born 1985, Alta born 1989 and Marelie born 1992. Hannes is a facebook friend of the author.

Geldenhuys, J. C. M. Petty Officer of the South Africa Naval Service at the outbreak of World War 11. South Africa possessed no real naval vessels on the outbreak of war, but their strength consisted of three officers and three ratings. Geldenhuys was subordinate to Lieutenant-Commanders J. Dalgleish and F.J. Dean.

Geldenhuys, J.N. Died at Paardeberg during the Boer War. He was serving with the Wolmaranstad Kommando, under General S.P. du Toit.

Geldenhuys, J. N. (born? died 25th March 1945), Warrant Officer Class 11, killed in action during the closing stages of World War 11. Geldenhuys was a crew-member on a Liberator of No 34 Squadron, South African Air Force, piloted by Captain L.J. de Jager that was hit by flak during their bombing run on Villach. Villach was a key point on the railway line into Austria, which was attacked twice within four days. 50 heavies were very successful on the night of 25/26 March 1945, when the goods and transhipment depots were almost totally destroyed. Unfortunately, the flak was accurate. The Liberator was crewed by pilot plus a crew of eight. The other members of the crew killed in action were Lt.'s R.L. Chegwyn, P.M. Tylden-Wright, I.J. Doble, F/O R. Warrington, WO's J. Robbertse and W.A.J. Venter, and Sgt A.C. Phillips.

Geldenhuys, J.N.E. (born? died 4th August 1942), Sapper, killed Cairo and buried at Heliopolous cemetery. General Jannie Geldenhuys is photographed at the gravestone, in the formers book entitled "A General's Story".

Geldenhuys, Johannes Norval (born Vrede district, OFS 18th February 1918 - died Cape Town 22nd July 1964), minister of NG Kerk and author of theological and religious books, was the son of Jurie Johannes Geldenhuys and his wife Mabel Aletta Louw Norval. After matriculating at Vrede, Johannes studied at the University of Pretoria, before going to the University of Cambridge, England for 2 years, having been awarded an Elsie Ballot Scholarship. When he returned, he had his theological training in Pretoria, and was admitted to the ministry towards the end of 1943. The following year he was assistant minister in Pretoria North, and in 1945 went to Princeton USA where he obtained a Th.M. degree.

In 1947 he became secretary of publications for the Christian Students Association, but in 1948 he returned to be ordained and inducted as minister of Naboomspruit. Because of ill-health, however, he accepted (1949) the position as head of publications with the South African Bible Society (later known as the NG Kerk-uitgewers) in Cape Town, and from May of that year was Chief Compiler of the *Jaarboek van die Gerfedereerde Nederduitse Gerformeerde Kerk*. From 1952 he was the head of the new United Protestant Publishing and in 1963 became the general secretary of Church Publishers.

Although almost continuously in pain and forced to have several abdominal operations, he devoted all his energies to his great task. In a certain sense he was in the forefront of the Church's uphill struggle against a flood of undesirable literature, a struggle to which he made a positive contribution by establishing the monthly *Naweekpos*. This he maintained for ten years at personal financial sacrifice.

His works are of high scientific standard. His comment in English on the Gospel of St Luke was described overseas as the best in a hundred years, and another theological work *The supreme authority* (Marshal, Morton & Scott, Eng., 1953) was particularly well received. For the Protestantse Uitgewers he prepared a Family and Pulpit Bible, and was also responsible for final editing the epoch-making Afrikaans Bible, in three volumes, with explanatory annotations. In addition to theological works he wrote books on topical subjects and articles of a practical religious nature. These included *Die kommunistiese aanslag op die Kerk* (C.S.V., Stellenbosch, 1947), *Die Christen en politiek* (C.S.V., 1948) and *Ons grootste taak* (Stellenbosch, 1943) (child education). He also wrote several novels and scripts for good films he himself producing a number of fascinating films.

Despite his success as a writer he remained a modest and unassuming person. He served his church as an elder of the Groote Kerk congregation in Cape Town and notwithstanding the setbacks caused by his poor health remained both a cheerful idealist and an optimist. He was only forty-six years old when he died after another operation. Four of his six children of his marriage to Alida Paulina van Jaarsveld survived their father. There are photographs of him in *Die Kerkbode* of 9.9.1964; *Die Voorlighter* of September 1964 and *Die Jaarboek van die Ned. Geref. Kerk*, 1965.

Obituaries: *Die Burger*, 23.7.1964; *Cape Times*, 23.7.1964, *Die Volksblad*, 23.7.1964; *Die Kerkbode*, 9.9.1964; - R.VAN REENEN, Die onknakbare geeskrag van 'n "klein, vaal mannetjie'", *Die Burger*, 24.7.1964; - P.E.S. SMITH, 'Krag in swakheid volbring', *Die Koningsbode,* August 1964.

Geldenhuys, Jeanne (born George, Western Cape, 1 December 1961). Schooled at De Villiers Graaff, mother of Frans, Eugene and Cathy.

Geldenhuys, Joey (born 1883), fifth child of Hendrik Jacobus Geldenhuys – 1837, mentioned in the writers grandmothers Oorlogsherinneringe about the Anglo-Boer war 1899 - 1902

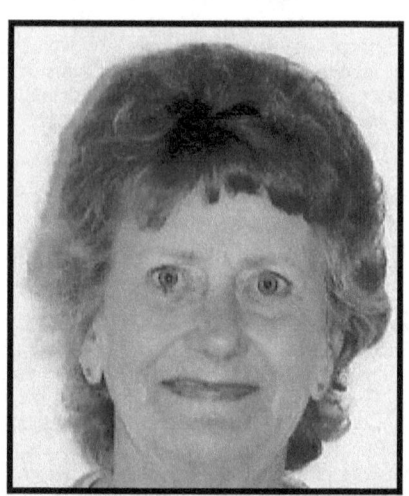

Geldenhuys, Joyce - detail already forgotten!

Geldenhuys, Judith (born 20th February 1812 and died 23rd June 1890). She was christened on the 30th March 1812 when six weeks old.

DICTIONARY OF FAMILY BIOGRAPHY

She married her cousin in Swellendam – Johannes Albertus Geldenhuys – our direct relative, born December 1807 and died on Doornbult Farm, Kroonstad 1894. She was the third daughter of Hendrik Jacobus Geldenhuys who was born in September 1785.

Geldenhuys, Julanda (born 15th July 1969), went to Hoërskool Heidelberg, Kaap – class of 1988, married André Engelbrecht born 4th February 1967. They married on 3rd October 1992, have two childen, a son Adriaan and a daughter Suzanne, and live in Swellendam. Julanda was an active faceboek 'FarmVille' game player with the writer in 2011.

Geldenhuys, Jurie

Geldenhuys, Jurie Johannes (was born at Onrusrivier 5th February 1940) and is a South African Insurance broker and business executive. He was the son of Jurie Johannes Geldenhuys and Maria Magdalena Groenewald. Jurie married Freda Johanna Fourie on 26th June 1965 and they have two sons and a daughter. Jurie received his education at De Villiers Graaff High School and obtained his B.Commerce degree at Stellenbosch University. He is the Managing Director of Santam Ltd, Cape Town, 1998.

Geldenhuys, Jurie (born Stanford 13th March 1958), son of Wessel Johannes and Corné Geldenhuys, married Nicoleen. They have three daughters, Jurita Mycroft, Nicolette Loubscher and Corné Olivier.

Geldenhuys, Jurie Johannes (born Durban, 1st December 1988), went to Gelofte Skool 2006, worked as a radar and sonar operator in the South African Navy, and lives in Durban. Facebook friend in 2011 – and his family branch still needs further research since Jurie Johannes was populatied by Hans Jacob – who fathered 18 children. Jurie is currently in a relationship with Ria Pretorius.

Geldenhuys, Kayla – another relative of Jurie Geldenhuys

Geldenhuys, Liane Muir (born Meyerton, Gauteng 20th July), went to Hoërskool Sasolburg and studied at Vereeniging Technical College. Married. Very good Facebook friend and games partner during 2011.

Geldenhuys, Lida (born Messina, Limpopo 7th October 1952), went to Hoërskool Edenvale. Married Smit, they have a daughter, Anneli Smit who is engaged to marry Gerhard van der Westhuizen from Ventersburg and lives in Pretoria; and Bellinda Geraldine Kruger. Friend but possibly relative of Annette Gallianos, nee Geldenhuys, who lives in Greece. Facebook friend in 2011.

Geldenhuys, Linette born 30th April 1964. See Johanna Elizabeth Kotzé – who is married to Hendrik Jacobus (Hennie) Geldenhuys.

Geldenhuys, Lou-Ann (born Gordons Bay 14 June 1992), younger sister to Andries Geldenhuys, born December 1984.

Geldenhuys, Liza (born 31st December 1964) is the eldest child of Gerhard Geldenhuys and Annaline Odendaal. She was christened on the 4th April 1965 at Stellenbosch-West and is a renown pianist who performs classical as well as light music. In Afrikaans music there is a song called *Lisa se Klavier* which was composed by Afrikaans rock singer "Koos Kombuis" (the stage name for André le Roux du Toit). This song has achieved something of a cult status amongst light Afrikaans songs. The song was composed by Koos Kombuis after he had heard her playing in her compartment in Cape Town in the late 1980's.

Gerhard kindly sent the author a recent article about Liza, Koos Kombuis and the song.

Geldenhuys, Louis Frederick Botes (born Aliwal North 22nd July 1940), son of James Henry and Louisa Frederick Botes, married Louisa Regina Knoop from Pretoria. They have 4 children – Louise, James Henry, Louis Botes and Mario.

Geldenhuys, Louis, born 17th October 1978, facebook friend in 2011, expressed an interest in the CD and book. Louis is married to Louise Geldenhuys.

Geldenhuys, Louise (born Johannesburg 5th May 1987), is the second child of Stuart William Geldenhuys and Joy Goldsworthy. She graduated witha B.Com degree and is now completing her Chartered Accountant qualification.

Geldenhuys Louise, born Brakenfell 20th August 1982, studied at Boland College Paarl, married to Louis Geldenhuys.

Geldenhuys, Louise (born Brakenfell 20th August 1982), studied at Boland College Paarl, married to Louis Geldenhuys.

Geldenhuys, Lourens (christened Malgasriver 30th March 1777), is a fifth generation Geldenhuys, Burgher of Stellenbosch, son of Johannes Albertus (1750) and Johanna le Roux (widow of Johannes Swart – 1748). Lourens got married in Cape Town on 15th April 1804 to Johanna Geertryda Gildenhuizen, who was the daughter of Stellenbosch burgher Hendrik Jacobus and Geertruida Grobbelaar. Not unlike Dunbar Moodie, he married a cousin/nephew, which was not uncommon in those days.

Lourens Dirk Cornelis Geldenhuys

DICTIONARY OF FAMILY BIOGRAPHY

Geldenhuys, Lourens Dirk Cornelis (born 23rd August 1836 - died 21st April 1891), founder of Geldenhuys Estate, son of Lourens (1811) and Elsie Sophia Prins of Heidelburg, and father of Rand pioneer and politician Lourens (1864). He was baptised in Swellendam 6th November 1836, married Elsie also in Swellendam, on 6th March 1854. They settled in the Transvaal Republiek when the gold reef was discovered. His grandson, Frans Eduard (1889 –1961) became an agriculturist, journalist and diplomat of note. He died in Johannesburg on 21st April 1891

Geldenhuys, Lourens (Louw). (Born Klip River, Heidelberg district, Tvl 6th December 1864 – died Emmarentia, Johannesburg district, 31st August 1929) Rand pioneer, businessman, politician, and farmer, was the son of Lourens Dirk Cornelius Geldenhuys, and his wife Elsie Sophia Prins.

In 1878 Lourens was 14 years old when the family moved from the Heidelberg district to the farm Wilgespruit on the East Rand, where his father, together with Frederick Struben, discovered that the Main Reef crosses the farm. On selling the farm to Struben, the Lourens family settled at Elandsfontein in the Krugersdorp district, where Lourens senior and his three sons hired the mineral rights, started a new search for gold and here they again made an important gold find. Lourens was one of the few original inhabitants of the Witwatersrand who played an important part in the discovery and development of the goldfields. Because of his intuition in money matters he became a wealthy man. It was easy for him to establish firm friendships with the newcomers.

Lourens met with J.B. Robinson (later Sir Robinson – and sponsored by Alfred Beit), the owner of Langlaagte, Cecil John Rhodes, C. Rudd, H. Nourse (lessee of Turfontein) and Field Cornet Meyer on 5th August 1886 to a public meeting, to favour all farms being declared public diggings.

Gold was also found on what later became known as the Geldenhuys Estate, Elandsfontein No 1. Lourens and his eldest brother Frans Eduard bought the farm Braamfontein, where they hoped to find the Clifton Reef. When this failed they divided the farm and Lourens named his part of the subdivision after his wife Emmarentia. Later, this farm was cut up and further subdivided into residential areas, as well as the West Park Cemetery. Being an estate agent and town developer he was one of the few Afrikaners who were able to reach the top rung of the financial ladder. His success lay in his ability to overcome the Afrikaners' lack of business acumen and capital.

The Geldenhuys Estate is now an extensive area of smallholdings in the municipal area of Bedfordview and the magisterial district of Germiston. It lies about 8 to 11 km east of the Johannesburg City Hall, astride the road to Jan Smuts International Airport. It was laid out on the farm Elandsfontein and bears the name of his father - Lourens Dirk Cornelis Geldenhuys. It is used chiefly for vegetable growing and poultry-farming. The Geldenhuys Interchange on the N3 national road from Natal was constructed on the property.

In 1895 Lourens entered the political field for the first time when he was elected to the Tweede Volksraad, supporting General Piet Joubert as opposed to President S.J.P. Kruger. Lourens played an important role in the commission of inquiry into the consolidation of the gold laws. His first and only defeat in an election occurred in 1899 when General Ben Viljoen ousted him over the issue of selling alcohol to Natives - a policy that Lourens always strongly opposed.

When the Second Anglo-Boer War (1899-1902) broke out, he went to Natal with the Krugersdorp Commando, but surrendered after the occupation of Pretoria on 5th June 1900. After the war he was so affected by the lot of his improvised and unemployed fellow Afrikaners that he decided to provide work for them. Since a dam had to be built and orchards maintained on the farms Braamfontein and Emmarentia, he provided a large number of farmers with a good living and collected an annual amount of £ 1 450 in rents.

Lourens resumed his political career in 1910 when he was elected to stand for Vrededorp in the first Union Parliament. As a member of the South Africa Party (SAP) he was an ardent supporter of General Louis Botha and General J.C. Smuts, and in the 1915 election held Vrededorp for the SAP, but moved over to Johannesburg North in 1920. He retained his seat until his death, winning by only one vote in his last election in 1929. He was a member of the House of Assembly for nineteen years - a record for his time. His standpoint, always strong and his pleasantly persuasive style of debating commanded the respect of his fellow parliamentarians. The political struggle on the Rand in the twenties largely centred on him, with the National Party opposition over-eager to defeat this old stalwart of Botha and Smut's party. He also served on the Johannesburg City Council for many years.

As a churchman Lourens contributed a great deal. He was a member of the NG congregation in Johannesburg East from the date of its establishment and served on the Church Council for thirty years. He built a small church on his farm where regular services were held for the people in his district.

Always extremely generous to the church, the school, and the poor, Lourens never boasted of his wealth and gave willingly to the church and the school in the form of money and stands. The Afrikaans - medium Louw Geldenhuys Primary School in Linden, Johannesburg, was named after him. He was also a co-founder of the Langlaagte Orphanage of the N.G. Church, which at first bore his name. He was noted for his charity and integrity.

Lourens was buried on his farm Emmarentia by the Rev. Willem Nicol, in whose parish he had been an Elder. Approximately 1500 people, including General Jannie Smuts attended the funeral of this popular Afrikaner.

Lourens married Emmarentia (Margaretha) Botha on 9th February 1887 and had eight children. There is a photograph of him in S.A.W.W. (Infrc)

S.A.W.W. 1916 - Obituaries: *The Star* 31.8.1929; *Rand Daily Mail* 3.9.1929. - SESA Vol 5 C.T. 1972; - B.M. SCHOEMAN, *Parlementere verkiesings in Suid Afrika 1910-1976*, Pta 1977 - E.L.P. STALS (ed) *Afrikaners in die Goudstad* C.T. - Pta 1978.

Geldenhuys, Lourens. Boer War POW at Groenpunt. Lourens appears in a photograph with his brother Dirk and father also named Dirk. Also in the photograph is Hendrik Geldenhuys, believed to be a cousin rather than a brother to Dirk, because his features are dissimilar. Dot Serfontein wrote the caption in her excellent book *Keurskrif vir Kroonstad* but apart from naming the brothers Piet and Stoffel van Coller, offers no clue whether Lourens' father Dirk was the Rand pioneer and miner.

Geldenhuys, Lourens Pieter Arnoldus born 10th October 1835 in Swellendam and died in captivity in Ceylon, in the Colombo hospital on 22 January 1902. He was aged 66 years and 3 months when he died.

Geldenhuys, Loretta (born Kroonstad 28th March 1960), married Antony Smith and they have two sons, Jacques and Charles Lauton Smith.

Geldenhuys, Louw. Married to Meyerene and lives in Naboomspruit. Louw and Meyerene are friendly with Charles Brink's father. Charles is married to Chanli Bouwer, daughter of Delene Elizabeth Geldenhuys.

Geldenhuys, Lucas Marthinus (born 1st April 1941 in Caledon), married Alta Obbes born in Malmesbury on 9th July 1946. They are the parents of Jacobus 'Jaco' Geldenhuys born in Bellville on 28th March 1971.
See also website:

http://www.cs.sun.ac.za/~jaco

Geldenhuys, Lucille (born Vryburg 17th November 1988), went to Hoërskool Vryburg and studied at CUT Vrystaat Universiteit, class of 2008. Works as a photographer at Central Pix in Bloemfontein. In a relationship with Victor Fincham. Sibling brother is Andre Geldenhuys, in Johannesburg.

Geldenhuys, Lucy (born Durban 29th March 2009) is the first daughter to Pey Malan Geldenhuys and Eloise Howard. She immigrated to New Zealand whilst still only a mere three months old. Super hyper-active and learnt to operate an iphone and ipad before learning to talk. God's blessing to grandparents, especially Oumie (who can't wait to emigrate to Auckland).

Geldenhuys, M., was a pilot serving on No 3 Squadron, South African Air Force, on 10th November 1943. At that time, the squadron was based at Savoia, Eastern Mediterranean, and tasked with convoy protection and shipping standby as 25 ships and 5 escorts were passing en route Bengasi. Captain M. Geldenhuys was one of six Hurricane 11Cs pilots scrambled to intercept six Junker 88s and five Dornier 217s escorted by five fighters about to attack the ship convoy. A Captain R. Yeats attacked two Ju88s and sent one down, but after attacking another his screen frosted up and he lost contact with the enemy in the gathering darkness. A second Hurricane pilot fired at a Ju88 and saw it crash into the sea but did not claim a share.

Captain M. Geldenhuys led his section into an attack during which the pilots individually fired bursts at four Ju88s, one of which went into the sea. Another lost height, with port engine smoking, and a Do217 was also destroyed. The enemy single-engined aircraft made no attempt to intervene before the engagement had to be broken off because of darkness.

Much later, during October 1944, No 3 Squadron SAAF, as part of No 8 Wing, was based at Borghetto (Near Ancona and Florence, Italy), and by now equipped with Spitfire aircraft. Captain M. Geldenhuys is again mentioned as playing his full part in 8 Wing activities, in leading missions either against designated targets or on cabrank patrol.

Geldenhuys, Maria (born 1880, died July 1901), third child of Hendrik Jacobus Geldenhuys – 1837, grand aunt of the writer, who died during the Anglo-Boer War 1899 – 1902.

Geldenhuys, Maria Susanna Wilhelmina (born 27th May 1911 Rustpan, Bothaville, died 15th March 1995). She was the daughter of Johannes Albertus (born July 1877) and Anna Elisabeth Preller, and elder sister of Abram Carl Frederik Preller Geldenhuys. Married Theodorus van Rensen and had three children – Johan, Elizabeth (Libby) Adriana and Adrian Henry. She is photographed in Dot Serfontein's book "*Keurskrif vir Kroonstad*", appearing as dancers with a quartet. Aunt Minnie was tragically murdered in her Pretoria Rietondale home by a black gardener burglar.

Geldenhuys, Mariana (born Klerksdorp). She is the youngest daughter to Johannes Albertus Geldenhuys and Helena Frederika Steyn of Kroonstad. She married Johan Rautenbach and they currently live on the farm Vrugbaar. They have two children, Elaine born 5th May 1994 and Georg Frederik born 13th June 1997. Johan Rautenbach also owns the farm Uitkyk, on which his mother and step-father have retired. Interestingly, Uitkyk used to belong to Kil Dreyer, of Kroonstad fame.

Geldenhuys, Marile (born Christiana 21st September 1993), went to Gekombineerde Skool Christiana. Her sibling brothers are Stephan and Schikkie.

Geldenhuys, Margaretha Helene 'Marita' Brodie, born 21 December 1946 in Ermelo, Mapumalanga, South Africa, died 19 July 2013. Marita lived in Suva City, Central, Fiji. Marita married Donald 'Ross' Brodie born 29 January 1947 in Geraldine, New Zealand - but is presently separated from the father of her two children.

I got to know Marita through her eldest sister, Maureen (who are fourth-cousins, decendant from Dirk Cornelius Geldenhuys), and how pleased I was since Marita now has the most up-to-date and detailed 'Geldenhuys' MyHeritage site that the writer is aware of.

Marita was the child of Willem Geldenhuys and went to Ermelo High School in the Transvaal.

Marita was an exceptional artist of note with a very successful exhibition of her paintings which sold very well. Facebook pictures of her double-storied home in Fiji is awesome!

She had a son Shyane Brodie born 30 May 1973 in New Plymouth (New Zealand) and a daughter, Tonja born 1975 married to Luke Ian Fisher. Marita has two grandchildren from her daughter – Stevie Meriel Fisher born 2007 and Scarlett Robyn Fisher.

Marita's MyHeritage site is well worth a visit. Her sudden passing in July 2013 came as a shock and will be sorely missed. Although I never met her, I always felt very close to my fourth-cousin.

Geldenhuys, Mariza (born Riversdal, Western Cape 29th December 1988), daughter of Sorina Nefdt Geldenhuys, went to Langenhoven Hoërskool – class of 2007, and sister of Wedré. Worked at and was 2 I/C for American Swiss.

Geldenhuys, Martin
Actor / Filmaker of Martin Geldenhuys Productions

Geldenhuys, Marianne (born 15th July 1986), middle daughter of Izak George Geldenhuys and Hannelie Booysen. Elder sister is Suzanne and younger sibling is Liezel. She has two half-siblings Cabous and Lena – step mother being Wilna Bester. Mariaane is a Facebook friend since 2011 – and in a relationship with Jannis Louw.

Geldenhuys, Mauritz Herman Otto (born 26th March 1909). Also died in Potchefstroom, on 23rd March 1993 – three days short of his 84th birthday.

Geldenhuys, Martin Lourens (born 14 September 1985) is the son of Hannes and Magda of Heidelberg – all facebook friends. Martin studied medicine at Pretoria University and is a foreman on his fathers 'Geldenhuys Boerdery' farm in Heidelberg. Martin married Lourens.

Geldenhuys, Martinus Johannes

Geldenhuys, Monica (born Kraaifontein, Cape, 14th August 1986), went to Monument Park High School, lives in Stellenbosch and works in Admin with Cape PC Services.

Geldenhuys, Myrl Maureen (born Amersfoort, Ermelo district, Mpumalanga 11th October 1939), daughter of Willem Geldenhuys born 4th April 1913 and Sarah Johanna Louw 'Sally' Groenewald 1914-1989. Maureen married pharmacist Dr Albertus Martinus Trichardt born 30th December 1940. Dr Trichaardt is a descendant of Carolus Johannes Trichardt, the Voortrekker who found the Victoroia Falls before David Livingstone (he did not name them). Maureen is a MyHeritage and Facebook supported who shared family linkages with the writer. Many gaps were filled in!

Maureen is a descendant of Dirk Cornelius Geldenhuys

Geldenhuys, Meyerene. Meryerene is married to Louw – who are friendly with Charles Brink's father. Charles is married to Chanli Bouwer, daughter of Delene Elizabeth Geldenhuys. Genealogy connection and relationships still need to be established.

Geldenhuys, Michael Francis (born Witbank 25 March 1973). Went to Witbank Technical College and studied Engineering at Witbank Technical College. Michael married Susan and they have a daughter, Finette. Currently employed as a Field Service Technician with Joy Mining Machinery.

Geldenhuys, Michael Pieter (born Hermanus 28 September 1972). Went to Paul Roos Gymnasium. Married Adéle. Michael is a partner of 'Flip Geldenhuys Builders' and lives in Gansbaai, Western Cape. They have two children, Michael Conrad and Karli-Mari. Philip Geldenhuys is listed as a brother.

Geldenhuys, Mike (born 1882? Circa Boer War). Mike is pictured with the Winburg-kommando displaying an array of rifles used during the Anglo-Boer War of 1899-1902. He is shown standing, in the front row, holding his long Mannlicher, 8-mm (model 1888) rifle. It is not known whether he was the brother or cousin to Ou Dad Johannes Albertus Geldenhuys. Whilst his looks would suggest he could be the younger brother, his appearance especially with the beard would suggest an age much older than 18 to 20, if born 1882. Service with the Winburg Commando is also confusing.

Geldenhuys, Monica (born Krugersdorp 28th May 1945), is the youngest of three sisters born to Pieter Theunis Blomerus Geldenhuys and Johanna Helena Geldenhuys (note: her maiden name was also Geldenhuys, being the daughter of Barend Hermanus Geldenhuys born Graaff-Reinett 4th April 1869 and Jacoba Johanna Hendrina Theron). In July 2011, Monica joined MyHeritage website and wrote me as follows, in Afrikaans:

Beste Prop, Baie dankie vir al die moeite. Ja, dit lyk my die Geldenhuyse was 'n vrugbare lot - maar nou het hulle in die vroeër jare mos sommer 11/12 kinders gehad, en dan het die mans met die stamnaam ook nog baie maal 'n tweede en derde maal getrou met ook nog kinders by daardie vrouens. En dit maak die nasporing net soveel moeiliker.

My ma was Johanna Helena Geldenhuys (gebr.19/04/1914 te Potchefstroom – oorlede 25/05/98 te Roodepoort). Sy was die oudste van drie susters en een broer: die ander se name: Elizabeth Johanna (oorlede); Jacoba Hendrina (oorlede); Pieter (oorlede). Hulle ouers was: Barend Hermanus Geldenhuys (gebore 4/04/1869 te Graaff-Reinet - oorlede 1924 in Pelgrimsrus. Hy het deelgeneem aan die Anglo-Boere Oorlog en was Krygsgevangene in Ceylon. Daarna was hy gouddelwer in Pelgrimsrus (waar hy toe oorlede is) en Jacoba Johanna Hendrina Theron. Barend Hermanus was baie ouer as my ouma (JJH Theron) en sy is toe weer getroud met Nicolaas Daniël Geldenhuys. Nicolaas D Geldenhuys en Elizabeth Johanna (nee onbekend) het net een seun gehad en dit was my pa Pieter Theunis Blomerus Geldenhuys (gebore 17/10/1914 - 1975). Ek weet nie of Nicolaas Daniel en Barend Hermanus dalk neefs was en vandaar die huwelik tussen Jacoba Johanna Hendrina en Nicolaas Daniel toe albei hul maat verloor het nie. Nicolaas Daniel het geboer op Muiskraal... en volgens my suster se geheue - was dit in die Krugersdorp Distrik. My ma en pa het in Krugersdorp gewoon en werk en ons al drie dogters is daar gebore. My ouma Jacoba Johanna Hendrina is 'n derde maal getroud met 'n Scheepers (maar dit was reeds in hul senior jare) en het saam met my ouers in die huis in Krugersdorp gewoon. My susters is: Jacoba Johanna Hendrina (4/10/36 -); Elizabeth Johanna (26/11/40 -) .. my pa se ma se name ... en toe kom ek en die familiename is op!!! en word toe maar sommer Monica genoem (28/05/45 -). My ma was ook 'n tweede maal getroud met Christiaan Petrus Kotze - ook reeds oorlede.

Dit wil vir my lyk of bogenoemde. Geldenhuyse weer 'n heeltemal ander vertakking van die stamvader Albert Barends Gildenhuisz/Margaretha Hoefnagels was. Baie gekompliseerd! Maar dit is tog opvallend dat die familiename herhaaldelik voorkom, nê.

Ek en my man, Francois Slabber, het net drie dogters: Joalien (van Johanna Helena), Francis (na haar pa) en Petra (na my stiefpa CP Kotze). Hulle is almal nog in SA - dankie tog- en ons het ses kleinkinders. Ons woon in Knysna in die Suid-Kaap en hulle almal in Kaapstad. Francois is 'n CA en het nog sy eie praktyk en werk nog baie hard - wil ook nie ophou nie, want wat maak ons dan?

Ek hoop nie ek het jou deurmekaar gepraat nie, maar die goed is werklik baie interessant. Ons het 'n Familiebybel gehad met die hele stamboom voor in en my Oom

Pieter het dit ge erf na Ouma Jacoba Johanna Helena se dood. Sy oudste dogter het dit van haar pa geërf - maar heellaas het sy van die aardbol af verdwyn. Sy was nooit een vir familie-aangeleenthede nie en het gladnie in die ander familie se doen en late belanggestel nie. Dat so iemand nou die geskrifte moes kry, nê.

Sterkte verder met die navorsing.
Groete, Monica

She married Francois Slabber, a Chartered Accountant, in Knysna, and has three daughters (mentioned earlier), and six grandchildren.

Nefdt-Geldenhuys, Sorina (born 1st July), went to Hoërskool Langenhoven, and has two sons, Wedré and Jovan, and two daughters, Mariza and Sharika.

Geldenhuys, Mynhart (born Port Elizabeth 14th September 1963), went to Andrew Rabie school and is a Warrant Officer in the South African Police Service. He married Adele on 1st December 2001; they have two daughters, Lianca and Chante; and live in Port Elizabeth. He is also the father of Pieter Geldenhuys. Facebook friend in 2011.

Geldenhuys, Nicolette (born Stanford), one of three daughters of Jurie and Nicoleen Geldenhuys, married Nicholas Loubser. They have one child. Her siblings are Jurita Mycroft and Corné Olivier.

Geldenhuys, Okkie, married Baby Olivier, parents of Joleen Geldenhuys who married Hendrik van Aardt in Ladismith 6th July 1985.

Geldenhuys, Paul Preller (born Ndola, Zambia 15th December 1966 ab6c3d7e8f7g9h1i6j1k3), mechanic and fruit-juice manufacturer / distributor, boat builder and property developer, is the son of Johannes Albertus Geldenhuys (1940) and Julia Lillian Dippenaar.

Paul qualified as an artisan, married Karen de Waal in Johannesburg on 31st December 1988 and had two children – daughter Chanel and son Craig Jannie. Paul joined his father's fresh fruit juice manufacturing business at KwaMakuta/Amanzimtoti.

Paul was the specialist mechanic for Lance Froneman's "Waikiki'" moored at the Durban yacht mole – and was devastated when the charter vessel sank 5 kilometres outside the harbour mouth in late May 1999. He had maintained the two powerful diesel engines in first class condition and had also spent many man-hours on modifications and improvements. The boat sank within some seven minutes when the taking on of seawater was first noted – and settled some 65 to 70 metres below sea level. Many a happy hour was spent on deep sea fishing trips.

However, Lance Froneman subsequently purchased a replacement ocean going catamaran and selected Paul to sail the new acquisition Hakuna Matata from Langebaan on the Cape west coast to Durban. This was indeed an opportunity of a lifetime that Paul was only too pleased to exchange for his experience as a marine engineer. Paul then bought his own yacht, Goblet, and sailed it from Richards Bay to Durban.

When his father Jan acquired an interest in Wave Dancer, Paul became the only competent skipper on the converted Wave Master Dancer. However, the family relationship with Lance Froneman soured, and Paul then directed his energies in constructing quaint wooden chalets at Bush Babies Lodge. When this was completed, the potential to further develop the Bengu property materialised, and Paul then applied his multi-skills fully in the building / construction industries. However, it did not take long for his younger cousin Pey to seek his expertise in expediting the completion of the Durban North home that Pey and Eloise had bought.

Geldenhuys, Peter (born?), fund raiser, man with a mission.

This caring man is walking from Johannesburg to Cape Town to raise funds for a sick child. He was pounding the road somewhere between Colenso and Estcourt, in his solitary "walk for life". He was easily recognisable, as he continued on his way, with his 35kg backpack, crutches and fluttering South African flag. This dedicated man is busy walking between Johannesburg and Cape Town to raise funds for an eight year old Benoni girl, Lauren Banfield, who is suffering from Franconis Anaema, a form of leukaemia.

While Lauren undergoes intensive chemotherapy and radiation treatment, Peter walks between towns en route to Cape Town to help pay for her treatment. "The Banfield family faces a staggering R400 000 medical bill, of which they have raised R250 000, leaving a shortfall of R150 000," said Peter. Lauren's medical expenses include sourcing and obtaining bone marrow from Germany, paying the medical expenses of the donor, accessing the computer system for matching, and tests for donor compatibility, her bone marrow transplant, the extended stay in the ICU, 10 weeks instead of six due to complications, and private doctor's fees.

Peter carried a cell phone with him to facilitate anyone interested in donating money to assist the Banfield family. "There is nothing more enjoyable than having someone phone you when you are in the middle of nowhere, it helps raise your spirits." added Peter. The newspaper promotion showed Peter Geldenhuys with the flag mounted on his backpack, a spare crutch sticking out, floppy hat, and gloved hands clutching the crutches. This super-human endeavour, from a caring South African, warrants mention in this record of the Geldenhuys'.

Estcourt and Midlands News - Friday September 24, 1999.

Geldenhuys, Pey Malan (born Gwelo, Rhodesia 22nd December 1970 ab6c3d7e4f3g5h1i6j2k2), computer programmer and analyst, businessman and director of companies, is the son of Wg. Cdr. Preller Matt Geldenhuys AFZ (Rtd) (1943) and Susanna Catharina Malan.

Pey was schooled at Prospect, Kariba, Chiredzi, Cecil John Rhodes and Alexandra Boys' High in Pietermaritzburg. He qualified in computer data processing at Technikon Natal Durban. After completing his national service at No 5 South African Infantry Battalion Ladysmith, he, together with an army mate, established Annotech Software Consultants, based Durban.

He married Marion Muller in Welkom on 2nd April 1994. However, after an unfortunate miscarriage, they divorced. In spite of his asthmatic ailment, Pey excelled at sports, representing Natal at wave skiing. He competed in the Cape as well in Natal at National Championships level. He is also a sports organiser of note, coaching women hockey and including providing computerised time keeping for several events. Pey played a fair game of social squash as well as club rugby. He travelled to Boston for snow skiing. Pey also invested in a water ski boat and regularly caravanned at Wagendrift Dam to pursue his interests in water sports.

Pey teamed up with Marcelle Gilson and this partnership lasted seven years, till 2005. Webdynamix and the Peysoft software programmes were successfully developed. A lovely home was established at Umdloti, but Marcelle opted to terminate the partnership in April 2005, after having toured Brazil, Egypt, Israel, Malaya and New Zealand together. Pey also travelled to Spain, representing South Africa at Wave Skiing.

Then mid 2005 he met a wonderful woman, Eloise Howard, and they teamed up in November 2005. It did not take long for Pey to acknowledge his perfect match and they duly married on 27th April 2007. 116 Edgeley Road, Durban North was acquired – a place young Matthew Dylan could call home for a short while – before emigrating to New Zealand. Because Eloise had not travelled abroad, Pey kept his honeymoon plans secret till his wedding day.

Pey and Eloise flew up to the Victoria Falls, then on to Thailand. However, with morning sickness setting in, the honeymoon was a bit of an ordeal. Baby Jake was born on 18th December 2007, but died 12 days later on 30th December. Lucy Hope was born in Durban 29th March 2009 – with the family immigrating to Auckland, New Zealand.

DICTIONARY OF FAMILY BIOGRAPHY

The table below is intended as a quick navigational aid to trace his ancestry back over eleven Geldenhuys generations, and ten Malan generations. It would be nice if Pey and Eloise adds another generation to the list - - but if not, then that would also be fine.

GELDENHUYS		MALAN	
Albert Barends	c1640-1693	Jacques	1665-1742
Barend	1682-	David	1708-1792
Hendrik	1717-1770	Jacobus Johanus	1739-1806
Johannes Albertus	1750-	David	1765-1851
Lourens	1777-	Daniel Stephanus	1801-
Johannes Albertus	1807-1894	Hendrik Francois	1833-
Hendrik Jacobus	1849-1924	Hendrik Francois	1878-1959
Johannes Albertus	1877-1944	Francois Daniel	1907-1988
Abram Carl Frederik Preller	1916-1972	Susanna Catharina	1945
Preller Matt	1943-	Pey Malan	1970-
Pey Malan	1970-		

Geldenhuys, Philip (born 14th March 1980), related to Michael Pieter and Adéle Geldenhuys. Went to Kroonstad High School and works for Flip Geldenhuys Bouers in Gansbaai, Western Cape.

Geldenhuys, Pieter (born 18??), younger brother of the writers grandfather – Johannes Albertus, and second son of Hendrik Jacobus and Elizabeth Schikkerling (more affectionately known as "Oubaas and Bessie Geldenhuys". Ou Dad and Pieter deployed to the 'western front' at the outbreak of the Anglo-Boer War. He fought at the Battles of Belmont, Graspan and Magersfontein. He was captured, possibly at Paardekraal when Cronje surrendered, and sent to Umballa prisoner-of-war camp in India. His picture above appears in Dot Serfontein's book *Keurskrif vir Kroonstad*.

DICTIONARY OF FAMILY BIOGRAPHY

Geldenhuys, Pieter (born 8th February 1991), son of Mynhardt Geldenhuys and Sanette Worthington. His step-mother is Adele Geldenhuys of Port Elizabeth; went to Hoërskool Framesby – class of 2009; and Flight Academy - Class of 2012. The writer suspects that Adele is a step-mother, since his father, Mynhardt, married Adele on the 1st December 2001 – (and Pieter is certainly much older than the ten years since the marriage!)

Geldenhuys, P A. Born 2 January 1978. Studied at Calvinia. Lives in Oudshoorn, Western Cape. Married to Petra. Facebook friend since 2011.

Geldenhuys, Pieter David. Went to HTS Drostdy. Lives in Wolseley, Western Cape, South Africa. In a relationship with Elmé de Wet. Facebook friend since 2011.

Geldenhuys, Pieter Gabriël Jacobus born Riversdal 23rd December 1869, married Magdelena Johanna van Tonder, who owned a shop at Brandrivier in 1900, had three sons and three daughters. He is the grandfather to Pieter Geldenhuys (who contacted the author in March 2010). Pieter Gabriel farmed on Muiskraal in the Brandrivier or Riversdal district. Pieter had a younger brother, Adriaan, that left home to join a Free State commando during the Anglo-Boer War. After the war he acquired land in the Kroonstad area which he farmed.

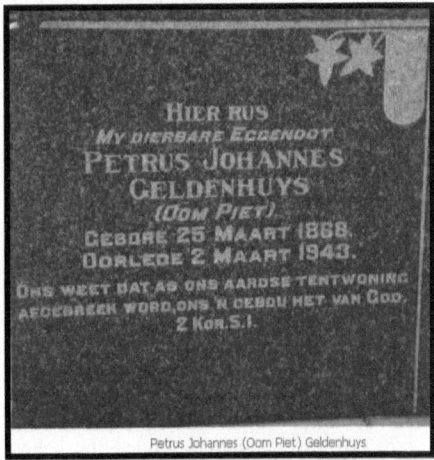

Petrus Johannes (Oom Piet) Geldenhuys

Geldenhuys, Petrus Johannes (born 25th March 1868 and died 2nd March 1943), known as "Oom Piet". Grave stone supplied by 4th-cousin Marita Brodie, nee Geldenhuys, from Fiji. Writer has often wondered whether Oom Piet was perhaps my grandfathers brother? Oudad was born in 1877, versus Oom Piet in 1868. Perhaps older cousin rather than younger brother?

Geldenhuys, Pieter Jacobus born in Cape Town in 1931 to Jozua Geldenhuys

Geldenhuys, Preller Matt (born Rustpan, Bothaville, OFS 20th February 1943), pilot, personnel and safety practitioner and Loss Control Manager with Masonite board manufacturer, is the son of Abram Carl Frederik Preller Geldenhuys (1916 – 1972) and his wife Matthia Martha Lotter.

Preller met Rina Malan when she enrolled at Thornhill High School in Gwelo. She had already befriended Delene at Fort Victoria's Andrew Louw farm school – Delene went to Chaplin and Rina joined her brothers Hendrik and Philip at Thornhill. Much hanky-panky occurred during the annual Gilbert and Sullivan productions at school. The first was 'Pirates of Penzance' which William S. Gilbert and Arthur Sullivan composed in 1880. In 1885 they also composed 'The Mikado' and when the school laid on the production, opportunities to 'cement' a long-term relationship developed! Also, during the Nyasaland (now Malawi) Emergency, the Cranwell Boys Hostel lads were expected to carry out "roving" patrols around the school grounds, armed with cricket and baseball bats. But instead spent their time, with rather feeble excuses, guarding all those lovely ladies in Holton Girls Hostel – more often than not balancing precariously on window sills groping their lady friends!

Preller Matt attested into the Royal Rhodesian Air Force in March 1962 and qualified for his Wings on 29th June 1963. Flying service was carried out on No 1 Squadron (Hunter aircraft), No 2 Squadron (Provost and Vampire), No 4 Squadron (Provost, Lynx and Trojan) and No 5 Squadron (Canberra aircraft). Successive appointments held included 'B' Flight Commander No 1 Squadron, 'A' Flight Commander No 5 Squadron, Strike 1, Officer Commanding Forward Airfield 2 - Kariba, Senior Air Representative Fire Force Charlie, Officer Commanding Forward Airfield 7 - Buffalo Range, Officer Commanding Administrative Wing Air Force Station Thornhill, Staff Officer Volunteer Reserve/Reserves 1, Officer Commanding (HQ) Unit/Personnel 1 and Staff Officer Personnel.

Special service qualifications included Instrument Rating Examiner, Day Fighter/Ground Attack/ Internal Security Pilot Attack Instructor, F95 PhotoReconnaissance Pilot, Graduate Senior Joint Warfare and Joint Service Coin Course. Preller Matt retired from the Air Force of Zimbabwe with the rank of Wing Commander on 15th June 1982.

Board manufacturer Masonite (Africa) Limited was joined as a Personnel Superintendent at their Estcourt Mill. After a seven-year spell in Pietermaritzburg for the Forestry Division, Preller Matt was promoted to Loss Control Manager at Estcourt. Masonite occludes include Employee Excellence awards in 1994 and 1998 and twice National Occupational Safety Association Safety Practitioner of the Year awards in 1996 and 1998.

Like my predecessor and namesake, Gustav S. Preller, I became fascinated late in life with early Geldenhuys/South African history – with emphasis on the Anglo-Boer War and genealogy. Although an early start had been made on *Nickel Cross* (1980's), it was only late 1999 that this novel was prompted with the first unpublished edition being dedicated to our pride and joy – Courtney Jelley. Research conducted at the Don Afrikaner Library in Durban snowballed to visits to the Estcourt and Pietermaritzburg Central libraries in order to peruse and extract from countless sources any material considered remotely relevant. The form and shape evolved as time went on! Fascination with research findings, and the urgency to collate the information in one document before it is 'too late', placed a severe burden on a very patient and forgiving loving wife. I trust our good Lord will provide Rina (stroke victim) with the mental capacity to appreciate the contents of these literary attempts. Pey's expertise and provision of Microsoft Word certainly facilitated easy editing – albeit one finger typing speed did not quite churn out what needed to be said quickly enough.

Like a Roman tragedy the onset of irreversible and incurable Alzheimer's disease has affected the quality of this documentary.

The degenerative memory and intellectual functioning has added an urgency to get to print before it is too late. It came as a no shock to recognise the tell tale symptoms like loss of short term memory, speech repetitions, misplacing objects and even forgetting names of family and friends. I found myself having a dictionary at hand just trying to name familiar objects and spelling simple words. As previously mentioned, I make no apology for obvious plagiarism. However, I trust that futures generations would find this record useful to assist in tracing their backgrounds.

The Paradox of our age - -
We have taller buildings, but short tempers
Wider freeways, but narrower viewpoints
We spend more, but have less;
We buy more, but we enjoy it less.
We have bigger houses but smaller families,
More conveniences but less time
We have more degrees, but less common sence,
More knowledge, but less judgement.
We have more experts, and more problems,
More medicines, but less wellness.
We build more computers to hold more information,
To produce more copies, but we have less communication.
We have multiplied our possessions, but reduce our values.
We talk too much, love too seldom and lie too often.
We have learned how to make a living, but not a life.
We have added years to life, not life to years.
We have been all the way to the moon and back, but have trouble crossing the street to meet the new neighbour.
We have conqcurred outer space, but not inner space.
We have done large things but not better things.
We have cleaned up the air, but polluted the same.
We have split the atom, but not our prejudice.
We have learned to rush, but not to wait,
We have more acquaintances, but fever friends,
We spend too recklessly, laugh too little, drive too fast, get angry too quickly, stay up too late, get up too tired, read too seldom, watch television too often and PRAY TOO SELDOM
The chorus of a song that brings a tear to the eye goes like this:-

Come live in me
All my life, take over
Come breath in me
And I will rise on eagle's wings

Words cannot express the joy and happiness that grandchildren bring to old folks like Oudad and Oumie – we thank God for his riches and blessings.

The message that I would like to pass on is this: - "The greatest thing that a father can do for his children is to love their mother.'

May God's light always shine on you Courtney, Brendan, Chanel, Craig, Matthew and Baby Lucy - to light up your paths and to lead you into righteousness. May the Lord's hand be upon you always and that you will continue to be a blessing to your mother and father for the length of your days

The final word must go to my darling Rina who has borne the brunt of her stroke afflictions for many years (about 15 – as at 2006), as well as providing me with the necessities of life. I trust God will spare her the burdens of coping with any additional hardships in the event of me predeceasing her.

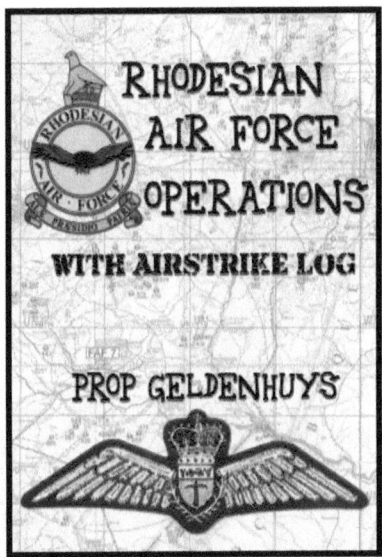

Geldenhuys, Quintin, born Klerksdorp, South Africa, , played for Italy in the World Rugby Cup in New Zealand.

Geldenhuys, Regardt (born 15th April 1977), has a relative or brother Bernard Geldenhuys. Married to Marile Badenhorst.

Geldenhuys, R owned part of Paardekraal, with the co-owner being S.J. Kaltwasser.

Geldenhuys, Renene Delene (born Gwelo, Rhodesia 8th August 1988). Nurse, mother of Courtney and Brendan, is the daughter of Preller Matt Geldenhuys and Susanna Catha'Rina' Malan.

Renene was schooled at Prospect; Kariba, Chiredzi, Gwelo Convent, Estcourt Senior, Pietermaritzburg Russell High and qualified as a nurse at Greys Hospital. She furthered her nursing experience in Britain and returned to South Africa to marry Dr. Grahame David Jelley.

Two days before her wedding, she was brutally assaulted near the Draycott turn-off. A frustrated school leaver slashed her car tyres, smashed the car windows and stabbed her four times – twice in her back and then twice in the chest. A passing motorist came to her assistance and rushed her off to the Estcourt hospital – to be discharged on the morning of her wedding!

Their wedding, at the Kevin Curren Champagne Sports resort in the Drakensberg was something really special – and whenever one hears the '*Amazing Grace*', we think of it being specially composed for Renene and Grahame – so much so that it is appropriate to repeat the words: -

AMAZING GRACE

Amazing grace, how sweet
The sound
That saved a wretch like me
I once was lost, but now I'm found
Was blind, but now I see.

'Twas grace that taught my
Heart to fear
And grace my fears relieved
How precious did that grace
Appear
The hour I first believed

Through many dangers, toils
And shares
I have already come, "'twas
Grace
That brought me safe thus
Far
And grace will lead me home

When we've been there ten
Thousand years
Bright shinning as the sun
We've no less days to sing
Gods praise
Than when we've first begun

Renene and Grahame made their home in Chiredzi where Grahame was the medical officer for Hippo Valley Sugar Estates. After a short while they set up their Clinic practice at Chipinge. Renene returned to the Lowveld town of Triangle for the birth of Courtney Sacha in September 1993, but had their second baby, Brendan Vaughan in Chipinge. They developed the Chipinge Clinic, made many friends, and built their own first home on a beautiful wooded plot overlooking a valley towards Mount Selinda. Grahame carried out a locum assignment in New Zealand in the late 1990's, and liked the country so much that the family decided to emigrate and settled in Westport, South Island.

In December 2002 Renene organised a once in a lifetime family re-union at Gentle Annie – at which our (and my sister Delene's) entire immediate family were present. Rina and I had both our children – Pey and Renene. Delene had both her children – Chanli and Rensha. Stu McColl had his son, and his mother – Dave and Joyce. Then there were also two close friends – Marcelle who partnered Pey, and Goffrey who partnered Joyce. Those that flew in from South Africa were I, Rina, Pey, Marcelle, Rensha and Dave. It was indeed a memorable re-union.

Our visit to New Zealand was made that much more special in that we were able to visit all the major cities and provinces – which obviously included the capital city Wellington as well as Auckland, North Island and Christchurch, South Island. It would be difficult to single out any one particular place – but we do have fond memories of Wanaka, Queenstown, Christchurch, Timaru, Dunedin, Invercargill, Te Anau, Franz Joseph glacier, Hokitika, Greymouth, Karamea, Pakawau, Motueka. Nelson, Blenheim and Kaikura. Places visited in North Island included Wanganui, Mount Egmont, Waitomo Caves, Whangarei, Russell, Rotorua and Taupo. We were fascinated by the larger than life corrugated iron sculptures at a quaint little place called Tirau. This was certainly a once-in-a-lifetime holiday on the other side of the globe.

Much credit also needs to be given Renene for the home schooling she did for young Courtney and Brendan. When they arrived in New Zealand, it was with a temporary work permit for husband Grahame to work as a locum. It befell Renene to acclimatise the children as Kiwis – culturally, socially and to fit into the educational system. Great job, Renene!

The Jelley's were well liked and respected by their adopted community. It was a tough decision to relocate to North Island at the end of 2003. They decided on Ohope in the Bay of Plenty and bought a lovely home big enough to accommodate Grahame's parents (who duly left Vancouver, Canada, during November 2005). Within a year husband Grahame bought the medical practice, Total Health, from his employer and renamed it Family Healthcare Ohope. Renene was instrumental in getting the practice to operate on a sound financial footing. Whilst not completely flush, they generously sponsored the writer and Oumie to an extended second New Zealand visit.

When Renene's brother Pey decided to marry lovely Eloise Howard, the Jelley's pulled out all stops to attend the wedding. Regretfully, Grahame could not make it – but made great personal sacrifice so that their children at least would meet with new cousin Matthew Dylan. Being the great organiser that Renene is, meant that many could heave a sigh of relief because Renene would sort out any problems in a jiffy. This particular trip thus prompted the writer to get this edition of the family history to all the nearest relatives.

Renene took up 'tramping' and joined the Nga-Tapuwae O-Taneatua Tramping Club in Wkakatane in 2008. Her article in the Footprint magazine reads as follows: "I took the plunge after seeing an article in the Beacon and joined the Tramping Club in April. My first day coinciding with the Sir Edmund Hilary commemorative walk on the 10 April where I was warmly welcomed into the group by Warner Haldane and Rhonda Boyle. They kindly looked out for me amongst all the others taking part in the ceremony and I enjoyed a beautiful clear day with the group.

"We also walked on further along the Toi walkway and into areas of White Horse Drive along the Waieww Stream. The beautiful days continued as I returned every Thursday and explored areas I would not normally have had the opportunity to enjoy – such as in the Totomas and Nukuhou Valley. As a family we have now joined the club as members and hopefully Grahame, my husband and my daughter Courtney (15) and my son Brendan (12) will one day join me on one of the tramps.

"The Thursday group is now familiar with me – camera in hand as I take pictures to send back to family in Africa. In many ways, I tramp for my mother who suffered a debilitating stroke at the age of 49, robbing her of her mobility and speech. I joke that I am her legs and the pictures are for her as she tramps with me in spirit. She has a digital photo frame which we update with all our experiences on the other side of the world.

"We initially came from Zimbabwe and moved to New Zealand in 2000. We lived in a tea and coffee farming area in the Eastern Highlands, bordering Mozambique and left our beloved country because of the political unrest and illegal farm occupations at the time. We settled in the South Island on the west coast for 4½ years and enjoyed the many walk-ways there, especially part of the Heaphy on the Karamea side and along the gold/coal mining towns of Charleston and Seddonville. We were sad to leave the good friends of the coast but pleased to make the Bay of Plenty our new home and continue to enjoy the warmer climate here.

"We look forward to continuing our association with the club and meeting more of the members. Thank you for making us feel so welcome".

Renene then took up a School Nurse position with Trident High School in Whakatane in 2008. For the November Staff Bulletin she wrote: My parents are my most inspirational persons – my mother for not letting a stroke and cancer at forty-nine limit her, and my father for writing five books after retirement and still undertaking more research. Three proud memories are the birth of my two children (now Jelley Teens), my experiences in Zimbabwe and New Zealand citizenship as a family.

Her advice for teachers: Everything that happens to you is your teacher. Best advice received: Words are seeds, we scatter as we go - from them sweet flowers or harmful weeds will grow. Something recommended: A walk along the beach / reflexology. What keeps you motivated: The downward spiral of boredom. Favourite book / movie: 'Out of Africa' / 'Prince of Tides'.

"The Upward Spiral" is worth repeating: Renewal is the principle and process that empowers us to move on an upward spiral of growth and change, of continuous improvement. Education of the conscience is vital to the truly proactive, highly effective leader. Conscience is the empowerment that sences our congruence or disparity with correct principles and lifts us towards them. Training and educating the conscience requires regular feasting on inspiring literature, thinking noble thoughts, and living in harmony with its small voice. Dag Hammarskjold, past Secretary-General of the United Nations, said, "He who wants to keep his garden tidy doesn't reserve a plot for weeds". The law of the harvest governs, we will always reap what we sow - - no more, no less. Moving along the upward spiral requires us to learn, commit and do on increasingly higher planes.

Geldenhuys, Renier (born Strand 9th November 1983), son of Chris Geldenhuys, with sibling sister Andrea. Cousin to Andries Geldenhuys. Went to Hoërskool President, class of 2001. Studied IT Management at Computer Career Training College.

Geldenhuys, Resje (born Durban, KwaZulu-Natal), went to Chisipiti Senior

School and Middleton Grange School, class or 2006, and studied English at the University of Otago. Lives in Coffd Harbour, New South Wales. Resje is with Tersia Geldenhuys, in the picture above.

Geldenhuys, Riaan (born 8th July 1965), son of Danie Geldenuys and Rita Conradie, sibling to Sonja and Ryno. Riaan is married to Elnarette and they have two children, Daniel named after his grandfather and Riandi – named after her father. They live in Someret-West.

Geldenhuys, Rian. Graphics artist and On-Line editor of the Boer War television Centenary documentary *"Empire and Eclipse"* screened on SABC TV during October 1999.

Geldenhuys, Rina (born 25th June 1986). Lives in Windhoek. Facebook friend in 2011. She is very keen to trace her Namibian ancestors and has an elder brother, Hendrik.

Geldenhuys, Ronald Olwen (died 18th April 1979), soldier in Number 1 Commando of the Rhodesian Light Infantry, with the rank of Trooper in Four Troop, killed in action with terrorists on 18th April 1979. Ronald features in the Rhodesian Roll of Honour, and is believed to be a distant relative of the author, who also served during the Rhodesian War. It is very likely that he was killed in the same action / contact in which 726942 Corporal van Niekerk, N.J., was also killed. Service Number 122175, tribute paid as the "Unknown Soldier" in the Preller M. Geldenhuys novel titled *Nickel Cross*.

Geldenhuys, Ruben (born Randfontein 5th January 1974), went to Wessel Maree and in a relationship with Hennie van Deventer (born Centurion 16th November 1974). He is a sales executive at iBurst. Friends with Eugene Geldenhuys who is married to Jan du Plessis.

Geldenhuys, Russell (born 29th March 1960), younger brother to Maureen, married "Corli" Jacoba Cornelia Opperman and they have two sons, Willem born 8 January 1986 Vrendaal and Allan, born 27TH January 1989

Geldenhuys, Ryno (born Somerset-West, 20th April 1970), son of Danie Geldenhuys born November 1938 and Rita Conradie. Siblings are Sonja and Riaan. Ryno went to Strand High School, married Heidi Brooks and they have two sons, Luka and Zach. Ryno is a broker / makelaar with Charis Brokers / Makelaars. Facebook friend in 2011.

DICTIONARY OF FAMILY BIOGRAPHY

Geldenhuys, Schikkie (born 19th May), went to Gekombineerse Skool Christina, and Kovsies. Lives in Sasolburg and is Head of Department at HTS Sasolburg. Sibling to Marile and Stephan

Geldenhuys, Shawn (born 26th February 1968). Married Chantelle Myburgh on 9th February 2002
Facebook friend, e-mail address - geldenhuys.shawn@gmail.com

Geldenhuys, Sebastiaan 'Basie' (born 7th September 1971), fourth son of Izak George 'Sakkie' of Sonneskyn, married Veronica Engelbrecht on 11 February and is the Managing Director of Proffessional Design Services in Nelspruit, Mpumalanga.

Geldenhuys, Simeon (born), son of Alta and Adri Geldenhuys.

Geldenhuys, Sonja (born Durbanville 19th June), daughter of Danie Geldenhuys and Rita Conradie. Schooled at Hoërskool

Stellenbosch, married to Hennie Delport. They have two children, Danita "Dee-Dee" born 1st November 1990 and Leandra, married to Pieter Hugo le Roux.

farm manager with Arborlaine Boerdery, Tweefontein. Steve is a facebook friend in 2011, and an avid Empires and Allies player on the internet.

Geldenhuys, Stephan (born Christiana, 5th August 1986), Studied at the University of the Free State, lives in Frankfort and has siblings Marile and Schikkie.

Geldenhuys, Stuart William (born Bulawayo, Rhodesia 18th September 1957), sugar farmer, eldest adopted son of Johannes Albertus Geldenhuys (1940) and Julia Lillian Dippenaar, married Joy Goldsworthy in Manzini, Swaziland on the 10.7.1980. They have two children – Ian Jannie and Louise both born in Johannesburg in 1986 and 1988.

Stuart never knew his biological father (an Italian named Peter Borruso, who died of cancer in Australia circa 1994), was raised by his adopted father on the Zambian Copperbelt and later in Swaziland. On leaving school he started his career farming in Swaziland where he managed a large estate. He encouraged and fully supported his sons' natural balls skills and set an outstanding example by representing Swaziland Districts at cricket and also being a keen rugby supporter.

Stuart continues to be employed in the Citrus industry in Swaziland.

Geldenhuys, Steve (born 11th March 1981), married Aniska and they have a two-year old daughter Lize. Steve went to Agricultural High School Oakdale and is a

DICTIONARY OF FAMILY BIOGRAPHY

Geldenhuys, Suzanne (born Pretoria), eldest daughter of Izak George Geldenhuys and Hannelie Booysen. Lives in Cape Town. Distant relative traced on Facebook. Her father then married Wilna Bester and half-siblings are thus Cabous and Lena Geldenhuys. Her younger sisters, by the same mother, are Marianne and Liezel.

Geldenhuys, Tersia – see also Resje, probably, and most likely, sisters.

Geldenhuys, Ulrich (born 27th October 1964), went to Helderberg High School, married Rita Bothma on her birthday – 2nd May – and lives in Middelburg, Mpumalanga. They have a son named Heinrich. Ulrich's brothers are Stephen Lee and Johan, and two sisters Delmarie Knierim and Ronel Kruger.

Geldenhuys, Teresa sister to Amanda Geldenhuys. Facebook friend.

Geldenhuys, Vanessa wife of André Geldenhuys, they have a daughter Charné and live in Rusternburg, North West province, South Africa.

Geldenhuys, Wedré (born Riversdale, Free State, 11 January), is the son of Sorina Nefdt Geldenhuys, studied Psychology at Stellenbosh and is in a relationship with Susan Vosloo. Brother to Mariza (and Jovan and Sharika).

Geldenhuys, Victor, went to Hoërskool Ermelo, class of 1970 and studied at UNISA.

Geldenhuys, Wb (born 26th October 1987), in a relationship with Angelique Pretorius.

DICTIONARY OF FAMILY BIOGRAPHY

Bam in Cape Town on 27th July 1793. Her ancestor was a German soldier from Schwerin who arrived in 1725 – and who had four children from a Ragel van die Kaap. My interpretation of "van die Kaap" relates to the imported slave women during Jan van Riebeek's time to entertain visiting soldiers. In those days, inter mixing of the races was not uncommon, providing the consenting partners were not heathen.

Geldenhuys, Zane (born 29th June 1988), son of Adri and Alta Geldenhuys, engaged to Estie Ferreira. Facebook friend in 2011, and co-game player - Empires and Allies as well as FarmVille. Profile photo of Zane with his fiance

Gildenhuis, Elizbe (born Pretoria, South Africa). Friends or relative of John, Tiaan and Irma.

Gerber, Rina (born Pietersburg 5th March 1942, died 25th May 2009), married Hendrik Francois Malan and bore him three sons, Philip born Pretoria 14th April 1973, Francois Daniel born 12th September 1976 and Eddie Deon born 24th March 1978.

Gildenhaus, Casper Heinrich, (born 1748), blacksmith and wagon driver (wadrywer), arrived about 1770 from Osnabruck. He was not related to the Geldenhuys stamvader Albert Barend Gildenhuisz. He married a Johanna Dorothea

Gildenhuys, Eric and Tanya (born 8th March 1983), loves surfing, married to Tanya

Gildenhuys from Port Elizabeth who went to Hoërskool Framesbury.

Gildenhuis, John (born Witbank 30th March 1969)

Gildenhuis, Irma (born Centurion, Gauteng 26th September 1965), went to Hoërskool Hendrina – class of 1983. Works as Accounts payable clerk at Afgri Bedryf.

Gildenhuisz, Barend (born Cape Town 6th September 1682) – see Geldenhuys - Barend, son of Albert Barends Gildenhuysz and Margaretha Hoefnagels, second generation descendant of the 'Stamvader".

Gildenhuys, Albertus Barend (born 30th September 1985), from Ohrigstad, studied at Coastal College and married Cheyenne van Niekerk. Albertus Barend appears to be named after the 'stamvader'! He works at Rosond Explorations in Ohrigstad.

Gildenhuis, Louise (born in Witbank 17th July 1977), went to Hendrina, married, and works at Lynette Gous and Associates. Relatives are Elizbe and Tiaan Gildenhuis. Facebook friend and Farmville neighbour in 2011.

Gildenhuys, Albie born 1st April 1973 in Hennenman in the Freestate, is a Facebook friend (2014) who still lives in Hennenman, as the Piling Consultant, owner and CEO of Gidenhuys GEO & Civils (Pty) Ltd. He has a daughter, Elisma and a son Albie Junior.

Gildenhuys, Bart, born 5th March 1988. Very private person.

Gildenhuys, Bernard (born Rustenburg 30th September 1985), studied at Coastal College, married Cheyenne van Niekerk, and lives in Rustenburg. Works for Rosond Exploration. Facebook friend in 2011.

Gildenhuys, Chris (born 19th April 1949), went to Paarl Boys High School and Stellenbosch. Lives in Velddrift, Western Cape and works at Marine Special Products. Married Celia Gildenhuys from Durban, Natal, on 16th August 1975. They have two sons, Christiaan and David.

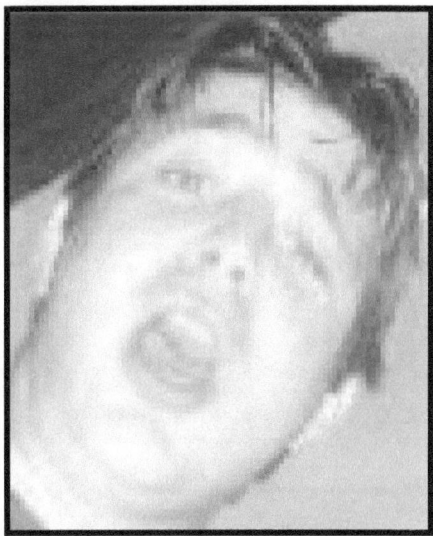

Gildenhuys, Christiaan (born), went to Tygerberg Hoërskool.

Gildenhuys, Clive Peter (born Hermanus, Western Cape 31st October 1987), in a relationship with Carlé Kuhn.

Gildenhuys, David (born 9th June 1977), lives in Cape Town

Gildenhuys, Elizma, born 5th February 1995 in Hennenman, model daughter of Albie Gildenhuys.

Gildenhuys, Johannes 'Jannie' (born Heidelberg, Western Cape 11th July 1929), well known South African actor

Gildenhuysen, Margaretha (christened Cape Town 6th October 1684), stam-moeder, seventh child of Albert Barends Gildenhuisz and Margaretha Hoefnagels who became "vryburgers" in 1661. Margaretha was the younger sister to the Geldenhuys ancestor Barend born in 1682. She married German Heinrich du Plooy on the 5.7.1704. He had arrived at the Cape in 1701, from Soest, Westfale. They had six children, including Hendrik Willem born 13th October 1707, and Albert Barend born 14th August 1712 – thereby becoming the "stam-moeder" of the du Plooy's! Margaretha married Philippus Richter on 10th June 1725. It is not known whether she became a 'stam-moeder' for a second time.

Gildenhuyzen, Elsje (christened Cape Town 11th May 1674), stam-moeder, first South African born child of Albert Barends Gildenhuisz of Bergstein in Westfale who arrived at the Cape in 1661, and Margaretha Hoefnagels of Leyden.

Elsje married Jacobus van der Heiden from Haarlem, Netherlands, in 1691. They had seven children – and became the stam-moeder of the van der Heiden's with the birth of their first son Jacobus. Jacobus married Aletta Nobel on 28th September 1717 and also had seven children.

Their second son, Andries, married Maria Odendaal on 11th January 1728, had 5 children and produced 11 grandchildren.

It is noteworthy to record that van der Heiden became a co-owner of the van der Stel farm Vergelegen. Jacobus, brother-in-law to Barend Gildenhausen, bought quarter shares – together with Malan and Cloete. Jacobus van der Heiden, according to Cor Pama (Die Groot Afrikaanse Familie Naamboek – 1983), also married Abigael Vroom on 24th February 1703 – daughter of Jacob Vroom and Margaretha Weimans, from Amsterdam – and they had four children. Jacobus's marriage to Elsje lasted from 1691 to some time before 1703 (the reason for the separation is unknown).

Gildenhuyzs, Matthys Johannes (born Swellendam 22nd April 1822), the son of Johanna Susanna Elizabeth Gildenhuizen (christened Stellenbosch 28th September 1785), is one, if not more, from uncertain parentage as well as ancestor. His father is unknown, and his mothers' father, also unknown, was given as "Juli v.d. K." – in those days taken to mean "male, from the Cape...".It is known that his grandmother, Geertruy Anna was christened on 28th September 1785, no record of "husband" found, but was the mother of Johanna Susanna! Three important facts emerge; (1) in those days mixed marriages, both legal and illegal, was not uncommon: (2) In 1656 the first slave was freed in order to marry a Dutchman; and (3) Dr. D.F. Du T. Malherbe observed in his *Stamregister van die Suid-Afrikaanse Volk,* and I quote 'In enkele gevalle is mense erg onthuts en teleurgesteld as hulle uitvind dat hul stammoeder van eeue gelede nie heeltemaal blank was nie. Ander is weer bang om te vêr in hul familiegeskiedenis terug te gaan uit vrees vir onthullings, Daar was destyds nie die sterke kleurbewustheid en afkeer teen bloedvermenging soos vandag nie en die Hollandse kerk het geen beswaar gehad om so 'n paar te trou nie. Dit was die heersende opvatting orals in die tyd, soos dit trouens vandag nog in ons oorsese stamlande bestaan, waar verbastering tussen wit en bruin en swart orals plaasvind.' – Unquote.

The above translates that some people are sceptical to research their origins because of earlier white, brown and black sexual partners, albeit accepted practise overseas. The Dutch church did not have a problem marrying people of colour so long as they had been 'baptised', plus being 'converted' Christians and were of "goeie gedrag" – or 'good behaviour'. Authors note: it is ironical that apartheid Prime Minister H.F. Verwoed wrote the foreword to the book! However, it would appear during the research conducted, that mixed marriages was thus not abnormal, both legal and illegal, in those earlier days. It should also be remembered that in the early slave trade days, the Dutch East India Company of Jan van Riebeek actually provided special slave quarters in order to 'service' all the visiting sailors to the Cape – hence the coloured population as we know it today.

Another snippet of gossip which research revealed concerns a certain Christina Francina who was born on the *Kaapse Duine* – or Cape dunes – on 7th March 1832; her father is recorded as a Hendrik A Gildenhuizen, 'married' unknown. The father is currently "unclassified"!

Research reveals some very interesting facts! Especially intermarriages - Geldenhuys with Geldenhuys' (at least six intermarriages, including twice in our own direct genealogical blood line), le Roux and Uys; Bouwer with le Roux; de Waal with Malan; Dippenaar with Dippenaars; le Roux with Lotter and Uys; Malan with Malans, Bouwer, le Roux and Preller; and Uys with Geldenhuys and le Roux! And that is not considering our immediate past.

Gill, Elsa

From Klerksdorp, wrote to the author with her fascinating Geldenhuys connection through her mother, Madelene, daughter of Frederik Gerhardus Geldenhuys and Getrude Augusta Maria Herder. She said:-

"Ek is Elsa Gill van Klerksdorp. Ek verstaan dat u 'n CD van die Geldenhuys genealogie beskikbaar het. My ma, Madelene was n Geldenhuys en sy het ons heelwat vertel van die plaashuis op Braamfontein waar my Oupa Frederik Gerhardus Geldenhuys en Ouma Getrude Augusta Maria Geldenhuys (geb Herder) vroeer jare gebly het.

Is dit moontlik dat ek n afskrif van die CD kan bekom? Ek het ook n afskrif van notas wat my Oumagrootjie, Judith Fredrika Salomina Geldenhuys geb Grobler geskryf het oor haar familie en kinderdae en hoe sy my Oupagrootjie Frans ontmoet het in Heidelberg,Transvaal en hoe hy 2 jaar later na haar pa se plaas toe is met die verskoning om n verlore perd te soek. Die uiteinde was dat hy nooit die perd gevind het nie maar eintlik net vir haar wou kom kuier het. Dit is interessant om te sien dat haar familie hier naby in Potchefstroom geboer het.

Laat my weet wat die koste daaraan verbonde is (met posgeld ingesluit) asseblief. Ek kan die geld via internet betaal en dan die deposito bewys aan u fax. Ek sal dus u bankbesonderhede daarvoor nodig he.

My adres is Posbus 6872, Flamwood, Klerksdorp 2572 en my email is egill@lantic.net.

Gilson, Marcelle (born Germiston 7th March 1971). Marcelle was the third of four children born to Dennis Michael Gilson (16th October 1940 – 11th March 1997) and Cathleen Elizabeth Potgieter (born 1st July 1942). Her grandfather died of a heart attack and was then adopted. Marcelle completed her primary schooling at Colin Mann, Lamton Germiston with the notable distinction of not missing one day during the entire duration. Her high school was completed at the Johannesburg Art, Ballet, Drama and Music School, specialising in Art.

Marcelle worked in the printing industry for ten years – typesetting. Her adopted father died of Cancer in 1997. She met illustrious handsome Pey Malan Geldenhuys on 10th July 1998. Pey hoodwinked Marcelle to relocate from Johannesburg to Durban to establish her own Web Dynamix business specialising in design and promotion of Web pages on the Internet. After the best seven years of her life, Marcelle surprisingly opted to terminate the relationship and moved out of the home that they both had built up.

Goldsworthy, Joy married Stuart William Geldenhuys on the 10th July 1957, in Manzini, Swaziland. Joy raised Ian Jannie, born Johannesburg 22nd February 1985, and Louise born two years later, on the 5th June 1987

Gooding, Adam married Tracy Bauden and they now have three children, Braydon, Katelyn and Marissa

DICTIONARY OF FAMILY BIOGRAPHY

Gooding, Cherie Jane (born Australia), daughter of Mark Gooding and Letitia Bezuidenhout.

Gooding, Dean Mark (born Biloela, Queensland, Australia 18th June 1984) second son of Mark Gooding and Letitia Bezuidenhout. Facebook friend in 2011 – and invited to join the MyHeritage Preller Geldenhuys website (e-mail address: deano_demon@hotmail.com

Gooding, Ronald Mark (born Warwick, Queensland, Australia 18th July 1943), son of Ronald Mark Gooding and Nancy Neilson. Mark married Letitia Bezuidenhout and they have five children – Adam, Cherie Jane, Dean Mark, Benjaman Luke and Braydon Lee.

Gooding, Ronald Mark, married Nancy Neilson. Son married Letitia Bezuidenhout.

Griffiths, Cherie (born Seychelles 29th April), grew up and trained as a teacher in New Zealand, from Kaiwaka, married . They have two children and live in Qatar.

DICTIONARY OF FAMILY BIOGRAPHY

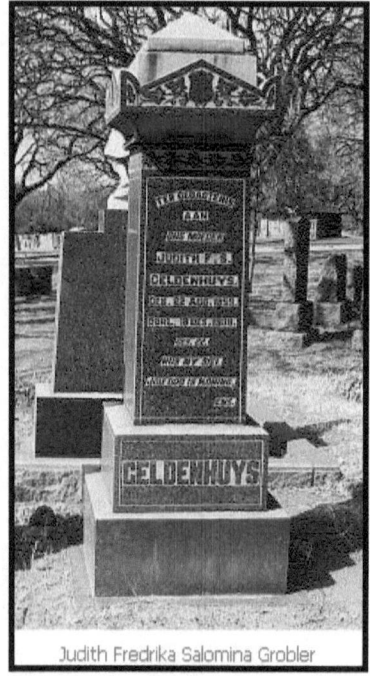

Judith Fredrika Salomina Grobler

Grobler, Judith Fredrika Salomina (born 22nd August 1859 and died 18th December 1938) married Frans Eduard Geldenhuys (1856-1934), who was one of the Rand pioneers.

Gurney, Nerissa Geldenhuis (born Whangarei, Northland, NewZealand, 10th November 1982), went to Whangarei Girls' High, married Eben Geldenhuis and lives in Hamilton. They have two daughters, Cleopatra and Joanna.

Harding, Monja (born 6th May), married Trevor Geldenhuis and lives in Sydney, Australia. They have two daughters, Monja Geldenhuis and Faith Dabin.

Haynes, Desirée – married Davyd McColl, only son of Stuart John McColl. Stu flew in from New Zealand to attend the wedding. They have a son, Kayden.

DICTIONARY OF FAMILY BIOGRAPHY

Howard crest

Howard, Dylan (Born Durban). Dylan is the younger brother to Eloise Howard – who married Pey Malan Geldenhuys in Durban, on 27th April 2007. Dylan is partnered with Mandy Pienaar – and they live in the Granny Flat on his parent's property.

Eloise gave her son the middle name Dylan, in honour of her younger brother. Dylan, like Pey, is fond of the outdoors and has enjoyed setting up their caravans alongside each other at Wagendrift Dam, just outside Estcourt.

Howard, Eloise (born Durban, 4th April 1972). Eloise is a Financial Advisor and Single Mom who teamed up with Pey Malan Geldenhuys, in November 2005. She is mom to Matthew Dylan, who was born on 3rd April 2001. Eloise is the eldest child of Steve Kenneth Howard and Ingrid Stella Estment – and inherited all her mothers' attributes. She is a very independent, strong-willed, assertive and ambitious woman who knows what she wants in life, and knows how to get it. She is determined and intends completing her degree in psychology – despite raising a highly energetic son and building a new home.

Eloise managed to make an honest broker out of Pey and they both decided to tie the knot on 27th April 2007. To cement the relationship they bought 116 Edgeley Road in Durban North and promptly proceeded to demolish the interior. They roped in their father (-in-law) and cousin Paul to reconstruct the ideal house they envisaged – a place that Matthew Dylan, and his sibling, could call home. The family - no everybody - is waiting to hear the outcome of Koh Samui!

The outcome turned out to be 'morning sickness' – with the birth of beautiful baby Jake in December! However, tragedy struck when 12-day old baby Jake died on 30th December 2009. Joy did eventually return to the family with the birth of a beautiful daughter, Lucy Hope, in Durban, on 29th March 2009.

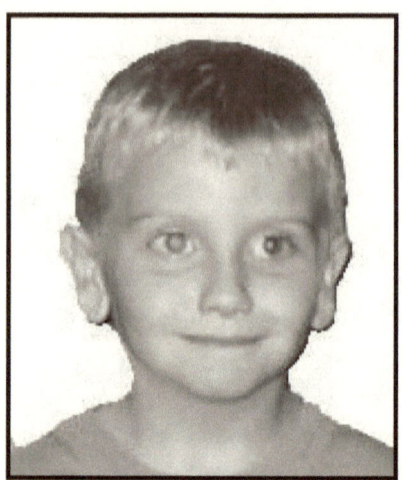

Howard, Kenneth Steve (born Durban 4th October 1947), is an Auto and Diesel-Electrician, father-in-law to Pey Geldenhuys and grandfather to Matthew Dylan. He was the firstborn child to James Alexander (Johnny) Howard and Mary Victoria Milton. Steve has two younger sisters, Eileen and June. He qualified as an engineer with Woodlands New Forest, Durban, met and married Ingrid Stella Estment on 6th June 1970. They have two children, Eloise and Dylan.

Steve settled in Athlone, Amanzimtoti and carried out extensive alterations and additions to his property. With his knowledge of electricity, he successfully wired his own housing additions. It is small wonder then that Pey Geldenhuys nabbed his father-in-law to wire his newly acquired property in Durban North.

Howard, Matthew Dylan (born Durban 3rd April 2001). Matthew is the son of Eloise Howard, fathered by David Sinton. Matthew was a gifted genius on pre-historic dinosaurs, at the tender age of four years. He could recognise the various types and correctly pronounce the names of the dinosaur types even before he developed the ability to read.

Matthew started his schooling at Maritz Brothers College, has settled in well and even managed to swim the whole length of the swimming pool at the Gala held in March 2007.

Matthew was adopted by Pey Malan Geldenhuys and as a result thereof, had his surname changed to Geldenhuys just prior to the family immigrating to New Zealand.

His first brother, Jake, died 12 days after birth. However, his next sibling, Lucy Hope, who was born in Durban on the 29th March 2009, was declared fully medical fit to undertake the long flight from Africa to New Zealand.

Jehle, Walter (born Stuttgart, Germany 16th May 1902) "stamvader", son of Julius von Jehle, arrived in 1951 from Germany and married Maria Otto on 6th December 1959. They had one son. The mystery whether the Jehle's are related to the Jelley's will be a future challenge for Brendan Vaughan to resolve!

DICTIONARY OF FAMILY BIOGRAPHY

Jelley crest

Jelley, Basil Owen, born in April 1912? and died in September ?, memorial stone next to 'Molly' Jelley

Jelley, Brenda Merle (born Salisbury) to Cecil William Gordon Jelley and Joyce Pamela Deeves, grandaunt to Courtney and Brendan Jelley. Brenda married Talbot, in Salisbury, Rhodesia, and moved to South Africa in 1983. In 1987 the family immigrated to Perth, Australia. Brenda is the half-sister to Brian and William Patterson Jelley.

Jelley, Brendan Vaughan (born Chipinge Zimbabwe 15th November 1996-) son of Dr. Grahame David Jelley and Renene Delene Geldenhuys, and grandson to proud William Jelley and Margaret Whiteley, as well as Preller Geldenhuys and Rina Malan. Brendan, like his two grandfathers, took an

early interest in aviation, and took great delight with the aircraft gift toys that he received. Like his elder sister, Brendan benefited immensely when his father took up a six-month locum appointment in New Zealand.

He started his schooling at St Canice in Westport, and then went to Ohope Beach School when his parents moved to the Bay of Plenty in North Island. He took music lessons in Westport, but it was tap dancing and drama that he did really well in. At Ohope Brendan helped produce and acted in a TV video production. He teamed up with his elder sister in the "Jelley Duo" to publicise their tap dancing skills. Brendan excelled at Speech and Drama – playing numerous roles in a variety of plays – more noteably Budsy Malone and Charlie Chaplin. Brendan also formed part of the Lighting Crew in the Whakatane High School production of Grease.

Like his sister Courtney, Brendan walked away with a fistful of prizes at the annual Tauranga performing arts competitions. These included winning the Mount Baptist prize for Bible reading and the J Loughlin prize and Lewis Cup for improvisation.

Brendan will always be very special for me. When Jake left us so unexpectedly, Brendan sent a specially designed Sorry card, which read: *Dear Pey, Eloise and Matthew, I am so sorry about little Jake. But he has gone to a better place now and may God look after him. He has blessed us all and is now looking over us. I never met him but still I will always love and hurt for you and him. Love from Brendan.* I picture was attached with Matthew holding Jake, sitting on the hospital bed, between Eloise and Pey. On the opposite side of the card, Brendan had neatly typed the following poem:-

I may never see Tomorrow, There's no guarantee,
And things that happened yesterday, Belong to history.
I cannot predict the future, I cannot change the past, I have just the present moment, I must treat it as my last.
I must exercise compassion, Help the fallen to their feet, Be a friend to the friendless, Make an empty life complete.

The unkind things I do totoday, May never be undone, Any friendships that I fail to win, May evermore be won.
I may not have another chance, On bended knee to pray, And I thank the Lord with humble heart, For giving one more day.

Brendan also also chose that lovely site outside Ohope, a wetland on Ohiwa harbour, specially dedicated as a memorial site to the memory of baby Jake, who blessed us all during those brief 12 days he spent on this earth.

His trip to Vanautu Island is one of the highlights of his young career. He is also one of the few family members who has undertaken a 'Zorb' ball roll down a hillside at Rotorua. His sailing up the east coast of Australia in the Pacific Pearl, and opportunity to scuba dive on the Great Barrier Reef will last a lifetime. Brendan has also taken to Saint John's development like a duck to water – with sights set on achieving the Grand Prior award.

In August 2014, the Whakatane News reprted the following tribute:- :*Hectic pace for Spirit Award winner – Whakatane High School deputy head boy Brendan Jelley maintains an impressive schedule.*

:*At school he's part of the 40 hour famine group, enviro group and school council and he leads the health committee, students against dangerous driving group and Interact committee. He'sthe co-choreographer of the school show* Footloose, *organiser of the school ball and last year he was the lead dancer and organiserof the school's Smokefree Rock Quest competition.*

"Outside of school, Brendan makes an impact. The Governor General presented Brendan with his Grand Priors Award, as a result of his commitment to St John, where he is a senior cadet and is now mentoring and training other cadets aged 8-17.

"He is one of ten cadets that created a five year plan for the Under 16 National St John programme and he was the media manager for St John Youth New Zealand at the International Cadet Camp and Competition in Sydney.

"Brendan is the Bay of Plenty Cadet of the Year and he works to engage with the community, andhelps organise events like competitions for badges, camps and fundraisers. And it was one of these fundraisers, a hair shaving and leg waxing

DICTIONARY OF FAMILY BIOGRAPHY

event that raised $3,000 for St John, CanTeen and Camp Quality.

"Add to this, Brendan had a lead role of 'CATS' and is helping to fundraise for this group's new facilities. He's also a member of the Whakatane District Youth Council, Not surprisingly Brendan is the winner of the Trustpower Whakatane District Youth Spirit Community Award.

"Run in conjunction with the Trustpower Whakatane District Awards, the Trustpower Youth Community Award recognises secondary school students' service to the school and the community. The Award is jointly run by the Whakatane District Council.

Local high schools were asked to recommend one student to be considered for the Award. As the winner Brendan received a trophy, a framed certificate and $500 prize money, He also made a $250 donation to a community group of his choice,"

Brendan is a 12th generation Geldenhuys, 11th generation Malan, 9th generation Moodie, 4th generation Whiteley and at least 4th generation Jelley (only four were researched in South Africa – but he is most likely a very latter Jelley when considering UK origins). For ease of reference, ancestors are as follows:-

GELDENHUYS	MALAN	MOODIE/WHITELEY	JELLEY
Albert Barends c1640-1693	Jacques 1665-1742	James Moodie 1757-1828	Thomas Jely 1472
Barend 1682-	David 1708-1792	Benjamin Moodie 1789-'38	Thomas Jely 1518
Hendrik 1717-1770	Jacobus Johanus 1739-1806	James BD Moodie 1819-'94	William Jellie 1673
Johannes Albertus 1750-	David 1765-1851	Margery Hester Moodie 1845	Andrew Jellie 1684
Lourens 1777-	Daniel Stephanus 1801-	Lucretia Maria Coleman 1865	William Jelly 1798
Johannes Albertus 1807-1894	Hendrik Francois 1833-	Len Whiteley 1893?	Godfrey Jelley c 1875
Hendrik Jacobus 1849-1924	Hendrik Francois 1878-1959	Percival Whiteley 1876	Charles Henry
Johannes Albertus 1877-1942	Francois Daniel 1907-1988	Alan Whiteley 1897-1989	Cecil William Gordon 1898
Abram C F Preller 1916-1972	Susanna Catharina 1945	Margaret Mary Elaine Whiteley 1935	William Paterson 1935-2009
Preller Matt 1943-	Renene Delene 1968-	Grahame David 1959	Grahame David 1959
Renene Delene 1968-	Brendan Vaughan 1996-	Brendan Vaughan 1996-	Brendan Vaughan 1996-
Brendan Vaughan 1996-			

DICTIONARY OF FAMILY BIOGRAPHY

Jelley, Brian Godfrey (born Salisbury, Rhodesia 11th March 1932), is the granduncle to Courtney and Brendan Jelley. Brian is the eldest son to Cecil William Gordon Jelley and Mary McRoberts Paterson. They lived in the Avenues, Salisbury, and during the Recession the family moved to South Africa where Brian's father managed a Trading Store at Glenhope in the Transkei. Brian's younger brother, William (grandfather to Courtney and Brendan) was born in Durban in 1935. The family then moved to Orange Grove Johannesburg, where Cecil Jelley, called Gordon, secured employment with African Explosives. In 1937, the firm transferred the family from Johannesburg back to Salisbury. They lived at 19 Bates Street – a house that Brian now passes daily some 53 years later! Brian started his schooling at the Convent School, and then went on to do his Standard 1 to Standard 4 at David Livingstone. Because the school did not have a standard 5, he then completed his junior schooling at Blakiston – named after a hero of the Mazoe Patrol. High Schooling was completed at Alan Wilson, which was, and still is, next to Prince Edward High School. Having qualified for his School Leaving Certificate he joined Mosenthalls Rhodesia Limited's Atlantic Petrol Company as a general clerk. He was then transferred internally to the building supplies department of Robertson Hudson as a salesman – who took over Mosenthalls when they closed down in 1960 (Robertson Hudson had their head office in Benoni, South Africa). The Salisbury office at that time had a staff of six, two whites and four blacks. The firm expanded in 1975 when Robertson Hudson combined with Mitchell Cotts from the United Kingdom – they traded as Robertson Hudson as a Member of the Mitchell Cotts' Group up until 1983. Then another group from Mitchell Cotts combined with Robertson Hudson to become Mitchell Cotts Engineering. In October 1996, the Engineering part was sold to Randalls Holdings and Brian Jelley retired on 1st February 1997 – after 36 years service. Up until 2006 Brian was still enjoying life to the full, still on retirement.

Brian Jelley carried out his National Service at the Drill Hall and Nkomo Barracks from 1952 to 1955. In 1961 he was called up for service with 8 Rhodesia Regiment and at age 38 was placed on Reserves. Then in 1973 Brian Jelley was called up again to serves in the Dad's Army during the Rhodesian War. He did two stints at Mukumbura in the RHU – Rhodesian Holding Unit – that later became the RDR – Rhodesia Defence Regiment. His duty whilst on the border was to protect the Cordon Sanitaire fence erectors along the Rhodesia Mozambique border – within which land mines were laid. In view of the small staff holding at his Mitchell Cotts business, Brian was then transferred to do his call-up stints at Army Headquarters in the Data Processing Unit, attached to 11 Signals Squadron at King George VI Barracks. He continued to serve there right up to the Zimbabwe elections – and when the results were announced of the Zanu PF landslide, burned his military uniforms to escape the witch-hunt that followed immediately afterwards. Brian says "Nobody ever came around to confront me for 'destroying' government property!"

Jelley, Cecil William Gordon (born Qumbo, Transkei 11th October 1898 - died 23rd June 1977) Great-grandfather to Courtney and Brendan Jelley. Poppa Gordon, although born in the Transkei, and whose father Valentine Godfrey is believed South African born, may have been of Irish descent. He married Mary McRobert Paterson (born Isipingo 1905) and they had Brian, born 1932, and William Paterson born 1935. Bill's mother died at the tender age of 38 - she had undergone a gallstone operation which was not entirely successful, and returned to Durban when further complications developed. Mary died 13th November 1943. In

1946, Poppa Gordon re-married, to Joyce Pamela Deeves.

Jelley, Courtney Sacha (born Triangle, Zimbabwe 13th September 1993-) beautiful, bright daughter of Dr. Grahame David Jelley (1959-) and Renene Delene Geldenhuys, and beloved granddaughter of Preller Matt Geldenhuys (1943-) and 'Rina' Susanna Catharina Malan.

Courtney was the most beautiful baby that Ou Dad had seen in twenty-five years. Not since 1968 had there been born such a joy to a grandparent. Oudad's father had given Renene a similar compliment, except that his time period was only 23 years because it related back to 1945. Mine covers a quarter of a century!

Courtney displayed above intelligence at a very early age, and despite a six-month visit to New Zealand when her father took up a locum position, she managed her continued schooling at home admirably. She acquired intelligible telephonist skills whilst still in nappies, so to speak. Her mature conversation never ceased to amaze Oumie and Oudad, so much so that Oumie would hobble to the phone at double quick time whenever Courtney surprised us with her delightful tales. We safely trust that having a female in the family has been a special blessing to Gran and Grandpa Jelley as well.

In fact, the opportunity to travel to New Zealand at such an early age only broadened her horizons and contributed to her rapid development in the adult world. Her ability to grasp a variety of complex issues simultaneously and focus her attention on a subject at hand never ceased to amaze those that she came in contact with. Her grounding at St Canices in Westport has been excellent and special gifts in speech, drama, music and tap and jazz dancing soon came to the fore. We trust that Courtney will inherit her mothers' presence of mind when it comes to caring for her brother Brendan's formative development. Renene did a magnificent job with her brother Pey – fighting his battles for him and preventing him from being exposed to bad influences.

Courtney started school at Mvurachena in Chipinge and went on to St Canices in Westport. She then went to Ohope Beach School in Ohope for one term and went on to Whakatane Intermediate. In December 2005 she starred as Dorothy in the Wizard of Oz. Her favourite subjects are maths and all technologies which include food technology, biotechnology, hard materials, soft materials, electronics and information computer technology. Her ambition is to become a Vet and if she can't be that she will fall back to Hairdressing. She would like to marry a cute, Christian man that cares about love, honesty, faith, hope, and her.

In February 2006, she wrote the following essay describing - *"My Holiday"* thus:-

This holiday I have done a lot. I have been spending my Christmas with my dad's side of grandparents. But it's not a holiday unless you go somewhere other then your town. So I went on a holiday during school. Yes I missed the first two weeks of school and went on holiday so that is what I am going to tell you about My Holiday.

It started on Saturday the 4th of February. We travelled four tiring hours in the car to Auckland - then another half-an-hour to Whangaparoa to our cousins. Our cousins are not really our cousins they are our second cousins. These are my cousins: Aunty Chan (Chanli) oh and you pronounce it shun, Uncle Charlie (Charles), Tal (the oldest), Nea (the next), Deu (after Nea), and Gem (the youngest).

We got there and said hello to everyone and unpacked. About fifteen minutes later Mom's Aunty (aunty Delene) arrived with mom's side of our grandparents. We showed them how we swing on the swings and showed them the tree house.

We call them Oumie and Oudad. Oudad is very fit but also has a Jelley Belly like dad. It is very sad because Oumie can't get around much so she can't see everything because she has had a stroke.

Mum and dad got to sleep in Tal's room and all the kids slept in the tree house. The tree house is amazing. It has lighting, and four person bunk bed. It has proper walls and a proper roof. It also has a door and a fly screen.

The next day on Sunday the 5th we went and did the Donut run which is what our cousins do when they have guests. They go to the donut shop and chose what we want and have that for breakfast. I got a cream donut. We spent the rest of the day at Stanmore Beach and had a picnic. I thought the water was ICE!!! Then we came back and watched Second Hand Lions with every one. Which was hilarious? Then we went to bed.

The next day on Monday the 6th instead of doing the Donut run we travelled one hour just to go to a beach called Tawharanui with waves so Uncle Charlie could surf. This beach was on a reserve and had lots of seaweed every where you went. There were also a lot of caves and rock pools you could go into. On our way back we stopped at the ice-cream shop that has thirty six flavours of ice-cream. I of course got Chocolate Mud which is chocolate ice-cream with choc chips and chocolate covered peanuts. Dad finished his ice-cream and went and got another one (which isn't helping his tummy) and I got another one to. Mum and dad went with Oumie and Oudad to Gulf Harbour while we kids jumped on the trampoline.

On Tuesday our cousins went to school as we packed to go travelling again. We got in the car and went to the Donut shop and I got a chocolate donut (not surprising) and a mince savoury. We ate that on the way to picking up the grandparents. After we picked them up it was another four tiring hours to Kerikeri. On the way there we stopped at a café called Utopia which was a really strange café. You sat in domes of different colours. Outside there was a pod that you could sit in and doodle. So we had some drinks there.

Then we got to Kerikeri which means dig dig because the Maori would dig for kumara in that particular place. Kerikeri is often referred to as The Cradle of the Nation and was the site of New Zealand's first true colonial settlement. We found the Top 10 and went in. But they didn't have our unit ready. So we went shopping and bought some groceries. By the time we got back the unit was ready. Brendan and I went and found the playground which was very unsafe. So we went and played ping pong. I wanted to see if there was a candy machine because I saw a drink machine. We found one and Brendan being him looked in the change box and found a dollar. So we shared it and bought a packet of chips that we shared.

After tea we went to the oldest stone building in New Zealand and had a look around that building. Then we went next door to the first house ever built in New Zealand and had a look around at that building. I learnt that the oldest buildings were the sole survivors of the musket wars of the 1820's. The mission house was built for the reverend John Butler in 1821. The house soon belonged to the Clarke family and then came the Kemp family, James and Charlotte and their decedents lived there. Until Ernest Kemp gave it to New Zealand's Historic Places Trust. You can have a look around the house and see how the Kemp's and other people lived. The stone building was built in 1832. The store was built for storing mission supplies in large amounts. The stone building is now a stone store that you can look around and buy all the historic things that they used there.

The next day on Wednesday the 8th we travelled to Pahia and went and found a place called Cooks Lookout Motel and settled in there. We had a look around the site and Brendan and I found the swimming pool and spa. We ran up to our unit, grabbed our togs, put them on and jumped in the pool. The water was really warm.

Then we went to the Waitangi Grounds and we went on a walk that took us to the biggest waka and had a look at it. I learnt that the waka was called Ngatokimatawhaorua and that it was 35 meters long. It would hold up to 76 warriors at a time. We then had to go back to the place where you pay because we watched a movie telling us all about the Treaty. We then walked to the flagstaff which marks exactly where it was signed. Next we went into the Whare and it was called Te Whare Runanga. It had fifty panels holding it up and two centre poles. It was built in 1940 a year after the Treaty. Then we went next door to the British residency which was called that before but is now called The Treaty house. The Treaty house was built for James Busby. James married Agnes and they had Sarah (their daughter) and John (their son) who lived in that house. James went away to sell Kauri Gum in USA and then war started so Agnes took the children and moved to Sydney. The Busby family returned in 1846 after it was used for base for the British Army. When James died ten years later, Agnes sold the house and garden and moved. For fifty years that place has been empty until Mr

Bledisloe Bought and gave it to the Treaty as a gift. The House had the actual treaty that was signed and it is hard to believe that they had neat handwriting.

That same night we went to a restaurant called The Sugarboat. It was an actual boat sitting in the water. It was really nice.

Then the day after that on Thursday the 9th we went on a car ferry to Russell. Also known as Kororaraka and it also is the old capital of New Zealand and drove around there. We first went to the Flagstaff at the top of Russell, that same pole was the same one Chief Hone Heke chopped down four times because the Union Jack was flying on that flagstaff. We went and had a look around the Russell museum and they had a mini version of the Endeavour and a big crayfish. Then we crossed the road and had a look at the first New Zealand church built. It has lots of gun shots and graves there from the wars.

Then we got an ice-cream hoped in the car and went back on the ferry to the motel. Brendan and I then had another swim and I started doing this essay mum is making us do because I am missing school.

The next day Friday the 10th we were going to Whangarei but first we stopped at Adventure Land. It was full of fun stuff like the Trapeze, Waterslide, Tightrope, Tarzan swings and the Magaslide that was blown up like a bouncy castle. My favourite was the trapeze which was at least five meters high and you had to swing for as long as you want and you let go and land on a big bouncy castle type thing. It is breathtaking. My next favourite thing was the tightrope. You had to walk along a tightrope for as long as you can. If you fall off you land on the same thing a bouncy castle. Then there was the mega slide which was awesome you would sit in a sack and go down so fast. Whoosh! Then there was the waterslide. It took a while to go fast because you had to get wet first and the only way you could do that is if you went down it first. Then came the Tarzan swings but I could never get past the first one so that is why it is my least favourite.

Then we got in the car and travelled an hour to Whangarei. We were staying at a Top 10 again. After tea we went to the shops and looked around by five o'clock I hadn't found Dick Smith Electronics but lots of expensive cameras. Then we got directions to find the Warehouse but how were we supposed to know where the Warehouse was. So we gave up. Then dad wanted to look at the boats and as we were going there I saw the Warehouse so we went there and then I saw it so I shouted "there's Dick Smith." So dad parked and Oudad and I went in there. I found the camera I was looking for and bought it. Oudad spoilt me and bought me a memory card so instead of forty pics I had nine hundred. And he also bought me some rechargeable batteries. So now I had a digital camera.

Then we went to some of friends of ours for dinner. They have a nice house with a great view. We just watched videos until dinner. By then I was really tired so I fell asleep. I woke up and we were in the car and then I fell asleep again. In the morning I was woken up by a flash because Oudad had taken a picture of me. I had to get dressed because we were going to The Cheesecake shop. We went there because our friends own it. We had lunch there well just a drink but we bought a quiche. Then we travelled about three and a half hours to Waiwera Thermal pools. We were going to meet our cousins there and we thought we were late but we were the first ones there. Aunty Chan was making muffins so that was why they were late. But we still had fun. I taught myself how to dive although I am still not sure of myself and I went down the Hydro slides but I wasn't allowed to go down the big, scary slide because I had earrings on and I couldn't take the off so I just kept on going on Squeeze the biggest one I could go on. Then we had to go so I got out my camera and got someone to take a picture of everyone together.

Then we headed back to their house and I was taking pictures of everyone and they were all asking me "Can I have a turn." And it was really getting annoying. We went and slept in the tree house. In the morning dad took us for a donut run while aunty Chan made pancakes. So we ate our donuts and came back to pancakes. After we were all full we said our goodbyes and we left for Ohope. Another four tiring hours in the car. We got home and said hello to Granny and Grandpa and Lady and Dotty. We showed Oumie and Oudad around the house and where their room was. They got Brendan's room and he is sleeping in my room. We are staying at home until Tuesday but on Monday I will go to school and I will get to see my friends and Miss Harris again I can't wait.

At school we did handwriting and Skills. We also did a maths test and a reading test. I think I did really well in the reading and in my maths I think I just passed. We also had a surfing lesson and learnt about the rips and waves. I have a lot of work to catch up on in the next week.

It's Tuesday and we are heading off to Whangarau Bay. We have rented a batch there and it is near a Macadamia Farm. We travelled to Opotiki and dad refuelled and we got an ice-cream. When got there and it was a really nice open plan building. It had a mezzanine floor and an excellent view of the bay because it was across from us. We would swim and play but most of the time it was boring. Apart from when we played Flight Simulator 2000. It is this really cool virtual flying game. You can choose your plane and take flying lessons. I'm a natural because on my first go without taking lessons I took off and landed well. We went to the Macadamia Farm and had an ice-cream there. Mum bought some chocolate macadamias and some roasted ones. They had heaps on their drive way.

It was beautiful there but I couldn't wait to get home. On Friday we eventually travelled home but first we went and had an ice-cream at the Macadamia farm. We got home changed into our togs and went to the beach. Brendan and I slept in the tent.

Courtney won the Tim Balme prize for characterisation in the 11 – 15-year age group and the Myra-Lou Cnnor Trophy for the highest mark in dramatic characterisation in the annual Tauranga performing arts competitions. She also won cups for the most marks and points in three non-scholarship classes. She was also first equal in the Edna Connor Memorial Cup for the highest marks for light verse classes, and the Anna Robinson prize for extract from a play. She was invited to perform in the celebration concert at the Baycourt Theatre – presenting her light verse poem *The Cookie Thief*. Courtney excelled at Whakatane High School – especially at Drama as in the June 2009 production of Grease, where she acted as Patty Simcox, one of the few named roles as one of The Pink Ladies. Another notable achievement during 2009 was the top award of the Grand Prior by St John's. St John's is the leading paramedics and Ambulance service in New Zealand.

Courtney also took up Karate and excelled at the sport, displaying excellent qualities of leadership.

Her visits to White Island, Fiji and the cruise up the east coast of Australia, had helped to mould her character, confidence and strong leadership qualities.

Courtney's reason for wanting to join the New Zealand Air Force: "Both my grandfathers on my maternal and paternal side served as pilots in the Royal Rhodesian Air force. My parents grew up on air force bases, so in turn I have grown up hearing stories which have inspired me to want to join. My father is a civilian medical officer and my mother is a professional nurse. I have always had an interest in medicine and having joined St John Youth in 2008 I have developed a passion for emergency medicine which has inspired me to join as a military medic.

My experience in St John has allowed me to gain essential emergency skills as well as discipline through Drill and pride through wearing the uniform of a respected organisation. I have also learnt to respect authority and gained valuable leadership skills through the organisation's ranking system. I have obtained my Grand Prior (the highest award a youth member can achieve) and hold the rank of Cadet Leader (the highest rank a youth member under the age of 18 can receive (equivalent to Warrant Officer in Military Cadets))

The core values gained in St John i.e empathy, integrity, professionalism, and teamwork are the same values I wish to maintain in the air force.

I am proud to have become a New Zealander and it would be an extreme privilege to serve the country." I have no doubt that Courtney will serve with distinction and be a credit to her adopted country.

Keep your eyes on Jesus, Courtney, for God will be with you and you will be a blessing to your parents for the length of their days.

Stop Press! Courtney has passed her Year 13 at Whakatane School and is about to embark on making her mark on life, as she awaits the outcome of her New Zealand Air Force application. Her St John's experience and qualifications will prove beneficial in her chosen profession.

Jelley, Grahame David (born Salisbury, Rhodesia 22nd March 1959), is a medical practitioner, eldest son of Wg. Cdr. William Paterson Jelley (born 1935, died 2009) and Margaret Mary Elaine Whiteley (a descendant of stamvader Benjamin Moodie), educated at Guinea Fowl School Gwelo and University of Cape Town. Practised at Edendale Pietermaritzburg, married Renene Delene Geldenhuys on 6th June 1992 in the beautiful Drakensberg setting at Champagne Sports and returned to Zimbabwe as MO for Hippo Valley at Chiredzi. Set up private practice at Chipinge.

Grahame and Renene carried out a locum spell in New Zealand, and liked it so much that they decided to take up a permanent job offer with Coastal Health in Westport, South Island. Westport was good for them – to settle down and acclimatise to the New Zealand culture. Grahame sponsored a family re-union at Gentle Annie – and the opportunity was taken to circumnavigate the whole Southern Island.

After a while, Grahame resigned his position. Despite a plea by the Westport Major to reconsider his decision, the KiwiJells took the bold move to relocate to the North Island, to a beautiful spot in the Bay of Plenty called Ohope. Grahame was contracted to Total Health Whakatane, but within a year he was faced with taking over the Ohope practice. Whilst growth expectations did not materialise it was a tough and daring decision to turn a marginal business around. With astute management and keeping his finger on the pulse, he was able to provide an above-average life style for his family. Within a short time he found the ideal relaxation of owning and sailing a tri-miran on Ohiwa harbour – which was virtually right on his doorstep. In fact, he could keep an eye on his boat from his kitchen window.

Clinical advisor awarded Fellowship in General Practice

Clinical advisor Grahame Jelley (left) receives his Fellowship in General Practice from Royal New Zealand College of General Practice President, Harry Pert.

Grahame received his Fellowship in General Practice from the President of the Royal New Zealand College of General Practice. This equates to a Senior Medical Officer, regarded as a Specialist in the field of General Practice.

Grahame has now been a GP for 22 years (as at going to print), worked in rural hospital practice post graduation in 1983, returned to Zimbabwe in 1990, then immigrated to New Zealand in 2000, working for the Buller Hospital and Buller Medical Services general practice in Westport.

He moved to Ohope in 2005 and subsequently to Whakatane, and has been a clinical advisor for Planning and Funding since February 2010; fot the wider Te Teo Herenga Waka team.

His generosity knows no bounds and we are truly blessed for the Sponsorship to New Zealand – and for taking the trouble to show us the whole of South Island plus most of North Island as well – during our previous three visits to their beautiful country.

Jelley, Keith Brian (born 19th November 1960, Salisbury, Rhodesia), youngest son of Wg. Cdr. William Paterson Jelley (born 1935, died 2009) and Margaret Mary Elaine Whiteley (a descendant of stamvader Benjamin Moodie), educated at Guinea Fowl School Gwelo and University of Cape Town. Keith immigrated to Canada and then relocated to Melbourne, Australia. Married Jean van Wyk. They do not have any children.

Jelley, Leonard William. A Field Reservist in the British South African Police, who was killed in action on 14th December 1979, during the Rhodesian War. Leonard William Jelley features in the Roll of Honour as published on the Internet, www.mazoe.com/rohaz.html, and also mentioned in Chas Lotter "Echoes of an African War".

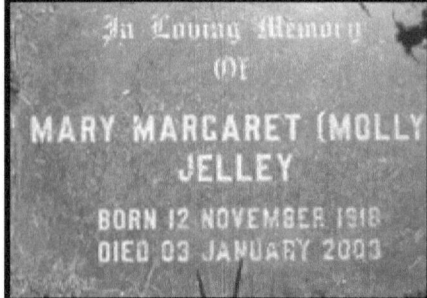

Jelley, Mary Margaret 'Molly' born 12th November 1918, died 3 January 2003, buried / cremated and commemorated at the Stellawood cemetery in Durban, South Africa.

Jelley, William Paterson (born Durban 6th July 1935, died Ohope, New Zealand 15th January 2009), was a retired pilot, son of Cecil William Gordon Jelley, born Transkei,, and Mary McRobert Paterson; grandfather of Courtney and Brendan. Married Margaret Mary Elaine Whiteley and had two sons, Grahame David and Keith Brian.

Bill Jelley joined the Rhodesian Air Force on Short Service Unit flying training course. In the early 1960's he flew twin engined Canberra's and by December 1966 commanded No 4 Squadron, Thornhill. On 19th January 1967 he flew with 'Prop' Preller Geldenhuys in Provost 305 to Bulawayo, followed by a Master Green instrument flying test on 26th May 1967. In July 1967 he stood in for Wingco Mick McLaren as OC Flying Wing Thornhill.

Bill Jelley commanded Prop Preller Matt Geldenhuys during Operation Nickel but handed No 4 Squadron over to Peter Cooke, in order to assume command of No 2 Vampire Squadron (August 1967). In October, a late afternoon border reconnaissance sortie was flown, landing shortly after dusk. Vampire drop tank trials were carried out the following month. During early January 1968, 60x20 millimetre cannon air to ground trials were conducted with Prop Geldenhuys. Operation Cauldron, from 18 to 23rd March 1968 was one of those highly successful counter insurgency operations that accounted for a major terrorist incursion from the Zambia/Mozambique border. The group was intercepted on the Angwa River and

3x60 lb squashhead rockets, plus 151x20 mm high explosive incendiary cannon airstrike was carried out. Both Vampires were dead on target, as confirmed by ciné camera recordings. In the ensuing ground contact, 1 RLI Trooper E. Ridge and 1 RAR Corporal Erisha was killed in action from gunshot wounds (RLI = Rhodesian Light Infantry; RAR = Rhodesian African Rifles). The School of Infantry, in Gwelo, named one of their auditoriums 'Cauldron'. Squadron Leader Bill Jelley also commanded the successful Operations Griffin and Mansion in July.

Operation Knuckle, from August 26 to September 11th 1968 was carried out at Bulawayo airfield. The city was treated to 55 minutes of spectacular formation flying by eight Vampire aircraft on the 8th. Boss Jell led the formation, with Prop Geldenhuys, as No 5, led the second 'box' of four Vampires.

On 3rd March 1969, Bill Jelley carried out 8x20 lb bombing trials, with Prop Geldenhuys. He handed over command of No 2 Squadron to Sqn Ldr Tol Janeke. By July 1972, he had been promoted to Wing Commander and appointed Officer Commanding Flying Wing, Air force Base New Sarum - as per Prop's flying logbook.

Bill's career in the Rhodesian Air Force was recorded in Bateleur thus: "I will follow it up later with a similar note on my experiences in civil aviation with the likes of Bob Blair, Rex Earp-Jones, Pat Meaddows-Taylor, Arthur Downs, Chris Wentworth, Mitch Stirling, Rod Wilson, Tim Kemp and others. Also later some brief notes on family and our move to Canada etc.

Joined No 6 Short Service Unit in March 1954 with Peter Cooke, Jerry Dunn, Mike Reynolds, Nils Prince, Humph Willows and Jock McKenna to name a few. Wings in 1955 and completed SSU February 1956. Jerry and I were selected for the last Provost Ferry, two sections of 4 aircraft, from the UK in December 1955 arriving in Salisbury on Christmas Day after a most fascinating ten day trip.

Peter, Jerry and I were offered Medium Service Commissions, which we accepted in March 1956. I was posted to No 3 Squadron flying Canadairs, Daks and Pembrokes etc until 1961. A Canberra conversion followed at Bassingbourne before being posted to No5 Squadron and later No 6 Squadron. In 1965 I was appointed Personal Staff Officer to the Chief of Air Staff Harold Hawkins which included that dramatic period of UDI and the days that followed. At my request I was sent to No 4 Squadron for a Flying Instructor Course on Provosts. Whilst at Thornhill, and to a lesser degree at New Sarum, I took an active part in Station sport administration, was Chairman of the Midlands Rugby Football Board and a member of the Rhodesian Rugby Football Union. I was appointed Officer Commanding No 4 Squadron on the posting out of Ken Edwards. With the introduction of the Trojan imminent, Peter Cooke was appointed OC No 4 Squadron and I was posted out as OC No 2 Squadron operating Vampires and Provosts. I had the privilege of leading the first live Vampire strike in the country with Prop Geldenhuys during Operation Cauldron in 1968. Officer Commanding Administrative Wing Thornhill followed before I was appointed Director of Air Intelligence at Air Headquarters. Promotion to Wing Commander and my appointment as Officer Commanding Flying Wing New Sarum in 1972 was the highlight of my Air Force career. During this period, as the war escalated and the operational demands on the Station increased, I spent many months as Acting Commanding Officer New Sarum following erratic appointments to this post. I was appointed Staff Officer Training at Air Force Headquarters in late1975 followed by selection and attendance at the SAAF Staff College at Voortrekker Hoogte in March 1976. I returned from Staff Course in December 1976 retaining the appointment as Staff Officer Training. Following ID Smith's acceptance of majority rule in September 1976, it was my opinion that the reason for my two sons being called up for the war, was nullified, so I considered retirement and emigration as an option. So after a very full, exciting and rewarding career, I retired from the Rhodesian Air Force on 30th June 1977. During those last six months of 1977, apart from studying for my civilian flying licence, I spent many hours flying Daks and Islanders as a reserve pilot, even got shot up a couple of times. Our family immigrated to South Africa in January 1978. So there you have it, 23 years of service life in that great little Air Force with all those wonderful people, on a thumbnail! I have promised the family that for posterity I will one day record the family history in simple form, which for obvious reasons, will be more personal and detailed."

Bill was only one of two pilots on his course – the other being Peter Cooke – that on completing pilot training on No 6 SSU, remained on a Medium Service engagement, and retired as Wing Commanders.

From South Africa, Bill and Margaret returned to Zimbabwe, settled at lovely Christon Bank, where they renewed their friendships with Peter and Anne Cooke. Bill and Margaret hosted several memorable Christmas family gatherings at which the Jelley's and Geldenhuys' cemented valued bonds. When their younger son immigrated to Vancouver, Canada, Bill and Margaret followed suit.

Then in November 2005 they chose to move to Ohope, New Zealand – to join his son Grahame and Renene.

A major family reunion was arranged for February 2006.

Jelley, Valentine Godfrey. Born in the Cape Colony – date unknown. He was a manager of a trading business. Married Mary Ann McKenzie (also born in the Cape Colony), great-great-grandfather to Courtney and Brendan Jelley. Godfrey was the father of Cecil William Gordon, born Qumbo, Transkei on 11th October 1898. Ancestors are possibly a Thomas Jely in 1472 Cl (Ess) and a Robert Jely in 1524. A Thomas Jelle held a tenement in Ayr, Scotland 1518 (Friars Ayr, p-81) and William Jellie is recorded in Cruikens, a parish of Carnwath, 1673 (Lanark C.R.). Andrew Jellie and his wife were residents in the parish of Fosse; Alfred 1909 was a British author and poet. Louise Isabel Jely (Kirkland 1910) was an American actress.

Johnson-Worboys, Heather, born 1931, is married to Alan Raymond Malcolm Whiteley, brother to Margaret Mary Elaine Whiteley.

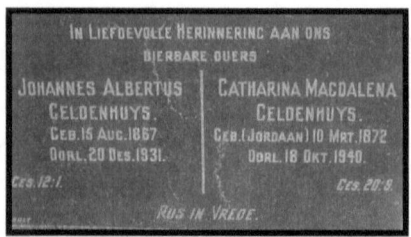

Jordaan, Catharina Magdalena (born 10th March 1872 and died 18th October 1940), married Johannes Albertus Geldenhuys (born 15th August 1867) . They were buried together, as per her gravestone.

Jordaan, Steyn – married 'Aunt Bess, the writers father's eldest sister – who farmed on the family farm, Rustpan, in Bothaville. Steyn Jordaan was buried on Rustpan.

Kala, Anton J went to Hoërskool Brandwag and lives in London, UK. Anton married Louise, grand-daughter to 'Ray' Alan Raymond Malcolm Whiteley, in Johannesburg on the 18th September 2011. Ray is the Uncle to Grahame Jelley.

DICTIONARY OF FAMILY BIOGRAPHY

Kleynhans, Vicky, born 20th July 1983, married to Brent Bezuidenhout.

Kloppers, Marriët (born 11 December 1979), married Jacobus Adriaan 'Kotie' Geldenhuys on 25th October 2008. Marriët is related to Hermann Erwin Rudibert 'Rudi', Izak George Geldenhuys and Lauretta Smith born Geldenhuys.

Knoop, Louisa Regina (born Pretoria 13th July 1944), married Louis Frederick Botes Geldenhuys born Aliwal North 22nd July 1940. They have four children.

Kruger, Dorothea 'Dot' Johanna (born 1930), married farmer Wynand Bezuidenhout, sister-in-law to Johannes Jurgens (Hansie), retiring to Mica Point, Kariba.

La Bella, Vinny (born Johannesburg 27th November 1963), went to Boksburg High School, class of 1979, married Sandra Simpkins and lives in Johannesburg where he works for Bateleur. Brother-in-law to Johan Bouwer.

le Roux crest

le Roux crest

le Roux, Aletta Magdalena Susanna (born Lichtenburg 1st September 1913, died Vereeniging 19th August 1997), married Francois Daniel Malan, mother of Susanna Catharina, who married Preller Matt Geldenhuys. Ouma Lettie bore five children and lived quite a hard life. She had been a farmer's wife for all of her married life, and always saw that her children were fed adequately. There was always food on the table, no matter the hardships. Her eldest daughter Lettie married a businessman Nick van Aardt. Next was Gerta, who married a tobacco farmer Hansie Bezuidenhout. Then eldest son Hendrik, named after his grandfather, married Rina. Then came the twins, Philip who married Elcora Bouwer and Rina mentioned above. Francois the youngest married Aletta Lock.

Lettie survived her husband Frans by nine years. She suffered a stroke, was hospitalised in Vereeniging, and died shortly thereafter. Being a resident of the Avondrus Oue Tehuis, Ds C Marais conducted the funeral service and she was laid to rest next to her husband in the cemetery outside Vereeniging. Paul bearers were Hendrik Malan, Phillip Malan, Frans Malan, Nic van Aardt, Preller Geldenhuys and grandson Francois Malan.

le Roux, Johannes (died 19th September 1944), famous Word War 11 fighter ace.

"Chris", as he was known to his friends, followed a similar path to that trodden by many South Africans and others from many nations, by volunteering for service with the Royal Air Force just before the outbreak of war. He had a dramatic start to his career as a fighter pilot with No 73 Squadron during operations in France in 1940, being shot down 12 times without recording one victory. So, when he joined No 91 Squadron in 1941 he had a lot of leeway to make up, and was very keen to redress the balance. He did not have too long to wait, for on 17th August 1941 his squadron was ordered to intercept enemy aircraft that were escorting a tanker east of Calais. Five aircraft from No 91 led by Flying Officer Paddy Barthropp joined forces with aircraft from No 72 and were soon in combat with approximately 20 Bf 109s. Barthropp, Pilot Officer Donahue and le Roux all sent German fighters to watery graves, so at least the South African had struck back.

The nature of patrol work upon which he was engaged took le Roux on low-level sweeps over the Channel and occupied France, so he quickly became accustomed to staffing anything he saw whilst over enemy territory. An early example of this came in late August when on the 26th he destroyed four Bf 109s on the airfield at Furnes/Coxyde, on the 29th a Bf 109 in the air near Calais, and on the following day supply barges off the same port.

Le Roux had lightning reactions and never a man to take unnecessary chances; this was well illustrated by an action on 30th October when, as he crossed the French coast, he encountered heavy and accurate anti-aircraft fire. Deciding that discretion was the better part of valour, he headed back out to sea where he attacked two flak-ships. Five days later he showed he had no preference for any type of target by first fighting an inconclusive combat with a Fokker-Wolf 190, then shooting at soldiers and lorries and, on the way home, strafing a ship nestling in Boulogne harbour!

By this time he had already received several congratulatory letters from his Air Officer Commanding as well as collecting a Distinguished Flying Cross on 4th October. His first tour ended in December, but he returned to No 91 Squadron as a Flight Commander the following autumn. On 31st October he shot down a pair of FW 190s that had bombed Canterbury, and this brought him another 'well done' letter from his AOC. In January he was posted to No 111 Sqn and moved to Algiers, where on the 19th he opened his North African account. This tour continued successfully until April when he returned to England, and was given command of No 602 Sqn and began his third operational tour on 8th July 1944. His first sortie on 12th July brought no aerial combat, but a blazing three-ton truck showed that he had not lost his touch or appetite for ground targets.

On 16th July 1944, both German and air forces under the Allies capitalised on the air superiority that had given them a tremendous edge during the June invasion. The Luftwaffe, however, was still far from beaten, and although initially their fighters, now mainly FW 190s, were not plentiful, they were more than capable of giving a good account of them both in air-to-air combat. And then, if successful in eluding the Allied fighter umbrella, in strafing troops and transport on the ground.

Allied pilots were also keen to "mix it" at all levels, and although some fighter pilots did not like going too near the ground, especially in aircraft like the Spitfire that was not primarily designed for the ground attack role, they did seek targets of opportunity. Then Sqn Ldr Johannes le Roux had his most historically significant moment. On the day in question, No 602 Sqn, which had moved with its Mk Vb and 1X Spitfires to France on 25th June, was briefed to carry out an armed reconnaissance in the battle area near Fleurs. They bounced six Bf 109s and the squadron commander soon sent one spinning to the ground; engaging a second, he saw hits on the enemy aircraft, then noticed a German staff car complete with motorcycle outrider weaving a solitary path along the narrow roads below.

Le Roux pulled his Spitfire into a wingover and screamed into the attack, a wry grin spreading across his face as he saw the car weaving to avoid his fire, then crashing into the ditch. He pulled his aircraft into a climb and rejoined his companions before heading for home. The man in the staff car had been Field Marshal Erwin Rommel, and his injuries were such that he had to be replaced as commander of the German forces on the Western Front. Le Roux had unwittingly come so close to killing the great German soldier who had such an illustrious war reputation. le Roux was already an ace (5 kills) and equally at home whether attacking air or ground targets.

His final victory came on 20th July when he shared a FW 190 with Flg Off Oliver, the remainder of the month being occupied with ground attack work. By now he had received two Bars to his original DFC and was once again 'rested' from operations. As is often the case, fate now took a hand and on 19th September 1944 this talented and popular South African was killed in an accident. He is officially credited with 22½ victories, of which 16½ were enemy aircraft destroyed in air-to-air combat. As well as these, there are countless trucks, small ships and of course, Rommel's staff car.

LIEBENBERG

Liebenberg crest

le Roux, Susanna Catharina 'Suster', sister to Aletta Magdalena Susanna le Roux, married Daniel Malan (two Malan brothers marrying the two le Roux sisters).

Liebenberg, Meisie, related to Julia Dippenaar, son of Lu, lives in London and came to South Africa for the funeral of her brother Piet. Meisie is married to Wayne Matthews

Liebenberg, Philip, brother to Meisie, married Yvonne, and lives in Winklespruit, Kwa-Zulu Natal. Philip is the eldest son of Julia's sister Louzya Dippenaar

Lock crest

Liebenberg, Tara, daughter of Philip and Yvonne, was married but now divorced – has two sons.

Lock, Anna, mother to Helena and Hugo. They farmed in the Enkeldoorn district of Rhodesia. Now lives in Vereeniging, with Frans and 'Kleinding' Elena Malan.

Lock, Helena 'Kleinding' (born Enkeldoorn) Maried Francois Daniel Malan. They have two children, Amanda and Francois Daniel. They settled in Vereeniging but in the late 2011's, retired to Uitkyk, where a most enjoyable and memorable sixtieth birday reunion was held for Frans. Kleinding is very close to her mother, Anna, and maintains very close relationships with her brothers Johan and Hugo. The photo above was taken in October 2011 – just prior to Rina (Susanna Catharina Malan) saying 'Adio Africa' and relocating to New Zealand.

Lock, Ina elder sister to Helena, married Ian Currin, who farms in the Mooi River area of Kwa-Zulu Natal.

Lock, Jacqueline Joan, born 20th July 2005 to Shelley Lock. She has an older brother Andrew Hugo, born in December 2005

Lock, Hugo (born ?) brother-in-law to Francois Daniel Malan. He has remained behind in Zimbabwe, and believed involved with crocodile farming in the Binga area of Lake Kariba.

Lock, Shelley Jacqueline (born Umtali 7th February 1978). Shelley grew up on Clare Farm, Inyazura, with her father Hugo Lock and mother Melanie, and later moved to Rooibult Farm in 1984. Junior schooling was Hillcrest and senior schooling at Peterhouse. On leaving school Shelley went to Goldenbreed Thoroughbred Stud and started her training in horses. A year later she flew to

England to continue her equine studies. Having completed her Stud Management course she took a job training the Queen's horses for four months. Wanting to further her studies she went to work for Ringfort Studies. She then had a bad accident six-months later, and returned to Zimbabwe to recuperate for nine months. She then returned to England and rode the International Show Jump circuit. Then furthering her studies she took a temporary job for nine months in Mombasa, Kenya. Then in 2004 her dream job materialised to manage a cross-breed stud farm in Bulawayo – but the dream was shattered eight months later when the farm was invaded by 'war veterans'. Shelley then moved to Harare to take a temporary landscaping job. On 4th December 2005 she bore her son, Andrew Hugo Lock. In 2006 Shelley was offered a job in Krugerdorp to manage a stud farm but resigned the position a year later because it was not the lifestyle she wanted for her son. She then moved to Mutare and on the 20th July 2005 she had her baby girl, Jacqueline Joan Lock. She is currently living in Mutare, running a transport company – but shortly due to relocate to Harare to wed the man of her life, Daniel Francois Briers.

Lötter crest

Lock, Tom, son of Hugo.

Lotter, Matthias (born Augsburg, Germany, died 1752), "Stamvader", arrived as a naval cadet midshipman in South Africa in 1734 with his German wife Susanna Roge. They had three children.

Matthias Lotter came from a family of gold and silversmiths. He became a burgher in 1735, a year after his arrival, and then resumed his trade as a silversmith.

On 16th November 1734 he married his second wife, Anna Dorothea van den Berg in the Cape. They had six children, including three sons; b1, b4 and b6. The first born was Johannes Casparus, in 1737, who married Johanna Catharina van Kerken. They had nine children. Fourth born was Christoffel, in 1744, and who married Susanna Sophie Jacobs. They had eleven children – Matthias Johannes (seven offspring), Christoffel (three offspring) and Willem Godfrey with five children. The last born was Willem Godfried, in 1748 and who married Helena Cornelisse and Wilhelmina Wentzel. He fathered ten children, including: -

Johannes George, in 1777, with six offspring,

Willem Godfried, in 1780, with five offspring,

Matthias, with four children, including Willem Godfried in 1808, and Lourens Johannes in 1812.

Carel David, who married Catharina Dorothea van Echten – they had Willem Godfried in 1811 and Salomon in 1814.

Matthias Lotter died in 1752. A Lotter also featured during the declaration of hostilities during the Anglo-Boer War. It is known that he, together with Scheepers, Kritzinger and Malan operated south of the Orange River, in the Colesberg – Noupoort district. (whereas de Wet operated in the Free State; Botha, Beyers and Viljoen in ZAR/Transvaal, De Le Rey/Kemp in Klerksdorp – Mafeking area; and Maritz/Jannie Smuts in north-western Cape). Further research will be needed to establish his contribution to the outcome of history.

Lotter, Matthia Martha (born Johannesburg 19th October 1916, died Johannesburg), married to Abram Carl Frederik Preller Geldenhuys, was the mother of Johannes Albertus born 1940; Preller Matt born 1943, Delene Elizabeth born 1945 and Dawn born 1949.

Her ancestor was Matthias Lotter who arrived at the Cape in 1734 as a midshipman. 'Prop' Preller Matt derived his second name from his mother who was called Matt, and also most likely from the 'Matt' in Matthias.

My mother was a good mother – I could not have wished for better. However, tragedy struck the family when the youngest child Dawn died when a disenchanted Swahili domestic set the thatched homestead alight. Jan and Delene fortunately managed to escape the inferno. My mother was not home – she had dropped my father off at the Chingola Copper Mine where he was on night shift – and was visiting me in hospital (admitted for malaria). Words cannot express a mothers sorrow on the loss of a child. My Mom sought solace in brandy but found closure impossible. This led to an attempted suicide when she stuck a loaded pistol into her mouth and pulled the trigger. The bullet deflected off her false teeth and shattered her jaw. She was rushed to the Mine hospital and luckily survived the suicide attempt. She never did get over the loss of Dawnie.

My parents left the Copperbelt and started general farming in the Fort Victoria district. This was a failed venture, leading to my father taking up temporary employment with the roads department (his mine 'Blasting Certificate' came in handy with building the road to Kyle Dam), and ultimately rejoining the South African Air Force as a Storeman. My father died in service, but my mother continued to life a good and fruitful – albeit very lonely – life. She eventually went to live with her sisters in Johannesburg – where she suffered a fatal heart attack.

Lotter, Matthias, arrived in 1734 from Augsburg Germany. Matthia Martha Lotter, who married Abram Carl Frederik Preller Geldenhuys, is the great-grandmother to Craig and Chanel Geldenhuys and Courtney and Brendan Jelley.

Loubcher, Nicolette, married Geldenhuys, facebook friend in 2011.

Lourens, Anelia (born Heidelberg, Gauteng, 9 September 1987), went to Hoër Volkskool in 2005 and studied with Centurion Akedemie till 2008. Anelia married Martin Lourens Geldenhuys and they live in Heidelberg where her husband is a foreman with Geldenhuys Boerdery.

MacRae, Alphonso (born 6th April 1931), married Carienie Geldenhuys – daughter of Hendrik Jacobus Geldenhuys. They live in California, USA.

Lourens, Maritza, married Philip Malan born Pretoria 14.4.1973, son of Hendrik Francois Malan and Rina Gerber.

Malan crest

Malan crest

Malan, Adolf (born 1910 - died September 1963), was a famous World War II Spitfire Fighter Ace. 'Sailor', as he was generally known, left the Royal Air Force in 1946 after a distinguished career as a fighter pilot and, before his early death from Parkinson's disease in September 1963, became National President of 'Torch Command', the ex-servicemen's anti-apartheid movement. He much preferred to be known for the work he carried out on behalf of this organisation than the estimated 34 victories that at one time placed him as the top-scoring Allied ace of the Second World War.

South African born 'Sailor' turned to the sea for his living, carrying out his early training on the *General Botha* training ship before becoming an officer in the Merchant Navy. At 25 he decided to seek further adventure and turned from the sea to the sky, enlisting in the then expanding Royal Air Force in 1935 and becoming a fighter pilot with No 74 Squadron flying Gauntlets. By 1938, Malan was a Flight Commander and demonstrated his natural flair for leadership by guiding his flight to victory in that year's Sir Phillip Sassoon Trophy.

'Sailor's' first taste of action came over the beaches of Dunkirk in May 1940, and within a week he had achieved 'ace' status with five confirmed and two probable's to his credit, which also brought the award of a DFC -Distinguished Flying Cross, in June. His all-round skill as a fighter pilot was ably demonstrated on the night of 19th June 1940, when he took off in his Spitfire to try to intercept German night raiders. The Spitfire was far from ideal as a night fighter, but Malan was such a master of his machine that he was able to fly it by instinct while searching the moonlit skies. His vigilance was rewarded, and he accounted for a pair of Heinkel He 111s within a 20-minute period before executing a perfect touch-down in the dark, no mean feat bearing in mind the narrow track of the Spitfire's undercarriage. These two night victories brought him an immediate Bar to his DFC.

In July, the Battle of Britain started in earnest, and on the 12th he shared a He 111 of 11/*KG* 53 with Pilot Officer Stevenson and Sgt Mould, a week later accounting for a Bf 109 of 11/*FG* 51. On 28th July he was engaged in combat with a Bf 109, the pilot of which nearly proved his match, but eventually the Spitfire pilot managed to get the upper hand and claimed a probable as the German fighter departed in a hurry towards France. It was later discovered that this Bf 109E-3 was being flown by Maj. Werner Moelders, the *Geschwader Kommander* of *FG* 51 who was to become the first Luftwaffe pilot to score 100 victories and whose total stood at 115 when he was killed in a flying accident in November 1941.

Two more 109s and a couple of Dornier 17s in August completed his tally for the Battle of Britain. During August, No 74, commander by now by Sqn Ldr Malan, was moved for a rest to Kirton-in-Lindsey where he wrote his famous "10 Rules of Air Fighting" (see Prop's Nickel Cross). This document that was circulated throughout the RAF and was still to be seen in some fighter pilots' crew rooms in Korea in the early 1950s when jets were engaged in aerial combat with each other for the first time.

No 74 returned to the south during the autumn and Malan led it into action from Biggin Hill, initially against high-level and low-level hit-and-run raiders, then in excursions across the Channel. By the end of 1940, his score stood at 18 and he was leading the Biggin Hill Wing. As the RAF carried the offensive to occupied Europe, Malan's wing was occupied with escort duties. And there were few chances of increasing personal scores, but in June the tempo increased and in just over a month he had accounted for 14

Bf 109s, his final kill of the war being achieved on 4th July 1941. At that time his total of 32 made him the top-scoring Allied ace, and by the time damaged and shared aircraft were taken into account, his final tally could well have been the 35 claimed in his biography.

In October he went to the USA on a goodwill mission, and whilst there gave many lectures and occasionally flew with instructors and pupils of the US Army Air Corps. On one such occasion he 'destroyed' 12 P 39 fighters with his camera gun in the space of just under 5 minutes! Returning to England, he instructed at the Central Gunnery School, Sutton Bridge, before being promoted to Group Captain and returning to Biggin Hill as Station Commander in January 1943. At the time of the Normandy Invasion in June 1944 he was commanding No 20 Fighter Wing and flew several sorties over the beachheads. The following month he took over as Commander of the Advanced Gunnery School, where he had five aces, including 'Screwball' Beurling, serving under him as instructors, a formidable line-up that must have imparted a great deal of confidence to the students.

Despite attending a Staff College course in 1945 which seemed to bode well for his future in the post-war RAF, he decided against a peacetime service career and returned to South Africa in 1946, becoming secretary to Harry Oppenheimer before, in 1950, starting his own sheep farm at Kimberley. His interest in 'Torch Command' gradually took more and more of his time, and he was not just an 'on paper' activist. Deteriorating health took its toll, but he put up a brave fight as one would expect from a man of such undoubted courage, but in the end lost his fight against the final enemy and died at the early age of 53.

The wise counsel of ACF Preller Geldenhuys comes to mind of "There are Bold pilots, and there are Old pilots, But there are few Old Bold pilots". 'Sailor' Adolf Malan was truly in the latter category - a man among men - whose exploits, together with those of le Roux, are recorded in this Geldenhuys history as a tribute for future generations.

Malan, Aletta Magdalena Susanna (born 9th October 1934), more affectionately called Lettie or Sussie, married Nicolaas Hendrik van Aardt who was born in Heilbron in the Orange Free State on 22nd November 1932. They have three children, the first named after her mother Aletta (Alta) Magdalena Susanna van Aardt was born in Lusaka 5th May 1955 (but registered in South Africa in 1967). She married Willem Adriaan Jacobus Oosthuisen and they had three children, all born in Salisbury; Yvette Marie born 6th October 1976, Liesl Adriaana born 27th July 1978 and Schalk Johannes born 31st August 1979.

Lettie's second child Hendrik Jacobus van Aardt was born in Lusaka on 18th May 1961 and got married in Ladismith, Cape Joleen Geldenhuys, born Ladismith 27th October 1957. They have two children, Nicolaas Daniel born in Bredasdorp on 25th August 1988 and Leane born in Alberton on 29th May 1987.

Lettie's third child Nicolene van Aardt was born in Salisbury on 3rd September 1966 and she got married in Alberton on 19th September 1987 to Reinier Olivier (born Sasolburg 22nd May 1965). They have two children; both were born in Johannesburg, Jaco on 9th February 1989 and Anneke born 16th November 1990.

Malan, Amanda (born Fort Victoria, Rhodesia 13 April 1974 and christened in the NG Kerk on the 5th May 1974), daughter of Francois Daniel Malan (1949) and Helena Alberta Lock. Amanda went to Vereeniging Hoërskool, class of 1992 and got her BA Hons in Recreation and Tourism from the Pietersburg University in 1996. Married fellow university graduate Charles Joseph Stopforth. They have three children, a daughter Dominique born 7th September 2001 and two sons, Michael born 15th August 2003 and Andrew born 6th January 2005. Amanda and Charles had a miraculous escape from a horrific vehicle accident while returning to Polokwane from Haenertsburg, Magoebaskloof on the morning of 14 June 2007. They settled in Polokwane, and have built up a beautiful Game Farm called Uitkyk / Mbizi. Amanda calls her Polokwane home her 'Temple of Grace', welcoming all friends and relatives to share in their blessings.

Malan, Daniel, married Susanna Catharina le Roux. Two brothers married two le Roux sisters – the other pair being Francois Daniel Malan that married Aletta Magdalena Susanna le Roux (mother to Rina Geldenhuys)

Malan, Daniel Francois. (born at Allesverloren, near Riebeek West on 22nd May 1874 and died at 'Morewag', Stellenbosch on 7th February 1959), statesman, church and cultural leader, was the second child in a family of four sons and two daughters. His parents were Daniël François Malan (12.6.1844 – 22.9.1908) and Anna Magdalena du Toit (5.5.1847-12.6.1893), both of whom came from the Wellington district and were descendants of the French Huguenots. After living in the Wamakersvallei they settled on the farm Allesverloren in January 1872, where they were friends and neighbours of the parents of Jan C. Smuts.

Malan, David. A brother-in-law of Jacobus Malan (of Morgenster), who was living on Vergelegen, caused a scandal that same year, 1788, by eloping with a slave woman: David Malan and she Zara, a slave belonging to Jurgen Radyn! They disappeared into the interior and after a time David was declared dead. However, he reappeared many years later, was reunited with his wife and settled on the eastern frontier. Riaan Malan refers to this episode in his book, *My Traitors Heart*.

Malan, David. Born Drakenstein 19.7.1708 and christened in Kaapstad (NG) 27.9.1708. Died 1792, having married in Paarl 17.4.1735 to Eleonora MELIUS who had been christened also in Paarl 28.4.1715. She died March 1750 and was the daughter of Johan Heinrich Melius and Hester Roux. David Malan married a second time, xx Paarl 22.11.1750 Elisabeth Marais in Paarl on the 22 November 1750 (she died in 1802 and was the daughter of Stephanus Marias and Maria Elisabeth de Villiers). David was the second generation Malan, and his descendant son was Jacobus Johannes, born in April 1739.

Malan, Eddie Deon, born Pretoria 12th March 1978, youngest son of Hendrik Malan and Rina Gerber. Eddie is married to Judine Grobbelaar and they have a baby son Lian Jandra. They live in Fairie Glen, Pretoria.

Malan, Elsa-Lou Cornelia (born Chiredzi, Rhodesia, on 20th November 1973), daughter of Philippus Johannes Malan and Elcora Bouwer, qualified as a Nurse and married doctor Willem Petrus (WP) Nel at the NG Kerk in Garsfontein, Pretoria, on 28th November 1998. They left South Africa to settle in Scotland.

Malan, Francois Daniel (born Lichtenburg 2nd October 1907- died Vereeniging 3 April 1988), farmer, seventh generation descendant of Jacques and son of Hendrik Francois (1879-1959) and Getruida Johanna van Eeden. FD married Aletta Magdalena Susanna le Roux; they had six children.

As a young boere seun, he remembered seeing Haley's Comet in 1910, and the 1914 "Rebellie" SAP versus Nat boer versus boer, and broer versus broer, and growing up on a farm without the benefit of formal schooling. Farm chores included herding sheep, milking cows, tending the vegetable garden (with produce which his father sold as a cash crop) and collecting daily a bag of "kraal mis" – cow dung, as fuel for the coal stove. All the brothers took turns attending school in a shed on the neighbour's farm; and when your turn came around, you needed to take a 25 litre paraffin can along to serve as seating. Schooling cycles only lasted six-months in the year, either because of farming chores but more often than not because of teacher transfers. First was a Miss Neethling, who was replaced by a Mnr Schalkwyk – who also only lasted for six months. After another short spell, formal schooling ceased at Standard Five - - farming in those days was more important in order to acquire survival skills. Besides, most of the education was biblical studies and "*Kweper lat*" punishment!

He farmed at Rusthof in 1941, then for Beyers at Bega 1951-54 and immigrated to Southern Rhodesia to farm tobacco at Chinditu, in the Gutu area. He moved around quite a lot – to Trickling Waters, Kombisa, Blackstone, and Knutsford Farms – earning a living for the farmers he worked for. For a while he also made bricks for SP Burger at Chiredzi in the Lowveld. He manufactured concrete products, paving, water canals and bricks His happiest days were with Louis Ferreira in the Beatrice and Chipinga areas of Rhodesia.

He retired to Lichtenburg, and after a while relocated to Vereeniging when his youngest so, Frans, managed to get a flat for him. Frans Malan senior, and his wife Lettie, both died and were buried in Vereeniging, Oom Frans in 1988 and Lettie much later. He was the writer's admired father-in-law - - and whose father, Hendrik Malan, was a rapportryer in the Boere Oorlog.

The following is Pa Malan's fascinating story in his own words:-

Dit was my lewens toestand - Opaandrang van my kinders dat ek 'n boek moet skryf van my lewens loopbaan dit wil my voor kom of ek 'n opstand teen my Skepper gaan wees. Om al my tee spoed wat ek in my lewe gehad het, alles wat ek in hierdie boek gaan skryf is die waarheid - daar is nie aanlassings nie maar om terug te kom van 80 jaar tot een jaar gaan daar baie fratse wees wat nie gemeld is nie aangesien dat ek 'n ongeletterd man is en dat daar baie woorde is wat dalk nie reg gespel is nie (julle moet dit reg maak).

In die jaar 1 Oktober 1907 is daar op die plaas Rietgat 'n kindjie gebore en die dag toe hy sy ogies oop gemaak het, weinig het hy geweet watter donker toekoms vir hom voor lê. Hy sal 'n arm man bly en swoeg en spartel vir 'n lewe. Rykdom en geld was nie vir hom bedoel nie, maar God het ons altyd bygestaan en gehelp. Toe ek 3 jaar oud was het ek die Haley's komeet (1910) gesien in die Ooste. 'n Helder ster met 'n geweldige rooi aan. Die jare stap toe aan, ek word groot in armoede, leef net van pap en melk en in 1914 breek die Rebellie uit. Boer teen boer en broer teen broer. Dit was toe Sap en Nat oorlog.

Dit is toe in die tyd dat ons ouers besluit het daar vir ons 'n begins van skool gemaak moet word. Ons loop toe op die plaas rond soos wilde meerkatte, maar ons moes al die plaaswerk behartig. Koeie melk en versorg, die skape versorg en bedags spit ons in die tuin, want my Pa het groente verkoop. Die middag moes ons sorg vir 'n sak vol beesmis vir die kool stoofie om pap mee te kook. Dan kom al die boere se kinders se skooldae. Op die buurman se plaas was 'n ou huis. Vier van ons broers dra toe daardie more elkeen 'n parafien kassie skool toe. Dit was om op te sit. Daar aangekom, staan daar toe 'n tafel, 'n swart bord en 'n kas in die skool. Ons kry toe elkeen 'n lei en 'n griffie om mee te skryf. Boeke en potlode was nog nie daar nie. 'n Mejuffrou Neethling was ons onderwyseres, na ses maande word sy verplaas. Ons loop toe vir 6 maande weer rond op die plaas en intussen gebeur my eerste drama. Ons was besig om koeie te melk. My broer Daan het gemelk en ek het vir Vlêrmuis, met die wit bles, vas gehou met 'n riem. Sy het twee sulke gaffel horings gehad. Toe my broer klaar gemelk het, moes ek haar los maak. Toe vaar die duiwel in haar en sy bevlieg my, steek haar een horing in my broekie in, skeur hom oop van onder tot bo en klowe my middel deur tussen my twee bene.

Ek hol toe huis toe en gaan lê toe op 'n bedjie en die bloed loop vol stroom. My ouers het die middag vir bure gaan kuier met 'n donkiekar. Toe hulle terug kom vertel hulle vir my ouers dat Vlermuis my oop gekloof het. Hulle hardloop die huis binne en kry my in 'n bad bloed. Daar word my Pa toe flou, want hy kon nie mens bloed weerstaan nie. In daardie dae was daar nog nie dokters nie. My Ma het my gedokter met Vaselien. So lê ek toe op my rug vir 17 dae en die wond het toe weer aanmekaar gegroei.

Toe is ek weer skool toe, en 'n Van Schalkwyk was toe ons onderwyser. Ek het meer onder die kweperlat deurgeloop, wou nie leer nie. Na 6 maande word hy ook verplaas en ons loop weer vir 6 maande rond op die plaas. Ons moes maar die span osse dryf en oestyd meilies oes. Al wat plaaswerk was moes ons seuns doen, want daar was nie 'n swartman op die plaas nie. Toe is ons weer terug skooltoe. My niggie, Ann Malan, was toe ons onderwyseres, ook maar net weer vir 6 maande, en toe weer sonder skool. Toe kom daar 'n meneer Momsen as onderwyser. Daar het ek elke dag straf moes uitskryf, en loop maar elke dag deur met die kweperlat. My geleerdheid was net dat ek alles uit die Bybel geleer het. Toe ek 2 weke in standerd 5 was, haal my Pa my uit die skool. Die onderwyser raas en blaas maar my Pa is baas.

Ploegtyd met sweep in die hand dryf ek die osse aan en saai meilies. Toe word ons land met springkane geslaan vir 3 jaar. Baie dae het hulle die son verduister en in 1918 breek daardie vreeslike siekte uit, "Die Griep", wat oor die hele wêreld duisende mense se lewens ge-eis het. Ons familie het gelukkig nie siek geword nie. Ons moes elke dag wilde aalwyn ryt beukes vossie en blougomblare wat gekook was, drink en 'n toelappie met 'n knoffel huisie om die nek dra, dit was om die kieme van ons af te hou.

In dieselfde jaar is ons sussie gebore, maar sy het net 24 dae geleef. Op die foto staan ons by die graffie. Op nommer een sien julle die hele familie, toe was armoede orde van die dag, geen geld of kos nie.

Daarna wyk ons uit na die delwery, op soek na die blink klippies. Ek noem eerste al die plekke waar ons gedelf het, Pitfontein, Omega, Sterkfontein, Bethal, Uanana, Witklip, Elands putte en ten laaste Grasfontein. Daar het ons darem 'n sink huisie gehad, maar al die plekke het ons onder 'n bokwa op graspolle geslaap. Ons het net 'n karrige kombersie oor ons gehad en het pap uit die pot en koffie uit die kan gedrink. Ons koffie het bestaan uit gebrande boersensels en patats. Ek meld hier 'n foto geneem op Grasfontein.

Ons was om en by 3 jaar op die delwery, 6 maande by die huis en 6 maande op die delwery. Daar het ons as kinders al ons gesondheid weg gegooi, kap met pikke en sif die grond en as daar 'n wassie klaar is dan word dit gewas. As daar 'n diamantjie te voorskyn kom, dan gaan die geld net so vir die paaiemente op die plaas en kos en klere vir die familie. Ons seuns het nooit 'n pennie gekry nie.

Ek kom terug na Bethal delwery toe. Die regering het 'n sink gebou opgesit vir skoolgaande kinders, waar ons Sondae kerk gehad het. Daar het 'n klok op paal gehang vir die kerk doeleindes en as die kerk uitkom dan klim ek die paal op en haal die klok af en dra dit 3 myl ver, waar die volgende Sondag se diens dan sal wees. Sommer agter 'n slaghuis. Ek kry dan vir die vervoer van die klok 1 shilling en 'n sikspens en dit het maar hard gegaan om daardie geld by die kolekte bymekaar te kry.

Saterdag middag het ons altyd ons hempie en broekie gewas wat vol modder en sand was, sonder seep. As dit klaar gewas was dan loer ons of daar nie meisie mense naby is nie. Dan hardloop ons kaalbas uit om ons klere op te hang. Wanneer dit droog is dan word dit gelap en stop, tabaksakkies word gebruik om die gate mee toe te stop. Jou broek en hemp is so gestop van lap dat jy naderhand nie weet van watter materiaal dit van gemaak is nie. God dank, ons was altyd geseen met gesondheid en werk kon ons nie onderkry nie.

Nou gaan ek na Grasfontein toe. Die rykste delwery maar net op seker plekke. Toe moes dit gepen word, 6 myl moes ons hardloop deur rowwe veld en uitstaande klippe. Ons was die eerste dag 22 duisend hardlopers van oor die hele wêreld. Toe ou meneer Tool die proklamasie aflees, voordat die vlag val, toe spring daar 'n steenbok op uit die hoe gras en almal hardloop om die bok te vang. Gevolglik was dit 'n vals risiko, toe trek die regering al die penne op. Dit was drie lorries vol en na 14 dae vind die regte risiko toe plaas en was toe in die 40 duisend hardlopers.

Die aarde het gedreun met al die voete op die aarde, toe ons weggespring het. Armoede was baie groot en ons Malan seuns was uithaler hardlopers. My Pa verhuur ons dan aan ander mense vir 5 pond as ons die aangewese plekke pen. By die pennery was daar altyd vuis gevegte want 'n "claim" was 15 x 15 tree groot en elkeen druk sy penne in soos hy goed dink. Dan gebeur dit ook dat 'n ander persoon binne jou "claim" sy pen insteek. Wat dan gedoen ? Hardloop en pluk sy pen uit en gooi dit baie ver weg.

Dit is dan waar die bakleiery plaasvind. Dan na die pennery soek ons dan na 'n oop val stukkie grond waar ons op gaan delf, want ons Pa het daardie 5 pond dringend nodig. Ons kon ryk mense vandag gewees het as daardie "claims" aan ons behoort het.

Daardie middag na die pennery was die aarde onder 'n stofwolk, al wat leef en beef grawe in die aarde en die Jode sit winkels op. Die diamand kopers sit klein huisies op waar hulle elke Vrydag dan diamante koop. Toe word daar groot water tenke op pale opgerig. Water vir die wasmasjiene, en die delwerssit 'n sink of sak huisie op vir hulle families. Alles was maar in gehawende toestand om te sien waar groot families, waar groot meisies ook by was.

Na berekening het hulle met die begin gesê dat daar om en by 40 000 mense daar was, meeste was swartmense, Indiërs, Italianers, Grieke Jode Afrikaaners en Engelse. Al die nasies van die wêreld. Die ou mense wat oud en gedaan was het toe darem 'n wa en donkies gehad waarmee hulle water aangery het vir die masjiene. Dit was vir die arme donkies net hel want hulle moes snags ook in die tuig slaap en sy tuig het bestaan uit 'n buiteband van 'n fiets en doringdraad was die stringe.

Toe kom die lorries in en hulle ry toe die water aan. Gevolglik sit die arme mense met die donkiewaens sonder 'n inkomste, toe was armoede die orde van die dag, ou mense met families. Daar loop toe honderde donkies rond op die delwery. Wat die ou mense toe gedoen het, hulle jaag toe hulle eie donkies 12 myl ver na Lichtenburg se skut en dan kry hy 1 shilling en 'n sikspens vir dryfgeld. Die skut het elke maand 'n veiling gehou. Daar was gevalle dat 12 na 14 donkies vir 2 shillings en 'n sikspens vir die hele trop verkoop was.

Hulle vind toe uit dat daar 'n fout met die water is. Die gesondheids-inspekteur kom toe ondersoek instel en hulle ondek toe in die veertig pasgebore babatjies in daardie water tenke is. Nou kan julle self dink in watter soort van 'n lewe ons ons bevind het. In die middag gaan soek ons in die veld rond na donkie mis om ons pap water mee te kook. Die pap het behoorlik na donkie mis geruik ! Mag die liewe Vader help dat daar nooit weer so 'n delwery kom nie.

Toe ons stukkie grond uitgewerk was het ons gaan pik slaan op 'n bankbestuurder se grond, waarvoor ons 1 pond per week gekry het. Dit het toe gehelp dat ons toe vir onsself skoene en klere kon koop, en 'n fiets. Toe sy grond uitgewerk was, het ons koers gevat huiswaards, want daardie lewe kon ons nie meer staan nie. Die armoede en ellende was te veel en kon dit nie meer aanskou nie.

Op die plaas het ons maar weer elke dag se roetine gewerk, en nogmaals gewerk. Ons Pa sê toe dat ons 'n blaas orkes moet koop en ons bestel toe die instrumente vanaf Duitsland (kyk foto nommer 3)   Daar is 6 broers, 'n meneer Wrogeman, ons leier, en 'n meneer Bosman.

Toe duik daar weer nuwe dinge op. My Pa sê toe ons broers moet bymekaar bly en die plaas van 310 morge is te klein. Hy soek toe groter grond. Ek en my Pa klim toe die trein na Suidwes Afrika (Namibia) toe. 'n Meneer Rautenbach kry ons toe op die stasie, Okasiesie, en ons laat vat na die groot plaas. Foto is geneem op die plaas en net daar besluit my Pa dat ek daar moet bly om daardie land se maniere te leer. Ek was toe 'n mannetjie wat al verloof was. Foto is Grootrivier by Upington waar die treinspoor oorloop. Ek het daar vir die twee oumense gewerk. Vir 'n ronde jaar het ek 12 000 hektaar draad gespan. Ek het toe 'n klompie koeie en bokke gekoop en verkoop. Elke Saterdag op Omoeroevo 'n paar pond botter verkoop vir sakgeld en intussen kry my Pa nie sy grond verkoop nie.

Upington - Die oumense kom toe in opstand teen my en vloek my uit net omdat my Pa nie kon koop nie. Ek vat toe die trein terug huistoe, want in daardie jaar het ek geen jongmense gesien nie. By die huis gekom, kry ek werk by 'n meneer Voorendyk vir 10 shillings 'n maand en 'n deel uit die oes. Dit is toe trousiekte my byt.

Ek koop to 'n No. 7 Dover koolstofie, 'n tafel, 3 stoele en 'n dubbel bed, 'n perde karretjie en 'n paar stukkies eetgereedskap. Ek kon nie meer koop nie, want die geld was so skaars soos hoender tande en op die 20ste Desember 1932 staan ons twee voor die preekstoel. Na die troue is ons reguit plaas toe, en daardie eerste nag sal ek nooit vergeet nie. Die nag toe ek wakker word sien ek die kers brand en julle Ma sit en lees uit die Bybel. Die helder trane loop oor haar wange. Die rede daarvoor was dat sy in so 'n huis moes instap met daardie karrige ou huisraadjies waarmee ons begin het.

Ek kry toe darem 'n verhoging tot 1 pond en 5 shillings per maand. Intussen plant ek meilies en kyk na die geregistreede Afrikaner beeste. Om alles te kroon kom ou Voorendyk met sy hele familie daar aan en dan bly hulle maklik agt dae daar. Hulle bring toe niks kos saam nie en eet ons bietjie kos op. Net voor hy ry, gooi hy 2 shillings en sikspens op die tafel, dis nou vir al die kos wat hulle ge-eet het!

Toe my mielies in die saad kom, was dit 'n bietjie droogte en ou Voorendyk maak die hekke oop en jaag al sy beeste in my mielies in. Dit het toe met 'n groot woorde wisseling beteken dat ek weer in die wa-pad was. Ek haal net hier aan dat julle Ma toe 'n miskraam gehad het, en was dit 'n gesukkel om haar in Lichtenburg te kry. 'n Meneer Smit het ons gehelp en dit is toe dat ek by hom gaan boer het. Ook net vir 'n jaar, want sy seun kom toe boer.

Voor ons troue het ek op 'n ander plaas van meneer Voorendyk gewerk om 'n deel uit die oes en 10 shillings per maand te kry. My huisie was 'n sink huisie. Ek eet die pap uit die pot en koffie uit die ketel, sonder enige byvoegsels. As ek soggens lande toe gaan, hang ek my klere aan die windpomp se pyp waar die water uitloop. Dit was my manier van klere was, die windpomp doen die waswerk. Daar eindig my storie met meneer Voorendyk.

Ek het 'n spannetjie osse, 'n ploeg en 'n eg gehad. Daarmee ploeg en boer ons op Rietgat, 8 myl vanaf Lichtenburg. Ek het 'n redelike oes daardie jaar gewen en ons trek toe na my ouers toe. Ek bou toe 'n vertrek huisie en ploeg op die aangrensende plaas om 'n deel, maar intussen kry my Pa weer in sy kop om 'n groot plaas te koop. Ons hele familie vat toe eendag die pad na die Molopo (foto nommer 10 dui aan waar ons by 'n droe kameelboom staan). Weinig het ek geweet wat daar vir ons voorle. My Pa koop toe 'n plaas 10 000 morg groot sonder water. Ons moes toe klaarmaak vir die groot trek. Lettie is toe ook intussen gebore. Ek bou toe vir my 'n motorwiel wa en koop 10 Spanse donkies en verkoop al my ploeg gereedskap en ruil die osse vir aanteel beeste. Dit was toe die jaar 1936 waar die groot trek toe plaasvind. Ek laai die karrige huisraad op die waentjie en die hoender en hans skaaplam kom toe saam.

Die vroumense bly toe eers agter, want ons moes toe eers trek en hulle sal later gehaal word. Ek gee toe vir julle Ma 2 shillings en 6 pennies, en ek hou 1 shilling en 6 pennies vir myself. Dit was ons rykdom. So val ons toe in die land van melk en heuning soos hulle gesê het. Ons trek toe ses dae met die beeste en ek met die donkiewa. Ek weet nie eers waar ons gaan beland nie, want op die plaas moet nog eers geboor word.

Die Molopo het daardie jaar goed reen gehad en daar was groot kuile water. Ons stop toe by die eerste kuil en maak krale. Ek kap toe pale om 10 - 10 voet plate op te spyker en die mure maak ek toe met polmiet, 'n soort riet. Ja, dit was die begin van ons smarte. Mens en dier drink die kuile se water wat wemel van larwes en dat ons daar nie maagkoors en malaria opgedoen het nie, was net aan Gods bestuuring.

Ek voeg hier 'n teksie by wat toepassing is -

"Wanneer ek moeg en tam is, is my gemoed vol kommer.
Waneer die daaglikse probleme my gemoed versober, wanneer
kul wat die naaste moet wees.
Voel soos mense onbekend,
is daar een na wie ek my altyd wend.
Ek weet God is naby my."

Ons het nie lank by die kuil gestaan nie, toe is die water al gedaan. Weer is ons oppad na 'n ander kuil toe. Ek onthou nog alles baie goed. My eerste room tjekie was 1 shilling en 'n sikspens. Nou vra julle my hoe moet ek 'n huis met daardie geld onderhou en nog die swartman daaruit betaal? Toe daardie kuil ook droog is, trek ons verder na die plaas Wargrove, slaan huis op en gaan maar aan. Ons kan toe nog nie die donker kant van die lewe aanvaar nie.

Intussen word julle Ma se Pa siek in Lichtenburg aan maag kanker en ons moes gaan hand bysit. Ek kry toe werk in die meule vir 10 pond per maand, ek moes opdok vir die huis se kos en intussen is julle Ma geopereer vir blindederm. Gerta is toe ook intussen gebore en was omtrent 6 maande oud toe my Skoonpa oorlede is. Na die begrafnis is ons weer terug en ons trek toe na 'n meneer Barnard se plaas met 'n groot kuil water. Weer die ou roetine, huis opsit en aangaan met die lewe.

Daarna trek ons na Bray, slaan pondokkie op en moes wag vir 'n boor masjien. Toe die boor masjien arriveer, klim ek op my ou waentjie en donkies om hout aan te ry vir die stoom boor. Dit was 24 myl na die plaas toe. Ek laat julle Ma en 2 kinders agter, wat hulle elke dag ge-eet het weet ek nie, God weet alleen. Wanneer ek nie kan begryp nie, wanneer dit lyk as of niks en niemand die lewe kan beheer nie, wanneer ons beste pogings faal en ons staan daar gestroop en kaal sal die wete altyd by my bly. Ek weet God is naby my.

Ek en 2 van my broers is by die boor. Een broer gee water aan vir die stoom ketel, ek ry hout aan en saam met my swartman en my een broer kap die hout stukkend vir die boor masjien. Ek en vrou en twee kinders is toe al ses maande van mekaar af weg en al wat kom is water in die boorgat wat al 500 voet in die harde rots geboor is.

Toe een môre gebeur die tragieste ding in my lewe. Nou kon julle self dink hoe moes ek gevoel het. My Pa kom toe daar aan, kry my oppad met 'n vrag hout en sê vir my ek kan maar die hout afgooi, hy het handdoek ingegooi. Sy geld is gedaan en hy het die groot plaas terug gegee.

"Wanneer die skemer daal en ek die nag moet ingaan, weet ek seker dat ek ookal gaan. Daarom leef ek gelukkig en bly, want God is naby my."

'n Meneer Lawia het toe 7 myl verder geboor en toe water gekry. Ek kon toe by hom water kry vir die diere, maar ek sit toe 'n grasdakkiehuisie by die droe boorgat op en ek gaan haal my diere en familie. Sien geen mens of kraai nie maar almal is gesond en sterk. Ons boer in die lewe net vorentoe. Toe trek ons na meneer Lawia toe om nader aan die water te wees, laai die grasdakhuisie op my wa; en sit hom op pale en pleister die hout toe met mis en klei. Ons lewens was altyd in God se hande.

"Waar ons ookal daal en dwaal, verbreek niks my liede bande, maar ons geloof moet sterk wees, dan staan ons nooit alleen. Van Sy liefde wat alles vermag, is ons nooit vervreem. Wanneer al die kommer en sorge te veel word vir jou. Krag by Hom is hoop en nuwe moed. God is met jou elke dag."

Op 'n goeie aand kom meneer Wills daaraan, die eienaar van die meule wat ek in gewerk het in Lichtenburg, en hy sê toe dat ek vir hom moet kom boer. Ek kon my koeie melk en my roomgeld is myne. Ek moes na sy melkery omsien en is toe 10 pond per maand betaal.

Ek groet my vrou en kinders en hy neem my na Lichtenburg waar ek 'n trop beeste by die 300 en 7 perde en 'n pak-donkie moet af trek na sy plaas, 28 myl anderkant Bray. Dit was 'n bitter trek en snags moet die diere opgepas word. Daar het net een nag 'n donder storm op ons los gebars. Die vreeslikste donder slae. Ek het my in my ou seiltjie toe gedraai en die stormwater het al om my gespoel. Ons mieliemeel was pap nat, gevolglik was ons toe sonder kos. Ek het toe maar, toe ons by die plaas aankom. 'n stukkie brood en meel gebedel, tussen my en 3 swartmanne. Ons was 14 dae op die pad. Ek onthou nog goed, ons het op Kersdag met die trek beeste in Lichtenburg begin.

Ons land toe veilig daar aan en julle Ma en die kinders was toe al reeds daar. Hulle het met die donkie waentjie getrek. Ons bou toe 'n paal huisie, waar die mure met mis en klei toe gepleister was. Toe word daar geboor en oor die 400 voet kry ons toe water. Die stene word toe gemaak en 'n huis word gebou. Dit was toe die eerste keer wat ons toe in 'n ordentelike huis kon in trek. Maar voor ons in getrek het, nog in die paal huisie kry julle Ma toe malaria en al die volk. Ek moes toe elke dag die 40 koeie alleen melk. Een kaffir se vrou is toe aan die koors dood. 12 uur het ek dan klaar gemelk en dan gaan versorg ek vir julle Ma en die twee kinders.

En sy het die dood in die oe gestaar. Dan gaan room ek die melk, was die roomafskeier en kom vier uur eers in die huis. Toe wonder ek baie dae of ek die regte ding aangevang het, want toe begin die druk my swaar kry.

Maar toe leef ons op die nuwe plek baie lekker. Dit gaan toe alles voor die wind. Op die plaas was om en by 1600 osse en oor die 300 koeie wat elke môre gemelk moes word. Het toe 17 kaffirs onder my gehad en ek het elke môre self die roomer gedraai. Twee na drie en twintig 5 gallon kanne room - onthou dit was nie my room nie, dit was Mnr Wills sin - myne was maar om en by 1 gallon room. Daarvoor het ons huis benodighede gekoop en met die 10 pond koop ek beeste voor.

Dit was toe in die jaar 1938 toe die groot wereld oorlog uit gebreek het. Maar die boerdery gaan nog sy gang en dit is waar Lettie by 'n Mnr Labeshagne begin skool gaan het.

Ek kom terug na 1937 toe ons nog in die paal huisie gebly het. Toe het my vrou verwag en Mnr Wills neem haar na Lichtenburg vir die bevalling. Ek bly agter om toe te sien na die boerdery toe kry ek 'n blindederm aanval en die ou baas jaag met my na Lichtenburg. Ek is toe geopereer en daardie dae moes 'n mens 14 dae op sy rug bly lê.

Die dag toe ek uit kom toe is dit julle Ma wat geboorte moet gee. Kry die vroedvrou in en daar gebeur dit dat sy die kindjie se nekkie gebreek het - gevolglik het ons kindjie nooit die lig gesien nie. Dit was 1 Augustus 1937. Ek gaan toe terug plaas toe na die nuwe huis.

Rusthof was die plaas se naam en daar kry ek malaria. Daar was 'n kleurling met sy gesin op die plaas en sy vrou het bedags vir my sop gemaak wat ek kon eet. Toe hoor julle Ma van my siekte en sy kom toe eendag daaraan. Ek is toe nog in die bed maar ek het darem herstel.

Toe breek die Wereld 1938 se oorlog uit.

Die boerdery gaan maar aan en ek werk soos 'n slaaf, niks kom my breek of onder kry nie en ek kon nie moeg word nie. In 1942 breek die droogte uit. Tussen my en meneer Wills het daar om en by 600 beeste gevrek en op die 7de Februarie kry ons die eerste reën. Al die varke het gevrek want daar was nie melk nie. Ons het toe nie eers koffie melk nie.

Toe laat my swaer Tom Muller vir my weet dat hy vir my 'n model A Ford karretjie wat 80 pond sal kos. Ek vra toe vir meneer Wills 4 dae verlof om die karretjie te gaan haal. Op die vierde aand arriveer ons op die plaas en meneer Wills kom toe die volgende môre daar aan - ek ontmoet hom toe in die kraal - en dit is toe net daar dat hy vir my sê ek moet die einde van die maand die plaas verlaat! Met geen rede nie! Ek sê toe net "Baie dankie".

Twee dae later kom hy daar aan en hy sê my hy is baie spyt wat hy gedoen het ; ek kan maar nog aan bly. Toe sê ek vir hom "Gaan vra vir my vrou". Hy sê toe dat hy baie spyt is en dit is toe julle Ma vir hom sê dat ek vir hom as 'n slaaf 4 jaar gewerk het en nooit was daar vir my een dag verlof gegin nie en net hierdie vier dae om 'n karretjie te gaan haal steek jy my man soos 'n kaffir in die pad ! Julle Ma sê toe "Dankie, ons trek".

Al weer in die pad - sal daar dan nie 'n einde aan kom nie? Dit lyk al behoorlik of daar "TREK" op my voorkop geskrywe staan !

Ons kry toe plek by 'n meneer Sarel Naude. Die plaas se naam is "Bega". Nou kan my kinders saam met my begin dink van al ons daarop volgende trek jare. Ons trek toe in 'n grasdak huis met paal muure wat toe gepleister is met mis en klei. Dit was toe in die jaar 1943.

My een broer Daan en meneer Roth het toe 'n plaas gekoop waarop my een broer Frikkie waar geneem het. Een aand kom een van sy werksvolk daar aan gehardloop om en by 14 myl van waar ons bly en hy kom toe sê dat my broer skierlik dood is. Ons jaag toe soentoe en ek en 'n meneer Hyser lê hom toe uit en ek jaag toe 7 myl daar vandaan na die naaste telefoon om my ouers en broers in Lichtenburg te vertel. En was dit 'n gesukkel om petrol koepons in die hande te kry - want dit was in die hartjie van die oorlog !

Na twee dae kom die lykswa daar aan en ons gaan agterna vir die begafnis in die distrik van Lichtenburg. Toe kom my broer Daan na my toe en vra toe dat ek moet by kom oorneem op sy plaas "Crowa".

Al weer trek ! Gelukkig het ek nog murg in my liggaam gehad wat nog nie gekrak was nie. Daar aan gekom , bou 'n nuwe huis en boer voorentoe. Lettie en Gerta was toe op Vergeleegen in die skool, maar daar kon Gerta nie aanpas nie. Eindelaaste na Lichtenburg se skool en hulle woon in by julle Ma se Ma. Intussen is Hendrik gebore en alles gaan toe voorspoedig.

My buurman Flip Swart en ek jag toe hyeanas, 'n gevaarlike dier want hy het die sterkste kaake van al die wilde diere. Ons vang hulle met kaal hande. Een is gestuur na Johannesburg se dieretuin en een na Pretoria sin. Een is op die werf dood deur beseerings. Een more kom my kaffir daar aan en vertel my dat die wilde honde onder my kalwers maai. Ek jaag toe daar na toe reg in die bedding van die Molopo Rivier - daar skiet ek toe sewetien kalwers dood want hulle was vreeslik verskeur. My koeie het destyds in die Protektoraat gewei en dan het dit verskeie keere koeie kraal toe gekom waar van die hele maag af geskeur is of die derms sleep agter die dier uit geplok is deur die wilde honde.

In tussen verkoop my broer sy deel van sy plaas aan meneer Roth. Ek meld hier die tweeling was al daar (Flip en Rina). Toe kom meneer Roth se skoonseun en hy se hy kom nou boer - ek moet vir my 'n ander plek soek - al weer trek! Ek koop toe 'n 10 morg plot in Vanderbylpark. Sal maar in een van die fabrieke gaan werk soek. In Lichtenburg huur ek 'n huis en ek koop toe 'n boormasjien. Intussen verkoop ek al my diere 179 in getal vir 'n bedrag van 900 pond (vandag betaal ons vir een bees daardie geld!).

Ek begin toe boor maar as daar 'n ding is waar jy onder die brood lyn leef is om 'n lewe uit 'n boormajien te maak. Ek boor een gat en dan weer vir drie maande wag voordat weer 'n gat gestamp word. Ek sit toe vir ons 'n groot sink huis op die plot op en ons verkas soentoe. Lettie in die Tegniese skool en Gerta en Hendrik in die Laer skool. Ja, in tussen is Frans toe ook gebore in Lichtenburg.

Ek kry toe werk in Vecor in die fabriek. Kry 3 shillings en 6 pennies per uur. Toe kom daar 'n Jood by my en sê ek moet vir hom kom boer. Hy gaan nege duisende hoenders aan hou en ek kry 'n deel. Dinge klink toe baie belowend en ek gee my job op - en ons trek al weer.

Daar aan gekom was daar in die 50 hoenders en elke weekend kom sy vriende daar aan en dan word daar hoenders geslag. Toe die hoenders klaar is toe sê die jood dat hy bankrot is - ek moet loop. Al weer terug trek na die sink huis en soek werk, wat maar nie gekry kan word nie.

Toe kry my famielie vir my werk by 'n engineering werke. Al weer trek na Lichtenburg, huur 'n huis in Burgersdorp en ek begin werk teen 10 pond per week. Dit was nie 'n honderd jaar toe daag daar 'n meneer Nic Maree op en hy vra of ek nie vir hom wil kom boer op Bega waar ek alreeds was. Ek val vir die aanbod en ons trek al weer. Daar aangekom het ons nie eers kos om te eet nie. Daar was baie tortel duiwe - dan stel ek 'n wip en ons vang en slag die duiwe vir 'n bietjie vleis vir die ligaam. Elke trek beland ons in armoede!

Ek gaan nou 'n paar jaar terug. Dit val my nou by in daardie drama moet julle weet. Toe op soek na water was in die bulte. Toe gee julle Ma een more die wasgoed vir die meid om te gaan was waar sy besig was om water warem te maak. Al die wasgoed was in 'n hemp gestop. Terwyl sy die roomer was kom daar 'n werdwaalde windjie en gooi 'n flammetjie op die hemp. Toe alles uit gebrand het sien sy dit eers. Julle Ma, Lettie en ek het net die klere aan ons bas. Toe kom my oudste broer daaraan en deur jammerte loop die trane oor sy wange. Hy gee vir julle Ma 10 shillings en sê dit is al wat hy het - sy moet maar 'n rokkie vir Lettie koop.

Kinders, ek getuig voor die Aller hoogste dat alles in hierdie boek waar is. En dit is nog nie die einde nie want ons lewe lê nog voor.

Ons is weer terug op Bega. Oom Nic Maree leen my 400 pond om beeste te koop en ek kon toe darem weer room verkoop.

Intussen is Nic en Lettie getroud, Gerta werk op Gerdou in die kooperasie en Hendrik, Flip en Rina is in die koshuis op Bray. Ek kry toe maag koors en worstel met die dood. Die dokter het nie vir my hoop gehad nie, maar deur die genade herstel ek. Maar toe was al my tande los in my mond en ek laat toe die hele klomp uit trek.

Toe vreet die hyeanas my kalwers op. Gelukkig het ek hom dood geskiet.

Op 'n goeie dag daag daar 'n meneer Bester en Oom Erens Kruger daar aan en net daar praat Oom Erens en ek oor Rhodesia - en dat ek vir hom moet kom boer. En was dit 'n gesukkel om al ons immegrasie papiere in orde te kry, want Bega en Pretoria was vêr van mekaar. Alles het net deur briewe plaas gevind.

Toe alles in orde was vertel ek vir Oom Nic Maree my storie. Hy het behoorlik gehuil soos 'n kind. Toe kry ek 'n meneer Nel se lorrie om my trek deur te vat en dit beteken ons trek al weer. Ons slaap die eerste nag in Mafeking, die tweede nag in Ventersdorp, die derde nag by Potgietersrus, die vierde nag op Beitbrug en die vyfde nag by Oom Erens Kruger se plaas.

Nou kom boer ek met tabak en al wat ek van tabakboerdery weet is om dit te rook ! Maar ek valkard in die onderneming. Die drie kinders is op Chatsworth in die skool. Toe verskuif ons hulle na Andrew Louw skool waar Frans fice begin skool gaan.

Intussen doen ek balharsia op wat net iets vreeslik is, en daar na kry ek 'n kwaadaardige gewas op my oor. Ek jaag toe na Kroonstad om dit te laat uittrek. En nie lank daarna nie weer een aan my nek - weer jaag ek na Kroonstad.

Ons boer toe lekker en ek koop toe vir my 'n trekker en ander gereedskap. Na ses jaar toe kom Oom Erens se skoonseun vir my sê hy wil nou kom boer en ek moet vir my 'n ander plek soek. Maar intussen is Hansie en Gerta getroud en ek huur toe 'n plaas by 'n meneer Manie Venter.

Ons trek al weer - na Kombisa - en die kinders gaan toe in Gwelo skool. Ek kry toe 100 koeie by die koelkamers en dit was my redding gewees want die tabak het elke keer 'n siekte op getel dat daar maar 'n karige oes tevoorskyn. Dit het so vir twee jaar aangehou toe trek ons al weer na 'n meneer Danie Nel se plaas en daar trek die pes my tabak weer by. Ek verkoop maar my jong kalwers om aan die lewe te bly en die Land Bank wil my net elke dag uitverkoop.

Dit gaan toe weer bitter swaar want om 4 kinders in die koshuis te onderhou vra net geld en waar kom dit vandaan ? Dit was toe daardie tyd dat Frans hom in die oog geskiet het met 'n windbiks.

Ons trek toe al weer na Trickling Waters op 'n meneer Kashula se plaas maar dinge wou nie uit werk nie. Ek moes kom 25% van die oes af gee en 790 rente vir die Landbank op my kunsmus. Flip en Rina kry toe werk by die koelkamers en Frans nog op die skool.

Ek was net 'n jaar daar toe kry ek werk by 'n meneer Burger in Chiredzi teen 20 pond per week. Dit wil sê ons trek toe al weer en ek gee al my gereedskap vir Hansie, en daar gaan ons. Ons staan in 'n karavaan tussen die hoope steene - eet meer sement en sand as kos ! Toe gee die Ou Baas vir ons 'n huis en hy stuur 'n lorrie om ons huisraad te gaan laai.

Intussen kry Flip werk in die suiker meule en Rina by N.Richards en Hendrik flenter rond van plek tot plek. Daar kon ek toe my agter stalige skulde afbetaal en dit is toe dat Pey en Rina getrou het en vestig hulle in Gwelo waar hulle vir Frans vry losies gegee het. Toe Frans sy skool loopbaan voltooi het kom werk hy in die Standard Bank in Chiredzi en loeseer by ons in die huis. Na vier jaar by meneer Burger was Chiredzi feitlik klaar op gebou en daar was nie meer opset vir stene nie.

Ek werk toe die ou se bou dedryf en ek moes op Chisembanzi gaan sement blokke maak vir Roberts Construction. Toe dit klaar is het ek na Chipinga gaan water kanale maak en toe dit klaar is toe moes ek weer die hase pad vat. Ek kry toe 'n plaas by meneer Ferreira waar ek koeie kon aankoop en room stuur vir 'n inkomste. Dit het toe al moeiliker geword en die geldjies gedaan.

Toe koop Nic 'n plaasie in die distrik Beatrice en ek trek toe al weer met my paar goedtjies. Koop 'n ou trekker en planter en plant meilies en stuur 'n bietjie room weg. Toe word julle Ma baie siek en beland in die hospitaal vir amper 4 maande. Kon net nie uitvind wat sy mekeer nie en sy stry met die dood. Uiteidelik vind hulle uit dat dit 'n vreemde virus in haar bloed was. Ek kry toe 'n kwaad aardige gewas bo op my hand en moes toe die ding toe ook laat verwyder.

Ek knap die huis mooi op - sit 'n varanda op, pleister buite af, bou 'n kombuis aan en ek sit die hele huisplafonne in. Na alles klaar was toe verkoop Nic die plaas aan 'n meneer Rassie De Klerk. Al weer trek , verkoop my skape en die paar koeie en ons trek na meneer Hannes Jacobs toe in 'n groot huis met 'n grasdak.

Daar bly ons toe baie lekker. Die twee mense was dierbaar - ons betaal nie eers krag nie en hulle hou ons yskas vol vleis - alles verniet. Ons sal hulle prys so lank as wat ons leef.

Intussen verplaas die bank vir Frans na Fort Victoria en Marendellas en toe na Salisbury. Toe breek die terroriste oorlog uit. Flip, Frans, Pey en Hansie is in die bos, hulle lewe was elke dag in gevaar en ons het net elke dag gevrees dat hulle die grasdak in die brand kan steek. Gevolglik dit was maar net 'n senuwee lewe. Ons het net altyd gebid vir veiligheid in die bos.

Kinders, my storie gaan nou ten einde - en die boek is nog nie vol nie ! Nou kan julle ook pratse en snaakse dinge wat intussen gebeur het ook in hierdie boek skryf wat ons famielie lewe baie intersant kan maak.

In tussen het Flip en Elcora getrek na Groblersdal. Hy en sy stief Pa boer toe saam maar daar wou dinge ook nie uit werk nie. Hy kry toe 'n heenkoome by meneer Kobus de Villiers, en dit is toe dat hulle besluit dat ons na hulle toe moet trek. So gesê, so gedoen. Ons kry al ons immegrasie papiere in orde en hulle kry meneer de Villiers se lorrie om ons trek te kom haal. Gevolglik verkoop ons een derde van ons meubels en ons trek al weer.

Sal daar dan nooit 'n einde aan trek kom nie ? Ons was nie lank daar dat meneer de Villiers vir Flip se dat hy sy dienste nie meer nodig het nie. Gelukkig het Flip 'n goeie vriend gehad - Chris Cordier - en hy werk toe in Matubatuba se suiker meule en Flip kontak hom dat hy vir hom moet uitkyk vir 'n job. Dit gebeur toe dat Flip toe daar geholpe raak.

Ons verkoop toe weer een derde van ons huis raad so dat beide van ons ons huisraad in die vervoer wa kon gaan. Ja, en daar trek ons al weer. Daar aangekom en ons woon in by die kinders.

Na 'n ruk trek ons in by Chris Cordier en sy vrou en ons doen aansoek by die Regering vir pension. Ek boer by die magistraat en Predekant maar al wat gehelp word is ons. Julle Ma word toe baie siek en ons besluit toe om by oorleede Willie Naude gaan kuier - goeie vriende van Vanderbyl se dae.

Hulle bly toe by die monding van die Toegela Rivier. Daar word julle Ma baie siek en ons roep toe vir Dr Chirts in en hy sê toe dat dit brongietes en inflamasie is. Ons het hom twee maal laat in roep. Willie en Janette was baie goed vir ons - ons sit toe gehawend sonder 'n pennie maar ons bly by hulle gratis want hulle wil niks hê nie.

Lettie het vir ons telke maale geld gestuur van af Port Elizabeth. Oorlede Wilie werk toe en ek loop maar bedags langs die strand met 'n vis stok. In die drie maande het ek net een ou vissie gevang ! Julle Ma het toe herstel en ons besluit toe om weer terug te gaan na die Cordiers toe. Ons was daar om en by een maand toe bel die Posmeesteres een middag en sê my sy wil my sien.

Daar aan gekom deel sy my mee dat ons twee ou mense se pension is toe gestaan. Nou dink ons vinnig om ons eie sit plekkie te bekom en daar in dan besluit ons gaan terug na Lichtenburg. Bestel toe 'n pak wa en ons laai ons meubels en ons val in die lang pad. Al weer trek na Lichtenburg - hier waar ek gebore is, gedoop is, aangeneem is, getroud is, al ons kinders is hier gebore en gedoop is en Lettie is hier getroud. Ek voeg hier by dat dit ons voorspoedigste jare van ons lewe was.

Want die regeering sorg vir ons kan ons darem die huis rente betaal, die krag en water, die telefoon en kos en petrol vir die kerk. Dit gaan van maand tot maand so aan tot alles klaar betaal is dan is ons platsak ; maar God dank ons kry die geld om by alles by te kom. Ons het die 28 ste Oktober hier in getrek en julle Ma en ek werk nog soos esels.

Maar daar was gedurig 'n pyn in my sei dan sê ek altyd vir julle Ma ek sweer hulle het my blinde derm nie uit gehaal nie. Maar toe tref die grootste teleurstelling vir my. Ons armoede en al die trekery was nie so 'n groot slag wat vir my getref het (ek meld net hier dat ons op hierdie stadium al 31 keer getrek het) en ons het gedink dat dit die einde van ons trek jaare is maar nou het daar weer 'n nuwe ding voor 'n dag ge kom dat ons dalk weer sal moet trek. Waar gaan ons met al ons huisraad herberg kry ?

Kinders my storie loop ten einde en as julle dink dat dit die moeite sal werd wees om alles te boekstaaf - so nie gooi die boek in die as emmer. As daar dinge by julle sal byval wat gebeur het toe julle nog saam in die huis was, dan meld julle dit in hierdie boek. Wat my betref, daar is baie dinge wat met ons gebeur het wat ek na 80 jaar nie kan byval nie.

Nou kom die vreeslikste slag in my lewe wat ek tot vandag nie kan aan pas nie. Op die dag van die elfde Oktober het Hansie my na Klerksdorp se hospitaal geneem vir 'n ondersoek. Daar ondersoek Dr Jooste my en daar hoor ek by hom wat 'n verwronge mens laat word het – hy meld toe dat ek kanker in my prostaatklier het en dat hulle niks daaraan kan doen nie. Dit kan nie verwyder word nie, ek moes toe 'n klein operasietjie ondergaan waar hy my verseker het dat dit sal veroorsaak dat dit nie verder sal versprei.

Maar elke derde trek hulle van my bloed, elke keer was die antwoord konstant. Maar die laaste verslag het hulle my gesê dat dit nou besig is om in my heupe en lewer besig is om te versprei. Kinders hier sit ek elke dag geknak en vol pyne dag en nag. Mag God my genaadig wees en krag gee om hierdie stryd te kan weerstaan.

Francois Daniel Malan
Aletta Magdalena Susanna Malan

Ek verwys na No 1 foto wat my bygeval het wat vergeete gebly het. Ek noem hier my ouers en broers se name en geboortes en sterf syfer aan.

My Pa: Gebore 14 de Desember 1878, en het 83 jaar oud geword (oorlede 29 Mei 1959).
My Ma: Gebore 5 de February 1883, en het 72 68 jaar oud geword (oorlede 6 Aug 1951).

Nou kom ek by al my broers van oud tot jonk :-
Hendrik Francois - Gebore 16 February April 1904 oorlede 6 Augustus 1960
Frederik Jackobus - Gebore 27 Julie 1905 oorlede 20 Augutus1943
Daniel Stefanus - Gebore 13 Augustus 1906 oorlede 4 Aug September 1982
Francois Daniel - Gebore 2 Oktober 1907 oorlede April 1988
Willem Stefanus - Gebore 13 Oktober 1908 oorlede 9 Maart 1975
David Johannes Jakob - Gebore 28 Oktober 1910 oorlede 9 April 1984
Gert Johannes - Gebore 16 April 1912 toe laating
Jacobus Bernandus- Gebore 15 Augustus 1916 oorlede 20 Maart 1981
Heila Magdalena - Gebore 11 Julie 1918 oorlede 7 Augustus1918
Felix Festus - Gebore 29 Maart 1920 toe laating
Gideon Van Eeden - Gebore 26 Oktober 1924 toe laaste.

Julle sal merk dat daar maar min maande verskil is met al ons geboortes (Pey voeg by - daar was nie TV in daardie dae nie!)

Dan wil ek hier in melt van ons feisel wat die krure mee gestamp was - in 'n kanon koel se dop wat in die Eerste Wereld Oorlog gebruik was. In die stamper is 'n pen wat trokke se buffers aan mekaar hou. Die kind wat dit eendag gaan neem moet dit met goud laat oorblaas vir 'n ornament in die huis.

En ek melt hier die hoorlosie gaan na Frans toe - dit bly in die stam naam. Die Horlosie is op vandag se datem 28 January 1987 al 44 jaar in ons besit. Die ouderdom kon nie vasgestel word nie , maar kennise meen dat hy al 'n paar honderd jaar oud is."
(Written by F.D. Malan – 28th January 1987),

One year later, he died. Francois Daniel Malan, born 2 October 1907, died 3rd April 1988, at the age of 80 years and six months

The whole of his family was at his bedside in the Vereeniging hospital when he died of heart failure. His funeral service was conducted by Dominee JJ Redelinghyus in the Ned. Geref. Kerk Herman Steyn. Coffin bearers were Boet Malan, Phil Malan, Frans Malan, Nic van Aardt, Pey Geldenhuys and Johan Bezuidenhout. He was buried in the cemetery outside Vereeniging.

benevolence towards his ailing parents. Not only did Frans attend to their accommodation and survival needs, but also faced with the un-envious task of burying both parents.

Preller is indebted to Frans for supplying the Malan Genealogy and in no small measure for embarking on this family heritage.

Malan, Francois Daniel (born Lichtenburg 7th February 1949), soldier, banker, scrap dealer, auctioneer and businessman. Youngest son of Franscois Daniel Malan (190-198) and Aletta Magdalena Susanna le Poux. Elder sister "Rina" married Preller Matt Geldenhuys.

Frans was schooled at Thornhill High in Gwelo and joined the Standard Bank. Despite frequent Army call-ups during the Rhodesian War, he progressed rapidly to become the Branch Manager at Chipinga. Frans also gained rapid and justifiable promotion in the Rhodesian Territorial Force Army, rising to Company Commander. In this capacity, he was called up for up to 230 days, out of 365, for active service.

He married Helena Alberta Lock in Enkeldorn, on 5th February 1972, and they had two children – a natural athlete Amanda, on 13th April 1974, and Francois Daniel on 24th December 1976. Amanda was born in Fort Victoria and Francois at Salisbury. Frans immigrated to South Africa and became the Financial Director of a metal dealer in Meyerton. His kindred are indebted for his

Malan, Francois Daniel (born Salisbury 12th February 1976), ninth generation Malan, son of Frans(cois) Daniel and Helena Alberta Lock, married Adele du Plessis on the 8th May 1999 in Vereeniging.

Malan, Francois Stephanus (born Bovlei, near Wellington, 12th March 1871 - died Cape Town, 31st December 1941), editor, politician and cabinet minister, was the second child of Daniel Gerhardus Malan (20th October 1848 – 21st July 1926), a teacher who became a farmer at Dal Josafat, and Elizabeth Johanna Malan (20.10.1848 – 21.7.1926). Malan was therefore of Huguenot descent on both sides: his parents were the fifth and sixth generation, respectively, of Huguenot refugee, Jacques Malan, who arrived in South Africa in 1689.

Of the fourteen children in the family only seven reached maturity. In 1874 the family moved from Dal Josafat to the farm, Leeuwenjacht, in Agter-Paarl South. Malan was educated at a farm school and matriculated at the boys' high school in 1889. In 1892 he obtained a BA degree in mathematics and science at Stellenbosch, followed by a LL.B degree at Cambridge. On 1.8.1895 he was admitted to the Cape bar as an advocate but in November took on the editorship of Ons Land – the mouthpiece of the Afrikaner Bond.

In September 1897 he married Johanna Brummer (died 1926). They had two sons and two daughters. In 1928 he married his second wife, Anna Elizabeth Attwell (died 1967), a sister of his first wife.

In 1900 Malan was elected unopposed as Malmesbury Member of the Legislative Assembly and prime minister of the Cape, without a break, until 1924. In 1927 he was elected to the Senate and he remained a senator until his death – from 1940 to 1941 he was president of the senate. Malan died in the closing hours of 1941 and was buried at the Woltemade cemetery after a state funeral on 2.1.1942. A charcoal portrait of Malan is in the Africana museum, Johannesburg.

Johann Fredrick Preller wrote the biography as it appears in the DSAB – Dictionary of South African Biography, published 1968. Preller also edited 'Die konvensie-dagboek van sy edelagbare Francois Stephanus Malan, 1908-1909': (van Riebeeck Society, no. 32), Cape Town, 1951. Incidentally, Preller Matt Geldenhuys married Susanna Catharina Malan in 1966!

sister of Rina (who married Preller Geldenhuys). Gerta married farmer Hansie Johannes Jurgen Bezuidenhout. They were the parents of Johan "Bez" Bezuidenhout (of Special Forces SAS fame). Hansie owned Anker in the Tengwe Block between Karoi and Sinoia and was a very active forefront tobacco farmer as well as a PATU – BSA Police Anti-Terrorist Unit. Their second child Letitia, married Australian Mark Gooding and they set up their home down under to raise a rather large farming family by modern day standards. A third child, Francois, studied in Britain but returned to Zimbabwe to pursue a civil flying career. Both Hansie and Johan "Bez" distinguished themselves during the Rhodesian War.

On retiring from active farming, Hansie and Gerta had a magnificent home built at Mica Point, on the shores of Lake Kariba. During one of the Air Force re-union gatherings, the Bezuidenhouts kindly hosted the Geldenhuys family. Courtney and Brendan Jelley may one day choose to renew their early memories of this particularly memorable experience.

Hansie and Gerta sold their Kariba home and retired to Qalisa Retirement village in Bulawayo, in 2004.

Malan, Hendrik Francois (born Tulbagh 1833, died in Lichtenburg). Rina's great grandfather – genealogy number b6c3d2e5f2. Married Anna Magarita Malan in Tulbach – and settled in the Lichtenburg district, where all of Rina's immediate relatives were born. They had four children – Daniel Stephanus, Anna E who married a Moolman, David Jacobus, and Elizabeth who married a Joubert, and their fifth child also named Hendrik Francois

Malan, Hendrik Francois (born 14.12.1878, died 29.5.1959). Anglo-Boer War "Rapportryer", mentioned in dispatches. He married Getruida Johanna, who was born on 5th February 1883, and died 6th August 1951. They had eleven children – ten boys with the only daughter Heila Magdalena, born 11th July 1918, died on 7th August 1918 when she was a mere 27 days old. The fourth son, Francois Daniel, born 2nd October 1907, was the writer's wife Rina's beloved father.

Malan, "Gerta" Gertruida Johanna. born Lichtenburg 27th December 1936 and christened Lichtenburg (NG) 24th January 1937. She became a farmer's wife, and elder

Malan, Jacques (Stamvader - born St Martini D'Aigues, France 1665 - died in Stellenbosch in 1742). He was a farmer and the Huguenot refugee Stamvader of the Malan descendants. Discrepancies exist on birth date – some records reflect "gebore ca. 1672 [although 1665 seems the more popular date], van Merindol naby Avignon in Provence of van La Motte-d'Aigues (albei in Suidoos Frankryk)" – quoted literately from one of the references researched. Jacques arrived in the ship *Berg China* on 4th August 1688. On 18th October 1694 he became the owner of the Franschhoek farm he named "La Motte" – which he sold in 1719 to his step-son Pierre Jourdan. In 1709 he purchased "Morgenster", one of the four sub-divisions of "Welgelegen", the property of Adriaan van der Stel (authors note: perhaps *Vergelegen* – see Barend Gildenhuisz !?). Jacques was involved in Adam Tas's struggle against the corruption of the government of Willem Adriaan van der Stel – see also Barend Geldenhuys, Jacobus van den Heiden and Henning Huising.

In 1699 he married Elisabeth (Isabeau) le Long, widow of Jean Jourdan (Jordaan). They had 7 children. Jacobus, Catharina and Jacob – firstborn, fifth and seventh all died young. Daniel, third born and more so sixthborn David produced most of the South African descendants. Jacques was a wealthy farmer, and by 1733 he had 32 slaves, 50 horses, 140 cattle and 900 sheep. He was a member of the Stellenbosch church council for many years. In 1717 he supervised the transport of building stone and wood for the building of a new church at Stellenbosch. Isabeau died in 1736 and Jacques six years later in 1742. Both were buried in the same grave in the Stellenbosch church.

Notable Malan's are sixth generation Francois Stephanus (1871-1941) and ninth generation Susanna Catharina (1945)

Malan, Hendrik (born on Guy Fawkes Day 5th November 1943).

Hendrik is the first son of Francois Daniel Malan and Aletta Magdalena Susanna le Roux. He is the eldest brother of Rina, who married Preller Matt Geldenhuys. Hendrik also married a "Rina" Gerber who had three girls and a boy. She bore him three sons. Her own son 'Dons' Johannes was killed in the line of duty in the SA Police. They currently live in Pretoria. Hendrik's three sons are Philip, Francois Daniel and Eddie Deon. Rina Gerber died in 2009 – within months of the Malan Re-union that youngest brother Frans had arranged in Pietersburg.

Malan, Hercules Official Genealogist of the Malan-Family – contactable at Louis Bokstraat 4 Universitas, Bloemfontein 9301 (Telephone 051-5220664 / Fax 051-5221610 – as at July 1997; by kind favour of Frans Malan)

Malan, Jacobus Johannes (Born Paarl 10th April 1739 and died 19th August 1806). He married Anna Aletta Retief in Paarl in September 1762 (she was born there on 18th July1744 - died 18th April 1795 and was the daughter of Francois Retief and Anna Marais. Remarried in Cape Town on 19th June 1796 to Aletta Bosman who died November 1809 and was the daughter of Hermanus Bosman and Maria Marias. Jacobus was a farmer in the Palmeit Valleij, Drakenstein.

Malan, Philip Johannes, (born 1933) Philip is the son of Daniel Stefanus Malan, born 13 August 1906, who was the elder brother of Francios Daniel Malan (father of Susanna Catharina who married Preller Geldenhuys).

Philip married Ria Venter and they have two children, son currently in England, and a daughter Salome living in Bothas Hill, Hillcrest.

Philip joined the Internal Affairs Department as a District Assistant and saw Rhodesian War service in Plumtree, Filabuzi. His father-in-law farmed in the Chatsworth area and after leaving Intaf. Philip took up general farming, retiring to the Natal South Coast – Palm Beach, near Port Edward.

Malan, Philip Johannes, (born Lichtenburg, Transvaal 5th March 1945) son of Francois Daniel Malan and Aletta Magdalena Susanna le Roux. Phil is the twin-brother of Rina (who married Preller Matt Geldenhuys).

As a National Serviceman on call-up Philip will not quickly forget 14th September 1964. He was passing through Gwelo on his motorcycle en route for Army call-up, when he met with an unfortunate accident. Preller managed to wrangle a general low flying sortie in Provost 302 for him. After kitting him out with the necessary flying gear, the intrepid airman took to the wild blue yonder. He certainly appeared to enjoy the tree hopping, but did not take a liking to the aerobatics. He was trying to remain conscious during high 'g' manoeuvres, but when the smell of avgas entered the cockpit pilot Geldenhuys had a problem scraping the second hand carrots off the instrument panel. Airsickness affects are at its worst after the event, because the resultant migraine headaches, which sets in whenever a stomach is emptied. Despite Preller being kind to his brother-in-law by curtailing the sortie to a mere thirty-five minutes, Phil has been getting his back ever since.

Phil has a great sense of humour. Some people just have the right knack to remember and tell jokes. He is also a great practical joker. But jokes aside, the following Natal newspaper article is the sort of tale that Phil would be able to raise a laugh in mixed company. It really is a genuine, true story published in a respectable newspaper. I quote "The Cape Times report that the Baden Club at Montague, which allegedly bars blacks, now sells a brandy called *Fokol*. The label proclaims that it is a Fokol Antique full strength brandy. 'You can depend on Fokol these days, because nearly everyday everyone promises you Fokol as nearly everyone in the new South Africa possesses Fokol. You have no option these days but to believe Fokol. Most people regularly enjoy Fokol because there is nothing better, and it actually makes Fokol DIFFERENCE. Specially manufactured by people who own Fokol for people who could not care about Fokol in a country where money is worth Fokol".

Phil is also a musician of note, playing a variety of instruments – guitar and piano accordion mainly. In the 1998's the band Hardland Boereorkes cut a CD titled "*Hier's die Hardland*" in which Phil composed and played two songs called *Die Vosperdsetees* and *Die Jodewals*.

Phil is just as well known for his poetry, as he is for his musical talents. One poem, on Rina (and his) birthday in 2007, brought much snot and trane. There is a Right Time for Everything – what else can I say (he also composed "Rhodesia----In Memory of those who fell" which can be found at page 73):-

What a Lady

I would like to share with others this day,
My love for a wonderful lady.
In fact I have always loved her so.
Ever since she was a little baby.

We always got on so well together,
Right from the time we were small.
No matter what the two of us did,
We always had a terrific ball.

Between us never passed a word in anger,
We did not fight, or scold, or blame,
We always handled our petty differences,
With love and care, never shame.

We went through school, always friends,
Never very far from one another.
When ever she was hurt or maybe sad,
I was there for her like a brother.

Through school and into adult hood,
We stood by each other over the years.
She fell in love with my best friend,
And married him with eyes full of tears.

They were so happy; it showed in her face,
Despite the responsibilities she now carried.
But even then we were always close,
She also cried the day I got married.

Then one fateful day misfortune struck,
Half her body paralysed through a stroke.
I fought the tears and tried to be brave.
But it was not long before I broke.

I will never forget how much I cried.
Overwhelmed by sorrow, I felt drained.
She always played a big part in my life.
How could I help? I felt chained.

She could not speak, yet we understood.
The expression of acceptance plain on her face.
No big deal, there is no need to cry.
GOD will share with us his amazing grace.

She has learned to do things no matter how tough,
So much courage and faith is wonderful to see.
To many a person she's been an inspiration,
There is someone who really admires her, it's me.

My admiration and thanks go to her life long mate,
Who has stood by her through all these years,
He never once flinched from his responsibility,
Despite the hardship, heartbreak and tears .

I salute you both for what you've been through .
And so we all learn from one another .
I thank the LORD for his wonderful mercy.
I am so proud to be your twin brother !!!

Malan, Philip son of Hendrik Malan and Rina Gerber. He attended the Frans Malan 60th birthday re-union at Uitkyk game farm in Polokwane, hosted by Charles Stopforth and Amanda Malan.

Malan, Roux Daniel, (born Grobblersdal 5th July 1971) is the son of Phil Malan and Elcora Bouwer. Roux married Lesley Ann Reeve born Boksburg 11th November 1977. They married in Boksburg on the 25th October 1966, and currently live in Pretoria.

Malan, Susanna Catharina (born Lichtenburg, Tvl. 5th March 1945-), twin daughter of Francois Daniel Malan (1907-1988) and Aletta Magdalena Susanna le Roux. As a farmer's daughter, went to Andrew Louw farm school in Fort Victoria, Rhodesia where she befriended Delene Elizabeth Geldenhuys. Nicknamed Rina or Boudtjies at school. Completed high school at Thornhill, Gwelo where Preller Matt Geldenhuys fell in love with this sporty boeremeisie. Bore two lovely children and despite stricken with breast cancer and a crippling stroke in March 1993, inspired and saved many souls for the Kingdom of God.

Rina's early childhood was spent in Lichtenburg and remembers the family immigrating to Rhodesia to farm at Trickling Waters in the Chatsworth district. She recalled the incident when the car stalled on the mine railway track that runs through Messina – the train screeched to a halt, but could not avoid the collision that followed! The frightful experience was enough to turn the car around and head straight back to the Transvaal; but with much intrepidation, the family decided to press on with establishing a new life in the wilds of a newly developing country. She and her twin brother Philip started their schooling at Chatsworth and completed primary at Andrew Louw farm school. Both then joined their elder brother Hendrik at Thornhill High in Gwelo.

Rina excelled at athletics and sports, winning the Victrix Ludorum for running, long jump and medley-relays: all kaalvoet and with her head cocked to one side. She also represented the school at Hockey and

Tennis. As a star performer/singer she acquitted herself admirably in the Gilbert and Sullivan school productions in The Pirates of Penzance, The Mikado and Iolante. Rina was also a Prefect in the only girl's hostel, Holton (named after a Royal Air Force base in Britain). On leaving school, she worked for the Cold Storage Commission in Fort Victoria, then relocated to Chiredzi where she worked for N. Richards and Coy. After a respectful one year courtship, she married her schoolboy sweetheart, in Fort Victoria and then settled in Gwelo.

Air Force postings meant relocations to Salisbury, back to Gwelo, Kariba, Buffalo Range and quite a few Gwelo / Salisbury moves in between. Both children were born in Gwelo – Renene Delene on 8th August 1968 and Pey Malan on 22nd December 1970. Renene proved to be a particularly bright scholar, but never-the-less complained that she had lost count of just how many different schools that she was required to attend. Pey did not do too badly himself – and both qualified for their National Diplomas – Renene in Nursing and Pey in Computer Data Processing.

Rina became a devout Christian, long before her disabling Stroke, but more so subsequent to the misfortune. She is most content when able to spend every wakeful moment in praise and worship. Her inspiration has led many a lost soul to salvation. Her cup runneth over.

On the 1st June 1990, Rina wrote a letter to God. It reads as follows:

"Dearest Father,

I come before you today in the name of Jesus. And Lord, I am writing you this letter to let you know what is on my heart.

Father what I want in life is not wealth and all those things that go with it. All I am asking you today is a home with contentment. A home that can be shared with love. But above all is my desire to have you as first in our lives. Lord, when I saw on Wednesday night how that family got together to worship you and to pray together. My heart just went out with such a longing for our family to be like that. Not just Prop and myself but for Pey and Renene; Delene and her family and Jan and Julie + Paul and Karen. Father where the main topic when we get together would be about you. So heal their hearts as well as mine: Its like a canal and only you can have a hand in it. Change us I pray.

Father then there is that desire for me something more than just going to church and me reading my Bible, and not getting an answer. It is as if what ever I am reading just don't seem to have an anointing on me – that I have been blinded and cannot hear. Father I don't want to be conformed to this world. But please I pray that I can hear and be a doer of Your word. Change my heart.

Father I want to be like Gal 5.22 – a Spirit of love, joy, peace, patience, kindness, goodness faithfulness, gentleness and self content. Lord I claim that for all those I mentioned today.

Help us to be strong in the Lord and his mighty power. I put on my full armour of God and take a stand against you devil, in the name of Jesus.

I love you Lord and I lift up my voice to worship you.

Amen"

I wept - - Amen and Amen!

Matthews, Wayne, husband of Meisie Liebenberg – related to Julia Lillian Dippenaar (wife of Jan Geldenhuys)

McColl crest

McColl, Andrew (born in Govan, Glasgow, UK 19th November 1858). Entered Royal Navy as a rating and served until 11th April 1890. Armourer. Obtained his discharge at Simonstown in order to join the Rhodesian Pioneer Corps artillery – appointed Trooper (Armourer) and posted to 'C' Troop in June. He was sentenced to 3 extra guards and stoppage of grog for 2 weeks for being drunk and resisting escort, 11th July. Sentenced to 3 extra guards and fine £1 for being asleep on guard, 3 September.

He was re-engaged in R.N. 10th November 1891, and served until 1st December 1898. Re-engaged yet again on 5th January 1899 and served until 28th December 1908 – retired with the rank of Chief Armourer.

His relationship to Stu McColl is uncertain. Information gained was from author Robert Cary's book The Pioneer Corps, which also mentions Margaret Mary Elaine Whiteley, married to William Jelley and their two sons, Graham David and Keith Brian.

McColl, Davyd John Charles (born Johannesburg 18th March 1978), only son of Stuart John McColl and Eve Elizabeth Boxall. Went to Glenwood High School. Married Desirée Haynes. Senior Developer at Derivco.

McColl, Isis, born in Bulawayo, Zimbabwe and lives in Glasgow, UK. Uncertain relationship.

McColl, Joyce Edith (born Matchett), affectionately known as Ma McColl – mother of Stuart John McColl, and grandmother of Davyd John Charles.

McRoberts, Mary, passed away 13th November 1943 aged 38 years, related via Margaret Mary Elaine Jelley nee Whiteley.

McColl, Stuart John (born Bromley, Kent UK 27th March 1949) was the only son of Peter John and Joyce Edith Matchett), self-employed Electronics Engineer. Married Eve Elisabeth Boxall and had a son Davyd John Charles born Johannesburg 18th March 1978) Married Delene Elizabeth Geldenhuys 26th September 1991 and emigrated to Whangaparaoa New Zealand August 2000. Realised the ambition which was formulated since being a 12 year-old in Television Broadcasting. They purchased a home in Elliston Crescent and then sold the property after carrying out several modifications and improvements.

Stu and Delene have now moved to new accommodation in Beach Haven, North Shore City of Auckland and plan to retire perhaps to a smallholding suitable for the planting and marketing of limes.

A very enjoyable and memorable trip up the 90-Mile Beach and bus stop-over at Cape Reinga was had during February 2010. Other highlights included a visit to the Kauri Museum, Gumdiggers marsh and a train ride, with lunch, through a small town called Kawakawa.

Mocke, Pieter married Leanie van Aardt. Pieter is an electrical engineer and works for Eskom. They live in Tygervallei

Moodie crest

Moodie, Benjamin (born Melsetter 1st January 1789 - died Westfield, Port Alfred 2nd April 1856), "Stamvader", pioneer, trader, coloniser and eldest son of James Moodie – Last Laird of Melsetter, Scotland, and his wife Elizabeth Dunbar. James and Elizabeth had six children: four sons and two daughters.

Benjamin was born on New Year's Day at Melsetter, Orkney Islands off Scotland. He married Margaret Malcolmsen in 1817 and they had 4 sons and 4 daughters.

In February 1817 his father transferred to him as tenth laird the heavily mortgaged property, Melsetter. About this time he and a partner, a Cape Town merchant, decided to subsidise the passage to the Cape of some displaced, skilled Scottish labourers. On 5th May 1817 he sailed with the first fifty of them. Subsequently his partner left him in the lurch and he was forced to sell Melsetter. This, however, did not yield the money necessary and he could not continue the scheme; but he himself emigrated with his family to the Cape Colony.

In 1817 he bought the farm Melkhoutboom near Swellendam and by subsequent purchases developed this property into a large family farm called Grootvaders Bosch. He was, however, essentially a coloniser and in 1840, on the initiative of Gibbon Wakefield, he was entrusted with the execution of a new emigration scheme which, however, also failed owing to lack of financial support.

He married Susan Barnett in 1841 and died at Westfield Port Alfred 2nd April 1856, aged 71. In 1951 his descendants erected a monument to his memory on a coppie overlooking the Breede River.

He was an ancestor to Courtney Sacha and Brendan Vaughan Jelley (grandchildren of Prop and Rina Geldenhuys). He is related in 9 steps – via Margaret Jelley born Margaret Mary Elaine Whiteley.

Moodie, Donald (born Melsetter, Orkney Islands 25th June 1794 - died Doorn Kop, Klip River district, Pietermaritzburg, Natal 27th August 1861), retired naval officer, government secretary, Natal administrator, and Settler's House owner - the Moodies of Melsetter. A younger brother of Benjamin Moodie, he was the son of James Moodie, who claimed descent from Harold Mutadi, Norse Earl of Orkney.

After serving in the navy, mainly in the Mediterranean, Donald became a lieutenant on half-payin 1816. Donald arrived or emigrated to South Africa as one of the 1820 Settlers. He married Elizabeth Sophia Pigot (died 26th October 1881) on 29th March 1824 in Albanie in the Cape (daughter of Major George Pigot). Their third son, George Benjamin Dunbar, was instrumental in persuading his cousin Thomas, to lead the Moodie Trek to Melsetter in Rhodesia.

In 1825 he became acting resident magistrate at Port Francis and three years later, of Grahamstown. From 1830 to 1834 he served as protector of slaves for the eastern districts. In 1838 he secured a grant enabling him to compile from early records an 'authentic history of the Colony and its relations with native tribes'.

In 1840, Donald Moodie, as the Recorder for Natal, purchased the "Old House" Museum, behind the Gables, described as Lot 3 Block Ba. He sold the house in 1849 to Byrne emigration settlers who arrived in 57 ships 1849 – 1851. The property changed hands for 100 pounds and a piano! 813 the Gables was purchased by Preller Geldenhuys for R109 000! (Who bought Illovo Beach property – as well as Jan and daughter-in-law Joy Goldsworthy Geldenhuys – which is the river mouth along which the Byrne settlement had settled nearly 150 years previously).

He had 12 years' Cape service in colonial administration. On the establishment of the Natal Government in 1845 he became secretary, treasurer-general, and registrar of deeds. He was also a member of the Land Commission. Until 1850 he was the virtual ruler of Natal. Behind an appearance of amiability and graceful manners he concealed an inflexible will and a memory for affronts that was almost vindictive (observation made in Dr John Clark's *Natal Settler-Agent* – the career of John Moreland, agent for the Byrne emigration-scheme of 1849-51). To a great extent, Donald Moodie was the man who, as Napoleon said of Sir Sydney Smith at Acre, made Moreland and Byrne "miss their destiny".

Related by marriage to the Shepstones, he was the most influential of the clique of permanent officials who conducted the affairs of Natal, and was to be the real ruler of the government for the crucial period during which Moreland attempted to make a success of the emigration scheme. As a member of the Land Commission, Donald Moodie was the man behind setting the upset or reserve price on Natal Crown land at four shillings per acre – when the value was more like one shilling, double the price of similar land in the Cape and four to six shillings and ninepence per acre for a select plot at the Umgeni mouth.

On 5th July 1850, Donald was in Durban when the *Minerva* arrived with 287 Byrne emigrants and shipwrecked at the foot of the Bluff. As an ex-lieutenant of the Royal Navy he rendered valuable help in the rescue of passengers and crew of the 987-ton ship which broke up completely. Moreland had bought 31,000 acres of land in six blocks on the Illovo River, and settled the passengers of the Lady Bruce, Edward, Conquering Hero and Sandwich. In Byrnetown, he located the passengers of the Minerva and Henrietta. Today both localities comprise the Richmond area. All told, Byrne sent 20 ships to Natal.

On 21st February 1857 Donald was elected to the legislative council as second member for Durban – whilst on retirement on his Doorn Kop farm in the Klip River district – and was the first Speaker of that same council.

It is a historical fact a D. Pigot-Moodie was the owner of the stately house "Westbrooke", next to Groote Schuur, and who is renowned for supplying the current for the first electric street lamp in the Cape Peninsula in 1886. The street lamp had been installed at Rondebosch – it was placed at the top of the fountain in the main road near St. Paul's Church. D. Pigot Moodie had presented the fountain with a drinking trough for horses to the Rondebosch municipality. The lighting plant at Westbrooke supplied the current to the lamp, which was incorporated in the cast iron decoration above the circular trough – where travellers stopped to water their horses. The trough is still there and still bears the name by which several generations of Capetonians have known it – The Fountain.

Donald Moodie died on 27th August 1861, at the age of 67. The obituary in the Natal Witness stated that much of the public clamour against Moodie was based on misinformation. He was described as amiable, scholarly, and graceful in all his intercourse; he was esteemed and beloved by many an old colonist. He was the founder of the Assurance & Trust Society and also the president of the Natal Society.

Moodie, George Benjamin Dunbar (born Pietermaritzburg 8th July 1861-Kenilworth Melsetter 9th March 1897), pioneer, visionary, son of William James Dunbar, grandson of Donald Moodie (1794-1861) and his wife Elizabeth Sophia Pigot. Dunbar Moodie is recognised as a man of vision, as it was entirely due to his original efforts that the first settlement of Melsetter took place.

Dunbar married Sarah Maria Moodie at Victoria, Southern Rhodesia on 24th October 1892, the daughter of Groot Tom (as) Moodie and Cecilia Jacomina Robbertse. They had three children; Cecilia Barbara Lovemore, Leander Starr Jameson (deceased) and

George Benjamin Dunbar, born three weeks before Dunbar died of Malaria.

In 1890 Dunbar Moodie arrived by boat in Beira and travelled up the Pungwe River, and then overland to Macequece and on to the Penhalonga valley in Manicaland, where he established his camp as manager of the Sabie Ophir Gold Mining Company. Dr (later Sir) Leander Starr Jameson had been with the Pioneer Corps who had raised the Union Flag at Fort Salisbury on 12th September 1890 – and later that month arrived at Dunbar's camp on their way to find an eastern seaport for Rhodesia. Dunbar assisted Jameson by recruiting thirty carriers from nearby kraals, with the liberal aid of his already sjambok. Later that year Jameson, together with Dennis Doyle routed via Penhalonga to collect Dunbar (who had resigned from the mining company). And the three set out on horseback, with the carriers, on their long trek southwards.

On 19th January 1891 they crossed the Umvumvumvu River and, as they approached the higher ground near the Chimanimani Mountains, Dunbar was very taken with the agricultural prospects and looked at the country with a view of bringing settlers to this fertile area. Later, the same year, Dunbar met with Cecil John Rhodes for support to establish the Melsetter settlement. Dunbar Moodie embarked on a boat for Durban, from where he travelled to Bethlehem in the Orange Free State, and to his cousins there he unfolded his tale of the rich farming prospects of Gazaland. Farming in the Free State had not prospered Dunbar's cousin Thomas – who was easily persuaded to consider the prospect to emigrate. Dunbar did not accompany Thomas; he went via Beira and Umtali to Salisbury, and expected to join up with Thomas well inside Rhodesia shortly after his arrival there in August.

He had great difficulty in locating the trek, and it was two weeks later, after he had ridden 450 miles on horseback, that he found them barely out of Bechuanaland (Botswana). He married Groot Tom's daughter en route through Fort Victoria. The trek ended when they reached Waterfall on 4th January 1893. Dunbar established himself with his newly wedded wife (and second cousin) Sarah on Kenilworth – and others also settled around the Chipinga area.

In August 1893, Free State Fouriesburg farmer Marthinus Martin arrived at Waterfall on an exploratory trip, and was given a great reception by the Moodies. Dunbar, as the Company representative, took them round on a visit of inspection. They rode over towards the Nyahode River and the Chimanimani Mountains, and travelled across Lemon Kop and Cecilton. After ten days' riding Marthinus Martin chose a farm to be named Rocklands. He returned to Fouriesburg to arrange the Martin Trek, which followed and reached Waterfall on 17th October 1894.

As the new pioneers were making their way to Rocklands, Dunbar dispatched a police officer with a letter commandeering all the men to come with their rifles and ammunition and provisions for eight days to withstand a Portuguese army which planned to take over Gazaland. They responded, setting off to Kenilworth in pouring rain. After the eight days, they arrived back at the Trek, wet, hungry and tired, and without having had the privilege of meeting with the Portuguese.

The railway line from Beira towards Umtali had by then reached Chimoio – from where supplies were obtained by carriers. From the outset Dunbar Moodie pressed for the Company to build the Umtali-Melsetter wagon road. He stressed that it was a matter of great importance, as the settlers needed roads to travel on. In January 1895 the road was surveyed and laying commenced. By June wagons could get through although the journey took many weeks

The district was administered from the B.S.A. Company headquarters on Dunbar Moodie's farm Kenilworth, where pole-and-dagga huts were the Government offices and a police force of thirteen was stationed. From 1893 Dunbar was what he himself termed Pooh-Bah: Native Commissioner, Justice of the Peace, Magistrate and Administrator of Gazaland. He was also the Postal agent, and each quarter a relay of runners carried despatches and post; the runners could reach Umtali in three days in favourable weather, but with the erratic service letters from Salisbury were often answered from Kenilworth many weeks later. In 1895 Dunbar was relieved of his official appointments.

Controversy arose over the 3000 morgen allotments, in terms of the Certificates of Rights, made by Dunbar. It was said that wherever one went, that the ground belonged to some Moodie or other – and that Dunbar had by then had 4000 morgen surveyed in excess of his grant of 27 000 morgen. Dunbar was also accused of charging high fees for checking beacons for farmers, and some farmers had to leave, as they were unable to meet these unreasonable demands.

Meanwhile, the centre of the settlement gradually became definitely the Chimanimani area, closely filled by the Martin Trek, and the feeling grew that the township should be established there. The original idea was to move the township only, but somehow the name came with the move, and the township to the south, which had been pegged out but not developed, became Chipinga. The few Moodie trekkers who were still there disliked the fact that the name Melsetter was being taken from them, but they were outnumbered and their spokesman, Dunbar, had quarrelled with the magistrate. After consideration of various sites on Rocklands, Cecilton and Fairfield, G.F. Heyn's farm Dunbarton was chosen. Some difficulty was experienced because in April, when the idea was mooted of placing a township in that vicinity, Dunbar Moodie immediately beaconed off these farms for his own benefit and appropriated the ground without having any legal right to it and said that he would question anyone's right to interfere with his distribution. The two recently appointed local administrators were removed in rapid succession.

The Magistrate at Tuli, Longden, was dispatched, and was installed at Kenilworth – and was immediately involved in the tangled problem of the transfer of the township. In early 1896, Melsetter Township, a tiny cluster of pole-and-dagga huts, 5000' above sea level, in a beautiful, remote and not easily accessible corner of Rhodesia, was established.

Moodie, James (1757-1856). Last (9th) Laird of Melsetter, father of "Stamvader" Benjamin who arrived at the Cape in 1817. His wife, who died 1798, was the daughter of Captain Thomas Dunbar and his wife Janet (daughter of Sir William Dunbar of Mempriggs, Scotland).

Moodie, Thomas (born Grootvadersbosch, Swellendam 29th November 1839 - died Waterfall, Chipinga, Rhodesia 30th April 1894). He was the Melsetter pioneer, farmer and early Rhodesian settler. Thomas was persuaded by his younger cousin Dunbar to lead the Moodie Trek during their meeting held in March 1891. Dunbar made the necessary arrangements and on 5th May 1892 Thomas left Bethlehem with a caravan of 16 wagons on the long trek to the north.

Four months had confidently been allowed for the Moodie trek to travel from Bethlehem to Gazaland, but such were the hazards and hardships of the trek that it took them four months to reach the Rhodesian border only, and another four months of weary trekking before they crossed the Sabi River. By the time the Trek reached Fort Victoria there was dissension about leadership, their ultimate destination, and various other matters, and so the party split up and the majority took up land between Fort Victoria and Salisbury.

Seven wagons only, with fourteen men, four women and three children, left Fort Victoria to travel to their goal in the east. The journey was full of incident and hardship: a road had to be found and negotiated, the Sabi river had to be crossed, the Driespanberg (up whose steep slopes it was necessary to use three spans of oxen for each wagon) had to be surmounted, there was a threat of tsetse fly, and nearly all members of the party were ill with malaria. They overcame all the difficulties, and the trek ended when they reached Waterfall on 4th January 1893, where Thomas Moodie settled with his family. Ernst du Plessis, the dependable second-in-command of the trek, chose Clearwater for his farm, where his son and grandson still live as at 1972. Dunbar established himself and his wife Sarah on Kenilworth farm, and the others also settled around the Chipinga area.

The Trekkers arrival was followed by a sad tale of hardship, struggles and death, and it was particularly sad for all that Thomas Moodie, their wise, courageous and strong leader, died before the end of that first year, and was buried on Waterfall Farm. Dr. D.F.du T. Malherbe affectionately referred to Thomas as 'Groot Tom' in the Stamregister van die Suid-Afrikaanse Volk.

Louis Ferreira established Mayfield and Knutsford – the latter being farmed by Frans and Lettie Malan, who were the parents of Rina Geldenhuys. Knutsford was located on the Lusitu river valley, and faced the Chimanimani Mountains to its north-east.

Motke, Pieter (born), married Lianie van Aardt in Waenhuiskraal on the 8th October 2011.

Mueller crest

Mueller, Marion Janine (born Malawi 17th July 1970). First wife of Pey Malan Geldenhuys. Mags as she was generally known, completed her education at Wartburg Kirshof. Her parents, Hannes and Valerie married and divorced three times. Pey and Mags got married in Welkom and returned to The Gables flat in Durban. After an unfortunate miscarriage they separated amicably and decided to divorce on 17th January 1997.

Muir-Geldenhuys, Liane (born 20th July), from Meyerton, Gauteng: studied at Vereeniging Technical College.

Muirhead crest

DICTIONARY OF FAMILY BIOGRAPHY

Muirhead, Byron (born 7th April 1995) is the eldest son of Neill Muirhead and Lynn Brink.

Muirhead, Bevan Glyn (born New Zealand 21st October 2000). His parents live in Hamilton.

Bevan shared a memorable birthday celebration with his slightly younger cousin Gem Brink in October 2011. Bevan Glyn Muirhead is a nephew of the husband of a niece. I trust his elder cousins will explain this relationship to him?

Muirhead, Kim Chanelle (born Durban, KwaZulu-Natal 23rd May 1992), went to St. Paul's Collegiate School, lives in Hamilton, New Zealand.

Affectionally known as Nelle, always very welcome in the Brink's home, and makes a huge inpact on all her cousins. She is indeed a lovely person, unknowingly a blessing to the Geldenhuys family as well.

Christmas 2011 holds many pleasant surprises, like trying to figure out that her relationship to the writer is 'a niece of the husband of a niece'!

Muirhead, Lynn (actually born Brink, in Pretoria, 1st September 1965), married Neill Wynn Muirhead.

Muirhead, Neil Wynn (born in England, UK, 12th February 1961), married Lynn Brink. They have three children, already mentioned. Neil Wynn Muirhead is a brother-in-law of the husband of a niece

Murray, Jordan Elizabeth (born Sandton Clinic, Randburg, Johannesburg, South Africa 18th January 1999), daughter of Stephen James Murray and Carol Brink born 16th June 1970, who is the younger sister to Charles Roy Brink (Chanli Bouwer's husband)

Mussell crest

DICTIONARY OF FAMILY BIOGRAPHY

Mussell, Christina, daughter of Pierre and Angela Varikas.

Mussell, Josua,

Mussell, Maurice, married June Howard (born 14th June 1953), uncle and aunt to Eloise Geldenhuys (nee Howard). Pierre Mussell, married to Angela (nee Varikas, I suspect), lives in Gold Coast, Queensland. Maurice and June live in Durban, South Africa.

Mussell, Pierre married Angela (Varikas) on 8th February 1998 and live on the Gold Coast, Queensland, Australia. They have two children, Josua and Christina. Pierre is the son of Maurice Mussell and June Howard – and cousin to Eloise and Pey Geldenhuys.

DICTIONARY OF FAMILY BIOGRAPHY

Myburgh, Chantelle (born 5th November), from Uitenhage, Eastern Cape; married Shawn Geldenhuys on 9th February 2002. They have a daughter, Chanté. Blue Bulls supporter. Facebook friend in 2011.

Nel crest

Nel, Willem Petrus (Snr), married Magdalena Maria Nel, parents of Dr Willem Petrus Nel who married the writer's niece, Elsa-Lou Cornelia Malan on 28th November 1998.

Nel, Willem Petrus 'WP' (born Berchley, Kempton Park, Johannesburg, on 20th February 1972), met nurse Elsa-Lou Malan and married her in Pretoria at the Garsfontein NG Kerk on the 28th November 1998. Willem practiced as a locum in Scotland and decided to to settle there.

Neilson, Nancy, married Ronald Mark Gooding, whose son married Letitia Bezuidenhout.

Noetje, Renaldo, married Melda Geldenhuis. Facebook friends in 2011.

DICTIONARY OF FAMILY BIOGRAPHY

Olivier crest

Olivier, Jaco (born) son of Reneir Olivier and Nicolene van Aardt.

Olivier, Anneke (born) daughter of Renier Olivier and Nicolene van Aardt.

Olivier, A Charles (born 15th March 1892, died 16th August 1965, married Johanna who lived more than 100 years - grandparents of Joleen Geldenhuys.

Olivier, Renier (born 22nd May), married Nicolene van Aardt

Aardt– they had three children; Yvette Marie born 6th October 1976, Liesl Adriaana born 27th July 1978 and Schalk Johannes born 31st August 1979, all born in Salisbury.

Oosthuisen, Yvette Marie (born Salisbury 6th October 1976), the eldest of three children, as aforementioned.

Oosthuisen, Liesl Adriaana (born Salisbury 27th July 1978), second daughter of Willem Adriaan Jacobus and Alta van Aardt. The two other siblings are Sckalk Johannes born 31st August 1979, and Yvette Marie born 6th October 1976. Liesl married Cobus de Villiers and they have three sons, Jacques born 23rd April 2003, Adriaan born 28th January 2005 and Ben born 19th April 2008.

Oosthuisen, Schalk Johannes (born Salisbury) 31st August 1979,

Page crest

Page, Mark is in a relationship with Courtney Sacha Jelley. OuPey trusts that it is proper, and all above board! The caption says it all: and the three 'birdies' in the Page coat of arms may just whisper in ones ear.

Pelley, Pamela from Sacremento, CA, writes: My name is Pamela Perry, born Townsend.
My mother was Maria Magdalena Townsend (born Geldenhuys) Her father was Nicholas George Johannes Geldenhuys His father was Nicholas George Antonie born in Caledon. He was raised by an uncle and aunt so we do

Oosthuisen, Willem Adriaan Jacobus Farmer in the Beatrice area, married Alta van

not know if he was illegitimate. Swart family seems to be associated with him?

He had his own wagon and began trading and lived on a farm Graafwater in the district of Britstown.

He married Maria Magdalena van Heerden of Murraysburg and my grandfather NGJ was born in 1894. This branch of the family, ultimately settled in Kuruman.

I am trying to find out the names of my grandfather's siblings as they are bound to be family names. Perhaps I can connect that way. I had a look at the Swart almost incestuous relationship with the Geldenhuys crowd in almost evry generation!!! My great grandmother was a le Roux and there are some connections there as well so in some respects we are cousins sveral times over.

I am including my brother and my cousin in this discussion. I have to say that my mother contended that 2 of her uncles had "glas oe"
(glass eyes), meaning that the eyes were those of mixed blood. South Africans are very descriptive in their speech and writing, (we have produced fabulous authors), so the contrast of the skin and eye colour is probably what glass eyes described. I have always had dark skin which I am sure harkens back to my ancestors. As about three-quarters of my ancestry can be traced back to the days of slavery in the Cape, I surely have a good dose. My fathers, grandfather and mother gave an injection of lily white from Britain, but the rest, as was stated by Floors van Jaarsveld, is a mixture.

I lived in Pretoria at the time of the Floors van Jaarsveld thesis, what a furore that caused at Unisa. It was just at the time when the Broederbond and the "pure Afrikaans" was reaching it's zenith and on top of it, in Pretoria the capital!!!! Poor man was tarred and feathered by Eugene Terrebalanche and the like!! It was a kind of awakening for some, uneasy, but it struck a chord.

Then there was the family (seemingly white)that belonged to the Hervormde CHurch (the really intense church) who produced a son that was for all intents and purposes a "coloured" child. His two younger siblings had the glass eyes and but not the very tight curly hair.

What misery that family and especially the boy endured. They put him into a private English school in Pretoria and put him into the boy scouts. I remember the boy never took his cap off, always trying to hide his hair. How cruel humans are. Eventually the boy was given up for adoption at about age 10, to family in the Cape.

That could not heal the wound to the boys life or to his blood family but it appeased the the "whites". I think of this painful chapter often, it is a wound in all the souls of South Africans.

Thank you for your valuable contribution. I think it is very important for all South Africans to re-visit their past, we can nevr erase the past but surely it will lead to new understanding and more humanity. It is like Christianity in a way, fighting the battle every day to be better people, South Africans should think every day of their past especially when confronted with the crime that is raging. I do believe that the former 'untouchables" also need to come to a realization, we can only keep trying to bring them to that realization. I see the same thing in the US.

The one ingredient, which is sorely lacking, is discipline and self-discipline. The discipline part was so evident in the former "bad old good days" or perhaps "the good old bad days". The wrong kind of freedom is rampant here and in so many places in the world.

Can one be truly happy without self-discipline?

Pienaar, Mandy is the daughter of Mary-Anne; and the partner of Dylan Howard (who is the brother-in-law to Pey Malan Geldenhuys).

Pienaar, Tammy, sister to Mandy

Porter, Cayden, Bianca's son, grandson to Vivian Belfour-Cunningham (born Carr).

Porter, Chad married Bianca Belfour-Cunningham and is the father of Cayden

Preller crest

Preller crest

Preller, Abraham (born Bothaville 26th April 1987), class of 2005 at Grey College School, studied B.Ing Mechanical Engineering at North-West University. Son of Abri, siblings are Tina and Ivan. Lives in Potchefstroom. Engaged to marry Alecia Strydom.

Preller, Abri (born Pretoria 4th October 1960), studied B.Sc Agric (Plant production) at the Univerisity of Pretoria, lives in Bothaville and family includes Abraham, Ivan, Tina and Sulindie. Abri is a Facebook friend in 2011.

Preller, Alexis (born Pretoria 1911 - died Pretoria 1975) Painter. Inconclusive research as to his parent, but reasoned to be a fifth generation Preller and descendant of Johan Frederik Preller and Carel Friedrich Preller (1809-1870). As a painter, P. was encouraged by Jacob Pierneef, studied in London, later in Paris. He was powerfully affected by his years as a prisoner of war in Italy, and by his visits to Europe as well as to the Congo (Zaire), Zanzibar (Tanzania), the Seychelles and Egypt.

His first important government commission (1953) was for a mural painting for the Revenue Office, Johannesburg; his monumental mural in the Pretoria Provincial Administration Building was completed in 1955. Preller developed an individual, bold, formal style of painting, with striking imagery and symbolism drawn from his African background, from mythology and from his personal experiences. Preller worked in seclusion on his Transvaal farm. He died a month after one of his most successful exhibitions.

The following extract is worth inserting, despite obvious duplications: Art Education:

Alexis Preller studied art in 1934 at Westminster School of Art, London, under Mark Getler. Then in 1937 studied at Grande Chaumiere, Paris, under Othon Frieze. Nine years later, in 1946 went to London and Paris on a study-tour, and in 1953 carried out a second study-tour of Italy and Egypt.

Short Artist Biography:-

1911 to 1934 Alexis Preller was educated at Pretoria Boys High School, active in theatrical ventures; after completing school Alexis Preller worked for some time as a clerk before persuading his family to allow him to seek a future in the arts.

1934 Encouraged by his lifelong friend, Norman Eaton, Alexis Preller set off for London; there JH Pierneef advised him to enroll at Westminster School; with guidance from Gertler he made the choice of painting as his career.

1935 Returned to Pretoria via East Coast of Africa, held his first art exhibition; early works were emotional with strong colour and distortion.

1937 On return from further studies in Paris Alexis Preller stayed for a while in Swaziland painting continuously; exhibited in Johannesburg; referred to in Press as 'South African Gauguin'.

1938 Alexis Preller joined the New Group, included on its first art exhibition.

1939 Set out on a safari into the Congo; impressed by tribal ritual and sculptures; stirred by witnessing erupting volcanoes; outbreak of war brought him back to Pretoria.

1940 to 1943 Alexis Preller joined the Field Ambulance Corps, POW in North Africa and Italy until 1943; returned to South Africa and exhibited in Johannesburg; recollections of war experiences influenced his paintings; development of 'urn-heads' and surrealistic imagery; beginning of Blue Period

1944 Builds 'Ygdrasil', his studio designed by Norman Eaton.

1946 Again in Europe; study in Museums concentrating on Greek sculpture; phase of extensive self-exploration and imaginative translation of themes for Alexis Preller.

1948 Appearance of book, 'Alexis Preller' by Christi Truter, with autobiographical introduction.

1948 to 1949 Visits to Zanzibar and Seychelles Islands followed by many paintings; urgency of earlier expression followed by greater serenity; palette mellows toward Brown Period; development of previous themes relating to 'Ndebele Culture'; member of International Art Club, South Africa.

1953 Alexis Preller received Molteno Award; mural commissioned for Johannesburg offices of Receiver of Revenue; trip to Italy, where he studied frescoes in Florence and Arezzo; much impressed and influenced by Piero della Francesca; on return-trip visited Egypt, hieratic expression of that ancient culture had lasting impact on his work.

1954 Moved to a farm near Hartebeespoort Dam.

1955 Alexis Preller awarded Medal of Honour of South African Akademie.

1955 to 1958 Period of hieratic figure compositions; development of individual formal idioms and mythological symbolism.

1958 Last one-man exhibition Johannesburg; won national Univleis Competition.

1962 Several avenues explored: abstract symbolism, informalism and culmination of Quattrocento-style conceptions.

1965 Beginning of Gold Period; controversy regarding both new abstract and continued figurative expression, but great demand for all his paintings.

1968 Trip to Greece and Italy; began his autobiography.

1969 Alexis Preller experiments with 'intaglio' painting using moulded fibre-glass.

1971 Travels in Greece and Italy.

1972 Prestige Retrospective Exhibition, Pretoria Art Museum, prompted renewed exploration of several earlier themes.

1973 Began building 'Mudif' , a guest house in Middle Eastern Marsh-Arab tradition; filming of documentary production co-directed by Esme Berman and Edgar Bold interrupted by Preller's ill health - completed 1974.

1975 Last Exhibition, Johannesburg; died of heart attack.

Art Exhibitions:- 1935 Alexis Preller's first one-man art exhibition, Pretoria; 1936 Empire Art Exhibition, Johannesburg; 1938 New Group Exhibition, Cape Town and subsequent exhibitions; 1948 Overseas exhibition of South African Art, Tate Gallery; 1952 Van Riebeeck Tercent Exhibition, Cape Town; 1954 and 1956 Venice Biennale; 1966 Republic Fest Exhibition, Pretoria; 1972 Prestige Retrospective Exhibition, Pretoria Art Museum; 1973 Sao Paulo Biennale.

Public Art Collections:- South African National Art Gallery, Cape Town; Johannesburg Art Gallery; Pretoria Art

Museum; Durban Art Gallery; William Humphreys Art Gallery, Kimberley; King George VI Art Gallery, Port Elizabeth; Ann Bryant Art Gallery, East London; Hester Rupert Museum; Africana Museum, Johannesburg; Rembrandt Art Foundation; University of Wits Art Gallery; UNISA; Sandton Municipal Collection.

Source:- Berman, E. 1994. *Art & Artists of South Africa*. Southern Book Publishers.

Preller, Anna "Lizzie" Elizabeth (born 23rd February 1879 died 5th April 1976), Boer-War Concentration Camp survivor, daughter of Abraham Christoffel Naude Preller and Helletta Lephina Botha, married Johannes Albertus Geldenhuys on 27th June 1899. She was named after her grandmother, Anna Elizabeth Dreyer, who married Bothaville founder Theunis Louis Botha.

OuMam "Lizzie", as she was affectionately known, wrote about her experiences in the concentration camps in a book that was published April 1954 titled *Die Oorlogsherinneringe van Lizzie Geldenhuys*. It was the reason that prompted her grandson Preller Matt to write *Nickel Cross*, followed subsequently by documenting this work.

OuMam Lizzie was a neice of Gustav Schoeman Preller. Amongst the collected works of Preller Matt is a letter which Gustav wrote to Oumam, dated 26th June 1939, just prior to World War 2 as the Registrar of Burgers for war service. In the letter, Gustav writes about his regret to decline the invitation of a visit to Rustpan because of his unwelcome appointment in his old age; concern that the Japanese or the Italians, or both, declaring war. And his pending trip to Bloemfontein to establish a Free State Burger Union; and interestingly enough, that he had completed the family tree, except for the Naudé's".

OuMam Lizzie had six children. The first, Helletta Levina, was a victim of the British Concentration camp during the Boer War. The last, a son, Abram Carl Frederik Preller, was born at the family farm Rustpan, on 2nd August 1916. She lived to a ripe old age and died in 1976, aged 97.

'n Boerebruilof – a boer wedding – from Dot Serfontein's *Amper Onse Mense*.

"Abraham Christoffel Naudé Preller was delighted that cold winter's morning on 27th June 1899, when his daughter Lizzie – one of the most beautiful ladies from the Onder-Vals – married Jannie Geldenhuys.

Around the white-washed stone-church of the small town Bothaville the esteemed of the North-West Free State stood. The men were dressed in neat tailored suits, with heavy watch-chains in the embroidered waistcoat pockets; the beards are lopped, the hair curls smeared with springbuck fat and pressed into shape with scented water. The women are standing in groups, with their umbrellas on their shoulders, shielding them from the cold southerly wind. Their watered jaconet velvety gowns, gathered and full of tucks and pleats, the unmistaken camphor smells of distinction. Moreover hooded carts, 'spaaiders', coaches, carriages and landaus massed together, polished and with the coachmen dutifully in front of their horses. All around the church square all the shops, the police station, the post office and the blacksmith's shop was closed. Even the school closed early for the day so that mister Bosman, the teacher, and his wife Daisy could attend the wedding.

Oom Japie van Rensburg, the spiritual leader of the neighbourhood, was there; Herman Claasen from Graspan, Hendrik Lourens of Verlaatspruit, Dolf van Wyk – descendant of Long Piet van Wyk, the first who came to live here and one of the first owners of Gladdedrif, the farm on which Bothaville was laid out six years before the wedding – and definitely also Abraham Preller's two friends, Karel Coetzee and Barend Greyling. They were his colleagues on the town board and had six years previously supported him in the drawn-out negotiations with the Free State government to declare this place the town. The wives of

Barend, Karel and Abraham most probably wore golden broaches which their men-folk would have brought for them from Bloemfontein when they were there with the Bothaville petition.

Even Martinus and Cornelius Beukes from Kroonstad, and Hartley from Klerksdorp, highly esteemed and respected solicitors in their black frocks, starched collars and shoe-lace covers would have been there, because they handled the legal work, and very likely did the scheming that led to the breakthrough in the unpalatable struggle between Preller and his friends who wanted the town at Gladdedrif and Anthonie Goosen, Jan Richter and others who wanted the town higher up next to the Vals River. Briefly, all the important people in the surrounding districts and from Bothaville, or Botharania, like Preller wanted to call the town, was that day at the wedding – or gave their written apologies to the Prellers.

It speaks volumes for a man like Preller who in the space of ten years did not have a bean to his name when he worked behind the counter of Coulsen's shop in Kroonstad. Preller's father, Carl Frederik Preller, had in the muddy past in the Transvaal, had just a little too much to say about the ineffective administration of the Zuid Afrikaansche Republic – and when he opened his eyes he had his ground at Wonderboom near Pretoria confiscated and had to flee as a bankrupt fugitive to the Free State. His son Abraham started work as a shop clerk in Kroonstad and in 1876 married Helletta Lephina Botha, the daughter of Theuns Botha and Anna Dreyer, both large land-owners in the Onder-Vals. It made Abraham Preller a wealthy and influential, but not a self explanatory respected man. The scales in a rural district move slower and subtle than that, but in the passage of time he for other reasons aligned with the core bearing layer of the community. He was justice of the peace, one of the few who could draft testimonials and settle deceased estates, write official letters and make court presentations.

Abraham Preller was one of those who could take the initiative when it was decided to establish another town westwards along the Vals River as a connection between the recently established mine digging towns of Kimberley and Klerksdorp. For him the preferred place was his wife's inheritance from her father, Theuns Botha, the farm Gladdedrift. With a little legal knowledge, knavery and perseverance, he presented the Free State government in 1893 with the accomplished fact of the layout of Bothrania – already surveyed and provided with water: Botha-, named after his father-in-law, r-, after Hartley in Klerksdorp, and –nia, after his wife Lephina, who incidentally died before she could enjoy any of these privileges.

By the time his lovely daughter Lizzie married Jannie Geldenhuys, he was already with his third wife, hardly older than Lizzie. He was a member of the Town board, member of the church council, Veldcornet – field cornet, and a man just prior to the Anglo-Boer war that was listened to.

At this wedding his father-in-law, wealthy Theuns Botha who possessed everything here once upon a time, was an important figure. Despite his sixty years his reddish brown hair showed no signs of greying, and his smooth skin no wrinkles. Perhaps he wore, like the portrait of him that remained preserved, an elegant brown alpaca suit with silk facings around the sleeves and lapels, his snow-white round collared shirt, his red silk tie and his shoes made with genuine American leather, without laces or holes. Like many of those families still do today, he most likely spoke forcibly, with his left hand at his side and his right forefinger pointed, his head cocked to one side, his eyes glaring under the dense eyebrows. At best he was not too pleased with the skinny, poor boy which his grand-daughter was marrying.

If there was anybody who arrived at the last minute, in a light buggy or "sjees" (fail; expel, send down) as it was then called, it would have been Wilhelm van der Lingen, the well travelled, imposing preacher from Kroonstad, his beard trimmed square on his chest, hair curled backwards and his large tender eyes still full of the ardency of the drive.

The horse that pulled his buggy would have been a thoroughbred with the delicate gait, and Dominee could tell you precisely how long the journey had taken him. Dominee van der Lingen was known as an authority of horses, and frenzied lover of best stallions and elegantly modern English draught-animals. Spiritual sermons were founded on equestrian subjects. After an hour long talk regarding horses the congregations spiritual wellbeing was overflowing, the tithes collected and peace was made with ones neighbour.

It was surely Jan van Blommenstein that was the first to notice that the bridal car pulled away from his raw brick house where his wife Liz was busy dressing the bride. Jan van Blommenstein was a life long friend to

Preller, and the man who ran the mail service from Kroonstad to Bothaville. His wife Liz was mother to the various children out of the Preller marriages, and was also the convenor of the wedding that day. It assured her of significant status and brought in a handsome income for the family.

The wedding guests wait outside the church until the first blue horses of Jan Steyn appears at the church gates – his pride horses with colourful ribbons and ostrich feathers on the heads.

Jan Steyn, the owner of Lace Mine, a diamond mine near Bothaville, with his striped dress-coat, light brown trousers and white gloves, is in control of the reins. When he entered through the church gate the thin wheels of the black, landau cut grooves in the lose sand, spluttering the stone poles with stones.

How lovely Lizzie Preller looked in her white mervilleux wedding gown, on the arm of her father as the wedding march was played on the peddle-organ, as she approached the groom – beautiful in the sense of well-formed, but also beautiful because at that moment the inheritance of a proud ancestors was visible in her young face; the grey eyes of the Preller's, prominent high forehead and nose-bridge which rises high above the eyes, the slim, bony and nervous traits of the Dreyers, the blossom complexion of the Naudé's and the fiery manner of the Botha's.

Dot Serfontein (the writer) got to know Lizzie when she was already in her nineties, and from this bodily beauty the crux still discernible – still the bright eyes, the pride, and the vigilant spirit. She was then a truly Boer-aristocrat. The wedding service was conducted by Pastor Donges, the father of the latter Minister, and it was undoubtedly drawn out, because this minister was known amongst the older generation as an exegete and rationalist. The sermon could be thought out ever so carefully, but Duintjies as he was known by, would easily argue the merits of his own annotations, which resulted in the public worship being stretched to beyond lunch times. Not that anybody held it against him! The old forefathers were a lot more patient with their learned people than they are today.

After the service by ds. Donges, the bridal procession head out to the grand Preller homestead, on their part of Gladdedrif, which they called De Bank. If it rained, it did not dampen the spirit of anybody because the homestead on De Bank was the largest in the whole Onder-Vals. A Frenchman, Emile, and a Hollander, Jan de Wachter, had broken and cut the sandstone into large bricks and sent them to start building the house. But the task was so enormous that after a year they just disappeared. A second builder, Willem Knoetze, took another three years to complete this house, which was burnt down by the British during the Anglo-Boer War. Helletta Lephina, for whom Abraham Preller had built the house for, did not live long enough to see it through to completion. A second wife, with adolescent children, came and died; only a third – young wife, Johanna Wessels – got the heavy hangings and wall paper sent by train from the Cape, served the meals around the enormous walnut tree table and there gave birth to children. Helletta Lephina did her duty with the large abstract oil painting in the lounge.

All the rooms were decorated with anything that was green in the winter months. The young folk crowded around the tables lay with cake, biscuits, milk tart and sugared fruit. The three storied bridal cake was decorated with silver leaves and artistic icing, very luxurious and unusual for that time. The Preller's had ordered the cake from Fichardt in Bloemfontein and had it sent by mail coach from Kroonstad after being railed. The cake had to withstand the rough road and bumpy drifts.

The guests thong in the long, broad passages, the pantry, the living rooms and on the spacious verandah. The young men serve ginger-beer and warm wine-punch, and frolic with the maidens. The bridal couple, together with the older family members and prominent persons from the district sit at the dining room table, with side tables. Here lengthy speeches and toasts are made on both sides of the families, because weddings were one of the important platforms for public speakers in those days; and it was celebrated with very good Cape wines and imported gin. A heavy meal of suckling pig, lambs-pie, yellow rice and steamed potatoes is brought inside. A full-bodied sweet adorns the centre of the table, steaming in its 'witblits' (bootleg), cinnamon, sugar and lemon peels – so intoxicating that's its aroma was enough to take ones breath away.

By the light large, heavy hanging lamps with its glass shades hanging from the broad yellow-wood ceiling, the feast was eaten. They were the people who had tamed the wild tributaries of the Vals River, laid out their church and town, managed it and annually dispatched their council meting reports to Bloemfontein by coach and horses. They would be welcomed by Cornelis Wessels, waiting for them at the impressive pillars of the Raadsaal – Government Chambers, where they would partake of a presentable meal, and discuss news reports with the smooth advocate Abraham Fischer.

But times were a changing; it would even give way to the most thoughtless. One just had to look at the balmy Italian who dressed himself in a black waiter's suit, with a white cooks-hat, and who dramatically introduced himself in broken Afrikaans as Emilio Castignani. He claims to be the bridegroom's best friend. He serves, he encourages, he praises the aroma of the servings, the ladies clothing, and the men's tobacco. He tells jokes, he approves the weighty hypothesis of the speakers proposing toasts, he hums Italian street music, he murmurs and strikes his hand against his chest and over his heart when there is spoken of the brides brilliant future and how lovely and elegant she looks.

Before the Cape wine began to have its effect there must have been certain guest who took exception to the impudent Italian at such a classy Boer-wedding, and whispered amongst themselves that the foreigners from Kimberley and Johannesburg were infiltrating everywhere.

Kimberley brought in a flood of Uitlanders and loafers in 1871 to the West-Free State with the fever to prospect for anything. Before long the Sandvelders found that Frans de Raedt discovered coal at Vierfontein, and polluted their clean drifts with pitch black coal wagons en route to Kimberley. They had hardly come to accept this when gold was discovered at Johannesburg. Then the fat was in the fire, and this brought in a stream of riff-raff from the North. Everywhere around Klerksdorp little mines sprung up, with miners gallivanting and using God's name in vain in the bars and at the gambling tables.

On a day a prospector is found sitting at the road to Rondebossie, the farm of Jan Steyn, and watches how the ants remove grains just like at Kimberley. Before Jan Steyn could say 'knife', a diamond mine was established on his farm. De Beers pounded on him and bought the ground from under him, and now he is rich Jan Steyn who travels with the boastful span of horses and landau – so whispers the people – ostensibly specially to hire a cart and horses to go to the Cape on 'business'. There in front of the barmaid he lights his pipe with five pound notes.

Near Jan Steyn's mine, Lacemine, were two Italians Renaldo and Cicero Castignani who had a small shop. The Italian who was at the smart Boer-wedding was Emilio, the third brother who had recently emigrated from Italy.

Emilio Castignani was one of the astonishing fortune-seekers which the gold fever had offloaded in the Sandveld. When Jannie and Lizzie Geldenhuys got married, Emilio was only a couple of months in the country. But before the outbreak of the Anglo-Boer War, there were already rumours that he was involved with diamond smuggling. During the War, all activity at the Lace-Mine ceased, but shortly thereafter he was caught by detectives with diamonds in his possession. And so he was the first white man to be detained in the new prison cells of Kroonstad's new prison. The shocked Sandvelders hid their faces over the shame and decided that the last evil had arrived.

On the day that Emilio was caught, he sobbingly embraced his two Bantu assistants, and took his leave in unintelligible broken Afrikaans – Italian – Sesotho. This was not strange, because his association with nation was naturally not clipped their wings by the Afrikaner's inbred reserved ness.

The day he was arraigned he played the role of his wrath was kindled by unjust behaviour and argued every point the witnesses put forward. Eventually an investigation on site was ordered and he was taken under guard to his shop. There the court found that a door mentioned in evidence did not exist, that the cupboards in which the detectives found the diamonds did not have drawers; that the windows that were on the left was now on the right. The case was dismissed outright. Afterwards it was found that Emilio at the parting from his workers hastily instructed them to plaster up a middle door, to break down a window and a side wall, to white wash the walls and remove certain furniture.

Emilio was never again prosecuted. He moved his small farm shop to Bothaville and later joined the British community in Kroonstad which stayed behind after the War, and made the town a business centre. His legendary vitality, the unconventional confrontations and his cold-blooded business transactions, amongst the blood-thirsty, would even in a modern setting be the subject of debate, yet he was Mayor of Bothaville and of Kroonstad for many years. He was the only man who was mayor of both towns simultaneously. When he eventually died at a ripe old age, he left his third wife and all his children as very wealthy, god-fearing and totally Afrikaans converted. Buildings, hotels and streets are named after him in both towns.

Often, as is frequently told, the mayors of the surrounding towns would meet in Bothaville. As the resident Mayor he would give the welcoming address. In the middle of his speech he would suddenly stop, shriek, take a gulp of water and declare formally: "I am sorry gentlemen, but I cannot continue this speech. My young wife is waiting for me at home. Enjoy yourselves in any way you please." He pushed his chair aside, and pole-upright with long strides leave the assembly hall.

Yes, Lizzie and Jannie Geldenhuys had a distinctly spectacular wedding but perhaps the Geldenhuys's were not so impressed. That would have been Oubaas and Bessie Geldenhuys, Jannie's parents, Aap and Meraai Geldenhuys, Hendrik and Nelie Geldenhuys, his uncles, and his cousins Jurie, Lang Jan, Jan Stael, Dik Willem and Tol and others. Although the Geldenhuyse in those years could not compete one on one with the Bothas as far as property were concerned, or compared with the legal beaver Preller's, they did consider themselves a step above the average. Their farms were between the fertile Renoster and Vals rivers towards Kroonstad, and although they also had sand-veldt farms, they wouldn't dream to brag about it.

The Sandveld as Bothaville and surrounds were originally noted for, had in modern times with the use of fertilizer became famous as the mielie – quadrangle. Then it was a desert type region with a hard distasteful tussock territory. The grass grew as it had done in earlier years in Kroonstad. Then the old folk usually sent the ewes with their young sons and a trustworthy servant to go there to lamb. After a month or three the poisonous plants had sprouted, the grass lost its nourishment and the sheep had to return.

Mielies did not want to grow there, because the ground was too deficient of phosphate. A lot of people who lived there stayed in small groups, un-baptised, unmarried and in wretchedness and poverty huddled or herded together, intermarried and became mentally retarded. There was for example a group who /which dug their homes in the banks around a large pan, and were given the name "*Appeldammers*" – Apple dammars, for years a synonym for everything that was deplorable and inferior. The useable portions were the Vals River and its rivulets, and further west the Vaal River with its tributaries. That was the home of the Preller's wedding guests, but for the Kroonstaders it was not remotely not unusual. They had most likely calmly and self-assuredly participated in the festivities.

Dot Serfontein could imagine that the conversation amongst the men folk was troublesome and boring over the recent rinderpest with its shocking stock losses and the gloomy political circumstances: in Pretoria this is said, and in Bloemfontein that. But the burghers who had attended the 1899 target-shooting where the Free State government had issued everybody with one hundred mauser bullets, with the strict instruction under no circumstances to use it, and where they got hour long lectures over bodily and head by experienced Majuba-marksmen, could they reach their own conclusions.

The Geldenhuyse would have politely but without interest, listened. According to the journal that Jannie kept later during the War, was his people not unduly locked into the political situation of their time. They would apparently have considered it not "kosher" to trouble such a festive opportunity with insoluble problems.

Dutifully from a front-room they would already the light prancing of the concertina, and wait their turn to slip out one at a time to join the fray. They all had the English and Boer concertinas, the guitar and the new-fangled banjo which they played, and were fond of dancing. Not just reeling. They were masters of the mazurka and the lancers and knew that a person could in the spaciousness of the De Bank homestead execute such a dance with taste and precision.

Abraham Preller could also hear the concertina, but he stubbornly confined his conversation to land matters. His house, his virtuous house is being subjected to worldly music for the first time in its existence. What could he do but pretend that he could not hear it. He places his hand peremptory on his young wife's knee so that she would perhaps in her youthful indifference not keep time with the music. It was considerate of him, or so he thought, to build a house for Jannie and Lizzie just across the large homestead, over the depression, because he would keep a firm hand on the rudder. He sees how the groom ushers his bride out the door in the direction of the shriek music.

In the front-room the bridle couple are boisterously welcomed, and everybody stands back so that they could grace the dance-floor. Jannie gallantly takes a bow in front of his wife. His courting is of the highest order; relaxed and charming. He twirls her across the dance floor. He is an accomplished dancer, but he adjusts his footsteps to his clumsy bride. She only knows the steps from hearsay. Her knowledge of music was gained at college – the organ and piano – and the crazes she had learned to play, was church music (she was the church organist of the town up to the time of her marriage, and here and there a popular Victorian hit like *"Over the Waves", "Silent Confession"* and *"Whispering Hope"*. Sang they did, out of the Sankey and the old *"Globe"* song albums.

The time arrives, after a few dances – everybody knows it. The youngsters look forward to the moment with eagerness; the elderly remind themselves with melancholy. The bridal couple must depart for the nuptial couch. Lizzie is helped to get on top of the round table. Jannie holds her hand. She is blindfolded, and turns in circles. Al the single couple's crowd around the table – she has to throw her bouquet for somebody to catch it. For a young girl it is virtually impossible with all the young bachelors with arms outstretched. Young men grab the girls around their waists and hoist them in the air. Even if she does not catch the bouquet, just being held is something. Few of them realised at the privilege of catching the bouquet because it meant surviving the War and still being able to marry.

Lizzie disappears unnoticed, changes out of her wedding dress and meets Jannie at the back door. The light from the kitchen shines on a brand new half-tent carriage with springbuck leather cushions and a brand new harness. Even the pair of brown coach-horses she does not recognise. Everything looked beautiful, exciting and prosperous. A year later she would be pregnant, and flee apprehensively in it from the British army.

They sit close together as the horses set course down the white moonlit track. About a mile from the large house, across a hollow where a few 'katbos' – cat bush – are present stands a four-roomed house which they have already christened *"Katbos View"*.

They unlock the front door, and he carries her since time immemorial across the threshold, and lights the candle. Then he returns to stable the horse. She dresses with her printed calico nightgown and heavy embroidery, combs her long white hair and plaits it. He proceeds to the lounge and modestly sits in an easy-chair until she is finished. He takes care that the knotted quilt is properly tucked in around her when she climbed into the feather-bed, because he loves her and would always in future ensure that she is protected.

And if there was a search light in every window of the big house, or the continuous rain dripped though a hole onto the floor smeared with cow-dung, or whether this was said in Pretoria, or that in Bloemfontein, the love in Katbos View was young and sweet and enough for a life time together.

The above two stories was written by Dot Serfontein in her book **Amper Onse Mense**, which the writer has translated into English, for the benefit of his descendants. It is not often that one discovers such a priceless gem: A historical record of ones own grandparents, which one could forward to one's own grandchildren. May this survive another 100 years – for *their* grandchildren.

An interesting conclusion that Dot Serfontein found in her **Keurskrif vir Kroonstad** is that only another Geldenhuys was good enough to marry a Geldenhuys. No wonder there were twelve inter-marriages! (Preller M Geldenhuys, Durban, 11 November 2005)

Oumam lived in Bothaville until her death on 5th April 1976. She was buried next to my grandfather on Rustpan. The following is inscribed on her headstone *"Hier rus moeder, tot die dag breek".*

Die Oorlogsherinneringe van Lizzie Geldenhuys Limited edition published 20.4.1954. Amper Onse Mense - Dot Serfontein. Keurskrif vir Kroonstad – Dot Serfontein. Bothaville en sy Mense – v.d. Schyff and Van Eeden

Preller, Bertus (born 6th July), son of Kaai and Maryna Preller, married Liesl and father of Jeane Preller. Bertus studied at the University of the Orange Free State, lives in Cape Town and is a Family ans Divorce Law Attorney at Abrahams and Gross Attorneys.

Preller, Bob, born in Krugersdorp in South Africa in 1947 and together with his parents trans-located to the Northern Transvaal in 1954, now known as Limpopo Province.

After his studies, he spent most of his life in the financial world, but was always directly or indirectly involved in wildlife conservation. He travelled extensively in and through the Bushveld regions of South Africa, during which time he developed a love for the wild animals and birds of his country, but more particularly a passion for the Gentle Giants of South Africa, the African Elephant.

He has been a Honourary game ranger for many years in various regions. Since his first encounters with Elephant, as a young boy, his fascination grew into a lifelong obsession to understand and fathom the spirit and behaviour of these highly intelligent animals. He and his wife Annette lived amongst the elephant for four years in the Bushveld, after which they lived near the Tsitsikama forests in the Southern Cape, during which time he had close interaction with elephant night and day, often spending endless hours in their presence.

His dreams and ambitions to further explore the forests of Central Africa where the forest elephant (Loxidonta cyclotis) occur, will hopefully be realized, and allow him to share this information with others who are passionate about the elephantom species.

Bob and his wife Annette presently live in Pretoria, and together they enjoy the wonders of nature.

Preller, Carl, eldest son of Kaai and Maryna Preller.

Preller, Charles Arthur

Birth: 1853
Death: Apr. 5, 1885

English silk salesman. His body was found in a trunk in Room 144 of the Old Southern Hotel in St. Louis, Missouri. Preller became acquainted with Hugh Brooks, a.k.a. Walter Maxwell, on board the steamship Cephalonia on their way to America. Brooks was without means, but Preller was generous and the pair arranged to proceed to Australia after having seen the United States. Preller rejoined Brooks in St. Louis, where they were last seen together on Easter Sunday 1885. The next day Brooks left the hotel alone, leaving two trunks and a handbag behind. Disguising himself, he headed for San Francisco to sail to New Zealand a few days later. Suspicions were confirmed at the Southern Hotel when the abandoned trunks were opened. The body of Preller was found in one of the trunks with a note attached reading: "So perish all traitors to the great cause." It was felt that this note was left to make the crime appear an act of vengence on the part of the Fenian Brotherhood, a very active group at the time, with many Irish-Americans sympathizers in the United States. However, Brooks was captured in Australia and returned to the United States to stand trial for his cold-blooded crime. His defense was that Preller died under the influence of chloroform, but that murder was never intended. Brooks claimed that he administered chloroform at Preller's request in order to insert a catheter into his urethra, but the fatal results caused him to strip Preller's body and place it in the trunk. After taking steps to evade the authorities and prevent his identification and taking all of Preller's money, he fled in the hope of escaping arrest and trial. He claimed that his subsequent conduct was due to mental distress and liquor. On the night of June 4th the case was submitted to the jury and on the following morning a verdict of guilty was returned. Brooks appealed to the Supreme Court for a new trial, but the governor declined to intervene and Brooks was hanged on August 10, 1888.

Burial:
Bellefontaine Cemetery

Preller, Dain (born Durban, KZN-Natal, 23rd June 1984), son of Roland Preller and Portia Cloete.

Preller, Friedrich (1804-1878), German painter, whos paintings are in the Metropolitan Museum of Art, New York City. The sef portrait is shown above

Preller, Gustav Schoeman (born Pretoria, 4th October 1879 - died Pelindaba, Pretoria district, 6th October 1943), journalist, champion of Afrikaans, writer, critic and historian, was the son of Komdt. Robert Clunie Logie Preller (1846 – 1916), of Klipdrift, a farm in the district of Pretoria, and his wife, Stephina Schoeman, daughter of Komdt-Gen. Stephanus Schoeman. Preller's great-grandfather, Johan Friedrich Preller, of Halle-an-der-Saale, Germany, who came to the Cape as a soldier in 1787, was the first South African ancestor of the Preller family.

In 1898 Preller married Johanna Christina Pretorius, second daughter of Lt-Col. Henning P.N. Pretorius, commandant of the Transvaal State artillery, who was a grandson of Piet Retief and of Piet Pretorius, brother of Komdt. Gen. A.W.J. Pretorius. Three sons were born.

In 1878 Preller's parents moved to Paardekop, in the Standerton district, and from 1887 onward Preller went to school at Standerton. In 1891 the family returned to Pretoria. Where Preller was employed as a shop assistant, an attorney's clerk, a clerk and, before the Second Anglo-Boer War, as chief clerk in the department of mines. At the beginning of the war, when his father was fighting on the Colesberg front with his uncle, Gen. Hendrik Schoeman, Preller, serving in the State artillery, took part in major battles in

Natal: Dundee (a battle he described in one of his works), Modderspruit, Colenso and Platrand (Wagon Hill), Ladismith (6.1.1900). By May 1900 Preller was back in Pretoria to help the state attorney J.C. Smuts, move the government's gold bars to safety. He continued to serve in the artillery, and was the war correspondent of *De Volksstem* and *De Zoutpansberg Wachter*, Pietersburg. Four months before peace he was taken prisoner near Ermelo and sent to India. *Ons parool: dae uit die dagboek van 'n krygsgevange* (Cape Town, 1938) recounts Preller's experiences as a prisoner of war.

Discouraged in September 1902 at not being able to resume his work with the department of mines after his release, Preller intended to accompany the Rev. Louis Vorster as an immigrant to Argentina. He gave up his plans when Eugene N. Marais asked him to become the editor of *Land en Volk*. That was the beginning of Preller's career as an Afrikaans journalist. From 1902 to 1936 he was successively editor of *Land en Volk* (1902-03), assistant editor (1903-24) and editor (1924-25) of *De Volksstem* (later *Die Volkstem*), men like J.H.H. de Waal in the chief editor of *Ons Vaderland* (later *Die Vaderland*) from 1925 to 1936. In 1928 he declined the editorship of *Die Volksblad* (Bloemfontein).

Preller distinguished himself as a versatile journalist. A brilliant reporter with an unusual flair for news, he remains unsurpassed in his best leading articles. Although he was one of the most gifted journalists of his day, he was, by modern standards, not very successful as an editor: he was too much of an individualist, was not an organiser, and, technically, was too attached to old-fashioned methods and ideas.

The Afrikaners' changing circumstances after 1902 and their love of their language paved the way for the growth of Afrikaans. Writing in *De Goede Hoop*, *De Afrikaner* and *De Volkstem*, men like J.H.H. de Waal in the south, J.S.M. Rabie in Natal, and Preller, himself in the north advocated the acceptance of Afrikaans as a written language. But the most rousing plea was Preller's. Encouraged by his support, the *Tweede Afrikaanse Taalbeweging* ('Second language movement') grew apace, and he became one of its greatest leaders.

The stimulus for Preller was J.H. ('Onze Jan') Hofmeyr's speech *Is 't ons ernst?* Which he made at Stellenbosch on 6.3.1905. Hofmeyr accurately summarised the faults of 'our language' as used in churches, in schools, by the government and by people generally. To this Preller gave a most positive reply in a series of articles, *Laat 't ons toch ernst wezen! Een voorstel te handhaving en veredeling van het Afrikaans als schrijftaal* in *De Volkstem* (19.4.1905 – 14.6.1905, published as a brochure in July 1905).

In this *Taalbeweging* manifesto Preller became the first person openly submit, in the leading Transvaal newspapers, a closely reasoned plea for Afrikaans. To Hofmeyr's question, which concerned *Dutch*, he replied with the plea that his fellow countrymen should take *Afrikaans* seriously. While Hofmeyr's attitude was negative, Preller was historically accurate and positive; he maintained that, unlike Dutch and English, both of which were foreign languages. Afrikaans was the only language that had a chance of surviving in South Africa because, unlike the other two languages, it was a deeply rooted, living language, which could not be destroyed.

After the publication of Preller's plea and two days before he called for the forming of a society for the advancement of Afrikaans, Eugene Marias's poem 'Winternag' was published in *Land en Volk* (reprinted in *De Volkstem* on 5.7.1905). Preller immediately used this poem to show what, in the hands of an able poet, could be done with a despised 'kitchen' language.

In his call for an Afrikaans society Preller showed how it could be formed. He captured public interest by publishing provocative articles and letters from his readers. Above all, he was tactful; to persuade the Afrikaners – his first aim – he advised them to speak and write Afrikaans, to learn Dutch and to read both. As an encouragement, he started a short story competition: 'Wie kan stories skryf'?'

Inevitably, a storm of criticism greeted Preller's appeal. The arguments of its opponents were that Afrikaans was a patois, that it had no literature and that, as a written language, it hardly stood a chance against English. Preller was so sure of his case that he was able to listen patiently and to deal with arguments in a logical and considered manner.

In his struggle for his language and the identity of his people, Preller appealed to both reason and sentiment. His call for a language society met with general approval; preliminary committees were formed in Pretoria and Bloemfontein with instructions to draw up a programme for discussion by the proposed society, particularly in regard to spelling.

On 13.12.1905 about thirty supporters of Afrikaans met in *De Volkstem's* office under the chairmanship of Dr N.M. Hoogenhout to found the Afrikaanse Taalgenootskap (A.T.G.). Hoogenout became the chairman of the committee, which was elected, while the other members were Preller, A.J. van der Walt, H. Visscher, N.J. de Wet, Izak van Heerden (secretary) and F.T. Nicholson. In addition, the following were asked to become members: H.C. Jorissen, Dr D.F. Malan, Dr J.D. du Toit, S.W. Pienaar, the Rev. W. Postma, Joh. Visscher, J.S.M. Rabie and the Rev. P.C. Snyman.

In 1909 Preller helped to found the Zuid-Afrikaanse Akademie voor Taal, Letterkunde (Letteren) en Kunst (now the Suid-Afrikaanse Akademie vir Wetenskap en Kuns), of which he remained an active member until his death. From 1913 to 1925 and from 1925 to 1927 he was secretary to the Akademie, and later elected an honorary member, this being a mark of appreciation of his services to Afrikaans. In 1913 he delivered the first Afrikaans address to the Akademie.

In 1910 Preller was one of the founders of *Die Brandwag*, he and Dr W.M.R. Malherbe becoming joint editors on the 31.5.1910, and after Malherbe had resigned Preller was sole editor until February 1922, when the periodical was discontinued. This magazine was of incalculable value in the language struggle and often contained the first literary work of many new writers.

Preller was also a pioneer literary critic. Although he was influenced by the *Tagtigers* (a group of Dutch poets of the eighties), his individual judgements were sound and he tried to be objective.

In his reviews, which appeared in *De Volkstem* and *Die Brandwag*, he urged writers to use Afrikaans in conveying experiences both subtle and profound. Preller was the leading critic in the Afrikaanse Taalgenoodskap. Through his study of Dutch literature and of the products of the *Eeste* ('First language movement') and *Tweede Taalbeweging,* Preller developed into an able critic. Emulating the *Tagtigers*, he attacked everybody who disgraced his language; he destroyed pretensions, which gave a false picture of the language and of experience.

Preller was the first critic honestly to appraise Afrikaans literature with literary insight. He found nothing that was lasting, uplifting and good in the work of Melt Brink; he pointed out the shortcomings of J.H.H. de Waal's *Johannes van Wyk* (cf. His 'Persoonlike appresiasie van J.H.H. de Waal s'n Johannes van Wyk'; *De Volkstem*, 19.8.1906), and gave his views on how an historical novel should be written; he also introduced his people to *Die vlakte en ander gedigte* by J.F.E. Celliers. This is perhaps the clearest evidence that as a critic, he was in advance of his time. Among the other works that he reviewed during 1908-09 were: *By die monument* (Totius), *Verse van Potgieterstrek* (Totius), *Die revier* and *Karoo blommetjies* (D.F. Malherbe). His mature experiences of life, his erudition, his vision, his idealism and his wisdom make his contributions both significant and inspiring.

From his critiques, including those of the play Susanna Reyniers (A. Francken), of Afrikaanse verhale (J.G. Engela), of Die eselkakebeen (Dr O'Kulis) and of Stompies: 'n bundle stories, rympies en toneelspeletjies in die Afrikaanse taal (de Waal), it became clear that Preller did not hesitate to expose all the errors which offended his pride in his language and his people. Although too prone to regard a work of art as organic, he was the first serious and penetrating critic in Afrikaans.

Preller also demonstrated the poetic expressiveness of Afrikaans. His poem 'As die soeklig van die wagskip', a remarkable translation of Joubert Reitz's 'When the searchlight from the gunboat', appeared in the introduction to the *Vlakte* collection. Two of his poems appeared in *De Volkstem* (30.8.1905); the melancholy 'Hoe lang?' and the rather more hopeful 'More'. *De Volkstem* of 5.9.1906 also contained 'Te wees, of nie te wees', his translation of 'To be or not to be'.

In March 1907 he helped to found the Afrikaans-Hollandse Toneelvereniging, which remained in existence until 1918 and of which he was the chairman. He produced translations from English and French: Augusta Gregory's *Spreading the news*, adapted in Afrikaans as *Hoe die nieuws versprei het*; Thomas Brandon's *Charley's aunt* as the popular *Piet s'n tante* (1908); and Emily Zola's *Les heritiers de Rabourdin as Erasmus s'n erfgename*.

As a journalist Preller dealt daily with correspondence that was a hotchpotch of Dutch, Afrikaans and English. He fully realised that the standard of Afrikaans prose was still very low. When judging the short story competition, he asserted that to develop and refine the written language a writer should not simply tell a story; he should have experienced what he had tried to convey, because only then would his readers be able to share what he had to express.

But Preller did not only advise younger writers; he set them an example through his own work. On 13.12.1905 the first of a series of articles on Piet Retief was published in *De Volkstem*. Through this he wanted to prove that Afrikaans could also be used for the sciences and arts as Marias and Celliers had used it for poetry.

Preller's prose style was clear, concise and individual. Some of his best prose, uniting literary and scientific excellence, is in historical works of his such as his biographies of Trichardt and Pretorius and his war memoirs, particularly *Oorlogsmag*, which as prose has the qualities of a classic.

Preller was the first conscious stylist in Afrikaans literature. His language was larded with foreign words, but he also used new words and combination of words, including his own coinage, which he combined with racy colloquialism. He was, however, too prone to use Dutch when a good, vigorous Afrikaans expression would have served his purpose equally well. In spite of such irregularities and oddities, Preller used Afrikaans distinctively, forcefully and evocatively.

Not only as a champion of Afrikaans and a writer, Preller also made important contributions towards the development of Afrikaans historiography.

Apart from his collaboration with Dr F.V. Engelenburg in publishing *Onze krijgsofficieren* (Pretoria, 1904), a photograph-album containing brief biographical sketches of Boer officers who fought in the Second Anglo-Boer War and *Paul Kruger's afkomst en familie* (Pretoria, 1904), a brief occasional publication issued in the years that President S.J.P. Kruger died, Preller became known as a historian when his series of articles, 'Piet Retief; lewenskets naar nieuwste gegevens bewerk', appeared in the *De Volkstem* (13.12.1905 to 6.1.1906). These articles, which were continually being supplemented and improved, appeared in book form in 1906, and in 1920 the tenth edition was published. Once he had begun, he became so fascinated by the research into and the writing of his country's history that he devoted to this task the little spare time he had as a journalist; later he declared that, as a journalist, politics was his occupation, while history was his life.

After his retirement as a newspaper editor he was appointed government historian of South Africa from 1.3.1936 and until his death applied himself to the writing of history.

He devoted most of his time to two periods which were peaks in the history of the Boer nation; the period of the Great Trek and the migrations westward and northward which followed it; and the Second Anglo-Boer War, 1899-1902.

Preller wrote the following works on Boer migration during the nineteenth century: *Piet Retief: lewensgeskiedenis van die grote Voortrekker* (Pretoria, 1906*); Baanbrekers: 'n hoofstuk uit die voorgeskiedenis van Transvaal* (Pretoria, 1915), reprinted later in *Oorlogs- oormag en ander sketse en verhale* (Cape Town, 1923); an introduction to *Dagboek van Louis Trichardt, 1836-1838* (edited and annotated by Preller, Bloemfontein, 1917; *Voortrekkermense*, a collection of documents on the history of the Great Trek (6 volumes; Cape Town, 1918-25 and 1938); *Voortrekker-wetgewing: notule van die Natalse volksraad, 1839-1845* (Pretoria, 1942); 'Die Retief-Dingaan-ooreenkoms'. In *Annale van die Universiteit van Stellenbosch*, IIB, no. 1 (Cape Town, 1942), later included in *Sketse en opstelle* (Pretoria, 1828); *Hoe ons aan Dingaansdag kom: Jan Bantjies se dagverhaal van die winkommando* (Bloemfontein, 1828, reprinted in *Voortrekkermense*, VI); *Die Grobler-moord* (2 v.; Pretoria, 1930); *Andries Pretorius: lewensbeskrywing van die Voortrekker-kommandant-generaal* (Johannesburg, 1937); *Ou-Pretoria: sakelike verhaal van die stad se Voortrekkerperiode* (Pretoria, 1938; English edition: *Old Pretoria*; Pretoria, 1938; and *Voortrekker van Suidwes* (Cape Town, 1941).

Preller dealt with the Second Anglo-Boer War in *Kaptein Hindon: oorlogsavonture* van 'n baas-verkenner (Pretoria, 1916); Generaal Botha: 'n paar besonderhede en 'n paar foto's, 27 September 1862 – 27 Augustus 1919 (1919; later partly reprinted in Historiese opstelle); Oorlogsoormag en ander sketse en verhale (Cape Town, 1923); Ons parool: dae uit die dagboek van 'n krygsgevangene (Cape Town 1938); Scheepers se dagboek en die stryd in Kaapland, I Oktober 1901-18 Januarie 1902 (Cape Town. 1938); Talana: die drie generaalsslag by Dundee, met lewenskets van Generaal Daniel Erasmus (Cape Town, 1942).

Preller also wrote on other subjects: *Agt jaar s'n politiek: skoon geskiedenis van die Suid-Afrikaanse Nationale party, 1902-1910* (Pretoria, 1910); under the pen-name 'Knop'); 'Suid-Afrika s'n Boere republiek: 'n historiese resume' (1919); included in Preller and C.J. Langenhoven's *Twee geskiedkundige opstelle* (Cape Town, 1919); *Historiese opstelle* (Pretoria, 1925) and *Sketse en opstelle* (Pretoria 1928), two works containing various essays, including his views on history; *Ons goud roman: die Marias-dagboek* (1849-1865), Pretoria, 1935 (English edition: *Argonauts of the Rand*); *Daglemier in Suid-Afrika; oorsig van die geskiedenis van Suid-Afrika van die vroegste tye tot 1881* (Pretoria, 1937; English edition: *Day-dawn in South Africa); Geskiedenis van die Krugerstandbeeld* (Pretoria, 1939); and *Lobengula: the tragedy of a Matabele king* (Johannesburg, 1963).

Preller also collected numerous documents, statements, reminiscences, diaries and portraits. As archivist of the A.T.G.- Afrikaanse Taalgenoodskap he appealed to readers of *Die Brandwag* from 1910 to send to the editor of the magazine all unpublished historical documents. In this manner he obtained much material concerning the A.T.G., the Afrikaans-Hollandse Toneelvereniging, the Unie van Debatsvereniginge, and other related organisations. During his long association with *De Volkstem* he also collected and kept in files a great amount of historical information which forms the comprehensive Preller collection in the Transvaal archives, Pretoria, and is an important source for researchers.

Through his choice of his two special spheres of research, as well as his approach to and presentation of history, Gustav showed himself pre-eminently a national historian. He began to write in Afrikaans at a time when most historical publications were in English.

He wanted, firstly, to show the opponents of Afrikaans what could be done with a 'kitchen language' and, secondly, to make his people aware of their own language during a period of Anglicisation after the Second Anglo-Boer War.

His explicit aim was to acquaint his despondent countrymen with their heroic past, so that their pride in that past might restore their courage and their hope for the future; he led them to a discovery of their past. Thus, for example, he saw the Great Trek as a nation's quest for freedom. Objectivity was not his main concern. His approach, he maintained, was as objective as was consistent with his duty as an Afrikaner. This accounts for many of the criticism in his historical work.

To him history was not the actions of 'a generation of Titans or a generation of great intellectuals', but of 'a great many small people like us'. To him history was made by the will of the masses under the dispensation of God. Thus he considered history the biography of nations. But he did not ignore the individual's part in history; this is clear from his biographical work and his view of Retief as a 'conscious founder of the Afrikaner nation'. To Gustav history should be a lesson to present and future generations so that they would not make the same mistakes as their predecessors.

In spite of his figurative and forceful style, and his remarkable narrative and descriptive gifts, Gustav's historiography was not the work of a trained historian. Too often his original research was faulty; he made errors about dates and facts, and often included an overwhelming number of superfluous details. Because of his eagerness to give a national interpretation of history, he often ignored incidents which had no bearing on Afrikaner development, and sometimes did injustice to personalities he did not consider heroes.

Despite the aforementioned observations, Gustav Preller secured himself a special reputation as the first Afrikaans historian to make his nation aware of its past. In 1930 the University of Stellenbosch recognised his work with an honorary doctorate, while he was also honoured in Holland, where he was made a member of the Historisch Genootschap, Utrecht, and the Maatschappij der Nederlandse Letterkunde, Leiden.

Gustav was reserved, modest and courteous; he devoted his life to study and writing, using his many gifts to further

Afrikaner ideals. In his last years he wrote various historical articles for *Die Huisgenoot*, dealing, for example, with the controversy on the discovery of the Witwatersrand main reef; he also wrote articles for the special editions on the Great Trek (1936 and 1938). He lived to see the symbolic Ossewatrek (1938) and was a guest speaker on the Day of the Covenant that year.

In 1939 he was summoned from his farm and appointed Registrar of Burgers for World War 2. On 26th June 1939 he wrote to Oudad Johannes Albertus Geldenhuys and "Nig. Lizzie" that he had completed the family tree, and also his concern that the Japanese and Italians will be joining the War.

Gustav Schoeman Preller died on his farm near Hartebeespoort and was buried there in the family graveyard, where his friend Eugene Marais also lies buried. A plaque was unveiled on his grave in 1947.

; Transvaal archives, Pretoria: Preller collection; - J.H.J. VAN AS, 'Hy het sy merk gemaak', *Ons Vaderland*, 5.12.1930; - EUGENE MARIAS, 'Gustav Preller', *Ons Vaderland*, 5.12.1930; - A.M. VAN SCHOOR, article *Die Huisenoot*, 29.5.1931; - RUD P. VISSER, 'Vier-en-twintig jaar koerant-ontwikkeling onder drie redakteurs', *Die Vaderland*, 2.7.1963; - D.W. KRUGER, 'Die geskiedskrywing oor die Groot Trek', *Koers*, Dec. 1938; 'G.S. Preller as geskiedskrywer', *Koers*, June 1944; - G.S. PRELLER, 'Ons stig 'n tydskrif . . .", *Die Huisgenoot*, 28.6.1940; 'Laat 't ons toch ernst wezen', repr. In *H. Ann.*, Oct 1952; - D.J. OPPERMAN, 'G.S. Preller as kritikus', *Die Huisgenoot*, 8.11.1940; - F.V. LATEGAN, 'Gustav Preller: Piet Retief', *O.E.B.*, Sept 1943; - Obituaries: *Die Vaderland*, 6.10.1943; *Die Transvaler*, 7.10.1943; *Die Burger*, 7.10.1943; *Die Volkstem*, 8.10.1943; - H.S. PRETORIUS, 'Rede by Preller se begrafnis', *Die Transvaler*, 8.10.1943; -*Die Huisgenoot*, 22.10.1943 (art. Harm Oost, J.P. la Grange Lombard, J.M.H. Viljoen); - 'Dr Preller se werke', *Die Huisgenoot*, 29.10.1943 (full bibliog.); - J.F.W. GROSSKOPF, 'Ons Afrikaanse geskiedskrywer, *Die Volkstem*, 1.12.1943; - J.R. MALAN, 'Preller as kunstenaar met verwysing na sy mensbeelding, verhaalkuns, taal en styl' (Unp. M.A. thesis, Unisa (P.U.C.) 1943; - P.C. SCHOONEES, Die prosa van die Tweede Afrikaanse Beweging. 3rd ed. C.T. 1943; - H.B. THOM, 'Dr Gustav Preller, 1875-1943', *T.W.K.*, Mar. 1945; - A.J. ANTONITES, `Die Afrikaanse taalstryd in Transvaal, 1910-1922' (Unp M.A. thesis, U.W., 1945); J.S. DU PLESSIS, 'Dr Gustav Preller as historikus van die Groot Trek' (Unp. M.A. th., Unisa (P.U.C.), 1946; `Gustav Schoeman Preller:4.10.1875-6.10.1943. Sy geskiedskrywing' , *Historia*, Oct. 1956; - E.C. PIENAAR, Die triomf van Afrikaans: historiese oorsig van die wording, ontwikkeling, skriftelike gebruik en geleidelike erkenning van ons taal. C.T., 1946; - P.J. NIENABER, 'Aantekeninge i.v.m. Gustav Preller' *H. Ann.*, Oct. 1952; - D.J. OPPERMAN, 'Preller en sy studiebronne', *Standpunte*, Dec. 1952; - J. BOUWS, 'Gustav Preller en die Afrikaanse musiek', *S.A. Musiekonderwyser*, 7.12.1954; - T.H. LE ROUX, 'Vyftig jaar Afrikaans', *T.W.K.* Oct 1955; 'Gustav Preller as bouer aan ons taal', *H. Ann.*, Dec 1965; `Die Afrikaans van Gustav Preller', *T.W.K.*, Sept. 1966; - RINIE STEAD. `Gustav Preller – 'n huldeblyk', *Lantern*, Sept. 1961; - F.A. VAN JAARSVELD, Ou en nuwe wee in die Suid-Afrikaanse geskiedskrywing (Comm. Unisa, A.16). Pta., 1961; - C.F.J. MULLER, `Die Groot Trek', hervertolking van ons geskiedenis. (Comm. Unisa, B.19). Pta., 1963; - J.J. OBERHOLSTER, 'Die neerslag van die romantiek op ons geskiedskrywing – Gustav S. Preller', *T.G.W.*, Dec. 1966-Mar. 1967.

Preller, J.C a decendant of Voortrekker Piet Retief – great-granddaughter helped lay the foundation stone to the Voortrekker Monument.

The Voortrekker Monument is a monument in the city of Pretoria, South Africa. The massive granite structure, built to honour the Voortrekkers who left the Cape Colony between 1835 and 1854, was designed by the architect Gerard Moerdijk who had the ideal to design a "monument that would stand a thousand years to describe the history and the meaning of the Great Trek to its descendants". It can be seen from almost any location in the city, as it is seated on a hilltop.

Construction started on 13 July 1937 with a sod turning ceremony performed by chairman of the SVK, Advocate Ernest George Jansen, on what later became known as Monument Hill. On 16 December 1938 the cornerstone was laid by three descendants of some of the Voortrekker leaders: Mrs. J.C. Muller (granddaughter of Andries Pretorius), Mrs. K.F. Ackerman (great-granddaughter of Hendrik Potgieter) and Mrs. J.C. Preller (great-granddaughter of Piet Retief).

http://www.360cities.net/image/voortrekker-monument-north-roof

Preller, James (born 1961) is the childrens' book author of the Jigsaw Jones Mysteries, which are published by Scholastic Corporation. It appears that James is the youngest of seven children, and has two older brothers and four older sisters. He grew up in Wantagh, New York and went to college in Oneonta, New York. After graduating from college in 1983, James Preller was employed as a waiter for one year before being hired as a copywriter by Scholastic Corporation, where he was introduced (through their books to many notable children's authors. James Preller published his first book, entitled *Maxx Trax: Avalanche Rescue* in 1986. Since that time James Preller has written a variety of books, and has written under a number of pen names, including Mitzy Kafka, James Patrick, and Izzy Bonkers. James lives in Delmar, New York with his wife Lisa and their three children, Nicolas, Gavin and Maggie.

Preller, Johann Friedrich (1764-14.12.1825), stamvader, soldier and later hunter, from Halle a.d. Saale, son of Johann Friedrich Preller and Johanna Dorothea Philemon.

In 1794, Preller was employed by butcher Frederik van Reenen as a cattle buyer, and became a citizen of Graaff-Reinet in 1813. He married Zacharia Chistina de Beer 23rd November 1794 – she was born 7th November 1777 and died 6th March 1845. They had seven children, two sons and five daughters. The first son, was unmarried and died aged 26, and the last son, Carel Friedrich, had 15 children. Preller died in 1825, either 20th July or 14th December (writers note; - discrepancies found during research into exact dates from different sources was not uncommon!).

Preller, Ivan (born Bothaville 22nd November 1993), youngest son of Abri Preller. Goes to Potchefstroom Gymnasium. Sibling to Abraham and Tina Preller

Preller, Johan Frederik (circa 1967), M.A. assistant director of Archives, Pretoria, fourth or fifth generation descendant of Johann Friedrich Preller (stamvader) and Zacharia Christina de Beer. Ancestors were Carel Friedrich 1809-1870 and Johan Frederik of either Pietermaritzburg 13th September 1855 or twin born to Mauritz Herman Otto Preller born Beaufort-Wes 3rd July 1840.

Preller was a contributor to 'Dictionary of South African Biography' – DSAB – as edited by W.J. de Kock, M.A., B.Ed. (Cape Town), D.Phil. (Stell), sometime professor of history, University College of the Western Cape in 1968. He contributed by writing the biography of Francois Stephanus Malan, which appears in edited form in this biographical record.

DICTIONARY OF FAMILY BIOGRAPHY

Preller, Jon-Jon (born East London, Eastern Cape, on 23 November 1981), son of Roland Preller and Portia. Jon-Jon has two other brothers, Dain and Rhett. Jon-Jon was schooled at Bloemfontein College, and lives in East London. Roland Preller manages the MyHeritage Preller site – well worth a visit [I used it extensively for Preller genealogy and useful 'smart matches' facility.

Preller, Kaai (born 25th May), married Maryna, father of Carl, Bertus and Alesta, and grandfather to Jeane, Ryno, Herman and Henno. Studied at the University of the Free State and interested in Athletics coaching. Facebook friend in 2011.

Preller, Karen (born Erwitte, Germany, 2nd March 1983), lives in Duisburg, Germany. Facebook friends of Kirsten Preller and Roland Preller (and the writer, in 2011).

Preller, Kirsten (born Erwitte, Germany), High schooled at Realschule Anröchte and lives in Magdeburg, working for Uniklinikum Magdeburg.

Preller, Kirsten (born Enwitte, Germany 15th April 1980), sister to Karin Preller, living in Magdeburg, Germany. Kirsten has worked at Uniklinikum. Facebook friend in 2011.

Preller, Mark Anthony (born Windhoek, Namibia, 7th March 1985), son of Nicholas Fraser. Studying professional acting for camera at City Varsity. Lives in Cape Town, Western Cape.

Preller, Lara Nieuwoudt (born), Facebook acquaintance 2011.

Preller, Paul (born Uqchlen, 24th April 1954), studied at St. Agnes Pedaqoqische Academie and lives in Rosmalen, North Brabant province, Netherlands.

DICTIONARY OF FAMILY BIOGRAPHY

Elizabeth Geldenhuys aged 66
Johannes Albertus Geldenhuys
  born 8.7.1877 died 28.5.1944
Pieter Christian Gideon Steyn Jordaan
  born 10.10.1901 died 31.12.1963
Anna Elizabeth (Preller) Geldenhuys
  born 23.2.1879, died 5.4.1976

Preller, Paul T (born Windhoek, 9th February 1986), son of Nicholas Fraser and Sonja Preller. Studied STCW 95 at Cape Pininsula University of Technology. Lives in Windhoek, Namibia and is a Management and Tour Guide at Baqatelle Kalahari Game Ranch.

Preller, Petrus Johannes (born 21st June 1847, died Rustpan 5th February 1923). Petrus Johannes was the first person to be buried in the small Rustpan cemetery. He has a substantial concrete tomb and it is believed he was one of the original Preller farmers in the district. He was aged 55 when the Boer War ended in 1902.
  Petrus Johannes is recorded as a bachelor in the writers genealogical records – and it is believed it was him who ceded Rustpan farm to OuMam Lizzie Preller.
Rustpan's homestead was built in 1880, with walls 15 feet high and 18 inches thick. The house was burnt down by the British during the Anglo-Boer War. At the cessation of hostilities, Jannie Geldenhuys and Lizzie Preller moved there (Rustpan was her "erfgrond"), and in 1904 the farm of 3455 morgan was lent to three persons – Johanna Maria Botha, Johannes (Jannie) Albertus Geldenhuys, and Carel (Charlie) Friedrich Preller.

The graves, in order of burial dates, on Rustpan are as follows:-
Petrus Johannes Preller
  born 21.6.1847 died 5.2.1923
Hendrik Jacobus Geldenhuys born 5.7.1849 died 12.12.1930

Preller, Rhett (born Bloemfontein 11 December 1990), son of Roland Preller and Portia. Went to Sentraal Hoërskool, and lives in East London, Eastern Cape.

Preller, Rita, lives in Baltimore, Maryland, USA. Psychotherapist, specialising in the treatment for alcohol and substance abuse, eating disorders, sex-addiction, co-dependency for adults, adolescents and couples.

297

Preller, Robert Clunie (born 5th April 1846 - died 8th April 1943), of Klipdrift, a farm in the district of Pretoria (some records state he was born 5th May 1846, in Pietermaritzburg!). He married his wife, Stephina Schoeman, on 14th December 1874, the daughter of Komdt-Gen. Stephanus Schoeman. As a Kommandant during the Boer War, he commanded the Pretoria-Randkommando. He was the father of Gustav S Preller, journalist, champion of Afrikaans, writer, critic and historian. Preller's grandfather, Johan Friedrich Preller, of Halle-an-der-Saale, Germany, who came to the Cape as a soldier in 1787, was the first South African ancestor of the Preller family.

Kmdt. Preller operated mainly in the Southern Free State front – notably the Colesberg and Philippolis areas and is quoted extensively by Professor Fransjohan Pretorius, historian at the University of Pretoria, in his "*Kommandolewe Tydens die Anglo-Boereoorlog 1899-1902*", which was published by Human and Rousseau in 1991. In fact, it is believed that Kmdt Preller also served as the "Landdros of Philippolis" and Chairman of the "Krygsraad" during November 1899 / January 1900, when he sentenced a burger to fourteen days imprisonment or the payment of a £5 fine for drunkenness.

Kmdt Preller is quoted in Dr JEH Grobler's *The War Reporter* as being 'recalled to Pretoria and relieved of his command' after General Koos de la Rey found him responsible for causing dissention amongst the boer officers when General Stephanus Schoeman was 'replaced' by the promotion of Commandant H.R. Lemmer as chief commandant to take charge of the Southern Front.

However, Preller did return to the Southern Front and on the 7th September 1901 he was wounded in the Colesberg area, captured and sent to Shajahanpur in India as a prisoner-of-war.

Preller, Robert H

On 12th June 1940, only two days after Italy declared war, three Hartbees of No 11 Squadron, under Major B H Preller (No 11 Squadron being one of the three original squadrons which the SAAF had earlier dispatched to Kenya), set off on an offensive reconnaissance over Italian Somaliland. The purpose was to locate enemy aerodromes near the Kenyan border. They flew from Nairobi to Garissa where they refuelled before traversing the waterless bush and semi-desert of the Northern Frontier Districts that separated the cultivated areas of the Highlands of Kenya from the Italian sector of East Africa. Their mission was a success, as was a raid by JU 86's bombers of No 12 Squadron the following day over the Italian aerodromes at Kismayu, Jelib and Afmadu in Somaliland.

These SAAF initiatives were something of impertinence considering the relative sizes of the warring factions. In all, there were only about forty SAAF aircraft in Kenya, lined up against an estimated three hundred IAF aircraft, albeit that they were spread over the length and breadth of the Italian Empire, embracing Somaliland, Abyssinia and Eritrea.

Towards the end of 1940, the SAAF Squadrons had established themselves at strategic places in Kenya, carrying out softening up programmes preparatory to the invasion of Italian-held territory. No 11 Bomber Squadron, under Major Bob Preller, which had started off with Hartbees, was now using Fairey Battles operating from Archer's Post.

To reach their targets the pilots of No 11 Squadron would leave their bases in the Kenya Highlands and refuel at advance fields in the bush, often sleeping out for the night under the wings of their aircraft before taking off at first light. This sustained programme of air attacks was continued ruthlessly, smashing planes on the ground, and damaging aerodromes, railways, transport and fuel stacks.

The ports of Mogadishu and Kismayu in Somaliland became favourite targets of No 11 squadron. It was on a recce in the area of the latter that Squadron Commander Bob Preller and his crews were involved in a near disastrous incident that won Preller the DFC - the <u>first</u> SAAF decoration of the War. After photographing Kismayu, Preller had turned inland to have a look at Afmadu aerodrome. There his crew took more photos and after that he shot up an Italian plane on the ground in a series of low-level passes. A bullet from ground fire hit the radiator of the Battle and out poured the glycol. Within a few miles the engine seized. Preller made a hazardous landing among trees well inside enemy territory.

The three airmen set fire to the plane after removing the compass and film and set off with only one water bottle between them. While an intensive air search was made for them, the three made their way through the bush suffering dreadful privation. Tormented by thirst and starving, they staggered on for days. After a week, when they had been posted as "missing" Preller told Air Corporals Petterson and Ackermann to remain at a waterhole, in an endeavour to recover some of their strength while he continued alone. Twelve days after the crash, Preller was spotted by a Rhodesian Air Force plane jogging slowly along on a camel on the road between Garissa and Libol. A truck and an ambulance were ordered out, and they picked up Preller, weak, suffering from severe sunburn and blistered feet. He was able to direct the rescue party to the waterhole where the two corporals lay exhausted.

Preller was awarded the DFC with a citation for "imbuing his squadron with his own offensive spirit to a remarkable degree", and for bringing back "very valuable exposed film of enemy military objectives."

Preller, Roland John (born Bloemfontein, Free State, 22nd November 1954), son of Beverly Anthony Preller and Alice Francis Vos. Went to Christian Brothers College in Bloemfontein, married Portia Cloete and lives in East London, Eastern Cape. Facebook friend in 2011 and manages the Preller website.

Preller, Tasmin (born Volksrust, 16th January 1988), daughter of Douglas Bruce Preller and Erica de Vos. Schooled at Voksrust Hoërskool – class of 2005 and studied at Medunsa – class of 2008.

Preller, Tessa (born Volksrust), lives in Pretoria.

Preller, Tina, born Bothaville?, daughter of Abri and sibling to Abraham and Ivan Preller. Music teacher in Potchefstroom

Preller, Tracy-Leigh (born 21st October), daughter of Charles Walker Preller and June Hazel Torlage. She has an older sibling, Robert Mervyn, born 27th October 1971 – and they are great-grandchilden of 'Charlie' Preller, the writers grandmothers, brother, who served with my grandfather during the Anglo-Boer War of 1899-1902. Tracy-Leigh is thus a 'MyHeritage' relative: 2nd cousin once removed.

Pretorius crest

Pretorius, Jacomine Geldenhuys (born Kimberley 23rd February 1980), schooled at Hoërskool Diamantveld, class of 1998. Studied Education of Music Theory at North West University – Bmus – married Beukes Geldenhuys on 13th December 2008, lives in Centurion, Gauteng and manages Old Mondoro Bush Camp with her husband.

Prinsloo, Yolande (born South Africa 15th November 1974), married John Robert Brink in Krugersdorp on 18th October 1988. They have a son, Joshua Dean Brink, born 18th December 2002.

Reeve, Lesley Ann (born Boksburg, Transvaal 11th November 1973) married Roux Daniel Malan on the 25th October 1979.
Lesley Ann Malan [Reeve] is the wife of a nephew of the wife to the author.

Pretorius, Debbie-Ann (born 9th December 1980), married Gilbert Jacobus Geldenhuis on the 15th March 2009. She had two children, Jaun-Pierre born 1st April 2002 in Cape Town and Chrisna born 28th May 2005, in Mosselbay.

Retief, Piet. Voortrekker – related to the Prellers. He was murdered by Zulu King Dingaan, which then resulted in the Battle of Blood River, the Convenent of 16 December, and the building and commemoration of the Voortrekker Monument in Pretoria.

In October 1837, Piet Retief, Voortrekker Leader at the time, visited Dingaan at the Royal Kraal. Retief was in high spirits at the prospect of negotiating a land deal for his people with Dingaan. In November 1837, about 1000 Voortrekker wagons started the descent down the Drakensberg from the Orange Free State into Natal. Dingaan asked Piet Retief for a token of their friendly intentions. Some of Dingaan's cattle had been stolen by Chief Sekonyela and his tribesmen. He asked Retief to recover them. Retief and his party of 69 men recovered 700 head of cattle, 63 horses and a few rifles.

The party arrived at uMgundlovu (which means, "the secret place of the elephant".) on 3 February 1838. On the following day, a treaty was signed, whereby Dingaan ceded all the land south of the Thukela River, as far as the Mzimvubu River, in the Transkei, to the Voortrekkers

On 6 February, Retief and his party were treated to a farewell dance by the Zulu impis. They were told to leave their firearms outside the royal kraal. Suddenly, when the dancing had reached a frenzied climax, Dingaan leapt to his feet and shouted "bambani laba bathakathi!" ("Kill the wizards!") The men were totally overpowered and dragged away to a hill called kwaMatiwane, named after a chief who had been killed there. Retief and his men were savagely butchered to death. The general opinion as to the reason why they were killed is because for some obscure reason, they withheld some of the cattle recovered from Chief Sekonyela.

During the Battle of Blood River on December 1838, the assassination of Retief and his men was avenged. The victorious Voortrekkers finally arrived at uMgundgundlovu on 20 th December, 1838. The Zulu capital was deserted and ablaze with fire. They found the skeletal remains of Retief and his party. A memorial to mark the spot where they were buried was later built. The huts in the original "city" have been rebuilt on their foundations, and restored.

On a hill overlooking uMgundgundlovu, in 1838, the Reverend Francis Owen tried to negotiate the establishment of a permanent mission station. Also from this hill, he was witness to the cruel slaying of Retief and his men on that fateful day.

Robertse, Hendrina, mother-in-law to Adrian van Rensen.

DICTIONARY OF FAMILY BIOGRAPHY

Robertse, Tersia, married Adrian van Rensen, and lives in Pretoria.

Schikkerling, Elizabeth Born 5th March 1858 and died 4 September 1924. Married 'OuBaas' Hendrik Jacobus born 5th July 1849, on the 2nd March 1874. Names appear on the family chart inherited by Hennie Geldenhuys - - and also in Dot Serfonteins 'Keurskrif vir Kroonstad' – which the author obtained from the Kroonstad Municipality. OuBaas – or Grootvader as appears on the gravestone, is buried on Rustpan farm, in the Bothaville district.

Scotson, Gill's mother, daughter married John Preller.

Scotson, Gillian (born Sittingbourne 13th April 1955), went to East Secondary School and Victoria Park High School, class of 1969, married John Preller on 15th June 1991. They live in Port Elizabeth, Eastern Cape. Facebook friend in 2011.

Siek, Anna Margaretha (born 13th March 1695), the eldest of three children of Johann Siek, who died in 1715 and arrived from Bremen, Germany, with his wife Geertruyd Helm.
Anna married Barend Gildenhuysen on 31st August 1710, had seven children and became the Stammoeder of our branch of the Geldenhuys family. Whilst tracing her background, it was discovered that she also married Michael Otto on 1st March 1722, and also had another seven children by him. Otto arrived at the Cape in 1714 from Stettin, Germany.
It is most likely that the popular Geldenhuys female Christian names originate from her and her mother – Geertruyda and Margaretha.
With her second marriage to Michael Otto, Malherbe's Stamregister lists her as the stammoeder of the Otto's as well. Otto died in 1743.

303

DICTIONARY OF FAMILY BIOGRAPHY

Simpkins crest

Kilamanjaro several times. Married Johan Bouwer – see Debra Bouwer entry earlier alphabetically.

Simpkins, Sandra (born 28 May 1964), elder sister of Debra – who married Johan Bouwer. Sandra married Vinny La Bella, born Johannesburg 27th November 1963 and, who still lives there.

Simpkins, Debra (born 26th December 1966), went to University of Natal, Sociology in 1988, then University of Port Elizabeth in 1989 – Sociology MA, studied MBA at Edinburgh University Herriott Watt in 2000 and Ancient Egyptian Studies, Honours, at University of South Africa. Owner of Nomadic Adventures and has climbed Mount

Simpkins, Sue – mother of Debra, who married Johannes Jacobus Francois Bouwer.

Sinton crest

Sinton, Alasdair, lives in Nairobi, Kenya.

Sinton, David James (born Kenya 27th March 1975) is the biological father of Matthew Dylan Howard Geldenhuys. David's parents are David Murray and Trish Sinton who settled in Australia. Pey Malan Geldenhuys adopted Matthew shortly after he married Eloise Howard.

Sinton, David Murray (born 18th October 1947) married Trish. They are parents of David James born 1975. They visited Auckland during the Rugby World Cop in 2011 – and took young Matthew to see the match where Wales beat Australia.

Sinton, David Scott (born 5th September 1924) is the younger son of James Scott and Zoe Anderson, who arrived in 1920. His elder sibling is John Scott, born 11th February 1921. David married Gillian Macaulay in 1953.

Sinton, James Scott arrived in South Africa from Harpenden, England, in 1920, with his bride of two years Zoe Anderson, from Pietermaritzburg.

Sinton, Mark and Cherie are from Kaiwaka, New Zealand but live in Qatar. Cherie was born a Griffiths, in Seychelles, on 29th April (no year given on Facebook), brought up and trained as a teacher in New Zealand. They have two children.

Sinton, Neil is a nephew of Murray Sinton (who is the grandfather to Matthew Dylan Geldenhuys), and lives in London. Julia Sinton born 13th April is also a relative, but relationships have not been established at the time of going to print.

Steenkamp crest

Stoltz crest

Steenkamp, Maatje Catharina Jacoba (born 17th June 1887 and died 27th October 1918), married Dirk Cornelius Geldenhuys and they had four children; Angela Adriana de Jager, Mercia Phillys, Willem and Ruben Benjamin. Maatje was the daughter of Willem Steenkamp and Annie de Jager.

Stoltz, Anneke (born Krugersdorp 24th October 1969). Anneke married Barend Petrus Geldenhuys, born 13th April 1973, and they have two sons, Barend Petrus and Izak Jacobus, both born in Krugersdorp repectively on 27th December 1993 and 3rd March 2000.

Stopforth crest

went to Westvalia Hoërskool Klerksdorp, class of 1991, and obtained his BA Hons degree in Environmental Science at the University of North West in 1975. He enjoys his rugby, having played for SA Universities U/21 and Leopards (North West province) 1994-95).

The Stopforths arrived in the Knysna area, from Scotland, and still have the "Stopforth huis" in George / Knysna.

Stopforth, Dominique, born 7th September 2000, to Amanda Malan and Charles Joseph Stopforth. Dominique is the eldest of three children – the other two, boys, being Michael born 15th August 2002 and Andrew, born 6th January 2006. All three children are attending the Pietersburg Oos Laerskool.

Stopforth, Charles Joseph (born 14th June 1973), son of Charles Joseph Stopforth senior, married Amanda Malan. They have three children, a daughter and two sons, and live in the Pietersburg / Polokwane area in the Northern Transvaal. Charles has built up a lucrative game farm, Uitkyk / Mbizi. Charles

Stopforth, Pieter Johannes (born 7th October 1968), son of Charles Stopforth and Cornelia van Biljon. Brother to Celesté born 28th August 1967 and Jeanette Stopforth, born Pietersburg 2nd August 1968. Pieter is currently a teacher / deputy head at the Tom Naude Technical school in Polokwane.

Thomas crest

Thomas, Lesley Ann (born 1950), married Erens Lodewyk Johannes Venter (born 1946). Lesley and Ernie have three children.

Tsirindanis, Joy nee Geldenhuys. Facebook friend. Still looking forward to follow up relationship.

Thompson, Dan married Bianca Belfour-Cunningham (daughter of Vivian Carr) and they have a son with the unusual name of Rhayla-Rayne

Trichardt, Louis – Voortrekker (born ?, died Delagoa Bay – Lourenco Marques / Maputo). Extract from Gedenks genootskap – reads in Afrikaans as follows:

Die Louis Trichardt Gedenktuin in Josina Machel straat in Maputo herdenk 'n uiters belangrike mylpaal in die geskiedenis van die Afrikaner. Om dié rede het die Genootskap Louis Trichardt wat deur die Erfenisstigting bestuur word, besluit om 'n bedrag van meer as R90 000 te spandeer aan die opknap en herstel van verskeie elemente op die terrein. Die Erfenisstigting ontvang geen staatssubsidie nie en moet self fondse genereer vir projekte op terreine wat onder sy beheer val.

Die besluit is geneem in opvolging van die herstel van die mosaiek-kaart wat deel van die tuin vorm en wat in 2011 teen 'n bedrag van meer as R35 000 gerestoureer is. Die huidige herstelwerk sluit onder andere herstelwerk aan die erg beskadigde trappe en die waterpomp, skoonmaak van die wit marmer vloer asook die -paneel waarop die ossewa uitgebeeld word, herstelwerk van graniet, die verf van alle mure, die hetstel en skoonmaak van al die klipplaveisel en die aanlê van water na die grag om die mosaiekkaart in.

Maar waarom is die gedenktuin van soveel kultuurhistoriese waarde? Op 13 April 1838 het Louis Trichardt, na vele struikelblokke en die gevreesde malaria, waaraan meer as die helfte van die geselskap gesterf het, vanuit die Kaapkolonie in Delagoabaai aangekom. Daar het hulle eers hul nege waens onder 'n groot vyeboom uitgespan maar later uitgesprei oor die gebied. Martha, Trichardt se vrou, sterf op 1 Mei 1838 aan malaria. Na haar dood en dié van ander in die geselskap besef Trichardt dat hy nie weer oor land sou kon wegtrek nie en stuur 'n brief na die Trekkers in Port Natal (Durban) om 'n skip na Delagoabaai te stuur om hulle te kom haal. Hy self sterf op 25 Oktober 1838. Op 3 Julie 1839 bereik die *Mazeppa*Delagoabaai. Die 25 oorlewende Voortrekkers en drie bediendes kom op 19 Julie 1839 in Port Natal aan waar hulle by ander Voortrekkers aansluit.

Trichardt was die enigste Voortrekkerleier wat 'n dagboek van sy trek nagelaat het. Gustav S. Preller het *Die Dagboek van Louis Trichardt* in 1917 uitgegee.

See also Gustav Preller

van Aardt, Leane (born Alberton 29th May 1987), daughter of Hendrik van Aardt and Joleen Geldenhuys.

van Aardt crest

van Aardt, Gerrit Jansz (born Delft, Nederland, 11th June 1671). He was the grandson of Gerrit Gerritsz van Aert / veraert /van der Aert born circa 1595.

van Aardt, Nicolaas Hendrik (born Heilbron, Free State 22nd November 1932), second of eight children of Hendrik Jacobus van Aardt and Magdalena Christina Nel. Nic married Aletta Magdalena Susanna Malan – eldest sister to 'Rina' Susanna Catharina who married Preller Matt Geldenhuys.

Nic and Lettie had three children:-
'Alta' Aletta Magdalena Susanna, born Lusaka 5th May 1955, married Willem

Adriaan Jacobus Oosthuisen – they also had three children; Yvette Marie born 6th October 1976, Liesl Adriaana born 27th July 1978 and Sckalk Johannes born 31st August 1979, all born in Salisbury.

Hendrik Jacobus born Lusaka 18th May 1961, married Joelene Geldenhuys in Ladismith, Cape; they had two children, Leane born Alberton 29th May 1987 and Nicolaas Daniel born Bredasdorp 25th August 1988.

Nicolene born Salisbury 3rd September 1966 married Reinier Olivier in Alberton; they had two children, Jaco born Johannesburg 9th February 1989 and Anneke born 16th November 1990, also in Johannesburg.

van Aardt, Alta (born Lusaka 5th May 1955), eldest daughter to Lettie Malan and Nic van Aardt. Alta married Willem Oosthuizen, born Salisbury 16th November 1947. They had three children, Yvette Marié born 6th October 1976 (and died 25th May), Liesl Adriana born 27th June 1978 and Schalk Johannes born 31 August 1979.

The following wedding picture was supplied by Gerta Malan Bezuidenhout, during the Adio Africa trip to Bulawayo.

van Aardt, Hendrik Jacobus (born Lusaka 18th May 1961) son of Nic van Aardt and Lettie Malan, went to Bothashof School in Salisbury, Rhodesia. He married Joleen Geldenhuys born Ladismith 27th October 1957. They married in Ladismith 6th July 1985 and have two children, Nicolas Daniel born

Bredasdorp 25th August 1988 and Leanie born Alberton 29th May 1987.

van Aardt, Leanie (born 29th May 1987), went to Bredasdorp high school and Stellenbosch University where she obtained her B.Sc Bio-chemical research. She married electrical engineer Pieter Motke on the 8th October 2011 in Waenhuiskraal, and lives in Tygervallei.

van Aardt, Nicolaas Daniel (born Bredasdorp, southern Cape 25th August 1988), son of Hendrik Jacobus and Joleen Geldenhuys. This photo of Danie with his parents, and sister who graduated, was taken end of 2009.

van Aardt, Nicolene (born Salisbury 3rd September 1966), married Renier Olivier and have two children, Jaco and Anneke, both born in Johannesburg. Nicolene became a single-mum who has done an admirable job in singlehandedly raising two fine upstanding youngsters any parent will be very proud of.

Nicolene married Andre du Plooy, in Bredasdorp, in December 2012.

van der Walt, Adele (born Johannesburg 9th March 1968), married Johan Bezuidenhout. The had two sons, Aiden born Johannesburg 10th October 1998 and died 13th March 2008; and Jared born Johannesburg.

van Rensen, Elizabeth 'Libby' (born) Cousin to Jan and Preller Geldenhuys, daughter to Theo van Rensen and Mienie Geldenhuys. Lives in Pretoria, with her son Christopher. Libby spends most of her 'holidays' in Thailand, having inherited the passion of the far east from her parents, when they were alive. Libby invited Johannes Albertus Geldenhuys and his wife, Julia nee Dippenaar, twice but once in 2004, to tour around Thailand. In 2011, she went back for a three-month stay, touring around the islands in a boat. This was her ninth visit to Thailand! Christopher's health is deteriorating rapidly, so Libby now spends most of her time providing frail care to her son – Bekkers muscular dystrophy sufferer. Libby is also very close to her younger brother Adrian (who has now moved into the lovely cottage he build behind his main house in Pretoria).

van Rensen, Adrian, younger brother to Elizabeth, married to and lives in Pretoria. Adrian is an expert on palms. The elder brother is Johan. Their mothers murder by a domestic servant badly affected the whole family.

van Rensen, Johan a cousin who grew up in Pretoria. Brother to Libby.

van Rensen, Theodore, married 'Mienie' Maria Susanna Wilhelmina Geldenhuys, father of cousin 'Libby' Elizabeth.

van Rensen, Louise her married name, married to Johan.

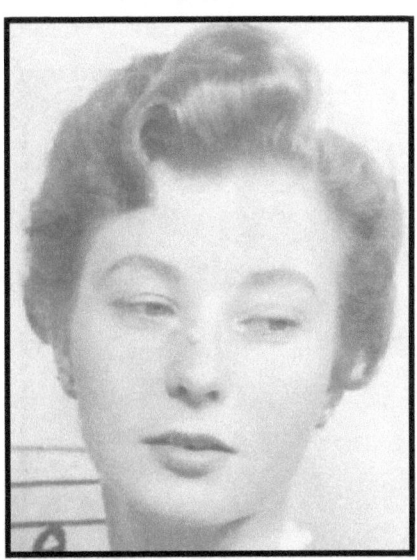

van Rooyen, Mona Daphne married Schalk Reginald Brink who was born 8th November 1933 and died 23rd February 1988.

van Wyk crest

van Wyk, Jean, married Keith Brian Jelley on the 1st August 2002, in Vancouver, British Columbia, Canada.
    He loves me
    He loves me not
    He loves me
    So we're tying the knot
At the University Golf Club, Vancouver.

Keith and Jean managed to get employment for Bill at an Apartment Complex, and later assisted them to re-locate to New Zealand [while Keith and Jean moved to Melbourne in Australia.

Varikas, Angela married Pierre Mussell on 8th February 1998. They live in Gold Coast, Queensland, Australia. Related to Maurice Mussell and June Howard from Durban, and thus also related to Pey Geldenhuys and Eloise Howard, who live in Auckland, New Zealand?.

Venter crest

Venter, Benjamin Louis, a pilot, first officer on long-haul Boeing 777. Son of Erens Venter.

Venter, Erens Lodewyk Johannes (born 1946) Pilot, Agriculturist, Poultry Farmer in the Greytown, New Hanover district of Kwa-Zulu Natal. Fourth child of Venter.

Ernie was educated at Thornhill High School 1961-65, joinedthe Engineers and was attached to Support Commando of the RLI where he was exposed to flying. Joined the Air Force despite reservations from his parents, advanced to first solo on Provost aircraft but resigned some what prematurely from No 24 Pilot Training Course before completion of his Basic Flying School. Ernie love of flying did not forsake him, he invested in a Microlight and build a landing strip on his poultry farm.

Ernie married lover of horses, Lesley Ann Thomas, born 1950. They have three children, a son Gustaf Thomas who is in England, a second son Benjamin Louis, who is a pilot for Air Emirates (with over 6400 hours, currently a first officer on the longhaul Boeing 777) and a daughter Yvonne Julie, twin of Ben, who is a Commercial pilot with an instructors rating, operating out of Grand Central and Lanseria.

In 2007 Ernie arranged a mini THS / Malan family re-union on his farm, at which his elder brother Japie again met up with Rina Malan and her husband Prop Geldenhuys.

Venter, Heinrich (Hendrik) (born 21st April 1663, died 2nd May 1713), a Taylor from Hameln, Duitsland, married Anna Viljoen (Villon), born 19th May 1678 and died 11th May 1713. Hendrik is the Stamvader of the Venters, and probably settled in South Africa at the time of Jan van Riebeeck.

Heinrich was a taylor at Stellenbosch, became the owner of the farm Nazaret on the Krommerivier on the 22nd February 1690 which he sold to his brother-in-law Johannes Viljoen in 1710. He then bought the farm Vleeschbank near Hermon Station on the Bergrivier. (SO of Riebeekskasteel 25.8.1704 – 2.5.1713).

Venter, Hermanus Johannes Smartenryk Venter born 3 March 1902 died 3 March 1972 (note: birth and death date were both on the third of March), married Salomina Adriana van Heerden born 13 April 1909 died 15 August 1973. He was knowm as Manie Venter – who hired a Chatsworth farm to the author's father-in-law Frans Malan: His sons Japie and Erns went to school with the author – Thornhill High School in Gwelo. The author courted Rina Malan while she lived at Kombisa farm. Ria Venter, the elder sister to Japie, married Rina's cousin – Philipus Johannes Malan (elder brother to Francois Daniel Malan).

Venter, Japie (born 1944)
Japie Venter went to Thornhill High School Gwelo, where he befriended Prop Geldenhuys. His elder sister married Rina Malan's cousin, Philip Malan – son of Daan Malan.

Venter, Yuonne Julie, twin-daughter of Erens Venter – sharing the families love of flying.

Venter, Ria (born 1940) second child of Hermanus Johannes Smartenryk Venter who was born in 1902 (and died 1972). Ria married Philipus Johannes Malan, born and they had a son and a daughter Salome.

Waldeck, Alwyn related to Libby Beukes born Elizabeth van Rensen

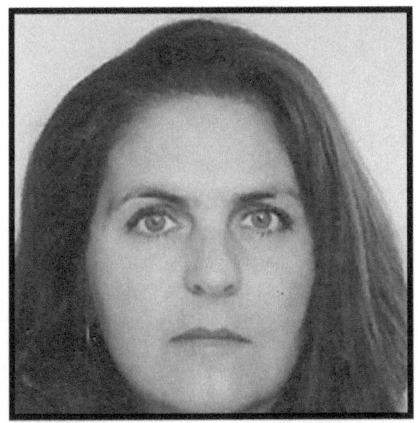

Waldeck, Caryn – daughter of writers cousin Libby Beukes (nee van Rensen). Facebook friend in 2011.

Waldek, Caryn, grand-daughter to Libby Beukes? [Writer regets this issue was not resolved during the Adio Africa sojourn during October 2011.

Waldeck, Erin – granddaughter to Libby Beukes, who has made a name for herself with rock climbing.

Walls, Mary daughter to Lieutenant General Peter Walls, related via 14 steps through the Margaret Jelley and Brian McQueen families.

Walls, Peter, Lt. General, historical figure in the Rhodesian War. Commanded combined operstions.

Whiteley, Alan (born in Yorkshire, UK) married Stella Nesta Arnott on 12th August 1929, parents of Alan Raymond Malcolm and Margaret Mary Elaine – and great-grandparents of Courtney Sacha and Brendan Vaughan Jelley.

Alan was brought up in Paarl, Cape. He served in the R.A.F. during the First World War, and acted as Link Instructor in the Rhodesian Air Force in the Second World War. He joined the Salisbury Municipality in 1928, Town Clerk's and Town Treasurer's Department, retiring after 30 years service.

Whiteley crest

Whiteley, Leonard, born 1894 and died 20 January 1965, married Hilda born 1903 and died 4 December 1965.

DICTIONARY OF FAMILY BIOGRAPHY

Whiteley, Margaret Mary Elaine (born 16th December 1935). Sixth generation descendant of James Moodie, the last Laird of Melsetter. Married William Paterson Jelley and had two sons. Grahame David qualified as a medical practitioner and married Renene Delene Geldenhuys, and Keith Brian a computer expert who immigrated to Canada with Jean van Wyk and then relocated to Melbourne, Australia.

Margaret became a proud grandmother with the birth of Courtney Sacha, and was doubly blessed when Brendan Vaughan was born.

Whitely, Alan Raymond Malcolm (born 9th February 1931), brother to 'Marjel' Margaret Mary Elaine Whiteley, walked his granddaughter Louise down the aisle to marry Anton J Kata in Johannesburg on 18th September 2011.

Ray married his wife Heather Johnson-Worboys on 15th December 1956. They have three children, Janet Mary born 6th August 1959, Helen Jean born 30th April 1962 and Irene Heather born 1st February 1967. They moved to the UK about five years ago in 2007, to join family there.

Wigston, Jessie – mother to Valerie, who married Francois Bezuidenhout

Wigston, Valerie (born 17 September), went to Vainona High School, married Francois Bezuidenhout.

Wolfaardt, Ester, grandmother to Nicolas Hendrik van Aardt.

Worthington, Sanette (born approx 4th May 1961), celebrated her 50th in May 2011; and is the mother of Pieter Geldenhuys, born 8th February 1991. Pieters' father, Mynhardt, married Adele on the 1st December 2001. Sanette and Mynhardt thus separated some time before 2001, when Pieter was a mere 10 years old.

Zara (Slave). A slave woman belonging to Jurgen Radyn caused a scandal in 1788, by eloping with David Malan (brother-in-law of Jacobus Malan). Jacobus Malan was the owner of Morgenster, and he bought Vergelegen in 1788. Why or how come Jacobus's brother-in-law David, with same surname, was living at Vergelegen at that time is not known. They disappeared into the interior and after a time David was declared dead. However, he reappeared many years later, was reunited with his wife and settled on the eastern frontier. Riaan Malan refers to this episode in his book, *My Traitors Heart*.

THIS ENDS VOLUME 1

VOLUME 2 consists of the genealogy listings and the Index for both Volume 1 and Volume 2

GELDENHUYS GENEALOGY

12 Generations

Volume Two

PRELLER MATT GELDENHUYS

VOLUME 2

CONTENTS

GELDENHUYS GENEALOGY 1650 to 2010+

Contents

STAMREGISTER / FAMILY REGISTER	10
RELATIONSHIP WITH DISTANT RELATIVES	14
NAME CHANGES	15
SOUTH AFRICAN SURNAMES and THEIR MEANINGS	18
PERSONALITIES AND PLACES OF INTEREST	23
BLOOD RIVER and THE VOW	36
THE BOER-BASOTHO WARS	38
KROONSTAD & BOTHAVILLE HISTORY	39
FIRST ANGLO-BOER WAR	41
ANGLO-BOER WAR of 1899-1902	45
WORLD WAR II 1939-1945	63
RHODESIA – ZIMBABWE WAR 1967 –1980	68
MASONITE (AFRICA) LIMITED	73
THE KIWIS – NEW ZEALANDERS	78
MALAN REUNION	81
ADIO AFRICA – FAREWELL	92
DICTIONARY OF FAMILY BIOGRAPHY	100

VOLUME 2 310

GEDCOM INSERT	325
ABBREVIATED GENEALOGIES	383
GELDENHUYS, MALAN and PRELLER GENEALOGY	383
JELLEY	431
MALAN	434
PRELLER	442
RELATIONSHIP CHART	451
RELATIONSHIP WITH DISTANT RELATIVES	451
RELATIONSHIP TO PRELLER GELDENHUYS	451
GELDENHUYS INTERMARRIAGES	486

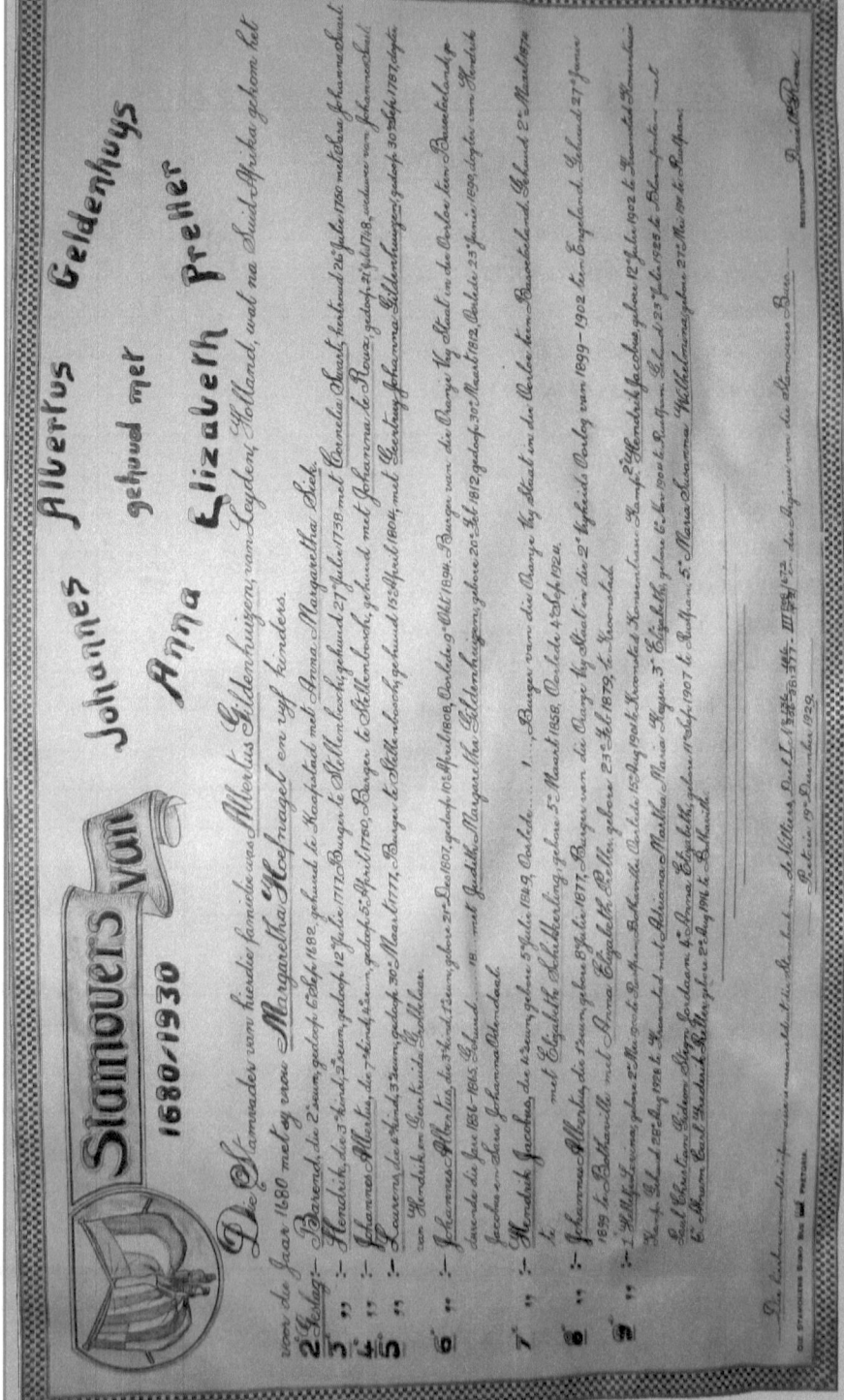

The preceding family heirloom reads as follows:

STAMOUERS van Johannes Albertus Geldenhuys
Gehuud met Anna Elizabeth Preller
1680 – 1930

Die Stamvader van hierdie familie was Albertus Gildenhuizen, van Leyden, Holland, wat na Suid Afrika gekom het voor die Jaar 1680 met sy vrou Margaretha Hoefnagels en vyf kinders.

2de Geslag:- Barend, die 2de seun, gedoop 6de Sep 1682, gehuudte Kaapstad met Anna Margaretha Siek

3de Geslag:- Hendrik, die 3de kind, 2de seun, gedoop 12de Julie 1717. Burger te Stellenbosch, gehuud 27ste Julie 1738 met Cornelia Swart, hertroud 26ste Julie met Sara Johanna Swart.

4de Geslag:- Johannes Albertus, die 7de kind, 4de seun, gedoop 5de April 1750, Burger te Stellenbosch, gehuud met Johanna le Roux, gedoop 21ste Julie 1748, widow of Johannes Swart.

5de Geslag:- Lourens, die 4de kind, 3de seun, baptised 30ste Maart 1777, Burger te Stellenbosch, gehuud 15de April 1804, with Geertruy Johanna Gildenhuizen, gedoop 30ste Sep 1787, dogter van Hendrik en Geertuida Grobbelaar

6de Geslag:- Johannes Albertus, die 3de kind, 1st seun, gebore 21ste Dec 1807, gedoop 10de April 1808, Oorlede 9de Okt 1894. Burger van die Oranje Vry Staat in die Oorloe teen Basoetoeland, gedurende die Jare 1856 - 1865. Gehuud ..18.. met Judith Margaretha Gildenhuizen, gebore 20th Feb 1812, gedoop 30ste Maart 1812, Oorlede 23ste Junie 1890, dogter van Hendrik Jacobus en Sara Johanna Odendaal.

7de Geslag:- Hendrik Jacobus, die 4de seun, gebore 5de Julie 1849, Oorlede ..19.., Burger van die Oranje Vry Staat in die Oorloe teen Basoetoe Maart 1874 te . . met Elizabeth Schikkerling, gebore 5de Maart 1858, Oorlede 4de Sep 1924.

8ste Geslag:- Johannes Albertus, die 1ste seun, gebore 8ste Julie 1877, Burger van die Oranje Vry Staatin die 2de Vryheids Oorlog van 1899 – 1902 teen Engeland. Gehuud 27th Junie 1899 te Bothaville met Anna Elizabeth Preller, gebore 23ste Feb 1879, te Kroonstad.

9de Geslag:- Helletje Levina, gebore 2de Mei 1900 te Rustpan, Bothaville, Oorlede 15de Aug 1901 te Kroonstad Konsentrasie Kamp, 2de Hendrik Jacobus, gebore 12de Julie 1902 te Kroonstad Konsentrasie Kamp, Gehuud 28th August 1928 te Kroonstad met Adriana Martha Maria Keyser. 3rd Elizabeth gebore 6 Nov 1904 te Rustpan. Gehuud 23ste Julie 1925 te Bloemfontein met Paul Christiaan Gideon Steyn Jordaan. 4de Anna Elizabeth, gebore 11de Sep 1907 te Rustpan. 5th Maria Susanna Wilhelmina gebore 27ste Mei 1911 te Ruspan. 6de Abram Carl Frederik Preller gebore 2de Aug 1916 te Bothaville

---

Die - - - informasie versamel uit die Stamboek van de Villiers, Deel 1 No 136/286-98, 186/277. III 808/1402/672 in die Argriewe van die Stamouers Bura - - - Pretoria 19de Desember 1929 - - - - Bestuurder: Daniel P. Re?

Geldenhuys Family Tree

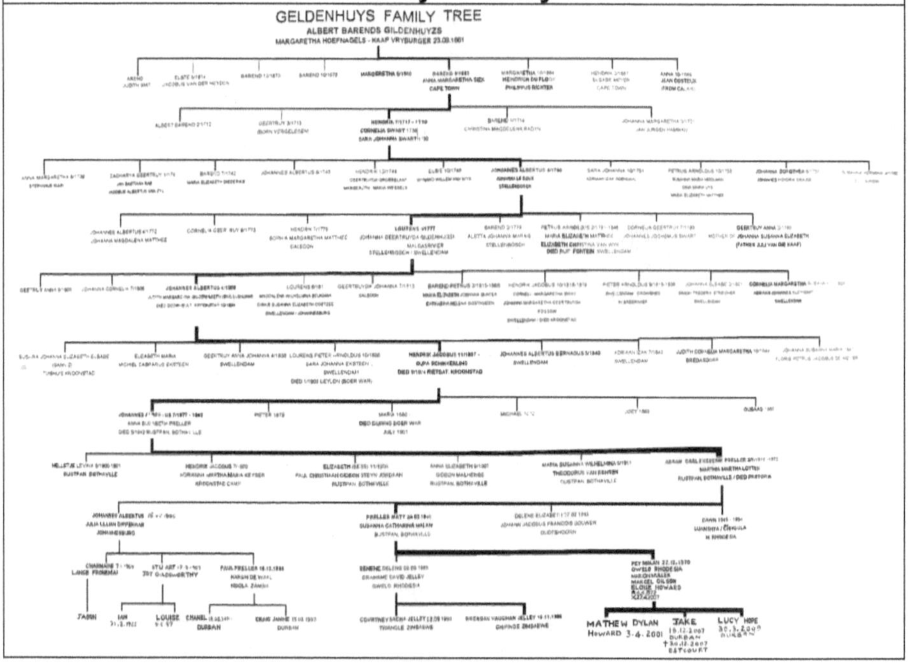

Preller Geldenhuys extract

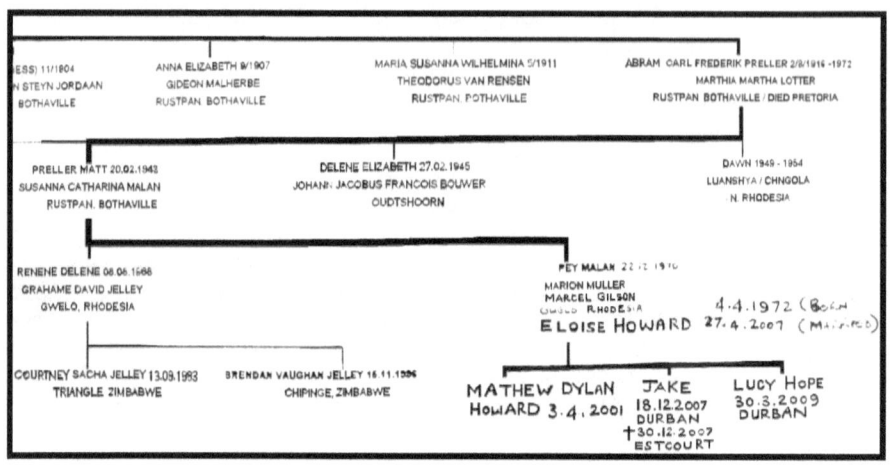

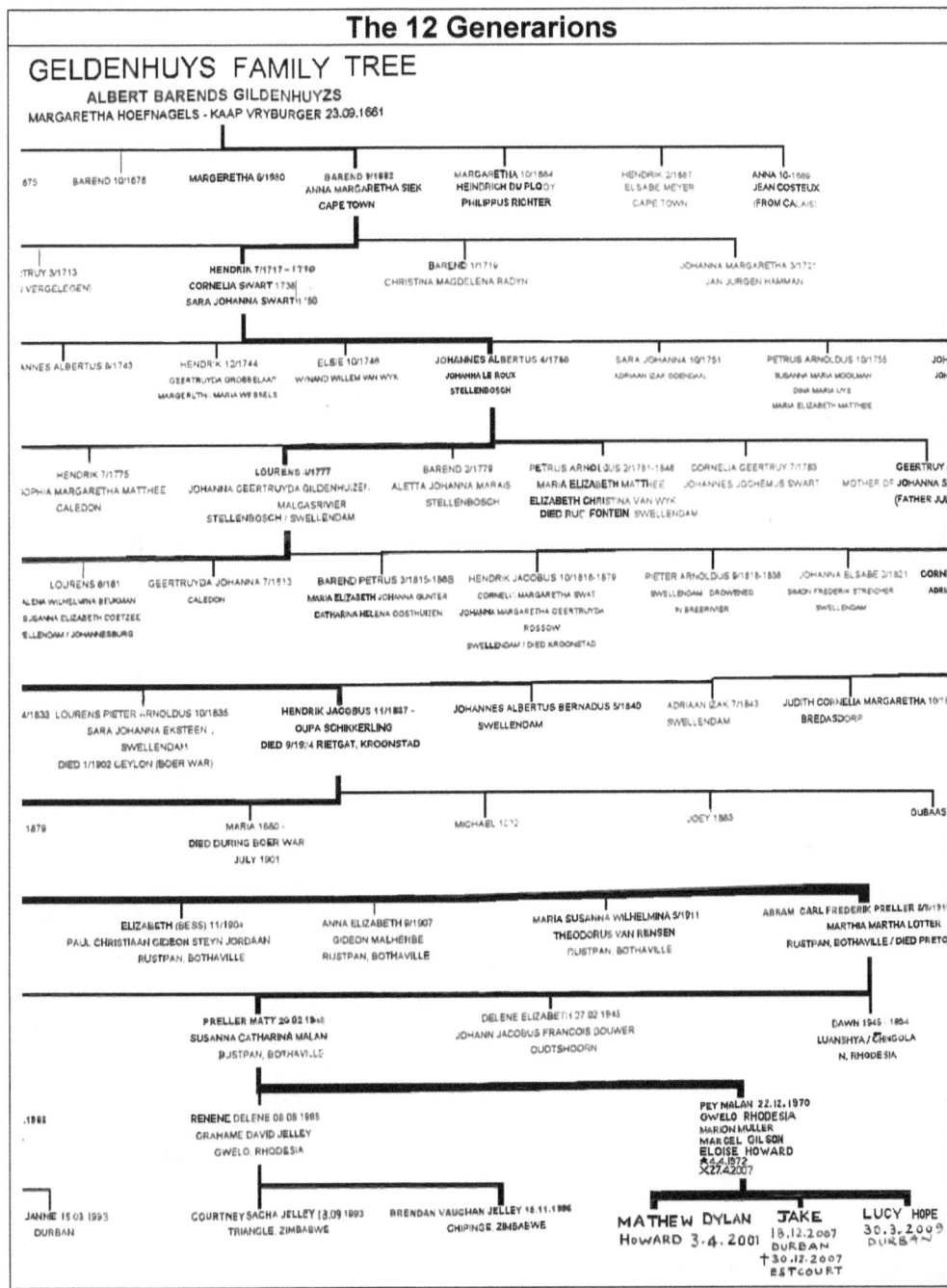

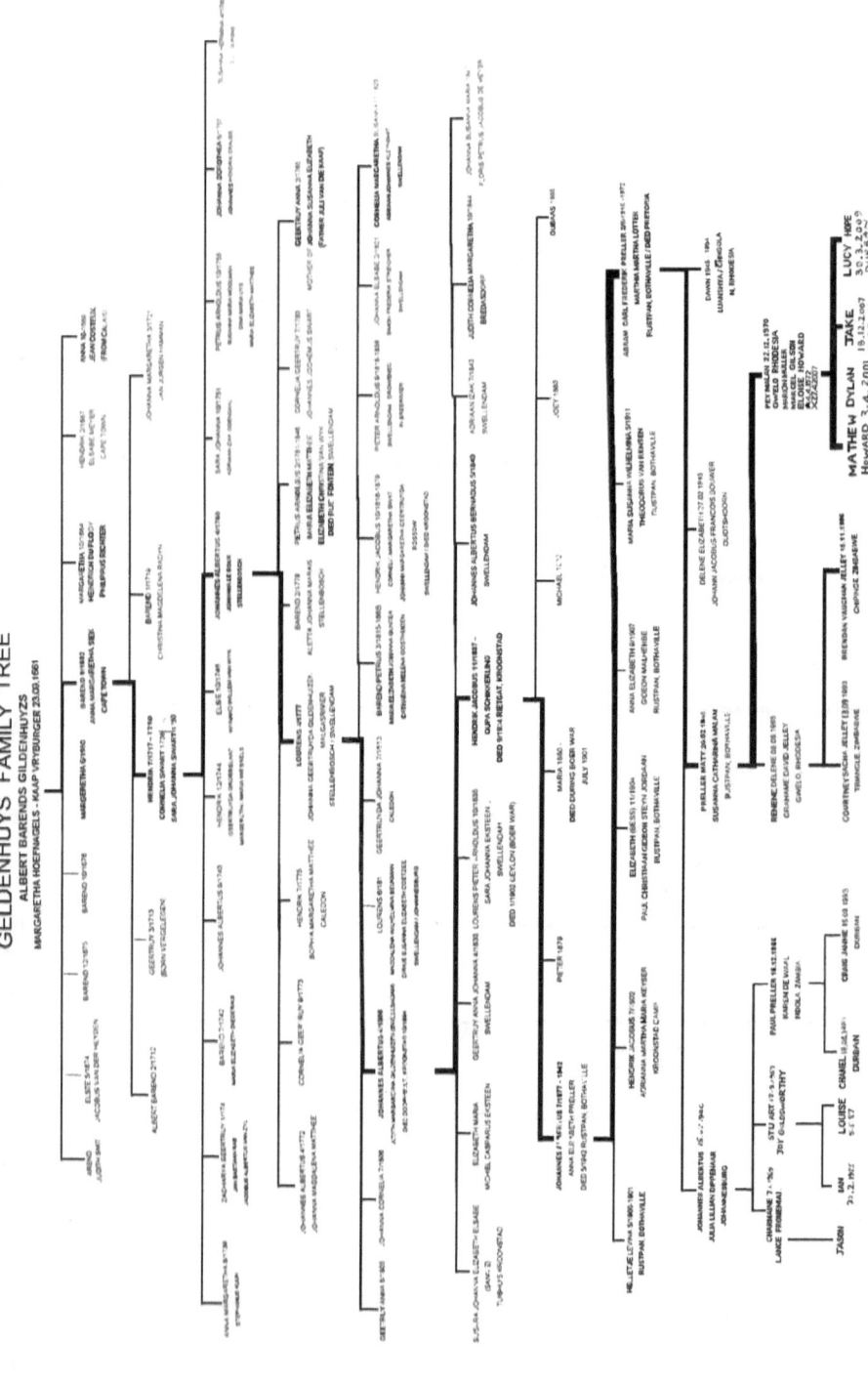

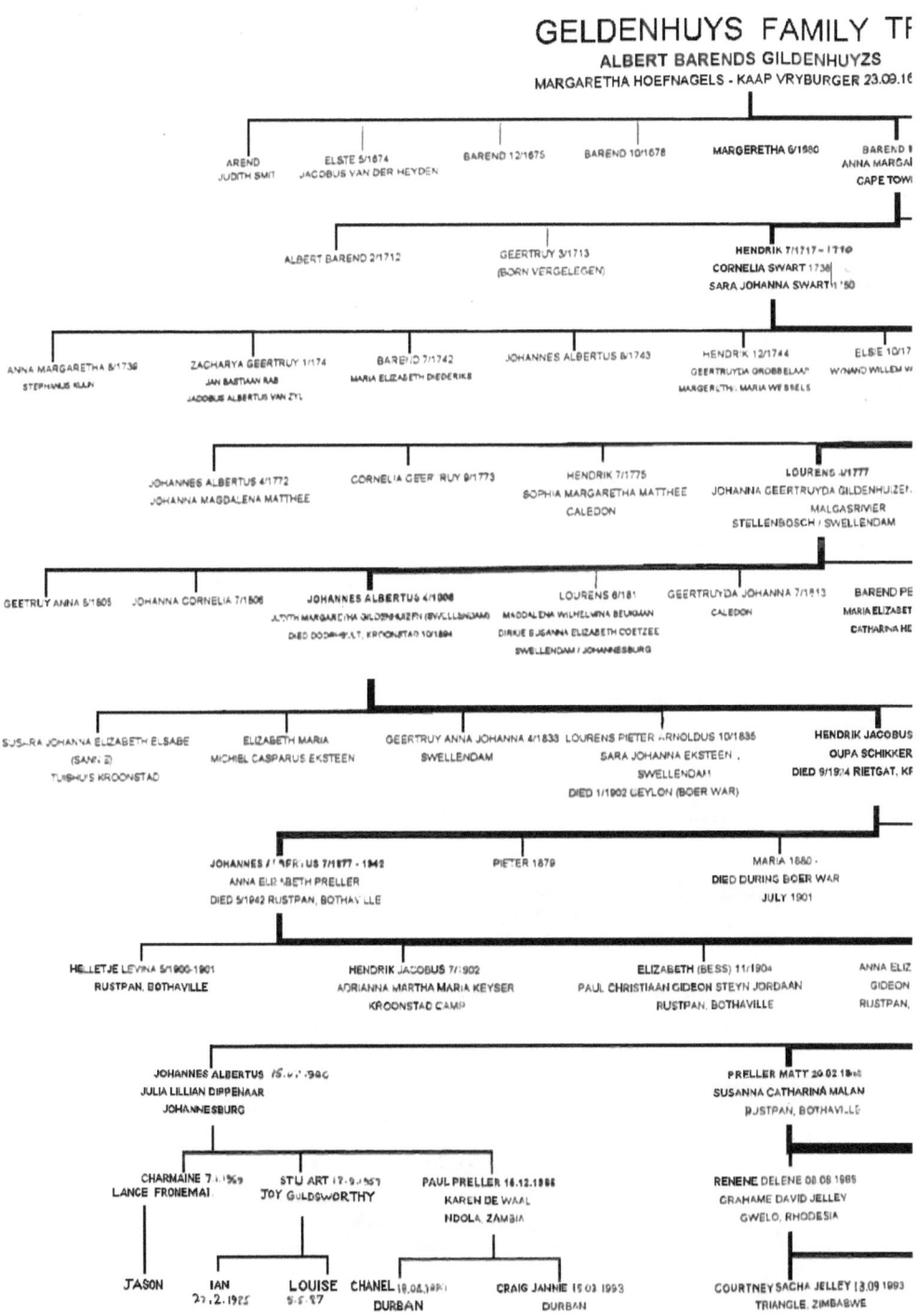

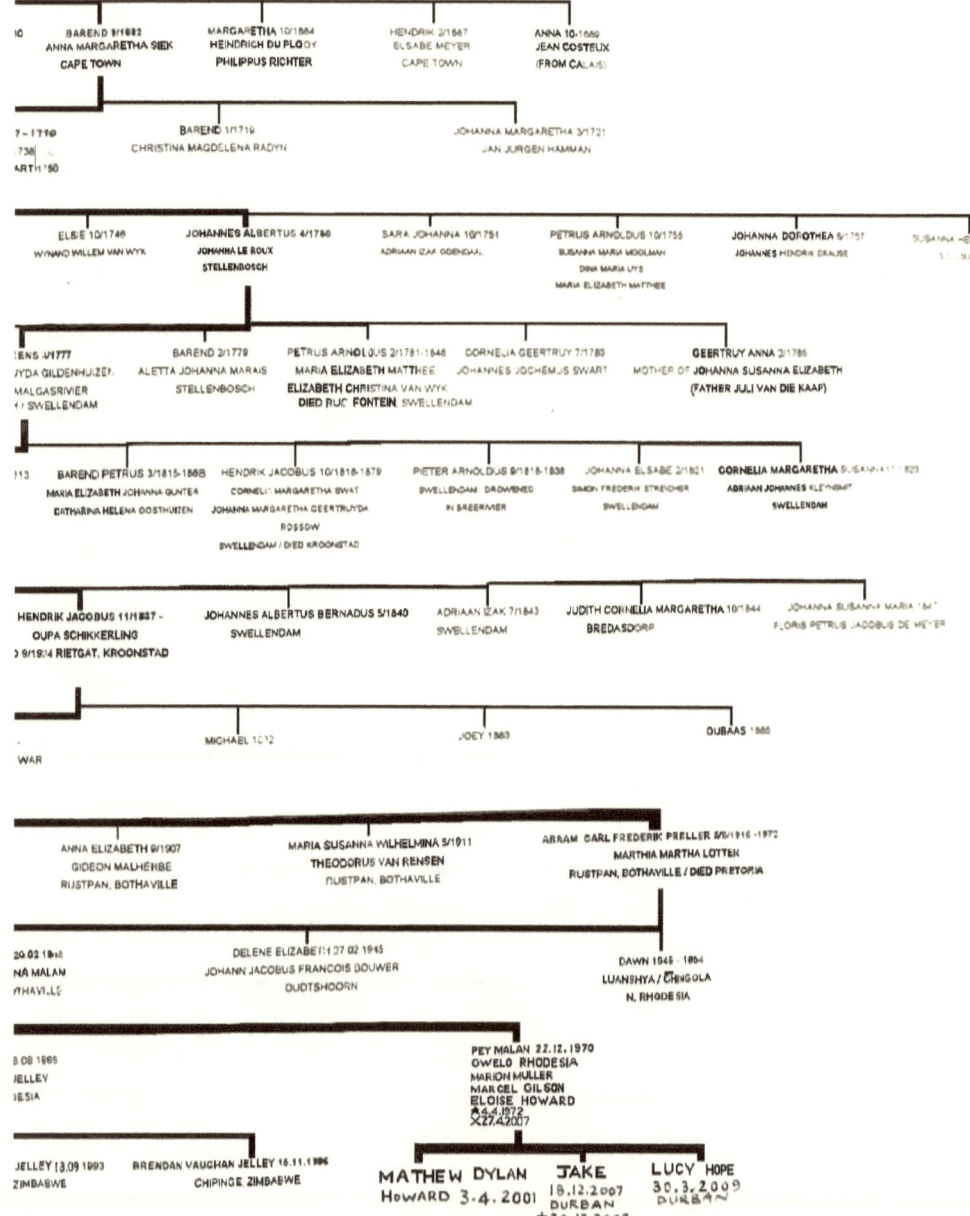

Preller Geldenhuys extract

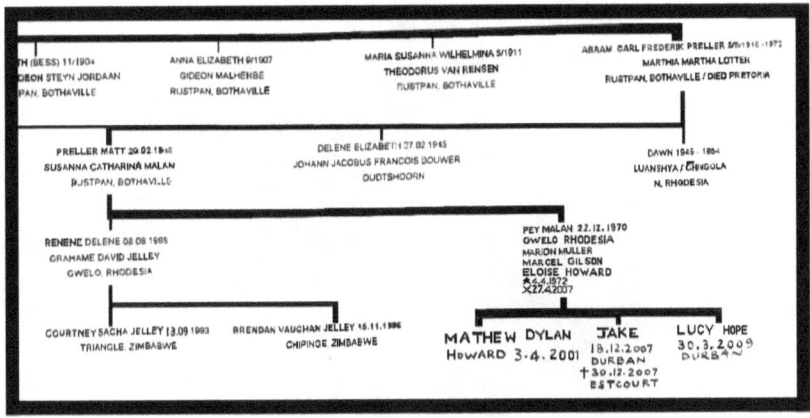

BOOKS

Rhodesian Air Force Operations with Air Strike Log – 2007

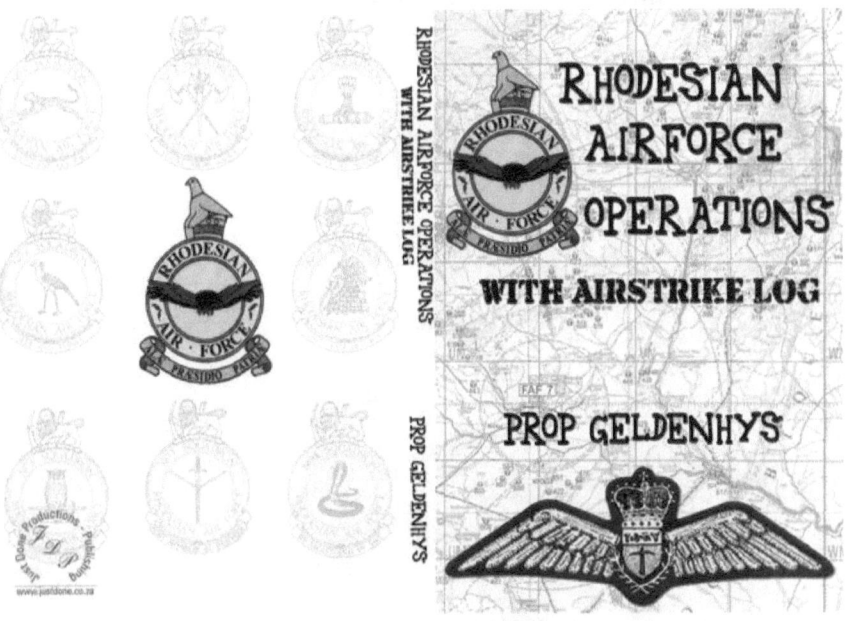

Nickel Cross – published 2006 and 2007

Operation Miracle – published 2008

Operation Miracle

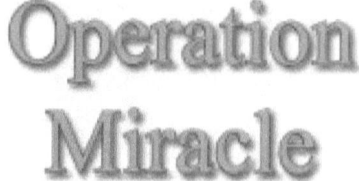

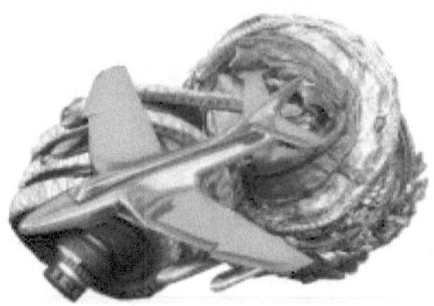

Geldenhuys, Manser and McKenzie

Rhodesian War Casualties and Air Force Memorials – published 2009

Rhodesian War Casualties – A5 sized published in 2009

The Anglo-Boer War Diaries of Jan Geldenhuys – published 2010

Rhodesian Memorials – published 2009

The cry down the generations of 'Lest we forget' rings even more poignantly for the survivors of Rhodesia, many of whom are so far from home and whose country lives only in their memories. If those memories are not captured and published, Rhodesian society will disappear, forgotten. Time passes so rapidly. Already a child born in 1980 is 29 years old and has no direct experience of Rhodesia.

In this and his other books, Prop Geldenhuys supplies not just information of where the memorials are, where names of the lost are to be found, but he has inspired others to join him in seeking out aircraft crash sites in Mozambique and solving other mysteries. The record can never be complete, but, with the aid of the indefatigable Prop, many gaps in it are filled. His consolidation of the rolls of honour, compiled from many sources is of value in itself. Certainly what he has provided will be mined by historians henceforth. - Dr J.R.T. Wood

RHODESIAN MEMORIALS

RHODESIAN ROLL OF HONOUR

ROLL OF HONOUR 1965 TO 1979   PROP GELDENHUYS

Geldenhuys Genealogy – published September 2011

GELDENHUYS

GENEALOGY
12 Generations

PRELLER MATT GELDENHUYS

Volume 2 – published November 2011

GEDCOM INSERT

(Kindly provided by Publisher John Dovey)

REGISTER NUMBERING EXAMPLE

The following example shows the most common numbering conventions which can appear in the register report. Your register may print some or all of these numbers and symbols depending upon which report options you select.

--------------- Example Only ----------------

1. **John**^{3} **Smith**^{6} [17] (Robert^2, Scott^1) born 17 Feb 1849 in New York, NY, died 3 Jan 1930^7. He married 30 Jun 1870 **Mary Jones**, daughter of Albert and Samantha Wiggins.

Their children were:

+   2   **Bobby**^{4} [43]
       3   **Susan**^{4} [44], born 25 Dec 1871.

---

^{6}Smith Family Bible, p. 2
^{7}U.S. Social Security Death Index

Explanation:

John^3 John Smith is a third generation ancestor (^{3}).
Smith^6 Citation^6 referring to source of information.
[17]   Record Identification Number (RIN)
died 3 Jan 1930^7 Citation^7 referring to source of information for this event.
(Robert^2, Scott^1)   Lineage: John is son of Robert. Robert is son of Scott.

+   2   **Bobby**^{4} [43]
        Bobby had issue (+). His paragraph number is two (2), he is the first child in the family, and of the fourth (^{4}) generation. Bobby's RIN number is [43].

Another example, for Preller Matt Geldenhuys – see ***Generation 11*** – as follows:

11111111112. Preller Matt^{11} **GELDENHUYS Wg Cdr (Rtd)** [1] (Abram Carl Frederik Preller^{10}, Johannes (Jan) Albertus^9, Hendrik Jacobus^8, Johannes Albertus^7, Lourens^6, Johannes Albertus^5, Hendrik (c3)^4, Barend^3, Albert Barends Gildenhuisz^2, Bernd Gildenhausen^1), born 20 Feb 1943 in Bothaville, OFS, South Africa. He married on 5 Mar 1966 in Fort Victoria, Rhodesia **Susanna Catharina (MALAN) GELDENHUYS** [2], born 5 Mar 1945 in Lichtenburg, Tvl, South Africa, daughter of Francois Daniel Malan [11] and Aletta Magdalena Susanna le Roux [12].

10 X 1 = 10 generations; 2 =2nd child; 11 = 11th generation, [1] = RIN = Record Identification Number; 10 = 10th generation, my father ACFP, 9 = my grandfather, 9th generation; and so on and so forth.

---------------- Example Only ----------------

Descendants of Bernd Gildenhausen GELDENHUYS and Elsken VON COESFELD

1. **Bernd Gildenhausen**[1] **GELDENHUYS** [193], born abt 1610 in Burgsteinfurt, Westfalen, Duitsland; died unknow in possibly Germany. He married in suspect Burgsteinfurt, Westfalen, Germany **Elsken (VON COESFELD) GELDENHUYS** [194], born in unknown - possibly Germany; died 12 May 1680 in unknown - possibly Germany.

Children of Bernd Gildenhausen GELDENHUYS and Elsken VON COESFELD were as follows:

+   11   Albert Barends Gildenhuisz[2] **GELDENHUYS** [138], born abt 1630 in Burgsteinfurt, Wesfale, Duitsland; died abt 1693 in Kaapstad (Cape Town), South Africa. He married **Margaretha HOEFNAGELS** [139].

Generation 2

11. Albert Barends Gildenhuisz[2] **GELDENHUYS** [138] (Bernd Gildenhausen[1]), born abt 1630 in Burgsteinfurt, Wesfale, Duitsland; died abt 1693 in Kaapstad (Cape Town), South Africa. He married on 28 Mar 1649 in Legden, Netherlands **Margaretha (HOEFNAGELS) GELDENHUYS** [139], born 28 Mar 1649 in Legden, Westfalen, Netherlands; died 1689 or 1713 in Kaapstad (Cape Town), South Africa, daughter of Arend HOEFNAGELS [1488] and Grietje CORNELIS [1489].

Notes for Albert Barends Gildenhuisz GELDENHUYS
    Some dates suggest 1628 as date of birth in Netherlands

    Albert returned to the Cape with is wife and newborn son, Arend

    Sailor onboard the ship 'Princesse Royale'

    (a death in Netherlands in 1649 is given in some reports)

    Albert returned to Europe to marry Margaretha Hoefnagels (1649? - 1689). Stammoeder of the Geldenhuys family

Children of Albert Barends Gildenhuisz GELDENHUYS and Margaretha HOEFNAGELS were as follows:

+   111   **Barend**[3] **GELDENHUYS** [137], born 6 Sep 1682 in Kaapstad / Cape Town, South Africa; died 1721 in Cape, South Africa. He married **Anna Margaretha SIEK** [195].

+   112   **Arend Gildenhuisz**[3] **GELDENHUYS** [222], born abt 1673 in Legden, Netherlands. He married **Judith SMIT (SCHMIDT)** [223].

+   113   **Elsje Gildenhuisz**[3] **GELDENHUYS** [233], born 11 May 1674 in Kaapstad / Cape Town, South Africa. She married **Jacobus VAN DER HEIDEN** [234].

    114   **Margaretha**[3] **GELDENHUYS** [242], born 9 Jun 1680 in Kaapstad / Cape Town, South; died abt 1684.

    115   **Margaretha**[3] **GELDENHUYS** [243], born 6 Oct 1684. She married (1) on 5 Jul 1704 **Heinrich DU PLOOY** [248]; (2) on 10 Jun 1725 **Philippus RICHTER** [249], born in Soest.

+ 116 Hendrik (b8)[3] **GELDENHUYS** [244], born 2 Feb 1687 in Kaapstad / Cape Town, South Africa. He married **Elsabe MEYER** [247].

117 Anna[3] **GELDENHUYS** [245], born 6 Oct 1689. She married on 22 May 1712 in Kaapstad / Cape Town, South Africa **Jean COSTEUX** [246], born in Calais, France.

Generation 3

111. Barend[3] **GELDENHUYS** [137] (Albert Barends Gildenhuisz[2], Bernd Gildenhausen[1]), born 6 Sep 1682 in Kaapstad / Cape Town, South Africa; died 1721 in Cape, South Africa. He married on 31 Aug 1710 in Unknown - possibly Cape Town **Anna Margaretha (SIEK) GELDENHUYS** [195], born 13 Mar 1685 in Kaapstad (Cape Town), South Africa; died in Unknown - possibly Cape Town, daughter of Johan SIEK [196] and Geertruy HELMS [197].

Notes for Barend GELDENHUYS
Some records have date as 9th, and not the 6th

Died young (date 1678 or perhaps later, needs verification)

Margaretha had a subsequent son, also named Barend in 1682.

Also died young - most probably 1678, but could be before 1682

Children of Barend GELDENHUYS and Anna Margaretha SIEK were as follows:

+ 1111 Hendrik (c3)[4] **GELDENHUYS** [136], born 12 Jul 1717 in Cape Town (Kaapstad), South Africa; died 6 Aug 1770. He married (1) **Cornelia SWART** [190]; (2) **Sara Johanna SWART** [252].

1112 Albert Barend[4] **GELDENHUYS** [250], born 21 Feb 1712.

1113 Geertruy[4] **GELDENHUYS** [251], born 24 Mar 1712.

+ 1114 Barend[4] **GELDENHUYS** [474], born 22 Jan 1719; died 1771. He married **Christina Magdalena RADYN** [475].

1115 Johanna Margaretha[4] **GELDENHUYS** [925], born 1720. She married on 12 Jan 1738 **Jan Jurgen HAMMAN** [926], born 1705 in Staucha, Dresdan, Germany; died 1788 in South Africa.

112. Arend Gildenhuisz[3] **GELDENHUYS** [222] (Albert Barends Gildenhuisz[2], Bernd Gildenhausen[1]), born abt 1673 in Legden, Netherlands. He married on 28 Dec 1698 in kaapstad / Cape Town, South Africa **Judith (SMIT (SCHMIDT)) GELDENHUYS** [223], born abt 1672; died 1713, daughter of Heinrich SCHMIDT [224].

Children of Arend Gildenhuisz GELDENHUYS and Judith SMIT (SCHMIDT) were as follows:

1121 Margrijet Gildehuijsen[4] **GELDENHUYS** [225], born 11 Apr 1700 in Stellenbosse and Drakenstein, Cape, South.

1122 Margaretha[4] **GELDENHUYS** [226], born 10 Dec 1702 in Kaapstad / Cape Town, South Africa; died 18 Mar 1770. She married on 20 Oct 1725 in Stellenbosch, Cape, South Africa **Jan LOUW** [227], born 10 Oct 1674 in Kaapstad / Cape Town, Louwvleitt, South Africa; died 18 Mar 1770 in Stellenbosch, Cape, South Africa. Notes: Oranje, near Hopetown, have Doopregister records (Prop-PMG) Stammoeder of Karen Geldenhuys nee de Waal

1123 Henricus Geldenhuisz ab1c3[4] **GELDENHUYS** [228], born 16 Aug 1705 in Cape, South Africa.

1124 Elsje[4] GELDENHUYS [229], born 15 Jul 1708 in Cape, South Africa. Notes: See 'Geldenhuys Genealogy' by Preller Geldenhuys

1125 Albert Barentse[4] GELDENHUYS [230], born 22 Sep 1709 in Cape, South Africa. Notes: Geldenhuys Genealogy - Preller Geldenhuys

1126 Jacobus[4] GELDENHUYS [231], born 19 Jun 1712.

1127 Johanna[4] GELDENHUYS [232], born 21 Apr 1720 in Cape Colony, South Africa; died in Cape Colony, South Africa.

113. Elsje Gildenhuisz[3] GELDENHUYS [233] (Albert Barends Gildenhuisz[2], Bernd Gildenhausen[1]), born 11 May 1674 in Kaapstad / Cape Town, South Africa. She married in 1691 **Jacobus VAN DER HEIDEN** [234], born 1670 in Haarlem; died 1726 in Possibly Stellenbosch area, son of Andries VAN DER HEIDEN [276] and Hester KYPER [277].

Notes for Jacobus VAN DER HEIDEN
Brother-in-law to co-owner of Vergelegen - Barend Geldenhuys

Children of Elsje Gildenhuisz GELDENHUYS and Jacobus VAN DER HEIDEN were as follows:

1131 Anna[4] VAN DER HEIDEN [274], born 1694 in Cape, South Africa.

1132 Jacobus[4] VAN DER HEIDEN [275], born 1695 in Cape Town, South Africa.

116. Hendrik (b8)[3] GELDENHUYS [244] (Albert Barends Gildenhuisz[2], Bernd Gildenhausen[1]), born 2 Feb 1687 in Kaapstad / Cape Town, South Africa. He married on 11 Oct 1711 in Possibly Cape Town **Elsabe (MEYER) GELDENHUYS** [247], born 31 Mar 1697 in Cape Colony, South Africa; died 1721 in South Africa.

Notes for Elsabe MEYER
Seems at age 14, she was very young (compared to her husband)

Children of Hendrik (b8) GELDENHUYS and Elsabe MEYER were as follows:

1161 Susanna Margaretha[4] GELDENHUYS [927], born 1715.

+ 1162 Hendrik Albertus[4] GELDENHUYS [928], born 6 Jun 1717. He married **Elizabeth TAILLEFER** [932].

1163 Gerrit[4] GELDENHUYS [929], born 11 Dec 1718.

1164 Susanna Jacoba[4] GELDENHUYS [930], born 2 Nov 1721. She married on 8 Sep 1748 **Guilliam Hendrik HEEMS** [931].

Generation 4

1111. Hendrik (c3)⁴ GELDENHUYS [136] (Barend³, Albert Barends Gildenhuisz², Bernd Gildenhausen¹), born 12 Jul 1717 in Cape Town (Kaapstad), South Africa; died 6 Aug 1770. He married (1) **Cornelia (SWART) GELDENHUYS** [190], born 4 Feb 1720 in Cape Town (Kaapstad), South Africa; died 11 Apr 1750 in Swellendam, Cape, South Africa; (2) on 26 Jul 1750 **Sara Johanna (SWART)** GELDENHUYS [252].

Notes for Hendrik (c3) GELDENHUYS
married Cornelia Swart

7th child, Johannes Albertus, was born two months before second marriage to Sara (sister to Cornelia?)

married Sara Johanna Swart

ab6c3

Notes for Cornelia SWART
Cornelia Swart died Swellendam Apr 11 1750.

her sister (or cousin?), Sara Johanna, married Hendrik in July 1750

Speculation: Possibly died with childbirth (of her son Johannes Albertus on Apr 5 1750?)

Notes for Sara Johanna SWART
Cornelia Swart was first wife to Hendrik

Re-marriage to Sara Johanna Swart

Children of Hendrik (c3) GELDENHUYS and Cornelia SWART were as follows:

+ 11111 **Johannes Albertus⁵ GELDENHUYS** [135], born 5 Apr 1750 in South Africa; died c? 1785 in South Africa. He married **Johanna LE ROUX** [189].
+ 11112 **Petrus Arnoldus - d10⁵ GELDENHUYS** [140], born 5 Oct 1755 in South Africa; christened 5 Oct 1755 in Stellenbosch, Cape Colony, South Africa; died 25 Mar 1836 in South Africa. He married **Dina Maria UYS** [141].
  11113 **Anna Margaretha⁵ GELDENHUYS** [256], born 30 Aug 1739. She married on 15 Feb 1756 **Stephanus KUUN** [262].
  11114 **Zacharya Geertruy (Gildenhuizen)⁵ GELDENHUYS** [257], born 15 Jan 1741 in Cape, South Africa; died in South Africa. She married (1) on 1 Nov 1761 **Jan Bastiaan Rabie RABIE** [263]; (2) on 25 Dec 1763 **Jacobus Albertus VAN ZYL** [264].
+ 11115 **Barend⁵ GELDENHUYS** [258], born 1 Jul 1742. He married **Maria Elizabeth DIEDERIKS** [265].
  11116 **Johannes Albertus⁵ GELDENHUYS** [259], born 25 Aug 1743.
+ 11117 **Hendrik⁵ GELDENHUYS** [260], born 13 Dec 1744. He married (1) **Geertruyda GROBBELAAR** [1437]; (2) **Margaretha Maria WESSELS** [1448].
  11118 **Elsie⁵ GELDENHUYS** [261], born 9 Oct 1746.

Children of Hendrik (c3) GELDENHUYS and Sara Johanna SWART were as follows:

  11119 **Sara Johanna⁵ GELDENHUYS** [253], born 31 Oct 1751; died 26 Aug 1836.

1111A Cornelia Margaretha^5 GELDENHUYS [254], born 12 Aug 1753.
+ 1111B PetrusD Arnoldus - duplicated branch^5 GELDENHUYS [255], born 5 Oct 1755; died 25 Mar 1839. He married (1) **Susanna Maria MOOLMAN** [635]; (2) **Dina Maria UYS** [638].

1114. Barend^4 **GELDENHUYS** [474] (Barend^3, Albert Barends Gildenhuisz^2, Bernd Gildenhausen^1), born 22 Jan 1719; died 1771. He married **Christina Magdalena (RADYN) GELDENHUYS** [475].

Children of Barend GELDENHUYS and Christina Magdalena RADYN were as follows:
+ 11141 **Barend**^{5} **GELDENHUYS** [476], born 1 Jul 1742. He married **Geertruyda Susanna WESSELS** [679].
+ 11142 **Jurie Johannes**^{5} **GELDENHUYS** [477], born 6 Sep 1744; died 19 Nov 1777. He married **Anna FOURIE** [703].
+ 11143 **Albert Hendrik**^{5} **GELDENHUYS** [478], born 10 Jul 1746. He married **Maria Dorothea RADYN** [482].
  11144 **Petrus Arnoldus**^{5} **GELDENHUYS** [479], born 9 Aug 1750.
  11145 **Anna Margaretha**^{5} **GELDENHUYS** [480], born 10 Sep 1752.
+ 11146 **Jacobus**^{5} **GELDENHUYS** [842], born 13 Feb 1759. He married **Maria Chistina TESNER** [843].
  11147 **Maria Margaretha**^{5} **GELDENHUYS** [911], born 15 Jul 1759.
  11148 **Christina Margaretha**^{5} **GELDENHUYS** [912], born 12 Apr 1762.
  11149 **Susanna Elizabeth**^{5} **GELDENHUYS** [913], born 7 Oct 1764.
+ 1114A **Hendrik Andries**^{5} **GELDENHUYS** [915], born 6 Oct 1771. He married **Elsabe SWART** [916].

1162. Hendrik Albertus^4 **GELDENHUYS** [928] (Hendrik (b8)^3, Albert Barends Gildenhuisz^2, Bernd Gildenhausen^1), born 6 Jun 1717. He married on 7 Nov 1738 **Elizabeth (TAILLEFER) GELDENHUYS** [932].

Children of Hendrik Albertus GELDENHUYS and Elizabeth TAILLEFER were as follows:
  11621 **Elsabe**^{5} **GELDENHUYS** [933], born 1738. She married in Dec 1757 **Paul Henricus EKSTEEN** [934], born 1737, son of Heinrich Oswald EKSTEEN [1897].
+ 11622 **Jan Hendrik**^{5} **GELDENHUYS** [935], born 6 Apr 1777. He married **Helena Gerharda KEULDER** [936].
  11623 **Petrus**^{5} **GELDENHUYS** [938], born 18 Dec 1740.
+ 11624 **Hendrik**^{5} **GELDENHUYS** [939], born 16 Sep 1742. He married **Margaretha Johanna VAN AARDE** [940].
  11625 **Maria Elizabeth**^{5} **GELDENHUYS** [1052], born 21 Jun 1744.
  11626 **Susanna Jacoba**^{5} **GELDENHUYS** [1053], born 22 May 1746.
+ 11627 **Albert Barend**^{5} **GELDENHUYS** [1054], born 8 Sep 1748; died in Zoutekloof, Cape District. He married **Sophia Catharina LOUBSER** [1056].
+ 11628 **Guilliam Hendrik**^{5} **GELDENHUYS** [1055], born 13 Dec 1750. He married **Helena Maria WALTERS** [1095].

Generation 5

11111. Johannes Albertus[5] **GELDENHUYS** [135] (Hendrik (c3)[4], Barend[3], Albert Barends Gildenhuisz[2], Bernd Gildenhausen[1]), born 5 Apr 1750 in South Africa; died c? 1785 in South Africa. He married **Johanna (LE ROUX) GELDENHUYS** [189], born 21 Jul 1748; died in Swellendam, Cape, South Africa.

Notes for Johannes Albertus GELDENHUYS
    Burgher of Stellenbosch

    ab6c3d7

Notes for Johanna LE ROUX
    widow of Johannes Swart

    Children of Johannes Albertus GELDENHUYS and Johanna LE ROUX were as follows:

+   **111111**   **Lourens**[6] **GELDENHUYS** [134], born 30 Mar 1777 in Malgasriver, South Africa; died 1843 in South Africa. He married **Johanna Geertruyda GILDENHUIZEN** [188].
+   **111112**   **Johannes Albertus**[6] **GELDENHUYS** [552], born 5 Apr 1772. He married **Johanna MATTHEE** [564].
    111113   **Cornelia Geertruy**[6] **GELDENHUYS** [553], born 3 Sep 1773.
    111114   **Hendrik**[6] **GELDENHUYS** [554], born 30 Jul 1775.
+   **111115**   **Barend**[6] **GELDENHUYS** [555], born 17 Feb 1779 in Stellenbosch, Cape Colony, South Africa. He married **Aletta Johanna MARAIS** [594].
+   **111116**   **Petrus Arnoldus**[6] **GELDENHUYS** [556], born 25 Feb 1781; died 27 Jun 1846 in Rustfontein, Swellendam, South Africa. He married (1) **Maria Elizabeth MATTHEE** [598]; (2) **Elizabeth Christina VAN WYK** [634].
+   **111117**   **Geertruy Anna**[6] **GELDENHUYS** [558], born 28 Sep 1785. She married **NN NN** [559].

11112. Petrus Arnoldus - d10[5] **GELDENHUYS** [140] (Hendrik (c3)[4], Barend[3], Albert Barends Gildenhuisz[2], Bernd Gildenhausen[1]), born 5 Oct 1755 in South Africa; christened 5 Oct 1755 in Stellenbosch, Cape Colony, South Africa; died 25 Mar 1836 in South Africa. He married on 3 May 1778 **Dina Maria (UYS) GELDENHUYS** [141], born in South Africa; died 25 Mar 1839 in South Africa.

Notes for Petrus Arnoldus - d10 GELDENHUYS
    some dates given as 1839, and not 1836

    Children of Petrus Arnoldus - d10 GELDENHUYS and Dina Maria UYS were as follows:
+   **111121**   **Petrus Arnoldus - e5**[6] **GELDENHUYS** [142], born 21 Jul 1785 in Stellenbosch, Cape Colony, South Africa; died in South Africa. He married **Cornelia Johanna KLEYNSMIT** [143].

11115. Barend[5] **GELDENHUYS** [258] (Hendrik (c3)[4], Barend[3], Albert Barends Gildenhuisz[2], Bernd Gildenhausen[1]), born 1 Jul 1742. He married on 12 Jan 1766 **Maria Elizabeth (DIEDERIKS) GELDENHUYS** [265].

    Children of Barend GELDENHUYS and Maria Elizabeth DIEDERIKS were as follows:
    111151   **Martha**[6] **GELDENHUYS** [266], born 10 May 1767.

111152 Cornelia[6] GELDENHUYS [267], born 30 Sep 1768.
111153 Maria Elizabeth[6] GELDENHUYS [268], born 2 Sep 1770.
111154 Barend[6] GELDENHUYS [269], born 19 Feb 1775; died 26 Mar 1841.
111155 Anna Dorothea[6] GELDENHUYS [270], born 22 Mar 1777.
111156 Susanna Geertruyda[6] GELDENHUYS [271], born 2 May 1779.
111157 Hester Johanna[6] GELDENHUYS [272], born 4 Nov 1781.
111158 Sara Magdalena[6] GELDENHUYS [273], born 18 Dec 1785.

11117. Hendrik[5] GELDENHUYS [260] (Hendrik (c3)[4], Barend[3], Albert Barends Gildenhuisz[2], Bernd Gildenhausen[1]), born 13 Dec 1744. He married (1) **Geertruyda (GROBBELAAR)** GELDENHUYS [1437], born 22 Sep 1753 in Drakenstein, Cape Colony, South Africa; died 17 Apr 1837 in Swellendam, Cape Colony, South Africa; (2) on 18 Jan 1801 **Margaretha Maria (WESSELS)** GELDENHUYS [1448], born in Cape Colony, South Africa; died 1801 in Cape Colony, South Africa.

Children of Hendrik GELDENHUYS and Geertruyda GROBBELAAR were as follows:
111171 Cornelia Margaretha[6] GELDENHUYS [1438], born 19 Feb 1775 in Swellendam, Cape Colony, South Africa; died 24 May 1839 in Rviersonderend, Cape Province, South Africa. She married **Dirk HUMAN** [1439].
111172 Susanna Maria[6] GELDENHUYS [1440], born 1 Jan 1790.
111173 Elisabeth Catharina[6] GELDENHUYS [1441], born 13 Apr 1783. She married **Pieter Gerhardus HUMAN** [1461].
+ 111174 Hendrik Jacobus[6] GELDENHUYS [1442], born 18 Sep 1785; died 2 Apr 1861. He married **Sara Johanna ODENDAAL** [1462].
111175 Geertruy Johanna[6] GELDENHUYS [1443], born 9 Sep 1787 in Swellendam, Cape Colony, South Africa; died 25 May 1888.
111176 Susanna Dorothea[6] GELDENHUYS [1444], born 3 Mar 1790; died 19 Jan 1863. She married **Jan Cornelis SWART** [2004].
111177 Elsie Johanna[6] GELDENHUYS [1445], born 1 Nov 1792; died 24 Mar 1857.
111178 Pieter Arnoldus[6] GELDENHUYS [1446], born 15 Feb 1795; died 3 Mar 1852 in Burgersdorp.
111179 Anna Maria[6] GELDENHUYS [1447], born 14 Oct 1798.

Children of Hendrik GELDENHUYS and Margaretha Maria WESSELS were as follows:
+ 11117A Wynand Hendrik[6] GELDENHUYS [1449], born 11 Nov 1801. He married **Elsabe Cornelia MATTHEE** [1450].

1111B. PetrusD Arnoldus - duplicated branch[5] GELDENHUYS [255] (Hendrik (c3)[4], Barend[3], Albert Barends Gildenhuisz[2], Bernd Gildenhausen[1]), born 5 Oct 1755; died 25 Mar 1839. He married (1) on 23 Aug 1772 **Susanna Maria (MOOLMAN)** GELDENHUYS [635], born 1754; (2) on 3 May 1778 **Dina Maria (UYS)** GELDENHUYS [638].

Notes for PetrusD Arnoldus - duplicated branch GELDENHUYS
ab6c3d10

Children of PetrusD Arnoldus - duplicated branch GELDENHUYS and Susanna Maria MOOLMAN were as follows:
1111B1 Christina Magdalena[6] GELDENHUYS [636], born 10 Oct 1773 in Stellenbosch, Cape Colony, South Africa; died 27 Aug 1839. She married **Jan Hendrik BADENHORST** [1949], born 1771; christened 7 Jul 1771.
1111B2 Catharina Elizabeth[6] GELDENHUYS [637], born 29 Oct 1775.

Children of PetrusD Arnoldus - duplicated branch GELDENHUYS and Dina Maria UYS were as follows:

1111B3 Susanna Hermina^6 GELDENHUYS [639], born 16 Jan 1780.

1111B4 Hendrik Petrus^6 GELDENHUYS [640], born 10 Mar 1782; died 20 Jun 1869.

+ 1111B5 Petrus Arnoldus^6 GELDENHUYS [641], born 21 Jul 1785. He married Cornelia Johanna KLEYNSMIT [653].

1111B6 Sara Johanna^6 GELDENHUYS [642], born 13 Apr 1788. She married in Jun 1809 in Swellendam, Cape, South Africa **Cornelis Janse UYS** [652].

1111B7 Dina Maria^6 GELDENHUYS [643], born 24 Jan 1790. She married **H J LOURENS** [651].

1111B8 Cornelia Susanna^6 GELDENHUYS [644], born 26 Feb 1792. She married **D C LOURENS** [650].

1111B9 Maria Catharina^6 GELDENHUYS [645], born 11 Oct 1795. She married **J J TALJAARD** [649].

1111BA Johanna Dorothea^6 GELDENHUYS [646], born 14 Oct 1798. She married **C P LOURENS** [648].

1111BB Dirk Cornelis^6 GELDENHUYS [647], born 4 Oct 1801.

11141. Barend^5 GELDENHUYS [476] (Barend^4, Barend^3, Albert Barends Gildenhuisz^2, Bernd Gildenhausen^1), born 1 Jul 1742. He married on 8 Dec 1768 **Geertruyda Susanna (WESSELS)** GELDENHUYS [679], born 11 Sep 1746 in South Africa; died in South Africa, daughter of Wessel WESSELS [1895] and Susanna ODENDAAL [1896].

Children of Barend GELDENHUYS and Geertruyda Susanna WESSELS were as follows:

111411 Christina Geertruyda^6 GELDENHUYS [680], born 29 Oct 1769. She married on 14 Nov 1790 **Frans Hendrik BADENHORST** [681].

111412 Susanna Margaretha^6 GELDENHUYS [682], born 7 Jul 1771. She married on 22 Nov 1789 **Petrus Johannes BADENHORST** [689].

111413 Barend^6 GELDENHUYS [683], born 6 Feb 1774.

+ 111414 Wessel Johannes^6 GELDENHUYS [684], born 1 Oct 1775. He married **Anna Geertryda Gildenhuizen GELDENHUYS** [690].

111415 Jacobus^6 GELDENHUYS [685], born 29 Jun 1777.

111416 Maria Johanna^6 GELDENHUYS [686], born 19 Nov 1790.

111417 Jurgen Johannes^6 GELDENHUYS [687], born 23 Mar 1783.

111418 Geertruyda Maria^6 GELDENHUYS [688], born 26 Jun 1785.

+ 111419 Wessel Johannes^6 GELDENHUYS [740], born 1 Oct 1775. He married **Anna Geertruyda Gildenhuizen GELDENHUYS** [743].

11141A Geertruyda Elizabeth^6 GELDENHUYS [741], born 15 Nov 1778.

11141B Maria Johanna^6 GELDENHUYS [742], born 19 Nov 1780.

11142. Jurie Johannes^5 GELDENHUYS [477] (Barend^4, Barend^3, Albert Barends Gildenhuisz^2, Bernd Gildenhausen^1), born 6 Sep 1744; died 19 Nov 1777. He married on 28 Apr 1771 **Anna (FOURIE)** GELDENHUYS [703], born 1752 in Stellenbosch, Cape, South Africa; died 20 Jul 1840.

Children of Jurie Johannes GELDENHUYS and Anna FOURIE were as follows:

+ 111421 Barend^6 GELDENHUYS [704], born 5 Jul 1772 in Cape Colony, South Africa; christened 5 Jul 1772; died 1819. He married **Elsebe SWART** [755].

111422 Elizabeth Johanna⁶ GELDENHUYS [705], born 6 Feb 1774. She married **Wessel WESSELS** [739].
+ 111423 Jurgen Johannes⁶ GELDENHUYS [706], born 8 Apr 1776. He married **Elizabeth Luytjie SWART** [707].

11143. Albert Hendrik⁵ GELDENHUYS [478] (Barend⁴, Barend³, Albert Barends Gildenhuisz², Bernd Gildenhausen¹), born 10 Jul 1746. He married on 28 Mar 1779 **Maria Dorothea (RADYN) GELDENHUYS** [482].

Children of Albert Hendrik GELDENHUYS and Maria Dorothea RADYN were as follows:
111431 Anna Dorothea⁶ GELDENHUYS [483], born 26 Feb 1780. She married **Wessel Johannes GILDENHUIZEN (GELDENHUYS)** [486].
111432 Christina Magdalena⁶ GELDENHUYS [484], born 19 Jan 1783.
+ 111433 Barend Petrus⁶ GELDENHUYS [487], born 1 Jan 1792. He married **Anna Maria LE ROUX** [488].
111434 Christina Maria⁶ GELDENHUYS [491], born 3 Aug 1794 in Caledon, Western Cape, South Africa; died 1837. She married on 4 May 1817 in Caledon, Western Cape, South Africa **Stephanus Jacobus BOTHA** [492].
111435 Albert Hendrik⁶ GELDENHUYS [493], born 29 Jan 1797.
+ 111436 Jurgen Johannes⁶ GELDENHUYS [494], born 14 Oct 1798. He married **Elizabeth Debora BOTHA** [495].
111437 Albert Hendrik⁶ GELDENHUYS [501], born 4 Oct 1891.

11146. Jacobus⁵ GELDENHUYS [842] (Barend⁴, Barend³, Albert Barends Gildenhuisz², Bernd Gildenhausen¹), born 13 Feb 1759. He married **Maria Chistina (TESNER) GELDENHUYS** [843], born 10 Mar 1757, daughter of Heinrich TESNER [846] and Francina CORDIER [847].

Children of Jacobus GELDENHUYS and Maria Chistina TESNER were as follows:
111461 Christina Magdalena⁶ GELDENHUYS [844], born 4 Feb 1781. She married on 9 May 1804 in Cape Town, South Africa **Barend Hendrik BEUKES** [853].
+ 111462 Jacobus⁶ GELDENHUYS [848]. He married **Geertruyda SWART** [854].
+ 111463 Hendrik Andries⁶ GELDENHUYS [849], born 28 Dec 1794. He married **Sachararya Magdalena VAN DEVENTER** [888].
+ 111464 Barend Petrus⁶ GELDENHUYS [850], born 25 Oct 1797. He married **Anna Christina GROENEWALD** [851].

1114A. Hendrik Andries⁵ GELDENHUYS [915] (Barend⁴, Barend³, Albert Barends Gildenhuisz², Bernd Gildenhausen¹), born 6 Oct 1771. He married on 23 Feb 1806 in Stellenbosch, Cape, South Africa **Elsabe (SWART) GELDENHUYS** [916], born 6 Feb 1777.

Children of Hendrik Andries GELDENHUYS and Elsabe SWART were as follows:
+ 1114A1 Barend Hendrik⁶ GELDENHUYS [917], born 20 Sep 1809; died 22 Aug 1878 in Bethlehem, OFS, South Africa. He married (1) **Anna Catharina MULDER** [918]; (2) **Anna Maria SMIT** [922]; (3) **Margaretha Maria SCHEEPERS** [923].

11622. Jan Hendrik⁵ GELDENHUYS [935] (Hendrik Albertus⁴, Hendrik (b8)³, Albert Barends Gildenhuisz², Bernd Gildenhausen¹), born 6 Apr 1777. He married on 19 Sep 1802 in Cape Town, South Africa **Helena Gerharda (KEULDER) GELDENHUYS** [936].

Children of Jan Hendrik GELDENHUYS and Helena Gerharda KEULDER were as follows:
    116221   Hendrik Johannes⁶ GELDENHUYS [937], born 25 Dec 1803.

11624. Hendrik⁵ GELDENHUYS [939] (Hendrik Albertus⁴, Hendrik (b8)³, Albert Barends Gildenhuisz², Bernd Gildenhausen¹), born 16 Sep 1742. He married on 5 May 1773 **Margaretha Johanna (VAN AARDE) GELDENHUYS** [940].

Children of Hendrik GELDENHUYS and Margaretha Johanna VAN AARDE were as follows:
    116241   **Elizabeth Elsabe⁶ GELDENHUYS** [941], born 20 Mar 1774. She married **Theodorus Louis KRIEL** [942].
+   116242   **Jan Hendrik⁶ GELDENHUYS** [943], born 6 Apr 1777. He married **Helena Gerharda KEULDER** [944].
+   116243   **Hendrik Albertus⁶ GELDENHUYS** [946], born 15 Nov 1778. He married **Rachel Marie JORDAAN** [947].
    116244   **Jacobus Carel⁶ GELDENHUYS** [958], born 12 Mar 1780.
+   116245   **Petrus Guilaume⁶ GELDENHUYS** [959], born 4 Nov 1781. He married **Maria Catharina REYNEKE** [960].
+   116246   **Abraham Jacobus⁶ GELDENHUYS** [977]. He married **Martha Louisa LE ROUX** [985].
    116247   **Susanna Petronella⁶ GELDENHUYS** [978], born 20 Mar 1785. She married on 5 Dec 1802 **Adam Johannes REYNEKE** [1015].
    116248   **Martha Jacoba⁶ GELDENHUYS** [979], born 26 Nov 1786. She married **Carel Lodewyk VAN DER MERWE** [1016].
+   116249   **Albert Barend⁶ GELDENHUYS** [980], born 17 Aug 1788. He married **Susanna Elizabeth LE ROUX** [1017].
    11624A   **Margaretha Louisa Elizabeth⁶ GELDENHUYS** [981], born 4 Sep 1791.
+   11624B   **Guilliam (or Gideon) Theodorus⁶ GELDENHUYS** [982], born 20 Oct 1793. He married **Martha Maria DU TOIT** [1020].
+   11624C   **Theodorus Louis Hermanus⁶ GELDENHUYS** [983], born 20 Mar 1796. He married **Elizabeth Rachel DE VILLIERS** [1036].
    11624D   **Barend Hendrik⁶ GELDENHUYS** [984], born 5 Aug 1798.

11627. Albert Barend⁵ GELDENHUYS [1054] (Hendrik Albertus⁴, Hendrik (b8)³, Albert Barends Gildenhuisz², Bernd Gildenhausen¹), born 8 Sep 1748; died in Zoutekloof, Cape District. He married on 23 Apr 1784 **Sophia Catharina (LOUBSER) GELDENHUYS** [1056], born 1756; died 15 Nov 1836.

Children of Albert Barend GELDENHUYS and Sophia Catharina LOUBSER were as follows:
+   116271   **Hendrik Albertus⁶ GELDENHUYS** [1057], born 13 May 1781; died Aug 1836. He married **Hilletje Aletta SMIT** [1064].
+   116272   **Pieter Johannes⁶ GELDENHUYS** [1058], born 10 Nov 1782. He married **Sibella Jacoba JORDAAN** [1081].
+   116273   **Albert Barend⁶ GELDENHUYS** [1059], born 16 May 1784. He married **Anna Catharina Hendrina VAN DYK** [1089].

116274 Johannes Albertus⁶ GELDENHUYS [1060], born 13 Aug 1786.
116275 Elizabeth Maria Helena⁶ GELDENHUYS [1061], born 6 Apr 1788.
116276 Johanna Hendrina⁶ GELDENHUYS [1062], born 14 Apr 1790.
116277 Guilliam Hendrik⁶ GELDENHUYS [1063], born 1 Feb 1795.

11628. Guilliam Hendrik⁵ GELDENHUYS [1055] (Hendrik Albertus⁴, Hendrik (b8)³, Albert Barends Gildenhuisz², Bernd Gildenhausen¹), born 13 Dec 1750. He married on 9 Nov 1772 **Helena Maria (WALTERS) GELDENHUYS** [1095].

Children of Guilliam Hendrik GELDENHUYS and Helena Maria WALTERS were as follows:
+ 116281 **Hendrik Albertus⁶** GELDENHUYS [1096], born 14 Mar 1779. He married **Johanna Magdalena BRUYNZWART** [1098].
   116282 **Maria Margaretha⁶** GELDENHUYS [1097], born 31 Dec 1780.

Generation 6

111111. Lourens⁶ GELDENHUYS [134] (Johannes Albertus⁵, Hendrik (c3)⁴, Barend³, Albert Barends Gildenhuisz², Bernd Gildenhausen¹), born 30 Mar 1777 in Malgasriver, South Africa; died 1843 in South Africa. He married on 4 Apr 1804 in Cape Town, South Africa **Johanna Geertruyda (GILDENHUIZEN) GELDENHUYS** [188], born 30 Sep 1787; died 25 May 1888.

Notes for Lourens GELDENHUYS
Johanna Geetruyda Gildenhuizen - is cousin to Uncle Hendrik Jacobus Gildenhuizen and Geetruida Grobbelaar

Notes for Johanna Geertruyda GILDENHUIZEN
daughter of Hendrik Geldenhuys and Geertruyda Grobbelaar

Children of Lourens GELDENHUYS and Johanna Geertruyda GILDENHUIZEN were as follows:
+ 1111111 **Johannes Albertus⁷** GELDENHUYS [10], born 21 Dec 1807 in Stellenbosch or Swellendam, South Africa; died 9 Oct 1894 in Doornbult, Kroonstad, OFS, South Africa. He married **Judith Margaretha GILDENHUIZEN** [187].
   1111112 **Geertruy Anna⁷** GELDENHUYS [502], born 8 Aug 1805.
   1111113 **Johanna Cornelia⁷** GELDENHUYS [503], born 6 Jul 1806.
+ 1111114 **Lourens⁷** GELDENHUYS [504], born 12 Jun 1811. He married (1) **Dirkie Susanna Elizabeth COETZEE** [545]; (2) **Dirkie Susanna Elizabeth COETZEE** [588].
   1111115 **Geertruyda Johanna⁷** GELDENHUYS [505], born 24 Jul 1813; died 1888.
+ 1111116 **Barend Petrus⁷** GELDENHUYS [506], born 3 Mar 1815 in Caledon, Western Cape, South Africa; died 4 Apr 1868 in Holfontein, Kroonstad, South Africa. He married (1) **Maria Elizabeth Johanna GUNTER** [527]; (2) **Catharina Helena OOSTHUIZEN** [536].
+ 1111117 **Hendrik Jacobus⁷** GELDENHUYS [507], born 10 Oct 1816 in Swellendam, Cape, South Africa; died 4 May 1879 in Kroonstad, OFS, South Africa. He married (1) **Cornelia Margaretha SWART** [512]; (2) **Johanna Margaretha Geertruyda ROSSOUW** [517].
   1111118 **Pieter Arnoldus⁷** GELDENHUYS [508], born 6 Sep 1818 in Swellendam, Cape, South Africa; died 1 Dec 1838 in Drowned in Breerivier - aged 20.
   1111119 **Johanna Elsabe⁷** GELDENHUYS [509], born 4 Feb 1821 in Swellendam, Cape, South Africa. She married on 27 Jan 1838 in Swellendam, Cape, South

Africa **Simon Frederik STREICHER** [563], born 9 Nov 1819 in Potjeskraal, Swellendam, Cape, South Africa; died 16 Aug 1882 in Uitulugt, Swellendam, Cape, South Africa.

111111A **Cornelia Margaretha Susanna**[7] **GELDENHUYS** [510], born 4 Nov 1823 in Swellendam, Cape, South Africa. She married on 20 Nov 1836 in Swellendam, Cape, South Africa **Adriaan Johannes KLEYNSMIT** [511].

111112. Johannes Albertus[6] **GELDENHUYS** [552] (Johannes Albertus[5], Hendrik (c3)[4], Barend[3], Albert Barends Gildenhuisz[2], Bernd Gildenhausen[1]), born 5 Apr 1772. He married on 20 Sep 1801 **Johanna (MATTHEE) GELDENHUYS** [564].

Children of Johannes Albertus GELDENHUYS and Johanna MATTHEE were as follows:

+ 1111121 **Johannes Albertus**[7] **GELDENHUYS** [565], born 20 Feb 1803. He married **Johanna Susanna BESTER** [566].
  1111122 **Elizabeth Maria**[7] **GELDENHUYS** [574], born 2 Dec 1804.
+ 1111123 **Johanna Susanna**[7] **GELDENHUYS** [575], born 31 Aug 1808. She married **Christoffel Christiaan HEYNE** [576].
  1111124 **Cornelia Geertruy**[7] **GELDENHUYS** [578], born 17 Apr 1808. She married on 29 Dec 1833 in Caledon, Western Cape, South Africa **Petrus Johannes GERMISHUYSEN** [579].
+ 1111125 **Elias Jacobus**[7] **GELDENHUYS** [580], born 11 Aug 1809. He married **Elizabeth Helena SWART** [581].

111115. Barend[6] **GELDENHUYS** [555] (Johannes Albertus[5], Hendrik (c3)[4], Barend[3], Albert Barends Gildenhuisz[2], Bernd Gildenhausen[1]), born 17 Feb 1779 in Stellenbosch, Cape Colony, South Africa. He married **Aletta Johanna (MARAIS) GELDENHUYS** [594], born 14 Apr 1787 in Stellenbosch, Cape Colony, South Africa.

Children of Barend GELDENHUYS and Aletta Johanna MARAIS were as follows:
1111151 **Johanna Aletta**[7] **GELDENHUYS** [595], born 25 Dec 1806.
1111152 **Maria Elizabeth**[7] **GELDENHUYS** [596], born 14 Sep 1813 in Tulbagh, Cape, South Africa.
1111153 **Aletta Petronella**[7] **GELDENHUYS** [597], born 13 Jun 1815 in Tulbagh, Cape, South Africa.

111116. Petrus Arnoldus[6] **GELDENHUYS** [556] (Johannes Albertus[5], Hendrik (c3)[4], Barend[3], Albert Barends Gildenhuisz[2], Bernd Gildenhausen[1]), born 25 Feb 1781; died 27 Jun 1846 in Rustfontein, Swellendam, South Africa. He married (1) on 8 Jan 1804 in Cape Town, South Africa **Maria Elizabeth (MATTHEE) GELDENHUYS** [598]; (2) on 4 Apr 1838 in Caledon, Western Cape, South Africa **Elizabeth Christina (VAN WYK) GELDENHUYS** [634].

Notes for Elizabeth Christina VAN WYK
widow of Wessel Wessels

Children of Petrus Arnoldus GELDENHUYS and Maria Elizabeth MATTHEE were as follows:
1111161 **Maria Elizabeth**[7] **GELDENHUYS** [599], born 23 Dec 1804.
+ 1111162 **Johannes Albertus**[7] **GELDENHUYS** [600], born 14 Sep 1806. He married **Anna Christina Elizabeth SWART** [619].
1111163 **Johanna Margaretha**[7] **GELDENHUYS** [601], born 4 Oct 1807.

1111164 Cornelia Geertruy[7] **GELDENHUYS** [602], born 2 Jul 1809.

1111165 Geertruyda Anna Johanna[7] **GELDENHUYS** [603], born 15 Sep 1811 in Caledon, Western Cape, South Africa.

1111166 Sara Johanna[7] **GELDENHUYS** [604], born 22 Aug 1813 in Caledon, Western Cape, South Africa.

+ 1111167 Petrus Arnoldus[7] **GELDENHUYS** [605], born 24 Aug 1815 in Caledon, Western Cape, South Africa; died 23 Apr 1846 in Vogelvallei, Caledon, Cape, South Africa. He married **Maria Magdalena SWART** [612].

1111168 Sophia Margaretha[7] **GELDENHUYS** [606], born 14 Aug 1817 in Caledon, Western Cape, South Africa.

1111169 Anna Susanna[7] **GELDENHUYS** [607], born 23 Jun 1819 in Caledon, Western Cape, South Africa; died 16 Jun 1878 in Winburg, OFS, South Africa. She married **Johanna Albertus WESSELS** [611].

111116A Maria Magdalena[7] **GELDENHUYS** [608], born 7 Apr 1821 in Caledon, Western Cape, South Africa.

111116B Elias Caledon[7] **GELDENHUYS** [609], born 23 May 1824.

111116C Hendrik Johannes[7] **GELDENHUYS** [610], born 3 Dec 1825 in Caledon, Western Cape, South Africa.

111117. Geertruy Anna[6] **GELDENHUYS** [558] (Johannes Albertus[5], Hendrik (c3)[4], Barend[3], Albert Barends Gildenhuisz[2], Bernd Gildenhausen[1]), born 28 Sep 1785. She married **NN NN** [559].

Children of Geertruy Anna GELDENHUYS and NN NN were as follows:
+ 1111171 Johanna Susanna Elizabeth[7] **GELDENHUYS** [560], born 27 Oct 1799 in Stellenbosch, Cape, South Africa. She married **NN (FATHER - JULI VAN DIE KAAP** [561].

111121. Petrus Arnoldus - e5[6] **GELDENHUYS** [142] (Petrus Arnoldus - d10[5], Hendrik (c3)[4], Barend[3], Albert Barends Gildenhuisz[2], Bernd Gildenhausen[1]), born 21 Jul 1785 in Stellenbosch, Cape Colony, South Africa; died in South Africa. He married on 2 Mar 1806 in Swellendam, Cape, South Africa **Cornelia Johanna (KLEYNSMIT)** GELDENHUYS [143], born 1785 in South Africa.

Children of Petrus Arnoldus - e5 GELDENHUYS and Cornelia Johanna KLEYNSMIT were as follows:
+ 1111211 Adrian Johannes - f2[7] **GELDENHUYS** [144], born 23 Apr 1810 in Swellendam, Cape, South Africa; died 26 Oct 1867 in Heidelberg, Cape, South Africa. He married **Elsabe Dina LOURENS - B3C5D2E?** [145].

1111212 Petrus Arnoldus[7] **GELDENHUYS** [1894], born 30 Jul 1808 in South Africa.

111174. Hendrik Jacobus[6] **GELDENHUYS** [1442] (Hendrik[5], Hendrik (c3)[4], Barend[3], Albert Barends Gildenhuisz[2], Bernd Gildenhausen[1]), born 18 Sep 1785; died 2 Apr 1861. He married on 6 Apr 1806 in Swellendam, Cape Colony, South Africa **Sara Johanna (ODENDAAL)** GELDENHUYS [1462], born 30 Mar 1783; died in Cape Town, Cape Colony, South, daughter of Adriaan Izaak ODENDAAL [1463] and Sara Johanna (Gildenhuyzen) GELDENHUYS [1464].

Children of Hendrik Jacobus GELDENHUYS and Sara Johanna ODENDAAL were as follows:

1111741 Sara Johanna[7] **GELDENHUYS** [1465], born 3 Mar 1807.

1111742 Geertruy Anna[7] GELDENHUYS [1466], born 1 Oct 1809.

1111743 Judith Margaretha[7] GELDENHUYS [1467], born 20 Feb 1812; died 23 Jun 1890. She married on 6 May 1827 in Swellendam, Cape Colony, South Africa **Johannes Albertus (Gildenhuizen) GELDENHUYS** [1468], died 23 Jun 1890.

1111744 Cornelia Margaretha[7] GELDENHUYS [1469], born 9 Aug 1814 in Swellendam, Cape Colony, South Africa; died 9 Nov 1858 in Modderriver, OFS, South Africa. She married (1) on 1 Jun 1834 in Swellendam, Cape Colony, South Africa **Petrus Johannes BADENHORST** [1473]; (2) **Gert Johannes VAN DEN HEVER** [1474].

+ 1111745 Hendrik Jacobus[7] GELDENHUYS [1470], born 2 Dec 1816 in Swellendam, Cape Colony, South Africa; died 1 Jul 1857 in Roodeport, Winburg, OFS, South Africa. He married (1) **Jacoba Margaretha SWART** [1475]; (2) **Cornelia Geertruyda Dina HUMAN** [1478].

1111746 Susanna Maria[7] GELDENHUYS [1471], born 30 Jan 1821 in Swellendam, Cape Colony, South Africa.

1111747 Adriaan Izaak[7] GELDENHUYS [1472], born 18 Sep 1823 in Swellendam, Cape Colony, South Africa.

11117A. Wynand Hendrik[6] **GELDENHUYS** [1449] (Hendrik[5], Hendrik (c3)[4], Barend[3], Albert Barends Gildenhuisz[2], Bernd Gildenhausen[1]), born 11 Nov 1801. He married **Elsabe Cornelia (MATTHEE) GELDENHUYS** [1450].

Children of Wynand Hendrik GELDENHUYS and Elsabe Cornelia MATTHEE were as follows:

11117A1 Elizabeth Maria[7] GELDENHUYS [1451], born 7 Mar 1826.

11117A2 Hendrik[7] GELDENHUYS [1452], born 28 Aug 1827.

11117A3 Margaretha Maria[7] GELDENHUYS [1453], born 12 Jun 1829.

11117A4 Elias Jacobus[7] GELDENHUYS [1454], born 1 Jul 1832.

11117A5 Elsabe Cornelia Geertruy Anna[7] GELDENHUYS [1455], born 1 Jan 1835.

11117A6 Wynand Hendrik Johannes[7] GELDENHUYS [1456], born 26 Aug 1836.

11117A7 Sophia Margaretha[7] GELDENHUYS [1457], born 28 Sep 1838 in Caledon.

11117A8 Hendrik Johannes[7] GELDENHUYS [1458], born 6 Nov 1840 in Bredasdorp.

11117A9 Johanna Cornelia[7] GELDENHUYS [1459], born 18 Aug 1843 in Bredasdorp.

11117AA Abraham Johannes[7] GELDENHUYS [1460], born 18 May 1845 in Bredasdorp.

1111B5. Petrus Arnoldus[6] **GELDENHUYS** [641] (PetrusD Arnoldus - duplicated branch[5], Hendrik (c3)[4], Barend[3], Albert Barends Gildenhuisz[2], Bernd Gildenhausen[1]), born 21 Jul 1785. He married on 2 Mar 1806 in Swellendam, Cape, South Africa **Cornelia Johanna (KLEYNSMIT) GELDENHUYS** [653].

Children of Petrus Arnoldus GELDENHUYS and Cornelia Johanna KLEYNSMIT were as follows:

+ 1111B51 Petrus Arnoldus[7] GELDENHUYS [654], born 30 Jul 1808. He married **Anna Christina DE JAGER** [656].

+ 1111B52 Adriaan Johannes[7] GELDENHUYS [655], born 23 Apr 1810; died 1867. He married **Elsabe Dina LOURENS** [664].

111414. Wessel Johannes[6] **GELDENHUYS** [684] (Barend[5], Barend[4], Barend[3], Albert Barends Gildenhuisz[2], Bernd Gildenhausen[1]), born 1 Oct 1775. He married **Anna Geertryda Gildenhuizen (GELDENHUYS) GELDENHUYS** [690].

Children of Wessel Johannes GELDENHUYS and Anna Geertryda Gildenhuizen GELDENHUYS were as follows:

1114141 Maria Aletta[7] GELDENHUYS [691], born 17 Apr 1808. She married on 3 Oct 1824 in Swellendam, Cape, South Africa **Gerrit VAN DEVENTER** [701].

1114142 Geertruyda Susanna[7] GELDENHUYS [692], born 18 Nov 1810.

+ 1114143 Barend Petrus Johannes[7] GELDENHUYS [693], born 6 Sep 1812 in Caledon, Western Cape, South Africa. He married (1) **Anna Judith Geertruyda KUUN** [696]; (2) **Anna Judith Geertruyda KUUN** [750].

1114144 Christina Maria Geertruy[7] GELDENHUYS [694], born 20 Mar 1817 in Caledon, Western Cape, South Africa.

1114145 Elizabeth Dorothea Magdalena[7] GELDENHUYS [695], born 27 Jun 1819 in Caledon, Western Cape, South Africa. She married on 20 Apr 1838 in Caledon, Western Cape, South Africa **Barend Petrus FOURIE** [702].

111419. Wessel Johannes[6] GELDENHUYS [740] (Barend[5], Barend[4], Barend[3], Albert Barends Gildenhuisz[2], Bernd Gildenhausen[1]), born 1 Oct 1775. He married on 24 Nov 1805 in Stellenbosch, Cape, South Africa **Anna Geertruyda Gildenhuizen (GELDENHUYS) GELDENHUYS** [743].

Children of Wessel Johannes GELDENHUYS and Anna Geertruyda Gildenhuizen GELDENHUYS were as follows:

1114191 Maria Aletta[7] GELDENHUYS [744], born 17 Apr 1808. She married on 3 Oct 1824 in Swellendam, Cape, South Africa **Gerrit VAN DEVENTER** [749].

1114192 Geertruyda Susanna[7] GELDENHUYS [745], born 11 Nov 1810.

1114193 Barend Petrus Johannes[7] GELDENHUYS [693], born 6 Sep 1812 in Caledon, Western Cape, South Africa. He married (1) on 9 May 1830 in Caledon, Western Cape, South Africa **Anna Judith Geertruyda KUUN** [696]; (2) on 9 May 1830 in Caledon, Western Cape, South Africa **Anna Judith Geertruyda KUUN** [750].

1114194 Christina Maria Geertruy[7] GELDENHUYS [694], born 20 Mar 1817 in Caledon, Western Cape, South Africa.

1114195 Elizabeth Dorothea Magdalena[7] GELDENHUYS [695], born 27 Jun 1819 in Caledon, Western Cape, South Africa. She married on 20 Apr 1838 in Caledon, Western Cape, South Africa **Barend Petrus FOURIE** [702].

111421. Barend[6] GELDENHUYS [704] (Jurie Johannes[5], Barend[4], Barend[3], Albert Barends Gildenhuisz[2], Bernd Gildenhausen[1]), born 5 Jul 1772 in Cape Colony, South Africa; christened 5 Jul 1772; died 1819. He married on 21 Sep 1800 in Cape Town, South Africa **Elsebe (SWART) GELDENHUYS** [755].

Children of Barend GELDENHUYS and Elsebe SWART were as follows:

1114211 Anna Christina Elizabeth[7] GELDENHUYS [756], born 18 Jan 1801.

+ 1114212 Petrus Lafras[7] GELDENHUYS [757], born 20 Feb 1803. He married **Johanna Christina GERMISHUIZEN** [766].

+ 1114213 Jurie Johannes[7] GELDENHUYS [758], born 9 Dec 1804. He married **Cornelia Geertruyda Gildenhuizen GELDENHUYS** [780].

1114214 Geertruy Johanna[7] GELDENHUYS [759], born 14 Sep 1806. She married on 2 May 1824 in Swellendam, Cape, South Africa **Hendrik Johannes FOURIE** [782], born 7 Aug 1802.

1114215 Elizabeth Johanna[7] GELDENHUYS [760], born 28 Sep 1808.

1114216 Elsabe Cornelia[7] GELDENHUYS [761], born 7 Oct 1810.

1114217 Catharina Elizabeth[7] **GELDENHUYS** [762], born 21 Jul 1813 in Caledon, Western Cape, South Africa.

+ 1114218 Barend Hermanus[7] **GELDENHUYS** [763], born 23 Jun 1815 in Caledon, Western Cape, South Africa; died 1840. He married **Margaretha Maria MAREE** [783].

1114219 Elizabeth Maria[7] **GELDENHUYS** [764], born 9 Aug 1817 in Caledon, Western Cape, South Africa.

111421A Johannes Albertus[7] **GELDENHUYS** [765], born 31 Jul 1819 in Caledon, Western Cape, South Africa.

111423. Jurgen Johannes[6] **GELDENHUYS** [706] (Jurie Johannes[5], Barend[4], Barend[3], Albert Barends Gildenhuisz[2], Bernd Gildenhausen[1]), born 8 Apr 1776. He married on 21 Sep 1800 **Elizabeth Luytjie (SWART) GELDENHUYS** [707].

Children of Jurgen Johannes GELDENHUYS and Elizabeth Luytjie SWART were as follows:

1114231 Jurgen Johannes[7] **GELDENHUYS** [708], born 12 Sep 1802. Notes: Twin, died young

+ 1114232 Johannes Joachimus[7] **GELDENHUYS** [709], born 12 Sep 1802; died 20 Feb 1874 in Heidelberg, Cape, South Africa. He married (1) **Sara Johanna KLEYNSMIT** [711]; (2) **Maria Francina VAN DYK** [730]; (3) **Magdalena Johanna LOUW** [734].

+ 1114233 Jurgen Johannes[7] **GELDENHUYS** [710], born 6 Jul 1806. He married (1) **Dina Maria Kleynsmit (---)** [797]; (2) **Elizabeth Catharina BLOEM** [804].

111433. Barend Petrus[6] **GELDENHUYS** [487] (Albert Hendrik[5], Barend[4], Barend[3], Albert Barends Gildenhuisz[2], Bernd Gildenhausen[1]), born 1 Jan 1792. He married **Anna Maria (LE ROUX) GELDENHUYS** [488].

Children of Barend Petrus GELDENHUYS and Anna Maria LE ROUX were as follows:

+ 1114331 Albert Hendrik[7] **GELDENHUYS** [489], born 23 Dec 1816. He married **Anna Geertruyda Fredrika OTTO** [490].

1114332 Gabriel Stephanus le Roux[7] **GELDENHUYS** [830], born 15 Oct 1818 in Caledon, Western Cape, South Africa.

1114333 Margaretha Agatha Johanna[7] **GELDENHUYS** [831], born 10 Apr 1821 in Caledon, Western Cape, South Africa.

1114334 Gabriel Petrus Stephanus[7] **GELDENHUYS** [832], born 15 Mar 1823 in Caledon, Western Cape, South Africa.

1114335 Maria Dorothea Catharina Petronella[7] **GELDENHUYS** [833], born 23 Jan 1828 in Caledon, Western Cape, South Africa.

1114336 Anna Maria Margaretha Alberta[7] **GELDENHUYS** [834], born 3 Apr 1830 in Caledon, Western Cape, South Africa.

1114337 Barend Petrus Johannes[7] **GELDENHUYS** [835], born 6 Aug 1832 in Caledon, Western Cape, South Africa.

1114338 Petrus Jurie Hendrik[7] **GELDENHUYS** [836], born 12 Jan 1835 in Caledon, Western Cape, South Africa.

1114339 Jurie Petrus Wessel[7] **GELDENHUYS** [837], born 10 Jul 1838 in Caledon, Western Cape, South Africa.

111436. Jurgen Johannes[6] **GELDENHUYS** [494] (Albert Hendrik[5], Barend[4], Barend[3], Albert Barends Gildenhuisz[2], Bernd Gildenhausen[1]), born 14 Oct 1798. He married on 2 Apr 1822 in Caledon, Western Cape, South Africa **Elizabeth Debora (BOTHA) GELDENHUYS** [495].

Children of Jurgen Johannes GELDENHUYS and Elizabeth Debora BOTHA were as follows:

1114361 **Albert Hendrik Stephanus**[7] **GELDENHUYS** [496], born 10 Oct 1822 in Caledon, Western Cape, South Africa.

1114362 **Catharina Maria Johanna**[7] **GELDENHUYS** [497], born 13 Mar 1824 in Caledon, Western Cape, South Africa.

1114363 **Maria Dorothea Elizabeth**[7] **GELDENHUYS** [498], born 19 Nov 1826 in Caledon, Western Cape, South Africa.

1114364 **Stephanus Jacobus Johannes**[7] **GELDENHUYS** [499], born 19 Nov 1830 in Caledon, Western Cape, South Africa.

1114365 **Margaretha Christina Maria**[7] **GELDENHUYS** [500], born 5 Apr 1835 in Caledon, Western Cape, South Africa.

111462. Jacobus[6] **GELDENHUYS** [848] (Jacobus[5], Barend[4], Barend[3], Albert Barends Gildenhuisz[2], Bernd Gildenhausen[1]). He married **Geertruyda (SWART) GELDENHUYS** [854], born 22 Sep 1793.

Children of Jacobus GELDENHUYS and Geertruyda SWART were as follows:

1114621 **Christina Geertruyda Maria**[7] **GELDENHUYS** [855], born 9 Jun 1813 in Caledon, Western Cape, South Africa. She married on 6 Jan 1838 in Caledon, Western Cape, South Africa **Petrus Johannes BENEKE** [877].

+ 1114622 **Jacobus Jacob Hendrik**[7] **GELDENHUYS** [856], born 30 Jun 1815 in Caledon, Western Cape, South Africa. He married **Anna Francina Elizabeth GRESSE** [878].

1114623 **Maria Chistina**[7] **GELDENHUYS** [857], born 29 Sep 1817 in Caledon, Western Cape, South Africa. She married **Hendricus Petrus BENEKE** [876].

+ 1114624 **Nicolaas Johannes**[7] **GELDENHUYS** [858], born 21 Jan 1820 in Caledon, Western Cape, South Africa. He married **Martha Johanna GRESSE** [868].

1114625 **Barend Petrus**[7] **GELDENHUYS** [859], born 22 May 1822 in Caledon, Western Cape, South Africa. He married on 4 Apr 1850 in Caledon, Western Cape, South Africa **Cornelia Susanna ERWEE** [867], born 1833.

1114626 **Philip Rudolph**[7] **GELDENHUYS** [860], born 3 Feb 1825 in Caledon, Western Cape, South Africa.

1114627 **Lucas Marthinus**[7] **GELDENHUYS** [861], born 15 Aug 1827 in Caledon, Western Cape, South Africa.

1114628 **Geertruyda Johanna**[7] **GELDENHUYS** [862], born 28 Sep 1829. She married **Paul Lodewyk KUHN** [866].

1114629 **Hendrik Andries**[7] **GELDENHUYS** [863], born 31 Oct 1831 in Caledon, Western Cape, South Africa.

111462A **Jacomina Geertruyda**[7] **GELDENHUYS** [864], born 17 Sep 1834 in Caledon, Western Cape, South Africa. She married on 8 May 1862 in Caledon, Western Cape, South Africa **Johannes Jurie COOPER** [865].

111463. Hendrik Andries[6] **GELDENHUYS** [849] (Jacobus[5], Barend[4], Barend[3], Albert Barends Gildenhuisz[2], Bernd Gildenhausen[1]), born 28 Dec 1794. He married on 5 May 1821 **Sachararya Magdalena (VAN DEVENTER) GELDENHUYS** [888].

Children of Hendrik Andries GELDENHUYS and Sachararya Magdalena VAN DEVENTER were as follows:

    1114631 Maria Chistina Catharina^7 GELDENHUYS [889], born 8 Feb 1822 in Caledon, Western Cape, South Africa.

    1114632 Catharina Maria Christina^7 GELDENHUYS [890], born 20 Jan 1824 in Caledon, Western Cape, South Africa.

    1114633 Elizabeth Johanna Magdalena^7 GELDENHUYS [891], born 31 Jan 1825 in Caledon, Western Cape, South Africa.

+   **1114634** HendriK Andries^7 GELDENHUYS [892], born 4 Apr 1827 in Caledon, Western Cape, South Africa. He married **Elizabeth Magdalena UNGERER** [894].

    1114635 Magdalena Jacoba^7 GELDENHUYS [893], born 5 Aug 1829 in Caledon, Western Cape, South Africa.

111464. Barend Petrus^6 GELDENHUYS [850] (Jacobus^5, Barend^4, Barend^3, Albert Barends Gildenhuisz^2, Bernd Gildenhausen^1), born 25 Oct 1797. He married on 2 Apr 1820 in Caledon, Western Cape, South Africa **Anna Christina (GROENEWALD) GELDENHUYS** [851].

Children of Barend Petrus GELDENHUYS and Anna Christina GROENEWALD were as follows:

    1114641 Jacobus Johannes^7 GELDENHUYS [852], born 14 Aug 1822 in Caledon, Western Cape, South Africa.

    1114642 Catharina Maria Christina^7 GELDENHUYS [897], born 20 Jan 1824 in Caledon, Western Cape, South Africa.

    1114643 Maria Chistina^7 GELDENHUYS [898], born 1 Nov 1825 in Caledon, Western Cape, South Africa.

    1114644 Anna Christina Geertruyda^7 GELDENHUYS [899], born 16 Dec 1827 in Caledon, Western Cape, South Africa.

+   **1114645** Hendrik Andries^7 GELDENHUYS [900], born 3 Dec 1829 in Caledon, Western Cape, South Africa. He married **Maria Johanna COOPER** [905].

    1114646 Christina Francina Johanna^7 GELDENHUYS [901], born 23 Sep 1831 in Caledon, Western Cape, South Africa.

+   **1114647** Barend Petrus^7 GELDENHUYS [902], born 5 Sep 1833 in Caledon, Western Cape, South Africa. He married **Beatrix Geertruyda GERBER** [908].

    1114648 Coenraad Johannes^7 GELDENHUYS [903], born 1 Jun 1835 in Caledon, Western Cape, South Africa.

    1114649 Johannes Hermanus^7 GELDENHUYS [904], born 18 Dec 1839 in Caledon, Western Cape, South Africa.

1114A1. Barend Hendrik^6 GELDENHUYS [917] (Hendrik Andries^5, Barend^4, Barend^3, Albert Barends Gildenhuisz^2, Bernd Gildenhausen^1), born 20 Sep 1809; died 22 Aug 1878 in Bethlehem, OFS, South Africa. He married (1) on 28 Aug 1836 in Caledon, Western Cape, South Africa **Anna Catharina (MULDER) GELDENHUYS** [918]; (2) **Anna Maria (SMIT) GELDENHUYS** [922]; (3) **Margaretha Maria (SCHEEPERS) GELDENHUYS** [923].

Children of Barend Hendrik GELDENHUYS and Anna Catharina MULDER were as follows:

    1114A11 Christiaan Cornelis^7 GELDENHUYS [919].

    1114A12 Philip R(udolph?)^7 GELDENHUYS [920].

    1114A13 Cornelis Johannes^7 GELDENHUYS [921].

Children of Barend Hendrik GELDENHUYS and Margaretha Maria SCHEEPERS were as follows:

1114A14 Jan Hendrik[7] **GELDENHUYS** [924], born 8 May 1852 in Sneeuberg, Graaff-Reinet, Cape, South Africa; died 15 Jun 1867. Notes: Aged15

116242. Jan Hendrik[6] **GELDENHUYS** [943] (Hendrik[5], Hendrik Albertus[4], Hendrik (b8)[3], Albert Barends Gildenhuisz[2], Bernd Gildenhausen[1]), born 6 Apr 1777. He married on 19 Sep 1802 in Cape Town, South Africa **Helena Gerharda (KEULDER) GELDENHUYS** [944].

Children of Jan Hendrik GELDENHUYS and Helena Gerharda KEULDER were as follows:

    1162421   Hendrik Johannes[7] GELDENHUYS [945], born 25 Dec 1803.

116243. Hendrik Albertus[6] **GELDENHUYS** [946] (Hendrik[5], Hendrik Albertus[4], Hendrik (b8)[3], Albert Barends Gildenhuisz[2], Bernd Gildenhausen[1]), born 15 Nov 1778. He married **Rachel Marie (JORDAAN) GELDENHUYS** [947].

Children of Hendrik Albertus GELDENHUYS and Rachel Marie JORDAAN were as follows:

    1162431   Hendrik Albertus[7] GELDENHUYS [948], born 11 Oct 1801.
    1162432   Gesina[7] GELDENHUYS [949], born 2 Sep 1804.
    1162433   Margaretha Johanna Martha[7] GELDENHUYS [950], born 2 Feb 1806. She married on 4 Oct 1821 in Stellenbosch, Cape, South Africa **Stephanus JORDAAN** [951].
    1162434   Petrus Johannes[7] GELDENHUYS [952], born 12 Aug 1810. He married on 8 Nov 1835 in Swartland, Cape, South Africa **Catharina Jacoba BASSON** [953].
    1162435   Rachel Maria[7] GELDENHUYS [954], born 14 Feb 1813. She married on 8 Jul 1832 in Paarl, Western Cape, South Africa **Hendrik Johannes (GILDENHUIZEN) GELDENHUYS** [955], born 29 Apr 1810, son of Albert Barend (GILDENHUIZEN) GELDENHUYS [956 and Susanna Elizabeth LE ROUX [957].

116245. Petrus Guilaume[6] **GELDENHUYS** [959] (Hendrik[5], Hendrik Albertus[4], Hendrik (b8)[3], Albert Barends Gildenhuisz[2], Bernd Gildenhausen[1]), born 4 Nov 1781. He married on 24 Apr 1803 in Cape Town, South Africa **Maria Catharina (REYNEKE) GELDENHUYS** [960].

Children of Petrus Guilaume GELDENHUYS and Maria Catharina REYNEKE were as follows:

    1162451   Magdalena Catharina[7] GELDENHUYS [961], born 6 Nov 1804.
    1162452   Hendrik Johannes[7] GELDENHUYS [962], born 28 Sep 1806.
    1162453   Margaretha Johanna Elizabeth[7] GELDENHUYS [963], born 2 Apr 1809.
    1162454   Petrus Guilliam[7] GELDENHUYS [964], born 16 May 1812.
    1162455   Casparus Abraham[7] GELDENHUYS [965], born 9 Oct 1814.
    1162456   Elizabeth Elsabe Hendrina[7] GELDENHUYS [966], born 27 Oct 1816.
+   **1162457**   Johannes Jacobus Carel[7] GELDENHUYS [967], born 29 Aug 1819. He married **Johanna Adriana MULLHOLLAND** [970].
    1162458   Charles Jacobus[7] GELDENHUYS [968], born 30 Apr 1822 in Swartland, Cape, South Africa.
    1162459   Susanna Petronella[7] GELDENHUYS [969], born 10 May 1826 in Swartland, Cape, South Africa.

116246. Abraham Jacobus⁶ GELDENHUYS [977] (Hendrik⁵, Hendrik Albertus⁴, Hendrik (b8)³, Albert Barends Gildenhuisz², Bernd Gildenhausen¹). He married on 23 Oct 1803 in Cape Town, South Africa **Martha Louisa (LE ROUX) GELDENHUYS** [985], daughter of Abraham LE ROUX [986].

Children of Abraham Jacobus GELDENHUYS and Martha Louisa LE ROUX were as follows:

    1162461   Hendrik Johannes⁷ GELDENHUYS [987], born 26 Dec 1804.
    1162462   Anna Magdalena⁷ GELDENHUYS [988], born 10 Apr 1807.
+   1162463   Abraham Josua⁷ GELDENHUYS [989], born 25 Dec 1808. He married **Margaretha Johanna Elizabeth (GILDENHUIZEN) GELDENHUYS** [1000].
    1162464   Maria Johanna Petronella⁷ GELDENHUYS [990], born 22 Jul 1810.
    1162465   Martha Louisa⁷ GELDENHUYS [991], born 21 Jul 1812.
    1162466   David Jacobus⁷ GELDENHUYS [992], born 30 Mar 1815 in Paarl, Western Cape, South Africa.
    1162467   Petrus Guillaume⁷ GELDENHUYS [993], born 20 May 1817 in Paarl, Western Cape, South Africa.
    1162468   Albert Barend⁷ GELDENHUYS [994], born 16 May 1819 in Paarl, Western Cape, South Africa.
    1162469   Theodorus Louis⁷ GELDENHUYS [995], born 16 May 1820 in Paarl, Western Cape, South Africa.
    116246A   Magdalena Francina⁷ GELDENHUYS [996], born 10 May 1823 in Paarl, Western Cape, South Africa.
    116246B   Roelof Gabriel Thomas⁷ GELDENHUYS [997], born 8 Jan 1825 in Cape Town, South Africa.
    116246C   Elizabeth Elsabe⁷ GELDENHUYS [998], born 25 Jun 1828 in Paarl, Western Cape, South Africa. She married on 8 Jan 1855 in Prins Albert, South Africa **Carel Hendrik Francois KEULDER** [999].

116249. Albert Barend⁶ GELDENHUYS [980] (Hendrik⁵, Hendrik Albertus⁴, Hendrik (b8)³, Albert Barends Gildenhuisz², Bernd Gildenhausen¹), born 17 Aug 1788. He married on 11 Oct 1808 in Stellenbosch, Cape, South Africa **Susanna Elizabeth (LE ROUX) GELDENHUYS** [1017].

Children of Albert Barend GELDENHUYS and Susanna Elizabeth LE ROUX were as follows:

    1162491   Hendrik Johannes⁷ GELDENHUYS [1018], born 29 Apr 1810 in Paarl, Western Cape, South Africa. He married on 8 Jul 1832 in Paarl, Western Cape, South Africa **Rachel Maria Gildenhuisen GELDENHUYS** [1019].

11624B. Guilliam (or Gideon) Theodorus⁶ GELDENHUYS [982] (Hendrik⁵, Hendrik Albertus⁴, Hendrik (b8)³, Albert Barends Gildenhuisz², Bernd Gildenhausen¹), born 20 Oct 1793. He married **Martha Maria (DU TOIT) GELDENHUYS** [1020], daughter of Pieter DU TOIT [1021].

Children of Guilliam (or Gideon) Theodorus GELDENHUYS and Martha Maria DU TOIT were as follows:

+   11624B1   Hendrik Abraham Johannes⁷ GELDENHUYS [1022], born 17 Sep 1815 in Paarl, Western Cape, South Africa. He married **Johanna Catharina GROBBELAAR** [1027].
    11624B2   Pieter Albertus Cornelis⁷ GELDENHUYS [1023], born 6 Aug 1817 in Paarl, Western Cape, South Africa.

11624B3 David Jacobus Abraham⁷ GELDENHUYS [1024], born 18 Jun 1820 in Paarl, Western Cape, South Africa.

11624B4 Pieter David⁷ GELDENHUYS [1025], born 6 Jan 1822 in Paarl, Western Cape, South Africa.

11624B5 Gideon Theodorus⁷ GELDENHUYS [1026], born 29 Oct 1826 in Paarl, Western Cape, South Africa.

11624C. Theodorus Louis Hermanus⁶ GELDENHUYS [983] (Hendrik⁵, Hendrik Albertus⁴, Hendrik (b8)³, Albert Barends Gildenhuisz², Bernd Gildenhausen¹), born 20 Mar 1796. He married in Sep 1818 in Paarl, Western Cape, South Africa **Elizabeth Rachel (DE VILLIERS) GELDENHUYS** [1036], daughter of Piet Daniel DE VILLIERS [1037].

Children of Theodorus Louis Hermanus GELDENHUYS and Elizabeth Rachel DE VILLIERS were as follows:

11624C1 Johanna Jacoba⁷ GELDENHUYS [1038], born 9 Aug 1819 in Paarl, Western Cape, South Africa.

11624C2 Elizabeth Rachel⁷ GELDENHUYS [1039], born 13 May 1823 in Paarl, Western Cape, South Africa.

11624C3 Hendrik⁷ GELDENHUYS [1040], born 15 Jun 1825 in Paarl, Western Cape, South Africa.

11624C4 Susanna Petronella⁷ GELDENHUYS [1041], born 4 May 1827 in Paarl, Western Cape, South Africa.

+ **11624C5 Pieter Daniel⁷ GELDENHUYS** [1042], born 21 Nov 1828 in Franschoek, Cape, South Africa; died 23 Dec 1889. He married **Susanna Margaretha NIGRINI** [1043].

116271. Hendrik Albertus⁶ GELDENHUYS [1057] (Albert Barend⁵, Hendrik Albertus⁴, Hendrik (b8)³, Albert Barends Gildenhuisz², Bernd Gildenhausen¹), born 13 May 1781; died Aug 1836. He married on 29 Mar 1801 in Cape Town, South Africa **Hilletje Aletta (SMIT) GELDENHUYS** [1064].

Children of Hendrik Albertus GELDENHUYS and Hilletje Aletta SMIT were as follows:

+ **1162711 Albert Barend⁷ GELDENHUYS** [1065], born 25 Jul 1802. He married **Helena Johanna VAN SCHALKWYK** [1072].

1162712 Johanna Hendrika Maria⁷ GELDENHUYS [1066], born 13 Jan 1805. She married on 4 Mar 1821 in Tulbagh, Cape, South Africa **Gideon VAN DYK** [1071], born 19 Jul 1802 in Swartland, Cape, South Africa.

1162713 Sophia Catharina⁷ GELDENHUYS [1067], born 17 Jul 1808.

1162714 Sophia Sibella Helina⁷ GELDENHUYS [1068], born 30 Jun 1811.

1162715 Christoffel Christiaan⁷ GELDENHUYS [1069], born 20 Feb 1814. He married on 7 Oct 1838 in Swartland, Cape, South Africa **Anna Susanna Wilhelmina SERDYN** [1070].

116272. Pieter Johannes⁶ GELDENHUYS [1058] (Albert Barend⁵, Hendrik Albertus⁴, Hendrik (b8)³, Albert Barends Gildenhuisz², Bernd Gildenhausen¹), born 10 Nov 1782. He married on 28 Oct 1810 in Stellenbosch, Cape, South Africa **Sibella Jacoba (JORDAAN) GELDENHUYS** [1081].

Children of Pieter Johannes GELDENHUYS and Sibella Jacoba JORDAAN were as follows:

1162721 Albertus Barend⁷ GELDENHUYS [1082], born 5 May 1811.

1162722　Johanna Maria[7] GELDENHUYS [1083], born 28 Mar 1813.
1162723　Pieter Johannes[7] GELDENHUYS [1084], born 18 Dec 1814.
1162724　Adriaan[7] GELDENHUYS [1085], born 4 May 1817.
1162725　Pieter Johannes[7] GELDENHUYS [1086], born 3 Dec 1826.
1162726　Stephanus Nicolaas[7] GELDENHUYS [1087], born 11 Oct 1829.
1162727　Hendrik Oostwald Loubser[7] GELDENHUYS [1088], born 14 Oct 1831 in Cape Town, South Africa.

116273. Albert Barend[6] GELDENHUYS [1059] (Albert Barend[5], Hendrik Albertus[4], Hendrik (b8)[3], Albert Barends Gildenhuisz[2], Bernd Gildenhausen[1]), born 16 May 1784. He married on 7 Mar 1812 in Tulbagh, Cape, South Africa **Anna Catharina Hendrina (VAN DYK) GELDENHUYS** [1089].

Children of Albert Barend GELDENHUYS and Anna Catharina Hendrina VAN DYK were as follows:
1162731　Hilletje Aletta Johanna[7] GELDENHUYS [1090], born 24 Jan 1813.
1162732　Sophia Catharina Elizabeth[7] GELDENHUYS [1091], born 9 Jul 1815. Notes: Possibly died young - older sister got same names
1162733　Sophia Catharina Elizabeth[7] GELDENHUYS [1092], born 29 Sep 1816. Notes: Twin to Anna Catharina Hendrika Named after older sister - possibly died very young
1162734　Anna Catharina Hendrina[7] GELDENHUYS [1093], born 29 Sep 1816. Notes: Twin to Sophia Catharina Elizabeth
1162735　Elizabeth Maria Susanna[7] GELDENHUYS [1094], born 18 Apr 1824.

116281. Hendrik Albertus[6] GELDENHUYS [1096] (Guilliam Hendrik[5], Hendrik Albertus[4], Hendrik (b8)[3], Albert Barends Gildenhuisz[2], Bernd Gildenhausen[1]), born 14 Mar 1779. He married on 6 Jan 1806 in Stellenbosch, Cape, South Africa **Johanna Magdalena (BRUYNZWART) GELDENHUYS** [1098], daughter of Bartholomeus BRUYNZWART [1099].

Children of Hendrik Albertus GELDENHUYS and Johanna Magdalena BRUYNZWART were as follows:
1162811　Maria Elizabeth[7] GELDENHUYS [1100], born 9 Aug 1807.
1162812　Guilliam Petrus[7] GELDENHUYS [1101], born 31 Dec 1809.
1162813　Susanna Jacoba[7] GELDENHUYS [1102], born 18 Feb 1811 in Paarl, Western Cape, South Africa; died 13 Jun 1852 in Paarl, Western Cape, South Africa. She married **Jacobus Arnoldus LOUW** [1126], born 8 Jun 1802 in Swartland, Cape, South Africa; died 29 Jan 1856 in Paarl, Cape Colony, South Africa, son of Albertus Wynand LOUW [1127] and Johanna Magdalena BAARD [1128].
1162814　Alida Johanna[7] GELDENHUYS [1103], born 14 Mar 1813.
1162815　Guilliam Hendrik[7] GELDENHUYS [1104], born 6 Mar 1815 in Paarl, Western Cape, South Africa.
+ 1162816　Hendrik Marthinus[7] GELDENHUYS [1105], born 30 Sep 1818 in Paarl, Western Cape, South Africa; died 4 Dec 1897 in Bloemfontein, OFS, South Africa. He married **Margaretha Georgina Fredrika RORICH** [1110].
1162817　Guilliam Jacob[7] GELDENHUYS [1106], born 25 Aug 1820 in Paarl, Western Cape, South Africa.
1162818　Pietus Taillefer[7] GELDENHUYS [1107], born 22 Mar 1823.
1162819　Helena Johanna[7] GELDENHUYS [1108], born 16 Jul 1825 in Paarl, Western Cape, South Africa.

116281A Albert Barend[7] GELDENHUYS [1109], born 5 Jun 1828 in Paarl, Western Cape, South Africa.

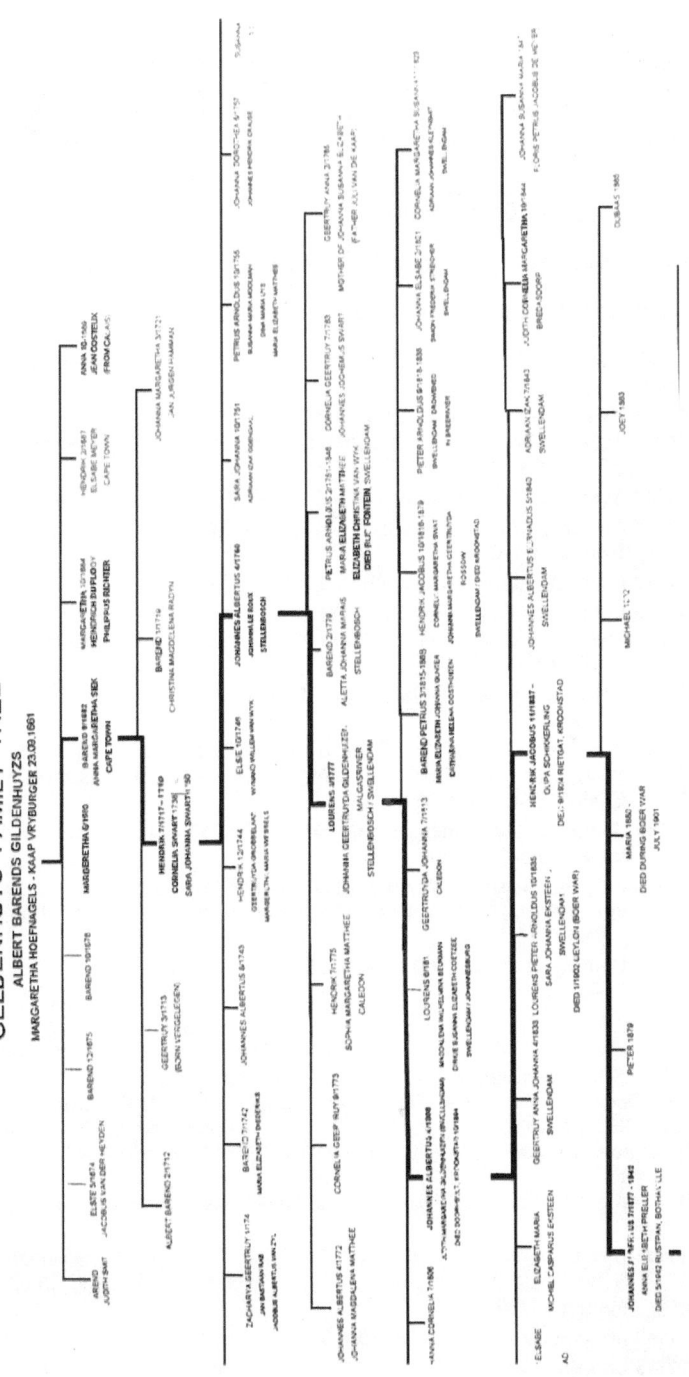

Generation 7

1111111. Johannes Albertus[7] GELDENHUYS [10] (Lourens[6], Johannes Albertus[5], Hendrik (c3)[4], Barend[3], Albert Barends Gildenhuisz[2], Bernd Gildenhausen[1]), born 21 Dec 1807 in Stellenbosch or Swellendam, South Africa; died 9 Oct 1894 in Doornbult, Kroonstad, OFS, South Africa. He married on 6 May 1827 in Swellendam, Cape, South Africa **Judith Margaretha (GILDENHUIZEN) GELDENHUYS** [187], born 20 Feb 1812; died 23 Jun 1890.

Notes for Johannes Albertus GELDENHUYS
    Judith Margaretha Gildenhuisen - his cousin

    Fought in the Basoeteland War of 1856-1865

    Fought in the Basoeteland War 1856-1865

    Children of Johannes Albertus GELDENHUYS and Judith Margaretha GILDENHUIZEN were as follows:

+   **11111111 Hendrik Jacobus[8] GELDENHUYS** [8], born 17 Nov 1837 in South Africa; died 4 Sep 1924 in Rietgat, Kroonstad, OFS, South Africa. He married **Elizabeth SCHIKKERLING** [31].

    11111112 Susara Johanna Elizabeth Elsabe[8] GELDENHUYS [74].

    11111113 Geertruy Anna Johanna[8] GELDENHUYS [86], born 4 Apr 1833 in Swellendam, Cape.

    11111114 Elizabeth Maria[8] GELDENHUYS [1716].

+   **11111115 Lourens Pieter Arnoldus[8] GELDENHUYS** [1717], born 10 Oct 1835 in Swellendam, Cape; died 22 Jan 1902 in Ceylon. He married **Sara Johanna EKSTEEN** [1718].

    11111116 Johannes Albertus Bernardus[8] GELDENHUYS [1726], born 5 May 1840 in Swellendam, Cape.

+   **11111117 Adriaan Izak 'Aap'[8] GELDENHUYS** [1727], born 22 Jul 1843; died 1 Jan 1904 in Kroonstad, Free State, South Africa. He married **Maria Susanna Wilhelmina SCHICKERLING** [1728].

    11111118 Judith Cornelia Margaretha[8] GELDENHUYS [1755], born 12 Oct 1844 in Bredasdorp, Cape, South Africa.

+   **11111119 Johanna Susanna Maria[8] GELDENHUYS** [1756], born 1847; died 6 Jun 1881 in Harrismith, South Africa. She married **Floris Petrus Jacobus DE MEYER** [1758].

    1111111A Hendrik Jacobus[8] GELDENHUYS [1757], born 5 Jul 1849.

1111114. Lourens[7] GELDENHUYS [504] (Lourens[6], Johannes Albertus[5], Hendrik (c3)[4], Barend[3], Albert Barends Gildenhuisz[2], Bernd Gildenhausen[1]), born 12 Jun 1811. He married (1) on 30 Dec 1844 in Swellendam, Cape, South Africa **Dirkie Susanna Elizabeth (COETZEE) GELDENHUYS** [545], died Apr 21 189x in Johannesburg, Tvl, South Africa; (2) **Dirkie Susanna Elizabeth (COETZEE) GELDENHUYS** [588], died 21 Apr 1899.

    Children of Lourens GELDENHUYS and Dirkie Susanna Elizabeth COETZEE were as follows:

+   **11111141 Dirk Cornelis[8] GELDENHUYS** [546], born 1 Jan 1858 in Heidelberg, Transvaal, South Africa; died 31 Aug 1929 in Johannesburg, Gauteng, South Africa. He married **NN NN** [1810].

    11111142 Maria Elizabeth[8] GELDENHUYS [547], born 15 Nov 1860.

    11111143 Lourens[8] GELDENHUYS [548], born 6 Dec 1864 in Heidelberg, Tvl, South Africa.

11111144 Magdalena Wilhelmina[8] **GELDENHUYS** [549], born 9 Jan 1871. She married **Joseph P KOK** [550].

Children of Lourens GELDENHUYS and Dirkie Susanna Elizabeth COETZEE were as follows:
11111145 Dirk Cornelis[8] **GELDENHUYS** [546], born 1 Jan 1858 in Heidelberg, Transvaal, South Africa; died 31 Aug 1929 in Johannesburg, Gauteng, South Africa. He married **NN NN** [1810]. Notes: Some dates given as Jan 1, and not Jan 5
11111146 Maria Elizabeth[8] **GELDENHUYS** [590], born 15 Nov 1860.
11111147 Lourens[8] **GELDENHUYS** [591], born 6 Dec 1864 in Heidelberg, Tvl, South Africa.
11111148 Magdalena Wilhelmina[8] **GELDENHUYS** [592], born 9 Jan 1871. She married **Joseph P KOK** [593].

1111116. Barend Petrus[7] **GELDENHUYS** [506] (Lourens[6], Johannes Albertus[5], Hendrik (c3)[4], Barend[3], Albert Barends Gildenhuisz[2], Bernd Gildenhausen[1]), born 3 Mar 1815 in Caledon, Western Cape, South Africa; died 4 Apr 1868 in Holfontein, Kroonstad, South Africa. He married (1) on 22 Jul 1838 in Swellendam, Cape, South Africa **Maria Elizabeth Johanna (GUNTER) GELDENHUYS** [527], died 28 Jun 1862; (2) **Catharina Helena (OOSTHUIZEN) GELDENHUYS** [536].

Children of Barend Petrus GELDENHUYS and Maria Elizabeth Johanna GUNTER were as follows:
11111161 Jacoba Margaretha[8] **GELDENHUYS** [528], born 2 Aug 1839 in Swellendam, Cape, South Africa.
11111162 Geertruida Johanna[8] **GELDENHUYS** [529], born 6 Apr 1841.
11111163 Maria Elizabeth Magdalena Johanna[8] **GELDENHUYS** [530], born 4 Aug 1843. She married on 6 May 1861 in Kroonstad, OFS, South Africa **Jan Hendrik COETZEE** [544].
11111164 Geertruyda Johanna Elizabeth[8] **GELDENHUYS** [531], born 9 Sep 1846 in Swellendam, Cape, South Africa. She married **Johan Christian Lambrecht COETZEE** [543].
11111165 Jacoba Margaretha[8] **GELDENHUYS** [532], born 21 Aug 1849 in Swellendam, Cape, South Africa. She married on 1 Mar 1869 in Kroonstad, OFS, South Africa **George Diederick PRINSLOO** [542].
11111166 Barendina Petronella[8] **GELDENHUYS** [533], born 22 Jun 1852 in Swellendam, Cape, South Africa. She married on 18 Dec 1871 in Kroonstad, OFS, South Africa **Petrus Cornelis BOUWER** [541].
11111167 Cornelis Janse[8] **GELDENHUYS** [534], born 5 Sep 1855 in Winburg, OFS, South Africa.
11111168 Lourens Johannes Albertus[8] **GELDENHUYS** [535], born abt 1858; died 15 Apr 1864 in Kroonstad, OFS, South Africa.

Children of Barend Petrus GELDENHUYS and Catharina Helena OOSTHUIZEN were as follows:
11111169 Elizabeth Helena[8] **GELDENHUYS** [537]. She married on 30 Apr 1881 in Middelburg, Transvaal, South Africa **Jacobus Nicolaas MATTHEE** [540].
1111116A Barend Petrus[8] **GELDENHUYS** [538], born 20 May 1864 in Kroonstad, OFS, South Africa.
1111116B Johannes Albertus[8] **GELDENHUYS** [539], born 15 Aug 1867 in Potchefstroom, Transvaal, South Africa.

1111117. Hendrik Jacobus[7] **GELDENHUYS** [507] (Lourens[6], Johannes Albertus[5], Hendrik (c3)[4], Barend[3], Albert Barends Gildenhuisz[2], Bernd Gildenhausen[1]), born 10 Oct 1816 in Swellendam, Cape, South Africa; died 4 May 1879 in Kroonstad, OFS, South Africa. He married (1) on 27 Dec 1835 in Swellendam, Cape, South Africa **Cornelia Margaretha (SWART) GELDENHUYS** [512]; (2) **Johanna Margaretha Geertruyda (ROSSOUW) GELDENHUYS** [517].

Children of Hendrik Jacobus GELDENHUYS and Cornelia Margaretha SWART were as follows:

11111171 **Lourens**[8] **GELDENHUYS** [513], born 31 May 1837 in Swellendam, Cape, South Africa.

11111172 **Susanna Dorothea**[8] **GELDENHUYS** [514], born 6 Oct 1848 in Swellendam, Cape, South Africa.

11111173 **Sophia Barendina Jacoba**[8] **GELDENHUYS** [515].

11111174 **Geertruyda Johanna**[8] **GELDENHUYS** [516].

Children of Hendrik Jacobus GELDENHUYS and Johanna Margaretha Geertruyda ROSSOUW were as follows:

11111175 **Geertruyda Johanna**[8] **GELDENHUYS** [518].

11111176 **Johanna Christina**[8] **GELDENHUYS** [519].

11111177 **Hendrina Jacoba**[8] **GELDENHUYS** [520].

11111178 **Jacoba Maria**[8] **GELDENHUYS** [521].

11111179 **Judith Margaretha**[8] **GELDENHUYS** [522].

1111117A **Hendrik Jacobus**[8] **GELDENHUYS** [523].

1111117B **Susanna Johanna**[8] **GELDENHUYS** [524].

1111117C **Johannes Albertus**[8] **GELDENHUYS** [525].

1111117D **Barend Petrus**[8] **GELDENHUYS** [526].

1111121. Johannes Albertus[7] **GELDENHUYS** [565] (Johannes Albertus[6], Johannes Albertus[5], Hendrik (c3)[4], Barend[3], Albert Barends Gildenhuisz[2], Bernd Gildenhausen[1]), born 20 Feb 1803. He married on 2 Mar 1828 in Swellendam, Cape, South Africa **Johanna Susanna (BESTER) GELDENHUYS** [566].

Children of Johannes Albertus GELDENHUYS and Johanna Susanna BESTER were as follows:

11111211 **Johannes Albertus**[8] **GELDENHUYS** [567], born 22 Mar 1829 in Caledon, Western Cape, South Africa.

11111212 **Francina Johanna**[8] **GELDENHUYS** [568], born 8 Feb 1831 in Caledon, Western Cape, South Africa.

11111213 **Willem Johannes**[8] **GELDENHUYS** [569], born 31 Jan 1833 in Caledon, Western Cape, South Africa.

11111214 **Elias Jacobus**[8] **GELDENHUYS** [570], born 11 Aug 1834 in Caledon, Western Cape, South Africa.

11111215 **Johanna Magdalena Susanna**[8] **GELDENHUYS** [571], born 19 Aug 1836 in Caledon, Western Cape, South Africa.

11111216 **Hendrik Jacobus**[8] **GELDENHUYS** [572], born 9 Mar 1841 in Bredasdorp, Cape, South Africa.

11111217 **Petrus Jacobus**[8] **GELDENHUYS** [573], born 24 Nov 1842 in Bredasdorp, Cape, South Africa.

1111123. Johanna Susanna⁷ GELDENHUYS [575] (Johannes Albertus⁶, Johannes Albertus⁵, Hendrik (c3)⁴, Barend³, Albert Barends Gildenhuisz², Bernd Gildenhausen¹), born 31 Aug 1808. She married in Caledon, Western Cape, South Africa **Christoffel Christiaan HEYNE** [576].

Children of Johanna Susanna GELDENHUYS and Christoffel Christiaan HEYNE were as follows:
 11111231 Matthys Johannes⁸ HEYNE [577], born 22 Apr 1822 in Swellendam, Cape, South Africa.

1111125. Elias Jacobus⁷ GELDENHUYS [580] (Johannes Albertus⁶, Johannes Albertus⁵, Hendrik (c3)⁴, Barend³, Albert Barends Gildenhuisz², Bernd Gildenhausen¹), born 11 Aug 1809. He married on 3 Mar 1831 in Caledon, Western Cape, South Africa **Elizabeth Helena (SWART)** GELDENHUYS [581].

Children of Elias Jacobus GELDENHUYS and Elizabeth Helena SWART were as follows:
 11111251 Johanna Magdalena⁸ GELDENHUYS [582], born 15 Mar 1836 in Caledon, Western Cape, South Africa.
 11111252 Elizabeth Helena⁸ GELDENHUYS [583], born 11 Mar 1839 in Bredasdorp, Cape, South Africa.
 11111253 Johannes Albertus⁸ GELDENHUYS [584], born 19 Dec 1841 in Bredasdorp, Cape, South Africa.
 11111254 Hendrik Daniel⁸ GELDENHUYS [585], born 4 Sep 1844 in Bredasdorp, Cape, South Africa.
 11111255 Maria Catharina⁸ GELDENHUYS [586], born 25 Mar 1833 in Caledon, Cape, South Africa.
 11111256 Cornelia Geertruida Anna⁸ GELDENHUYS [587], born 1 Jun 1847 in Bredasdorp, Cape, South Africa.

1111162. Johannes Albertus⁷ GELDENHUYS [600] (Petrus Arnoldus⁶, Johannes Albertus⁵, Hendrik (c3)⁴, Barend³, Albert Barends Gildenhuisz², Bernd Gildenhausen¹), born 14 Sep 1806. He married on 2 May 1830 in Caledon, Western Cape, South Africa **Anna Christina Elizabeth (SWART)** GELDENHUYS [619].

Children of Johannes Albertus GELDENHUYS and Anna Christina Elizabeth SWART were as follows:
+ **11111621 Petrus Arnoldus⁸ GELDENHUYS** [620], born 21 Jul 1831 in Caledon, Western Cape, South Africa; died 4 Apr 1887 in Stanford. He married **Mathilda Marietta BEHR** [621].

1111167. Petrus Arnoldus⁷ GELDENHUYS [605] (Petrus Arnoldus⁶, Johannes Albertus⁵, Hendrik (c3)⁴, Barend³, Albert Barends Gildenhuisz², Bernd Gildenhausen¹), born 24 Aug 1815 in Caledon, Western Cape, South Africa; died 23 Apr 1846 in Vogelvallei, Caledon, Cape, South Africa. He married **Maria Magdalena (SWART)** GELDENHUYS [612], daughter of Hans Jacob SWART [613] and Catharina Elizabeth MOOLMAN [614].

Children of Petrus Arnoldus GELDENHUYS and Maria Magdalena SWART were as follows:
 11111671 Catharina Elizabeth⁸ GELDENHUYS [615], born 12 Jan 1837 in Caledon, Western Cape, South Africa.

11111672 **Petrus Arnoldus Jacobus**[8] **GELDENHUYS** [616], born 11 Sep 1838 in Caledon, Western Cape, South Africa.

11111673 **Hans Jacob**[8] **GELDENHUYS** [617], born 15 Jan 1841 in Caledon, Western Cape, South Africa.

11111674 **Johannes Albertus Jochemus**[8] **GELDENHUYS** [618], born 25 Jun 1843 in Bredasdorp, Cape, South Africa.

1111171. Johanna Susanna Elizabeth[7] **GELDENHUYS** [560] (Geertruy Anna[6] GELDENHUYS, Johannes Albertus[5], Hendrik (c3)[4], Barend[3], Albert Barends Gildenhuisz[2], Bernd Gildenhausen[1]), born 27 Oct 1799 in Stellenbosch, Cape, South Africa. She married **NN (FATHER - JULI VAN DIE KAAP** [561].

Children of Johanna Susanna Elizabeth GELDENHUYS and NN (FATHER - JULI VAN DIE KAAP) were as follows:

11111711 **Matthys Johannes**[8] **(GILDENHUIZEN) GELDENHUYS** [562], born 22 Apr 1822 in Swellendam, Cape, South Africa.

1111211. Adrian Johannes - f2[7] **GELDENHUYS** [144] (Petrus Arnoldus - e5[6], Petrus Arnoldus - d10[5], Hendrik (c3)[4], Barend[3], Albert Barends Gildenhuisz[2], Bernd Gildenhausen[1]), born 23 Apr 1810 in Swellendam, Cape, South Africa; died 26 Oct 1867 in Heidelberg, Cape, South Africa. He married on 18 Jan 1835 in Swellendam, Cape, South Africa **Elsabe Dina (LOURENS - B3C5D2E?) GELDENHUYS** [145], born in South Africa; died in South Africa.

Children of Adrian Johannes - f2 GELDENHUYS and Elsabe Dina LOURENS - b3c5d2e? were as follows:

+ 11112111 **Gerhardus Bernardus - g7**[8] **GELDENHUYS** [146], born 25 Dec 1850; died 18 Sep 1936 in Heidelberg, Cape, South Africa. He married unknown.

11112112 **Christina Elizabeth**[8] **GELDENHUYS** [666], born 7 Oct 1838 in Swellendam, Cape, South Africa; christened 17 Feb 1839 in Swellendam, Cape Colony, South Africa. She married **Lourens Johannes PRINSLOO** [2031]. Notes: b6c3d10e5f2g2

11112113 **Cornelia Johanna**[8] **GELDENHUYS** [1890].

11112114 **Petrus Arnoldus**[8] **GELDENHUYS** [1891]. Notes: b6c3d10e5f2g1

+ 11112115 **Adriaan Johannes**[8] **GELDENHUYS** [668], born 2 Oct 1843 in Swellendam, Cape, South Africa; christened 8 Jan 1844 in Swellendam, Cape Colony, South Africa. He married **Petronella Wilhelmina PRINSLOO** [669].

11112116 **Cornelis Janse**[8] **GELDENHUYS** [1893].

+ 11112117 **Mattys Johannes Lourens**[8] **GELDENHUYS** [2032], born 12 Jul 1841; christened 4 Oct 1841 in Swellendam, Cape Colony, South Africa. He married **Francina Frederika PRINSLOO** [2033].

1111745. Hendrik Jacobus[7] **GELDENHUYS** [1470] (Hendrik Jacobus[6], Hendrik[5], Hendrik (c3)[4], Barend[3], Albert Barends Gildenhuisz[2], Bernd Gildenhausen[1]), born 2 Dec 1816 in Swellendam, Cape Colony, South Africa; died 1 Jul 1857 in Roodeport, Winburg, OFS, South Africa. He married (1) on 2 Aug 1835 in Swellendam, Cape Colony, South Africa **Jacoba Margaretha (SWART) GELDENHUYS** [1475]; (2) on 3 Jan 1842 in Bredasdorp **Cornelia Geertruyda Dina (HUMAN) GELDENHUYS** [1478].

Children of Hendrik Jacobus GELDENHUYS and Jacoba Margaretha SWART were as follows:

11117451 Elsa Johanna[8] **GELDENHUYS** [1476], born 7 Feb 1837 in Swellendam, Cape Colony, South Africa.

11117452 Sara Johanna[8] **GELDENHUYS** [1477].

Children of Hendrik Jacobus GELDENHUYS and Cornelia Geertruyda Dina HUMAN were as follows:

11117453 Anna Jacoba Susanna[8] **GELDENHUYS** [1479], born 21 Apr 1843 in Swellendam, Cape Colony, South Africa.

11117454 Hendrik Jacobus[8] **GELDENHUYS** [1480], born 23 Oct 1844 in Swellendam, Cape Colony, South Africa.

11117455 Cornelia Geertruyda Margaretha[8] **GELDENHUYS** [1481], born 17 May 1849 in Winburg.

11117456 Susanna Margaretha[8] **GELDENHUYS** [1482], born 25 Apr 1851 in Winburg.

11117457 Geertruy Anna Elizabeth[8] **GELDENHUYS** [1483], born 22 Jul 1853 in Winburg.

11117458 Judith Margaretha Elsabe[8] **GELDENHUYS** [1484], born 22 Apr 1855 in Winburg.

11117459 Susanna Maria Margaretha[8] **GELDENHUYS** [1485], born 27 Apr 1857 in Winburg.

1111745A Johannes Urbanus[8] **GELDENHUYS** [1486].

1111B51. Petrus Arnoldus[7] **GELDENHUYS** [654] (Petrus Arnoldus[6], PetrusD Arnoldus - duplicated branch[5], Hendrik (c3)[4], Barend[3], Albert Barends Gildenhuisz[2], Bernd Gildenhausen[1]), born 30 Jul 1808. He married on 16 Jan 1831 in Swellendam, Cape, South Africa **Anna Christina (DE JAGER) GELDENHUYS** [656].

Children of Petrus Arnoldus GELDENHUYS and Anna Christina DE JAGER were as follows:

1111B511 Christina Johanna[8] **GELDENHUYS** [657], born 10 Feb 1833 in Swellendam, Cape, South Africa.

1111B512 Cornelia Johanna[8] **GELDENHUYS** [658], born 17 Apr 1834 in Swellendam, Cape, South Africa.

1111B513 Petrus Arnoldus[8] **GELDENHUYS** [659], born 20 May 1836 in Swellendam, Cape, South Africa.

1111B514 Frederik Johannes Jacobus[8] **GELDENHUYS** [660], born 7 Nov 1837 in Swellendam, Cape, South Africa.

1111B515 Anna Catharina[8] **GELDENHUYS** [661], born 7 Sep 1840 in Swellendam, Cape, South Africa.

1111B516 Maria Catharina[8] **GELDENHUYS** [662], born 10 Jul 1843 in Swellendam, Cape, South Africa.

1111B517 Albertus Bernardus[8] **GELDENHUYS** [663], born 19 Apr 1846 in Swellendam, Cape, South Africa.

1111B52. Adriaan Johannes[7] **GELDENHUYS** [655] (Petrus Arnoldus[6], PetrusD Arnoldus - duplicated branch[5], Hendrik (c3)[4], Barend[3], Albert Barends Gildenhuisz[2], Bernd Gildenhausen[1]), born 23 Apr 1810; died 1867. He married on 18 Jan 1835 in Swellendam, Cape, South Africa **Elsabe Dina (LOURENS) GELDENHUYS** [664].

Children of Adriaan Johannes GELDENHUYS and Elsabe Dina LOURENS were as follows:

1111B521 Petrus Arnoldus[8] **GELDENHUYS** [665], born 18 Jul 1836.

1111B522 Christina Elizabeth[8] **GELDENHUYS** [666], born 7 Oct 1838 in Swellendam, Cape, South Africa; christened 17 Feb 1839 in Swellendam, Cape Colony, South Africa. She married **Lourens Johannes PRINSLOO** [2031]. Notes: b6c3d10e5f2g2

1111B523 Matthys Johannes Lourens[8] **GELDENHUYS** [667], born 12 Jul 1841 in Swellendam, Cape, South Africa.

1111B524 Adriaan Johannes[8] **GELDENHUYS** [668], born 2 Oct 1843 in Swellendam, Cape, South Africa; christened 8 Jan 1844 in Swellendam, Cape Colony, South Africa. He married on 30 Jan 1860 in Heidelberg, Cape, South Africa **Petronella Wilhelmina PRINSLOO** [669].

1114143. Barend Petrus Johannes[7] **GELDENHUYS** [693] (Wessel Johannes[6], Barend[5], Barend[4], Barend[3], Albert Barends Gildenhuisz[2], Bernd Gildenhausen[1]), born 6 Sep 1812 in Caledon, Western Cape, South Africa. He married (1) on 9 May 1830 in Caledon, Western Cape, South Africa **Anna Judith Geertruyda (KUUN) GELDENHUYS** [696]; (2) on 9 May 1830 in Caledon, Western Cape, South Africa **Anna Judith Geertruyda (KUUN) GELDENHUYS** [750].

Children of Barend Petrus Johannes GELDENHUYS and Anna Judith Geertruyda KUUN were as follows:

11141431 Wessel Johannes Willem[8] **GELDENHUYS** [697], born 5 Mar 1832 in Caledon, Western Cape, South Africa.

11141432 Cornelia Christina Johanna[8] **GELDENHUYS** [698], born 25 Dec 1833 in Caledon, Western Cape, South Africa.

11141433 Anna Geertruyda Elizabeth[8] **GELDENHUYS** [699], born 11 Mar 1836 in Caledon, Western Cape, South Africa.

11141434 Christina Berlina Geertruyda[8] **GELDENHUYS** [700], born 18 Jul 1838 in Caledon, Western Cape, South Africa.

Children of Barend Petrus Johannes GELDENHUYS and Anna Judith Geertruyda KUUN were as follows:

11141435 Wessel Johannes Willem[8] **GELDENHUYS** [751], born 5 Mar 1832 in Caledon, Western Cape, South Africa.

11141436 Cornelia Christina Johanna[8] **GELDENHUYS** [698], born 25 Dec 1833 in Caledon, Western Cape, South Africa.

11141437 Anna Geertruyda Elizabeth[8] **GELDENHUYS** [699], born 11 Mar 1836 in Caledon, Western Cape, South Africa.

11141438 Christina Berlina Geertruyda[8] **GELDENHUYS** [754], born 18 Jul 1838 in Caledon, Western Cape, South Africa.

1114212. Petrus Lafras[7] **GELDENHUYS** [757] (Barend[6], Jurie Johannes[5], Barend[4], Barend[3], Albert Barends Gildenhuisz[2], Bernd Gildenhausen[1]), born 20 Feb 1803. He married on 13 Dec 1818 in Stellenbosch, Cape, South Africa **Johanna Christina (GERMISHUIZEN) GELDENHUYS** [766].

Children of Petrus Lafras GELDENHUYS and Johanna Christina GERMISHUIZEN were as follows:

11142121 Elizabeth Johanna Wesselina[8] **GELDENHUYS** [767], born 18 Jul 1823 in Caledon, Western Cape, South Africa.

11142122 Elsabe Johanna Wesselina[8] **GELDENHUYS** [768], born 18 Jul 1823 in Caledon, Western Cape, South Africa.

11142123 **Johanna Geertruyda Cornelia Susanna**[8] **GELDENHUYS** [769], born 15 Jul 1825 in Caledon, Western Cape, South Africa.

11142124 **Anna Christina Elizabeth Cornelia**[8] **GELDENHUYS** [770], born 18 Jun 1827 in Caledon, Western Cape, South Africa.

11142125 **Teda Magdalena**[8] **GELDENHUYS** [771], born 3 Mar 1829 in Caledon, Western Cape, South Africa.

11142126 **Petrus Lafras Daniel**[8] **GELDENHUYS** [772], born 31 Aug 1832 in Caledon, Western Cape, South Africa.

11142127 **Wilhelmina Johanna Hendrina**[8] **GELDENHUYS** [773], born 6 Mar 1835 in Caledon, Western Cape, South Africa.

11142128 **Aletta Catharina Elizabeth**[8] **GELDENHUYS** [774], born 8 Oct 1837 in Caledon, Western Cape, South Africa. She married on 13 Sep 1858 in Heidelberg, Cape, South Africa **Matthys Wilhelm BEYERS** [776], born 1 Aug 1830 in Potteberg, Swellendam, Cape Province, South Africa; died 1883 in South Africa.

+ 11142129 **Barend Hermanus Nicolaas**[8] **GELDENHUYS** [775], born 28 Apr 1840 in Bredasdorp, Cape, South Africa. He married **Anna Sophia Aletta BEESLAAR** [777].

1114213. Jurie Johannes[7] **GELDENHUYS** [758] (Barend[6], Jurie Johannes[5], Barend[4], Barend[3], Albert Barends Gildenhuisz[2], Bernd Gildenhausen[1]), born 9 Dec 1804. He married on 2 Mar 1828 in Somerset-Wes, Cape, South Africa **Cornelia Geertruyda Gildenhuizen (GELDENHUYS) GELDENHUYS** [780].

Children of Jurie Johannes GELDENHUYS and Cornelia Geertruyda Gildenhuizen GELDENHUYS were as follows:

11142131 **Johanna Magdalena**[8] **GELDENHUYS** [781], born 4 Jan 1829 in Caledon, Western Cape, South Africa.

1114218. Barend Hermanus[7] **GELDENHUYS** [763] (Barend[6], Jurie Johannes[5], Barend[4], Barend[3], Albert Barends Gildenhuisz[2], Bernd Gildenhausen[1]), born 23 Jun 1815 in Caledon, Western Cape, South Africa; died 1840. He married on 15 Nov 1834 in Caledon, Western Cape, South Africa **Margaretha Maria (MAREE) GELDENHUYS** [783].

Children of Barend Hermanus GELDENHUYS and Margaretha Maria MAREE were as follows:

+ 11142181 **Barend Johannes Hermanus**[8] **GELDENHUYS** [784], born 6 Feb 1837 in Caledon, Western Cape, South Africa; died 1940 in Transvaal, South Africa. He married **Elizabeth Maria MULLER** [789].

11142182 **Burgent Christiaan**[8] **GELDENHUYS** [785], born 28 Jun 1838 in Caledon, Western Cape, South Africa; died Apr 1895 in Bloedrivier, wyk Marabastad, distr. Zoutpansberg, Transvaal, South Africa.

11142183 **Pieter Lucas Jacobus**[8] **GELDENHUYS** [786], born 3 Feb 1840 in Caledon, Western Cape, South Africa.

11142184 **Margaretha Judik Maria**[8] **GELDENHUYS** [787], born 13 Sep 1842 in Caledon, Western Cape, South Africa.

11142185 **Elena Catharina**[8] **GELDENHUYS** [788], born 3 Jun 1844 in Caledon, Western Cape, South Africa.

1114232. Johannes Joachimus[7] **GELDENHUYS** [709] (Jurgen Johannes[6], Jurie Johannes[5], Barend[4], Barend[3], Albert Barends Gildenhuisz[2], Bernd Gildenhausen[1]), born 12 Sep 1802; died 20 Feb 1874 in Heidelberg, Cape, South Africa. He married (1) on 5 Nov 1826 in

Swellendam, Cape, South Africa **Sara Johanna (KLEYNSMIT)** GELDENHUYS [711], died 8 Jun 1845; (2) on 12 Jan 1846 in Bredasdorp, Cape, South Africa **Maria Francina (VAN DYK)** GELDENHUYS [730], died 6 Jun 1849; (3) on 21 Jan 1850 in Swellendam, Cape, South Africa **Magdalena Johanna (LOUW)** GELDENHUYS [734], born 1815; died 28 Dec 1899, daughter of Daniel Johannes LOUW [735] and Susanna Johanna NN [736].

Children of Johannes Joachimus GELDENHUYS and Sara Johanna KLEYNSMIT were as follows:

11142321 Maria Catharina[8] **GELDENHUYS** [712], born 18 Aug 1827. She married on 21 Oct 1827 in Caledon, Western Cape, South Africa **Johannes Matthys EBERSOHN** [720].

11142322 Elsabe Luytje[8] **GELDENHUYS** [713], born 28 Mar 1830. She married on 25 Jul 1830 in Swellendam, Cape, South Africa **W L EBERSOHN** [721].

11142323 Jurie Johannes[8] **GELDENHUYS** [714], born 9 Jul 1833 in Swellendam, Cape, South Africa.

11142324 Sara Johanna[8] **GELDENHUYS** [715], born 25 Apr 1835 in Swellendam, Cape, South Africa. She married on 12 Jan 1857 in Heidelberg, Cape, South Africa **Jacobus Hendrik ODENDAAL** [722].

11142325 Cornelia Johanna Alberta[8] **GELDENHUYS** [716], born 4 Aug 1837 in Swellendam, Cape, South Africa. She married **George David Cornelis BEYERS** [723], born 20 Oct 1831; died 26 Oct 1895 in Heilbron, Orange Free State, South Africa, son of Johannes David BEYERS [728] and Johanna Magdalena LOURENS [729].

11142326 Susanna Hermina[8] **GELDENHUYS** [717], born 1 Aug 1840 in Swellendam, Cape, South Africa. She married on 13 Apr 1857 in Heidelberg, Cape, South Africa **Johannes Frederik UYS** [724], son of Cornelis Janse UYS [725].

11142327 Dina Maria Elizabeth[8] **GELDENHUYS** [718], born 3 Oct 1842 in Swellendam, Cape, South Africa. She married **G A VAN NIEKERK** [726].

11142328 Johanna Jochemina[8] **GELDENHUYS** [719], born 28 Apr 1845 in Swellendam, Cape, South Africa. She married on 24 Mar 1862 in Heidelberg, Cape, South Africa **Albertus Bernardus VAN RENSBURG** [727].

Children of Johannes Joachimus GELDENHUYS and Maria Francina VAN DYK were as follows:

11142329 Burgert Wynand[8] **GELDENHUYS** [731], born 16 Oct 1846 in Swellendam, Cape, South Africa.

1114232A Johannes Joachemus[8] **GELDENHUYS** [732], born 3 Jan 1849 in Swellendam, Cape, South Africa; christened 2 Feb 1849 in Swellendam, Cape, South Africa. He married in 1877 in Swellendam, Cape, South Africa **Elsabe SWART** [733]. Notes: Volksraadlid

Children of Johannes Joachimus GELDENHUYS and Magdalena Johanna LOUW were as follows:

1114232B Daniel Johannes[8] **GELDENHUYS** [737], born 23 Jun 1852 in Swellendam, Cape, South Africa.

1114232C Hans Jacob[8] **GELDENHUYS** [738], born 7 May 1855 in Swellendam, Cape, South Africa.

1114233. Jurgen Johannes[7] **GELDENHUYS** [710] (Jurgen Johannes[6], Jurie Johannes[5], Barend[4], Barend[3], Albert Barends Gildenhuisz[2], Bernd Gildenhausen[1]), born 6 Jul 1806. He married (1) on 5 Nov 1826 **Dina Maria Kleynsmit** GELDENHUYS [797]; (2) on 23 Nov 1839 in Swellendam, Cape, South Africa **Elizabeth Catharina (BLOEM)** GELDENHUYS [804].

Children of Jurgen Johannes GELDENHUYS and Dina Maria Kleynsmit were as follows:

11142331 **Jurie Johannes**[8] **GELDENHUYS** [798], born 14 Sep 1827 in Caledon, Western Cape, South Africa.

11142332 **Adriaan Hendrik**[8] **GELDENHUYS** [799], born 28 Jan 1830 in Caledon, Western Cape, South Africa.

11142333 **Maria Catharina Magdalena**[8] **GELDENHUYS** [800], born 15 May 1852 in Caledon, Western Cape, South Africa.

11142334 **Johannes Joachemus**[8] **GELDENHUYS** [801], born 2 Aug 1834 in Caledon, Western Cape, South Africa.

11142335 **Elsabe Luitje**[8] **GELDENHUYS** [802], born 3 Sep 1836 in Swellendam, Cape, South Africa.

11142336 **Dina Maria**[8] **GELDENHUYS** [803], born 8 Jul 1838 in Swellendam, Cape, South Africa.

Children of Jurgen Johannes GELDENHUYS and Elizabeth Catharina BLOEM were as follows:

11142337 **Anna Margaretha**[8] **GELDENHUYS** [805], born 25 Aug 1840 in Swellendam, Cape, South Africa.

+ 11142338 **Hans Jacob**[8] **GELDENHUYS** [806], born 1 Sep 1842 in Swellendam, Cape, South Africa; died 10 Aug 1899 in Marquard, South Africa. He married (1) **Gesina Catharina DE JAGER** [807]; (2) **Maria Elizabeth Susanna LUWES** [823].

1114331. Albert Hendrik[7] **GELDENHUYS** [489] (Barend Petrus[6], Albert Hendrik[5], Barend[4], Barend[3], Albert Barends Gildenhuisz[2], Bernd Gildenhausen[1]), born 23 Dec 1816. He married on 4 Nov 1838 in Stellenbosch **Anna Geertruyda Fredrika (OTTO) GELDENHUYS** [490], born 1818, daughter of Hendrik OTTO [841].

Children of Albert Hendrik GELDENHUYS and Anna Geertruyda Fredrika OTTO were as follows:

11143311 **Barend Petrus Albertus**[8] **GELDENHUYS** [838], born 13 Jul 1840 in Caledon, Western Cape, South Africa.

11143312 **Hendrik Gabriel Johannes Stephanus**[8] **GELDENHUYS** [839], born 4 Aug 1842 in Caledon, Western Cape, South Africa.

11143313 **Elizabeth Johanna**[8] **GELDENHUYS** [840], born 30 May 1844 in Caledon, Western Cape, South Africa.

1114622. Jacobus Jacob Hendrik[7] **GELDENHUYS** [856] (Jacobus[6], Jacobus[5], Barend[4], Barend[3], Albert Barends Gildenhuisz[2], Bernd Gildenhausen[1]), born 30 Jun 1815 in Caledon, Western Cape, South Africa. He married **Anna Francina Elizabeth (GRESSE) GELDENHUYS** [878].

Children of Jacobus Jacob Hendrik GELDENHUYS and Anna Francina Elizabeth GRESSE were as follows:

11146221 **Jacobus**[8] **GELDENHUYS** [879], born 23 Sep 1839 in Caledon, Western Cape, South Africa.

11146222 **Martha Johanna**[8] **GELDENHUYS** [880], born 26 Sep 1842 in Caledon, Western Cape, South Africa.

11146223 **Geertruyda Jacoba**[8] **GELDENHUYS** [881], born 20 Oct 1844 in Caledon, Western Cape, South Africa.

11146224 **Frans Lodewyk**[8] **GELDENHUYS** [882], born 11 Mar 1847 in Caledon, Western Cape, South Africa. He married on 10 Sep 1877 in Victoria-West, Cape, South Africa **Francina Jacoba LATSKY** [887].

11146225 **Jacobus Hendrik**[8] **GELDENHUYS** [883], born 21 Aug 1849 in Caledon, Western Cape, South Africa.

11146226 **Nicolaas Johannes**[8] **GELDENHUYS** [884], born 24 Nov 1851 in Caledon, Western Cape, South Africa.

11146227 **Anna Catharina Cornelia Susanna**[8] **GELDENHUYS** [885], born 24 Oct 1854.

11146228 **Judith Christina Elizabeth**[8] **GELDENHUYS** [886], born 10 Jan 1857 in Caledon, Western Cape, South Africa.

1114624. Nicolaas Johannes[7] **GELDENHUYS** [858] (Jacobus[6], Jacobus[5], Barend[4], Barend[3], Albert Barends Gildenhuisz[2], Bernd Gildenhausen[1]), born 21 Jan 1820 in Caledon, Western Cape, South Africa. He married on 29 Apr 1844 in Caledon, Western Cape, South Africa **Martha Johanna (GRESSE) GELDENHUYS** [868], daughter of Frans Lodewyk GRESSE [869].

Children of Nicolaas Johannes GELDENHUYS and Martha Johanna GRESSE were as follows:

11146241 **Jacobus**[8] **GELDENHUYS** [870], born 14 Apr 1845 in Caledon, Western Cape, South Africa.

11146242 **Martha Johanna**[8] **GELDENHUYS** [871], born 2 Sep 1847 in Caledon, Western Cape, South Africa.

11146243 **Frans Lodewyk**[8] **GELDENHUYS** [872], born 27 Aug 1849 in Caledon, Western Cape, South Africa.

11146244 **Geertruyda Wilhelmina**[8] **GELDENHUYS** [873], born 12 May 1852 in Caledon, Western Cape, South Africa.

11146245 **Nicolaas Johannes**[8] **GELDENHUYS** [874], born 5 Dec 1854 in Caledon, Western Cape, South Africa.

11146246 **Judith Wilhelmina**[8] **GELDENHUYS** [875], born 17 May 1857 in Caledon, Western Cape, South Africa.

1114634. HendriK Andries[7] **GELDENHUYS** [892] (Hendrik Andries[6], Jacobus[5], Barend[4], Barend[3], Albert Barends Gildenhuisz[2], Bernd Gildenhausen[1]), born 4 Apr 1827 in Caledon, Western Cape, South Africa. He married **Elizabeth Magdalena (UNGERER) GELDENHUYS** [894].

Children of HendriK Andries GELDENHUYS and Elizabeth Magdalena UNGERER were as follows:

11146341 **HendriK Andries**[8] **GELDENHUYS** [895], born 1 Oct 1863 in George, Cape, South Africa.

11146342 **Johan Diederik Ungerer**[8] **GELDENHUYS** [896], born 6 Oct 1865 in George, Cape, South Africa.

1114645. Hendrik Andries[7] **GELDENHUYS** [900] (Barend Petrus[6], Jacobus[5], Barend[4], Barend[3], Albert Barends Gildenhuisz[2], Bernd Gildenhausen[1]), born 3 Dec 1829 in Caledon, Western Cape, South Africa. He married on 3 Nov 1856 **Maria Johanna (COOPER) GELDENHUYS** [905].

Children of Hendrik Andries GELDENHUYS and Maria Johanna COOPER were as follows:

11146451 Hendrik Andries[8] **GELDENHUYS** [906], born 1860. He married on 29 Apr 1890 in Caledon, Western Cape, South Africa **Susanna Johanna COOPER** [907].

1114647. Barend Petrus[7] **GELDENHUYS** [902] (Barend Petrus[6], Jacobus[5], Barend[4], Barend[3], Albert Barends Gildenhuisz[2], Bernd Gildenhausen[1]), born 5 Sep 1833 in Caledon, Western Cape, South Africa. He married **Beatrix Geertruyda (GERBER) GELDENHUYS** [908].

Children of Barend Petrus GELDENHUYS and Beatrix Geertruyda GERBER were as follows:
- **11146471 Anna Christina Geertruyda**[8] **GELDENHUYS** [909], born 10 Aug 1860 in George, Cape, South Africa.
- **11146472 Frans Jacobus Anthonie**[8] **GELDENHUYS** [910], born 17 Aug 1862 in George, Cape, South Africa.

1162457. Johannes Jacobus Carel[7] **GELDENHUYS** [967] (Petrus Guilaume[6], Hendrik[5], Hendrik Albertus[4], Hendrik (b8)[3], Albert Barends Gildenhuisz[2], Bernd Gildenhausen[1]), born 29 Aug 1819. He married on 9 Dec 1845 in Wellington, Cape, South Africa **Johanna Adriana (MULLHOLLAND) GELDENHUYS** [970].

Children of Johannes Jacobus Carel GELDENHUYS and Johanna Adriana MULLHOLLAND were as follows:
- **11624571 Magdalena Catharina Susanna**[8] **GELDENHUYS** [971], born 12 Dec 1847 in Victoria-West, Cape, South Africa.
- **11624572 Johanna Maria (or Adriana)**[8] **GELDENHUYS** [972], born 1850.
- **11624573 Margaretha Johanna Elizabeth**[8] **GELDENHUYS** [973], born 21 Sep 1854 in Victoria-West, Cape, South Africa.
- **11624574 Martha Maria**[8] **GELDENHUYS** [974], born 10 Nov 1856 in Victoria-West, Cape, South Africa.
- **11624575 Petrus Gideon**[8] **GELDENHUYS** [975], born 12 Jun 1862 in Victoria-West, Cape, South Africa.
- **11624576 Martha Johanna Jacoba**[8] **GELDENHUYS** [976], born 4 May 1865 in Victoria-West, Cape, South Africa.

1162463. Abraham Josua[7] **GELDENHUYS** [989] (Abraham Jacobus[6], Hendrik[5], Hendrik Albertus[4], Hendrik (b8)[3], Albert Barends Gildenhuisz[2], Bernd Gildenhausen[1]), born 25 Dec 1808. He married on 6 Oct 1832 in Paarl, Western Cape, South Africa **Margaretha Johanna Elizabeth ((GILDENHUIZEN) GELDENHUYS) GELDENHUYS** [1000], born 2 Apr 1809, daughter of Petrus Guillaume (GILDENHUIZEN) GELDENHUYS [1012 and Maria Catharina REYNEKE [1013].

Notes for Margaretha Johanna Elizabeth (GILDENHUIZEN) GELDENHUYS
daughter of Petrus Guillaume Geldenhuys and Maria Catharina Reyneke

Children of Abraham Josua GELDENHUYS and Margaretha Johanna Elizabeth (GILDENHUIZEN) GELDENHUYS were as follows:
+ **11624631 Abraham Jacobus**[8] **GELDENHUYS** [1001], born 16 Jul 1835; died 29 Aug 1907 in Willowmore, South Africa. He married (1) **Anna Catharina Margaretha VAN VUUREN** [1004]; (2) **Susara Johanna VAN VUUREN** [1011].
- **11624632 Martha Louisa**[8] **GELDENHUYS** [1002], born 1841; died 3 Jul 1874 in Winburg, OFS, South Africa. She married on 16 Dec 1861 in Beauford-Wes, Cape, South Africa **Adam BARNARD** [1003].

11624B1. Hendrik Abraham Johannes^7 GELDENHUYS [1022] (Guilliam (or Gideon) Theodorus^6, Hendrik^5, Hendrik Albertus^4, Hendrik (b8)^3, Albert Barends Gildenhuisz^2, Bernd Gildenhausen^1), born 17 Sep 1815 in Paarl, Western Cape, South Africa. He married on 6 Sep 1836 in Paarl, Western Cape, South Africa **Johanna Catharina (GROBBELAAR) GELDENHUYS** [1027], born 1818, daughter of Evert GROBBELAAR [1028].

Children of Hendrik Abraham Johannes GELDENHUYS and Johanna Catharina GROBBELAAR were as follows:

    11624B11 Margaretha Maria^8 GELDENHUYS [1029].

+   **11624B12 Hendrik Abraham Johannes^8 GELDENHUYS** [1030], born 1848; died 5 Feb 1881 in Boshof. He married **Geertruyda Wouttrina KRIEL** [1031].

11624C5. Pieter Daniel^7 GELDENHUYS [1042] (Theodorus Louis Hermanus^6, Hendrik^5, Hendrik Albertus^4, Hendrik (b8)^3, Albert Barends Gildenhuisz^2, Bernd Gildenhausen^1), born 21 Nov 1828 in Franschoek, Cape, South Africa; died 23 Dec 1889. He married **Susanna Margaretha (NIGRINI) GELDENHUYS** [1043], died 2 Jan 1863.

Children of Pieter Daniel GELDENHUYS and Susanna Margaretha NIGRINI were as follows:

    11624C51 Pieter Daniel^8 GELDENHUYS [1044].
    11624C52 Johannes Albertus^8 GELDENHUYS [1045].
    11624C53 Maria Sophia^8 GELDENHUYS [1046], born 30 May 1859 in Villiersdorp, South Africa.
    11624C54 Johanna Christina Amelia^8 GELDENHUYS [1047], born 7 Jun 1861 in Villiersdorp, South Africa.
    11624C55 Christina Aletta^8 GELDENHUYS [1048].
    11624C56 Francois Lodewyk Johannes^8 GELDENHUYS [1049].
    11624C57 Petronella Daniellina Johanna^8 GELDENHUYS [1050].
    11624C58 Daniel Johannes^8 GELDENHUYS [1051].

1162711. Albert Barend^7 GELDENHUYS [1065] (Hendrik Albertus^6, Albert Barend^5, Hendrik Albertus^4, Hendrik (b8)^3, Albert Barends Gildenhuisz^2, Bernd Gildenhausen^1), born 25 Jul 1802. He married on 3 Feb 1822 in Swartland, Cape, South Africa **Helena Johanna (VAN SCHALKWYK) GELDENHUYS** [1072].

Children of Albert Barend GELDENHUYS and Helena Johanna VAN SCHALKWYK were as follows:

    11627111 Hilletje Aletta Hendrina^8 GELDENHUYS [1073], born 6 Jul 1823. She married on 7 Oct 1838 in Swartland, Cape, South Africa **Christaan Samuel Frederik SMIT** [1080].
    11627112 Hendrik Albertus^8 GELDENHUYS [1074], born 31 Jul 1825.
    11627113 Theunis Gerhardus^8 GELDENHUYS [1075], born 15 Apr 1827.
    11627114 Albert Barend^8 GELDENHUYS [1076], born 12 Jul 1829.
    11627115 Dirk Johannes^8 GELDENHUYS [1077], born 12 Jul 1829.
    11627116 Christoffel Christiaan^8 GELDENHUYS [1078], born 1831. He married on 13 Apr 1865 in Piketberg, Cape, South Africa **Catharina Helena Johanna LUCAS** [1079].

1162816. Hendrik Marthinus⁷ GELDENHUYS [1105] (Hendrik Albertus⁶, Guilliam Hendrik⁵, Hendrik Albertus⁴, Hendrik (b8)³, Albert Barends Gildenhuisz², Bernd Gildenhausen¹), born 30 Sep 1818 in Paarl, Western Cape, South Africa; died 4 Dec 1897 in Bloemfontein, OFS, South Africa. He married on 8 Jun 1844 in Paarl, Western Cape, South Africa **Margaretha Georgina Fredrika (RORICH) GELDENHUYS** [1110].

    Children of Hendrik Marthinus GELDENHUYS and Margaretha Georgina Fredrika RORICH were as follows:
- 11628161 Johanna Magdalena⁸ GELDENHUYS [1111], born 19 Nov 1849 in Paarl, Western Cape, South Africa.
- 11628162 Margaretha Fredrika⁸ GELDENHUYS [1112], born 4 Mar 1851 in Paarl, Western Cape, South Africa.
- + 11628163 Hendrik Albertus⁸ GELDENHUYS [1113], born 25 Mar 1853 in Paarl, Western Cape, South Africa; died 4 Dec 1897 in Blesbokfontein. He married **Anna Magdalena Elizabeth LOULO** [1115].
- 11628164 Margaretha Fredrika⁸ GELDENHUYS [1114], born 26 Oct 1855 in Paarl, Western Cape, South Africa.

Generation 8

11111111. Hendrik Jacobus⁸ GELDENHUYS [8] (Johannes Albertus⁷, Lourens⁶, Johannes Albertus⁵, Hendrik (c3)⁴, Barend³, Albert Barends Gildenhuisz², Bernd Gildenhausen¹), born 17 Nov 1837 in South Africa; died 4 Sep 1924 in Rietgat, Kroonstad, OFS, South Africa. He married **Elizabeth (SCHIKKERLING) GELDENHUYS** [31], born 5 Mar 1858 in South Africa; died in South Africa.

    Children of Hendrik Jacobus GELDENHUYS and Elizabeth SCHIKKERLING were as follows:
- + 111111111 Johannes (Jan) Albertus⁹ GELDENHUYS [7], born 8 Jul 1877 in Kroonstad, OFS, South Africa; died 28 May 1944 in Rustpan, Bothaville, OFS, South Africa; buried in Rustpan, Bothaville, OFS. He married **Anna Elisabeth (Lizzie) PRELLER** [9].
- 111111112 Pieter⁹ GELDENHUYS [69], born 1879.
- 111111113 Maria⁹ GELDENHUYS [70], born 1880; died Jul 1901.
- 111111114 Michael⁹ GELDENHUYS [71], born 1882.
- 111111115 Joey⁹ GELDENHUYS [72], born 1883.
- 111111116 Oubaas⁹ GELDENHUYS [73], born 1885.

11111115. Lourens Pieter Arnoldus⁸ GELDENHUYS [1717] (Johannes Albertus⁷, Lourens⁶, Johannes Albertus⁵, Hendrik (c3)⁴, Barend³, Albert Barends Gildenhuisz², Bernd Gildenhausen¹), born 10 Oct 1835 in Swellendam, Cape; died 22 Jan 1902 in Ceylon. He married **Sara Johanna (EKSTEEN) GELDENHUYS** [1718].

    Children of Lourens Pieter Arnoldus GELDENHUYS and Sara Johanna EKSTEEN were as follows:
- 111111151 Johannes Albertus⁹ GELDENHUYS [1719], born 6 Jun 1860 in Kroonstad, Free State, South Africa.
- 111111152 Susanna Maria⁹ GELDENHUYS [1720].
- 111111153 Michael Casparus⁹ GELDENHUYS [1721]. He married **Sannie BLOEMMENSTEIN** [1722].
- 111111154 Sara Johanna⁹ GELDENHUYS [1723].

111111155 Judith Margaretha⁹ GELDENHUYS [1724].
111111156 Lourens Pieter⁹ GELDENHUYS [1725].

11111117. Adriaan Izak 'Aap'⁸ GELDENHUYS [1727] (Johannes Albertus⁷, Lourens⁶, Johannes Albertus⁵, Hendrik (c3)⁴, Barend³, Albert Barends Gildenhuisz², Bernd Gildenhausen¹), born 22 Jul 1843; died 1 Jan 1904 in Kroonstad, Free State, South Africa. He married **Maria Susanna Wilhelmina (SCHICKERLING) GELDENHUYS** [1728], born 13 Oct 1855 in Potchefstroom, Transvaal, South Africa; died 25 Sep 1890.

Notes for Adriaan Izak 'Aap' GELDENHUYS
Fought in the Anglo-Boer war, taken prisoner and sent to India POW Camps

Children of Adriaan Izak 'Aap' GELDENHUYS and Maria Susanna Wilhelmina SCHICKERLING were as follows:
+ **111111171 Izak George⁹ GELDENHUYS** [1729]. He married **Debora VILJOEN** [1730].

11111119. Johanna Susanna Maria⁸ GELDENHUYS [1756] (Johannes Albertus⁷, Lourens⁶, Johannes Albertus⁵, Hendrik (c3)⁴, Barend³, Albert Barends Gildenhuisz², Bernd Gildenhausen¹), born 1847; died 6 Jun 1881 in Harrismith, South Africa. She married **Floris Petrus Jacobus DE MEYER** [1758].

Children of Johanna Susanna Maria GELDENHUYS and Floris Petrus Jacobus DE MEYER were as follows:
111111191 Olof Abram Jacobus⁹ DE MEYER [1759], born 1880 in Harrismith, South Africa.

11111141. Dirk Cornelis⁸ GELDENHUYS [546] (Lourens⁷, Lourens⁶, Johannes Albertus⁵, Hendrik (c3)⁴, Barend³, Albert Barends Gildenhuisz², Bernd Gildenhausen¹), born 1 Jan 1858 in Heidelberg, Transvaal, South Africa; died 31 Aug 1929 in Johannesburg, Gauteng, South Africa. He married **NN (NN) GELDENHUYS** [1810].

Notes for Dirk Cornelis GELDENHUYS
Some dates given as Jan 1, and not Jan 5

Children of Dirk Cornelis GELDENHUYS and NN NN were as follows:
+ **111111411 Laurie 'Lorrie'⁹ GELDENHUYS** [1811]. He married **Ada PRINGLE** [1815].
111111412 Frank⁹ GELDENHUYS [1812].
+ **111111413 Dirk Cornelis⁹ GELDENHUYS** [1813], died 1965. He married **Maatjie Catharina Jacoba STEENKAMP** [1817].
111111414 Danie⁹ GELDENHUYS [1814].

11111621. Petrus Arnoldus⁸ GELDENHUYS [620] (Johannes Albertus⁷, Petrus Arnoldus⁶, Johannes Albertus⁵, Hendrik (c3)⁴, Barend³, Albert Barends Gildenhuisz², Bernd Gildenhausen¹), born 21 Jul 1831 in Caledon, Western Cape, South Africa; died 4 Apr 1887 in Stanford. He married on 8 May 1852 in Bredasdorp, Cape, South Africa **Mathilda Marietta (BEHR) GELDENHUYS** [621], born 12 Dec 1836 in Cape Town, South Africa.

Children of Petrus Arnoldus GELDENHUYS and Mathilda Marietta BEHR were as follows:
111116211 Anna Christina⁹ GELDENHUYS [622]. She married **P WILLEMSE** [631].

111116212 Jan Willemse Alexander⁹ GELDENHUYS [623].
111116213 Zacharyas Johannes Wessel⁹ GELDENHUYS [624].
111116214 Mathilda Marietta⁹ GELDENHUYS [625]. She married **Jacob DU TOIT** [632].
111116215 Hans Jacob Stanford⁹ GELDENHUYS [626].
111116216 Elias Jacobus⁹ GELDENHUYS [627].
111116217 Hendrik Jacobus⁹ GELDENHUYS [628].
111116218 Johanna Christina⁹ GELDENHUYS [629]. She married **J P H VERMEULEN** [633].
111116219 Petrus Arnoldus⁹ GELDENHUYS [630].

11112111. Gerhardus Bernardus - g7⁸ GELDENHUYS [146] (Adrian Johannes - f2⁷, Petrus Arnoldus - e5⁶, Petrus Arnoldus - d10⁵, Hendrik (c3)⁴, Barend³, Albert Barends Gildenhuisz², Bernd Gildenhausen¹), born 25 Dec 1850; died 18 Sep 1936 in Heidelberg, Cape, South Africa. He married on 25 Jan 1910 in Swellendam, Cape, South Africa unknown.

Children of Gerhardus Bernardus - g7 GELDENHUYS were as follows:
+ 111121111 **Gerhardus Bernardus - h4⁹ GELDENHUYS** [147], born 12 Aug 1878 in Heidelberg, Cape, South Africa; died 16 May 1964 in Heidelberg, Cape, South Africa. He married **Susanna Maria Elizabeth BESTER** [148].

11112115. Adriaan Johannes⁸ GELDENHUYS [668] (Adrian Johannes - f2⁷, Petrus Arnoldus - e5⁶, Petrus Arnoldus - d10⁵, Hendrik (c3)⁴, Barend³, Albert Barends Gildenhuisz², Bernd Gildenhausen¹), born 2 Oct 1843 in Swellendam, Cape, South Africa; christened 8 Jan 1844 in Swellendam, Cape Colony, South Africa. He married on 30 Jan 1860 in Heidelberg, Cape, South Africa **Petronella Wilhelmina (PRINSLOO) GELDENHUYS** [669].

Children of Adriaan Johannes GELDENHUYS and Petronella Wilhelmina PRINSLOO were as follows:
+ 111121151 **Adriaan Johannes⁹ GELDENHUYS** [670], born 1867; died 8 Dec 1898 in Kroonstad, OFS, South Africa. He married **Martha Susanna VAN BILJON** [671].

11112117. Mattys Johannes Lourens⁸ GELDENHUYS [2032] (Adrian Johannes - f2⁷, Petrus Arnoldus - e5⁶, Petrus Arnoldus - d10⁵, Hendrik (c3)⁴, Barend³, Albert Barends Gildenhuisz², Bernd Gildenhausen¹), born 12 Jul 1841; christened 4 Oct 1841 in Swellendam, Cape Colony, South Africa. He married on 28 Jun 1864 in Heidelberg, Cape Colony, South Africa **Francina Frederika (PRINSLOO) GELDENHUYS** [2033].

Children of Mattys Johannes Lourens GELDENHUYS and Francina Frederika PRINSLOO were as follows:
111121171 **Elizabeth Susanna Johanna⁹ GELDENHUYS** [2034], born 2 Mar 1865; christened 9 Apr 1865 in Heidelberg, Cape Colony, South Africa.
111121172 **Elsabe Barendina Francina⁹ GELDENHUYS** [2035], born 2 Aug 1867; christened 1 Sep 1867 in Heidelberg, Cape Colony, South Africa; died 6 Oct 1940 in Heidelberg, Cape Colony, South Africa. She married on 21 Nov 1886 in Heidelberg, Cape Colony, South Africa **Hendrik Albertus SWART** [2036], born 21 Jan 1865; died 14 Oct 1940; buried in Heidelberg, Cape Colony, South Africa. Notes: married Hendrik Albertus Swart genealogy number b3c3d3e3f2g3h1

111121173 Susanna Johanna Maria[9] **GELDENHUYS** [2037], born 27 May 1870; christened 19 Jul 1870. Notes: apparently un-married

111121174 Christina Elizabeth Cornelia[9] **GELDENHUYS** [2038], born 1 Oct 1872; christened 10 Nov 1872 in Heidelberg, Cape Colony, South Africa.

111121175 Martina Jacoba[9] **GELDENHUYS** [2039], born 26 Jun 1875; christened 15 Aug 1875 in Heidelberg, Cape Colony, South Africa.

111121176 Adriaan Johannes[9] **GELDENHUYS** [2040], born 12 Aug 1877 in Heidelberg, Cape Colony, South Africa; christened 9 Sep 1877 in Heidelberg, Cape Colony, South Africa. Notes: b6c3d10e5f2g3h6

111121177 Johanna Cornelia[9] **GELDENHUYS** [2041], born 26 Nov 1878; christened 26 Jan 1879 in Heidelberg, Cape Colony, South Africa.

11142129. Barend Hermanus Nicolaas[8] **GELDENHUYS** [775] (Petrus Lafras[7], Barend[6], Jurie Johannes[5], Barend[4], Barend[3], Albert Barends Gildenhuisz[2], Bernd Gildenhausen[1]), born 28 Apr 1840 in Bredasdorp, Cape, South Africa. He married on 16 Dec 1863 in Villiersdorp, South Africa **Anna Sophia Aletta (BEESLAAR) GELDENHUYS** [777], daughter of J F BEESLAAR [779].

Children of Barend Hermanus Nicolaas GELDENHUYS and Anna Sophia Aletta BEESLAAR were as follows:

111421291 Johanna Christina Magdalena[9] **GELDENHUYS** [778], born 20 Aug 1864 in Villiersdorp, South Africa.

11142181. Barend Johannes Hermanus[8] **GELDENHUYS** [784] (Barend Hermanus[7], Barend[6], Jurie Johannes[5], Barend[4], Barend[3], Albert Barends Gildenhuisz[2], Bernd Gildenhausen[1]), born 6 Feb 1837 in Caledon, Western Cape, South Africa; died 1940 in Transvaal, South Africa. He married **Elizabeth Maria (MULLER) GELDENHUYS** [789], born Mar 1846 in Graaff-Reinet, Cape, South Africa; died 14 Apr 1895 in Oberholzer, Transvaal, South Africa.

Children of Barend Johannes Hermanus GELDENHUYS and Elizabeth Maria MULLER were as follows:

111421811 Elizabeth Maria[9] **GELDENHUYS** [790], born 17 Dec 1869; died 1895 in South Africa.

111421812 Jakobus Muller[9] **GELDENHUYS** [791], born 29 Dec 1873; died 1895 in South Africa.

111421813 Margaretha Maria[9] **GELDENHUYS** [792], born 12 May 1877; died 1895 in South Africa.

111421814 Barend Hermanus[9] **GELDENHUYS** [793], born 14 Jun 1878; died 16 Oct 1916.

111421815 Frederik[9] **GELDENHUYS** [794], born 19 Oct 1879; died 1895 in South Africa.

111421816 Pieter Burger[9] **GELDENHUYS** [795], born 18 Jan 1884; died 1910 in South Africa. He married **P N Geldenhuyzen NN** [796].

11142338. Hans Jacob[8] **GELDENHUYS** [806] (Jurgen Johannes[7], Jurgen Johannes[6], Jurie Johannes[5], Barend[4], Barend[3], Albert Barends Gildenhuisz[2], Bernd Gildenhausen[1]), born 1 Sep 1842 in Swellendam, Cape, South Africa; died 10 Aug 1899 in Marquard, South Africa. He married (1) on 10 Feb 1862 in Heidelberg, Cape, South Africa **Gesina Catharina (DE JAGER) GELDENHUYS** [807], daughter of Carel Pieter DE JAGER [822]; (2) **Maria Elizabeth Susanna (LUWES) GELDENHUYS** [823], born 9 Jun 1851; died 18 Oct 1920.

Notes for Maria Elizabeth Susanna LUWES

Widow of Jacobus Johannes Wentzel

Children of Hans Jacob GELDENHUYS and Gesina Catharina DE JAGER were as follows:
- 111423381 Jurie Johannes[9] GELDENHUYS [808].
- 111423382 Carel Pieter[9] GELDENHUYS [809].
- 111423383 Gesina Catharina[9] GELDENHUYS [810].
- 111423384 Elizabeth Catharina Christina[9] GELDENHUYS [811].
- 111423385 Jacoba Catharina[9] GELDENHUYS [812].
- 111423386 Hans Jacob Blom[9] GELDENHUYS [813]. He married **Anna Maria HOGEWIND** [820], died 1932.
- 111423387 Hendrik Petrus[9] GELDENHUYS [814].
- 111423388 Andries Johannes[9] GELDENHUYS [815], born 6 May 1875; christened 3 Oct 1875 in Ficksburg, OFS, South Africa.
- 111423389 Hester Johanna[9] GELDENHUYS [816].
- 11142338A Wybrand Hebershausen[9] GELDENHUYS [817].
- 11142338B Johanna Elizabeth Catharina[9] GELDENHUYS [818]. She married **Hendrik Johannes LACOCK** [821], born 15 Dec 1868; died 5 Sep 1952.
- 11142338C Jacobus Petrus Cornelis[9] GELDENHUYS [819].

Children of Hans Jacob GELDENHUYS and Maria Elizabeth Susanna LUWES were as follows:
- 11142338D Maria Elizabeth Susanna[9] GELDENHUYS [824].
- 11142338E Adriana Alberta[9] GELDENHUYS [825].
- 11142338F Elsabe Johanna Jacomina[9] GELDENHUYS [826].
- 11142338G Anna Margaretha Magdalena[9] GELDENHUYS [827].
- 11142338H Adriaan Hendrik[9] GELDENHUYS [828].
- 11142338I Andries Lodewicus Stephanus[9] GELDENHUYS [829].

11624631. Abraham Jacobus[8] GELDENHUYS [1001] (Abraham Josua[7], Abraham Jacobus[6], Hendrik[5], Hendrik Albertus[4], Hendrik (b8)[3], Albert Barends Gildenhuisz[2], Bernd Gildenhausen[1]), born 16 Jul 1835; died 29 Aug 1907 in Willowmore, South Africa. He married (1) on 20 Jul 1868 in Willowmore, South Africa **Anna Catharina Margaretha (VAN VUUREN) GELDENHUYS** [1004], born 1848; died 2 Jun 1879 in Kromkuil, Willowmore, South Africa; (2) on 19 Dec 1887 in Willowmore, South Africa **Susara Johanna (VAN VUUREN) GELDENHUYS** [1011].

Children of Abraham Jacobus GELDENHUYS and Anna Catharina Margaretha VAN VUUREN were as follows:
- 116246311 Johanna Jacomina Maria[9] GELDENHUYS [1005], born 7 May 1869 in Willowmore, South Africa.
- 116246312 Margaretha Johanna Elizabeth[9] GELDENHUYS [1006], born 22 Dec 1870.
- 116246313 Abraham Jacobus Josua[9] GELDENHUYS [1007], born 7 Jun 1872 in Willowmore, South Africa.
- 116246314 Anna Catharina Louisa Jacoba[9] GELDENHUYS [1008], born 7 Jun 1872 in Willowmore, South Africa.
- 116246315 Matthys Petrus Lourens[9] GELDENHUYS [1010], born 24 Dec 1878 in Willowmore, South Africa.
- 116246316 Stephanus Johannes Lourens[9] GELDENHUYS [1014], born 2 Oct 1877 in Willowmore, South Africa.

11624B12. Hendrik Abraham Johannes[8] **GELDENHUYS** [1030] (Hendrik Abraham Johannes[7], Guilliam (or Gideon) Theodorus[6], Hendrik[5], Hendrik Albertus[4], Hendrik (b8)[3], Albert Barends Gildenhuisz[2], Bernd Gildenhausen[1]), born 1848; died 5 Feb 1881 in Boshof. He married **Geertruyda Wouttrina (KRIEL) GELDENHUYS** [1031].

Children of Hendrik Abraham Johannes GELDENHUYS and Geertruyda Wouttrina KRIEL were as follows:
  11624B121 Hendrik Abraham Johannes[9] **GELDENHUYS** [1032], born 20 Jul 1871.
  11624B122 Johanna Nicolaas[9] **GELDENHUYS** [1033], born 12 Nov 1873.
  11624B123 Evert Johannes[9] **GELDENHUYS** [1034], born 30 Sep 1876.
  11624B124 Dirk Jacobus[9] **GELDENHUYS** [1035], born 4 Mar 1880.

11628163. Hendrik Albertus[8] **GELDENHUYS** [1113] (Hendrik Marthinus[7], Hendrik Albertus[6], Guilliam Hendrik[5], Hendrik Albertus[4], Hendrik (b8)[3], Albert Barends Gildenhuisz[2], Bernd Gildenhausen[1]), born 25 Mar 1853 in Paarl, Western Cape, South Africa; died 4 Dec 1897 in Blesbokfontein. He married **Anna Magdalena Elizabeth (LOULO) GELDENHUYS** [1115].

Children of Hendrik Albertus GELDENHUYS and Anna Magdalena Elizabeth LOULO were as follows:
  116281631 Hendrik Marthinus[9] **GELDENHUYS** [1116].
  116281632 Jan Adriaan[9] **GELDENHUYS** [1117].
  116281633 Anna Magdalena[9] **GELDENHUYS** [1118].
  116281634 Cornelis Michael[9] **GELDENHUYS** [1119].
+ **116281635** Siebert Frederik[9] **GELDENHUYS** [1120]. He married **Johanna VERMAAK** [1121].

Generation 9

111111111. Johannes (Jan) Albertus[9] **GELDENHUYS** [7] (Hendrik Jacobus[8], Johannes Albertus[7], Lourens[6], Johannes Albertus[5], Hendrik (c3)[4], Barend[3], Albert Barends Gildenhuisz[2], Bernd Gildenhausen[1]), born 8 Jul 1877 in Kroonstad, OFS, South Africa; died 28 May 1944 in Rustpan, Bothaville, OFS, South Africa; buried in Rustpan, Bothaville, OFS. He married **Anna Elisabeth (Lizzie) (PRELLER) GELDENHUYS** [9], born 23 Feb 1879 in Free State, South Africa; died 1976 in Rustpan, Bothaville, OFS, South Africa; buried in Rustpan, Bothaville, OFS, South Africa, daughter of Abraham Christofel Naude Christoffel PRELLER [29] and Helletta Lephina BOTHA [28].

Notes for Johannes (Jan) Albertus GELDENHUYS
    Fought the British in the Anglo-Boer War - Western Front of the Orange Free State. Was taken POW and shipped to Umballa, India

Children of Johannes (Jan) Albertus GELDENHUYS and Anna Elisabeth (Lizzie) PRELLER were as follows:
  1111111111 Helletta Lephina[10] **GELDENHUYS** [38], born 2 May 1900 in De Bank, Bothaville; died 15 Aug 1901 in Kroonstad Concentration Camp.
+ **1111111112** Hendrik Jacobus[10] **GELDENHUYS** [39], born 12 Jul 1902 in Kroonstad Concentration Camp; died 1967 in Normandy, Bothaville. He married **Adrianna Marta Maria (Max) KEYZER** [75].
+ **1111111113** Elizabeth (Bess)[10] **GELDENHUYS** [40], born 6 Nov 1904 in Rustpan, Bothaville, OFS. She married Steyn Jordaan.

1111111114 **Anna Elizabeth**[10] GELDENHUYS [41], born 11 Sep 1904 in Rustpan, Bothaville, OFS.

+ 1111111115 **Maria Susanna Wilhelmina**[10] GELDENHUYS [42], born 27 May 1911 in Rustpan, Bothaville, OFS; died 15 Mar 1995 in Rietondale, Pretoria, Transvaal. She married **Theodore Johan VAN RENSEN** [80].

+ 1111111116 **Abram Carl Frederik Preller**[10] GELDENHUYS [5], born 2 Aug 1916 in Bothaville, OFS, South Africa; died 13 Feb 1972 in Pretoria - Voortrekkerhoogte, South Africa; buried in Cremated - Pretoria. He married **Mattia Martha LOTTER** [6].

111111171. Izak George[9] GELDENHUYS [1729] (Adriaan Izak 'Aap'[8], Johannes Albertus[7], Lourens[6], Johannes Albertus[5], Hendrik (c3)[4], Barend[3], Albert Barends Gildenhuisz[2], Bernd Gildenhausen[1]). He married **Debora (VILJOEN)** GELDENHUYS [1730], born 1901.

Children of Izak George GELDENHUYS and Debora VILJOEN were as follows:

+ 1111111711 **Adriaan Izak 'Attie'**[10] GELDENHUYS [1731]. He married **Koeks NN NN KOEKS** [1740].
+ 1111111712 **Jacobus Strydom 'Kotie Sr'**[10] GELDENHUYS [1732], born 1 Nov 1929 in Kroonstad, Free State, South Africa; died 29 Aug 2008 in Pretoria, South Africa. He married **Ernestine Marlene STEINBACH** [1734].
+ 1111111713 **Izak George 'Sakkie'**[10] GELDENHUYS [1733]. He married **NN WESSELS** [1760].

111111411. Laurie 'Lorrie'[9] GELDENHUYS [1811] (Dirk Cornelis[8], Lourens[7], Lourens[6], Johannes Albertus[5], Hendrik (c3)[4], Barend[3], Albert Barends Gildenhuisz[2], Bernd Gildenhausen[1]). He married **Ada (PRINGLE)** GELDENHUYS [1815].

Children of Laurie 'Lorrie' GELDENHUYS and Ada PRINGLE were as follows:
1111114111 **Patricia 'Patsi'**[10] GELDENHUYS [1816].

111111413. Dirk Cornelis[9] GELDENHUYS [1813] (Dirk Cornelis[8], Lourens[7], Lourens[6], Johannes Albertus[5], Hendrik (c3)[4], Barend[3], Albert Barends Gildenhuisz[2], Bernd Gildenhausen[1]), died 1965. He married **Maatjie Catharina Jacoba (STEENKAMP)** GELDENHUYS [1817], born 17 Jun 1887; died 27 Oct 1918, daughter of Willem STEENKAMP [1823] and Annie DE JAGER [1824].

Children of Dirk Cornelis GELDENHUYS and Maatjie Catharina Jacoba STEENKAMP were as follows:

+ 1111114131 **Angela Adriana de Jager**[10] GELDENHUYS [1770], born 18 Apr 1908. She married (1) **Oscar BOHM** [1778]; (2) **George GILLESPIE** [1779].
1111114132 **Mercia Phillus**[10] GELDENHUYS [1819], born 1911; christened 1911. Notes: Name also spelled with 'y and i' as in Phillys / Phillis.
+ 1111114133 **Willem**[10] GELDENHUYS [1820], born 4 Apr 1913; died 19 Jul 1988 in Pongola, South Africa. He married **Sarah Johanna Louw 'Sally' GROENEWALD** [1822].
+ 1111114134 **Ruben Benjamin**[10] GELDENHUYS [1821], born 29 May 1916; died 24 Apr 1987. He married **Dorothy HURST** [1860].

111121111. Gerhardus Bernardus - h4^9 **GELDENHUYS** [147] (Gerhardus Bernardus - g7^8, Adrian Johannes - f2^7, Petrus Arnoldus - e5^6, Petrus Arnoldus - d10^5, Hendrik (c3)^4, Barend^3, Albert Barends Gildenhuisz^2, Bernd Gildenhausen^1), born 12 Aug 1878 in Heidelberg, Cape, South Africa; died 16 May 1964 in Heidelberg, Cape, South Africa. He married on 25 Jan 1910 in Swellendam, Cape, South Africa **Susanna Maria Elizabeth (BESTER) GELDENHUYS** [148], born 16 Sep 1886 in Heidelberg, Cape, South Africa; died 24 Aug 1978 in Heidelberg, Cape, South Africa.

Children of Gerhardus Bernardus - h4 GELDENHUYS and Susanna Maria Elizabeth BESTER were as follows:
+ **1111211111 Gerhardus Bernardus - i1**^{10} **GELDENHUYS** [149], born 13 Aug 1910 in Heidelberg, Cape, South Africa; died 17 Oct 1976 in Groote Schuur hospital, Cape Town, South Africa; buried in Heidelberg, Cape, South Africa. He married **Henrika Francina CLOETE** [150].

111121151. Adriaan Johannes^9 **GELDENHUYS** [670] (Adriaan Johannes^8, Adrian Johannes - f2^7, Petrus Arnoldus - e5^6, Petrus Arnoldus - d10^5, Hendrik (c3)^4, Barend^3, Albert Barends Gildenhuisz^2, Bernd Gildenhausen^1), born 1867; died 8 Dec 1898 in Kroonstad, OFS, South Africa. He married **Martha Susanna (VAN BILJON) GELDENHUYS** [671].

Children of Adriaan Johannes GELDENHUYS and Martha Susanna VAN BILJON were as follows:
 1111211511 Martha Jacoba Aletta^{10} GELDENHUYS [672].
 1111211512 Petronella Wilhelmina^{10} GELDENHUYS [673].
 1111211513 Adriaan Johannes^{10} GELDENHUYS [674].
 1111211514 Eenst Hendrik Schalk^{10} GELDENHUYS [675].

116281635. Siebert Frederik^9 **GELDENHUYS** [1120] (Hendrik Albertus^8, Hendrik Marthinus^7, Hendrik Albertus^6, Guilliam Hendrik^5, Hendrik Albertus^4, Hendrik (b8)^3, Albert Barends Gildenhuisz^2, Bernd Gildenhausen^1). He married **Johanna (VERMAAK) GELDENHUYS** [1121].

Children of Siebert Frederik GELDENHUYS and Johanna VERMAAK were as follows:
 1162816351 Francina^{10} GELDENHUYS [1122].
 1162816352 Anna^{10} GELDENHUYS [1123]. She married **NN BUYS** [1125].
 1162816353 Hendrik^{10} GELDENHUYS [1124].

Generation 10

1111111111. Helletje Levina GELDENHUYS, born 2 May 1900, died 15 Aug 1900.

1111111112. Hendrik Jacobus^{10} **GELDENHUYS** [39] (Johannes (Jan) Albertus^9, Hendrik Jacobus^8, Johannes Albertus^7, Lourens^6, Johannes Albertus^5, Hendrik (c3)^4, Barend^3, Albert Barends Gildenhuisz^2, Bernd Gildenhausen^1), born 12 Jul 1902 in Kroonstad Concentration Camp; died 1967 in Normandy, Bothaville. He married on 28 Aug 1928 in Kroonstad, OFS **Adrianna Marta Maria (Max) (KEYZER) GELDENHUYS** [75].

Children of Hendrik Jacobus GELDENHUYS and Adrianna Marta Maria (Max) KEYZER were as follows:
 11111111121 Catharina Susanna (Carien)^{11} GELDENHUYS [76], born 1 Oct 1931.

+ 1111111122 **Johannes Albertus (Jannie)**[11] **GELDENHUYS** [77], born 15 Mar 1937; died 3 May 1985 in Welgelegen, OFS. He married unknown.

1111111113. Elizabeth (Bess)[10] **GELDENHUYS** [40] (Johannes (Jan) Albertus[9], Hendrik Jacobus[8], Johannes Albertus[7], Lourens[6], Johannes Albertus[5], Hendrik (c3)[4], Barend[3], Albert Barends Gildenhuisz[2], Bernd Gildenhausen[1]), born 6 Nov 1904 in Rustpan, Bothaville, OFS. She married on 23 Jul 1925 in Bloemfontein, OFS unknown.

Children of Elizabeth (Bess) GELDENHUYS were as follows:
1111111131 **Paul**[11] **JORDAAN** [78].
1111111132 **Jannie**[11] **JORDAAN** [79].

1111111114. Maria Susanna Wilhelmina[10] **GELDENHUYS** [42] (Johannes (Jan) Albertus[9], Hendrik Jacobus[8], Johannes Albertus[7], Lourens[6], Johannes Albertus[5], Hendrik (c3)[4], Barend[3], Albert Barends Gildenhuisz[2], Bernd Gildenhausen[1]), born 27 May 1911 in Rustpan, Bothaville, OFS; died 15 Mar 1995 in Rietondale, Pretoria, Transvaal. She married **Theodore Johan VAN RENSEN** [80], born 27 Jan 1913 in Bloemfontein, OFS; died 23 Jan 1983 in Pretoria, Transvaal, son of Johan J VAN RENSEN [449] and Adrianna [450].

Children of Maria Susanna Wilhelmina GELDENHUYS and Theodore Johan VAN RENSEN were as follows:
+ 1111111141 **Elizabeth (Libby) Adriana**[11] **VAN RENSEN** [81], born 8 Nov 1941 in Cape Town. She married (1) **Ralph Arnold DUNCKERS** [451]; (2) **Johannes Christjan BEUKES** [458].
1111111142 **Johan**[11] **VAN RENSEN** [82], born 15 Sep 1944 in Cape Town.
1111111143 **Adrian Henry**[11] **VAN RENSEN** [83], born 7 Jan 1949 in Kroonstad, OFS.

1111111116. Abram Carl Frederik Preller[10] **GELDENHUYS** [5] (Johannes (Jan) Albertus[9], Hendrik Jacobus[8], Johannes Albertus[7], Lourens[6], Johannes Albertus[5], Hendrik (c3)[4], Barend[3], Albert Barends Gildenhuisz[2], Bernd Gildenhausen[1]), born 2 Aug 1916 in Bothaville, OFS, South Africa; died 13 Feb 1972 in Pretoria - Voortrekkerhoogte, South Africa; buried in Cremated - Pretoria. He married in 1940 **Mattia Martha (LOTTER) GELDENHUYS** [6], born 19 Oct 1916 in Johannesburg, Tvl, South Africa; died 1987 in Johannesburg, South Africa; buried in Cremated, Johannesburg, South Africa, daughter of Jan LOTTER [551] and NN NN [1921].

Notes for Abram Carl Frederik Preller GELDENHUYS
Served as a pilot for the duration of the war (South African Air Force)

Children of Abram Carl Frederik Preller GELDENHUYS and Mattia Martha LOTTER were as follows:
+ 1111111161 **Johannes Albertus**[11] **GELDENHUYS** [36], born 15 Aug 1940 in Johannesburg, Tvl. He married **Julia Lillian DIPPENAAR** [43].
+ 1111111162 **Preller Matt**[11] **GELDENHUYS Wg Cdr (Rtd)** [1], born 20 Feb 1943 in Bothaville, OFS, South Africa. He married **Susanna Catharina MALAN** [2].
+ 1111111163 **Delene Elizabeth**[11] **GELDENHUYS** [37], born 27 Feb 1945 in Oudshoorn, Cape. She married (1) **Johannes Jacobus Francois BOUWER** [235]; (2) **Stuart John MCCOLL** [236].
1111111164 **Dawn (Dawnie)**[11] **GELDENHUYS** [1279], born 1949 in Luanshya, Northern Rhodesia, now Zambia, Africa; died 13 Aug 1954 in Musenga Plots, Chingola,

Northern Rhodesia, now Zambia, Africa; buried in Chingola, Zambia. Notes: All things Bright and Beautiful

1111111711. Adriaan Izak 'Attie'[10] **GELDENHUYS** [1731] (Izak George[9], Adriaan Izak 'Aap'[8], Johannes Albertus[7], Lourens[6], Johannes Albertus[5], Hendrik (c3)[4], Barend[3], Albert Barends Gildenhuisz[2], Bernd Gildenhausen[1]). He married **Koeks NN (NN KOEKS)** GELDENHUYS [1740].

Children of Adriaan Izak 'Attie' GELDENHUYS and Koeks NN NN KOEKS were as follows:
   11111117111 Jacobus ' Kosie'[11] **GELDENHUYS** [1741].
   11111117112 Debora 'Debbie'[11] **GELDENHUYS** [1742].

1111111712. Jacobus Strydom 'Kotie Sr'[10] **GELDENHUYS** [1732] (Izak George[9], Adriaan Izak 'Aap'[8], Johannes Albertus[7], Lourens[6], Johannes Albertus[5], Hendrik (c3)[4], Barend[3], Albert Barends Gildenhuisz[2], Bernd Gildenhausen[1]), born 1 Nov 1929 in Kroonstad, Free State, South Africa; died 29 Aug 2008 in Pretoria, South Africa. He married **Ernestine Marlene (STEINBACH) GELDENHUYS** [1734], born 8 Sep 1934 in Clocolan; died 26 Mar 2002 in Nylstroom, Transvaal, South Africa.

Children of Jacobus Strydom 'Kotie Sr' GELDENHUYS and Ernestine Marlene STEINBACH were as follows:
+ **11111117121** Izak George[11] **GELDENHUYS** [1735], born 10 Jul 1958 in Kroonstad, Free State, South Africa. He married (1) **Hannelie BOOYSEN** [1743]; (2) **Wilna BESTER** [1747].
+ **11111117122** Lauretta[11] **GELDENHUYS** [1736], born 28 Mar 1960 in Kroonstad, Free State, South Africa. She married **Antony SMITH** [1750].
+ **11111117123** Hermann Erwin Rudibert 'Rudi'[11] **GELDENHUYS** [1737], born 8 Sep 1964 in Pretoria, South Africa. He married (1) **Deirdre TAPSON - ADOPTED BURNS** [1753]; (2) **Annelie STRYDOM** [1754].
   11111117124 Jacobus Adriaan 'Kotie Jr'[11] **GELDENHUYS** [1738], born 4 May 1973. He married on 25 Oct 2008 **Marriët KLOPPERS** [1739], born 11 Dec 1979.

1111111713. Izak George 'Sakkie'[10] **GELDENHUYS** [1733] (Izak George[9], Adriaan Izak 'Aap'[8], Johannes Albertus[7], Lourens[6], Johannes Albertus[5], Hendrik (c3)[4], Barend[3], Albert Barends Gildenhuisz[2], Bernd Gildenhausen[1]). He married **NN (WESSELS)** GELDENHUYS [1760].

Children of Izak George 'Sakkie' GELDENHUYS and NN WESSELS were as follows:
11111117131 Izak[11] **GELDENHUYS** [1761].
11111117132 Jurie[11] **GELDENHUYS** [1762].
11111117133 Adriaan 'Attie'[11] **GELDENHUYS** [1763].
11111117134 Sebastiaan 'Basie'[11] **GELDENHUYS** [1764]. He married on 11 Feb 2004 **Veronica ENGELBRECHT** [1765]. Notes: Hang-gliding (see Facebook)

1111114131. Angela Adriana de Jager[10] **GELDENHUYS** [1770] (Dirk Cornelis[9], Dirk Cornelis[8], Lourens[7], Lourens[6], Johannes Albertus[5], Hendrik (c3)[4], Barend[3], Albert Barends Gildenhuisz[2], Bernd Gildenhausen[1]), born 18 Apr 1908. She married (1) **Oscar BOHM** [1778]; (2) **George GILLESPIE** [1779].

Children of Angela Adriana de Jager GELDENHUYS and George GILLESPIE were as follows:
11111141311 Ian[11] **GILLESPIE** [1780].

1111114133. Willem[10] **GELDENHUYS** [1820] (Dirk Cornelis[9], Dirk Cornelis[8], Lourens[7], Lourens[6], Johannes Albertus[5], Hendrik (c3)[4], Barend[3], Albert Barends Gildenhuisz[2], Bernd Gildenhausen[1]), born 4 Apr 1913; died 19 Jul 1988 in Pongola, South Africa. He married **Sarah Johanna Louw 'Sally'** (**GROENEWALD**) GELDENHUYS [1822], born 22 Apr 1914 in Farm "Beltresna", Amersfoort, Mpumalanga, South Africa; died 1 Mar 1989 in Durban, South Africa; buried in Pongola cemetary, Transvaal.

Notes for Sarah Johanna Louw 'Sally' GROENEWALD
"Sally Cycad" - collector of cycads

Had the largest collection of Cycads from all over the world

Children of Willem GELDENHUYS and Sarah Johanna Louw 'Sally' GROENEWALD were as follows:
+ **11111141331 Myrl Maureen**[11] **GELDENHUYS** [1825], born 11 Oct 1938 in Amersfoort, Ermelo district, Mpumalanga, South Afr. She married (1) **Duncan Allan SMITH** [1829]; (2) **Albertus Marthinus TRICHARDT** [1834].
  11111141332 Willem Steenkamp[11] **GELDENHUYS** [1826], born 4 Nov 1943 in Amersfoort, Ermelo district, Mpumalanga, South Afr.
+ **11111141333 Margareth Helene 'Marita'**[11] **GELDENHUYS** [1827], born 21 Dec 1946. She married **Donald 'Ross' BRODIE** [1791].
+ **11111141334 Wanda**[11] **GELDENHUYS** [1828], born 21 May 1949 in Ermelo, Mpumalanga, South Africa. She married **Adriaan Johannes STRYDOM** [1858].

1111114134. Ruben Benjamin[10] **GELDENHUYS** [1821] (Dirk Cornelis[9], Dirk Cornelis[8], Lourens[7], Lourens[6], Johannes Albertus[5], Hendrik (c3)[4], Barend[3], Albert Barends Gildenhuisz[2], Bernd Gildenhausen[1]), born 29 May 1916; died 24 Apr 1987. He married **Dorothy** (**HURST**) GELDENHUYS [1860], born 5 Sep 1919; died 27 Aug 2002.

Children of Ruben Benjamin GELDENHUYS and Dorothy HURST were as follows:
+ **11111141341 Ruben Neville**[11] **GELDENHUYS** [1861], born 18 Mar 1940. He married **Joan COLLETT** [1795].
  11111141342 Lorraine[11] **GELDENHUYS** [1862], born 12 Aug 1942.
+ **11111141343 Allan Derek**[11] **GELDENHUYS** [1804], born 4 Nov 1949 in Ermelo, Mpumalanga, South Africa. He married **Linda Magdalene GEERE** [1806].
  11111141344 Raymond[11] **GELDENHUYS** [1864], born 4 Aug 1952.
  11111141345 Cheryl[11] **GELDENHUYS** [1776], born 24 Mar 1955.

1111211111. Gerhardus Bernardus - i1[10] **GELDENHUYS** [149] (Gerhardus Bernardus - h4[9], Gerhardus Bernardus - g7[8], Adrian Johannes - f2[7], Petrus Arnoldus - e5[6], Petrus Arnoldus - d10[5], Hendrik (c3)[4], Barend[3], Albert Barends Gildenhuisz[2], Bernd Gildenhausen[1]), born 13 Aug 1910 in Heidelberg, Cape, South Africa; died 17 Oct 1976 in Groote Schuur hospital, Cape Town, South Africa; buried in Heidelberg, Cape, South Africa. He married **Henrika Francina** (**CLOETE**) GELDENHUYS [150], born 30 Nov 1908 in Wynberg, Cape, South Africa; died in South Africa.

Children of Gerhardus Bernardus - i1 GELDENHUYS and Henrika Francina CLOETE were as follows:

+ 11112111111Gerhard - j1[11] **GELDENHUYS** [151], born 19 Nov 1937 in Worcester, Cape, South Africa. He married **Annaline ODENDAAL** [152].

Generation 11

11111111111. Johannes Albertus[11] **GELDENHUYS** [36] (Abram Carl Frederik Preller[10], Johannes (Jan) Albertus[9], Hendrik Jacobus[8], Johannes Albertus[7], Lourens[6], Johannes Albertus[5], Hendrik (c3)[4], Barend[3], Albert Barends Gildenhuisz[2], Bernd Gildenhausen[1]), born 15 Aug 1940 in Johannesburg, Tvl. He married on 27 Mar 1964 in Luanshya, Northern Rhodesia (now Zambia) **Julia Lillian (DIPPENAAR) GELDENHUYS** [43], born 12 Jul 1936 in Ficksburg, OFS, daughter of Johannes Petrus DIPPENAAR [44] and Louzya Christina DE BRUYN [45].

Notes for Johannes Albertus GELDENHUYS
Celebrated his 70th birthday with his immediate family, including Delene who came from New Zealand

Children of Johannes Albertus GELDENHUYS and Julia Lillian DIPPENAAR were as follows:

+ 111111111121 **Stuart William**[12] **GELDENHUYS** [46], born 18 Sep 1957 in Bulawayo, Rhodesia. He married **Joy GOLDSWORTHY** [49].
+ 111111111122 **Charmaine**[12] **GELDENHUYS** [47], born 7 Jan 1960. She married **Lance FRONEMAN** [51].
+ 111111111123 **Paul Preller**[12] **GELDENHUYS** [48], born 15 Dec 1966 in Ndola, Zambia. He married **Karen DE WAAL** [53].

11111111112. Preller Matt[11] **GELDENHUYS Wg Cdr (Rtd)** [1] (Abram Carl Frederik Preller[10], Johannes (Jan) Albertus[9], Hendrik Jacobus[8], Johannes Albertus[7], Lourens[6], Johannes Albertus[5], Hendrik (c3)[4], Barend[3], Albert Barends Gildenhuisz[2], Bernd Gildenhausen[1]), born 20 Feb 1943 in Bothaville, OFS, South Africa. He married on 5 Mar 1966 in Fort Victoria, Rhodesia **Susanna Catharina (MALAN) GELDENHUYS** [2], born 5 Mar 1945 in Lichtenburg, Tvl, South Africa, daughter of Francois Daniel MALAN [11] and Aletta Magdalena Susanna LE ROUX [12].

Notes for Preller Matt GELDENHUYS Wg Cdr (Rtd)
Born at Rustpan, family farm in the Free State

Air Force pilot

Children of Preller Matt GELDENHUYS Wg Cdr (Rtd) and Susanna Catharina MALAN were as follows:

+ 111111111111 **Renene Delene**[12] **GELDENHUYS** [3], born 8 Aug 1968 in Gwelo, Rhodesia now Zimbabwe. She married **Grahame David JELLEY** [13].
+ 111111111112 **Pey Malan**[12] **GELDENHUYS** [4], born 22 Dec 1970 in Gwelo, Rhodesia, South Africa. He married (1) **Eloise HOWARD** [18]; (2) **Marion MULLER** [404].

11111111113. Delene Elizabeth[11] **GELDENHUYS** [37] (Abram Carl Frederik Preller[10], Johannes (Jan) Albertus[9], Hendrik Jacobus[8], Johannes Albertus[7], Lourens[6], Johannes Albertus[5], Hendrik (c3)[4], Barend[3], Albert Barends Gildenhuisz[2], Bernd Gildenhausen[1]), born 27 Feb 1945 in Oudshoorn, Cape. She married (1) in Pretoria, South Africa **Johannes Jacobus Francois BOUWER** [235], born 19 Dec 1943 in Pretoria, South Africa, son of Willem BOUWER [1281] and Marie [1317]; (2) on 26 Sep 1991 **Stuart John MCCOLL** [236], born 27 Mar 1949 in Bromley, Kent, United Kingdom, son of Peter John MCCOLL [237] and Joyce Edith MATCHETT [1274].

Notes for Delene Elizabeth GELDENHUYS
Later divorced

Second marriage to Stuart John McColl

Accosted in her home by evil Afs, emigrated to New Zealand

Relocated to North Shore, Auckland

Moved to new home

Accosted a second time - had her gold necklace ripped off in broad daylight. Thief absconded down an alleyway

Notes for Stuart John MCCOLL
Eve Elisabeth Boxall, and had Davyd John Charkes, born March 1978

Re-married Delene Elizabeth Bouwer, nee Geldenhuys

Children of Delene Elizabeth GELDENHUYS and Johannes Jacobus Francois BOUWER were as follows:
+ **111111111131 Chanli**[12] **BOUWER** [62], born 12 Oct 1970 in Vereeniging, Gauteng, Tvl. She married **Charles Roy BRINK** [64].
   111111111132 Rensha[12] **BOUWER** [63], born 15 Feb 1972 in Salisbury, Rhodesia. She married **Craig BROWN** [1280].

11111111132. Johannes Albertus (Jannie)[11] **GELDENHUYS** [77] (Hendrik Jacobus[10], Johannes (Jan) Albertus[9], Hendrik Jacobus[8], Johannes Albertus[7], Lourens[6], Johannes Albertus[5], Hendrik (c3)[4], Barend[3], Albert Barends Gildenhuisz[2], Bernd Gildenhausen[1]), born 15 Mar 1937; died 3 May 1985 in Welgelegen, OFS. He married unknown.

Children of Johannes Albertus (Jannie) GELDENHUYS were as follows:
+ **111111111321 Hendrik Jacobus (Hennie)**[12] **GELDENHUYS** [154], born 1 Aug 1964 in Bothaville, OFS, South Africa. He married **Johanna Elizabeth (Linette) KOTZÉ** [155].

11111111161. Elizabeth (Libby) Adriana[11] **VAN RENSEN** [81] (Maria Susanna Wilhelmina[10] GELDENHUYS, Johannes (Jan) Albertus[9], Hendrik Jacobus[8], Johannes Albertus[7], Lourens[6], Johannes Albertus[5], Hendrik (c3)[4], Barend[3], Albert Barends Gildenhuisz[2], Bernd Gildenhausen[1]), born 8 Nov 1941 in Cape Town. She married (1) in 1962 in Pretoria, South Africa **Ralph Arnold DUNCKERS** [451], born 1943, son of Wilbur DUNCKERS [452] and Grace NN [453]; (2) in 1979 in Pretoria, South Africa **Johannes Christjan BEUKES** [458], born 27 Apr 1947 in Potchefstroom, Transvaal, South Africa.

Notes for Elizabeth (Libby) Adriana VAN RENSEN
Holds school Freestyle swimming record - not broken as at 2010

Libby divorsed Arnold Dunckers and married Beukes. She has a second son, Christopher

Children of Elizabeth (Libby) Adriana VAN RENSEN and Ralph Arnold DUNCKERS were as follows:
+ 111111111611 **Caryn Sandra**^{12} **DUNCKERS** [84], born 20 Nov 1963 in Pretoria, South Africa. She married **Alwyn WALDECK** [454].
+ 111111111612 **Brandon Arne**^{12} **DUNCKERS** [85], born 20 Jul 1965 in Pretoria, Transvaal. He married **Karen BOTHA** [456].

Children of Elizabeth (Libby) Adriana VAN RENSEN and Johannes Christjan BEUKES were as follows:
111111111613 **Christopher**^{12} **BEUKES** [459], born 4 Aug 1983 in Pretoria, South Africa.

11111117121. Izak George^{11} **GELDENHUYS** [1735] (Jacobus Strydom 'Kotie Sr'^{10}, Izak George^9, Adriaan Izak 'Aap'^{8}, Johannes Albertus^7, Lourens^6, Johannes Albertus^5, Hendrik (c3)^4, Barend^3, Albert Barends Gildenhuisz^2, Bernd Gildenhausen^1), born 10 Jul 1958 in Kroonstad, Free State, South Africa. He married (1) **Hannelie (BOOYSEN) GELDENHUYS** [1743]; (2) **Wilna (BESTER) GELDENHUYS** [1747].

Children of Izak George GELDENHUYS and Hannelie BOOYSEN were as follows:
111111171211 **Suzanne**^{12} **GELDENHUYS** [1744].
111111171212 **Marianne**^{12} **GELDENHUYS** [1745], born 15 Jul 1986.
111111171213 **Leizel**^{12} **GELDENHUYS** [1746].

Children of Izak George GELDENHUYS and Wilna BESTER were as follows:
111111171214 **Cabous**^{12} **GELDENHUYS** [1748], born 10 Feb 1998.
111111171215 **Lena**^{12} **GELDENHUYS** [1749].

11111117122. Lauretta^{11} **GELDENHUYS** [1736] (Jacobus Strydom 'Kotie Sr'^{10}, Izak George^9, Adriaan Izak 'Aap'^{8}, Johannes Albertus^7, Lourens^6, Johannes Albertus^5, Hendrik (c3)^4, Barend^3, Albert Barends Gildenhuisz^2, Bernd Gildenhausen^1), born 28 Mar 1960 in Kroonstad, Free State, South Africa. She married **Antony SMITH** [1750].

Children of Lauretta GELDENHUYS and Antony SMITH were as follows:
111111171221 **Charles Lauton**^{12} **SMITH** [1751].
111111171222 **Jacques**^{12} **SMITH** [1752].

11111117123. Hermann Erwin Rudibert 'Rudi'^{11} **GELDENHUYS** [1737] (Jacobus Strydom 'Kotie Sr'^{10}, Izak George^9, Adriaan Izak 'Aap'^{8}, Johannes Albertus^7, Lourens^6, Johannes Albertus^5, Hendrik (c3)^4, Barend^3, Albert Barends Gildenhuisz^2, Bernd Gildenhausen^1), born 8 Sep 1964 in Pretoria, South Africa. He married (1) **Deirdre (TAPSON - ADOPTED BURNS) GELDENHUYS** [1753], born 5 Mar 1967 in Salisbury, Rhodesia - now Harare, Zimbabwe, daughter of Gerry BURNS [2043]; (2) **Annelie (STRYDOM) GELDENHUYS** [1754], born 24 May 1971.

Notes for Deirdre TAPSON - ADOPTED BURNS
Born Tapson, but adopted by Gerry Burns

maiden name was Tapson, but adopted by Gerry Burns

First marriage to Rudi (Hermann Erwin Rudibert) Geldenhuys

2nd marriage to Dougie Stylianou

3rd marriage to Jan Bezuidenhout (father of Andrea 'Annie')

Children of Hermann Erwin Rudibert 'Rudi' GELDENHUYS and Deirdre TAPSON - ADOPTED BURNS were as follows:
111111171231Adriaan^{12} GELDENHUYS [2042], born 18 Apr 1993.

11111141331. Myrl Maureen^{11} GELDENHUYS [1825] (Willem^{10}, Dirk Cornelis^{9}, Dirk Cornelis^{8}, Lourens^{7}, Lourens^{6}, Johannes Albertus^{5}, Hendrik (c3)^{4}, Barend^{3}, Albert Barends Gildenhuisz^{2}, Bernd Gildenhausen^{1}), born 11 Oct 1938 in Amersfoort, Ermelo district, Mpumalanga, South Afr. She married (1) **Duncan Allan SMITH** [1829]; (2) on 11 Oct 1962 in Pretoria **Albertus Marthinus TRICHARDT** [1834], born 30 Dec 1940 in Bethal, son of Albertus Marthinus TRICHARDT [1849] and Susanna Catharina Margaretha DE VILLIERS [1850].

Children of Myrl Maureen GELDENHUYS and Duncan Allan SMITH were as follows:
+ **111111413311Russell Allan^{12} GELDENHUYS** [1830], born 29 Mar 1960. He married **Jacoba Cornelia 'Corli' OPPERMAN** [1831].

Children of Myrl Maureen GELDENHUYS and Albertus Marthinus TRICHARDT were as follows:
+ **111111413312 Albertus Marthinus "Bertie"^{12} TRICHARDT** [1835], born 20 Mar 1967 in Kroonstad hospital, Free State, South Africa. He married **Carolyn WOODLEY** [1838].
+ **111111413313 Michelle^{12} TRICHARDT** [1836], born 27 Nov 1968 in Piet Retief, South Africa. She married (1) **Eugene Constante GELDENHUYS** [1841]; (2) **Izak Francois MULDER** [1844].
+ **111111413314 Willem Geldenhuys^{12} TRICHARDT** [1837], born 12 Feb 1971 in Durban, South Africa. He married **Kelley Anne BROWN** [1847].

11111141333. Margareth Helene 'Marita'^{11} GELDENHUYS [1827] (Willem^{10}, Dirk Cornelis^{9}, Dirk Cornelis^{8}, Lourens^{7}, Lourens^{6}, Johannes Albertus^{5}, Hendrik (c3)^{4}, Barend^{3}, Albert Barends Gildenhuisz^{2}, Bernd Gildenhausen^{1}), born 21 Dec 1946. She married on 11 Mar 1972 in New Plymouth, New Zealand **Donald 'Ross' BRODIE** [1791], born 29 Jan 1947 in Geraldine, New Zealand, son of Nan Ngaire [1880.

Children of Margareth Helene 'Marita' GELDENHUYS and Donald 'Ross' BRODIE were as follows:
111111413331Shayne Ross^{12} BRODIE [1792], born 30 May 1973 in New Plymouth, New Zealand. He married on 20 Sep 2003 in New Zealand **Talei Lisi 'Torika' BJORN** [1793], born 29 Aug 1978.

11111141334. Wanda^{11} GELDENHUYS [1828] (Willem^{10}, Dirk Cornelis^{9}, Dirk Cornelis^{8}, Lourens^{7}, Lourens^{6}, Johannes Albertus^{5}, Hendrik (c3)^{4}, Barend^{3}, Albert Barends Gildenhuisz^{2}, Bernd Gildenhausen^{1}), born 21 May 1949 in Ermelo, Mpumalanga, South Africa. She married on 1 Apr 1972 **Adriaan Johannes STRYDOM** [1858], born 25 Sep 1947 in Pretoria, South Africa.

Children of Wanda GELDENHUYS and Adriaan Johannes STRYDOM were as follows:
111111413341 Riaan Geldenhuys[12] STRYDOM [1859], born 15 Jan 1981; died 7 Mar 2010 in Wellington, Cape, South Africa.

11111141341. Ruben Neville[11] GELDENHUYS [1861] (Ruben Benjamin[10], Dirk Cornelis[9], Dirk Cornelis[8], Lourens[7], Lourens[6], Johannes Albertus[5], Hendrik (c3)[4], Barend[3], Albert Barends Gildenhuisz[2], Bernd Gildenhausen[1]), born 18 Mar 1940. He married on 5 Jun 1965 **Joan (COLLETT) GELDENHUYS** [1795], born 11 Feb 1943.

Children of Ruben Neville GELDENHUYS and Joan COLLETT were as follows:
111111413411 Garth Patrick[12] GELDENHUYS [1871], born 11 Jul 1966; died 14 Oct 1995.
111111413412 Andrew Mark[12] GELDENHUYS [1797], born 13 Aug 1967. He married (1) on 4 Sep 1971 **Michelle RODRIQUES** [1800], born 15 Sep 1971; (2) **Michelle RODRIQUES** [1875], born 15 Sep 1971.
111111413413 Veronica Joan[12] GELDENHUYS [1873], born 1 Oct 1970.
+ 111111413414 Barbara Ann[12] GELDENHUYS [1799], born 22 Jan 1975. She married (1) **Jason Neil KRAHNER** [1801]; (2) **Jason Neil KRAHNER** [1876].

11111141343. Allan Derek[11] GELDENHUYS [1804] (Ruben Benjamin[10], Dirk Cornelis[9], Dirk Cornelis[8], Lourens[7], Lourens[6], Johannes Albertus[5], Hendrik (c3)[4], Barend[3], Albert Barends Gildenhuisz[2], Bernd Gildenhausen[1]), born 4 Nov 1949 in Ermelo, Mpumalanga, South Africa. He married **Linda Magdalene (GEERE) GELDENHUYS** [1806], born 12 May 1954.

Children of Allan Derek GELDENHUYS and Linda Magdalene GEERE were as follows:
111111413431 Oonagh Lorraine[12] GELDENHUYS [1807], born 2 May 1984 in Vancover, Canada.
111111413432 Simon David[12] GELDENHUYS [1808], born 16 Feb 1987 in Vancover, Canada.
111111413433 Anna Maria[12] GELDENHUYS [1809], born 27 Mar 1992 in Belevue, WA, USA.
111111413434 Oonagh Lorraine[12] GELDENHUYS [1867], born 2 May 1984 in Vancover, Canada. She married **Chris MAHNKE** [1937].
111111413435 Simon David[12] GELDENHUYS [1868], born 16 Feb 1987 in Vancover, Canada.

11112111111. Gerhard - j1[11] GELDENHUYS [151] (Gerhardus Bernardus - i1[10], Gerhardus Bernardus - h4[9], Gerhardus Bernardus - g7[8], Adrian Johannes - f2[7], Petrus Arnoldus - e5[6], Petrus Arnoldus - d10[5], Hendrik (c3)[4], Barend[3], Albert Barends Gildenhuisz[2], Bernd Gildenhausen[1]), born 19 Nov 1937 in Worcester, Cape, South Africa. He married on 14 Dec 1963 in Heidelberg, Cape, South Africa **Annaline (ODENDAAL) GELDENHUYS** [152], born 14 Oct 1940 in Heidelberg, Cape, South Africa.

Children of Gerhard - j1 GELDENHUYS and Annaline ODENDAAL were as follows:
111121111111 Lisa[12] GELDENHUYS [153], born 31 Dec 1964 in Stellenbosch, Cape, South Africa. Notes: Pianist - Lisa se Klavier composed by Koos Kombuis

Generation 12

111111111111. Renene Delene[12] **GELDENHUYS** [3] (Preller Matt[11], Abram Carl Frederik Preller[10], Johannes (Jan) Albertus[9], Hendrik Jacobus[8], Johannes Albertus[7], Lourens[6], Johannes Albertus[5], Hendrik (c3)[4], Barend[3], Albert Barends Gildenhuisz[2], Bernd Gildenhausen[1]), born 8 Aug 1968 in Gwelo, Rhodesia now Zimbabwe. She married on 6 Jun 1992 in Drakensberg **Grahame David JELLEY** [13], born 22 Mar 1959 in Salisbury, Rhodesia, now Zimbabwe, son of William Patterson JELLEY [14] and Margaret Mary Elaine WHITELEY [60].

Children of Renene Delene GELDENHUYS and Grahame David JELLEY were as follows:
   1111111111111 Courtney Sacha[13] **JELLEY** [16], born 13 Sep 1993 in Triangle, Zimbabwe.
      Notes: Awarded coveted Grand Prior qualification
   1111111111112 Brendan Vaughan[13] **JELLEY** [17], born 15 Nov 1996 in Chipinge, Zimbabwe.

111111111112. Pey Malan[12] **GELDENHUYS** [4] (Preller Matt[11], Abram Carl Frederik Preller[10], Johannes (Jan) Albertus[9], Hendrik Jacobus[8], Johannes Albertus[7], Lourens[6], Johannes Albertus[5], Hendrik (c3)[4], Barend[3], Albert Barends Gildenhuisz[2], Bernd Gildenhausen[1]), born 22 Dec 1970 in Gwelo, Rhodesia, South Africa. He married (1) on 27 Apr 2007 in Durban **Eloise (HOWARD) GELDENHUYS** [18], born 4 Apr 1972 in Durban, South Africa, daughter of Kenneth Steve HOWARD [22] and Ingrid Stella ESTMENT [25]; (2) on 2 Apr 1994 in Welkom, Free State, South Africa **Marion (MULLER) GELDENHUYS** [404].

Notes for Pey Malan GELDENHUYS
   Completed national service with No 5 South African Infantry Battalion

Children of Pey Malan GELDENHUYS and Eloise HOWARD were as follows:
   1111111111121 Matthew Dylan (Howard)[13] **GELDENHUYS** [19], born 3 Apr 2001 in Durban, South Africa.
   1111111111122 Jake[13] **GELDENHUYS** [20], born 18 Dec 2007 in Durban, South Africa; died 30 Dec 2007 in Estcourt, South Africa; buried in Cremated, Durban, South Africa.
   1111111111123 Lucy Hope[13] **GELDENHUYS** [21], born 29 Mar 2009 in Durban, South Africa.

111111111121. Stuart William[12] **GELDENHUYS** [46] (Johannes Albertus[11], Abram Carl Frederik Preller[10], Johannes (Jan) Albertus[9], Hendrik Jacobus[8], Johannes Albertus[7], Lourens[6], Johannes Albertus[5], Hendrik (c3)[4], Barend[3], Albert Barends Gildenhuisz[2], Bernd Gildenhausen[1]), born 18 Sep 1957 in Bulawayo, Rhodesia. He married **Joy (GOLDSWORTHY) GELDENHUYS** [49].

Children of Stuart William GELDENHUYS and Joy GOLDSWORTHY were as follows:
   1111111111211 Ian Jannie[13] **GELDENHUYS** [50], born 22 Feb 1985 in Johannesburg, Tvl.
   1111111111212 Louise[13] **GELDENHUYS** [57], born 5 Jun 1987.

111111111122. Charmaine[12] **GELDENHUYS** [47] (Johannes Albertus[11], Abram Carl Frederik Preller[10], Johannes (Jan) Albertus[9], Hendrik Jacobus[8], Johannes Albertus[7], Lourens[6], Johannes Albertus[5], Hendrik (c3)[4], Barend[3], Albert Barends Gildenhuisz[2], Bernd

Gildenhausen[1]), born 7 Jan 1960. She married **Lance FRONEMAN** [51], son of Mardel BELJOHN [1935].

Children of Charmaine GELDENHUYS and Lance FRONEMAN were as follows:
1111111111221Jason[13] **FRONEMAN** [52], born 4 Jan 1996 in Midrand, Gauteng.

111111111123. Paul Preller[12] **GELDENHUYS** [48] (Johannes Albertus[11], Abram Carl Frederik Preller[10], Johannes (Jan) Albertus[9], Hendrik Jacobus[8], Johannes Albertus[7], Lourens[6], Johannes Albertus[5], Hendrik (c3)[4], Barend[3], Albert Barends Gildenhuisz[2], Bernd Gildenhausen[1]), born 15 Dec 1966 in Ndola, Zambia. He married **Karen** (**DE WAAL**) GELDENHUYS [53], born 29 May 1966 in Vanderbylpark, Transvaal, South Africa, daughter of Jan Gerhardus DE WAAL [54] and Johanna Elizabeth 'Joey' CLOETE [133].

Notes for Karen DE WAAL
      Twin sister to Susan

Children of Paul Preller GELDENHUYS and Karen DE WAAL were as follows:
1111111111231Chanel[13] **GELDENHUYS** [55], born 18 Apr 1990 in Durban, Natal.
1111111111232Craig Jannie[13] **GELDENHUYS** [56], born 15 Mar 1994 in Durban, Natal.

111111111131. Chanli[12] **BOUWER** [62] (Delene Elizabeth[11] GELDENHUYS, Abram Carl Frederik Preller[10], Johannes (Jan) Albertus[9], Hendrik Jacobus[8], Johannes Albertus[7], Lourens[6], Johannes Albertus[5], Hendrik (c3)[4], Barend[3], Albert Barends Gildenhuisz[2], Bernd Gildenhausen[1]), born 12 Oct 1970 in Vereeniging, Gauteng, Tvl. She married on 6 Feb 1993 **Charles Roy BRINK** [64], born 1 Jan 1961 in Pretoria, Transvaal, son of Schalk Reginald BRINK [163] and Mona Daphne VAN ROOYEN [185].

Children of Chanli BOUWER and Charles Roy BRINK were as follows:
1111111111311Tal J[13] **BRINK** [65], born 26 Aug 1995 in Tauranga, BOP, New Zealand.
1111111111312Nea D[13] **BRINK** [66], born 27 Feb 1998 in Waitakere, New Zealand.
1111111111313Deu G[13] **BRINK** [67], born 7 Nov 1999 in Auckland, New Zealand.
1111111111314Gem[13] **BRINK** [68], born 17 Oct 2001 in Auckland, New Zealand.

111111111321. Hendrik Jacobus (Hennie)[12] **GELDENHUYS** [154] (Johannes Albertus (Jannie)[11], Hendrik Jacobus[10], Johannes (Jan) Albertus[9], Hendrik Jacobus[8], Johannes Albertus[7], Lourens[6], Johannes Albertus[5], Hendrik (c3)[4], Barend[3], Albert Barends Gildenhuisz[2], Bernd Gildenhausen[1]), born 1 Aug 1964 in Bothaville, OFS, South Africa. He married **Johanna Elizabeth (Linette)** (**KOTZÉ**) GELDENHUYS [155], born in Theunisen, Free State, South Africa.

Children of Hendrik Jacobus (Hennie) GELDENHUYS and Johanna Elizabeth (Linette) KOTZÉ were as follows:
1111111113211Johannes (Jannie) Albertus[13] **GELDENHUYS** [156], born 6 Feb 1989 in Bothaville, OFS, South Africa.

111111111611. Caryn Sandra[12] **DUNCKERS** [84] (Elizabeth (Libby) Adriana[11] VAN RENSEN, Maria Susanna Wilhelmina[10] GELDENHUYS, Johannes (Jan) Albertus[9], Hendrik Jacobus[8], Johannes Albertus[7], Lourens[6], Johannes Albertus[5], Hendrik (c3)[4], Barend[3], Albert Barends

Gildenhuisz², Bernd Gildenhausen¹), born 20 Nov 1963 in Pretoria, South Africa. She married **Alwyn WALDECK** [454].

Children of Caryn Sandra DUNCKERS and Alwyn WALDECK were as follows:
1111111116111   Eran¹³ **WALDECK** [455], born 9 Jul 1997 in Johannesburg, Tvl.

111111111612. Brandon Arne¹² **DUNCKERS** [85] (Elizabeth (Libby) Adriana¹¹ VAN RENSEN, Maria Susanna Wilhelmina¹⁰ GELDENHUYS, Johannes (Jan) Albertus⁹, Hendrik Jacobus⁸, Johannes Albertus⁷, Lourens⁶, Johannes Albertus⁵, Hendrik (c3)⁴, Barend³, Albert Barends Gildenhuisz², Bernd Gildenhausen¹), born 20 Jul 1965 in Pretoria, Transvaal. He married **Karen (BOTHA) DUNCKERS** [456].

Children of Brandon Arne DUNCKERS and Karen BOTHA were as follows:
1111111116121   Arne¹³ **DUNCKERS** [457], born 4 Mar 1986.   Notes: Relationship report: Arne is 'Prop' Prellers first cousin, twice removed (her gran, Libby and I are cousins)

111111413311. Russell Allan¹² **GELDENHUYS** [1830] (Myrl Maureen¹¹ GELDENHUYS, Willem¹⁰, Dirk Cornelis⁹, Dirk Cornelis⁸, Lourens⁷, Lourens⁶, Johannes Albertus⁵, Hendrik (c3)⁴, Barend³, Albert Barends Gildenhuisz², Bernd Gildenhausen¹), born 29 Mar 1960. He married in Pongola **Jacoba Cornelia 'Corli' (OPPERMAN) GELDENHUYS** [1831], born 27 May 1963 in Piet Retief, daughter of Phillipus Albertus OPPERMAN [1998] and Alida Jacoba Cornelia OOSTHUIZEN [1999].

Children of Russell Allan GELDENHUYS and Jacoba Cornelia 'Corli' OPPERMAN were as follows:
1111114133111 **Willem 'Willie'**¹³ **GELDENHUYS** [1832], born 8 Jan 1986 in Pongola, Natal, South Africa.
1111114133112**Allan**¹³ **GELDENHUYS** [1833], born 27 Jan 1989 in Pongola, Natal, South Africa.

111111413312. Albertus Marthinus "Bertie"¹² **TRICHARDT** [1835] (Myrl Maureen¹¹ GELDENHUYS, Willem¹⁰, Dirk Cornelis⁹, Dirk Cornelis⁸, Lourens⁷, Lourens⁶, Johannes Albertus⁵, Hendrik (c3)⁴, Barend³, Albert Barends Gildenhuisz², Bernd Gildenhausen¹), born 20 Mar 1967 in Kroonstad hospital, Free State, South Africa. He married in Durban **Carolyn (WOODLEY) TRICHARDT** [1838], born 3 Feb 1967.

Children of Albertus Marthinus "Bertie" TRICHARDT and Carolyn WOODLEY were as follows:
1111114133121**Mathew Carl**¹³ **TRICHARDT** [1839], born 1997.
1111114133122**Cameron Michael**¹³ **TRICHARDT** [1840], born 31 Mar 2000.

111111413313. Michelle¹² **TRICHARDT** [1836] (Myrl Maureen¹¹ GELDENHUYS, Willem¹⁰, Dirk Cornelis⁹, Dirk Cornelis⁸, Lourens⁷, Lourens⁶, Johannes Albertus⁵, Hendrik (c3)⁴, Barend³, Albert Barends Gildenhuisz², Bernd Gildenhausen¹), born 27 Nov 1968 in Piet Retief, South Africa.   She married (1) **Eugene Constante GELDENHUYS** [1841], born 5 May 1965 in Standerton, South Africa, son of Sarel Johannes GELDENHUYS [1985] and Letizia Clelia Ester BOGGIO BOZZO [1986]; (2) **Izak Francois MULDER** [1844], born 13 Feb 1966.

Children of Michelle TRICHARDT and Eugene Constante GELDENHUYS were as follows:
1111114133131   Zandalee[13] **GELDENHUYS** [1842], born 29 Apr 1992.
1111114133132   **Micayla Angelique**[13] **GELDENHUYS** [1843], born 11 Oct 1994.

Children of Michelle TRICHARDT and Izak Francois MULDER were as follows:
1111114133133   **Keanu Brandon**[13] **MULDER** [1845], born 12 May 2003.
1111114133134   **Francois Gustav**[13] **MULDER** [1846], born 14 Jun 2001.

111111413314. Willem Geldenhuys[12] **TRICHARDT** [1837] (Myrl Maureen[11] GELDENHUYS, Willem[10], Dirk Cornelis[9], Dirk Cornelis[8], Lourens[7], Lourens[6], Johannes Albertus[5], Hendrik (c3)[4], Barend[3], Albert Barends Gildenhuisz[2], Bernd Gildenhausen[1]), born 12 Feb 1971 in Durban, South Africa. He married on 19 Mar in London, England **Kelley Anne** (**BROWN**) TRICHARDT [1847].

Children of Willem Geldenhuys TRICHARDT and Kelley Anne BROWN were as follows:
1111114133141   **Connor William**[13] **TRICHARDT** [1848].

111111413414. Barbara Ann[12] **GELDENHUYS** [1799] (Ruben Neville[11], Ruben Benjamin[10], Dirk Cornelis[9], Dirk Cornelis[8], Lourens[7], Lourens[6], Johannes Albertus[5], Hendrik (c3)[4], Barend[3], Albert Barends Gildenhuisz[2], Bernd Gildenhausen[1]), born 22 Jan 1975. She married (1) **Jason Neil KRAHNER** [1801], born 18 Dec 1972; (2) **Jason Neil KRAHNER** [1876], born 18 Dec 1972.

Children of Barbara Ann GELDENHUYS and Jason Neil KRAHNER were as follows:
1111114134141   **Leah Ann**[13] **KRAHNER** [1802], born 4 Oct 2004.
1111114134142   **Campbell Fred**[13] **KRAHNER** [1803], born 18 Feb 2007.

GELDENHUYS FAMILY TREE

ALBERT BARENDS GILDENHUYZS
MARGARETHA HOEFNAGELS - KAAP VERBURGER 23.02.1691

FAMILY TREE – 12 GENERATIONS

ABBREVIATED GENEALOGIES

GELDENHUYS, MALAN and PRELLER GENEALOGY

Readers, take note: This is but an abbreviated genealogy. The detailed genealogy is listed at the back of this book.

GELDENHUYS GENEALOGY

a1   Albert Barends Gildenhuizen
      Born   1640? Burgsteinfurt, Westfale, Duitsland
      Married   1660? Margaretha Hoefnagels, Legden, Holland
      Died   1693   Cape Town

DETAILED GENEALOGIES

b6   **BAREND GILDENHUIZEN ab6**
Born   6.9.1682 Cape Town
Married 31.8.1710 Anna Margaretha Siek, Cape Town (christened 1685)

c3   **HENDRIK GILDENHUISZ ab6c3**
Born   12.7.1717
Married   27.7.1738   Cornelia Swart
               26.7.1750   Sara Johanna Swart
Died   6.8.1770

d7   **JOHANNES ALBERTUS GILDENHUISZ ab6c3d7**
Born   5.4.1750
Married   Johanna le Roux widow of Johannes Swart = 21.7.1748

e8   **LOURENS GILDENHUISZ ab6c3d7e8**
Born   30.3.1777   Malgasrivier
Married   15.4.1804   Johanna Gertruyda Gildenhuizen, CT. (Hendrik Jacobus)

f7   **JOHANNES ALBERTUS GELDENHUYS ab6c3d7e8f7**
Born   21.12.1807   Swellendam = 10.4.1808
Married   6.5.1827   Judith Margaretha Gildenhuizen
Died   9.10.1894   Kroonstad (62.6 yrs)

g9   **HENDRIK JACOBUS GELDENHUYS ab6c3d7e8f7g9**
Born   5.7.1849
Married   2.3.1874   Elizabeth Schikkerling
Died   12.12.1930 Bothaville, Rustpan (81)

h1   **JOHANNES ALBERTUS GELDENHUYS ab6c3d7e8f7g9h1**
Born   8.7.1877
Married   27.6.1899   Anna Elisabeth 'Lizzie' Preller
Died   28.5.1944   Bothaville, Rustpan (87)

i6   **ABRAHAM CAREL FREDRIK PRELLER GELDENHUYS ab6c3d7e8f7g9h1i6**
Born   2.8.1916   Rustpan, Bothaville, Oranje Vrystaat
Married   1940   Mattia Martha Lotter – Johannesburg *19.10.1916
Died   13.2.1972   Pretoria, Transvaal (55.6yrs)

j1   **JOHANNES ALBERTUS GELDENHUYS ab6c3d7e8f7g9h1i6j1**
Married 27.3.1964   Julia Lillian Dippenaar

k1   STUART GELDENHUYS

k2   CHARMAINE GELDENHUYS

k3   **PAUL PRELLER GELDENHUYS ab6c3d7e8f7g9h1i6j1k3**
Born   15.12.1966   Ndola, Zambia
Married   31.12.1988   Karen de Waal, Edenvale, JHB. (*29.5.1966 V.D.Byl)

         l1   CHANEL GELDENHUYS
               Born   18.4.1990   Durban

         l2   CRAIG JANNIE GELDENHUYS ab6c3d7e8f7g9h1i6j1k3l2
               Born   15.3.1993   Durban

j2   **PRELLER MATT GELDENHUYS**
Born   20.2.1943   Rustpan famielieplaas, Bothaville, O.F.S.
Married   5.3.1966   Susanna Catharina Malan – Fort Victoria, Rhodesia

- k1   **RENENE DELENE GELDENHUYS**
  - Born   8.8.1968   Gwelo, Rhodesia
  - Married   6.6.1992   Grahame David Jelley, Drakensberg

  - l1 **COURTNEY SACHA JELLEY**
    - Born   13.9.1993   Triangle, Zimbabwe

  - l2 **BRENDAN VAUGHAN JELLEY**
    - Born   15.11.1996   Chipinge, Zimbabwe

- k2   **PEY MALAN GELDENHUYS** ab6c3d7e4f3g5h1i6j2k2
  - Born   22.12.1970   Gwelo, Rhodesia (now Zimbabwe)
  - Married   2.4.1994   Marion Muller – Welkom
  -               27.4.2007   Eloise Howard - Durban

  - l1 **MATTHEW DYLAN HOWARD**
    - Born   3.4.2001   Durban (Step-son)

  - l2 **JAKE**
    - Born   18.12.2007   Durban
    - Died   30.12.2007   Estcourt

  - l3 **LUCY HOPE**
    - Born   29.3.2009   Durban

j3   **DELENE ELIZABETH GELDENHUYS**
Born 27.2.1945 Oudtshoorn
Married 2.6.1966 Johannes Jacobus Francois Bouwer, Pretoria
Married 26.9.1991 Stuart John McColl * 27.3.1949

- k1   **CHANLI G BOUWER**
  - Born   12.10.1970   Vereeniging
  - Married   06.02.1993   Charles Roy Brink

  - l1 **TAL J BRINK**
    - Born   26.8.1995   Tauranga, New Zealand

  - l2 **NEA D BRINK**
    - Born   27.2.1998   Waitakere, New Zealand

  - l3 **DEU G BRINK**
    - Born   07.11.1999   Auckland, New Zealand

  - l4 **GEM BRINK**
    - Born   17.10.2001   Auckland, New Zealand

- k2   **RENSHA BOUWER**
  - Born   15.2.1972   Salisbury, Rhodesia
  - Married   Craig Brown

j4   **DAWN GELDENHUYS**
Born   1949   Luanshya, Northern Rhodesia
Died   13.8.1954   Chingola

MALAN GENEALOGY

DETAILED GENEALOGIES

a1   JACQUES MALAN
     Born   1665   St Martini D'Aigues
     Married   1694   Isabeau le Long † 1736
     Died   1742   Stellenbosch

b6   DAVID MALAN
     Born   19.7.1708   Drakenstein
     Married   17.4.1735   Eleonora Melius † 1750
              22.11.1750   Elisabeth Marais
     Died   1792

c3   JACOBUS JOHANNES MALAN
     Born   10.4.1739   Paarl
     Married   5.9.1762   Anna Aletta Retief * 18.4.1744 † 4.1795
              19.6.1796   Aletta Bosman
     Died   19.8.1806

d2   DAVID MALAN
     Born   7.5.1765   Wellington
     Married   8.5.1791   Margarita Elizabeth Retief
     Died   4.8.1851   Tulbagh

e5   DANIEL STEPHANUS MALAN
     Born   26.5.1801   Tulbagh
     Married   2.9.1827   Elisabeth Magdalena Moller
     Died   9.11.1869   Tulbagh

f2   HENDRIK FRANCOIS MALAN
     Born   18.10.1833   Tulbagh
     Married 27.9.1858   Anna Margarita Du Toit
     Died   25.11.1912   Lichtenburg

g5   HENDRIK FRANCOIS MALAN
     Born   15.12.1879   Tulbagh
     Married   2.6.1903   Getruida Johanna van Eeden
     Died   29.5.1959   Lichtenburg

h4   FRANCOIS DANIEL MALAN
     Born   2.10.1907   Lichtenburg
     Married 20.12.1932   Aletta Magdalena Susanna le Roux
     Died   3.4.1988   Vereeniging

i5   SUSANNA CATHARINA MALAN
     Born   5.3.1945   Lichtenburg
     Married   5.3.1966   Preller Matt Geldenhuys – Fort Victoria, Rhodesia

j1   RENENE DELENE GELDENHUYS
     Born   8.8.1968   Gwelo, Rhodesia
     Married   6.6.1992   Grahame David Jelley - Drakensberg Natal
     l1 13.9.1993   Courtney Sacha
     l1 5.11.1996   Brendan Jelley

j2   PEY MALAN GELDENHUYS
     Born   22.12.1970   Gwelo, Rhodesia
     Married   2.4.1994   Marion Muller – Welkom
     Married   27.4.2007   Eloise Howard – Durban
            3.4.2001   Matthew Dylan Howard: Step-son
            18.12.2007   Baby Jake – Durban, died 30.12.2007

29.3.2009   Lucy Hope - Durban

PRELLER GENEALOGY

a1   JOHAN FREDERIK PRELLER
      Born   1764
      Married   23.11.1794   Zacharia Christina de Beer (*9.11.1794,† 6.3.1845)
      Died   14.12.1825

b7   CAREL FRIEDRICH PRELLER
      Born   11.10.1809
      Married 12.2.1830 Jacoba Petronella Heyneman († 7.3.1842)
      45 Maria Margaretha Naude (Pietermaritzburg, widow of CP Bothma) M.M. Strydom

c12   ABRAHAM CHRISTOFFEL NAUDE PRELLER
      Born   18.1.1853
      Married   ? Helletta Lephina Botha – died 7.8.1889
      Re-married   ? Maria Elizabeth Pretorius – died 21.9.1893
      Re-married   ? Johanna Magdalena Wessels
      Died   29.6.1907

d1   ANNA ELIZABETH PRELLER
      Born   23.2.1879
      Married   27.6.1899   Johannes Albertus Geldenhuys
      Died   1976   (aged 97)

e1 Helletta Levina – born 2.5.1900, died 15.8.1991
e2 Hendrik Jacobus Geldenhuys
      Born   12.7.1902
      Married   28.8.1928   Adrianna Martha Maria Keyser
e3 Elizabeth
      Born   6.11.1904
      Married   23.7.1925   Paul Christiaan Gideon Steyn Jordaan
e4 Anna Elizabeth
      Born   11.9.1907
      Married   ?   Gideon Malherbe
e5 Maria Susanna Wilhelmina
      Born   27.5.1911
      Married   ?   Theo van Rensen

e6   ABRAM CARL FREDERIK PRELLER GELDENHUYS
      Born   2.8.1916
      Married   ?   Matthia Martha Lotter
      Died   13.2.1972

f1   JOHANNES ALBERTUS GELDENHUYS
      Born   15.8.1940   Johannesburg
      Married 27.3.1964   Julia Lillian Dippenaar

      g3 PAUL PRELLER GELDENHUYS
          Born   15.12.1966   Ndola, Zambia
          Married   31.12.1988   Karen de Waal

          h1 CHANEL GELDENHUYS
              Born   18.4.1990   Durban

          h2 CRAIG JANNIE GELDENHUYS
              Born   15.3.1993   Durban

DETAILED GENEALOGIES

f2   PRELLER MATT GELDENHUYS
       Born   20.2.1943   Rustpan, Bothaville
       Married   5.3.1966   Susanna Catharina Malan – Fort Victoria

       g1 RENENE DELENE GELDENHUYS
           Born   8.8.1968   Gwelo, Rhodesia
           Married   6.6.1992   Grahame David Jelley - Drakensberg

           h1 COURTNEY SACHA JELLEY
              Born   13.9.1993   Triangle, Zimbabwe

           h2 BRENDAN VAUGHAN JELLEY
              Born   15.11.1996   Chipinge, Zimbabwe

       g2 PEY MALAN GELDENHUYS
           Born   22.12.1970   Gwelo, Rhodesia
           Married   2.4.1994   Marion Muller - Welkom
                                                       Eloise Howard – Durban

           h1 MATTHEW DYLAN HOWARD – surname changed to GELDENHUYS
              Born   3.4.2001   Durban (Step-son)

           h2 JAKE
              Born   18.12.2007   Durban
              Died   30.12.2007   Estcourt

           h3 LUCY HOPE
              Born   29.3.2009   Durban

f3   DELENE ELIZABETH GELDENHUYS
       Born   27.2.1945   Oudtshoorn
       Married   2.6.1966   Johannes Jacobus Francois Bouwer
       Married   26.9.1991   Stuart John McColl

       g1 CHANLI G BOUWER
           Born   12.10.1970   Vereeniging
           Married   6.2.1993   Charles Roy Brink

           h1 TAL J BRINK
              Born   27.8.1995   Tauranga, New Zealand

           h2 NEA D BRINK
              Born   27.2.1998   Waitakere, New Zealand

           h3 DEU G BRINK
              Born   07.11.1999   Auckland, New Zealand

           h4 GEM BRINK
              Born   17.10.2001   Auckland, New Zealand

       g2 RENSHA
           Born   15.2.1972   Salisbury, Rhodesia

MOODIE GENEALOGY

a1   JAMES MOODIE

	Born	1757	the last Laird of Melsetter, Scotland
	Married		Elizabeth Dunbar † 1798 had 4 boys and 2 girls
	Died	1828	(71yrs)

b1 BENJAMIN MOODIE
Born   1.1.1789   Melsetter, Orkney Islands, Scotland
Married   1817   Margaret Malcolmsen – had 4 boys and 4 girls
Remarried   1841   Susan Barnett (in London)
Died   2.4.1856   Westfield, Port Alfred (67yrs)

c1 JAMES BENJAMIN DONALD MOODIE
Born   26.5.1819   Scotland
Married   4.3.1836   Sara Maria Johanna van Zyl (1817-1897) Grahamstown 5 sons and 6 daughters
Died   4.12.1894   (75 yrs) Bethlehem O.F.S.

d6 MARGERY HESTER MOODIE
Born   4.12.1845
Married   16.3.1863   Edmund Francis Coleman (12.12.1836-16.1.1898) 1 boy+4 girls
Died   1937   (92 yrs)

e2 LUCRETIA MARIA COLEMAN
Born   15.8.1865
Married   3.3.1896   Sydney Nathaniel Arnott (28.11.1867-14.12.1924) 3+2
Died   13.10.1954   (89 yrs)

f4 STELLA NESTA ARNOTT
Born   27.5.1902
Married   12.8.1929   Alan Whiteley (11.10.1897-8.3.1989) 1 son + 1 d
Died   14.4.1985   (83 yrs)

g2 MARGARET MARY ELAINE WHITELEY
Born   16.12.1935   Salisbury, Rhodesia
Married 11.10.1958   William Paterson Jelley (6.7.1935) 2 sons

h1 GRAHAME DAVID JELLEY
Born   22.3.1959   Salisbury, Rhodesia
Married   6.6.1992   Renene Delene Geldenhuys (Gwelo 8.8.1968) 1s + 1d

i1 COURTNEY SACHA JELLEY
Born   13.9.1993   Triangle Zimbabwe

i2 BRENDAN VAUGHAN JELLEY
Born   15.11.1996

DETAILED GENEALOGIES

Genealogical Numbers: The genealogical number of the progenitor (i.e. The 'Stamvader' or 'family ancestor') of the family is "a", his children are numbered chronological "a1", "a2", "a3" etc.; his grandchildren are the "c" – generation, his great-grandchildren "d"; and then "e", "f" and so on and so forth. For example Pey Malan and Craig Jannie can be traced thus:-

    Pey – ab6c3d7e4f3g5h1i6j2k2
    Craig – ab6c3d7e4f3g5h1i6j1k1l2   12th generation Geldenhuys

The numbers that sometimes appear in brackets after the place and date of death refer to the person's age in years, months and days, e.g. † Kroonstad 30.5.1874 (65.4.8)

Abbreviations used:-
* - born   ~ - baptised   x – married   xx – second marriage   xxx – 3rd
   † - died   ÷ - divorced   c. - circa, about

GELDENHUYS/GELDENHUIZEN/GILDENHUISZ

Albert Barends Gildenhuisz / Gildenhuizen, Stamvader, *circa 1640, Burgsteinfurt, Westfale, x Legden 28.3.1649 Margaretha Hoefnagels. Ancestor was Johan ton Gyldenhaus in Westphalia in 1567.

b1   Arend * Legden, Netherlands ab1 x 28.12.1698 Cape Town Judith SMIT daughter of Heinrich Evert Schmidt of Ibbenbüren † 1713 xx 23.1.1718 Maria Dirkse
    c1 Margaretha ~ Kaapstad 11.4.1700 ab1c1 (must have died before 10 Dec 1702)
    c2 Margaretha ~ Kaapstad 10.12.1702 ab1c2 x 20.10.1725 Stellenbosch Jan LOUW * 10.10.1694 Cape Town "Louwvleit" † 18.3.1770 Stellenbosch
    c? Albert Barend * 1703/1704/1705 – possibly 1st son, died as a baby somewhere between 16.8.1705 and 22.9.1709, deducted from names of next two sons.
    c3 Henricus ~ 16.8.1705 ab1c3
    c4 Elsje ~ 15.7.1708 ab1c4
    c5 Albert Barend ~ 22.9.1709 ab1c5
    c6 Jacobus ~ 19.6.1712 ab1c6 x 14.8.1737 Anna Catharina KOEKEMOER
    c7 Johanna ~ 21.4.1720 ab1c7 x 29.12.1743 Jan DURAND
b2   Elsje ~ Kaapstad 11.5.1674 ab2 x 1691 Jacobus VAN DER HEIDEN (from Haarlem, Netherlands)
b3   Barend ~ 23.12.1675 ab3
b4   Barend ~ 27.10.1678 ab4
b5   Margaretha ~ Kaapstad 9.6.1680 ab5 † before Oct 1684? (next daughter given same name on 8.10.1684)
b6   **Barend** ~ Kaapstad 6.9.1682 ab6 x 31.8.1710 Anna Margaretha SIEK ~ Kaapstad 13.3.1685 daughter of Johann Siek † 1715 and Geertruy Helms of Bremen, Germany
    c1 Albert Barend ~ 21.2.1712 ab6c1

c2 Geertruy ~ 24.3.1713 ab6c2 – born at Vergelegen (previously owned by Willem Adriaan van der Stel)
c3 **Hendrik** ~ 12.7.1717 ab6c3 x 27.7.1738 Cornelia SWART * 4.2.1720 Cape Town † 11.4.1750 Swellendam xx 26.7.1750 Sara Johanna SWART * 31.10.1728 † Stellenbosch 6.8.1770
   d1 Anna Margaretha ~ 30.8.1739 ab6c3d1 x 15.2.1756 Stephanus KUUN
   d2 Zacharya Geertruy ~ 15.1.1741 ab6c3d2 x 1.11.1761 Jan Bastiaan RABIE xx 25.12.1763 Jacobus Albertus VAN ZYL
     e1 Christina Johanna van Zyl x Johannes Hendrik FOUCHE
     e2 Frederick Jacobus van Zyl x Johanna Wilhelmina STEYN
     e3 Geertruy van Zyl x Frederik Jacobus VAN EEDEN
       f1 Zacharia Geertruida van Eeden
       f2 Anna Francina
       f3 Maria Elizabeth
       f4 Cornelia Hendrina van Eeden x Martinus GOUS
       f5 Jacobus Albertus van Eeden
       f6 Frederick Jacobus van Eeden
       f7 Gideon Johannes van Eeden
       f8 Christina Johanna
       f9 Aletta
   d3 Barend ~ 1.7.1742 ab6c3d3 x 12.1.1766 Maria Elizabeth DIEDERIKS
     e1 Martha ~ 10.5.1767 ab6c3d3e1 x 24.7.1785 Johannes Lamberus COLYN
     e2 Cornelia ~30.9.1768 ab6c3d3e2
     e3 Maria Elizabeth Gildenhuijzen ~2.9.1770 ab6c3d3e3 x Jacob VAN EEDEN * 2.7.1758
       f1 Cornelia Dorothea van Eeden * 1.11.1797 † 1827 x 10.9.1815 Willem Adriaan CILLIERS
     e4 Barend ~ 19.2.1775 ab6c3d3e4 † 26.3.1841 x 2.12.1798 Maria Magdalena MAREE
       f1 Barend ~ 3.11.1799 ab6c3d3e4f1 † Gamka 26.3.1841 (41) x Caledon 21.4.1822 Geertruyda Johanna BADENHORST
         g1 Susanna Christina * 10.2.1823 ~ Caledon 16.3.1823 ab6c3d3e4f1g1
         g2 Maria Magdalena * 15.10.1824 ~ Caledon 12.12.1824 ab6c3d3e4f1g2
         g3 Christina Magdalena *11.9.1826 ~ Caledon 23.9.1826 ab6c3d3e4f1g3
         g4 Geertruyda Johanna * 16.9.1828 ~ Caledon 26.10.1828 ab6c3d3e4f1g4
         g5 Barend Leendert * 2.7.1830 ~ Caledon ab6c3d3e4f1g5
         g6 Jan Hendrik * 17.5.1832 ~ Caledon ab6c3d3e4f1g6
         g7 Daniel * 2.4.1834 ~ Caledon ab6c3d3e4f1g7
         g8 Pieter Arnoldus Hermanus * 7.1.1836 ~ Caledon 13.2.1836 ab6c3d3e4f1g8
         g9 Lucas Martinus * 8.12.1837 ~ Caledon 25.2.1838 ab6c3d3e4f1g9
         g10 Johanna Petronella Elizabeth * 12.9.1839 ~ Caledon 7.10.1839 ab6c3d3e4f1g10
         g11 Casper Hendrik Jurie Johannes * 16.7.1841 ~ Caledon 27.7.1841 ab6c3d3e4f1g11
     e5 Anna Dorothea ~ 22.3.1777 ab6c3d3e5 x Petrus Jacobus BEUKES
     e6 Susanna Geertruyda ~ 2.5.1779 ab6c3d3e6 x 25.9.1803 Alewyn Johannes SMIT
     e7 Hester Johanna ~ 4.11.1781 ab6c3d3e7 x Cape Town 9.2.1800 Philippus Johannes FOUCHE
     e8 Sara Magdalena ~ 18.12.1785 ab6c3d3e8 x Chritoffel Johannes WOLFAARD
   d4 Johannes Albertus ~ 25.8.1743 ab6c3d4
   d5 Hendrik ~ 13.12.1744 ab6c3d5 x 22.8.1773 Geertruyda GROBBELAAR xx 18.1.1801 Margaretha Maria WESSELS
     e1 Cornelia Margaretha ~ 19.2.1775 ab6c3d5e1 x 24.1.1796 Dirk HUMAN
     e2 Susanna Maria ~ 16.1.1790 ab6c3d5e2
     e3 Elizabeth Catharina ~ 13.4.1783 ab6c3d5e3 x 2.3.1806 Pieter Gelhardus HUMAN w.

DETAILED GENEALOGIES

e4 Hendrik Jacobus ~ 18.9.1785 ab6c3d5e4 † 2.4.1861 x Swellendam 6.4.1806 Sara Johanna ODENDAAL * 30.3.1783 † Cape Town (daughter of Adriaan Izaak Odendaal and Sara Johanna GILDENHUYZEN * 31.10.1751 † 26.8.1836)
  f1 Sara Johanna ~ 31.3.1807 ab6c3d5e4f1
  f2 Geertruy Anna ~ 1.10.1809 ab6c3d5e4f2 Swellendam † Kafferspoort, Hanover, Cape, 29.9.1881 x 1.4.1826 Swellendam Johannes Willem van ZYL * 1806 Nooitgedacht Sellendam † 13.11.1889 Dwaalfontein, Hanover (they had 9 children)
  f3 **Judith Margaretha** * 20.2.1812 ~ 30.3.1812 ab6c3d5e4f3 x Swellendam 6.5.1827 Johannes Albertus **GILDENHUIZEN** † 23.6.1890
  f4 Cornelia Margaretha * Swellendam 9.8.1814 ab6c3d5e4f4 † Modderrivier OFS 9.11.1858 x Swellendam 1.6.1834 Petrus Johannes BADENHORST xx Gert Johannes VAN DEN HEVER
  f5 Hendrik Jacobus * 2.12.1816 ~ Swellendam 12.1.1817 ab6c3d5e4f5 † Roodepoort, Winburg 1.7.1857 (40.6.-) x Swellendam 2.8.1835 Jacoba Margaretha SWART † 27.5.1841 xx Bredasdorp 3.1.1842 Cornelia Geertruyda Dina HUMAN (she xx Cornelius Muller)
    g1 Elsje Johanna * 7.2.1837 ~ Swellendam 3.7.1837 ab6c3d5e4f5g1
    g2 Sara Johanna ab6c3d5e4f5g2
    g3 Anna Jacoba Susanna * 21.4.1843 ~ Swellendam 3.4.1843 ab6c3d5e4f5g3
    g4 Hendrik Jacobus * 23.10.1844 ~ Swellendam 19.6.1845 ab6c3d5e4f5g4
    g5 Cornelia Geertruyda Margaretha * 17.5.1849 ~ Winburg 17.9.1849 ab6c3d5e4f5g5
    g6 Susanna Margaretha * 25.4.1851 ~ Winburg 25.5.1851 ab6c3d5e4f5g6
    g7 Geertruida Anna Elizabeth * 22.7.1853 ~ Winburg 12.11.1853 ab6c3d5e4f5g7
    g8 Judith Margaretha Elsabe * 22.4.1855 ~ Winburg 1.7.1855 ab6c3d5e4f5g8
    g9 Susanna Maria Margaretha * 27.4.1857 ~ Winburg 8.8.1857 ab6c3d5e4f5g9
    g? Johannes Urbanus ab6c3d5e4f5g?
  f6 Susanna Maria * 30.1.1821 ~ Swellendam ~ 8.4.1821 ab6c3d5e4f6
  f7 Adraan Izak * 18.9.1823 ~ Swellendam 7.12.1823 ab6c3d5e4f7
e5 Geertruy Johanna ~ 30.9.1787 ab6c3d5e5 x Cape Town 15.4.1804 **Lourens GILDENHUIZEN** ~ 30.3.1777 Malgasrivier ab6c3d7e4 (see below – son of Johannes Albertus and Johanna le Roux)
e6 Susanna Dorothea ~ 28.3.1790 ab6c3d5e6 † 19.1.1863 x Jan Cornelis SWART † 10.1.1836
e7 Elsie Johanna ~ 1.11. 1792 ab6c3d5e7 † 24.3.1857 x 3.9.1809 Nicolaas Barend SWART * .28.7.1785 † 11.3.1858
e8 Pieter Arnoldus ~ 15.2.1795 ab6c3d5e8 † Burgersdorp 30.3.1852 (57.5.2) x Caledon 3.10.1813 Catharina Magdalena KEMP
  f1 Johanna Christina * 22.12.1814 ~ Swellendam 5.2.1815 ab6c3d5e8f1 x Andries Petrus CRONJE
  f2 Hendrik Petrus * 22.3.1817 ~ Swellendam 8.6.1817 ab6c3d5e8f2
  f3 Petrus Johannes * 23.12.1819 ~ Swellendam 18.6.1820 ab6c3d5e8f3 † Deelkraal. Tvl. June 1866 x Sara Johanna CRONJE
    g1 Pieter Arnoldus * 14.9.1842
    g2 Jacobus * 30.8.1844 † Colesberg 7.10.1844
    g3 Hester Isabella * 24.4.1846 † Colesberg 2.8.1846 ? x F.G.C.C. WOLMARANS
    g4 Hendrik Petrus * 1849
    g5 Catharina Magdalena * 15.6.1850 † Deelkraal 13.8.1913 x Jacobus Martinus Johannes STEYN * 22.10.1845 †.27.9.1922
  f4 Geertruyda Johanna * 21.11.1822 ~ Swellendam 16.3.1823 ab6c3d5e8f4
  f5 Pieter Arnoldus * 13.3.1825 ~ Swellendam 22.5.1825 ab6c3d5e8f5
  f6 Catharina Magdalena * 24.9.1826 ~ Colesberg 14.1.1827 ab6c3d5e8f6
  f7 Pieter Arnoldus * 20.3.1830 ~ Colesberg 30.5.1830 ab6c3d5e8f7

                f8 Dirk ab6c3d5e8f8
            e9 Anna Maria ~ 14.10.1798 ab6c3d5e9 x Caledon 13.11.1814 Wessel Johannes BADENHORST
            e10 Wynand Hendrik ~ 15.11.1801 ab6c3d5e10 x Swellendam 5.12.1824 Esabe Cornelia MATTHEE
                f1 Elizabeth Maria * 7.3.1826 ~ Caledon 21.5.1826 ab6c3d5e10f1
                f2 Hendrik * 28.8.1827 ~ Caledon 6.1.1828 ab6c3d5e10f2
                f3 Margaretha Maria * 12.6.1829 ~ Caledon 6.2.1830 ab6c3d5e10f3
                f4 Elias Jacobus * 1.7.1832 ~ Caledon 3.2.1833 ab6c3d5e10f4
                f5 Esabe Cornelia Geertruy Anna * 11.1. 1835 ab6c3d5e10f5
                f6 Wynand Hendrik Johannes * 26.8.1836 ~ Caledon 20.11.1836 ab6c3d5e10f6
                f7 Sophia Margaretha * 28.9.1838 ~ Caledon 6.2.1839 ab6c3d5e10f7
                f8 Hendrik Johannes * 6.11.1840 ~ Bredasdorp 21.3.1841 ab6c3d5e10f8
                f9 Johanna Cornelia * 18.8.1843 ~ Bredasdorp 10.9.1843 ab6c3d5e10f9
                f10 Abraham Johannes * 18.5.1845 ~ Bredasdorp 29.3.1846 ab6c3d5e10f10
        d6 Elsie ~ 9.10.1746 ab6c3d6 x Wynand VAN WYK
    d7 **Johannes Albertus** ~ 5.4.1750 ab6c3d7 † c 1785 x Johanna LE ROUX wid. of Johannes Swart ~ 21.7.1748. Burgher of Stellenbosch
        e1 Johannes Albertus ~ 5.4.1772 ab6c3d7e1 x 20.9.1801 Johanna MATTHEE
            f1 Johannes Albertus ~ 20.2.1803 ab6c3d7e1f1 x Swellendam 2.3.1828 Johanna Susanna BESTER
                g1 Johannes Albertus * 22.3.1829 ~ Caledon 19.7.1829
                g2 Francina Johanna * 8.2.1831 ~ Caledon 31.7.1831
                g3 Willem Johannes * 31.1.1833 ~ Caledon 26.5.1833
                g4 Elias Jacobus * 11.8.1834 ~ Caledon 18.1.1835
                g5 Johanna Magdalena Susanna * 19.8.1836 ~ Caledon 8.1.1837
                g6 Hendrik Jacobus * 9.3.1841 ~ Bredasdorp 2.5.1841
                g7 Petrus Jacobus * 24.11.1842 ~ Bredasdorp 8.1.1843
            f2 Elizabeth Maria ~ 2.12.1804
            f3 Johanna Susanna ~ 31.8.1806 x Caledon Christoffel Christiaan HEYNE, is the mother of:
                g? Matthys Johannes * 22.4.1822 ~ Swellendam 31.8.1822
            f4 Cornelia Geertruy ~ 17.4.1808 widow, xx Caledon 29.12.1833 Petrus Johannes GERMISHUYSEN
            f5 Elias Jacobus ~ 11.8.1809 ab6c3d7e1f5 x Caledon 20.3.1831 Elizabeth Helena SWART
                g1 Maria Catharina * 25.3.1833 ~ Caledon 3.5.1833
                g2 Johanna Magdalena * 15.3.1836 ~ Caledon 1.10.1836
                g3 Elizabeth Helena * 11.3.1839 ~ Bredasdorp 14.7.1839
                g4 Johannes Albertus * 19.12.1841 ~ Bredasdorp 13.2.1842 ab6c3d7e1f5g4
                g5 Hendrik Daniel * 4.9.1844 ~ Bredasdorp 17.11.1844 ab6c3d7e1f5g5
                g6 Cornelia Geertruida Anna * 1.6.1847 ~ Bredasdorp ~ 28.7.1847
            f6 Geertruyda Anna * 27.3.1811 ~ Caledon 9.6.1811 x Caledon 19.2.1832 Michiel Burgert VAN DYK
            f7 Sara Johanna * 27.12. 1812 ~ Caledon 4.2.1813
            f8 Hendrik Johannes * 14.8.1814 ~ Caledon 25.9.1814 ab6c3d7e1f8
            f9 Sophia Margaretha * 14.5.1816 ~ Caledon 23.6.1816
            f10 Anna Susanna * 22.4.1818 ~ Caledon 12.7.1818
        e2 Cornelia Geertruy ~ 3.9.1773 ab6c3d7e2
        e3 Hendrik ~ 30.7.1775 ab6c3d7e3 x Caledon 6.2.1814 Sophia Margaretha MATTHEE
            f1 Johannes Albertus * 23.3.1815 ~ Caledon 23.4.1815 ab6c3d7e3f1
            f2 Elizabeth Maria * 16.4.1816 ~ Caledon 22.6.1816
            f3 Hendrik Johannes * 27.6.1817 ~ Caledon 10.8.1817 ab6c3d7e3f3 x Caledon 22.9.1838 Maria Francina VAN DYK
            f4 Johanna Magdalena * 18.3.1819 ~ Caledon 1.8.1819
            f5 Sophia Margaretha * 1.7.1820 ~ Caledon 16.7.1820
            f6 Elias Wynand * 2.6.1822 ~ Caledon 13.10.1822 ab6c3d7e3f6

DETAILED GENEALOGIES

f7 Margaretha Maria * 13.6.1824 ~ Caledon 25.7.1824
f8 Sara Johanna * 10.6.1826 ~ Caledon 27.8.1826
f9 Cornelia Geertruyda * 6.10.1827 ~ Caledon 6.1.1828
f10 Johannes Albertus * 23.7.1829 ~ Caledon 22.1.1830 ab6c3d7e3f10
f11 Louw Hermanus * 17.11.1831 ~ Caledon 6.2.1832 ab6c3d7e3f11
f12 Anna Susanna * 18.6.1833 ~ Caledon 4.10.1833
f13 Barend Johannes * 29.3.1835 ~ Caledon 25.10.1835 ab6c3d7e3f13

e4 **Lourens** ~ 30.3.1777 Malgasrivier ab6c3d7e4 x Cape Town 15.4.1804 Johanna Geertruyda **GILDENHUIZEN** (Hendrik Jacobus daughter, and Geertruida Grobbelaar). Burgher of Stellenbosch

f1 Geertruy Anna ~ 11.8.1805
f2 Johanna Cornelia ~ 6.7.1806
f3 **Johannes Albertus** *21.12.1807 ~10.4.1808 † Doornbult, Kroonstad 9.10.1894 (86.9.19) ab6c3d7e4f3 x Swellendam 6.5.1827 Judith Margaretha **GILDENHUIZEN** *20.2.1812 ~ 30.3.1812 † 23.6.1890. Fought in the Basoeteland War 1856-1865.

g1 Susara Johanna Elizabeth Elsabe
g2 Elizabeth Maria x Michiel Casparus EKSTEEN
g3 Geertruy Anna Johanna * 4.4.1833 ~ Swellendam 20.10.1833
g4 Lourens Pieter Arnoldus * 10.10.1835 ~ Swellendam 20.12.1835 ab6c3d7e4f3g4 † Ceylon 22.1.1902 Boer War POW (66.3.-) x Sara Johanna EKSTEEN

h1 Johannes Albertus * 6.6. 1860 ~ Kroonstad 5.7.1860 ab6c3d7e4f3g4h1 † "Klipfontein", district Winburg 30.8.1913 x Kroonstad Anna Elizabeth SCHICKERLING * 13.6.1866 ~ Potchefstroom 22.7.1866 (7th child of John Peter Schikerling * 1.6.1824 x Adriaana Wilhelmina Petronella MEYER
h2 Susanna Maria
h3 Michiel Casparus ab6c3d7e4f3g4h3 x Sannie BLOMMENSTEIN
h4 Sara Johanna
h5 Judith Margaretha * Kroonstad 16.3.1869 † Kroonstad 16.1.1859? (1959!!) x 15.6.1885 Jan Pieter SCHICKERLING * 17.5.1859 † Kroonstad 9.3.1930 Judith Margaretha GELDENHUYS
h6 Lourens Pieter ab6c3d7e4f3g4h6

g5 Hendrik Jacobus * 17.11.1837 ~ 5.7.1849? – died young or also married a Schickerling? Also possible 'Grootvader' or was buried at Rustpan (see g10)
g6 Johannes Albertus Bernardus * 5.5.1840 ~ Swellendam 2.8.1840 ab6c3d7e4f3g6
g7 Adriaan Izak * 22.7.1843 ~ Swellendam 5.3.1843 ab6c3d7e4f3g7 † Kroonstad 1.1.1904 x Kroonstad 11.3.1872 Maria Susanna Wilhelmina SCHICKERLING * 13.10.1855 Potchefstroom † 25.9.1890 or 15.12.1890 (her brother Henry Edward (Hendrik Eduard) * 22.8.1864 ~ Potchefstroom 21.9.1864 x Cornelia Gertruida Dina GELDENHUYS * Kroonstad June 1873 † Kroonstad 3.5.1923)

h1 Izak George ab6c3d7e4f3g7h1 † Kroonstad x Debora VILJOEN

i1 Adiaan Izak (Attie) – farmed Blesboklaagte
i2 Jacobus Strydom (Kotie Sr) * Kroonstad 1.11.1929 † 29.8.2008 x Ernestine Marlene STEINBACH * Clocolan, Free State 18.9. 1934. Kotie farmed Debsie at Renosterkop

j1 Izak George * 10.7.1958 Kroonstad x Hannelie BOOYSEN xx Wilna BESTER
k1 Suzanne
k2 Marianne
k3 Liezel (children of Hannelie Booysen)

                k4 Cabous (children of Wilna Bester)
                k5 Lena
            j2 Lauretta * Kroonstad 28.3.1960 x Pretoria Antony SMITH
                k1 Charles Lauton
                k2 Jacques
            j3 Hermann Erwin Rudibert 'Rudi' * Pretoria 18.9.1964 x Deirdre BURNS * 5.3.1967 xx Annelie
                k1 Adriaan * 18.4.1993
                k2 Andrea 'Annie' *
            j4 Jacobus Adriaan 'Kotie' * Pretoria 4.5.1973 ab6c3d7e4f3g7h?i2j4 x 25.10.2008 Marriët KLOPPERS * 11.12.1979 - lives in Melville, Pretoria
        i3 Izak George (Sakkie) of Sonneskyn
            j1 Izak
            j2 Jurie
            j3 Adriaan 'Attie'
            j4 Sebastiaan 'Basie' * Nelspruit, Mpumalanga 7.9.1971 x 11.2.2004 Veronica ENGELBRECHT
    g8 Judith Cornelia Margaretha * 12.10.1844 ~ Bredasdorp 4.1.1845
    g9 Johanna Susanna Maria * c.1847! Harrismith 6.6.1881 x Floris Petrus Jacobus DE MEYER
    g10 Hendrik Jacobus * 5.7.1849 – † Rietgat, Kroonstad 4.9.1924 buried Rustpan farm, Bothaville district ab6c3d7e4f3g10 x 2.3.1874 Elizabeth SCHICKERLING * 5.3.1858 † 4.9.1924/1944
        h1 **Johannes Albertus** * 8.7.1877 † Rustpan Bothaville 28.5.1944 ab6c3d7e4f3g10h1 x De Bank, Bothaville Anna Elizabeth PRELLER * 23.2.1879 † 5.4.1976.
            i1 Helletje Levina * 2.5.1900 Rustpan Bothaville † 15.8.1901 Kroonstad Concentration Camp
            i2 Hendrik Jacobus *12.7.1902 Kroonstad Camp x Kroonstad 28.8.1928 Adrianna Marta Maria (Max) xx 1956 Wedewee Jacomina Margaretha Beukes (nee BADENHORST) † 1967 Normandy
                j1 Catharina Susanna (Carienie) * 1.10.1931 x Alphonso MACRAE – Camarillo, California, USA
                j2 Johannes Albertus (Jannie) *15.3.1937 † Welgelegen 3.5.1985 x 11.3.1961 Helena Frederika STEYN Kroonstad (she re-married to Coen Wessels in May 1998).
                    k1 Hendrik Jacobus (Hennie) * 31.8.64 Bothaville x Johanna Elizabeth (Linette) KOTZÉ – Welgelegen. Currently farms Kromspruit, Ventersburg.
                        l1 Johannes Albertus * 6.2.1989 Bothaville
                        l2 Johanna Elizabeth (Joané) *3.5.1991 Bothaville
                    k2 Ernastina Helena (Esté) * 1966 Bothaville x Riaan STEYN – woon op plaas Sidestep, toe Aandster Bothaville.
                        l1 Henriëtte Steyn * 15.4.1987
                        l2 Adriaan Willem Steyn * 23.1.1992
                    k3 Mariana * 1968 Klerksdorp x Johan RAUTENBACH – woon op plaas Vrugbaar, Bothaville.
                        l1 Elaine Rautenbach * 5.5.1994
                        l2 Georg Frederick * 13.6.1997
            i3 Elizabeth (Bess) * 6.11.1904 Rustpan Bothaville †? x.23.7.1925 Bloemfontein Paul Christiaan Gideon Steyn JORDAAN.
                j1 Lulu x Ferreira
                j2 Paul Jordaan x Theresa THERON
                    k1 Marie Louise
                    k2 Elzet
                    k3 Juan
                j3 Jannie Jordaan (Johannes Albertus) x Sue BAM

DETAILED GENEALOGIES

k1 and k2 – Two adopted children
i4 Anna Elizabeth (Lilla) * 11.9.1907 Ruspan † 1993 x Gideon MALHERBE – van Stellenbosch
    j1 Willem x Louna
    j2 Jan x Peggy NN
    j3 Gideon (Dion)
i5 Maria Susanna Wilhelmina (Mini) * 27.5.1911 Rustpan † 15.3.1995 x Theodore Johan VAN RENSEN * Bloemfontein 27.1.1913 † 23.1.1983 – van Pretoria
    j1 Elisabeth (Libby) Adriana * Cape Town 8.11.1941 x 8.6.1962 Arnold DUNCKERS xx Beukes
        k1 Caryn Sandra * Pretoria 20.11.1963 x Pretoria 15.12.19?? Alwyn WALDECK
            l1 Eran * Johannesburg 9.7.1997
        k2 Brandon Arne * Pretoria 20.7.1965 x Karen BOTHA xx Jackie
        k3 Christopher * Pretoria
    j2 Johan – Pretoria * Cape Town 15.9.1944
    j3 Adrian Henry – Kroonstad * 7.1.1949
i6 **Abram Carl Frederik Preller** * Rustpan Bothaville 2.8.1916 † Pretoria 13.2.1972 ab6c3d7e4f3g10h1i6 x Johannesburg Matthia Martha LOTTER.* Johannesburg 19.10.1916
    j1 **Johannes Albertus** * Johannesburg 15.8.1940 ab6c3d7e4f3g10h1i6j1 x Luanshya 27.3.1964 Julia Lillian DIPPENAAR (Julia had Stuart and Charmaine by a previous marriage to Peter Borruso – both children were adopted by Jan)
        k1 Stuart William (Borruso but changed to Geldenhuys) * Bulawayo 8.9.1957 x Manzini, Swaziland 10.7.1980 Joy GOLDSWORTHY
            l1 Ian Jannie Geldenhuys * Johannesburg 22.2.1985
            l2 Louise * Johannesburg 5.6.1987
        k2 Charmaine * Salisbury, Rhodesia 7.1.1959 – Lance Froneman
            l1 Jason * Midrand 4.1.1996
        k3 Paul Preller * Ndola Zambia 15.12.1966 ab6c3d7e8f7g9h1i6j1k3 x Edenvale Johannesburg 31.12.1988 Karen DE WAAL * Vanderbylpark 29.5.1966
            l1 Chanel * Durban 18.4.1990
            l2 **Craig Jannie** * Durban 15.3.1993 ab6c3d7e8f7g10h1i6j1k3l2
    j2 **Preller Matt** * Ruspan Bothaville 20.2.1943 ab6c3d7e4f3g10h1i6j2 x Fort Victoria 5.3.1966 Susanna Catharina Malan
        k1 Renene Delene * Gwelo Rhodesia 88.8.1968 x Drakensberg 6.6.1992 Dr Grahame David JELLEY * Salisbury, Rhodesia 22.3.1959
            l1 Courtney Sacha JELLEY * Triangle, Zimbabwe 13.9.1993
            l2 **Brendan** Vaughan JELLEY * Chipinge, Zimbabwe 15.11.1996
        k2 Pey Malan * Gwelo 22.12.1970 ab6c3d7e4f3g10h1i6j2k2 x Welkom 2.4.1994 Marion MULLER xx Durban 27.4.2007 Eloise Howard

                    l1 Matthew Dylan Howard * Durban 3.4.2001 (Step-son)
                    l2 Jake * Durban 18.12.2007 † Estcourt 30.12.2007
                    l3 Lucy Hope * Durban 29.3.2009, emigrated to New Zealand
            j3 Delene Elizabeth * Oudtshoorn 27.2.1945 x Pretoria Johannes Jacobus Francois Bouwer * Pretoria 1943 xx 26.9.1991 Stuart John McColl * Bromley, Kent UK 27.3.1949
                k1 Chanli G Bouwer * Vereeniging 12.10.1970 x 6.2.1993 Charles Roy BRINK * 1.1.1961
                    l1 Tal J BRINK * Tauranga, New Zealand 26.8.1995
                    l2 Nea D BRINK * Waitakere, New Zealand 27.2.1998
                    l3 Deu G BRINK * Auckland, New Zealand 7.11.1999
                    l4 Gem BRINK * Auckland, New Zealand 17.10.2001
                k2 Rensha Bouwer * Salisbury 15.2.1972
            j4 Dawn * Luanshya c.1949 † Chingola Musenga Plots c. 13.8.1955
        h2 Bettie (named after her mother – Elizabeth Schikkerling)
        h3 Pieter * 1879
        h4 Maria * 1880 † July 1901 during Anglo-Boer War captivity
        h5 Michael * 1882 (could be an Uncle, or brothe named after an Uncler?)
        h6 Joey (Judith) * 1883 (believed named after her grandmother, Judith Gildenhuizen)
        h7 Hendry "Oubaas" *c.1885
        h8? Rose * 24 June 189?
f4 Lourens * 12.6.1811 ~ 7.7.1811 x Swellendam 11.5.1834 Magdalena Wilhelmina BEUKMAN xx Swellendam 30.12.1844 Dirkie Susanna Elizabeth COETZEE † Johannesburg 21.4.189?
    g1 Cornelia Petronella Margaretha * 5.6.1835 ~ Swellendam 19.7.1835
    g2 Lourens Dirk Cornelis * 23.8.1836 ~ Swellendam 6.11.1836 † Johannesburg 21.4.1891 x Swellendam 6.3.1854 Elsie Sophia PRINS of Heildelberg † 3.4.1896. Lourens bought Braamfontein farm but settled on Elandsfontein (now Bezuidenhout Valley), where he did find gold and floated the Geldenhuys Estates Gold Mining Company.
        h1 Frans Eduard * 9.5.1856 † 3.4.1896 ab6c3d7e4f4g2h1 (spelling of family name: Geldenhuys) x NN
            i1 Frans Eduard * Johannesburg 24.9.1889 † Pretoria 28.7.1961 x Stellenbosch 1921 Eunice Elizabeth JORDAAN * 1899
                j1 Elizabeth (Liebert) Jordaan * 16.2.1926 † 7.9.2010 x Prof. Christof F.J. MULLER
                j2 Frans Gert * 19.2.1922 † 1966, gynaecologist, Professor UP x Aletta LIEBENBERG
                    k1 Annamarie * 1955 † 2009
                    k2 Frans Eduard
                    k3 Gerhard
        h2 Dirk Cornelis * 5.1.1858 ab6c3d7e4f4g2h2 went farming in Ermelo x Maria Aletta Petronella OOSTHUISEN
            i1 Dirk Cornelis * Wilgerspruit 15.12.1982
            i2 Frans Eduard Doctor * 15.12.1889 Johannesburg † 28.7.1961 Pretoria x 1921 Stellenbosch Eunice Elizabeth Jordaan * 1899
                j1 Frans Gert Professor * 19.2.1922 † 1966 x Aletta LIEBENBERG
                    k1 Annamarie * 1955 † 2009
                    k2 Frans Eduard
                    k3 Gerhard
            i3 Elsie Sophia * 6.4.1892
            i4 Gerhardus Jacobus * 24.9.1894
            i5 Lourens Daniel * 5.1.1896 † Ermelo 24.6.1958 x Abigail ADENDORFF

DETAILED GENEALOGIES

i6 Maria Aletta Petronella * 21.10.1902
[i1 Frank]
[i2 Laurie 'Lorrie']
i7 Daniel Jacobus * 9.1.1906 x Ada PRINGLE
    j1 Patricia 'Patsi'
[i3 Danie]
i4 Dirk Cornelius † Boksburg 1965 x Maatje Catharina Jacoba STEENKAMP * 17.6.1887 † 27.10.1918 from the great flu epedemic
    j1 Angela Adriana de Jager * 18.4.1908 x Fred GILESPIE
    j2 Mercia Phillus * 1911 x Roux LOUW
        k1 Mercia
        k2 Averil OMally
        k3 Louw
    j3 Willem * 4.4.1913 † 19.7.1988 Interned Pongola x Sarah Johanna Louw 'Sally' GROENEWALD * 1914 † 1989
        k? Margaretha Helene 'Marita' x BRODIE
        k? Myrl Maureen * 11.10.1938 x Duncan Allan SMITH xx Dr Albertus Martinus TRICHARDT * 30.12.1940 (son of Albertus Martinus Trichardt and Susanna Catharina Margaretha de Villiers)
            l1 Russell Allan Geldenhuys * 29.3.1960 Vrendal(?) x 'Corli' Jacoba Cornelia OPPERMAN * 27.5.1963
                l1 Willem'Willie' * 8.1.1986 Vrendal, Western Cape
                l2 Allan * 27.1.1989
            l1 Albertus Martinus Trichardt * 20.3.1967 x Carolyn WOODLEY
                m1 Matthew Carl Trichardt * 1997
                m2 Cameron Michael Trichardt * 1997
    j4 Ruben Benjamin * 29.5.1916 † 24.4.1987 x Dorothy HURST * 5.9.1919 † 27.8.2002
        k1 Ruben Neville * 18.3.1940 x 5.6.1965 Joan COLLETT * 11.2.1943
            l1 Garth Patrick * 11.7.1966 † 14.10.1995
            l2 Andrew Mark * 13.1967 x 4.9.2004 Michelle RODRIQUES * 15.9.1971
            l3 Veronica Joan * 1.10.1970
            l4 Barbara-Ann * 22.1.1975 x Jason Neil KRAHNER * 18.12.1972
                m1 Leah Ann Krahner * 4.10.2004
                m2 Campbell Fred Krahner * 18.2.2007
        k2 Lorraine * 12.8.1942
        k3 Cheryl * 1955
h3 Maria Elizabeth * 15.11.1860 x J.L. VAN WYK or possibly van der MERWE?
h4 Lourens * Heidelberg Tvl 6.12.1864 ab6c3d7e4f4g2h4, member of Transvaal Volksraad † Johannesburg 31.8.1929 x 9.2.1887 Emmarentia Margaretha BOTHA * 1866 † 1938 (72). Suburb and Dam named after her (they had fifteen children of whom eight survived. Deaths were mainly due to diphtheria. It is known that he had three sons, Louw and Frans both built homes close by).
    i1 Emma – the eldest, settled in Worcester
    i? Frank * Heidelberg
    i? Marie x Edward van der MERWE, Marie lived in the Johannesburg 'old house'.
        j1 Louw Geldenhuys van der MERWE * 1936
    i? Frans x Judith Fredrika Salomina GROBBELAAR (their original home is now the Marks Park Clubhouse on the slopes of

Melville Koppies, overlooking Emmarentia Dam. See also Melville Koppies – MK – and history of Johannesburg).
j? Frederik Gerhardus x Gertrude Augusta Maria HERDER
k? Madelene x
l? Elsa GILL
i? Louw – and Frans built homes near Krugersdorp
i? another one of 15 children?
i? Jurie – to Louis Trichaardt, with brother Timo
i14 Eunice
i15 Timotheus 'Timo' x Elsa Jacoba COMBRINK * Aswegan 28.4.1905?
    j? Lourens 'Louw' * Louis Trichaardt 15.3.1937 x Louis Trichardt 3.3.1962 Meyerene VENTER * Louis Trichardt 11.6.1942 daughter of Johan Louis Venter * 12.8.1890 and Johanna Elizabeth Mulder * 15.10.1905
    k1 Lourene 28.10.1960 x Albert LIEBENBERG, relocated to Deneliquin, New South Wales, Australia
    k2 Lourens * 22.4.1964 x but divorced, moved to Australia
        l1 Kelsey-Tegan
        l2 Ashleigh-Lauren
        l3 Lourens Alexander
    k3 Elsabe * 19.10.1968 x Andre PIENAAR Naboomspruit
        l1 Nika
        l2 Ilke
        l3 Timo
    k4 Timo * 4.7.1973 x Tamany NEVIN – Mauritius
        l1 Emma Rachel
        l2 Hannah Lou
h5 Magdalena Wilhelmina * 9.1.1871 x Joseph P. KOK
g3 Geertruida Johanna * 6.2.1838 ~ Swellendam 2.4.1838 second marriage
g4 Dirk Christoffel ~ Swellendam
g5 Barbara Isabella * 11.3.1847 ~ Swellendam 2.5.1847
g6 Johannes Albertus * 7.6.1849 ~ Swellendam 14.9.1849
g7 Jacobus Hendrik Coetzee * 8.1.1852 ~ Swellendam 15.2.1852
f5 Geertruyda Johanna * 24.7.1813 ~ Caledon 3.10.1813 † 1888
f6 Barend Petrus * 3.3.1815 ~Caledon 2.4.1815 † Holfontein, Kroonstad 29.4.1868 x Swellendam 22.7.1838 Maria Elizabeth Johanna GUNTER † 28.6.1862 xx Catharina Helena OOSTHUIZEN
g1 Jacoba Margaretha * 2.8.1839 ~ Swellendam 3.11.1839
g2 Geertruida Johanna *6.4.1841 ~ Swellendam 6.6.1841
g3 Maria Elizabeth Magdalena Johanna * 4.8.1843 ~ Swellendam 29.10.1843 x Kroonstad 6.5.1861 Jan Hendrik COETZEE
g4 Geertruyda Johanna Elizabeth * 22.9.1846 ~ Swellendam 14.2.1847 x Johan Christian Lambrecht COETZEE
g5 Jacoba Margaretha * 21.8.1849 ~ Swellendam 23.12.1849 x Kroonstad 1.3.1869 George Diederick PRINSLOO
g6 Barendina Petronella * 22.6.1852 ~ Swellendam 23.7.1852 x Kroonstad 18.12.1871 Petrus Cornelis BOUWER
g7 Cornelis Janse * 5.9.1855 ~ Winburg 2.10.1855 x Heilbron 7.6.1880 Rachel Maria VAN COLLER
g8 Lourens Johannes Albertus * c. 1858 † Kroonstad 15.4.1864 (6 yr. old)
g9 Elizabeth Helena x Middelburg 30.4.1881 Jacobus Nicolaas MATTHEE
g10 Barend Petrus * 20.5.1864 ~ Kroonstad 18.6.1865
g11 Johannes Albertus * 15.8.1867 ~ Potchefstroom 26.8.1868 † 20.12.1931 x Catharina Magdalena JORDAAN * 10.3.1872 † 18.10.1940

DETAILED GENEALOGIES

    f7 Hendrik Jacobus * 10.10.1816 ~ Swellendam 24.22.1816 † Kroonstad 4.5.1879 (62.6.-) x Swellendam 27.12.1835 Cornelia Margaretha SWART xx Johanna Margaretha Geertruyda ROSSOUW
        g1 Lourens * 31.5.1837 ~ Swellendam 17.9.1837
        g2 Susanna Dorothea * 6.10.1848 ~ Swellendam 8.1.1849
        g3 Sophia Barendina Jacoba
        g4 Geertruyda Johanna
        g5 Johanna Christina
        g6 Hendrina Jacoba
        g7 Jacoba Maria
        g8 Judith Margaretha
        g9 Hendrik Jacobus
        g10 Susanna Johanna
            h11 Jan Johannes Albertus (suspect should read g11)
            h12 Barend Petrus – g12?
    f8 Pieter Arnoldus * 6.9.1818 ~ Swellendam 4.10.1818 † 1.12 1838, drowned in Breerivier (aged 20)
    f9 Johanna Elsabe * 4.2.1821 ~ Swellendam 25.2.1821 x Swellendam 27.1.1838 Simon Frederik STREICHER
    f10 Cornelia Margaretha Susanna * 4.11.1823 ~ Swellendam 22.7.1824 x Swellendam 20.11.1836 Adriaan Johannes KLEYNSMIT
e5 Barend ~ 17.2.1779 ab6c3d7e5 x Swellendam 24.11.1805 Aletta Johanna MARAIS
    f1 Johanna Aletta ~ 25.12.1806 x Tulbagh 8.10.1820 Wynand Petrus Johannes VILJOEN
    f2 Maria Elizabeth * 14.9.1813 ~ Tulbagh 20.2.1814
    f3 Aletta Petronella * 13.6.1815 ~ Tulbagh 29.10.1815
e6 Petrus Arnoldus ~ 25.2.1781 † Rustfontein, Swellendam 27.6.1846 x Cape Town 8.1.1804 Maria Elizabeth MATTHEE xx Caledon 20.4.1838 Elizabeth Christina VAN WYK, widow of Wessel Wessels
    f1 Maria Elizabeth ~ 23.12.1804
    f2 Johannes Albertus ~ 14.9.1806 x Caledon 2.5.1830 Anna Christina Elizabeth SWART (J-dg)
        g1 Petrus Arnoldus * 21.7.1831 ~ Caledon 23.10.1831 † Stanford 16.4.1887 (54.4. -) x Bredasdorp 8.5.1852 Mathilda Marietta BEHR
           h1 Anna Christina x P. WILLEMSE
           h2 Jan Willemse Alexander
           h3 Zacharyas Johannes Wessel
                i? Wessel Johannes 'Poekies' x Corne Joyce – from Stanford
                    j? Lydia
                    j? Jurie * 13.3.1958 x Nicoleen (daughter of Nicholas ?)
                        k1 Jurita x Mycroft
                        k? Nicolette x Nicholas Loubser
                        k? Corné * Vredenburg 24.4.1989 x Louis Olivier – email corne_g@yahoo.com
                    j? Jackie * Stanford
                    j? Nicky * 21.2.? x Amanda
                        k1 Conroy
                        k2 Wessel
                        k3 Nico
                    j? Dennis * Stanford
           h4 Mathilda Marietta * Cape Town 12.12.1836 x Jacob DU TOIT
           h5 Hans Jacob Stanford
           h6 Elias Jacobus
           h7 Hendrik Jacobus
           h8 Johanna Christina x J.P.H. VERMEULEN
           h9 Petrus Arnoldus

          f3 Johanna Margaretha ~ 4.10.1807 † before 27.6.1846 x Caledon 28.2.1830 Hans Jacob SWART * 10.3.1808 † Stanford 6.11.1862
          f4 Cornelia Geertruy ~ 2.7.1809
          f5 Geertruyda Anna Johanna * 15.9.1811 ~ Caledon
          f6 Sara Johanna * 22.8.1813 ~ Caledon 3.10.1813
          f7 Petrus Arnoldus * 24.8.1815 ~ Caledon 1.10.1815 † Vogelvallei, Caledon 23.4.1846 x Caledon 2.4.1836 Maria Magdalena SWART, daughter of Hans Jacob Swart and Catharina Elizabeth Moolman
            g1 Catharina Elizabeth * 12.1.1837 ~ Caledon 26.2.1837
            g2 Petrus Arnoldus Jacobus * 11.9.1838 ~ Caledon 23.12.1838
            g3 Hans Jacob * 15.1.1841 ~ Caledon 10.4.1841
            g4 Johannes Albertus Jochemus * 25.6.1843 ~ Bredasdorp 20.8.1843
            g5 Jurie Johannes Zacharias * 18.6.1845 ~ Bredasdorp 6.8.1845
          f8 Sophia Margaretha * 14.8.1817 ~ Caledon 21.9.1817
          f9 Anna Susanna * 23.6.1819 ~ Caledon 27.10.1819 † Winburg 16.6.1878 x Johannes Albertus WESSELS
          f10 Maria Maqdalena * 7.4.1821 ~ Caledon 14.10.1821
          f11 Elias Caledon 23.5.1824
          f12 Hendrik Johannes * 3.12.1825
          f13 Jacobus * 6.1.1821? ~ Caledon 21.5.1826
    e7 Cornelia Geertruy ~ 6.7.1783 x Johannes Jochemus SWART
    e8 Geertruy Anna ~ 28.9.1785, mother of:
        f1 Johanna Susanna Elizabeth ~ Stellenbosch 27.10 1799 (father given as Juli van die Kaap - from the Cape). A Johanna Susanna Gildenhuizen is the mother of Matthys Johannes * 22.4.1822 ~ Swellendam 31.8.1823
          g1 Matthys Johannes * 22.4.1822 ~ Swellendam 31.8.1823
  d8 Sara Johanna * 31.10.1751 ab6c3d8 † 26.8.1836 x 22.9.1776 Adriaan Izak ODENDAAL
  d9 Cornelia Margaretha ~ 12.8.1753 ab6c3d9 x 17.12.1781 Hermanus Adriaan COMBRINK
  d10 Petrus Arnoldus ~ 5.10.1755 ab6c3d10 x 23.8.1772 Susanna Maria MOOLMAN xx 3.5.1778 Dina Maria UYS † 25.3.1839 (77.6.3)
      e1 Christina Magdalena ~ 10.10.1773 † 27.8.1839 x 30.10.1791 Jan Hendrik BADENHORST
      e2 Catharina Elizabeth ~ 29.10.1775
      e3 Susanna Hermina ~ 16.1.1780 x 17.1.1796 Pieter Gerhardus HUMAN
      e4 Hendrik Petrus * 10.3.1782 ~ 7.7.1782 † 20.6.1869 x Cape Town 17.10.1802 Sara Johanna Louwrens † 15.11.1848 (63.8. -)
        f1 Susanna Hermina ~ 27.1.1805
        f2 Dina Maria ~ 2.3.1806 x Swellendam 2.9.1821 Hendrik Jacobus Lourens ~ 10.1.1789 † 9.7.1881
        f3 Sara Johanna ~ 24.12.1809
        f4 Susanna Hermina ~ 26.12.1811 x Swellendam 5.10.1828 Frans Johannes Cornelia CRONJE
        f5 Hendrik Petrus * 10.6.1816 ~ Swellendam 21.7.1816 x Swellendam 19.6.1836 Sara Johanna UYS
          g1 Sara Johanna * 19.4.1837 ~ Swellendam 3.7.1837
          g2 Hendrik Petrus * Melkbosch, Swellendam 20.6.1838 (Oom Hein) ~ Swellendam 2.9.1838 † Batticaloa, Ceylon (Sri Lanka) 21.5.1904 x Johanna Catharina STEYN (daughter of Daniel Jacobus Steyn and Johanna Catharina Lourens) * Bredasdorp 3.9.1840 † Pietermaritzburg Concentration Camp 10.9.1901 aged 61years 7 days.
            h1 Hendrik Petrus ("Boeta") * Cape province 1860 † 1962 x Marietjie
            h2 Johanna Catharina * Swellendam 1862/1863 † Standerton Refugee Camp 18.1.1902 aged 39 x Nicolaas Jacobus de WET † 1913 (he married Maria Aletta Petronella Cronjé after the Anglo-Boer War, and then later after she died he married Johanna's younger sister Susara Johanna.

DETAILED GENEALOGIES

i1 Pieter Jacobus * ca 1884 † Standerton Camp between Jul/Dec 1901 aged 7
i2 Hendrik Petrus * 1888 † Standerton Camp between Jan/June 1902 aged 4
i3 Johanna Catharina * 6.10.1889 x between 1902 and 1916 ROETS, probably Philippus Petrus who died 1928, then possibly xx van BREDA, Johannes Reinhardt (if so, they divorced 1939)
j4 Catharina Margarietha / Maria * 15.5.1893 x between 1902 and 1916 Machiel Christoffel PRETORIUS who †1956

h3 Susara Johanna * Swellendam Jan 1866 † 14.10.1933 (67yrs 9mths) x 1890? Ryno Johannes EKSTEEN † 1901 xx Nicolaas Jacobus de WET * 1860 † 18.4.1913 aged 52yrs 9 mths (was previously married to older sister Johanna Catharina who died in the Standerton Refugee Camp)
i1 Johanna Catharina EKSTEEN x Coenraad Lukas de WET † 1953
i2 Aletta Adriana EKSTEEN x BEYTEL

h4 Petrus Johannes * Swellendam 25.3.1868 † Pretoria hospital 2.3.1943 x Anna Margaretha GILDENHUYS * 16.5.1889 † Memel 14.7.1973

h5 Hermanus Hendrik ("Maans") x Swellendam 3.1871 † 5.11.1959 (aged 88 years 8 months) x before 1903 Sofia Dorothea Maria ("Baby") du TOIT * Swellendam 3.1871 † Hartebeesfontein farm OR Gansvlei district of Memel OR Vrede 5.4.1921 xx Sybella Elizabeth SCHMIDT

h6 Jacoba Maria ("Kootjie") * Vrede district 1872 † 1949 x Matthys Johannes EKSTEEN † in Natal 1939

h7 Daniel Jacobus Steyn * Hartebessfontein? 17.10.1878 † Middeldeel farm, Memel district 12.3.1960 x Maria Catharina Elizabeth ("Mollie") PRINSLOO * Free State 9.6.1893 † Memel 24.6.1973
i1 Maria Catharina Elizabeth ("Marietjie") * 14.12.1913 † 26/28.11.1992 x Frans Johannes GELDENHUYS * 10.4.1893 † 30.12.1958 xx Jan COLJEE * 1905 † 1976
j1 Maria Catharina Elizabeth ("Mollie") Geldenhuys x Gerrit ZIETSMAN (had three children, Gerhard, Matietjie and Frans)
i2 Johanna Catharina ("Hannie") * 20.7.1915 ~ 31.10.1915 † 3.2.2005 x Memel Johannes Frederick van koppe de VILLIERS * 28.10.1912 † 31.1.1959
j1 Gerhardus
j2 Daniel Jacobus Steyn * 22.11.1936 (older twin?) † before 1978
j3 Johannes Frederick van koppe * 22.11.1936 (younger twin?) x Durban 15.12.1962 Christine Elinor HICKMAN * 4.11.1940
j4 + j5 + j6
i3 Hendrik Petrus ("Hennie") * 28 May 1917 x Elizabeth Wilhelmina KOTZE xx Jacoba Mitha VOSLOO xxx Judith RYNEKE
i4 Francina Catharina Hendrika Paulina ("Sienie") * 21.5.1922 x Abraham Paul Stephanis von BENECKE
i5 Susara Johanna ("Sarie") * 28.4.1933 x Nicolaas BRITS

h8 Frans Johannes ≈ 1877 x after 4.12.1902 [War Claim. Aged 23 0n 4 Dec 1902]

h9 Sophia Dorothea ("Feitjie") * May 1882 (unmarried) † Vogelstruisfontein, Standerton district 15.7.1916 – aged 34 years and 2 months.

g3 Cornelis Janse * 3.5.1842 ~ Swellendam 17.7.1842 (brother of HPG – a.b6.c3.d10.e4.f5.g2 – the one who died in Ceylon)
g4 Dirk Cornelis * 6.5.1844 ~ Swellendam 11.8.1844
g5 Sara Johanna * 10.7.1849 ~ Swellendam 18.11.1849
g6 Dina Maria * 5.1.1851 ~ Swellendam 23.3.1851
g7 Frans Johannes * 28.11.1852/1853 ~ Swellendam 27.2.1853 † 14.5.1929 x Anna Margaretha DEGENAAR
h? Frans Johannes * 10.4.1893 Vrede † 30.12.1958 Newcastle x Margareha (perhaps intentionally spelt without the 't' in 'tha') Elizabeth

GELDENHUYS † 27.7.1937 xx Maria Catharina Elizabeth * 14.12.1913 † 26.11.1992
i? Maria Catharina Elizabeth

??? (missing link)
h?? Hendrik Petrus † 31.12.1960 x DE WET xx c 1930? Catharina Wilhelmina Maria BEUKES * 14.6.1904
   i1 Frans Johannes * 3.7.1905
      i2 Catharina Susanna Elizabeth * 8.7.1907?? x Willem Daniel van NIEKERK * 2.11.1897 † 7.6.1985 buried Utrecht
         j? Frans Johannes van Niekerk * 21.7.1944 x Ina Raubenheimer * 3.3.1947
            k? Willem Daniel van Niekerk * 24.8.1969 x 17.9.1994 Anna Magrietha de Klerk * 6.3.1971 Vanwyksvlei, Boesmanland, Karoo
               l1 Anita * 6.8.2001 Paarl, Cape
               l2 Lizelle * 11.12.2006 Paarl, Cape
   i3 Anna Margaretha * c 1909 x Nicholas Gerhardus Johannes OOSTHUIZEN * 9.11.1899
   i4 Jacobus Ignatius * 21.10.1910
   i5 Gertruida Jacoba x Michiel Josias BEUKES * 2.2.1917
   i6 Sara Johanna Josina x Johannes Stephanus VILJOEN * 23.9.1906
   i7 Hendrik Petrus * 7.9.1917
   i8 Susara Aletta Elizabeth x Gert Stephanus KOK * 24.10.1914
   i9 Dina Maria x Pieter George Slabbert van ZYL * 14.7.1911
   i10 Hermanus Christiaan Michiel * 8.8.1931
   i11 Catharina Wilhelmina Maria * 14.11.1934 x Paul Frans Petrus GELDENHUYS
   i12 Hendrika Petronella *4.6.1941

  g8 Cornelia Elizabeth * 27.7.1856 ~ Swellendam 7.12.1856 (sister of HPG – a.b6.c3.d10.e4.f5.g2 – the one who died in Ceylon)
  g9 Alida Maria * 15.12.1858 ~ Swellendam 17.5.1859
 f6 Cornelia Margaretha Susanna * 11.9.1819 ~ Swellendam 27.11.1819 x ?? xx Adriaan Johannes KLEYNSMIT
 f7 Dirkje Petronella * 19.12.1826 ~ Swellendam 25.2.1827
e5 Petrus Arnoldus ~ 21.7.1785 x Swellendam 2.3.1806 Cornelia Johanna KLEYNSMIT
 f1 Petrus Arnoldus ~ 30.7.1808 x Swellendam 16.1.1831 Anna Christina DE JAGER
  g1 Christina Johanna * 10.2.1833 ~ Swellendam 28.5.1833
  g2 Cornelia Johanna * 17.4.1834 ~ Swellendam 11.5.1834
  g3 Petrus Arnoldus * 20.5.1836 ~ Swellendam 31.6.1836
  g4 Frederik Johannes Jacobus * 7.11.1837 ~ Swellendam 26.11.1837
  g5 Anna Catharina * 7.9.1840 ~ Swellendam 11.10.1840
  g6 Maria Catharina * 10.7.1843 ~ Swellendam 3.9.1843
  g7 Albertus Bernardus * 19.4.1846 ~ Swellendam 7.7.1846
 f2 Adriaan Johannes ~ 22.4.1810 b6c3d10e5f2 † Heidelberg 26.10.1867 x Swellendam 18.1.1835 Elsabe Dina LOURENS (b3c5d2e?)
  g1 Petrus Arnoldus * 18.7.1836 ~ Swellendam 13.11.1836
  g2 Christina Elizabeth * 7.10.1838 ~ Swellendam 17.2.1839 x Lourens Johannes PRINSLOO
  g3 Mathys Johannes Lourens * 12.7.1841 ~ Swellendam 4.10.1841 x Heidelberg 28.6.1864 Francina Frederika PRINSLOO
   h1 Elizabeth Susanna Johanna * 2.3.1865 ~ Heidelberg 9.4.1865
   h2 Elsabe Barendina Francina * 2 August 1867 ~ Heidelberg 1.9.1867 † Heidelberg 6.10.1940 buried Heidelburg x Heidelberg 21.11.1886 Hendrik Albertus SWART (b3ced3e3f2g3h1) *

DETAILED GENEALOGIES

21.1.1865~ Heidelberg 16.12.1866 † 14.10.1940 buried Heidelberg

h3 Susanna Johanna Maria * 27.5.1870, ~ 19.7.1870, apparently un-married †

h4 Christina Elizabeth Cornelia * 1.10.1872 ~ Heidelberg 10.11.1872

h5 Martina Jacoba * 26.6.1875 ~ Heidelberg 15.8.1875

h6 Adriaan Johannes * 12.8.1877 ~ Heidelberg 9.9.1877

h7 Johanna Cornelia * 26.11.1878 ~ Heidelberg 26.1.1879

g4 Adriaan Johannes * 2.10.1843 ~ Swellendam 8.1.1844 x Heidelberg 30.1.1860 Petronella Wilhelmina PRINSLOO

h1 Adriaan Johannes * 21.3.1866 ~ Heidelberg 20.5.1866 [*1867? † Kroonstad 8.12.1898 x Martha Susanna VAN BILJON]
i1 Martha Jacoba Aletta
i2 Petronella Wilhelmina
i3 Adriaan Johannes
i4 Ernst Hendrik Schalk

h2 Elizabeth Susanna * 4.2.1868 ~ Heidelberg 29.3.1868 x Gustav Christian Carl MUHSFELDT * St Georg, Hamburg, Duitsland 5.1.1852 † Heidelberg 16.1.1916 buried Heidelburg (dentist)

h3 Martinus Johannes Jacobus * 13.7.1871 ~ Heidelberg 13.8.1871 x Andriesa Susara Jacoba SWART (b3cd3e3f2g3h9), * 24.5.1878
i1 Anna Magdalena * 11.4.1904 ~ Heidelberg 26.6.1904
i2 Richard John * 5.11.1909 ~ Heidelberg 13.3.1910

h4 Elsabe Dina Susanna * 24.5.1874 ~ Heidelberg 12.7.1874

h5 Petronella Wilhelmina * 3.8.1876 ~ Heidelberg 10.9.1876

g5 Cornelis Janse * 21.4.1846 ~ Swellendam 9.8.1846 x Heidelberg 2.8.1870 Magdalena Johanna VAN EEDEN

h1 Adriaan Johannes Bernardus * 25.1.1872 ~ Heidelberg 10.3.1872

g6 Cornelia Johanna * 12.11.1848 ~ Swellendam 11.2.1849, † young ?

g7 Gerhardus Bernardus * 25.12.1850 ~ Swellendam 27.4.1851 † Heidelnberg 23.1.1931 buried Heidelburg x Heidelberg 10.3.1874 Wesselina Martina Janse VAN RENSBURG * 30.8.1855 † Heidelberg 18.9.1936 burried Heidelberg

h1 Charlotte Maria *18.6.1874 ~ Heidelberg 2.8.1874 † Heidelberg 19.10.1953 buried Heidelberg x James Albert MITCHELL xx Willie van der MERWE

h2 Adriaan Johannes *20.11.1874 ~ Heidelberg 9.1.1876 (He fought in the Anglo-Boer War and was taken prisoner and sent to India. While his youngest brother Paul Kruger (h15)was still a baby in arms, the English troops came to search the house and when nobody could say where Apie was, they took his father who was locked up for the night at the Heidelberg Goal. After India, Apie went to Rhodesia and only returned temporarily in 1915. On the death of his first wife, his children were raised by family. He x Judith Susara Maria Catharina OLIVIER, from Rhodesia, † circa 1919 xx Miemie (Maria Susanna?) van NOORDWYK (sister of h10's wife)
i1 Hester Johanna x Johannes Cornelius BOSMAN (b7c4d3e9f5g7) * 1907
i2 Wesselina Martina * 28.9.1915 ~ Heidelberg 14.11.1915
j3 Gerhardus Cornelis *14.3.1917 ~ Heidelberg 13.5.1917
j4

h3 Michael Hillegard Janse van Rensburg * 5.3.1877 ~ Heidelberg 8.4.1877 x Maria Elizabeth Bester * circa 1880 † circa 1909 xx Heidelberg 3.5.1911 Margaretha Johanna Susanna ODENDAAL

i1 Sara Johanna Wilhelmina * 21.7.1902 ~ Heidelberg 21.12.1902 unmarried †
i2 Gerhardus Bernardus * 19.10.1903 ~ Heidelberg 20.12.1903
i3 Daniel Coenraad * 7.9.1905 ~ Heidelberg 15.10.1905 † Darling 1.6.1978 x Elizabeth Catharina ODENDAAL xx Engela
    ji Elizabeth Cathartina *1.3.1934 ~ Heidelberg 1.4.1934 various other children
i4 Wesselina Martina * 29.12.1907 ~ Heidelberg 10.5.1908
i5 Hilgard Michael Janse van Rensburg * 29.6.1909 ~ Heidelberg 12.9.1909
i6 Elizabeth Catherina * 7.5.1912 ~ Heidelberg 9.6.1912 x Billy Muller
i7 Charlotte Maria ~ Heidelberg 14.6.1914
i8 Margaretha Johanna Petronella Susanna * 14.9.1916 ~ Heidelberg 12.11.1916

h4 Gerhardus Bernardus * 12.8.1878 ~ Heidelberg 6.10.1878 † Heidelberg 16.5.1964 buried Heidelberg (was a butcher in Heidelberg, Cape. Commonly known as John, named by his first witness at his christening, John Thomas Moritz Engel) x Swellendam 25.1.1910 Susanna Maria Elizabeth BESTER * 16.9.1886 ~ Heidelberg 28.11.1886 † Heidelberg 24.8.1978 buried Heidelberg
  i1 Gert Bernardus * 13.8.1910 ~ Heidelberg 16.10.1910 † Groote Schuur hospital 17.10.1976 buried Heidelberg x Swellendam 30.3.1937 Henrika Francina Cloete * 30.11.1908 ~ Wynberg 23.6.1909
    j1 Gerhard * Worcester 19.11.1937 x Heidelberg 14.12.1963 Annaline ODENDAAL * Heidelberg 14.10.1940
      k1 Liza * 31.12.1964 ~ Stellenbosch-West 4.4.1965 x Jean JOUBERT * 29.6.1962 (ab8c1d8e5f7g5h2i1j3)
        l1 Jean-Daniel * 29.1.2000 ~ Pinelands 16.7.2000
        l2 Gerhard * 10.12.2001 ~ Stellenbosch-Central 7.4.2002
      k2 Henriëtte * 18.10.1966 ~ Stellenbosch-North 4.12.1966
      k3 Gerhard * Benoni 10.3.1970 ~ Boksburg-East 10.5.1970 x Vanessa Clark * 2.9.1974
        l1 Gerhard Robyn * 22.11.1997 ~ Stellenbosch-Central 7.7.2008
        l2 Mila Cecilia * 24.10.2007 ~ Stellenbosch-Central 6.7.2008
    j2 Suzette * Worcester 1.12.1941 x 29.10.1967 Rodney Theunis **GELDENHUYS** † 5.1.2002
  i2 Welhelm * 2.11.1911 ~ Heidelberg 10.12.1911 † suicide 9.11.1955
    i3 John * 3.4.1920 ~ Heidelberg 9.5.1920 † Roodepoort 15.3.1972 x Elizabeth Maria Cecilia le ROUX * 16.10.1931

h5 Elsabe Dina Maria * 24.8.1880 ~Heidelberg 13.10.1880 † 19.4.1952 x Andries van WYK
h6 Wesselina Martina Susanna * 12.12.1881 ~ Heidelberg 15.1.1882 (known as Baby) x Willem LOMBARD
h7 Matthys Johannes Lourens * 21.10.1883 ~ Heidelberg 2.12.1883 x Heidelberg 21.8.1906 Maria Johanna MATTHEE (from Lismore)
  i1 Susara Johanna Cornelia * 8.5.1907 x COETZEE
  i2 Wesselina Marthina * 25.1.1910 x OOSTHUIZEN
  i3 Gerhardus Benhardus * 6.1.1912 (?)
  i4 Matthys Johannes

DETAILED GENEALOGIES

i5 Magiel (twin of i4)
h8 Cornelis Ferdinand Janse * 29.5.1885 ~ Heidelberg 26.7.1885 † 21.8.1970 buried Heidelberg (choir singer of the NG church in Heidelberg, Cape) x Heidelberg 26.12.1916 Maria Magdalena de VILLIERS – no children.
h9 Petrus Arnoldus * 6.4.1887 ~ Heidelberg 12.6.1887 (farmer at Standerton) x Joey BOTHA
  j1) Gert
  j2) Ettie
  j3) Pietie - Three sons, Gert, Ettie and Pietie, one of whom was killed during World War II.
h10 Frans Frederick * 6.2.1889 ~ Heidelberg 21.4.1889 (farmed later at Vermaaklikheid) x Johanna Margaretha van NOORDWYK * circa 1890 † Vermaaklikheid 15.9.1978 (daughter of Jacobus Francois van Noordwyk and Maria Susanna de JAGER)
  i1 Gerhardus Bernardus * 17.3.1916 – unmarried
  i2 Maria Susanna * 12.10.1918 x CROUS
  i3 Jacobus Francois * 25.2.1921 – unmarried
  i4 Frans Frederik * 19.4.?, lived in Riversdale
  i5 Wesselina Martina * 23.3.?, x GELDENHUYS, lived in Oudtshoorn
  i6 Johanna Margaretha * 30.5.1934 x van DEVENTER
h11 Lourens Johannes * 22.10.1890 ~ Heidelberg 14.12.1890 † suicide – was a policeman in Johannesburg x Hilda PRETORIUS
  Ji)
  J2)
  J3) Three sons, one of whom was run over whilst still very young
h12 Dirk Johannes * 8.1.1892 ~ Heidelberg 1.5.1892 † Stilfontein 25.1.1976 buried Stilfontein (known as Sammy, farmed at Petrusburg) x Bettie UYS (widow of Uys) – no children, xx Rhoda ? later divorced. One son, Johan; xxx Bessie SADLER (WIDOW OF Sadler) † Dunnotar – no children
  i1 Johan
h13 Hermanus Wilhelm * 21.10.1893 ~ Heidelberg 10.12.1893 † Cape Town circa 1970 x Lizzie de DEER
  i1 Vida – lived in Zimbabwe
  i2 "Boetie" (Gert)
  i3 Elizabeth x Graham THIELE
h14 Christina Elizabeth Susanna * 1.8.1895 ~ Heidelberg 13.10.1895 – known as Violet - † Pretoria 6.12.1984 x Heidelberg August 1921 Alwyn Matthys TRUTER, farmer from Beaufort-West † Beaufort-West 1925 motor vehicle accident xx Heidelberg 6.6.1927 Thomas Louis Francois BURGER, policeman in Kimberley, later at de Beers, † Kimberley 24.3.1970 (a grandchild out of the first marriage is the Springbuck gymnast Alwyn Gerber)
h15 Paul Kruger * 9.1.1900 ~ Heidelberg 11.3.1900, lived later in Pretoria † 3.1.1955 x Pretoria 1922 Johanna Hendrina REYNDERS * 14.1.1900 (her father was killed during the Anglo-Boer War while she was six months old. Her stepfather was Cornelius Arnoldus Roos).
  i1 Maria Magdalena * Koster 1.11.1923 x Wynand Jurie de LANGE – no children

                    i2 Wesselina Martina * Cape Town 27.12.1925 x
                        Cornelius Jacob Daniel PRINSLOO – no children
                    i3 Gerhardus Cornelius * Pretoria 23.12.1939 x Launa
                        FRASER * Pretoria 9.3.1952
                        j1 Venita * Pretoria circa 1970
                        j2 Jakes * Durban circa 1974
                        j3 Francois * Pretoria 1979
            g8 Elsabe Dina Elizabeth Sofia * 9.1.1856 ~ Heidelberg 27.4.185
        e6 Sara Johanna ~ 13.4.1788 x Swellendam June 1809 Cornelis Janse UYS
        e7 Dina Maria ~ 24.1.1790 x H.J. LOURENS
        e8 Cornelia Susanna ~ 26.2.1792 x D.C. LOURENS
        e9. Maria Catharina ~ 11.10.1795 x J.J. TALJAARD
        e10 Johanna Dorothea ~ 14.10.1798 x C.P. LOURENS
        e11 Dirk Cornelis ~ 4.10.1801
    d11 Johanna Dorothea ~ 28.6.1757 ab6c3d11 x Johannes Hendrik CRAUSE
    d12 Susanna Hermina ~ 7.4.1760 ab6c3d12 x D.C. LOURENS
c4 Barend ~ 22.1.1719 x 6.8.1741 Christina Magdalena RADYN
    d1 Barend ~ 1.7.1742 x 8.12.1768 Geertruyda Susanna WESSELS
        e1 Christina Geertruyda ~ 29.10.1769 x 14.11.1790 Frans Hendrik BADENHORST
        e2 Susanna Margaretha ~ 7.7.1771 x 22.11.1789 Petrus Johannes BADENHORST
        e3 Barend ~ 6.2.1774
        e4 Wessel Johannes ~ 1.10.1775 x Stellenbosch 24.11.1805 Anna Geertruyda
            GILDENHUIZEN
            f1 Maria Aletta ~ 17.4.1808 x Swellendam 3.10.1824 Gerrit VAN DEVENTER
            f2 Geertruyda Susanna ~ 18.11.1810
            f3 Barend Petrus Johannes * 6.9.1812 ~ Caledon 21.9.1812 x Caledon
                9.5.1830 Anna Judith Geertruyda KUUN
                g1 Wessel Johannes Willem * 5.3.1832 ~ Caledon 1.4.1832
                g2 Cornelia Christina Johanna * 25.12.1833 ~ Caledon 23.2.1834
                g3 Anna Geertruyda Elizabeth * 11.3.1836 ~ Caledon 24.4.1836
                g4 Christina Berlina Geertruyda * 18.7.1838 ~ Caledon 23.9.1838
            f4 Christina Maria Geertruy * 20.3.1817 ~ Caledon 4.5.1817
            f5 Elizabeth Dorothea Magdalena * 27.6.1819 ~ Caledon 8.8.1819 x Caledon
                20.4.1838 Barend Petrus FOURIE
        e5 Jacobus ~ 29.6.1777
        e6 Geertruy Elizabeth ~ 15.11.1778
        e7 Maria Johanna ~ 19.11.1780
        e8 Jurgen Johannes ~ 23.3.1783
        e9 Geertruyda Maria ~ 26.6.1785
    d2 Jurie Johannes ~ 6.9.1744 † 1777 x 28.4.1771 Anna FOURIE * 1752 † 20.7.1840
        e1 Barend ~ 5.7.1772 x Cape Town 21.9.1800 Elsabe SWART
            f1 Anna Christina Elizabeth ~ 18.1.1801
            f2 Petrus Lafras ~ 20.2.1803 x Stellenbosch 13.12.1818 Johanna Christina
                GERMISHUIZEN
                g1 Elizabeth Wilhelmina Johanna * 15.9.1821 ~ Caledon 9.12.1821
                g2 Elsabe Johanna Wesselina * 18.7.1823 ~ Caledon 5.10.1823
                g3 Johanna Geertruyda Cornelia Susanna * 15.7.1825 ~ Caledon
                    12.10.1825
                g4 Anna Christina Elizabeth Cornelia * 18.6.1827 ~ Caledon 28.1.1828
                g5 Teda Magdalena * 30.3.1829 ~ Caledon 16.8.1829
                g6 Petrus Lafras Daniel * 31.8.1832 ~ Caledon 11.11.1832
                g7 Wilhelmina Johanna Hendrina * 6.3.1835 ~ Caledon 13.11.1835
                g8 Aletta Catharina Elizabeth * 8.10.1837 ~ Caledon 4.2.1838 x
                    Heidelberg 13.9.1858 Matthys Wilhelm BEYERS widower * 1.8.1830
                g9 Barend Hermanus Nicolaas * 28.4.1840 ~ Bredasdorp 15.11.1840 x
                    Villiersdorp 16.12.1863 Anna Sophia Aletta BEESLAAR (daughter of
                    J.F.)
                    h1 Johanna Christina Magdalena * 20.8.1864 ~ Villiersdorp
                        2.10.1860

DETAILED GENEALOGIES

g8 ? Pieter Daniel † Nelsrivier, Calvinia 23.12.1889 x 18.9.1855 Susanna Margaretha NIGRINI * 1830 † Villiersdorp 2.1.1863 xx widow THERON
    h1 Pieter Daniel
        i? Hendrik Willem van Eeden * 16.3.1919 x Anna Josephene Olivier * 4.12.1933
            j? Joleen * Ladismith, Cape * 27.10.1957 x Hendrik Jacobus van Aardt * Lusaka 18.5.1961.
                k1 Nicolaas Daniel * Bredasdorp 25.8.1988
                k2 Leane * Alberton 29.5.1987
    h2 Johannes Albertus
    h3 Maria Silphia * 30.5.1859 ~ Villiersdorp
    h4 Johanna Christina Amelia * 7.6.1861 ~ Villiersdorp 1.8.1861
    h5 Christina Alida
    h6 Francois Lodewyk Johannes
    h7 Petronella Danielina Johanna
    h8 Daniel Johannes
f3 Jurie Johannes ~ 9.12.1804 x Somerset-Wes 2.3.1828 Cornelia Geertruyda GILDENHUIZEN
    g1 Johanna Magdalena * 4.1.1829 ~ Caledon 15.4.1829
f4 Geertruy Johanna ~ 14.9.1806 x Swellendam 2.5.1824 Hendrik Johannes FOURIE
f5 Elizabeth Johanna ~ 28.9.1808
f6 Elsabe Cornelia ~ 7.10.1810
f7 Catharina Elizabeth * 21.7.1813 ~ Caledon 5.9.1813
f8 Barend Hermanus * 23.6.1815 ~ Caledon 20.8.1815 x Caledon 15.11.1834 Margaretha Maria MAREE
    g1 Barend Johannes Hermanus * 6.2.1837 ~ Caledon 9.4.1837
    g2 Burgent Christiaan * 28.6.1838 ~ Caledon 12.8.1838
    g3 Pieter Lucas Jacobus * 3.2.1840 ~ Caledon 18.5.1840
    g4 Margaretha Judik Maria * 13.9.1842 ~ Caledon 23.10.1842
    g5 Elena Catharina * 3.6.1844 ~ Caledon 10.11.1844
f9 Elizabeth Maria * 9.8.1817 ~ Caledon 26.10.1817
f10 Johannes Albertus * 31.7.1819 ~ Caledon 9.8.1819
e2 Elizabeth Johanna ~ 6.2.1774 x Wessel WESSELS
e3 Jurgen Johannes ~ 8.4.1776 x 21.9.1800 Elizabeth Luytje SWART
    f1 Jurgen Johannes ~ 12.9.1802 † young (twin)
    f2 Johannes Joachimus Gildenhuys ~ 12.9.1802 † Heidelberg 20.2.1874 (70.5. -)(Gerhard Geldenhuys records state * 17.2.1804 † 20.2.1874 – and this family kept the surname spelling as Gildenhuys) x Swellendam 5.11.1826 Sara Johanna KLEYNSMIT * 1805 † 8.6.1845 xx Bredasdorp 12.1.1846 Maria Johanna Francina VAN DYK * 18.10.1825 † 16.6.1849 xxx Swellendam 21.1.1850 Magdalena Johanna LOUW * 10.4.1815 † 28.12.1899 (84) daughter of Daniel Johannes and Susanna Johanna Louw
        g1 Maria Catharina * 18.8.1827 ~ Caledon 21.10 1827 x Johannes Matthys EBERSOHN
        g2 Elsabe Luytje * 28.3.1830 ~ Swellendam 25.7.1830 x Willem Ludolf EBERSOHN
        g3 Jurie Johannes * 9.7.1833 ~ Swellendam 1.9.1833
        g4 Sara Johanna * 25.4.1835 ~ Swellendam 14.6.1835 x Heidelberg 12.1.1857 Jacobus Hendrik ODENDAAL
        g5 Cornelia Johanna Alberta * 4.8.1837 ~ Swellendam 3.9.1837 x George David Cornelis BEYERS * 20.10.1831 † Parys 26.10.1831
        g6 Susanna Hermina * 1.8.1840 ~ Swellendam 6.9.1840 x Heidelberg 13.4.1857 Johannes Frederik UYS, son of Cornelis Janse Uys
        g7 Dina Maria Elizabeth * 3.10.1842 ~ Swellendam 26.8.1842 x G.A. van NIEKERK

g8 Johanna Jochemina * 28.4. 1845 ~ Swellendam 8.6.1845 x Heidelberg 24.3.1862 Albertus Bernardus van RENSBURG second marriage
g9 Burgert Wynand Gildenhuys * 16.10.1846 ~ Swellendam 22.11.1846 † 20.4.1916 ab6c4d2e3f2g9 x Maria Elizabeth STEYN * 8.10.1845 † 1.3.1936
    h1 Johannes Jochemus Gildenhuys * 19.3.1878 † 15.7.1946 ab6c4d2e3f2g9h1 x Heidelberg West Cape 22.12.1908 Alida Maria Catharina LOTZ * 15.1.1883 † 6.6.1962
        i1 Dina Margaretha * 26.9.1909
        i2 Burgert Wynand Gildenhuys * 16.10.1912 ab6c4d2e3f2g9h1j3
        i3 Maria Elizabeth * 28.12.1914 x Gert du PLESSIS
        i4 David Lotz Gildenhuys * 5.3.1917 † 22.8.1962 ab6c4d2e3f2g9h1i4 x Johanna von Hugel Joubert GUNTER * 2.4.1922 ab1c3d3e2f1g5
            j1 Johannes Jochemus Gildenhuys * 30.11.1947 ab6c4d2e3f2g9h1i4j1
            j2 Christiaan Frans Gildenhuys * 19.4.1949
            j3 David Lotz Gildenhuys * 8.9.1952 † 18.4.1976
            j4 Elizma Gildenhuys * 6.12.1961
        i5 Johannes Jochemus Gildenhuys * 31.8.1919 † 9.11.1992 x Elizabeth Gertruida de VRIES
            j1 Catharina Dorothea * 30.7.1949 x NN OOSTHUIZEN
        i6 Alida Johanna * 31.8.1919
        i7 Pieter Marthinus Gildenhuys * 12.11.1921 ab6c4d2e3f2g9h1i7 x Susara Cornelia OOSTHUIZEN
            j1 Johanna Margaretha * 24.4.1957
            j2 Pieter Marthinus Gildenhuys * 14.10.1958 ab6c4d2e3f2g9h1i7j2 x Jacqueline Catharina SLABBERT
                k1 Ebeth * 13.5.1982
                k2 Shanel * 21.7.1985
                k3 Jacqueline * 7.3.1988
            j3 Alida Maria * 25.1.1961
            j4 Wessel Johannes Gildenhuys * 31.3.1963 † Riversdale 15.8.1980 ab6c4d2e3f2g9h1j4
    h2 Johanna Magdalena *24.12.1879 x Attie de WAAL
    h3 Burgert Wynand Gildenhuys * 27.3.1882 † 15.11.1964 ab6c4d2e3f2g9h3 x Heidelberg 11.5.1909 Anna Ada Petronella HOPKINS * 12.5.1883 † 6.6.1960 ab6c5
        i1 Sarah * 18.12.1909 † 10.1.1979 x Heidelberg 28.11.1933 Jacobus Johannes UYS * 18.1.1885 † 5.10.1944 G255
        i2 Maria Elizabeth * 15.12.1913 † c 1994 x Philippus Lodewicus WESSELS † c 1991 ab2c2d4e4f7g10h1i1
        i3 Anna Yda * 19.5.1919 x Freddie FALCK
        i4 Burgert Wynand Gildenhuys * 2.10.1924 ab6c4d2e3f2g9h3i4
    h4 Maria Elizabeth * 4.12.1885 x Heidelberg West Cape 7.9.1909 Johan Adam Kunz UYS * 27.1.1885 † 30.9.1964 H260
        i1 Maria Elizabeth Uys * 16.5.1910 H260d1 x Heidelberg 29.3.1932 Pieter de WIT * 2.7.1903
        i2 Helena Kunz Uys * 30.1.1913 H260d2
        i3 Jacobus Lodewyk Uys * 8.12.1920 x Stellenbosch 3.2.1962 Margaretha Elizabeth Carolina van der MERWE * 21.12.1936
        i4 Burgert Gildenhuys Uys * 27.2.1927 x Cape Town Anna Margaretha OOSTHUIZEN

DETAILED GENEALOGIES

f2 – (as per Gerhard records, as follows) Johannes Joachimus GILDENHUYS * 17.2.1804 † 20.2.1874 ab6c4d2e3f2 x 21.1.1850 Swellendam Sara Johanna KLEYNSMIT * c 1805 † 8.6.1845 Swellendam ab2c8 xx 5.11.1826 Swellendam Johanna Francina van DYK * 18.10.1825 † 20.4.1916 ab6c4d2e3f2g9 xxx Magdalena Johanna LOUW * 10.41815 † 28.12.1899 ab5c1d1e1f2g7 (x Swellendam 21.1.1850 – same date as marriage of Sara Johanna Kleynsmit!)

    g1/g9 Burgent Wynand Gildenhuys * 16.10.1846 † 20.4.1916 ab6c4d2e3f2g9 x Maria Elizabeth STEYN * 8.10.1845 † 1.3.1936

    g2/g10 Johannes Jochemus Gildenhuys * 3.1.1849 ab6c4d2e3f2g10 x Elsabe SWART

g10 Johannes Jochemus * 3.1.1849 ~ Swellendam 11.2.1849 ab6c4d2e3f2g10 Volksraadslid x Swellendam 1877 Elsabe SWART third marriage

g11 Daniel Johannes * 23.6.1852 ~ Swellendam 13.8.1852

g12 Hans Jacob * 7.5.1855 ~ Swellendam 3.6.1855 † 26.1.1923 ab6c4d2e3f2g12 x c 1877 Christina Wilhelmina de WAAL * 25.1.1850 † 2.6.1894 ab2c7d1e2f13

    h1 Johannes Jochemus Gildenhuys * 2.9.1878 † 27.9.1956 ab6c4d2e3f2g12h1 x Ellie BEKKER

    h2 Pieter de Waal Gildenhuys * 27.5.1880 ab6c4d2e3f2g12h2 x Sienie SCHOEMAN

    h3 Daniel Jacob Gildenhuys * 23.9.1881 † 15.4.1966 ab6c4d2f2g12h3 x Heidelberg, West Cape 1.8.1911 Helena Jacomina UYS * 6.10.1886 † 9.3.1914 xx Annie TERBLANCHE xxx Gertruida du PLESSIS

        i1 Hans Jacob Gildenhuys * 14.8.1912 Strydenburg ab6c4d2e3f2g12h3i1 x 23.3.1940 Margaretha Magdalena COETZEE * 29.4.1915

            j1 Elizabeth Gildenhuys x Jacobus Johannes ENGELBRECHT

            j2 Daniel Jacob Gildenhuys x Ester Roos BARRY

                k1 Hans Jacob Gildenhuys ab6c4d2e3f2g12h3i1j2k1

                k2 Barry Gildenhuys

                k3 Elizabeth Gildenhuys

    h4 Burgent Wynand Gildenhuys * 12.7.1855 ab6c4d2e3f2g12h4 x Hetta SLABBERT

        i1 Johan Gildenhuys * c 1924 † c 1973 x Tienie Axelson

            j1 Karen Gildenhuys

            j2 Julie Gildenhuys

            j3 Marga Gildenhuys

    h5 Arend Jacobus Gildenhuys * 19.6.1887 ab6c4d2e3f2g12h5

    h6 Christina Wilhelmina de Waal Gildenhuys (daughter of Johanna Eksteen?) * 28.10.1896 (born 5 months after fathers marriage to Johanna) ab6c4d2e3f2g12h6 x William John Watt van JAARSVELD

    h7 Jacobus Johannes Eksteen Gildenhuys * 11.2.1898 † 11.9.1975 ab6c4d2e3f2g12h7 x Martha Hester Meyer * 1.8.1897 † 9.11.1986

    h8 Magdalena Johanna Gildenhuys * 4.6.1899

    h9 Hermanus de Waal Gildenhuys * 3.1.1902 † 21.11.1973 ab6c4d2e3f2g12h9

    h10 Johanna Maria Magdalena Gildenhuys * 24.3.1903 † 28.4.1977 ab6c4d2e3f2g12h10

    h11 Hans Maarten Luther Gildenhuys * 10.1.1906 † 24.5.1963 ab6c4d2e3f2g12h11 x 31.7.1937 Cape Town Ester de WET *21.1.1913

        i1 Hans Jacob Gildenhuys * 13.12.1938 ab6c4d2e3f2g12h11i1 x Anna Catharina Elizabeth BRINK

            j1 Hans Maartin Luther Gildenhuys * 2.7.1973

            j2 Hermanus Daniel Gildenhuys * 12.12.1978 ab6c4d2e3f2g12h11i1j2

        i2 Ena Gildenhuys * 21.9.1945 x Hendrik Daniel KANNEMEYER * 14.2.1947

    h12 Elizabeth Gildenhuys * 10.9.1907 ab6c4d2e3f2g12h12 x Frikkie THERON

    h13 Jacomina Aetta Gildenhuys * 29.11.1911 † 8.9.1987 ab6c4d2e3f2g12h13

f3 Jurgen Johannes ~ 6.7.1806 x 5.11.1826 Dina Maria KLEYNSMIT xx Swellendam 23.11.1839 Elizabeth Catharina BLOEM
  g1 Jurie Johannes Gildenhuys * 14.9.1827 ~ Caledon 21.10.1827 ab6c4d2e3f3g1 x 13.9.1847 Jacoba Elizabeth DE JAGER * 22.8.1829 ab9c3d4e5f1
    h1 Jurie Johannes Hendrik Gildenhuys * 7.7.1848 † 4.6.1902 ab6c4d2e3f3g1h1 x 30.12.1873 Sara Susanna Johanna PIENAAR * 17.8.1852 † 3.5.1884 xx 21.10.1884 Dina Elizabeth Johanna KOEN * 25.5.1882? (probably born 1862 and not 1882)
      i1 Jurie Johannes Gildenhuys * 3.9.1874 † 20.5.1905 ab6c4d2e3f3g1h1i1
      i2 Magdalena Maryna * 7.10.1876
      i3 Jacoba Elizabeth * 15.11.1878
      i4 Sara Susanna * 4.12.1880 † 21.4.1964 x 20.1.1903 Gerhardus Johannes Beukes KOEN * 3.8.1878 † 3.7.1919
      i5 Jacoba Elizabeth Koen (from second marriage) * 28.10.1885 x Marthys Johannes ODENDAAL * 18.10.1883 † 6.12.1918
      i6 Dina Elizabeth * 27.2.1887 x Marthinus Johannes GROENEWALD * 4.10.1886
      i7 Louisa * 20.4.1894 † 21.7.1972 x Sameul Lodewyk Theodorus de VILLIERS * 22.12.1885 † 4.9.1947
    h2 Louis Christiaan Johannes Gildenhuys * 24.11.1849 † 28.2.1865 ab6c4d2e3f3g1h2
    h3 Adriaan Hendrik Gildenhuys * 30.9.1851 † 1.9.1918 ab6c4d2e3f3g1h3 x 3.7.1876 Sophia Elizabeth de JAGER * 11.6.1859 † 16.9.1928
      i1 Jacoba Elizabeth * 12.5.1877 † 27.6.1949 x 10.1.1905 Hendrik J ODENDAAL * 10.12.1872 † 23.12.1946
      i2 Sophia Elizabeth Jacoba * 13.9.1878 † 18.6.1905 x 7.7.1903 Louis C A ODENDAAL * 25.1.1872
      i3 Jurie Johannes Gildenhuys * 7.1.1881 † 9.4.1935 ab6c4d2e3f3g1h3i3 x 26.6.1915 Mabel Aletta NORVAL * 8.9.1889 † 2.8.1977
        j1 Adriaan Hendrik Gildenhuys * 10.8.1916 † 10.5.1993 ab6c4d2e3f3g1h3i3j1 x 12.4.1941 Johanna Elizabeth Helena van WYK * 3.12.1921
          k1 Eleonora * 23.10.1942 x NN GEYSER
          k2 Mabel Aletta * 5.9.1944 x NN POTGIETER
          k3 Johanna Elizabeth * 3.12.1946 x NN GUTTER
          k3 Adriana * 27.3.1948
          k4 Maria Elizabeth * 3.2.1956 x NN van NIEKERK
        j2 Johannes Norval Gildenhuys * 18.2.1918 † 22.7.1964 ab6c4d2e3f3g1h3i3j2 x 4.1.1941 Alida Paulina van JAARSVELD * 7.7.1918 † 2.7.1994
          k1 Alida * 5.3.1943 † 30.10.1948
          k2 Jurie Johannes Deo Gildenhuys * 25.11.1944 † 29.6.1968 ab6c4d2e3f3g1h3i3j2k2
          k3 Jacobus Norval Gildenhuys * 1.9.1950 ab6c4d2e3f3g1h3i3j2k3 x Carin du TOIT * 6.11.1952
            l1 Johannes Norval Gildenhuys * 13.7.1982 ab6c4d2e3f3g1h3i3j2k3l1
            l2 Frieda * 30.3.1984
            l3 Jacques Gildenhuys * 16.4.1993
          k4 Adiaan Hendrik Gildenhuys * 6.4.1952 † 4.4.1968 ab6c4d2e3f3g1h3i3j2k4
          k5 Mabel Amora * 31.1.1954 x Pieter de WAAL * 18.4.1952
          k6 Albert Barend Gildenhuys * 23.2.1956 ab6c4d2e3f3g1h3i3j2k6 x Margaretha Johanna LAZARUS * 19.3.1959
            l1 Martha Alida * 19.1.1985
            l2 Jurie Norval Gildenhuys * 1.1.1988 ab6c4d2e3f3g1h3i3j2k6l2

DETAILED GENEALOGIES

   I3 Grethe * 1.10.1991
  j3 Jurie Johannes Gildenhuys * 5.6.1921 † 25.9.1965 ab6c4d2e3f3g1h3i3j3 x 2.2.1947 Elsie Susanna BADENHORST * 8.4.1924
    k1 Jurie Johannes Gildenhuys * 9.8.1948 ab6c4d2e3f3g1h3i3j3k1 x 22.1.1972 Johanna Adriana RIEKERT * 9.11.1950
     I1 Anna Cecilia * 6.3.1973
     I2 Elsie Susanna * 16.5.1974
     I3 Johanna Adriana * 22.11.1975
     I4 Jurie Johannes Riekert Gildenhuys * 3.2.1979 ab6c4d2e3f3g1h3i3j3k1l4
     I5 Elizabeth Louisa * 10.2.1983
    k2 Hendrik Jacobus Gildenhuys * 3.6.1950 ab6c4d2e3f3g1h3i3j3k2 x 20.11.1971 Anna Susanna STEYN * 2.5.1950
     I1 Annemien * 19.11.1974
     I2 Suzanne * 24.9.1977
     I3 Hendrik Badenhorst Gildenhuys * 18.2.1981 ab6c4d2e3f3g1h3i3j3k2l3
     I4 Jadien Gildenhuys * 25.2.1983
    k3 Dina Maria * 6.3.1952 x 29.11.1974 John Samuel Frederick BOTHA * 11.4.1952
    k4 Mabel Aletta * 8.4.1955 x 17.7.1976 Pieter Jozua ROSSOUW * 1.6.1955
  j4 Amy-Louise * 9.9.1924 x 25.3.1950 Willem du Toit MALAN * 29.9.1925
  j5 Sophia Elizabeth * 28.7.1926 x 22.3.1958 Christiaamn J ELS * 28.11.1923
 i4 Adriaan Hendrik Gildenhuys * 23.4.1884 † 9.5.1939 ab6c4d2e3f3g1h3i4 x Gesina Elizabeth Maria CRONJE * 8.9.1889
  j1 Dirkie Cornelia * 1.9.1911
  j2 Sophia Elizabeth Jacoba * 8.8.1915
  j3 Gesina Elizabeth Maria * 12.12.1917 † 24.5.1984
  j4 Jacoba Elizabeth * 23.10.1921
  j5 Johannes Petrus Cronje Gildenhuys ab6c4d2e3f3g1h3i4j5
 i5 Lourens Christiaan Gildenhuys * 20.3.1894 † 14.2.1996 ab6c4d2e3f3g1h3i5 x 20.3.1915 Dina Maria THERON * 5.8.1894 † 19.1.1980
  j1 Adriaan Hendrik Gildenhuys * 12.1.1918 † 14.2.1996 ab6c4d2e3f3g1h3i5j1 x 4.5.1940 Cecilia Johanna WOLFAARDT * 27.7.1920
   k1 Hester Germina * 18.2.1942
   k2 Dina Maria * 6.5.1943
   k3 Lourens Christiaan Gildenhuys * 19.11.1947 ab6c4d2e3f3g1h3i5j1k3 x 2.8.1969 Elsabe LUDDERD
    I1 Mariette * 29.6.1970
    I2 Andre Gildenhuys * 11.6.1971 ab6c4d2e3f3g1h3i5j1k3l2
   k4 Cecilia Johanna
  j2 Dina Maria * 10.12.1920 x 12.3.1040 Christiaan Erasmus WENTZEL * 7.7.1917
 h4 Lourens Christian Jacobus Gildenhuys * 4.9.1853 † 20.2.1931 ab6c4d2e3f3g1h4 x 18.8.1886 Hester Johanna de JAGER * 19.2.1870 † 9.1.1936

i1 Jurie Johannes Gildenhuys * 23.8.1887 † 19.4.1923 ab6c4d2e3f3g1h4i1 x 25.6.1912 Elizabeth Maria MASSYN * 25.6.1892 † 17.10.1979
   j1 Lourens Christiaan Gildenhuys * 13.2.1914 † 20.9.1987 ab6c4d2e3f3g1h4i1j1 x 1.11.1941 Hildegard WESSEL * 20.10.1920
      k1 Jurie Johannes Gildenhuys * 26.2.1943 x 10.11.1973 Elizabeth Josina Maria van STADEN * 5.4.1947
         l1 Lourens Christiaan Gildenhuys * 5.6.1974 ab6c4d2e3f3g1h4i1j1k1l1
         l2 Marthinus Petrus Gildenhuys * 14.10.1975 ab6c4d2e3f3g1h4i1j1k1l2
         l3 Lize-Marie * 3.9.1984
      k2 Maria Magaretha * 20.10.1946 x 19.10.1968 Alan John SAUNDERS * 23.3.1945
      k3 Elizabeth Maria * 20.10.1946 (a twin) x 26.9.1869 Johannes Wilhelmus Fourie JOUBERT * 22.3.1946
      k4 Carl August Gildenhuys * 18.11.1949 ab6c4d2e3f3g1h4i1j1k4 x 24.2.1973 Susanna Fransina Maria DAVEL * 30.5.1951
         l1 Lourens Christiaan Gildenhuys * 25.9.1974 ab6c4d2e3f3g1h4i1j1k4l1
         l2 Elizabeth Margaretha * 6.1.1977
         l3 Hilegard Gildenhuys * 23.9.1982
      k5 Hildegard Gildenhuys * 29.4.1957 x 20.12.1980 Johannes Jurgens van VREDEN * 3.11.1956
   j2 Frans Adam Gildenhuys * 31.3.1918 † 20.5.1971 ab6c4d2e3f3g1h4i1j2 x 7.6.1947 Magdalena Jacomina van VUUREN
      k1 Jurie Johannes Gildenhuys * 7.7.1948 ab6c4d2e3f3g1h4i1j2k1
      k2 Getruida Elizabeth * 31.3.1953 x 10.12.1977 Lucas Rudolph BOSHOF * 5.1.1954
   j3 Jurie Johannes Gildenhuys * 20.12.1920 † 2003 ab6c4d2e3f3g1h4i1j3 x 20.12.1945 Hendrina Susanna Joubert KRYNAUW * Stellenbosch 4.10.1922
      k1 Ester Maria * 24.10.1947 x 20.12.1945 Arthur Nightingale Pringle * 16.12.1944
      k2 Maria Elizabeth * 12.9.1949 x 27.9.1975 Andre du PLESSIS * 29.11.1950
      k3 Jurie Johannes Gildenhuys * 4.10.1952 † 31.8.1989 x 16.12.1976 Annemare ENGELBRECHT * 3.2.1956
         l1 Johanna Margaretha * 3.3.1980
         l2 Hendrina Susanna * 13.3.1982
         l3 Annie Elizabeth * 5.7.1984
      k4 Dawid Atonie Gildenhuys * 30.9.1954 † 1.2.1965
      k5 Lourens Christiaan Gildenhuys * 27.11.1955 x 15.12.1979 Hannaliza NEL * 23.12.1957
         l1 Jurie Johannes Gildenhuys * 12.8.1984
         l2 Zeneldi Hester* 2.5.1986
         l3 Loura Christi * 31.3.1989
      k6 Hendrina Susanna * 6.2.1957 x 14.8.1982 Hendrik Petrus WOLMARANS * 29.9.1954
      k7 Engela Johanna * 30.4.1960 x 24.9.1983 Frederik Strauss FRANKEN * 5.4.1960
      k8 Petro Christa * 25.5.1962 x 22.6.1985 Wessel Christiaan OOSTHUIZEN
   j4 Pieter Christiaan Gildenhuys * 20.12.1920
h5 Dina Johanna Gildenhuys *7.10.1855 x Koos ODENDAAL

DETAILED GENEALOGIES

h6 Jan Jochemus Gildenhuys *27.7.1857 † 2.2.1859
g2 Adriaan Hendrik * 28.1.1830 ~ Caledon 12.2.1830
g3 Maria Catharina Magdalena * 15.5.1832 ~ Caledon 2.9.1832
g4 Johannes Jochemus Gildenhuys * 2.8.1834 ~ Caledon 22.9.1834 ab6c4d2e3f3g4 x c. 1855 Martha Maria Jacoba de WIT * 6.3.1833 † 25.2.1870, Riversdale xx Heidelberg 3.1.1871 Susanna Maria Emerentia van RENSBURG * 3.9.1849 ab1c3d11e8f5
    h1 Jury Johannes Gildenhuys * 14.4.1857 † 19.1.1912 Riversdale ab6c4d2e3f3g4h1 x c.1859 Maria Catharina Sophia SWART † Riversdale 18.7.1931
        i1 Anna Margaretha * c. 1883 ab6c4d2e3f3g4h1i1 x Willem Daniel SNYMAN
        i2 Martha Margaretha * Riversdale 26.7.1885 † 21.4.1958 x Cornelis Godlieb Coenraad RALL * 27.6.1891
        i3 Jan Jochemus Gildenhuys * c. 1887 ab6c4d2e3f3g4h1i3 x Anna van WYK
        i4 Maria Catharina Sophia Gildenhuys * 30.9.1889 † Riversdale 25.1.1994 x Quinton Eusebius Bailey PAINTER * 20.3.1883 † Riversdale 16.3.1969
            j1 Maria Catharina Painter x 4.3.1911 † Riversdale 14.6.1949 x Johannes STEYN
            j2 Gerbrechta Elizabeth * 10.9.1914 x Jurie Johannes Wilhelm CRONJE
            j3 Quinton Bailey Painter * 11.6.1918 † Potchefstroom 12.3.1986 x Johanna Maria DE LEEUW * Willowmore 25.11.1926 † Saldanha 17.4.1985
            j4 Emmarentia x Norman Paul van GRAAN
        i5 Dina Maria Catharina * 1.7.1891 x Jacob van WYK
        i6 Matthys Lourens Gildenhuys * 23.1.1893
        i7 Elizabeth Maria * 14.1.1895 x Louis CROUS
        i8 Jurie Johannes Gildenhuys * 26.9.1897 † 16.7.1973 ab6c4d2e3f3g4h1i8 x 28.1.1930 Johanna Catharina Muller * 14.11.1896
            j1 Maria * 12.7.1931 † 22.10.1956 x Pieter Gerhardus Jacobus MEIRING * 4.1.1927
            j2 Johanna * 15.12.1932 x 6.8.1956 Carel Dixie NORVAL * Adelaide 6.11.1931
            j3 Muller Gildenhuys x c. 1933 x Nicolette DREYER
        i9 Susanna Maria Embrentia * 18.1.1903 † c.1987 x 31.3.1936 Johannes Jurie KASSELMAN * Riversdale 19.9.1899 † Parow 15.12.1979
            j1 Johannes Jurie Kasselman * Riversdale 1.3.1937 x Anna Isabella THERON * 4.1.1933
            j2 Jurie Paulus Kasselman * Parow 12.6.1944
            j3 Marianna Kasselman * 31.7.1945 x Jacobus Johannes van NOORDWYK
        i10 Bart Gildenhuys * c. 1905 ab6c4d2e3f3g4h1i10 x Cornelis van WYK
            j1 Marina Emerentia van Wyk * 7.10.1934 x 7.10.1961 Pieter Emelius STREICHER * 9.5.1932
            j2 Andre van Wyk
    h2 Martha Maria * 9.12.1858
    h3 Johannes Jochemus Antonie Gildenhuys * 10.2.1862 ab6c4d2e3f3g4h3 x Heidelberg 29.9.1885 Dirkje Cornelia OTTO
        i1 Cornelia Johanna Jurina Gildenhuys
        i2 Michael Daniel Gildenhuys

j3 Martha Maria Jacoba
j4 Cornelia Johanna
h4 Adriaan Hendrik Geldenhuys * 8.9.1863 ab6c4d2e3f3g4h4
h5 Dina Maria Catharina * 26.1.1867
h6 Pieter Gabriël Jacobus Geldenhuys * Riversdal 23.12.1869 ab6c4d2e3f3g4h6 † 3.3.1942 x Magdalena Johanna van TONDER * Barrydale 11.7.1869 † Mosselbaai 21-4-1957
    i1 First born died young
    i2 Jozua Geldenhuys * Riversdal 10.1.1897 † Kaapstad 14.2.1957 x Hester Catharina JORDAAN in 1929 * Barrydale 14.8.1898 † Kaapstad 29.5.1993
        j1 Aletta Magdalena * 22.8.1930 x Hendrik CILLIERS * 22.8.1927 Wolesley
            k1 Ester Cilliers
            k2 Ronel Cilliers
        j2 Pieter Jacobus * Cape Town 17.11.1931 ab6c4d2e3f3g4h6i2j2 x Kaapstad 9.12 1961 Ingrid du PLESSIS * 23.8.1936 Mafeking.
            k1 Erika * Kaapstad18. 10. 1962 x Kaapstad 23.2. 1990 Jacques Floris LOUW * Stellenbosch 11.5.1961
                l1 Ana-Mia * Kaapstad 23.12.1991
                l2 Max * Kaapstad 22.3.1993 † Kaapstad 21.7.1994
                l3 Reinhardt * Kaapstad 19.5.1995
            k2 Mariëtte * Kaapstad 20.11.1964
            k3 Christa * Kaapstad 19.7.1969
    i3 Pieter Gabriël
    i4 Jurie Johannes
    i5 Jacoba
    i6 Ria
    i7 Emma
h7 Johanna Catharina Gildenhuys (born to Susanna Maria Emerentia van Rensburg) * 22.2.1885 † 24.7.1960 x 4.1.1905 Johannes Jacobus Bartholomeus ZAAYMAN * 9.7.1880 † 29.8.1955
    i1 Susanna Maria Amerentia Saayman * 24.10.1905 † Port Elizabeth 13.11.1996 x Petrus Johannes CROUS * 24.5.1901 † 20.6.1974
        j1 Naomi Crous * c. 1938 x NN van der MERWE
        j2 Jan Crous * c. 1940 x R NN
        j3 Johanna Petronella Jacoba Crous * 30.9.1942 x Jacobus Johannes KOK * 10.2.1944
    i2 Fanny Zaayman * 24.6.1909 x Abraham Albertus UYS * 9.5.1908 ab1c1d4e2f2g9h6i2
        j1 Johanna Catharina Uys * 28.8.1940 ab1c1d4e2f2g9h6i2j1 x Willem van der VYVER
g5 Elsabe Luitje * 3.9.1836 ~ Swellendam
g6 Dina Maria * 8.7.1838 ~ Swellendam 12.8.1838 second marriage
g7 Anna Margaretha * 25.8.1840 ~ Swellendam 27.9.1840
g8 Hans Jacob * 1.9.1842 ~ Swellendam 3.10.1842 † Marquard 10.8.1899 ab6c4d2e3f3g8 x Heidelberg 10.2.1862 Gesina Catharina DE JAGER daughter of Carel Pieter de Jager † 1896 xx Maria Elizabeth Susanna LUWES * 9.6.1851 † 18.10.1920 widow of Jacobus Johannes Wentzel
    h1 Jurie Johannes
    h2 Carel Pieter
    h3 Gesina Catharina
    h4 Elizabeth Catharina Christina
    h5 Jacoba Catharina

DETAILED GENEALOGIES

        h6 Hans Jacob Blom x Anna Maria HOGEWIND 1932
        h7 Hendrik Petrus
        h8 Andries Johannes * 6.5.1875 ~ Ficksburg 3.10.1875
        h9 Hester Johanna
        h10 Wybrand Herbershausen
        h11 Johanna Elizabeth Catharina x Hendrik Johannes LACOCK * 15.12.1868 † 5.9.1952
        h12 Jacobus Petrus Cornelis
        h13 Maria Elizabeth Susanna
        h14 Adriana Albertha
        h15 Elsabe Johanna Jacomina
        h16 Anna Margaretha Magdalena
        h17 Adriaan Hendrik
        h18 Andries Lodewicus Stephanus
d3 Albert Hendrik ~ 10.7.1746
d4 Petrus Arnoldus ~ 9.8.1750
d5 Anna Margaretha ~ 10.9.1752
d6 Albert Hendrik ~ 21.7.1754 x 28.3.1779 Maria Dorothea RADYN
    e1 Anna Dorothea ~ 26.2.1780
    e2 Christina Magdalena ~ 19.1.1783
    e3 Maria Alberta * 24.3.1786
    e4 Anna Geertruy ~ 24.2.1788 x Wessel Johannes **GILDENHUIZEN**
    e5 Barend Petrus ~ 1.1.1792 x Caledon 7.4.1816 Anna Maria le ROUX
        f1 Albert Hendrik * 23.12.1816 ~ Caledon 23.2.1817 x Stellenbosch 4.11.1838 Anna Geertruyda Fredrika OTTO * 1818 (Hendrik-dg)
            g1 Barend Petrus Albertus * 13.7.1840 ~ Caledon 11.8.1840
            g2 Hendrik Gabriel Johannes Stephanus * 4.8.1842 ~ Caledon
            g3 Elizabeth Johanna * 30.5.1844 ~ Caledon 1.9.1844
        f2 Gabriel Stephanus le Roux * 15.10.1818 ~ Caledon 3.1.1819
        f3 Margaretha Agatha Johanna * 10.4.1821 ~ Caledon 17.6.1821
        f4 Gabriel Petrus Stephanus * 15.3.1823 ~Caledon 16.4.1823 x Sara Susanna DE KOCK
            g? Gabriel Petrus Stephanus * 29.10.1857
                h? Sarah Susanna * ? x 10.3.1849 ?
                i? Elaine * 6.11.1938 x Hans van de GROENENDAAL
                j? Susan * x MACKIE
            h? Gabriel Petrus * 26.11.1816 † 6.7.1946 (blackwater fever)
        f5 Maria Dorothea Catharina Petronella * 23.1.1828 ~ Caledon 15.6.1828
        f6 Anna Maria Margaretha Alberta * 3.4.1830 ~ Caledon 8.8.1830
        f7 Barend Petrus Johannes * 6.8.1832 ~ Caledon 4.11.1832
        f8 Petrus Jurie Hendrik * 12.1.1835 ~ Caledon 26.4.1835
        f9 Jurie Petrus Wessel * 10.7.1838 ~ Caledon 30.9.1838
    e6 Christina Maria ~ 3.8.1794 x Caledon 4.5.1817 Stephanus Jacobus BOTHA
    e7 Albert Hendrik ~ 29.1.1797
    e8 Jurgen Johannes ~ 14.10.1798 x Caledon 21.4.1822 Elizabeth Debora BOTHA
        f1 Albert Hendrik Stephanus * 10.10.1822 ~ Caledon 17.11.1822 x Getruida Petronella SWART † 1.11.1904 Jasfontein, Colesberg, North Cape; † 18.5.1894 Colesberg, Cape, South Africa.
            g1 Stephanus Johannes Jacobus Geldenhuis * 9.7.1863
            g2 Marthinus Johannes Geldenhuis * Caledon 28.2.1867, x Johanna Magrieta Willemina VILJOEN * Richmond 16.2.1874, † Cypherwater, Richmond, Cape 15.10.1930.
                h1 Albert Hendrik Geldenhuis * Richmond 7.10.1879, x Anna Catharina Susanna 1899-1984.
        f2 Catharina Maria Johanna * 13.3.1824 ~ Caledon 11.4.1824
        f3 Maria Dorothea Elizabeth * 19.11.1826 ~ Caledon 28.1.1827
        f4 Stephanus Jacobus Johannes * 19.11.1830 ~ Caledon 12.12.1830

    f5 Margaretha Christina Maria * 5.4.1835 ~ Caledon 31.5.1835
  e9 Albert Hendrik ~ 4.10.1801
d7 Jacobus ~ 13.2.1759 x Maria Christina TESNER ~ 10.3.1757 daughter of Heinrich Tesner and Francina Cordier xx Stellenbosch 7.5.1809 Elizabeth Christina WESSELS
 e1 Christina Magdalena ~ 4.2.1781
 e2 Christina Francina ~ 4.10.1789 x Cape Town 9.5.1804 Barend Hendrik BEUKES
 e3 Jacobus ~ 19.2.1719 † 6.2.1862 x Geertruyda SWART ~ 22.9.1793
  f1 Christina Geertruyda Maria * 9.6.1813 ~ Caledon 11.7.1813 x Caledon 6.1.1838 Petrus Johannes BENEKE
  f2 Jacobus Jacob Hendrik * 30.6.1815 ~ Caledon 10.9.1815 x Caledon 20.10.1838 Anna Francina Elizabeth GRESSE
   g1 Jacobus * 23.9.1839 ~ Caledon 20.10.1839
   g2 Martha Johanna * 26.9.1842 ~ Caledon 25.12.1842
   g3 Geertruyda Jacoba * 20.10.1844 ~ Caledon 5.1.1845
   g4 Frans Lodewyk * 11.3.1847 ~ Caledon 6.6.1847 x Victoria-West 10.9.1877 Francina Jacoba LATSKY
   g5 Jacobus Hendrik * 21.8.1849 ~ Caledon 20.1.1850
   g6 Nicolaas Johannes * 24.11.1851 ~ Caledon 16.2.1852
   g7 Anna Catharina Cornelia Susanna * 24.10.1854 ~ Caledon 3.12.1854
   g8 Judith Christina Elizabeth * 10.1.1857 ~ Caledon 22.3.1857
  f3 Maria Christina * 29.9.1817 ~ Caledon 23.11.1817 x Hendricus Petrus BENEKE
  f4 Nicolaas Johannes * 21.1.1820 ~ Caledon 2.4.1820 x Caledon 29.4.1844 Martha Johanna GRESSE (Frans Lodewyk's daughter)
   g1 Jacobus * 14.4.1845 ~ Caledon 13.7.1845
   g2 Martha Johanna * 2.9.1847 ~ Caledon 30.1.1848
   g3 Frans Lodewyk * 27.8.1849 ~ Caledon 16.12.1849
   g4 Geertruyda Wilhelmina * 12.5.1852 ~ Caledon 21.11.1852
   g5 Nicolaas Johannes * 5.12.1854 ~ Caledon 28.1.1855
   g6 Judith Wilhelmina * 17.5.1857 ~ Caledon 13.9.1857
  f5 Barend Petrus * 22.5.1822 ~ Caledon 3.11.1822 x Caledon 4.4.1850 Cornelia Susanna ERWEE * 1833
  f6 Philip Rudolph * 3.2.1825 ~ Caledon 11.9.1825
  f7 Lucas Marthinus * 15.8.1827 ~ Caledon 23.3.1828
  f8 Geertruyda Johanna * 28.9.1829 ~ Caledon 21.2.1830 x Paul Lodewyk KUHN
  f9 Hendrik Andries * 31.10.1831 ~ Caledon 3.4.1832
  f10 Jacomina Geertruyda * 17.9.1834 ~ Caledon 15.2.1835 x Caledon 8.5.1862 Johannes Jurie COOPER
 e4 Hendrik Andries ~ 28.12.1794 x Caledon 5.5.1821 Sacharya Magdalena VAN DEVENTER
  f1 Maria Christina Catharina * 8.2.1822 ~ Caledon 7.7.1822
  f2 Catharina Maria Christina * 20.1.1824 ~ Caledon 1.6.1824
  f3 Elizabeth Johanna Magdalena * 31.1.1825 ~ Caledon 12.6.1825
  f4 Hendrik Andries * 7.4.1827 ~ Caledon 9.9.1827 x Elizabeth Magdalena UNGERER
   g1 Hendrik Andries * 1.10.1863 ~ George 6.12.1863
   g2 Johan Diederik Ungerer * 6.10.1865 ~ George 18.2.1866
  f5 Magdalena Jacoba * 5.8.1829 ~ Caledon 2.4.1830
 e5 Barend Petrus ~ 25.10.1797 x Caledon 2.4.1820 Anna Christina GROENEWALD
  f1 Jacobus Johannes * 14.8.1822 ~ Caledon 27.10.1822
  f2 Catharina Maria Christina * 20.1.1824 ~ Caledon 1.6.1824
  f3 Maria Christina * 1.11.1825 ~ Caledon 15.1.1826
  f4 Anna Christina Geertruyda * 16.12.1827 ~ Caledon 20.4.1828
  f5 Hendrik Andries * 3.12.1829 ~ Caledon 21.2.1830 x 3.11.1856 Maria Johanna COOPER

DETAILED GENEALOGIES

g1 Hendrik Andries * 1860 x Caledon 29.4.1890 Susanna Johanna COOPER / or Delaina WARRINGTON
g2 Second child as guestimated by Prop – possibly a daughter named after her grandmother COOPER / or Warrington?
g3? Barend Petrus Lodewyk born Caledon 26.5.1866 † 8.5.1950 x Henrietta Wilhelmina Cornelia FRITZ * 18.5.1880 † 2.5.1960
    h1 Hendrik Andreas * 4.11.1900 † 13.6.1992 † 23.1.1933 x Marion van ZYL
    h2 Joseph * 13.1.1902 x Geldenhuys
    h3 Barend * 11.7.1903 † 11.1.1964
    h3 † with childbirth
    h4 Leinha * 2.8.1904 † 12.9.1996
    h5 Mary
    h6 Jan * 6.1.1907 † 4.3.1992 x Sannie du PLESSIS * 9.3.1912 † 29.10.1990
    h7 Koos * 17.6.1908 x Matt
    h8 James Henry * 9.2.1910
        i1 Anne * 2.11.1938
        i2 Louis Frederick Botes * Aliwal North 22.7.1940 x Pretoria 13.2.1965 Louisa Regina KNOOP * Pretoria 13.7.1944
            j1 Louise * Stellenbosch 26.2.1966 x 24.2.2000 Eben PIENAAR * 24.12.1971
                k1 Luan * 9.7.2004
                k2 Elandré * 17.4.2007
            j2 James Henry * Bellville 16.10.1967 x 24.3.1995 Ronel Christene ADRIAANSE * 25.2.1963
                k1 Danuelle * 18.5.1992
                k2 Lianke * 6.1.1997
            j3 Louis Botes * Pinelands 24.8.1969 x 28.9.1992 Stoffelina MM PRETORIUS * 27.11.1969
                k1 Louis * 28.1.1998
                k2 Stephanie * 4.6.1994
            j4 Mario * Aliwal-Noord 3.5.1974 x 6.4.2002 Yolande Buitendag * 13.7.1979
                k1 Logan * 24.6.2006
                k2 Jaden * 8.3.2009
        i3 Mary * 4.3.1942
        i4 Jimmy * 11.9.1943
        i5 Fred * 5.9.1945
        i6 Yvonne * 5.9.1945
        i7 Daphne * 3.9.1950
    h9 George * 22.11.1912 x Joey
    h10 Hettie
    h11 Christene
    h12 Bessie
    h13 Josephine
    h14 Nicolaas
f6 Christina Francina Johanna * 23.9.1831 ~ Caledon 25.12 1831
f7 Barend Petrus * 5.9.1833 ~ Caledon 4.10.1833 x Beatrix Geertruyda GERBER
    g1 Anna Christina Geertruyda * 10.8.1860 ~ George 25.11.1860
    g2 Frans Jacobus Anthonie * 17.8.1862 ~ George 23.11.1862
        h? Barend Petrus † c.1941 [Prop's guestimate – Ben's grandfather]
            i? Barend Petrus † c.1976 – lived in the Noupoort, District Christie, Kimberley area x Catarina / Catharina

       j1 Barend Petrus * c. 1947/48 † young
       j2 Antonie Michael * 17.12.1949 x Elsa VERMEULEN * 18.4.1953
        k1 Barend Petrus 'Ben' * 13.4.1973 x Anneke Stoltz * Krugersdorp 24.10.1969
        l1 Barend Petrus * Krugersdorp 27.12.1973
        l2 Izak Jacobus * Krugersdorp 3.3.200
       j3 Coenraad Johannes * 1961
     f8 Coenraad Johannes * 1.6.1835 ~ Caledon 5.7.1835
     f9 Johannes Hermanus * 18.12.1839 ~ Caledon 2.10.1840
 d8 Maria Margaretha ~ 15.7.1759 x 15.10.1775 Johannes OTTO
 d9 Christina Margaretha ~ 12.4.1762
 d10 Susanna Elizabeth ~ 7.10.1764 x 23.11.1783 Johannes SWART
 d11 Christina Geertruy ~ 11.10.1767 x 17.4.1785 Nicolaas SWART ~ 12.10.1760
 d12 Hendrik Andries ~ 6.10.1771 x Stellenbosch 23.2.1806 Elsabe SWART ~ 6.2.1777
  e1 Barend Hendrik ~ 20.9.1809 † Bethlehem 22.8.1878 (70.9. -) x Caledon 28.8.1836 Anna Catharina MULDER xx Anna Maria SMIT xxx Margaretha Maria SCHEEPERS
   f1 Christiaan Cornelis
   f2 Philip R.
   f3 Cornelis Johannes
   f4 Jan Hendrik * Sneeuberg, Graaff-Reinet 8.5.1852 † 15.6.1867 (15)
  e2 Sara Elsabe * 21.9.1810 ~ Caledon 21.4.1811
  e3 Christina Magdalena * 10.10.1812 ~ Caledon 22.11.1812
 c5 Johanna Margaretha ~ 22.3.1721 x 12.1.1738 Jan Jurgen HAMMAN
b7 Margaretha ~ 6.10.1684 X 5.7.1704 Heinrich DU PLOOY xx 10.6.1725 Philippus RICHTER (from Soest)
b8 Hendrik ~ Cape Town 2.2.1687 x 11.10.1711 Esabe MEYER
 c1 Susanna Margaretha ~ 15.12.1715
 c2 Hendrik Albertus ~ 6.6.1717 x 7.11.1738 Elizabeth TAILLEFER
  d1 Elsabe x Dec 1757 Paul Henricus EKSTEEN
  d2 Petrus ~ 18.12.1740
  d3 Hendrik ~ 16.9.1742 x 2.5.1773 Margaretha Johanna VAN AARDE
   e1 Elizabeth Elsabe ~ 20.3.1774 x Theodorus Louis KRIEL
   e2 Jan Hendrik ~ 6.4.1777 x Cape Town 19.9.1802 Helena Gerharda KEULDER
    f1 Hendrik Johannes ~ 25.12.1803
   e3 Hendrik Albertus ~ 15.11.1778 x Rachel Maria JORDAAN
    f1 Hendrik Albertus ~ 11.10.1801
    f2 Gesina ~ 2.9.1804
    f3 Margaretha Johanna Martha ~ 2.2.1806 x Stellenbosch 4.10.1821 Stephanus JORDAAN
    f4 Petrus Johannes ~ 12.8.1810 x Swartland 8.11.1835 Catharina Jacoba BASSON
    f5 Rachel Maria ~ 14.2.1813 x Paarl 8.7.1832 Hendrik Johannes GILDENHUIZEN ~ 29.4.1810 (son of Albert Barend and Susanna Elizabeth le Roux)
   e4 Jacobus Carel ~ 12.3.1780
   e5 Petrus Guillaume ~ 4.11.1781 x Cape Town 24.4.1803 Maria Catharina REYNEKE
    f1 Magdalena Catharina ~ 6.11.1804
    f2 Hendrik Johannes ~ 28.9.1806
    f3 Margaretha Johanna Elisabeth ~ 2.4.1809 x Paarl 6.10.1832 Abraham Josua GILDENHUIZEN ~25.12.1808 (son of Abraham Jacobus and Martha Louisa le Roux)
    f4 Petrus Guilliam ~ 16.5.1812
    f5 Casparus Abraham ~ 9.10.1814
    f6 Elizabeth Elsabe Hendrina ~ 27.10.1816
    f7 Johannes Jacobus Carel ~ 29.8.1819 x Wellington 9.12.1845 Johanna Adriana MULLHOLLAND
     g1 Magdalena Catharina Susanna * 12.12.1847 ~ Victoria-West 6.2.1848

DETAILED GENEALOGIES

   g2 Johanna Maria (or Adriana) * 1850
   g3 Margaretha Johanna Elizabeth * 21.9.1854 ~ Victoria-West 26.12.1854
   g4 Martha Maria * 10.11.1856 ~ Victoria-West 26.12.1856
   g5 Petrus Gideon * 12.6.1862 ~ Victoria-West 14.9.1862
   g6 Matha Johanna Jacoba * 4.5.1865 ~ Victoria-West 22.10.1865
  f8 Charles Jacobus *30.4.1822 ~ Swartland 22.6.1822
  f9 Susanna Petronella * 10.5.1826 ~ Swartland 26.10.1826
 e6 Abraham Jacobus x Cape Town 23.10.1803 Martha Louisa le ROUX (Abraham's daughter)
  f1 Hendrik Johannes ~ 26.12.1804
  f2 Anna Magdalena ~ 10.4.1807
  f3 **Abraham Josua** ~ 25.12.1808 x Paarl 6.10.1832 Margaretha Johanna Elizabeth **GILDENHUIZEN** ~2.4.1809 (daughter of Petrus Guillaume and Maria Catharina Reyneke
   g1 Abraham Jacobus * 16.7.1835 † Willowmore 29.8.1907 x Willowmore 20.7.1868 Anna Catharina Margaretha VAN VUUREN * 1848 † Kromkuil Willowmore 2.6.1879 (31) xx Willowmore 19.12.1887 Susara Johanna VAN VUUREN
    h1 Johanna Jacomina Maria * 7.5.1869 ~ Willowmore 9.1.1870
    h2 Margaretha Johanna Elizabeth * 22 12.1870 ~ Willowmore 9.4.1871 x Willowmore 21.10.1891 Hendrik P. EYBERS
    h3 Abraham Jacobus Josua * 7.6.1872 ~ Willowmore 25.8.1872
    h4 Anna Catharina Louisa Jacoba * 7.6.1872 ~ Willowmore 25.8.1872
    h5 Anna Catharina Louisa Jacoba * 16.9.1873 ~ Willowmore 21.12.1873
    h6 Stephanus Johannes Lourens * 2.10.1877 ~ Willowmore 23.12.1877
    h7 Matthys Petrus Lourens * 24.12.1878 ~ Willowmore 6.4.1879
   g2 Martha Louisa * c.1841 † Winburg 3.7.1874 x Beaufort-wes 16.12.1861 Adam BARNARD widower
  f4 Maria Johanna Petronella ~ 22.7.1810
  f5 Martha Louisa ~ 21.7.1812
  f6 David Jacobus * 30.3.1815 ~ Paarl 30.4.1815
  f7 Petrus Guillaume * 20.5.1817 ~ Paarl 18.6.1817
  f8 Albert Barend * 16.5.1819 ~ Paarl
  f9 Theodorus Louis * 16.5.1820 ~ Paarl 8.6.1820 x Susara Elizabeth VAN WYK
   g1 Abraham Jacobus † 7.12.1876 (21.5. -)
   g2 Catharina Johanna * 20.3.1864 ~ 5.4.1864
  f10 Magadalena Francina * 10.5.1823 ~ Paarl 14.6.1823
  f11 Roelof Gabriel Thomas * 8.1.1825 ~ Cape Town 27.2.1825
  f12 Elizabeth Elsabe * 25.6.1828 ~ Paarl 17.8.1828 x Prins Albert 8.1.1855 Carel Hendrik Francois KEULDER
 e7 Susanna Petronella ~ 20.3.1785 x 5.12.1802 Adam Johannes REYNEKE
 e8 Martha Jacoba ~ 26.11.1786 x Carel Lodewyk VAN DER MERWE
 e9 Albert Barend ~ 17.8.1788 x Stellenbosch 11.10.1808 Susanna Elizabeth le ROUX
  f1 Hendrik Johannes ~ 29.4.1810 x Paarl 8.7.1832 Rachel Maria **GILDENHUIZEN** (H-daughter)
 e10 Margaretha Louisa Elizabeth ~ 4.9.1791
 e11 Guilliam (or Gideon) Theodorus ~ 20.10.1793 x Martha Maria DU TOIT (Pieter's daughter)
  f1 Hendrik Abraham Johannes * 17.9.1815 ~ Paarl 8.10.1815 x Paarl 6.9.1835 Johanna Catharina GROBBELAAR * 1818 (Evert's daughter)
   g1 Margaretha Maria x Calvinia 3.10.1853 Pieter Jacobus MOMSEN
   g? Hendrik Abraham Johannes * 1848 † Boshof 5.2.1881 (33) x Geertruyda Wouttrina KRIEL
    h1 Hendrik Abraham Johannes * 20.7.1871
    h2 Johannes Nicolaas * 12.11.1873
    h3 Evert Johannes * 30.9.1876

                        h4 Dirk Jacobus * 4.3.1880
                f2 Pieter Albertus Cornelis * 6.8.1817 ~ Paarl 10.9.1817
                f3 David Jacobus Abraham * 18.6.1820 ~ Paarl 5.7.1820
                f4 Pieter David * 6.1.1822 ~ Paarl 12.2.1823
                f5 Gideon Theodorus * 29.10.1826 ~ Paarl
                    h1 Gideon Theodorus
                        i1 Gideon Theodorus
                        j1 Gideon Theodorus x FOURIE
                            kx Gideon Theodorus Geldenhuis x MARX
                                l1 Mellie
                            kx Melchoir Jacobus x Elsie Catharina RAUTENBACH
                                l1 Aletta
                                l2 Gideon Theodorus
                                l3 Chris x Barbara
                                l4 Flora x Andre MALHERBE
                                l5 Eunice Erica x Mark MARSHALL
                                l6 Melda Geldenhuis Nortje * 14.1.1976 x Renaldo NORTJE *
                                    3.4.1967 (son of Sophia † 2009)
                                    m1 Chelsea * 1997
                                    m2 Renaldo *
                                    m3 Almero * 200?
            e12 Theodorus Louis Hermanus ~ 20.3.1796 x Paarl Sept 1818 Elizabeth Rachel
                DE VILLIERS (Piet Daniel's daughter)
                f1 Johanna Jacoba * 9.8.1819 ~ Paarl 19.9.1819
                f2 Elizabeth Rachel * 13.5.1823 ~ Paarl 21.8.1823
                f3 Hendrik * 15.6.1825 ~ Paarl 17.7.1825
                f4 Susanna Petronella * 4.5.1827 ~ Paarl 1.7.1827
                f5 Pieter Daniel * 21.11.1828 ~ Franschoek 14.12.1828 † 23.12.1889 x Susanna
                    Margaretha NIGRINI † 2.1.1863
                    g1 Pieter Daniel
                    g2 Johannes Albertus
                    g3 Maria Sophia * 30.5.1859 ~ Villiersdorp 14.8.1859
                    g4 Johanna Christina Amelia * 7.6.1861 ~ Villiersdorp 11.8.1861
                    g5 Christina Aletta
                    g6 Francois Lodewyk Johannes
                    g7 Petronella Daniellina Johanna
                    g8 Daniel Johannes
            e13 Barend Hendrik ~5.8.1798
        d4 Maria Elizabeth ~ 21.6.1744
        d5 Susanna Jacoba ~ 22.5.1746
        d6 Albertus Barend ~ 8.9.1748 † Zoutekloof, Cape district x 23.4.1784 Sophia Catharina
            LOUBSER † 15.11.1836 (80)
            e1 Hendrik Albertus ~ 13.5.1781 † before 15.8.1836 x Cape Town 29.3.1801 Hilletje
                Aletta SMIT
                f1 Albert Barend ~ 25.7.1802 x Swartland 3.2.1822 Helena Johanna VAN
                    SCHALKWYK
                    g1 Hilletje Aletta Hendrina ~ 6.7.1823 x Swartland 7.10.1838 Christiaan
                        Samuel Frederik SMIT
                    g2 Hendrik Albertus ~ 31.7.1825
                    g3 Theunis Gerhardus ~ 15.4.1827
                    g4 Albert Barend ~ 12.7.1829 - twin
                    g5 Dirk Johannes ~ 12.7.1829 - twin
                    g6 Christoffel Christiaan * 1831 x Piketberg 13.4.1865 Catharina Helena
                        Johanna LUCAS
                f2 Johanna Hendrika Maria ~ 13.1.1805 x Tulbagh 4.3.1821 Gideon VAN DYK ~
                    Swartland 19.7.1802
                f3 Sophia Catharina ~ 17.7.1808
                f4 Sophia Sibella Helena ~ 30.6.1811
                f5 Christoffel Christiaan ~ 20.2.1814 x Swartland 7.10.1838 Anna Susanna
                    Wilhelmina SERDYN

DETAILED GENEALOGIES

    e2 Pieter Johannes ~ 10.11.1782 x Stellenbosch 28.10.1810 Sibella Jacoba JORDAAN
        f1 Albertus Barend ~ 5.5.1811
        f2 Johanna Maria ~ 28.3.1813
        f3 Pieter Johannes ~ 18.12.1814
        f4 Adriaan ~ 4.5.1817
        f5 Pieter Johannes ~ 3.12.1826
        f6 Stephanus Nicolaas ~ 11.10.1829
        f7 Hendrik Oostwald Loubser * 14.10.1831 ~ Cape Town 11.12.1831
    e3 Albert Barend ~ 16.5.1784 x Tulbagh 7.3.1812 Anna Catharina Hendrina VAN DYK
        f1 Hilletje Aletta Johanna ~ 24.1.1813 x Cape Town 4.3.1827 Petrus Arnoldus BRAND
        f2 Sophia Catharina Elizabeth ~ 9.7.1815
        f3 Sophia Catharina Elizabeth ~ 29.9.1816 - twins
        f4 Anna Catharina Hendrika ~ 29.9.1816 x 1831 F.J.T. BRAND
        f5 Elizabeth Maria Susanna ~ 18.4.1824
    e4 Johannes Albertus 13.8.1786
    e5 Elizabeth Maria Helena ~ 6.4.1788
    e6 Johanna Hendrina ~ 14.4.1790 x 25.9.1808 Johannes Frans PRINS
    e7 Guilliam Hendrik ~ 1.2.1795
  d7 Guilliam Hendrik ~ 13.12.1750 x 9.11.1772 Helena Maria WALTERS
    e1 Hendrik Albertus ~ 14.3.1779 x Stellenbosch 6.1.1806 Johanna Magdalena BRUYNZWART (Bartholomeus daughter)
        f1 Maria Elizabeth ~ 9.8.1807
        f2 Guilliam Petrus ~ 31.12.1809
        f3 Susanna Jacoba ~ 18.2.1811 † 13.6.1852 Paarl, Cape Town, x 17.4.1831 Paarl, Cape Town Jacobus Arnoldus LOUW 1802 – 1856 (son of Albertus Wynand LOUW 1969 - ? and Johanna Magdalena Baard
        f4 Alida Johanna ~ 14.3.1813
        f5 Guilliam Hendrik * 6.3.1815 ~ Paarl 4.3.1816
        f6 Hendrik Marthinus * 30.9.1818 ~ Paarl 18.10.1818 † Bloemfontein 4.12.1897 x Paarl 8.6.1844 Margaretha Georgina Fredrika RORICH
            g1 Johanna Magdalena * 19.11.1849 ~ Paarl 26.6.1850
            g2 Margaretha Fredrika * 4.3.1851 ~ Paarl 1.6.1851
            g3 Hendrik Albertus * 25.3.1853 ~ Paarl 11.9.1853 † Blesbokfontein 4.12.1897 (42) x Anna Magdalena Elizabeth LOULO
                h1 Hendrik Marthinus
                h2 Jan Adriaan
                h3 Anna Magdalena
                h4 Cornelis Michiel
                h5 Siebert Frederik x Johanna VERMAAK
                    i1 Francina
                    i2 Anna x BUYS
                    i3 Hendrik
            g4 Margaretha Fredrika * 26.10.1855 ~ Paarl 18.11.1855
        f7 Guilliam Jacob * 25.8.1820 ~ Paarl 17.9.1820
        f8 Petrus Taillefer * 22.3.1823 ~ 30.3.1823
        f9 Helena Johanna * 16.7.1825 ~ Paarl 31.7.1825
        f10 Albert Barend * 5.6.1828 ~ Paarl 27.6.1828
    e2 Maria Margaretha ~ 31.12.1780
  c3 Gerrit ~ 11.12.1718
  c4 Susanna Jacoba ~ 2.11.1721 x 8.9.1748 Guilliam Hendrik HEEMS
b9 Anna ~ 6.10.1689 x 22.5.1712 Jean COSTEUX from Calais

Unclassified Geldenhuys's

Aletta Geldenhuys
Abraham Barend Gildenhuizen x Cape Town 1.2.1835 Christina Margaretha Broodryk
Anna Cornelia Elizabeth Gildenhuizen (Petrus dg) x Sendingkerk Franschoek 18.8.1845 Johannes Hendrik Swart
Aletta Catharina Elizabeth Gildenhuizen x Heildelberg 13.9.1858 Matthys Willem Beyers * 1.8.1826 widow
Anna Levina Gildenhuizen * 10.1.1876 † Grabouw 20.3.1936
Barend C. Gildenhuizen (father Jan), x Stellenbosch 5.5.1805 Maria Margaretha Wessels
Barend Hermanus Gildenhuizen * c.1830 x Hester Jacoba Viljoen
b1 Jacobus Viljoen * 1857 † Ceylon 6.1.1901 (44.8. -) x Elsie Johanna DIPPENAAR
    c1 Judith Petronella
    c2 Barend Jacobus
    c3 Hester Jacoba
    c4 Johanna Elizabeth
    c5 Michael Christoffel
    c6 Jacobus Hermanus
    c7 Elizabeth Maria
    c8 Stephanus Johannes
    c9 Matthys Jacobus
    c10 Viljoen Enslin Ebenezer
Benardes Lambertus Geldenhuys * Sutherland 1909 - - father of Jakobus Willem
Catharina Elizabeth Cornelia Gildenhuizen x NN xx Caledon 20.11.1848 Alexander Hamilton
Catharina Helena Gildenhuizen x George 12.2.1848 Petrus Johannes Meiring widower
Christian Andrew Geldenhuis * 10.2.1915 † 13.6.1966 x Maria Magdalena Pretorius * 5.8.1918 † 18.8.1995
    b1 Dirk Jacobus Petrus Rocco * 25.9.1949
    b2 Jacobus Stefanus 'Cobus' * 31.3.1960
        c1 Werner * 28.7.1961 † 5.5.2006 x Naomi van Niekerk * 27.10.1980
            d1 Louw * 19.5.2003
        c2 Dewald * 17.10.1983
Christina Gildenhuizen * 17.7.1868 † Grabouw 9.7.1954
Christina Francina Gildenhuizen (H.A. daughter) ~ Engelse kerk, Wynberg 7.3.1832
Christina Elizabeth Gildenhuizen x Heidelberg 13.8.1860 Lourens Johannes Prinsloo
Christina Magdalena Gildenhuizen (J-dg) x Caledon 25.4.1830 Lucas Marius Pheiffer
Coenraad Johannes Gildenhuizen * 1836 x c. 1860 Johanna Hendrina Gericke * 1843
Cornelia Magdalena Gildenhuizen x Colesberg G.T. van der Heever
Cornelis Janse Gildenhuizen * 1847 x Heidelberg 2.8.1870 Magdalena Johanna van Eeden * 1850
Dina Catharina Johanna Petronella Gildenhuizen * 1841 x Willowmore 10.8.1865 Anthony Chatwind
Cornelia Johanna Gildenhuizen x c.1860 Jan Frederik Joliffe
Elizabeth Gildenhuizen x Caledon 4.9.1836 Hendrik Johannes Fourie
Elizabeth Dorothea Gildenhuizen x Caledon 20.4.1838 Barend Petrus Johannes Fourie
Elizabeth Maria Gildenhuizen x Michiel Casparus Eksteen
Elias Johannes Gildenhuizen x Riversdal 11.4.1859 Anna Regina Susara Kroone
Elsa Gill, daughter of Madeline Geldenhuys, granddaughter of Frederick Gerhardus Geldenhuys x Gertrude Augusta Maria Herder and great-granddaughter of Frans Geldenhuys x Judith Fredrika Salomina Grobler of Potchefstroom
G.Gildenhuizen x Helena Ruth Baumbach
    b1 Andre * 1962
    b2 Siegfried * 1965
    b3 Natasja * 1971
Gideon Cupidorus Gildenhuizen x Carolina Aletta Simon
b1 Pieter Daniel ~ Calvinia 5.2.1865
Hans Jacob Blom Gildenhuys * 1902 from Hofmeyr, Cape, x 1932 Anna Maria Hogewind: a granddaughter of stamvader Roelof Hogevind, who arrived 1897 from Smilde, Netherlands and who had married Jentina van der Werf in 1885 in Netherlands. Hans Jacob and Anna Hogewind had 8 children, including Dr. Roelof Jentinus Geldenhuys (named after his 'stamouers'). His son, Lucas, had a son Roelof born 24.2.1929, a dentist, x 14.3.1955 Febe Cloete.

DETAILED GENEALOGIES

Hendrik A Gildenhuizen x NN
    b1 Christina Francina * Kaapse Duine 7.3.1832
Johanna Heyla Susanna Gildenhuizen x Caledon 13.5.1844 Johannes Francois de Wet
Jacobus Viljoen Gildenhuizen * 1857 x Elsie Johanna Dippenaar
Joleen Geldenhuys * Ladismith 27.10.1957 x Hendrik Jacobus van Aardt * Lusaka 18.5.1951
    b1 Leane van Aardt * Alberton 29.5.1987
    b2 Nicolaas Daniel van Aardt * Bredasdorp 25.8.1988
Johanna Elizabeth Gildenhuizen x Fraserburg 15.12.1856 David Somon Johannes Toula xx Fraserburg 10.1.1860 Johannes Gerhardus Hoon
Johanna Gildenhuizen is the mother of: -
    b1 Johannes Petrus Gildenhuizen * 8.8.1819 ~ Caledon 1.1.1820
Johanna Magdalena Gildenhuizen x Kimberley 16.12.1872 James Nicol Cambell
Johanna Magdalena Cornelia Gildenhuizen * 1873 x Caledon 24.5.1892 George Wessels Cooper * 1871
Johanna Maria Hendrik Gildenhuizen (H.A.daughter) x 1820 Gideon van Dyk
Judith Magdalena Gildenhuizen x c.1870 Barend J.J. Vermaas
Lodewyk G.Gildenhuizen * 14.5.1868 † Grabouw 27.6.1938
Lourens Gildenhuizen * 1837 x Swellendam 20.10.1856 Johanna Christina Kemp
Margaretha Maria Gildenhuizen x Calvinia 3.10.1853 Pieter Jacobus Mommies
Maria Christina Gildenhuizen x Bredasdorp 13.8.1849 Willem Jacobus McDonald
Maria Catharina Gildenhuizen * 1843 x Uitenhage 3.6.1861 Daniel Petrus van Rooyen xx Willowmore, Petrus Willem Adriaan Nel
Maria Magdalena Gildenhuizen x Caledon 22.4.1844 James Milne
Matthys Johannes Gildenhuizen * 22.4.1822 ~ Swellendam 31.8.1823, son of Johanna Susanna Gildenhuizen
Matthys Johannes Lourens Gildenhuizen * 1842 x Heidelberg 28.6.1864 Francina Fredrika Prinsloo
Monica Geldenhuys * 28.5.1954, daughter of Pierter Theunis Blomerus Geldenhuys * 17.10.1914
Nicolaas Daniel Geldenhuys, farmed Muiskraal, Krugersdorp x Elizabeth Johanna
    b1 Pieter Theunis Blomerus * 17.10.1914 died 1975 x Johanna Helena Geldenhuys * 19.4.1914 died 25.5.1998 Roodepoort, daughter of Barend Hermanus Geldenhuys * Graaff-Reinet 4.4.1869 died Pilgrimsrest 1924 x Jacoba Johanna Hendrina Theron
        c1 Monica Geldenhuys * 28.5.1945 x Slabber
Nicolaas Daniel Gildenhuizen x Anna Gerharda Fourie
    b1 Jurie Johannes Gerhardus * Napier 1860 † Jacobsdal 25.11.1904 (45.8.23) x Anna Hester Margaretha Francina van Niekerk
        c1 Daniel Johannes Albertus * 28.2.1887
        c2 Anna Gerharda * 23.3.1889
        c3 Louisa Sophia * 22.3.1891
        c4 Ellen Johanna * 20.6.1894
        c5 Maria Elizabeth * 25.2.1897
Nicholas George Antonie Geldenhuys * 9.1867 Caledon and brought up by an Uncle and Aunt. Married Maria Magdalena van Heerden who was born 22.10.1864. He died 20.11.1941 on the farm Engeland, Kuruman.
    b1 Nicholas George Johannes Geldenhuys * 1894.
        c1 Maria Magdalena Geldenhuys x Townsend
            d1 Pamela x Perry
            d2 George Townsend
Petrus Arnoldus Gildenhuizen * 13.6.1824 ~ Swellendam 3.10.1834, son of Christina Magdalena Swart
Pieter Arnoldus Gildenhuizen x Susanna Catharina Snyman
    b1 Anna Margaretha * 27.4.1831 ~ Colesberg 28.5.1831
    b2 Anna Margaretha * 13.7.1835 ~ Colesberg 13.9.1835
    b3 Esaias Reynier * 14.2.1849 ~ Colesberg 17.6.1849
Rina Geldenhuys * Windhoek, Namibia

(Note: Professor Du T. Malherbe found that the Geldenhuys "rank order" in the G.R. - *Geslacht-Register der oude Kaapsche Familien* by C.C. De Villiers, is incorrect. This finding has not duly worried the writer - errors were also found in his works e.g. G.S. Preller married Johanna Pretorius in 1989).

DETAILED GENEALOGIES

BOTHA

Friedrich BOTH (later BOTHA) born Duitsland 4.3.1653 son of Michael BOTH and Susanna SAULUS arrived in the Cape from Wangenheim near Gotha, as a soldier in 1678. Five years later he got his burger rights and from 1686 he boarded with Jan Cornelisz. In 1692 he signed his name still 'Both' but in 1699 he signed as Botha. In the 'Opgraafrolle' the spelling Both, Boot and Botha appears. In the Cape it often happened that a person is called after the place of origin The fact that Friedrich Both originated from Gotha, this could have attributed that Friedrich Both from Gotha changed to Friedrich Botha.

a Friedrich Botha * 4.3.1653 x Stellenbosch 21.6.1717 Maria KICKERS, an orphan girl from Netherlands – and divorced wife of Jan Cornelisz.
    b1 Theunis * 15.4.1686

BOUWER

a1 Johann Ludwig, arrived 1724 from Kassel, Germany, x 19.2.1736 Cornelia BURGER
    b4 Jeremias Jes. * 1743 x 1765 Susanna VERMAAK
        c1 Jeremias Cornelis * Graaff-Reinet 1766 x Salomina A PIENAAR
            d1 Salomon * 1791 x Maria E OOSTHUIZEN
                e1 Daughter
                e2 Jeremias Cornelis * 1822

b11 Willem Christiaan * 1758 x 23.5.1784 Aletta Catharina NEL
   c1 Johannes Ludwig * 1785 x Sara Cornelia BOTHA
      d1 Pieter Willem Johannes * 1807
   c3 Pieter Willem Johannes * 1790 x Anna Susanna BOTHA
      d1 Willem Christiaan * 1810
b12 Petrus Frederik * 1760 x 6.1.1782 Regina Dorothea v.d.BANK
   c11 Willem Christiaan * 1803

      x1 Johannes Jacobus Francois * x Delene Elizabeth **Geldenhuys*** 27.2.1945 Oudtshoorn
         y1 Chanli * 12.10.1970 Vereeniging x Charles Roy BRINK *1.1.1961
            z1 Tal J * 27.8.1995 Tauranga, New Zealand
            z2 Nea D * 27.2.1998 Waitakere, New Zealand
            z3 Deu G * 7.11.1999 Auckland, New Zealand
            z4 Gem *17.10.2001 Auckland, New Zealand
         y1 Rensha * 15.2.1972 Salisbury, Rhodesia x Craig BROWN

BRINK

BRINK

a1 **Andries** x 13.7.1738 Sophia GROVE x 30.3.1749 Alida de Waal
   b1 Andries * 1739 x Magdalena ROSSOUW - 8 children
   b2 Jan Godlieb * 1741 x 29.7.1764 Susanna Maria de KOCK - 10 children
   b3 Johannes * 1753 x Maria E HENDRICKS and Susanna Justina FAURE - 14 children
   b11 Daniel * 1760 x 1788 Johanna van der SPUY - 11 children
   b12 Cornelis * 1762 x Sibella Eksteen and Magda lena C. STAAKMAN - 18 children
   b13 Arend * 1765 x 27.7.1788 Elisabeth EKSTEEN - 12 children
      c?Missing link
         d? Schalk Richard * 1864 † Johannesburg 11.12.1918 x Jane Sarah GLENN * 9.2.1866 † Johannesburg 12.11.1933
            e?Schalk Richard * 10.8.1891 † 13.5.1972 x Maud Nellie LIVERSAGE
               x1 Daphne x Arch Gerardy
               x2 Hazel x Cyril Stafford Schlemmer
               x3 Bendominee Maude (Bebe or Bendo) x Richard Alfred Earle Davey
               x4 Charles Richard
               x5 ?Schalk Reginald * 8.11.1933 † South Coast, KZ-Natal, South Africa 23.2.1988 x Mona Daphne van ROOYEN
                  ?y1 Richard * 21.1.1957, Johannesburg x 27.12.1980 Johannesburg, Brenda Joan MATHESON.
                     z1 Kellie Marie * 23.10.1981 Sandton Clinic, Ranburg
                     z2 Christie * 11.2.1988 Sandton Clinic, Randburg

DETAILED GENEALOGIES

?y2 Brian Reginald
?y3 Charles Roy*1.1.1960 x Chanli G BOUWER * 12.10.1970, daughter of Dr. Johannes Jacobus Francois Bouwer and Delene Elizabeth **Geldenhuys**
    z1 Tal J * 26.8.1995 Auckland, New Zealand
    z2 Nea D * 27.2.1998 Auckland, New Zealand
    z3 Deu G * 7.11.1999 Auckland, New Zealand
    z4 Gem * 17.10.2001 Auckland, New Zealand
?y4 John Robert * 28.8.1963 Pretoria x 18.10.1998 Krugerdorp Yolande PRINSLOO * 15.11.1974
    z1 Joshua Dean * 18.12.2002 Sandton Clinic, Randburg
?y5 Lynn x Neill Wynn MUIRHEAD
    z1 Kim Chanelle
    z2 Byron Neil
    z3 Bevan
?y6 Jenny * 7.10.1967 Pretoria, South Africa, x 7.5.1993 Alberton Roy Terence CULHANE
?y7 Carol * 16.6.1970 Ballito, Natal x Stephen James MURRAY
    Z1 Jordan Elizabeth Murray * 18.1.1999 Sandton Clinic, Randburg

COETSER / COETZER

Jacob Kutzer from Oostenryk, son of Wenzeslaus Kutzer arrived in 1709 as a soldier on board the Noordhoek from Wielingen. In 1713 he was a boer kneg and became a burger in 1714. He married Cornelia Helms on 15 September 1717 – she was the widow of Arie van Wyk. Jacob had a second marriage, to Susanna Snyman. It is believed he was the stamvader of Matthew Dylan and Lucy Hope Geldenhuys.

a Jacob Kutzer x Cornelia Helms xx Susanna SNYMAN
    b1 Johannes Jacobus ~ 24.5.1716 x 15.2.1739 Maria BOTHA xx 27.11.1746 Johanna NEL
        c1 Maria Anna ~ 13.12.1739 x 29.4.1759 J OOSTHUIZEN
        c2 Johanna Dorothea ~ 19.11.1747 x 23.3.1766 Jan Harmse LABUSCHAGNE
        c3 Cornelia ~ 26.1.1749 x 15.5.1770 Casper LABUSCHAGNE
        c4 Jacob ~ 2.4.1752
        c5 Pieter Willem ~ 12.8.1853 x 3.3.1782 Anna Susanna JORDAAN
            d1 Pieter Willem ~ 22.2.1785 x Elsie Dorothea COETZER (daughter of Wentzel Christoffel) xx Cradock 23.12.1832 Aletta Johanna GROBLER
                e1 Jacoba Johanna Aletta ~ 13.12.1807 x Graaff-Reinet 15.6.1823 Carolus ERASMUS

- e2 Pieter Willem ~ 7.5.1809 † 23.8.1875 (66.7.17) x Cradock 1.5.1836 Elizabeth Magdalena van HEERDEN
- e3 Wensel Christoffel * 27.8.1811 ~ Cradock 7.10.1811 † 18.10.1846 x Cradock 8.4.1833 Anna Susanna COETZER
  - f1 Pieter Willem
  - f2 Anna Maria
  - f3 Johannes Jacobus X Tarkastad 7.6.1869 Hester Johanna Maria SMIT
- e4 Anna Susanna * 6.10.1813 ~ Graaff-Reinet 20.2.1814
- e5 Gert Jacobus * 25.3.1817 ~ Cradock
- e6 Jacob Johan David * 30.10.1819 ~ 16.1.1820 x Cradock 12.8.1838 Anna Susanna JORDAAN
- e7 Willem Helm Johan * 27.11.1825 ~ Cradock 11.12.1825
- e8 Elsi Maria * 22.2.1828 ~ Cradock 7.4.1828
- d2 Johanna Jacoba ~ 22.2.1785 x J F SMIT
- d3 Elsie Dorothea ~ 7.2.1788 x 13.3.1803 Hendrik de BRYN
- d4 Magdalena Elizabeth ~ 13.2.1789
- d5 Johannes Jacobus ~ 7.4.1790 † Gelegenfontein, Aliwal-North 8.1.1856 (66.2.24) x Graaff-Reinet 17.12.1809 Elsie Maria COETZER xx Maria Dorothea Elizabeth van TONDER
  - e1 Anna Susanna ~ 22.5.1808
  - e2 Jacobus Johannes ~ 26.10.1810 x Cradock 7.2.1830 Catharina Maria SMITH
  - e3 Anna Susanna * 28.4.1814 ~ Graaff-Reinet 28.8.1814 x Cradock 6.7.1829 Jacobus Albertus COETZER
  - e4 Magdalena Elizabeth * 16.6.1816 ~ Graaff-Reinet 8.9.1816
  - e5 Johanna Cornelia * 16.4.1818 ~ Graaff-Reinet 21.6.1818
  - e6 Petrus Johannes Bartinus * 25.9.1819 ~ Cradock 16.1.1820
  - e7 Gert Jacobus Albertus * 11.1.1822 ~ Cradock 8.4.1822
  - e8 Johannes Jacobus * 27.12.1824 ~ Cradock 4.4.1825 x Martha Catharina GROBBELAAR † 27.8.1903
    - f1 Cornelia Johanna x Johannes Petrus du PLESSIS
    - f2 Martha Catharina (could be great-granmother to Eloise Howard?) x Charl Johannes du PLESSIS
    - f3 Johannes Jacobus
    - f4 Douw Gerbrand
  - e9 Wensel Christoffel * 7.2.1827 ~ Cradock 2.4.1827
  - e10 Wilhelm Helm Johannes *19.12.1829 ~ Cradock 17.1.1830
  - e11 Elsje Maria
  - e12 Cornelis Johannes * c.1842 x Geref. Kerk, Burgersdorp 25.11.1860 Maria Magdalena KRUGER * 1844
    - f1 Johannes Jacobus *1862 † 22.10.1888 (26.0.19) x Lasya Geertruyda de KLERK
      - g1 Cornelis Johannes
    - f2 Hendrik Gert Lodewyk * 23.2.1864 x Sophia Catharina GREYVENSTEYN (could be great-grandfather to Eloise Howard)
      - g1 ? Martha Petronella (nee du Plessis)
        - h? Ingrid Estment x Steve Howard
          - i1 Eloise (x) Dave Stilson xx Pey Malan Geldenhuys * 22.12.1970
            - j1 Matthew Dylan
            - j2 Jake
            - j3 Lucy Hope * Durban 29.3.2009
          - i2 Dylan
    - f3 Maria Dorothea Elizabeth * 12.6.1867
    - f4 Maria Magdalena Catharina * 2.9.1868
    - f5 Heyltje Johanna * 26.4.1869
    - f6 Cornelis Johannes * 26.6.1872
    - f7 Petrus Hendrik * 8.10.1874
    - f8 Johannes Hendrik * May 1876
    - f9 Susanna Lasya * 18.9.1878

DETAILED GENEALOGIES

       f10 Jacobus Albertus Johannes * 25.5.1880
       f11 Magdalena Elizabeth * 26.2.1882
       f12 Cornelia Johanna Magdalena * 15.4.1884
    e13 Jacob Jeremias x Burgersdorp 25.1.1864 Sarah Ellington JENKINSON
    e14 Johannes Hendrik
    e15 Barend Hendrik x Maria Dorothea Elizabeth NN
    e16 Casper Johannes David
d6 Gerit Jacobus ~ 13.1.1793
d7 Anna Susanna ~ 16.3.1794 x P S VAN HEERDEN
d8 Wensel Christoffel ~ 17.1.1797 x Cradock 15.11.1818 Elizabeth Helena van HEERDEN xx Cradock 14.4.1832 Maria Petronella POTGIETER widow of J H Steenkamp
    e1 Pieter Schalk Willem * 8.9.1820 ~ Cradock 2.10.1820
    e2 Carel Nicolas * 17.9.1822 ~ Cradock 29.9.1822
    e3 Wensel Christoffel * 16.4.1825 ~ Cradock 15.5.1825
    e4 Andries Hendrik * 1.3.1827 ~ Cradock 2.4.1827
    e5 Anna Susanna * 1.3.1827 ~ Cradock 2.4.1827
d9 Jacob Jeremias ~ 23.12.1798 x Graaff-Reinet 2.2.1817 Susanna Petronella du PLESSIS
    e1 Elizabeth Maria * 17.1.1818 ~ Cradock 8.3.1818
    e2 Anna Susanna * 23.9.1819~ Cradock 26.12.1819
    e3 Sara Johanna Magdalena ~ Cradock 20.10.1823
    e4 Pieter Willemse * 23.6.1828 ~ Cradock 14.9.1828
    e5 Johannes Jacobus * 27.2.1829 ~ Cradock 6.4.1829 (mother: Elizabeth Helena van Heerden)
d10 Casper Johannes ~ 10.11.1801 x Cradock 4.12.1820 Magdalena Johanna du PLESSIS
    e1 Pieter Willemse * 13.11.1821 ~ Cradock 26.12.1821 † 11.4.1892 (70) x Susanna Petronella Erasmus
       f1 Casper Johannes
       f2 Carel Stephanus
       f3 Pieter Willem Johannes
       f4 Petronella Wilhelmina x Thomas Johannes HOUGH
       f5 Hester Carolina x Rudolph Philippus Jacobus COETZER
       f6 Elizabeth Maria x Johannes Petrus BINGLE
       f7 Sara Johanna Aletta
       f8 Susanna Petronella
       f9 Magdalena Johanna Jacoba Petronella
    e2 Elizabeth Maria

DE WAAL

DE WAAL

a1 **Jan** * Netherland 3.1.1692 arrived 1715, x 3.5.1716 Elisabeth van ECK xx 24.3.1748 Anna Elisabeth DEMPERS
  b1 Jacoba * 1717 x 21.3.1756 Cornelis de LEEUW
    c7 Pieter * 1753 x 15.8.1773 Christina Magdalena BLANKENBERG
      d1 Arend * 1775 x 13.12.1793 Maria Margaretha BOSMAN
        e2 Pieter * 31.7.1798 x 7.2.1829 Susanna Geertruyda LOUW
          f4 Daniel * 15.10.1835 † 8.4.1884 x Rachel Susanna SCHOLTZ xx Rachel EKSTEEN
          f5 Pieter * 194.1837
          f7 Adriaan Jacobus * 21.8.1842 x Sophia EKSTEEN
          f9 David C * 25.11 1845 x 19.5.1869 Hester S HOFMEYR (sister of "Onse Jan")
          f10 Hermanus Lambertus * Paarl 27.2.1848 x Stellenbosch Elisabeth KRIGE
  b2 Arend * 15.10.1719 x 21.8.1740 Maria van BREDA
  b3 Cornelis * 1721 x 13.5.1742 Hilletje MOSTERT
  b8 Hendrik * 1732 x 23.5.1756 Elisabeth Judith LOUW

DIPPENAAR

a1 Johannes Marthinus Depner, arrived 1735 from Wehlau, East Prussia x 10.11.1748 Maria Magdalena SCHMIDT
  b1 Johannes Martinus * Stellenbosch 10.11.1748 x Elizabeth Johanna LIEBENBERG
    c1 Maria Magdalena ~ 1.7.1781 x Swartland 12.10.1806 Matthys Micheelse BASSON
    c2 Johannes Marthinus ~ 2.10.1784
  b2 Maria Catharina ~ Stellenbosch 12.9.1750 x 30.12.1770 Jurgen Paul KEYSER
  b3 Hester Margaretha ~ Tulbagh 21.5.1752 x 30.4.1777 Andries GOUS
  b4 Magdalena Adriana ~ Tulbagh 7.10.1753 x 23.4.1776 Johannes Cornelis BEUKES xx 13.9.1789 Johannes GROBBELAAR
  b5 Michael Christoffel ~ 2.12.1755 x 30.3.1777 Anna SMIT xx 29.2.1801 Maria Elizabeth ERASMUS
    c1 Johannes Marthinus ~ 8.3.1778
    c2 Rachel Maria ~ 28.4.1782 x Cape Town 4.10.1801 Barend Bartholomeus BURGER (Schalk Jacobus son)
    c3 Christiaan Jacobus ~ 8.5.1785
    c4 Anna Fredrika ~ 18.11.1787 x marriage court, Graaff-Rienet 6.4.1805 D.S. van der MERWE

DETAILED GENEALOGIES

c5 Maria Magdalena ~ 24.4.1791 x Graaff-Rienet 13.9.1812 Alwyn Jacobus BURGER
c6 **Alwyn Jacobus** ~ 13.7.1794 † Bloemfontein 9.12.1853 (60.11.20) x Graaff-Rienet 30.5.1813 Anna Sophia BURGER xx Graaff-Rienet 13.2.1852 Carolina Christina Johanna OOSTERHAGEN
   d1 Hester Sophia * 27.10.1816 ~ Graaff-Rienet 17.11.1816
   d2 Anna Maria * 5.3.1821 ~ Graaff-Rienet 25.3.1821
   d3 Michiel Christoffel * 10.5.1824 ~ Graaff-Rienet 20.6.1824 x Colesberg 13.3.1843 Susanna Elizabeth Cecilia MARKGRAAFF xx Jacoba Aletta BOTHA
     e1 Michiel Christoffel * 1.2.1844 ~ Winburg 6.5.1844
     e2 Hendrik Petrus * 1863 † Boshof 24.7.1895 x Geertruyda Petronella VAN NIEKERK
        f1 Jacoba Aletta * 8.10.1884
        f2 Geertruyda Petronella * 30.3.1887
        f3 Alewyn Jacobus * 25.4.1826 ~ Graaff-Rienet 3.7.1826
   d4 Alewyn Jacobus * 25.4.1826 ~ Graaff-Rienet 3.7.1826
   d5 **Schalk Willem** * 1.10.1827 ~ Graaff-Rienet 26.10.1827 † Bloemfontein x Christina Gesina Sophia VAN BILJON
     e1 Martha Jacoba Aletta
     e2 Alwyn Jacobus
     e3 Petrus Johannes
        f1 Johannes Petrus
           g1 Poppie x Doep BRITS
           g2 Anna Sophia
           g3 Hester
           g4 Martha
           g5 Cornelia
           g6 Schalk Willem
           g7 Pieter Johannes
           g8 Son
           g9 **Johannes Petrus** * 24.10.1898 † 1968 x Louzya Christina DE BRUYN * 30.11.1898 † 1970
              h1 Johanna Maria Barendina * 12.1.1918
              h2 Anna Johanna Sophia * 20.1.1920 * Gerald HABIG
                 i1 Carl Frederik
                 i2 John Peter
                 i3 Gerald
              h3 Louzya Christina * 30.8.1922 x Lukas LIEBENBERG xx Daniel VAN WYK xxx Les ROLINK
                 i1 Philip
                 i2 Piet
                 i3 Louzya Christina
                 i4 Louis
              h4 Alwyn Jacobus * 23.7.1924
              h5 Louis Hosia * 15.2.1929 x
                 i1 John Peter
              h6 Johanieta * 16.1.1931 x John William CARR
                 i1 Lucielle
                 i2 Sidney † 18 months
                 i3 Ronald
                 i4 Brian
                 i5 Vivian x Brian
              h7 Schalk Willem * 14.1.1933
                 i1 Arlene
                 i2 Janine
              h8 **Julia Lillian Dippenaar** *1936 x Peter BORRUSO † Australia xx Luanshya, Zambia 27.3.1964 Johannes Albertus GELDENHUYS *Johannesburg 15.8.1940

            i1 Stuart William * Bulawayo 18.9.1957 x Manzini, Swaziland 10.7.1980 Joy Goldsworty
            i2 Charmaine * Salisbury 7 January 1960, partnered Lance Froneman
                j1 Jason * Midrand 4.1.1996
            i3 **Paul Preller Geldenhuys** * Ndola, Zambia 15.12.1966 x 31.12.1988 Karen de Waal * Vanderbylpark 29.5.1966
              j1 Chanel Geldenhuys * Durban 18.4.1990
              j2 **Craig Jannie Geldenhuys** * Durban 15.3.1993
        e4 Anna Sophia
        e5 Schalk Willem
        e6 JS
        e7 HH
        e8
        e9
b6 Andries Petrus ~ Tulbagh 8.1.1758 x 17.1.1796 Gerbrecht Christina VOSTER 10 children
    c1 Johannes Marthinus ~ 19.3.1797 † Hollerivier, Vanrhynsdorp 2.7.1866 (69.4.19) x Johanna Sophia Magdalena ECKARD
        d1 Andreas Petrus 1824
        Johannes Hendricus 1827
    c3 Alwyn Jacobus ~ 20.4.1800 x Swartland 8.9.1822 Catharina Helena SMIT
        d3 Nicholas Michiel 1827
    c7 Michaelis Christoffel * 22.5.1808 ~12.3.1809 x Swartland 5.4.1835 Helena Johanna Jacoba SMIT 13 children
    c10 Barend Johannes 1818

ESTMENT

a Harry ESTMENT x Evelyn POLLARD
1 Frank
2 Bernard
3 May
4 Wharnie (as per Dr DF du T Malherbe – Stamregister van die Suid-Afrikaanse volk – no dates given)
Unclassified:
William Henry Estment * 1929/30 x Martha Petronelle (Floss) COETZER

DETAILED GENEALOGIES

GERBER

Stamvader was Frans Anton GERBER, arrived at the Cape in 1758 as a soldier from Epfig in Elsas on the "*Kroonenburg*" – became a burger in 1764, and a wagon maker in Stellenbosch. Married Catharina van DYK. Died in 1793

HOWARD

Edward Ford Howard † 1871 x Somerset-East 24.6.1837 Charlotte BRUTON * 8.6.1819 † Bloemfontein 1893 (Thomas-dg)
b1 Charlotte Anne * 13.1.1838 ~ Sommerset-East 19.3.1838

George Henry Howard * North America c. 1832 † Vogeldraai, Bethlehem 31.12.1872 (40), sailor, unmarried

Henry Howard x Lydia SMITH
b1 Henry Francis Christian * 12.8.1816 ~ Cape Town 13.10.1816

James Hibbert Howard x Somerset-East 4.2.1850 Maria Magdalena van der MERWE
b1 Margaret Alice * 8.3.1853 ~ Somerset-East 10.4.1853 x Cradock 9.4.1870 Hendrik Matthys STAPELBERG
b2 Anna Maria * 5.4.1856 ~ Glen Lynden 13.7.1856
b3 Charlotte Elizabeth * 1860 x Cradock 15.3.1875 Eduard van MEYEREN

John Haswell Howard x Susanna HOWARD xx Somerset-East 13.8.1849 Christina Anna (Johanna) VOOG
b1 Charlotte Elizabeth * Jul 1838 ~ Somerset-East 7.10.1838
    Second marriage
b2 James Hibbert * 24.1.1850 ~ Somerset-East 14.4.1850
b3 Susanna Anna * 28.8.1851 ~ Somerset-East 13.7.1854
b5 Charlotte Elizabeth * 16.2.1856 ~ Glen Lynden 13.7.1856

John Henry Howard x Somerset-East 29.3.1835 Harriet PEERS (Pierce)
b1 Henry * 9.12.1832 ~ Somerset-East 7.4.1835
b2 Harriet ~ Somerset-East 7.4.1835

b3 Jemima * 10.5.1839 ~ Cradock 13.10.1839

Joseph Howard, employed by William Duckitt in 1839

Thomas Howard * Cardiff, England 20.10.1853 son of James Howard and Maria Thomas x Cornelia NELL
b1 Llewellyn * Cape Town 18.1.1896 † East London x Vera Nellie LUGG
    c1 Kenneth John * Kenya 7.3.1932 x Moira E, NN
    c2 Philip Mowbray Llewellyn * Kenya 21.6.1933 x Marjorie Elsie RUSSELL * Pretoria 1.8.1937
        d1 Karen Vera * Pretoria 1.11.1959 x Leon RENAUD
        d2 Basil Glen * Pretoria 13.1.1966
        d3 Wendy Deborah * Pretoria 25.5.1973
    c3 Felicity May * Kenya 20.4.1937
b2 Cadwallader † young
b3 Kenneth Thomas * Claremont, Cape 1900, infantryman in the 4TH SA Infantry † France 17.4.1918 killed in action
b4 David * 1903 x Martha Catherine TOOLEY
    c1 David Thomas
    c2 Catherine Martha x Bernard BLOTAS
    c3 Evelyn Susan x Ian Leigh HUNT
b5 Leslie Gordon * 1906
b6 Gwenlilian Marwena * 1908 x Henry Walsham BRISTOW
b7 Elizabeth * 1910 x Edward John DARVALL
b8 Catherine Mary * 1914 x Frederick Rice Hamilton HOPLEY

William Howard * Aylesbury, Buckinghamshire 25.10.1776 † Port Elizabeth 27.1.1847 x Elizabeth NN * 1780 † Grahamstad 1825 xx 19.1.1827 Mary HILES * c. 1781 xxx 9.5.1834 Ann THARRATT * c. 1785
b1 John Henry * Buckinghamshire c. 1802 † Cradock 26.6.1850 x Harriett NN
b2 William * c.1804 († before 1845?)
    c1 William Howard x Dorothea Elizabeth HOMAN * 7.9.1834 † Rouxville 24.10.1879 daughter of Christiaan Jacobus Homan and Martha Maria Claasen (she xx Ernst Evert Brander)
        d1 Martha Maria ~ Burgersdorp 20.1.1852
        d2 Susanna * 22.6.1853 ~ Smithfield 29.10.1854 x 11.3.1872 Andries Johannes PEYPER (son of A.J.)
        d3 Jan Hassel
        d4 James Evert (author suspects that this could be the link to Kenneth Steve Howard
        d5 Chritiaan Jacob * 1.11.1859 ~ Aliwal-North 22.1.1860
        d6 William Ford * 15.9.1861 ~ Lady Grey 26.1.1862
        d7 Anna Sofia x Wepener 17.7.1883 Hendrik   Petrus Cornelius DIPPENAAR
        d8 Thomas Alfred
b3 Mary Ann * c. 1805 x c.1822 George HALLAM xx 20.4.1837 Richard WATSON * c.1801
b4 Thomas * London, England c 1809 † King William's Town 28.6.1835, unmarried
b5 Emily * 1819 x 19.9.1837 Henry JONES * c.1815
b6 Ester Arabella * Salem Hills c. 1823 † Grahamstown 1828 (refer P.M. Barnes: *Through the chequered path*)

Unclassified:
Charles Henry Howard * 1843 x OFS 20.7.1874 Anna Emerentia HUDSON * 29.9.1859 ~ Burgersdorp 8.1.1860 daughter of Richard Hudson and Anna Isabella Kotze
Henry Howard x Cradock 19.12.1852 Alida Sofia NIEUWENHUYS widow of J. Walker
Henry Howard x Cornelia Maria DELPORT (she xx Albanie 7.7.1856 William Gravett)
James Edward Howard * c.1857 x Burgersdorp 22.5.1875 Judith Jacoba Fredrika HAYWOOD * 24.8.1856 ~ Ladismith 18.1.1857 (daughter of John James)
James Hibbert Howard x Maria Elizabeth EDWARDS
    b1 Dorothea Elizabeth * 4.10.1893 ~ Barkley-East 19.11.1893
Michael Howard x Hester Jacoba LOTTERING

DETAILED GENEALOGIES

b1 Arnoldus * 16.10.1862 ~ Hopetown 2.10.1864

Thomas Percival Howard * Durban c. 1888 † Benoni 27.2.1931 (42.10), Storeman SAR x Laura NN
  b1 Phyllis Irene * 1813
  b2 Kennith Basil * 1914
  b3 Dennis Trevor * 1919
  b4 Reginald Cavell * 1927
  b? 'Johnny' James Alexander Howard * 7.8.1923 † 27.7.1968 x Mary Victoria MILTON * 28.9.1925 † 12.11.1991
    c? Kenneth Steve * Durban 4.10.1947 x Ingrid Stella ESTMENT * Johannesburg 1.9.1950
      d1 Eloise * Durban 4.4.1972 x Durban Pey Malan Geldenhuys * Gwelo, Rhodesia 22.12.1970
        e1 Matthew Dylan * Durban 3.4.2001 (father: David James Sinton * 27.3.1975)
        e2 Jake * Durban 18.12.2007 † Estcourt 30.12.2007
        e1 Lucy Hope * Durban 29.3.2009
      d2 Dylan * Durban

JELLEY

a1 Thomas Jely 1472
  b1 Thomas Jelle 1518, held a tenement in Ayr, Scotland (*Friars Ayr*, p.81)
    c1 Robert Jely 1524
      d1 William Jellie 1673 Cruikens, a parish of Carnwath (Lanark C.R.)
        e1 Andrew Jellie 1684, and his wife were residents in the parish of Borgue
          f1 William Jelly 1798 Creetown, was a mariner (Kirkcudbright)
            g1 Missing link
              h1 Godfrey Jelley c.1875 x Mary McKenzie
                i? Cecil William Gordon * 11.10.1898 † 23.6.1977 x Mary McRobert PATERSON * Isipingo 1902 † 13.11.1943 xx 1946 Joyce Pamela DEEVES
                  j1 Brian * 11.3.1932
                  j2 William Paterson * 6.7.1935 x 11.10.1958 Margaret Mary Elaine WHITELEY * 16.12.1935

         k1 Grahame David * 22.3.1959 x Drakensberg
             6.6.1992 Renene Delene **GELDENHUYS** *
             8.8.1968
             l1 **Courtney Sacha** * 13.9.1993 Triangle
             l2 **Brendan Vaughan** * 15.11.1996 Chipinge
         k2 Keith Brian

l? George Oliver Jeley 1909 British author and poet * Fosse Alfred
l? Louise Isabel Jelly 1910 American actress * Kirtland, Louise

LE ROUX

a Jean * c1667 x C1703 Jeanne MOUY * in France about 1686
c Johanna Le Roux ~ 21.7.1748 x Johannes SWART xx Johannes Albertus GILDENHUYZEN (Geldenhuys) ~ 5.4.1750, a burger of Stellenbosch and son of Hendrik GELDENHUYS and Cornelia SWART

Also: Susanna Catharina MALAN, daughter of Aletta Magdalena Susanna LE ROUX *1.9.1913 † 19.8.1997, married Preller Matt GELDENHUYS

Note also: brother to Jean, Gabriel le ROUX * 25.7.1669, in Blois, France – is also a stamvader of a very large Le Roux family.

LOTTER

DETAILED GENEALOGIES

a1 **Matthias**, arrived 1734 † 1752 x Susanna ROGE (3 children), xx 16.11.1736 Anna Dorethea VAN DEN BERG (6 children)
  b1 Johannes Casparus * 1737 x Johanna Catharina VAN KERKEN (9 children)
  b4 Christoffel * 1744 x Susanna Sophie JACOBS (11 children)
      c? Matthias Johannes – 7 children
      c? Christoffel – 3 children
      c? Willem Godfried – 5 children
  b6 Willem Godfried * 1748 x Helena CORNELISSE xx Wilhelmina WENTZEL (10 children)
  c? Johannes George * 1777 – 6 children
  c? Willem Godfried * 1780 – 5 children
  c? Matthias – 4 children
      d? Willem Godfried * 1808
      d? Lourens Johannes * 1812
  c? Carel David x 1810 Catharina Dorethea van ECHTEN
      d? Willem Godfried * 1811
      d? Salomon * 1814

        ? Jan Lotter
      g? Matthia Martha * Johannesburg 19.10.1916 † Johannesburg 1982 (66) x 1939 Abram Carl Frederik Preller GELDENHUYS
        h1 Johannes Albertus Geldenhuys * Johannesburg 15.8.1940 x Luanshya, N. Rhodesia 23.3.1964 Julia Lillian DIPPENAAR
          i1 Paul Preller Geldenhuys * Ndola, N.R. 15.12.1966 x Edenvale 31.12.1988 Karen DE WAAL * VanderByl Park 29.5.1966
            j1 Chanel * Durban 18.4.1990
            j2 **Craig Jannie Geldenhuys** * Durban 15.3.1993
        h2 Preller Matt Geldenhuys * Rustpan, Bothaville 20.2.1943 x Fort Victoria 5.3.1966 Susanna Catharina MALAN * Lichtenburg 5.3.1945
          i1 Renene Delene * Gwelo S. Rhodesia 8.8.1968 x Drakensberg 6.6.1992 Grahame David JELLEY * 22.3.1959
            j1 **Courtney Sacha** * Triangle 13.9.1993
            j2 **Brendan Vaughan Jelley** * Chipinge 16.11.1996
          i2 **Pey Malan Geldenhuys** ab6c3d7e4f3g5h1i6j2k2 * Gwelo, S. Rhodesia 22.12.1970 x Welkom 2.4.1994 Marion MULLER xx Durban 27.4.2007 Eloise HOWARD
            j1 Matthew Dylan Howard * Durban 3.4.2001 (Step-son)
            j2 Jake * Durban 18.12.2007 † Estcourt 30.12.2007
            j3 Lucy Hope * Durban 29.3.2009
        h3 Delene Elizabeth * 27.2.1945 Oudtshoorn x Pretoria 2.6.1966 Dr. Johannes Jacobus F BOUWER xx Durban Stuart John MCCOLL
          i1 Chanli * 12 10 1970 x Charles Roy BRINK * 1.1.1961
            j1 Tal J Brink *27.8.1995 Tauranga, New Zealand
            j2 Nea D * 27.2.1998 Waitakere, New Zealand
            j3 Deu G * 7.11.1999 Auckland, New Zealand
            j4 Gem * 17.10.2001 Auckland, New Zealand
          i2 Rensha * 15.2.1972 Salisbury, Rhodesia
        h4 Dawn * Luanshya N. Rhodesia 1949 † Musenga Plots, Chingola 13.8.1954

MALAN

MALAN

a1 **Jacques Malan** * 1665 St Martin-de-la-Brasque D'Aigues, France † Stellenbosch 1742, arrived 1688 from Merindol, near Avignon, Provence, France x Drakenstein 1699 Isabeau Elisabeth LE LONG * La Motte-d'Aigues 1668 † 1736 Stellenbosch. Jacques was the son of Antoine Mallan 1639 – 1688 and Isabeau VERDETTE 1649 – 1688. Jacques had 6 children
   b1 Jacobus * Drakenstein 2.7.1700 † young
   b2 Elisabeth Anna * Drakenstein 30.11.1701 = Stellenbosch (NG) 22.1.1702 x Stellenbosch 29.4.1725 Hermanus KRIEL * Hanau, Germany 1694 † Paarl xx 5.12.1745 Paarl Johann Caspar SCHLEE
   b3 Daniel * Drakenstein 11.9.1703 † Stellenbosch 25.1.1770 x Stellenbosch 8.8.1724 Maria VERDEAU (widow of Pieter Jourdan) * 1700 † 1750 daughter of Hercule VERDEAU and Maria Catharina HUIBEAUX xx Cape Town 13.12.1750 Emerentia STEYN (widow of Arnoud SCHEPHAUT) = Cape Town 21.3.1717 † 1762 daughter of Jacobus STEYN and Maria POTGIETER. He was a farmer at Morgenster, Hottentots-Holland – 13 children
      c3 Jacobus Hermanus * 1729 x 7.3.1756 Anna Elizabeth LOUW – 3 children
         d3 Daniel Josias * 1760 x 9.11.1783 Magdalena ODENDAAL – 5 children
            e2 Johannes Jacobus * 1786 x 7.10.1815 Sophia Margaretha van BRAKEL 3 children
               g1 Servaas
               g2 Hermanus Johannes Willem
      c4 Daniel Wynand * 1731 x 26.12.1753 Elsabe WIUM – 4 children
         f2 Hermanus Johannes * 1818 x Jeannetta de KOCK 4
         d3 Pieter * 1760 x Elisabeth REYNIERSE – 9 children
            e1 Daniel W * 1792 x 6.7.1816 Anna Maria FICK
               f1 Pieter Daniel * 1817
               f2 Christiaan Jacobus * 1820
               f4 Daniel W * 1827
            e4 Johannes Jacobus Reynierse
   b4 Maria * Drakenstein 6.4.1705 † 25.2.1780 x Stellenbosch 30.4.1724 Adriaan LOUW = Cape Town 12.11.1702 † Roggeveld 1772 son of Jacobus LOUW and Maria van BRAKEN
   b5 Catharina * Drakenstein 20.3.1707 = Paarl (NG) 15.5.1707 † young.
   b6 David * Drakenstein 19.7.1708 = Cape Town (NG) 27.9.1708 † 1792 x Paarl 17.4.1735 Eleonora MELIUS = Paarl 28.4.1715 † Mrt 1750 daughter of Johan Heinrich MELIUS

DETAILED GENEALOGIES

and Hester ROUX xx Paarl 22.11.1750 Elisabeth MARAIS = Paarl 23.12.1725 † 1802 daughter of Stephanus MARIAS and Maria Elisabeth de VILLIERS.
- c1 Hester Elisabeth * Paarl 4.3.1736 = Paarl (NG) 25.3.1736 † young.
- c2 Maria * Paarl 28.3.1737 = Paarl (NG) 7.4.1737 † young.
- c3 Jacobus **Johannes** * Paarl 10.4.1739 = Paarl (NG) 3.5.1739 † 19.8.1806 x Paarl 5.9.1762 Anna Aletta RETIEF * Paarl 18.7.1744 † 18.4.1795 daughter of Francois RETIEF and Anna MARAIS xx Cape Town 19.6.1796 Aletta BOSMAN = Paarl 2.12.1753 † Nov 1809 daughter of Hermanus BOSMAN and Maria MARIAS. Jacobus was a farmer in the Palmeit Valleij, Drakenstein
    - d1 Anna Aletta = Paarl (NG) 4.9.1763 † 1817 x Paarl 11.10.1789 Schalk Willem BURGER = 26.4.1750 son of Schalk Willem BURGER and Hester SMIT xx Cape Town 31.3.1799 Jacob EKSTEEN = 2.2.1750 son of Petrus Michiel EKSTEEN and Sophia CLOETE.
    - d2 **David** * 7.5.1765 Wellington † 4.8.1851 x 8.5.1791 Margarita Elizabeth RETIEF Tulbagh
        - e1 Jacobus Johannes * Paarl 8.2.1792 = Paarl (NG) 26.2.1792 † young (x Hester Johanna JOUBERT xx Hilletje Johanna BASSON – 12 children)
        - e2 Francois Daniel Johannes * Tulbagh 20.7.1794 = Tulbagh (NG) 18.3.1824 x Tulbagh 3.9.1820 Margaretha Johanna NAUDÉ * June 1802 † Tulbagh 25.12.1853 daughter of Jacob NAUDÉ and Martha RETIEF
        - e3 Jacobus Johannes * Tulbagh 25.8.1796 = Tulbagh (NG) 24.3.1799 † 1819 (not married)
        - e4 David Jacobus * Tulbagh 7.3.1799 = Tulbagh (NG) 24.3.1799 † 1819 (not married – died same year as elder brother) 1803 x Helena Alberta SMIT - 5 children
        - e5 **Daniel Stephanus** * Tulbagh 26.5.1801 = Tulbagh (NG) 11.6.1801 † Tulbagh 2.9.1827 x Tulbagh 2.9.1827 Elisabeth Magdalena MÖLLER * Tulbagh 30.10.1808 † Tulbagh 5.12.1872 daughter of Hendrik Francois MÖLLER and Anna Debora MARAIS (Farmer – Verrrekijker, Tulbagh)
            - f1 Anna Debora * Tulbagh 17.11.1828 = Tulbagh (NG) 14.12.1828 † jonk.
            - f2 David Jacobus * Tulbagh 3.3.1831 = Tulbagh (NG) 1.5.1831 † Tulbagh 14.1.1885 x Kruisvallei 27.7.1854 Margaretha Helena Frederika THERON * Tulbagh 1836 † Tulbagh 11.11.1876 daughter of Jacobus Francois THERON and Margaretha Johanna NAUDE xx Ceres 21.12.1877 Anna Gertruida Jacoba MARAIS * Ceres 14.7.1854. Farmer Verrekijker, Tulbagh
            - f3 Margaretha Elisabeth * Tulbagh 23.8.1832 = Tulbagh (NG) 21.10.1832 x Kruisvallei 9.5.1853 Izaak Willem NEETHLING * Tulbagh 28.10.1827 son of Frederik Jacobus NEETHLING and Hester Elizabeth MOLLER
            - f4 Hendrik **Francois** * Tulbagh 18.10.1833 = Tulbagh (NG) 3.11.1833 † Lichtenburg 25.11.1912 x Tulbagh 27.9.1858 Anna Margaretha Elizabeth DU TOIT †? Lichtenburg
                - g1 Daniel Stephanus * Tulbagh 2.2.1860 = Kruisvallei (NG) 18.3.1860 † 1938 x Johanna Catharina Wilhelmina THERON * Tulbagh 9.6.1871 † Lichtenburg 14.12.1895 daughter of Pieter Francois THERON and Elizabeth Petronella Retief xx Kimberley? Louisa Sophia PIRZENTHAL * Cradock Aug 1864 † Port Shepstone 29.1.1958 daughter of Johann Wilhelm PIRZENTHAL and Fredericka Mary NN
                - g2 Margaretha Johanna * Tulbagh 24.6.1863 + Kruisvallei (NG) 2.8.1863
                - g3 David Jacobus * Tulbagh 5.4.1867 = Kruisvallei (NG) 5.5.1867 x Lichtenburg 13.7.1909 Cornelia Maria VENTER * Ventersdorp 1889 † Lichtenburg 13.3.1941 daughter of Joseph Michiel VENTER

g4 Elizabeth Magdalena * Tulbagh 23.6.1874 = Kruisvallei (NG) 12.7.1874 x JOUBERT
g5 **Hendrik Francois** * Tulbagh 15.12.1879 = Kruisvallei (NG) 11.1.1880 † Lichtenburg 29.5.1959 (80) x Lichtenburg 2.6.1903 Getruida Johanna VAN EEDEN * Jacobsdal 5.2.1883 † Lichtenburg 6.8.1951 daughter of Frederik Jacobus VAN EEDEN and Heila Magdalena NN xx Lichtenburg? Anna Catharina TERBLANCHE (Farmer – Tweelingspruit, Lichtenburg).
    h1 Hendrik Francois * Lichtenburg 16.2.1904 = Lichtenburg (NG) 29.5.1904 † Lichtenburg 6.8.1960 x Zeerust 30.5.1953 Margaretha Isabella ROUX * Ventersdorp 12.7.1913 † Stellenbosch 18.9.1961 daughter of Paul ROUX and Hester Susanna CRONJE (Childless; Night guard)
    h2 Frederik Jakobus * Lichtenburg 27.7.1905 = Lichtenburg (H) 26.11.1905 † Vryburg 20.8.1943 x Lichtenburg 12.9.1933 Hester Cecelia le ROUX * Lichtenburg 6.12.1912 † Johannesburg 30.9.1935 daughter of Zacharias Petrus LE ROUX and Catharina Maria VENTER (Farmer – Doornhoek, Lichtenburg: childless)
    h3 Daniel Stefanus * Lichtenburg 13.8.1906 = Lichtenburg (H) 21.101906 † Rustenburg 4.9.1982 x Lichtenburg Susanna Catharina le ROUX * Lichtenburg 12.11.1910 † Rustenburg 16.10.1980 xx Rustenburg? Helina Elizabeth VAN DEN BERG * 30.12.1911 (Farmer – Waterkloof, Rustenburg).
        i1 Boet * x
        i2 Philip Johannes * x Ria Venter
    h4 **Francois Daniel** * Lichtenburg 1.10.1907 = Lichtenburg (NG) 19.1.1908 † Vereeniging 3.4.1988 x Lichtenburg 20.12.1932 Aletta Magdalena Susanna le ROUX * 1.9.1913 Lichtenburg † Vereeniging 19.8.1997
        i1 Aletta Magdalena Susanna * 9.10.1934 x Nicolaas Hendrik VAN AARDT * Heilbron OFS 22.11.1932 son of Hendrik Jacobus VAN AARDT and Magdalena Christina NEL
            j1 Aletta Magdalena Susanna van Aardt * Lusaka 5.5.1955 but registered in South Africa in 1967 x Willem Adriaan Jacobus Oosthuisen. They had three children, all born in Salisbury; Yvette Marie * 6.10.1976, Liesl Adriaana * 27.7.1978 and Schalk Johannes * 31.8.1979
            j2 Hendrik Jacobus van Aardt * Lusaka 18(5?).5.1961 x Ladismith, Cape Joleen **GELDENHUYS**. They had two children, Nicolaas Daniel * Bredasdorp 25.8.1988 and Leane * Alberton 29.5.1987.
            j3 Nicolene van Aardt * Salisbury 3.9.1966 x Alberton 19.9.1987 Reinier Olivier * Sasolburg 22.5.1965. They had two children, both born Johannesburg, Jaco * 9.2.1989 and Anneke * 16.11.1990
        i2 Gertruida Johanna * Lichtenburg 27.12.1936 = Lichtenburg (NG) 24.1.1937 x "Hansie" Johannes Jurgens Bezuidenhout
            j1 Johann Bezuidenhout xx Adele
            j2 Letitia Bezuidenhoudt x Mark Gooding – to Australia
            j3 Francois Bezuidenhoudt
        i3 Hendrik Francois * Lichtenburg 5.11.1943 (5 September?) = Lichtenburg (NG) 5.12.1943 x Rina

DETAILED GENEALOGIES

GERBER * Pietersburg 5.3.1942 (daughter of Salomon Ignatius Gerber and Magdalena Petronella)
    j1 Theresa (Tessa) * Pretoria 7.2.1963
    j2 Magda * Pretoria 20.4.1964
    j3 Gretha * Pretoria 2.5.1966
    j4 Johannes (Dons) * Pietersburg 25.5.1968 † 25.10.1970
    j5 Philip Malan * Pretoria 14.4.1973 x 3.5.1997 Maritza LOURENS
    j6 Francois Daniel Malan * 12.9.1976
    j7 Eddie Deon Malan * 24.3.1978
i4 Philippus Johannes * Lichtenburg 5.3.1945 = Lichtenburg 22.4.1945 x Groblersdal 3.10.1970 Elcora Bouwer * Groblersdal 26.10.1951
    j1 Roux Daniel * Groblersdal 5.7.1971 x Boksburg 25.10.1997 Lesley Ann REEVE * Boksburg 11.11.1973
    j2 Elsa-Lou Cornelia * Chiredzi 20.11.1973 x. Pretoria 28.11.1998 Willem Petrus Nel * Berchley, Kempton Park 20.2.1972
i5 Susanna **Catharina** * Lichtenburg 5.3.1945 = Lichtenburg (NG) 22.4.1945 x Fort Victoria 5.3.1966 Preller Matt **GELDENHUYS** * Bothaville 20.2.1943 son of Abram Carl Frederik Preller GELDENHUYS and Mathia Martha LOTTER
    j1 Renene Delene Geldenhuys * Gwelo 8.8.1968 x Drakensberg 6.6.1992 Grahame David Jelly 13.9.1993. They had two children; * Triangle 13.9.1993 Courtney Sacha Jelley and * Chipinge 15.11.1996 **Brendan Vaughan Jelley**
    j2 Pey **Malan Geldenhuys** * Gwelo 22.12.1970 ab6c3d7e4f3g5h1i6j2k2 x Welkom 2.4.1994 Marion Muller xx Durban 27.4.2007 Eloise Howard * Durban 4.4.1972
        k1 Matthew Dylan Howard * Durban 3.4.2001 (Step-son)
        k2 Jake * Durban 18.12.1970 † 30.12.1970
        k3 Lucy Hope * Durban 29.3.2009
i6 Francois Daniel * Lichtenburg 7.2.1949 = Lichtenburg (NG) 3.4.1949 x Enkeldoorn 5.2.1972 Helena Alberta LOCK * Enkeldoorn 14.5.1950 daughter of Willem LOCK and Anna Magdalena SMITH
    j1 Amanda * Fort Victoria 13.4.1974 = Fort Victoria (NG) 5.5.1974 x Charles STOPFORTH
    j2 Francois Daniel * Salisbury 24.12.1976 = Salisbury (NG) 17.4.1977 x Vereeniging 8.5.1999 Adele du Plessis
h5 Willem Stefanus * Lichtenburg 13.10.1908 = Lichtenburg (NG) 24.1.1909 † Klerksdorp 9.3.1975 x Lichtenburg? Isabella Catharina CONRADIE
h6 David Jacob * Lichtenburg 28.10.1910 = Lichtenburg (NG) 5.2.1911 † Johannesburg 9.4.1984 x Coligny 20.12.1938 Carolina Johanna Susanna CALITZ * Hartbeestfontein 6.1.1916 † Coligny 20.10.1983
h7 Gert Johannes * Lichtenburg 16.4.1912 = Lichtenburg (NG) 4.8.1912 † 2.2.1994 x Esma NN

h8 Jacobus Bernandus * Lichtenburg 15.8.1916 = Lichtenburg (NG) 3.11.1916 † Tzaneen 19.3.1981 x Kuruman? Hester Lecia SCHOEMAN * 14.9.1916.
h9 Heila Magdalena * 11.7.1918 † 7.8.1918
h10A Felix Festus * Lichtenburg 29.3.1920 = Lichtenburg (NG) 4.7.1920 † 14.10.1955
h11B Gideon Van Eeden * Lichtenburg 26.10.1924 = Lichtenburg (NG) 8.2.19.25 † Heidelberg, Tvl 17.12.1992 x Lichtenburg? Wilhelmina Johanna Maria MINNAAR * 10.10.1925
e6 Margaretha Elisabeth * Tulbagh 8.11.1803 = Tulbagh (NG) 27.11.1803 † Tulbagh 17.1.1866 x Worcester 1.11.1823 Jacobus Arnoldus Hugo * 3.2.1799 †   Tulbagh 11.2.1837 son of Petrus Francois HUGO and Margaretha Jacoba THERON
e7 a daughter * 1806 † young
e7 Carel Wynand * 1812 x Magdalena HUGO – 15 children
    f2 Wynand Charl x Margaretha Elisabeth JOUBERT
        g1 Wynand Charl * Beyersfontein, Murraysburg 16.8.1872 – famous Boer general, - to Tanganyika 1907
    f14 Abraham Hugo * 9.8.1860 x Hendrina JOUBERT, daughter of Boer General Piet Joubert
    f5 Anna Debora * Tulbagh 14.7.18.35 = Tulbagh (NG) 26.9.1835 † Tulbagh 23.12.1867 unmarried
    f6 Daniel Stephanus * Tulbagh 21.7.1837 = Tulbagh (NG) 27.8.1837 † young
    f7 Elisabeth Magdalena * Tulbagh 23.4.1840 = Tulbagh (NG) 29.11.1842 x Tulbagh 27.2.1867 Jan Petrus MARAIS
    f8 Daniel Stephanus * Tulbagh 21.1.1842 = Tulbagh (NG) 29.11.1842 † Tulbagh 15.5.1927 x Kruisvallei 7.11.1876 Maria Magdalena MÖLLER * Tulbagh 1855 † Tulbagh 9.10.1921 daughter of Charl Abraham MÖLLER and Maria Magdalena NN xx Kruisvallei 7.11.1922 Elizabeth Johanna Christina KOTZE * 1860
    f9 Francois Daniel * Tulbagh 6.2.1844 = Kruisvallei (NG) 25.2.1844 † Wolseley 26.12.1915 not married Farmer Verrekijker, Tulbagh
    f10A Hester Maria * Tulbagh 7.12.1848 = Kruisvallei (NG) 21.1.1849
    f11B Paul Johannes * Tulbagh 27.4.1852 = Kruisvallei (NG) 20.5.1852
d3 Lenora Elisabeth = Paarl (NG) 5.4.1767 † 1816 x Paarl Daniel Jeremias du TOIT = 18.5.1766 son of Andries du TOIT and Alida Margaretha MOLLER xx Stellenbosch 2.5.1812 Guillaume Jacobus GOOSEN = 23.8.1750 son of Cornelis GOOSEN and Wilhelmina Hendrina BERKMAN
d4 Maria = Paarl (NG) 25.11.1770 † 1774
d5 Jacobus Francois = Paarl (NG) 28.3.1773 † 1780.
d6 Daniel Johannes * Swartland 7.8.1775 = Swartland (NG) 3.9.1775 † 24 Riviere 21.12.1828 x Cape Town 11.5.1794 Rachel Elisabeth du PLESSIS = 9.5.1773 daughter of Jan Gabriel du PLESSIS and Rachel BLIGNAUT xx Stellenbosch 8.11.1807 Maria Christina LOUW * Paarl 5.1.1790 † Paarl 18.4.1833 daughter of Carel Wynand LOUW and Elsie Maria van der MERWE (Farmer – Eikelboom, Wellington)
d7 Maria Ester = Paarl (NG) 13.5.1781.
d8 Hester Margaretha * Swartland (NG) 28.10.1781
d9 Jacobus Francois * Wagenmakersvallei 15.6.1783 = Paarl (NG) 20.7.1783 † Wellington 17.5 1863 x Cape Town 31.10.1802 Maria Susanna ROSSOUW * 26.6.1785 † Wellington 6.10.1840 daughter of Gabriel ROSSOUW and Margaretha Magdalena Louw xx Charl Wynand LOUW and Elisabeth Maria van der MERWE (Farmer Groenfontein, Bovlei, Wellington).
c4 Daniel * Paarl 22.10.1741 = Paarl (NG) 12.11.1741 † Stellenbosch 10.3.1828 x Paarl 12.2.1763 Geertruida MARAIS * Paarl 26.3.1745 † 14.1.1784 daughter of Jacob MARAIS and Maria Elisabeth BOEIENS xx Stellenbosch 9.5.1784 Debora NAUDÉ * Paarl 19.9.1747 † 3.1.1831 daughter of Jacob NAUDÉ and Anna Susanna du TOIT (Farmer – Leeuwenvallei, Wellington).

DETAILED GENEALOGIES

c5 David * Paarl 11.9.1751 = Paarl (NG) 3.10.1751 † Somerset-East before 23.10.1824 x Paarl 27.10.1771 Elisabeth MALAN = Cape Town 21.10.1753 † Somerset-East 18.2.1842 daughter of Daniel MALAN and Emerentia STEYN; David took part in Slagtersnek (death and prison sentence) Farmer Buffelshoek, Zwagershoek, Somerset-East – 10 children
   d7 Jacobus * 1787 † 9.4.1838 with Voortrekker leaders Piet and Dirkie UYS, and two other Malans', x Margaretha Maria SWART xx Anna M.KLOPPER
      e1 David Ed * 1826 † 9.4.1838 (victim with his father at the massacre of P. UYS).
      e4 Hercules Philip * 2.11.1836 † 2.12.1899 (Boer-War). Rustenburg
   d9 Hercules Philip * 1792 † 1837, with Piet RETIEF, x Anna Maria BREED
      e1 David Daniel * 1816 † during Boer War x 1837? Anna Cornelia VILJOEN * 1815, farmed Strydfontein, Kroonstad area. They had 15 children, 10 daughters and 5 sons.
         f1-3 – Three daughters
         f4 Johanna Maria * 1845 x Willem SPANNENBERG (their descendants still live in Bothaville)
         f7 Jan Hendrik * 1851 x Anna Magdalena HATTING (lived on Bezuidenhoudskraal, district Rosendal – had two sons)
            g2 Francois * 1877 x Catharina DREYER (farmed Klipdrift, Bothaville)
               h? Jan (still lives in the Bothaville area)
         f9 Magdalena Margaretha * 1854 x Christiaan Loouwrens (Cul) DREYER 1851-1929
         f11 Jacob Jacobus † 1916 x Maria Alletta SERFONTEIN (they had 4 daughters and a son)
            g3 Dawid Daniel * 1903 † 1970 x Anna Susanna MARAIS * 1906 † 1968 lived on the Preller farm de Bank, Bothaville district.
               h1 Jacoba Magrieta * 1929 x Louis S. COETZEE (from Pretoria)
               h2 Jacob Jacobus (Jan) * 1933 x Anna Bronkhorst
               h3 Gert Lodewicus MARAIS (Gert) * 1935 x Helena (Ria) BURGER * 1934
               h4 David Daniel (Dawie) * 1943 x Joyce LINDEVELDT
               h5 Maria Magdalena (Milla) * 1944 x Andries van der WALT (Milla ia a nurse in Pretoria)
         f12 Martina Jacoba * 1860 x Hendrik Oostenwald LOUWRENS (farmed Verlaatspruit, Bothaville district)
      e2 Johannes Augustinus † aged 14, with Piet and Dirk UYS, at Italeni 9.4.1838
      e3 Hercules Philip, Komdt. in 1st Boer War 1880
      e4 Jacob ("Kaffer") Jacobus * 16.1.1820 † 19.1.191-, from Lydenburg, L.V. Z.A.R.
c6 Maria Elisabeth * Paarl 13.4.1754 = Paarl (NG) 5.5.1754 † Tygerberg 25.1.1841 x Paarl 10.2.1771 Hendrik Cornelis ENGELA = Swartland 3.11.1748 son of Jürgen Heinrich ENGELA and Anna van STADEN xx Cape Town 28.8.1791 David de VILLIERS = Paarl 13 4 1754 son of Pieter de VILLIERS and Elisabeth JOUBERT.
c7 Stephanus * Cape Town 16.12.1756 = Paarl (NG) 2.1.1757 † Cape Town 29.3.1836 x Swartland 9.2.1794 Margaretha Adelheyt HENDRIKS = 14.4.1765 daughter of Hieronymus HENDRIKS and Louisa SCHEFFER. Boer War Veldkornet and farmer – Kuiperskraal, Durbanville.
c8 Elisabeth Margaretha * Paarl 20.2. 1760 = Paarl (NG) 9.3.1760 † 3.6.1810 x Swartland 26.5.1776 Adriaan de NICKER = 3.10.1749 son of Pieter de NICKER and Johanna GREEFF xx Swartland 25.2.1781 Francois de VILLIERS * 14.8.1760 † 13.12.1830 son of Pieter de VILLIERS and Elisabeth JOUBERT
c9 Jacob * Paarl 21.11.1762 = Paarl (NG) 12.12.1762 † Cape Town 24.6.1843 x Cape Town 11.1.1784 Cornelia MOSTERT + 22.9.1765 daughter of Louis MOSTERT = 22.9.1765 daughter of Louis MOSTERT and Cornelia STRYDOM. Farmer Knorhoek, Hottentots-Holland. Later lived in Cape Town.
b7 Jacobus * Drakenstein 8.11.1710 = Cape Town (NG) 14.12.1710 † young

McCOLL

McColl SA Stamvader
  bx Missing link
    c1 Peter John x Joyce Edith Matchett
      d1 Stuart John * 1949 x xx xx Delene Elizabeth Geldenhuys (Bouwer divorsee)
        E1 Dayvd * 1991

MOODIE

a1 James Moodie * 1757 the last (9TH) Laird of Melsetter, Scotland † 1828 (71) x Elizabeth DUNBAR
  b1 **Benjamin** Moodie * 1.1.1789 Melsetter, Orkney Islands, Scotland † Westfield, Port Alfred 2.4.1856 (67) arrived 1817 x Scotland 1816 Margaret MALCOLMSEN † Grootvadersbosch 1838 xx London 1841 Susan BARNETT
    c1 **James Benjamin Donald** * Scotland 26.5.1819 † Bethlehem O.F.S., 4.12.1894 (75) x Grahamstown 4.3.1836 Sara Maria Johanna VAN ZYL (* 19.12.1817. †.20.7.1897)
      d1 Benjamin * Doornhoek, Burgersdorp 19.12.1836 † Egmont Rouxville 21.7.1877 x Dorothea Maria HENNING

DETAILED GENEALOGIES

  e1 James * Grootfontein, Craddock 10.2.1864 – captured at the Battle of Paardeberg, with Cronje, x Ladybrand Johanna Christina VAN ZYL
  f1 Benjamin * 25.1.1893
  f2 Hester Magdalena * 21.6.1903
  e2 Hester Magdalena * 10.12.1865 x Bloemfontein 2.9/1885 William DEALE
  e3 Donald Martin * 15.1.1867 † 3.9.1887 – unmarried
  e5 Thomas * Barletta, Ladybrand 19.5.1873 † 24.2.1947, captured with Cronje at Paardeberg, prisoner of war at St Helena, x 30.8.1915 Petronella Sophia PRETORIUS (7.1.1886 – 12.6.1963)
   f1 Benjamin * 15.8.1916 x 22.4.1943 Elizabeth Gertruyda THERON
    g1 Thomas * 1.8.1944
    g2 Stephen Theron * 22.10.1945
 d2 Thomas * Groortvadersbosch, Swellendam 29.11.1839 † Waterfall, Melsetter S.R. (Groot Tom of Moodie Trek fame) x Smithfield 24.8.1863 Cecilia Jacomina ROBBERTSE (* Somerset-East 20.6.1842)
  e2 Sarah Maria * 17.12.1866 x Fort Victoria S.R. George Benjamin Dunbar MOODIE (her cousin)
 d3 Donald Montgomery * Swellendam 7.4.1841 † Newcastle, Natal Sept 1897 x Mauritius 1869 Emma HADDON
 d6 **Margery Hester** * 4.12.1845 † 1937 (92) x 16.3.1863 Edmund Francis COLEMAN (* 12.12.1836 † 16.1.1898)
  e2 **Lucretia Maria Coleman** * 15.8.1865 † 13.10.1954 (89) x 3.3.1896 Sydney Nathaniel ARNOTT (28.11.1867-14.12.1924)
   f4 Stella Nesta Arnott * 27.5.1902 † 14.4.1985 (83) x 12.8.1929 Alan WHITELEY (* 11.10.1897 † 8.3.1989)
    g2 **Margaret Mary Elaine Whiteley*** 16.12.1935 x 11.10.1958 William Paterson JELLEY (6.7.1935)
     h1 **Grahame David Jelley** * 22.3.1959 Drakensberg 6.6.1992 Renene Delene **GELDENHUYS** * Gwelo 8.8.1968
      i1 **Courtney Sacha Jelley** * 13.9.1993 Triangle Zimbabwe
      i2 **Brendan Vaughan Jelley** * Chipinge 15.11.1996
b2 Thomas † 27.4.1824
b3 Donald * Melsetter, Scotland 25.6.1794 † Pietermaritzburg 27.8.1861, arrived in 1820, x Albany 29.3.1824 Elizabeth Sophia PIGOT † 26.10.1881
 c1 William James Dunbar * Port Francis, Cape Colony 13.11.1827 † 1875 x in Natal 28.9.1853 Clarissa Meek – 11 children
  d1 Donald Sutherland Dunbar * Pietermaritzburg 2.9.1855 † Pondoland 22.12.1875
  d2 Malcolm James Dunbar * 27.9 1857 † Battle of Isandlhana 22.1.1879
  d3 George Benjamin Dunbar * Pietermaritzburg 8.7.1861 † Melsetter, S. Rhodesia 9.3.1897, promoter of the Moodie-Trek to Rhodesia, x Fort Victoria 24.10.1892 Sarah Maria MOODIE (his second cousin and daughter of Groot Tom)
   e1 Cecilia Barbara Lovemore
   e2 Leander Starr Jameson (died in infancy)
   e3 George Benjamin Dunbar * 14.2.1897 – became the leader of the Natal Moodies 13.7.1903
  d4 William Alexander Dunbar * 8.12.63 x Standerton 29.11.86 Hester Helena Meyer
   e2 Hester Helena * 17.7.88
   e2 Hilda Mildred * 11.2.90
  d5 Norman Robert Dunbar * 6.8.63 – unmarried
  d6 Cuthbert John Dunbar * 24.2.67 – unmarried
  d7 Alan Patrick * 19.1.71 – unmarried
  d8 Charlotte Mary St. Clair x Fred Robert MOOR (later premier of Natal) – 7 children
   e1 Advocate St Clair
   e2 Cosmos

            e3 Leonore
            e4 Marion x 1903 Owen Walters
            e5 Shirley
            e6 Marjorie
         d9 Flora Agnes Strickland
         d10 Clara Jessie Maude x Richard Rimer
            e1 Guy
            e2 Grace
            e3 Joyce
   c2 George Pigot * Grahamstown 22.1.1829
   c3 Donald Hugh Menzies * Grahamstown 22.4.1830 x 1.5.1867 Maria Adriana Smuts – 18 children, including:
         d? Donald Alfred Pigot * Ladysmith 16.12.1868 – 2 children
            e1 Alfred Donald Robert
            e2 Vista Emma Ina
         d? William George Pigot * 11.5.85
   c6 John Bell * Graaff-Reinet 6.2.1836 † Pietermaritzburg 1876 x Anna Emily Hallett
      d1 Harry * 18.3.1869 x 1892 Lilla Turton
      e1 Donald * 1893
      e2 Dorothea 1896
      e3 Beatrice 1897
   c7 Duncan Campbell Francis * Cape Town 24.1.1838 † 1891 x 1874 Matilda Hunt
      d1 Harold Wedderburn * 21.9.1873 † 1898
   b4 John Wedderburn Dunbar * 1797 † 1869, arrived 1820, returned to London in 1829, * 4.4.1832 Susanna Strickland, family emigrated to Canada (wrote "Ten Years in S.A.")
   b5 Janet * Major Malcolm Nicholson
   b6 Henrietta * 1794 x 1818 Robert Heddle of Melsetter, † 2.7.1833

MUIRHEAD

A Wynne Muirhead x Majorie Hockaday
   b1 Neil Wynn x Lynn Brink
      c1 Kim
      c2 Byron Neil
      c3 Bevan
   b2 Glynn

ODENDAAL

Willem Odendaal, originally Wilhelm Odendall from Cologne, Germany, died 19.1.1732. In 1706 in the service of the Dutch East Company, later a burgher. He married 13.9.1711 Susanna BIEBOW, daughter of Detlev Biebow; remarried 11.11.1717 Judith NEL.

DETAILED GENEALOGIES

Ab6c9d6e4f10g1 Annaline Odendaal * Heidelberg 14.10.1940 x Heidelberg 14.12.1963 Gerhard GELDENHUYS * Worcester 19.11.1937, currently living in Stellenbosh. They have three children

k1 Liza Geldenhuys * 31.12.1964 ~ Stellenbosch-West 4.4.1965 x Jean JOUBERT (ab8c1d8e5f7g5h2i1j3) * 29.6.1962
l1 Jean Daniel Joubert * 29.1.2000 ~ Pinelands 16.7.2000
l2 Gerhard * 10.12.2001 ~ Stellenbosch-Central 7.4.2002
k2 Henriëtte * 18.10.1966 ~ Stellenbosch-North 4.12.1966
k3 Gerhard * 10.3.1970 ~ Boksburg-North 10.5.1970 x Vanessa Clark * 9.1974
l1 Gerhard Robyn * 22.11.1997 ~ Stellenbosch-Sentral 6.7.2008
l2 Mila Cecilia * 24.10.2007 ~ Stellenbosch-Central 6.7.2008

PRELLER

Johan Frederik Preller
1764 † 14.12.1825 x 23.11.1794 Zacharia Christina de Beer (*9.11.1777, † 6.3.1845)
b1 Dina Margaretha ~ 17.5.1798 † Claremont 1.12.1872 x 1822 Johannes Jacobus GERBER
b2 Maria Dorothea ~ 22.3.1861 † Claremont 1.12.1872 x 1822 Christiaan Johannes RABE
b3 Johann Friedrich * 24.10.1802 † 17.2.1829, bachelor.
b4 Aletta Margaretha * about 1804 † 31.5.1861, spinster.
b5 Catharina Francina * 13.1.1805 † 2.1.1876 x 1824 Robert Clunie LOGIE
b6 Anna Christina * 27.5.1808 † Ladismith 14.2.1876 x Ds Dirk van VELDEN
b7 Carel **Friedrich Preller** * Cape Town 11.10.1809 † Wonderheuvel, Kroonstad dist. 1.12.1870 x 12.2.1830 Jacoba Petronella HEYNEMAN † 7.3.1842 xx Pietermaritzburg 30.7.1845 Maria Margaretha NAUDE, widow of C.P. Bothma, † 7.3.1862: xxx M.M.STYDOM
c1 Johanna Susanna * 5.11.1830 x A.C. KEYTER
c2 Johann Friedrich * 25.2.1832 † Lydenburg Tvl 4.5.1863 x Pietermaritzburg 29.12.1852 Susanna Maria Salomina OTTO
d1 Karel Frederik * Pietermaritzburg 13.12.1853
d2 Johan Frederik * Pietermaritzburg 13.9.1855
d3 Gertruida Margaretha * Pietermaritzburg 10.7.1857
d4 Andries Otto * Pietermaritzburg 13.12.1858
c3 Zacharia Christina * 23.1.1834 † 8.9.1834 (aged 7 months)

c4 Johan Carel * 23.7.1838 † Pretoria 1.12.1883 x Potchefstroom 27.8.1860 Susanna Maria BOSMAN
   d1 Sara Susanna
   d2 Jacoba Petronella x Henry NOURSE
   d3 Carel Frederik
   d4 Leticia Hermina
   d5 Adelaide
   d6 Machida
   d7 Florence
c5 Mauritz Herman Otto * Beaufort-Wes 3.7.1840 x Anna Margaretha Elisabeth FURSTENBURG
   d1 Polly x P. HARTOG
   d2 Carry x W HARTOG
   d3 John Pieter Furstenburg
   d4 Robert   )
   d5 Mauritz Herman Otto   ) twins
   d6 Johan Friedrich   )
   d7 Carel Friedrich   ) twins
c6 Carel Friedrich *Beaufort-Wes 1841(?) † Pretoria 25.6.1903 x 11.3.1864 Anna Margaretha SCHOEMAN, widow Vercuil, daughter of Kommandant-General Stephanus Schoem4an
   d1 Gertina Johanna
   d2 Stephanus Carel
c7 Robert Clunie Logie * 5.5.1846 † 8.4.1916 x 14.12.1874 Stephanie Maria Aletta SCHOEMAN, daughter of Kommandant-General Stephanus Schoeman
   d1 Gustav **Schoeman** * 4.10.1875 † 6.10.1943 (68) x 1898 Johanna Christina PRETORIUS – 3 sons
   d2 Else Maria
   d3 Augusta Matilda
   d4 Winifred Letitia
   d5 Julia Margaret
   d6 Clunie Logie
   d7 Stephane Alberta
c8 Petrus Johannes * 21.7.1847. bachelor
c9 James Michael * 11.1.1849 † Nugget, Vredefort dist. 19.5.1907 x Louiza Gezina Maria van NIEKERK
   d1 Carel Frederik
   d2 Ferdinand Theodorus
   d3 Josephus van Niekerk Naude
   d4 Johan Reyno Benjamin
c10 Anna Maria Aletta Margaretha * 11.1.1849
c11 Zacharia Christina Carolina 4.10.1850
c12 Abraham Christoffel Naudé Preller * 18.1.1853 x? Helletta Lephina BOTHA † 7.8.1889 xx? Maria Elizabeth PRETORIUS † 21.9.1893 xx? Johanna Magdalena WESSELS † 29.6.1907 (daughter of Mattheus Gerhardus Wessels and Johanna Fronica Delport)
   d1 **Anna Elizabeth Preller*** 23.2.1879 † 5.5.1976 (aged 97) x 27.6.1899 **Johannes Albertus GELDENHUYS** † 28.5.1944
      e1 Helletta Levina * 2.5.1900, † Kroonstad, Boer War 15.8.1991
      e2 Hendrik Jacobus Geldenhuys * 12.7.1902 x 28.8.1928 Adrianna Martha Maria Keyser
      e3 Elizabeth x 6.11.1904 x 23.7.1925 Paul Christiaan Gideon Steyn Jordaan
      e4 Anna Elizabeth * 11.9.1907 x? Gideon Malherbe
      e5 Maria Susanna Wilhelmina * 27.5.1911 x? Theo van Rensen
      e6 Abram Carl Frederik Preller * Rustpan Bothaville 2.8.1916 † Pretoria 13.2.1972 x Johannesburg Matthia Martha LOTTER * Johannesburg 19.10.1916 † Johannesburg 1992 (76)?
         f1 Johannes Albertus * Johannesburg 15.8.1940 x Luanshya 27.3.1964 Julia Lillian DIPPENAAR

DETAILED GENEALOGIES

       g1 Paul Preller * Ndola Zambia 15.12.1966 x Edenvale Jhb 31.12.1988 Karen DE WAAL * Vanderbylpark 29.5.1966
          h1 Chanel * Durban 18.4.1990
          h2 Craig Jannie Geldenhuys * Durban 15.3.1993
   f2 **Preller Matt** * Rustpan Bothaville 20.2.1943 x Fort Victoria 5.3.1966 Susanna Catharina Malan
       g1 Renene Delene * Gwelo Rhodesia 88.8.1968 x Drakensberg 6.6.1992 Dr Grahame David JELLEY
          h1 **Courtney Sacha Jelley** * 13.9.1993 Triangle Zimbabwe
          h2 **Brendan Vaughan Jelley** * Chipinge 15.11.1996
       g2 **Pey Malan** * Gwelo 22.12.1970 x Welkom 2.4.1994 Marion MULLER xx Durban 27.4.2007 Eloise HOWARD
          h1 Matthew Dylan Howard * Durban 3.4.2001 (Step-son)
          h2 Jake * Durban 18.12.2007 † Estcourt 30.12.2007
          h3 Lucy Hope * Durban 29.3.2009
   f3 Delene Elizabeth * Oudtshoorn 27.2.1945 x Dr. Johannes Jacobus F BOUWER
       g1 Chanli G * 12.101970 x 6.2.1993 Charles Roy BRINK * 1.6.1961 Pretoria
          h1 Tal J Brink * 27.8.1995 New Zealand
          h2 Nea D * 27.2.1998 Auckland, New Zealand
          h3 Deu G * 7.11.1999 Auckland, New Zealand
          h4 Gem * 17.10.2001 Auckland, New Zealand
       g2 Rensha * 15.2.1972 Salisbury, Rhodesia
d2 Carel Friedrich (Charley) * 1881 † Kroonstad 1918 x Violet MUGGLETON
   e1 Elaine * 1911 x Rev J. Francis MACCREATH
   e2 Oscar x East London WALKER
d3 Theunis Louis * 1.1.1883 † 1.7.1884 (1 year and 6 months)
d4 Maria Margaretha *24.3.1887 † 17.5.1887 (2 months)
d5 Helletta Levina *7.8.1888 † 6.8.1889 (1 year and 4 months)
d6 Abraham Christofel Naude (Braam) * 1895 † 1963 x Johanna Margaretha Charlotte (Onnie) WESSELS * 1902 † 1975 (from Dealesville)
   e1 Johanna Wessels * 1927 – spinster
   e2 Francis Winnifred (Winnie) * 1930 x Quintus DEACON
   e3 Abram Christoffel Naude (Boet) * 1935 x Berenice BOTHA * 1933
       f1 Linda x Erwin UHLMANN
          g1 Antoinette
          g2 Michelle
       f2 Abraham * 1960 x Christine VISAGIE, farmed Palmietfontein, Bothaville.
          g1 Abraham Christofel Naude * 26.04.1987
          g2 Sulindie * 8.6.1990
          g3 Ivan * 22.11.1993
       f3 Karen * 1964 x Claus LIPPERT
          g1 Aninke
          g2 Fritz
       f4 Marie-Jeanne * 1969 x Johan KRUGER
       f5 Isle * 1971 x Deon GAUPNER
          g1 Lisa * 10.2.1994
d7 Johanna Fronica Magdalena (Joey) * 1896 † 1943 x Pieter C LUYT
d8 Maria Magdalena (Maraai) * 13.12.1899 † 5.4.1901 Kroonstad Concentration Camp, Anglo-Boer War.
d9 Mattheuwina Gerhardina Wessels (Matt) * 1903 x Dirk J BRINK
   e1 Johanna Magdalena (Madeleine)
   e2 Marthinus Cornelis (Martin)
   e3 Catharina Wilhelmina (Elna)
d10 Anna Carolina * 1905 † De Bank 1919

Unclassified Prellers':
Ancestors of Johanna Elizabeth JORDAAN * 1850 second wife of Carl Frederik Preller * 1853
1 Louis
2 Cornelia Christina
3 Susan
4 Johanna Elizabeth Carolina * 1897 † 1978
5 Louise Christina Adriata * 1901 † 1975
6 Carl / Charles Federick
7 Mauritz Herman Otto x Olivia Maria SANDENBERG (had 5 children)
   1 Alexis / Alexus * Pretoria 6.9.1911 † Pretoria 12.12.1975 (was famous artist and buried on his farm Dombeya near Britz.
   2 Alexis
   3 William Abraham
   4 Isaac Andrew
   5 Ester Wilhelmina Ann
   6 Kaiserine (Kay) Victoria

Winston Preller, resident Pinnacle Road, Orange 2800, NSW, Australia – email wepreller@bigpond.com

SCHICKERLING

a Johann Friedrich SCHICKERLING * Burg near Magdenburg, Pruisies-Sakse, Duitsland, arrived 1773 as a soldier; burger in 1780, † Kaapstad 6.8.1826 (son of Johann Conrad SCHICKERLING and Maria Elizabeth SEEGER) x 24.2.1782 Maria Magdalena MAARTENS (widow of George Carl KIRCHMANN; 8 children) ~ Luthurs Church, Kaapstad 24.8.1748 xx Kaapstad 25.10.1802 Maria Elizabeth MOCKE * Cape Town 11.9.1774 † Malmesbury 2.1.1866
    c? John Peter Schikerling * 1.6.1824 x Adriaana Wilhelmina Petronella MEYER
        d1 Maria Susanna Wilhelmina Schickerling * 13.10.1855 Potchefstroom †25.9.1890 or 15.12.1890 x Kroonstad 11.3.1872 Adriaan Izak GELDENHUYS † Kroonstad 1.1.1904
        d3 Jan Pieter Schickerling * 17.5.1859 † Kroonstad 9.3.1930 x 15.6.1885 Judith Margaretha GELDENHUYS * Kroonstad 16.3.1869 † Kroonstad 16.1.1859? (1959!!)
        d6 Henry Edward (Hendrik Eduard) * 22.8.1864 ~ Potchefstroom 21.9.1864 x Cornelia Gertruida Dina GELDENHUYS * Kroonstad June 1873 † Kroonstad 3.5.1923 xx van RENSBURG
        d7 Anna Elizabeth SCHICKERLING * 13.6.1866 ~ Potchefstroom 22.7.1866 x Kroonstad JOHANNES ALBERTUS GILDENHUYS (Geldenhuys) * Kroonstad 6.6.1860 † "Klipfontein", district Winburg 30.8.1913

DETAILED GENEALOGIES

SINTON

a1 James Scott Sinton, from Harpenden, England, arrived 1920 x c. 1918 Zoe ANDERSON from Pietermaritzburg
   b1 John Scott * 11.2.1921 x 15.12.1945 Coral Evelyn KELLAR
   b2 David Scott * 5.9.1924 x C.1953 Gillian MACAULAY
      c? David Murray * 18.10.1947 – father or David James? x Trish NN
         d? David James * (Kenya?) 27.3.1975
            e1 Matthew Dylan Howard * Durban 3.4.2001 (mother – Eloise Howard * Durban 4.4.1972)
Unclassified Sintons:
      c? Alisdair, elderly, lives in Nairobi, Kenya
         d? Neil Sinton, nephew of David Murray, lives in London.
      ?? Mark Sinton from Kaiwaka, New Zealand x Cherie Griffiths * Seychelles 29.4.??, brought up in New Zealand, has two children and lives in Qatar.
      ?? Julia Sinton * 13.4.?? – on Facebook

VAN AARDT

Nicolaas van Aardt x Aletta Magdalena MALAN
1 Alta * Lusaka, N. Rhodesia 5.5.1955 x 2.2.1975 Willem OOSTHUIZEN * Salisbury 16.11.1947
   1 Yvette Marié * Salisbury 6.10.1976 † 25.5.
   1 Cheyenne * 19.2.
      2 Liesl Adriana * Salisbury 27.6.78 x Cobus de VILLIERS * 23.9.1974
         1 Jacques * 23.4.2003
         2 Adriaan * 28.1.2005
         3 Ben * 19.4.2008
   3 Schalk Johannes * Salisbury 31.8.1979

2 Hendrik Jacobus * Lusaka 18.5.1951 x Joleen GELDENHUYS * Ladismith 27.10.1957, daughter of Hendrik Willem van Eden Geldenhuys
    1 Leane * Alberton 29.5.1987
    2 Nicolaas Daniel * Bredasdorp 25.8.1988
3 Nicolene x Renier OLIVIER

VAN HEERDEN

a Pieter Willem van Heerden, arrived onboard Popkens burgh in April 1701. † on his farm Weltevreden in 't Lant van Waveren, now Tulbach, 1763, aged over 80 years old x 1708 Magtilt van der Merwe † 1765, Weltevreden, Waveren
  b1 Willem * 1709

VENTER

DETAILED GENEALOGIES

a1 Heinrich (Hendrik) * 21.4.1663 † 2.5.1713 x Anna VILJOEN (Villon) * 19.5.1678 † 11.5.1713
   b5 Pieter * 1699 † 1761 x Hester NEL * 1706 † 1785
      c13 Hercules * 1750 x Anna Sophia Fick * 1766
         d7 Bernardus Gerhardus * 1794 x Johanna Catharina Maria OLIVIER * 1801 † 1827
            e11 Johannes Bernardus * 1838 † 1878 ab5c13d7e11 x Maria Elizabeth KLEYNHANS * 1836 † 1902
               f2 Carl Rudolph * 1863 ab5c13d7e11f2   x Wilhelmina Barendina KLEYNHANS * 1867
                  g7 Hermanus Johannes Smartenryk * 3.3.1902 † 3.3.1972 ab5c13d7e11f2g7 x Salomina Adriana van HEERDEN * 13.4.1909 † 15.8.1973
                     h1 Carel Rudolph * 16.8.27 ab5c13d7e11f2g7h1 † 30.1.1997 x Johanna Elizabeth (Baby) ROBBERTZE * 30.5.1930
                        i1 Susanna Lodewyka * 4.6.1953 x Barend Malan J. van NOORDWYK * 21.4.1953
                           j1 Martinus Rudolph (Martin) * 21.1.1977 x Jo-Ann (Jo) PEARSON
                           j2 Elizna Marelise * 19.4.1979 * 11.2.1977 Heinrich (Hein) BEXTER
                           j3 Thersia * 23.1.1984 x Morné GROBBELAAR *22.3.1981
                       i2 Salomina Adriana (Adri) * 24.4.1957 x Petrus Johannes (Pieter) MAASS
                           j1 Thersius 31.7.1982
                           j2 Arno * 24.9.94
i3 Carel Rudolph * 27.8.1962 ab5c13d7e11f2g7h1i3 x Gertruida Adriana (Ada) van ZYL
j1 Caitlin * 10.9.1996
j2 Van Zyl * 11.11.1997
i4 Elize * 21.5.1964 x Gunter van der WESTHUIZEN * 21.11.1962
j1 Jolise * 23.2.1995
j2 Schalk * 8.7.1998
h2 Elizabeth Christina (Bettie) * 23.4.1929
h3 Martinus Petrus Johannes (Tienie) * ab5c13d7e11f2g7h3
h4 Hermanus Johannes Smartenryk (Herman) * 8.2.1934
h5 Wilhelmina
h6 Salomina Adriana
h7 Maria Magdalena (Ria) * 10.4.1941 x Phillipus Johannes MALAN *
   i1 Hermanus *
   i2 Salomina *
h8 Elsie 'Ellie' * 26.2.1943 x Sarel Kotzé * 1.3.1938 (Potchefstroom)
h9 Japie * 194 ab5c13d7e11f2g7h9 x
h10 Erens Lodewyk Johannes Venter * 1946 ab5c13d7e11f2g7h10 x Lesley Ann THOMAS * 1950
   i1 Gustaf Thomas
   i2 Benjamin Louis * 1977
   i3 Yvonne Julie * 1979
h11 Bernardus Gerhardus (Bart) * ab5c13d7e11f2g7h12
h12 Anna Sophia Johanna (Annatjie) * 5.4.

WHITELEY

a1 William Whiteley * 2.4.1837 † 1932 (95), x Anna Maria Walker
    b1 Charles Henry * 2.1.1867 at Mirfield Yorkshire † 4.1952 (85), x 1894 Mary Kate Parkinson *22.1. 1868 at Leeds, Yorkshire † 29.1.1938 (70)
        c1 Walter * 23.4.1896 † 4.10.1989 x Mary Brown Broadbent * 4.8.1899
(a1 Len * 1893 Ripponden, Halifax, Yorkshire, England, - to Durban)
(a1 Percival * 23.2.1876 Sevenoaks, Kent - arrived 1899, x 18.11.1902 Katherine Mary FOSTER from Dulwich, England - 1 child)
        c2 Alan * Bridlington, Yorkshire UK 11.10.1897 † 8.3.1989 x 12. 8.1928 `* 27.5.1902 † 15.4.1985 (83)
            d1 Alan Raymond Malcolm *1931 x Heather Johnson-Worboys * 1931
                e1 Janet Mary * 1959 x 1981 Rob Killin
                    f1 Louise Clare * 1981
                e2 Helen Jean * 1962
                e3 Irene Heather * 1967
            d2 Margaret Mary Elaine * 16.12.1935 x 11.10.1958 William Paterson JELLEY * 6.7.1935
                e1 Grahame David * 22.3.1959 x Drakensberg 6.6.1992 Renene Delene **GELDENHUYS** * 8.8.1968 Gwelo
                    f1 Courtney Sacha * 13.9.1993 Triangle
                    f2 Brendan Vaughan * 15.11.1996 Chipinge
                e2 Keith Brian * Salisbury 19.11.1960 x Jean van Wyk
        c3 Percy * 1899 x 1931 Madelein Cooper) 1906

RELATIONSHIP CHART

RELATIONSHIP WITH DISTANT RELATIVES

The family tree below may assist to clarify relationships with distant relatives - especially where "removed" cousins occur. Note the diagonal relationship for easier understanding.

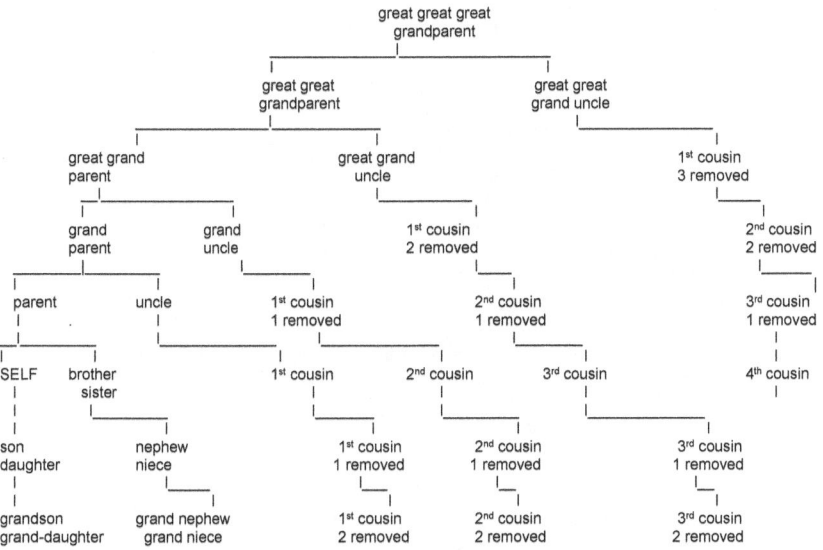

Tracing family, or working out your relationship with distant relatives can be difficult. The above chart will simplify the relationship for you.

RELATIONSHIP TO PRELLER GELDENHUYS

This listing is taken from the My Heritage website **- http://www.myheritage.com/site-72814171/preller-geldenhuys** - as at August 2011.

Preller Matt Geldenhuys is the home person
A Preller [Brugman] is related [8 steps]
A. (Benitti) Preller is a direct descendant of a great-great-grandfather
Abba Snowy is a first cousin
Abigael van der Heiden [Vroom] is related [11 steps]
Abraham (Abri) Preller is a 2nd cousin
Abraham Christofel Naude (Braam) Preller is a brother of a grandmother
Abraham Christofel Naude Christoffel Preller is a great-grandfather
Abraham Christofel Naude Preller is a 2nd cousin once removed
Abraham Daniel Bosman is a brother-in-law of a brother of a great-grandfather
Abraham Jacobus Geldenhuys is a 3rd cousin 5 times removed
Abraham Jacobus Josua Geldenhuys is a 6th cousin twice removed
Abraham Johannes Geldenhuys is a 2nd cousin 4 times removed

Abraham Josua Geldenhuys is a 4th cousin 4 times removed
Abraham le Roux is the father-in-law of a 3rd cousin 5 times removed
Abram Carl Frederik Preller Geldenhuys is the father
Abram Christofel Naude (Boet) Preller is a first cousin once removed (cousin of father)
Ada Geldenhuys [Pringle] is the wife of a 2nd cousin twice removed
Adelaide 'Ada' Simpson [Preller] is a first cousin twice removed (first cousin of grandmother)
Adam Barnard is the husband of a 5th cousin 3 times removed
Adam Daniel Gooding is a grandson of a sister of the wife
Adam Johannes Reyneke is the husband of a 3rd cousin 5 times removed
Adam Tas is related [12 steps]
Adele Bezuidenhout [van der Walt] is the wife of a nephew of the wife
Adele Malan [du Plessis] is the wife of a nephew of the wife
Adriaan 'Attie' Geldenhuys is a 3rd cousin
Adriaan de Villiers is a great-grandson of a sister-in-law
Adriaan Geldenhuys is a 3rd cousin once removed
Adriaan Geldenhuys is a 4th cousin 4 times removed
Adriaan Hendrik Geldenhuys is a 4th cousin 3 times removed
Adriaan Hendrik Geldenhuys is a 5th cousin twice removed
Adriaan Izaak Geldenhuys is a 2nd cousin 4 times removed
Adriaan Izaak Odendaal is the father-in-law of a 1st cousin 5 times removed
Adriaan Izak 'Aap' Geldenhuys is a brother of a great-grandfather
Adriaan Izak 'Attie' Geldenhuys is a 2nd cousin once removed
Adriaan Johannes (or Matthys Johannes?) Geldenhuys is a 3rd cousin 3 times removed
Adriaan Johannes Geldenhuys is a 4th cousin twice removed
Adriaan Johannes Geldenhuys is a direct descendant of a direct ancestor
Adriaan Johannes Geldenhuys is a great-grandson of a direct ancestor
Adriaan Johannes Kleynsmit is a brother-in-law of a great-great-grandfather
Adriaan Johannes Strydom is the husband of a 4th cousin
Adriaan Louw is related [10 steps]
Adrian Henry van Rensen is a first cousin
Adrian Johannes - f2 Geldenhuys is a 2nd cousin 4 times removed
Adrian van der Walt is a brother of a daughter-in-law of a sister-in-law
Adriana Alberta Geldenhuys is a 5th cousin twice removed
Adriana Groenewald is a niece of the wife of a cousin of the wife
Adriana Johanna Anderson [von Maltitz] is a direct ancestor of a grandson
Adriana Smit [Tol] is a direct ancestor   (8 generations; great-great-great-great-great-great-grandmother)
Adrianna Marta Maria (Max) Geldenhuys [Keyzer] is an aunt by marriage
Adrianna van Rensen is the mother of an uncle by marriage
Advocate St Clair Moor is a 3rd cousin 3 times removed of a son-in-law
Agnes Preller is a first cousin twice removed (first cousin of grandmother)

Aiden Bezuidenhoudt is a grandson of a sister of the wife
Alan Oscar Preller is a 2nd cousin
Alan Patrick Moodie is a 2nd cousin 4 times removed of a son-in-law
Alan Raymond Malcolm Whiteley is an uncle of the husband of a daughter
Alan Whiteley is a grandfather of the husband of a daughter
Albert Barend (Gildenhuizen) Geldenhuys is the father-in-law of a 4th cousin 4 times removed
Albert Barend Geldenhuys is a 2nd cousin 6 times removed
Albert Barend Geldenhuys is a 3rd cousin 5 times removed
Albert Barend Geldenhuys is a 4th cousin 4 times removed
Albert Barend Geldenhuys is a 5th cousin 3 times removed
Albert Barend Geldenhuys is a brother of a direct ancestor
Albert Barends Gildenhuisz Geldenhuys is a direct ancestor (9 generations; great-great-great-great-great-great-great-grandfather)
Albert Barentse Geldenhuys is a 1st cousin 7 times removed
Albert Hendrik Geldenhuys is a 1st cousin 6 times removed
Albert Hendrik Geldenhuys is a 2nd cousin 5 times removed
Albert Hendrik Geldenhuys is a 3rd cousin 4 times removed

Albert Hendrik Stephanus Geldenhuys is a 3rd cousin 4 times removed
Albertina Magdalena Trichardt [Hamman] is a grandmother of the husband of a 4th cousin
Albertus Barend Geldenhuys is a 4th cousin 4 times removed
Albertus Bernardus Geldenhuys is a direct descendant of a direct ancestor
Albertus Bernardus van Rensburg is the husband of a 4th cousin 3 times removed
Albertus Marthinus "Bertie" Trichardt is a 4th cousin once removed
Albertus Marthinus Trichardt is the father-in-law of a 4th cousin
Albertus Marthinus Trichardt is the husband of a 4th cousin
Albertus Wynand Louw is the father-in-law of a 4th cousin 4 times removed
Alda Elizabeth van der Westhuizen [van Heerden] is related [20 steps]
Aletta Catharina Elizabeth Beyers [Geldenhuys] is a 4th cousin 3 times removed
Aletta Johanna Geldenhuys [Marais] is a sister-in-law of a direct ancestor
Aletta Johanna van Heerden [Fouche] is related [15 steps]
Aletta Magdalena Susanna Malan [Le Roux] is the mother-in-law
Aletta Magdalena Susanna Oosthuisen [van Aardt] is a niece of the wife
Aletta Magdalena Susanna van Aardt [Malan] is a sister-in-law (sister of his wife)
Aletta Magrietha 'Alicia' Venter is related [8 steps]
Aletta Margaretha Preller is a sister of a great-grandfather of the father
Aletta Petronella Geldenhuys is a 1st cousin 4 times removed
Aletta van Heerden is related [13 steps]
Alewin Tol is a direct ancestor   (10 generations; great-great-great-great-great-great-great-great-grandfather)
Alexander Bennett McQueen is related [10 steps]
Alfred Bosman Preller is a first cousin twice removed (first cousin of grandmother)
Alfred Donald Robert Moodie is a 3rd cousin 3 times removed of a son-in-law
Alice Francis Preller [Vos] is the wife of a 3rd cousin
Alida Aletta van Dyk [Brits] is a direct ancestor   (7 generations; great-great-great-great-great-grandmother)
Alida de Waal is related [11 steps]
Alida Eksteen [van der Heiden] is a sister of a brother-in-law of a direct ancestor
Alida Jacoba Cornelia Opperman [Oosthuizen] is the mother-in-law of a 4th cousin once removed
Alida Johanna Geldenhuys is a 4th cousin 4 times removed
Allan Derek Geldenhuys is a 4th cousin
Allan Geldenhuys is a 4th cousin twice removed
Alwyn Jacobus Dippenaar is a 2nd cousin twice removed of the wife of the brother
Alwyn Jacobus Dippenaar is a brother of a great-grandfather of the wife of the brother
Alwyn Jacobus Dippenaar is a brother of the wife of the brother
Alwyn Jacobus Dippenaar is a direct ancestor of an wife of the brother
Alwyn Waldeck is the husband of a first cousin once removed
Amanda de Waal is a sister of a daughter-in-law of a brother
Amanda Stopforth [Malan] is a niece of the wife
Andre van Stryp is related [8 steps]
Andrea 'Annie' Bezuidenhout is a step-daughter of a 3rd cousin
Andrew Mark Geldenhuys is a 4th cousin once removed
Andrew Roos is a first cousin
Andries Jacobus van Heerden is related [17 steps]
Andries Johannes 'Andre' van Stryp is related [8 steps]
Andries Johannes Geldenhuys is a 5th cousin twice removed
Andries Lodewicus Stephanus Geldenhuys is a 5th cousin twice removed
Andries Otto Preller is a first cousin twice removed (first cousin of grandmother)
Andries van der Heiden is the father of a brother-in-law of a direct ancestor
Angela Adriana de Jager Gillespie [Geldenhuys] is a 3rd cousin once removed
Angelique Snowy is a first cousin
Aninke Lippert is a 2nd cousin once removed
Anna Aletta Malan [Retief] is a direct ancestor of the wife
Anna Buys [Geldenhuys] is a 7th cousin once removed
Anna Carolina Preller is a daughter of a great-grandfather
Anna Catharina Cornelia Susanna Geldenhuys is a 4th cousin 3 times removed

Anna Catharina Geldenhuys [Mulder] is the wife of a 2nd cousin 5 times removed
Anna Catharina Geldenhuys is a direct descendant of a direct ancestor
Anna Catharina Hendrina Brand [Geldenhuys] is a 4th cousin 4 times removed
Anna Catharina Hendrina Geldenhuys [van Dyk] is the wife of a 3rd cousin 5 times removed
Anna Catharina Louisa Jacoba Geldenhuys is a 6th cousin twice removed
Anna Catharina Margaretha Geldenhuys [van Vuuren] is the wife of a 5th cousin 3 times removed
Anna Catharina Maria van Heerden is related [17 steps]
Anna Christina Elizabeth Cornelia Geldenhuys is a 4th cousin 3 times removed
Anna Christina Elizabeth Geldenhuys [Swart] is the wife of a 1st cousin 4 times removed
Anna Christina Elizabeth Geldenhuys is a 3rd cousin 4 times removed
Anna Christina Geertruyda Geldenhuys is a 3rd cousin 4 times removed
Anna Christina Geertruyda Geldenhuys is a 4th cousin 3 times removed
Anna Christina Geldenhuys [de Jager] is related [11 steps]
Anna Christina Geldenhuys [Groenewald] is the wife of a 2nd cousin 5 times removed
Anna Christina van Velden [Preller] is a sister of a great-grandfather of the father
Anna Christina Willemse [Geldenhuys] is a 3rd cousin twice removed
Anna Costeux [Geldenhuys] is a sister of a direct ancestor
Anna Dippenaar [Smit] is a direct ancestor of an ex-wife of the brother
Anna Dorothea Geldenhuys is a 1st cousin 5 times removed
Anna Dorothea Geldenhuys is a 2nd cousin 5 times removed
Anna Elisabeth (Lizzie) Geldenhuys [Preller] is the paternal grandmother
Anna Elizabeth Botha [Dreyer] is a great-great-grandmother
Anna Elizabeth de Waal [Dempers] is a direct ancestor of the wife of a nephew
Anna Elizabeth Geldenhuys is an aunt (a sister of his father)
Anna Elizabeth Malan [Louw] is related [11 steps]
Anna Emily Moodie [Hallett] is related [11 steps]
Anna Francina Elizabeth Geldenhuys [Gresse] is the wife of a 3rd cousin 4 times removed
Anna Geertruy Gildenhuizen (Geldenhuys) is a 2nd cousin 5 times removed
Anna Geertruyda Elizabeth Geldenhuys is a 4th cousin 3 times removed
Anna Geertruyda Fredrika Geldenhuys [Otto] is the wife of a 3rd cousin 4 times removed
Anna Geertryda Gildenhuizen Geldenhuys is the wife of a 2nd cousin 5 times removed
Anna Geldenhuys [Fourie] is the wife of a 1st cousin 6 times removed
Anna Jacoba Susanna Geldenhuys is a 3rd cousin 3 times removed
Anna Johanna Barendina Dippenaar is a sister of the ex-wife of the brother
Anna Johanna Sophia Habig [Dippenaar] is a sister of the ex-wife of the brother
Anna Judith Geertruyda Geldenhuys [Kuun] is the wife of a 3rd cousin 4 times removed
Anna Liebenberg is a daughter-in-law of a sister of the ex-wife of the brother
Anna Lock is the mother of a sister-in-law of the wife
Anna Magdalena Burger [van Heerden] is related [11 steps]
Anna Magdalena Elizabeth Geldenhuys [Loulo] is the wife of a 5th cousin 3 times removed
Anna Magdalena Geldenhuys is a 4th cousin 4 times removed
Anna Magdalena Geldenhuys is a 6th cousin twice removed
Anna Margaretha Elisabeth Preller is a granddaughter of a great-great-grandfather
Anna Margaretha Elizabeth Elisabeth (Furstenburg) Preller [Furstenburg] is a daughter-in-law of a great-great-grandfather
Anna Margaretha Geldenhuys [Siek] is a direct ancestor (8 generations; great-great-great-great-great-great-grandmother)
Anna Margaretha Geldenhuys is a 1st cousin 6 times removed
Anna Margaretha Geldenhuys is a 4th cousin 3 times removed
Anna Margaretha Kuun [Geldenhuys] is a sister of a direct ancestor
Anna Margaretha Magdalena Geldenhuys is a 5th cousin twice removed
Anna Margaretha Malan [du Toit] is a great-grandmother of the wife
Anna Maria Dippenaar is a sister of a great-grandfather of the father of the ex-wife of the brother
Anna Maria Geldenhuys [Hogewind] is the wife of a 5th cousin twice removed
Anna Maria Geldenhuys [le Roux] is the wife of a 2nd cousin 5 times removed
Anna Maria Geldenhuys [Smit] is the wife of a 2nd cousin 5 times removed
Anna Maria Geldenhuys is a 1st cousin 5 times removed

Anna Maria Geldenhuys is a 4th cousin once removed
Anna Maria Malan [Fick] is related [13 steps]
Anna Maria Margaretha Alberta Geldenhuys is a 3rd cousin 4 times removed
Anna Maria Whiteley [Walker] is a great-great-grandmother of a son-in-law
Anna Ramertha van Heerden [Welgemoed] is related [17 steps]
Anna Retief [Marais] is a direct ancestor of the wife
Anna Sophia Aletta Geldenhuys [Beeslaar] is the wife of a 4th cousin 3 times removed
Anna Sophia Dippenaar [Burger] is a direct ancestor of an ex-wife of the brother
Anna Sophia Magdalena 'Ansie' van Stryp [Venter] is a niece of the wife of a cousin of the wife
Anna Sophia van Heerden [van der Merwe] is related [13 steps]
Anna Sophia van Heerden is related [12 steps]
Anna Sophia Venter [Fick] is related [10 steps]
Anna Sophia Venter [Griesel] is a sister-in-law of the wife of a cousin of the wife
Anna Susanna van Heerden [Coetzer] is related [15 steps]
Anna Susanna van Heerden [Erasmus] is related [16 steps]
Anna Susanna van Heerden is related [18 steps]
Anna Susanna Wessels [Geldenhuys] is a 1st cousin 4 times removed
Anna Susanna Wilhelmina Geldenhuys [Serdyn] is the wife of a 4th cousin 4 times removed
Anna van der Heiden is a 1st cousin 7 times removed
Anna van Heerden [Jordaan] is related [14 steps]
Anna Venter [Villion (Viljoen)] is related [12 steps]
Annaline Geldenhuys [Odendaal] is the wife of a 6th cousin
Anne Jubilee Preller is a great-granddaughter of a great-great-grandfather
Anneke Olivier is a granddaughter of a sister of the wife
Annelie Geldenhuys [Strydom] is the wife of a 3rd cousin
Annie Steenkamp [de Jager] is the mother-in-law of a 2nd cousin twice removed
Ansu van Stryp is related [8 steps]
Antoinette Henriette Preller [Friedrich] is the wife of a 2nd cousin once removed
Antony Smith is the husband of a 3rd cousin
Archibald Murray Anderson is a direct ancestor of a grandson
Arend de Waal is related [11 steps]
Arend Gildenhuisz Geldenhuys is a brother of a direct ancestor
Arend Hoefnagels is a direct ancestor   (10 generations; great-great-great-great-great-great-great-great-grandfather)
Ariaentgen Tijsz van der Piet [Pleunis] is a direct ancestor   (10 generations; great-great-great-great-great-great-great-grandmother)
Arlene Dippenaar is a niece of the ex-wife of a brother
Arne Dunckers is a 1st cousin twice removed
Arno Maass is related [8 steps]
Barbara Ann Krahner [Geldenhuys] is a 4th cousin once removed
Barbara Wilhelmina Brink is a sister of a grandfather of the husband of a niece
Barend Bartholomeus Burger is related [9 steps]
Barend Geldenhuys is a 1st cousin 5 times removed
Barend Geldenhuys is a 1st cousin 6 times removed
Barend Geldenhuys is a 2nd cousin 5 times removed
Barend Geldenhuys is a brother of a direct ancestor
Barend Geldenhuys is a direct ancestor   (8 generations; great-great-great-great-great-great-grandfather)
Barend Hendrik Beukes is the husband of a 2nd cousin 5 times removed
Barend Hendrik Geldenhuys is a 2nd cousin 5 times removed
Barend Hendrik Geldenhuys is a 3rd cousin 5 times removed
Barend Hermanus Geldenhuys is a 3rd cousin 4 times removed
Barend Hermanus Geldenhuys is a 5th cousin twice removed
Barend Hermanus Nicolaas Geldenhuys is a 4th cousin 3 times removed
Barend Johannes Hermanus Geldenhuys is a 4th cousin 3 times removed
Barend Johannes van Heerden is related [10 steps]
Barend Louwrens Cornelius Groenewald is related [9 steps]
Barend Malan J. van Noordwyk is related [8 steps]
Barend Petrus Albertus Geldenhuys is a 4th cousin 3 times removed

Barend Petrus Fourie is the husband of a 3rd cousin 4 times removed
Barend Petrus Geldenhuys is a 1st cousin 3 times removed
Barend Petrus Geldenhuys is a 2nd cousin 5 times removed
Barend Petrus Geldenhuys is a 3rd cousin 4 times removed
Barend Petrus Geldenhuys is a brother of a great-grandfather of the father
Barend Petrus Johannes Geldenhuys is a 3rd cousin 4 times removed
Barendina Petronella Bouwer [Geldenhuys] is a 1st cousin 3 times removed
Barry Luke Liebenberg is a grandson of a sister of an ex-wife of the brother
Bartholomeus Bruynzwart is the father-in-law of a 3rd cousin 5 times removed
Basil Jelley is a brother of a grandfather of the husband of a daughter
Beatrice Moodie is a 3rd cousin 3 times removed of a son-in-law
Beatrix Geertruyda Geldenhuys [Gerber] is the wife of a 3rd cousin 4 times removed
Ben de Villiers is a great-grandson of a sister-in-law
Bendomine Maude Brink is an aunt of the husband of a niece
Benjamin James Donald Lt Moodie is related [9 steps]
Benjamin Louis Venter is a nephew of the wife of a cousin of the wife
Benjamin Luke Gooding is a grandson of a sister of the wife
Benjamin Moodie is a 2nd cousin twice removed of a son-in-law
Benjamin Moodie is a brother of a great-grandmother of an in-law
Benjamin Moodie is a direct ancestor of a son-in-law
Bernardus Gerhardus Venter is related [9 steps]
Bernd Gildenhausen Geldenhuys is a direct ancestor (10 generations; great-great-great-great-great-great-great-great-grandfather)
Bernice Preller [Botha] is the wife of a first cousin once removed
Beryl Preller is a 3rd cousin
Bevan Glyn Muirhead is a nephew of the husband of a niece
Beverley Anne McQueen [Alexander] is related [11 steps]
Beverly Anthony Preller is a 3rd cousin
Bianca Porter [Cunningham] is a granddaughter of a sister of an ex-wife of the brother
Boet Malan is a cousin of the wife
Bonita Elizabeth Preller [Colesky] is the wife of a 2nd cousin
Brandon Arne Dunckers is a first cousin once removed (son of first cousin)
Brandon Gareth McQueen is related [11 steps]
Braydon Lee Gooding is a grandson of a sister of the wife
Brendan Vaughan Jelley is a grandson
Brent Bezuidenhout is a grandson of a sister of the wife
Brian Alexander McQueen is related [10 steps]
Brian Balfour-Cunningham is a son-in-law of a sister of the ex-wife of the brother
Brian Burger is a nephew of the wife of a nephew
Brian Carr is a nephew of the ex-wife of a brother
Brian Godfrey Jelley is an uncle of the husband of a daughter
Brian Liebenberg is a grandson of a sister of an ex-wife of the brother
Brian Reginal Brink is a brother of a son-in-law of a sister
Bronwynne Thomson [Bezuidenhout] is a granddaughter of a sister of the wife
Burgent Christiaan Geldenhuys is a 4th cousin 3 times removed
Burgert Wynand Geldenhuys is a 4th cousin 3 times removed
Burnette John Thorne is related [8 steps]
Byron Neil Muirhead is a nephew of the husband of a niece
C P Lourens is the husband of a granddaughter of a direct ancestor
C. Preller is a direct descendant of a great-great-grandfather
Cabous Geldenhuys is a 3rd cousin once removed
Caitlin Venter is related [8 steps]
Cameron Michael Trichardt is a 4th cousin twice removed
Campbell Fred Krahner is a 4th cousin twice removed
Capt Thomas of Grange Dunbar is a direct ancestor of a son-in-law
Carel Frederik Preller is a first cousin twice removed (first cousin of grandmother)
Carel Friedrich (Charley) Preller is a brother of a grandmother
Carel Friedrich Carl Preller is a great-great-grandfather
Carel Friedrich Preller is a son of a great-great-grandfather

Carel Hendrik Francois Keulder is the husband of a 4th cousin 4 times removed
Carel Jacobus van Heerden is related [13 steps]
Carel Jacobus van Heerden is related [15 steps]
Carel Lodewyk van der Merwe is the husband of a 3rd cousin 5 times removed
Carel Pieter de Jager is the father-in-law of a 4th cousin 3 times removed
Carel Pieter Geldenhuys is a 5th cousin twice removed
Carel Rudolph Venter is a brother-in-law of a cousin of the wife
Carel Rudolph Venter is a nephew of the wife of a cousin of the wife
Carel Sebastiaan van Heerden is a grandfather of the wife of a brother of a great-grandfather
Carel Sebastian van Heerden is related [10 steps]
Carel van Heerden is related [12 steps]
Carel van Heerden is related [13 steps]
Carel Willem van Heerden is related [15 steps]
Carl Frederik Habig is a nephew of the ex-wife of a brother
Carl Liebenberg is a grandson of a sister of an ex-wife of the brother
Carl Rudolph Venter is a grandfather of the wife of a cousin of the wife
Carlos Alberto Lopes de Oliveira is a son-in-law of a cousin of the wife
Carol Brink is a sister of a son-in-law of a sister
Carol Liebenberg [Ingle] is a daughter-in-law of a sister of the ex-wife of the brother
Carolina Christina Johanna Dippenaar [Oosterhagen] is related [8 steps]
Caroline Mary Adelaide Preller [Monck-Mason] is the wife of a first cousin twice removed
Caroline van der Walt [Wansbury] is a sister-in-law of the wife of a nephew of the wife
Carolus Johannes Trichardt is a grandfather of the husband of a 4th cousin
Carolus Johannes Trichardt is related [13 steps]
Carolyn Trichardt [Woodley] is the wife of a 4th cousin once removed
Caryn Sandra Waldeck [Dunckers] is a first cousin once removed (daughter of first cousin)
Casparus Abraham Geldenhuys is a 4th cousin 4 times removed
Catharina Elizabeth Geldenhuys is a 2nd cousin 3 times removed
Catharina Elizabeth Geldenhuys is a 3rd cousin 4 times removed
Catharina Elizabeth Geldenhuys is a granddaughter of a direct ancestor
Catharina Elizabeth Swart [Moolman] is the mother-in-law of a 1st cousin 4 times removed
Catharina Elizabeth van der Merwe [van Heerden] is related [11 steps]
Catharina Francina (Cato) (Catherine) Logie [Preller] is a sister of a great-grandfather of the father
Catharina Helena Geldenhuys [Oosthuizen] is a sister-in-law of a great-great-grandfather
Catharina Helena Johanna Geldenhuys [Lucas] is the wife of a 5th cousin 3 times removed
Catharina Helena Maria van Heerden [Geldenhuys] is related [17 steps]
Catharina Jacoba Geldenhuys [Basson] is the wife of a 4th cousin 4 times removed
Catharina Louisa van Heerden is related [10 steps]
Catharina Malan is related [9 steps]
Catharina Maria Christina Geldenhuys is a 3rd cousin 4 times removed
Catharina Maria Johanna Geldenhuys is a 3rd cousin 4 times removed
Catharina Susanna (Carienie) [Geldenhuys] is a first cousin
Catharina Wilhelmina (Elna) Brink is a granddaughter of a great-grandfather
Cayden Porter is a great-granddaughter of a sister of the ex-wife of the brother
Cecelia Jacomina Moodie [Robbertse] is related [8 steps]
Cecil William Gordon Jelley is a grandfather of the husband of a daughter
Cecilia Aletta van Heerden [van der Merwe] is related [14 steps]
Cecilia Barbara Lovemore Moodie is a 3rd cousin 3 times removed of a son-in-law
Cecilia Johanna Grobler [van Heerden] is related [20 steps]
Cedric Victor Heath is the husband of a 2nd cousin
Chad Porter is the husband of a granddaughter of a sister of the ex-wife of the brother
Chanel Geldenhuys is a granddaughter of a brother
Chanli Brink [Bouwer] is a niece
Charles Henry Whiteley is a great-grandfather of a son-in-law
Charles Jacobus Geldenhuys is a 4th cousin 4 times removed
Charles Lauton Smith is a 3rd cousin once removed
Charles Liversage is a great-great-grandfather of the husband of a niece
Charles Phillip Liversage is a great-grandfather of the husband of a niece

Charles Roy Brink is the husband of a niece
Charles Stopforth is the husband of a niece of the wife
Charles Vos is a brother-in-law of a 3rd cousin
Charles Walker Preller is a 2nd cousin
Charlotte Jane Sunshine Vos [Betteridge] is the mother-in-law of a 3rd cousin
Charlotte Mary St. Clair Moor [Moodie] is a 2nd cousin 4 times removed of a son-in-law
Charmain Froneman [Geldenhuys] is the wife of a first cousin once removed
Charmaine Geldenhuys is a niece
Cherie Jane Gooding is a granddaughter of a sister of the wife
Cheryl Geldenhuys is a 4th cousin
Cheyenne is a great-granddaughter of a sister-in-law
Chris Mahnke is the husband of a 4th cousin once removed
Christaan Samuel Frederik Smit is the husband of a 5th cousin 3 times removed
Christiaan Cornelis Geldenhuys is a 3rd cousin 4 times removed
Christiaan Jacobus Malan is a 4th cousin 3 times removed of the wife
Christiaan 'Koevoet' Human is a brother-in-law of the wife of a nephew
Christiaan Lourens Dreyer is a direct ancestor   (6 generations; great-great-great-great-grandfather)
Christiaan Rudolph van Heerden is related [20 steps]
Christina Aletta Geldenhuys is a 5th cousin 3 times removed
Christina Berlina Geertruyda Geldenhuys is a 4th cousin 3 times removed
Christina Dreyer [Steyn] is a direct ancestor   (6 generations; great-great-great-great-grandmother)
Christina Elizabeth Cornelia Geldenhuys is a 4th cousin twice removed
Christina Elizabeth Geldenhuys is a direct descendant of a direct ancestor
Christina Elizabeth Prinsloo [Geldenhuys] is a 3rd cousin 3 times removed
Christina Francina Beukes [Geldenhuys] is a 2nd cousin 5 times removed
Christina Francina Johanna Geldenhuys is a 3rd cousin 4 times removed
Christina Geertruy Swart [Geldenhuys] is a 1st cousin 6 times removed
Christina Geertruyda Badenhorst [Geldenhuys] is a 2nd cousin 5 times removed
Christina Geertruyda Maria Beneke [Geldenhuys] is a 3rd cousin 4 times removed
Christina Gesina Sophia Dippenaar [van Biljon] is a great-great-grandmother of an ex-wife of the brother
Christina Johanna Geldenhuys is a direct descendant of a direct ancestor
Christina Magdalena Badenhorst [Geldenhuys] is a granddaughter of a direct ancestor
Christina Magdalena Geldenhuys [Radyn] is a sister-in-law of a direct ancestor
Christina Magdalena Geldenhuys is a 2nd cousin 5 times removed
Christina Margaretha Geldenhuys is a 1st cousin 6 times removed
Christina Maria Botha [Geldenhuys] is a 2nd cousin 5 times removed
Christina Maria Geertruy Geldenhuys is a 3rd cousin 4 times removed
Christine Christina Magdalena Preller [Visagie] is the wife of a 2nd cousin
Christoffel Christiaan Geldenhuys is a 4th cousin 4 times removed
Christoffel Christiaan Geldenhuys is a 5th cousin 3 times removed
Christoffel Christiaan Heyne is the husband of a 1st cousin 4 times removed
Christoffel Johannes Francois van Heerden is related [17 steps]
Christopher Beukes is a first cousin once removed (son of first cousin)
Clara Jessie Maude Rimer [Moodie] is a 2nd cousin 4 times removed of a son-in-law
Clarissa Moodie [Meek] is related [11 steps]
Claudia Roos [Lotter] is an aunt (a sister of his mother)
Claus Lippert is the husband of a 2nd cousin
Clinton Thorne is related [8 steps]
Clive Froneman is a first cousin once removed (son of first cousin)
Clive Jnr ? Froneman is a 1st cousin twice removed
Clive van Biljon is a first cousin
Cloete Cloete is a grandfather of the wife of a nephew
Cobus de Villiers is the husband of a granddaughter of a sister-in-law
Coenraad Johannes Geldenhuys is a 3rd cousin 4 times removed
Colin David Preller is a 3rd cousin once removed
Colin Preller is a 3rd cousin twice removed

Connor William Trichardt is a 4th cousin twice removed
Coral Evelyn Sinton [Kellar] is related [7 steps]
Cornelia Christina Johanna Geldenhuys is a 4th cousin 3 times removed
Cornelia Geertruida Anna Geldenhuys is a 2nd cousin 3 times removed
Cornelia Geertruy Geldenhuys is a 1st cousin 4 times removed
Cornelia Geertruy Geldenhuys is a sister of a direct ancestor
Cornelia Geertruy Germishuysen [Geldenhuys] is a 1st cousin 4 times removed
Cornelia Geertruyda Dina Geldenhuys [Human] is the wife of a 2nd cousin 4 times removed
Cornelia Geertruyda Gildenhuizen Geldenhuys is the wife of a 3rd cousin 4 times removed
Cornelia Geertruyda Margaretha Geldenhuys is a 3rd cousin 3 times removed
Cornelia Geldenhuys [Swart] is a direct ancestor (7 generations; great-great-great-great-great-grandmother)
Cornelia Geldenhuys is a 1st cousin 5 times removed
Cornelia Johanna Alberta Beyers [Geldenhuys] is a 4th cousin 3 times removed
Cornelia Johanna Geldenhuys [Kleynsmit] is the wife of a 1st cousin 5 times removed
Cornelia Johanna Geldenhuys is a 3rd cousin 3 times removed
Cornelia Johanna Geldenhuys is a direct descendant of a direct ancestor
Cornelia Margaretha Combrink [Geldenhuys] is a daughter of a direct ancestor
Cornelia Margaretha Geldenhuys [Swart] is a sister-in-law of a great-great-grandfather
Cornelia Margaretha Geldenhuys is a 2nd cousin 4 times removed
Cornelia Margaretha Human [Geldenhuys] is a 1st cousin 5 times removed
Cornelia Margaretha Susanna Kleynsmit [Geldenhuys] is a sister of a great-grandfather of the father
Cornelia Susanna Geldenhuys [Erwee] is the wife of a 3rd cousin 4 times removed
Cornelia Susanna Gertruida Preller is a granddaughter of a great-great-grandfather
Cornelia Susanna Lourens [Geldenhuys] is a granddaughter of a direct ancestor
Cornelis de Waal is related [11 steps]
Cornelis Janse Geldenhuys is a 3rd cousin 3 times removed
Cornelis Janse Uys is the husband of a granddaughter of a direct ancestor
Cornelis Johannes Geldenhuys is a 3rd cousin 4 times removed
Cornelis Michael Geldenhuys is a 6th cousin twice removed
Cornelis Muller van Rooyen is a grandfather of the husband of a niece
Cornella Maria Liversage [Hard] is a great-grandmother of the husband of a niece
Cornie van Rooyen is an uncle of the husband of a niece
Cosmos Moor is a 3rd cousin 3 times removed of a son-in-law
Courtney Sacha Jelley is a granddaughter
Craig Brown is an ex-husband of the niece
Craig Jannie Geldenhuys is a grandson of a brother
Craig le Roux is related [9 steps]
Cuthbert John Dunbar Moodie is a 2nd cousin 4 times removed of a son-in-law
D C Lourens is the husband of a granddaughter of a direct ancestor
Dain Preller is a 3rd cousin twice removed
Dan Thomson is the husband of a granddaughter of a sister-in-law
Danie Geldenhuys is a 2nd cousin twice removed
Daniel de Waal is a direct ancestor of the wife of a nephew
Daniel Jacobus van Heerden is related [18 to 20 steps]
Daniel Johannes Geldenhuys is a 4th cousin 3 times removed
Daniel Johannes Geldenhuys is a 5th cousin 3 times removed
Daniel Johannes Louw is the father-in-law of a 3rd cousin 4 times removed
Daniel Josias Malan is a 2nd cousin 5 times removed of the wife
Daniel Malan is related [9 steps]
Daniel Pieter Jacobus (Petrus) de Waal is a great-grandfather of the wife of a nephew
Daniel Stefanus Malan is an uncle of the wife
Daniel Stephanus Malan is a great-great-grandfather of the wife
Daniel van Wyk xxx Rolink is the husband of a sister of the ex-wife of the brother
Daniel W Malan is a 3rd cousin 4 times removed of the wife
Daniel Wynand Malan is a 1st cousin 6 times removed of the wife
Daphne Brink is an aunt of the husband of a niece
Darcey van der Walt is a nephew of the wife of a nephew of the wife

Daughter Bezuidenhout is a great-granddaughter of a sister-in-law
Daughter NN Froneman is a 1st cousin twice removed
David Jacobus Abraham Geldenhuys is a 4th cousin 4 times removed
David Jacobus Geldenhuys is a 4th cousin 4 times removed
David James Sinton is the father of a grandson
David Johannes Malan is an uncle of the wife
David Malan is a direct ancestor of the wife
David Murray Sinton is the paternal grandfather of a grandson
David Scott Sinton is a great-grandfather of a grandson
David van Heerden is related [12 steps]
Davyd John Charles McColl is a son of the ex-husband of a sister
Dawn (Dawnie) Geldenhuys is a sister
Dean Mark Gooding is a grandson of a sister of the wife
Debbie Bouwer [Simpkins] is the wife of an ex-husband of the sister
Debora 'Debbie' Geldenhuys is a 3rd cousin
Debora Geldenhuys [Viljoen] is the wife of a first cousin twice removed
Deirdre Geldenhuys (xx Dougie Stylianou xxx Jan Bezuidenhout) [born Tapson – adopted by Gerry Burns] is the wife of a 3rd cousin
Delene Elizabeth Geldenhuys is a sister
Delene Elizabeth McColl [Geldenhuys / Bouwer divorcee] is a sister
Dennis van Rooyen is an uncle of the husband of a niece
Deon Gaupner is the husband of a 2nd cousin
Desire van der Walt [Price] is a sister-in-law of the wife of a nephew of the wife
Desirée McColl [Haynes] is a daughter-in-law of an ex-husband of the sister
Deu G Brink is a granddaughter of a sister
Dina Brits [Willemse] is a direct ancestor (8 generations; great-great-great-great-great-great-grandmother)
Dina Margaretha de Beer [van Dyk] is a direct ancestor (6 generations; great-great-great-great-grandmother)
Dina Margaretha Gerber [Preller] is a sister of a great-grandfather of the father
Dina Maria Elizabeth van Niekerk [Geldenhuys] is a 4th cousin 3 times removed
Dina Maria Geldenhuys [Uys] is a daughter-in-law of a direct ancestor
Dina Maria Geldenhuys is a 4th cousin 3 times removed
Dina Maria Kleynsmit Geldenhuys is the wife of a 3rd cousin 4 times removed
Dina Maria Lourens [Geldenhuys] is a granddaughter of a direct ancestor
Dirck Thonis van der Piet is a direct ancestor (10 generations; great-great-great-great-great-great-great-grandfather)
Dirk Cornelis Geldenhuys is a 1st cousin 3 times removed
Dirk Cornelis Geldenhuys is a 2nd cousin twice removed
Dirk Cornelis Geldenhuys is a grandson of a direct ancestor
Dirk Human is the husband of a 1st cousin 5 times removed
Dirk J Brink is a son-in-law of a great-grandfather
Dirk Jacobus Geldenhuys is a 6th cousin twice removed
Dirk Johannes Geldenhuys is a 5th cousin 3 times removed
Dirkie Susanna Elizabeth Geldenhuys [Coetzee] is a sister-in-law of a great-great-grandfather
Donald Alfred Pigot Moodie is a 2nd cousin 4 times removed of a son-in-law
Donald Hugh Menzies Moodie is a 1st cousin 5 times removed of a son-in-law
Donald Lt Moodie is related [9 steps]
Donald Martin Moodie is a 1st cousin 3 times removed of a son-in-law
Donald Montgomery Moodie is a brother of a great-grandmother of an in-law
Donald Moodie is a 3rd cousin 3 times removed of a son-in-law
Donald Moodie is related [9 steps]
Donald 'Ross' Brodie is the husband of a 4th cousin
Donald Sutherland Dunbar Moodie is a 2nd cousin 4 times removed of a son-in-law
Dorah Preller is a great-granddaughter of a great-great-grandfather
Dorothea Maria Moodie [Henning] is related [8 steps]
Dorothea Maria Smit [van Heerden] is related [10 steps]
Dorothie Moodie is a 3rd cousin 3 times removed of a son-in-law
Dorothy Geldenhuys [Hurst] is the wife of a 3rd cousin once removed

Dorothy Getrude Brink is a sister of a grandfather of the husband of a niece
Dougie Stylianou is related [9 steps]
Douglas Bruce Preller is a 3rd cousin once removed
Douw Gerbrand Grobler is related [21 steps]
Douw Gerbrand Grobler is related [21 steps]
Dr Con de Villiers is a grandfather of the husband of a 4th cousin
Ds Dirk van Velden is a brother-in-law of a great-great-grandfather
Duncan Allan Smith is the husband of a 4th cousin
Duncan Campbell Francis Moodie is a 1st cousin 5 times removed of a son-in-law
Dylan Howard is a brother of a daughter-in-law
Eddie Deon Malan is a nephew of the wife
Edmond Francis Coleman is a great-great-grandfather of a son-in-law
Eenst Hendrik Schalk Geldenhuys is a direct descendant of a direct ancestor
Elaine Parker MacCreath [Preller] is a first cousin once removed (cousin of father)
Elcora Malan [Bouwer] is a sister-in-law of the wife
Elena Catharina Geldenhuys is a 4th cousin 3 times removed
Eleonora Melius Malan is a direct ancestor of the wife
Elias Caledon Geldenhuys is a 1st cousin 4 times removed
Elias Jacobus Geldenhuys is a 1st cousin 4 times removed
Elias Jacobus Geldenhuys is a 2nd cousin 3 times removed
Elias Jacobus Geldenhuys is a 3rd cousin twice removed
Elisabeth Anna Malan is related [9 steps]
Elisabeth Catharina Human [Geldenhuys] is a 1st cousin 5 times removed
Elisabeth Johanna Dippenaar [Liebenberg] is related [10 steps]
Elisabeth Malan [Reynierse] is related [12 steps]
Elise Froneman [NN] is the wife of a first cousin once removed
Elizabeth (Bess) Geldenhuys is an aunt (a sister of his father)
Elizabeth (Libby) Adriana Dunckers [van Rensen] is a first cousin
Elizabeth Anderson [Smith] is a direct ancestor of a grandson
Elizabeth Catharina Christina Geldenhuys is a 5th cousin twice removed
Elizabeth Catharina Geldenhuys [Bloem] is the wife of a 3rd cousin 4 times removed
Elizabeth Christina 'Bettie' Groenewald [Venter] is a sister-in-law of a cousin of the wife
Elizabeth Christina Geldenhuys [van Wyk] is a sister-in-law of a direct ancestor
Elizabeth Christina Jacobs [van Heerden] is an aunt of the wife of a cousin of the wife
Elizabeth Christina van Heerden [Maree] is a grandmother of the wife of a cousin of the wife
Elizabeth de Waal [van Eck] is related [11 steps]
Elizabeth Debora Geldenhuys [Botha] is the wife of a 2nd cousin 5 times removed
Elizabeth Dorothea Magdalena Fourie [Geldenhuys] is a 3rd cousin 4 times removed
Elizabeth Elsabe Hendrina Geldenhuys is a 4th cousin 4 times removed
Elizabeth Elsabe Kriel [Geldenhuys] is a 3rd cousin 5 times removed
Elizabeth Francina 'Lizelle' Venter [Botha] is related [8 steps]
Elizabeth Geldenhuys [Schikkerling] is a great-grandmother
Elizabeth Geldenhuys [Taillefer] is the wife of a 1st cousin 7 times removed
Elizabeth Gertruida Preller [Venables] is the wife of a grandson of a great-great-grandfather
Elizabeth Gertruyda Moodie [Theron] is related [10 steps]
Elizabeth Helena Geldenhuys [Swart] is the wife of a 1st cousin 4 times removed
Elizabeth Helena Geldenhuys is a 2nd cousin 3 times removed
Elizabeth Helena Matthee [Geldenhuys] is a 1st cousin 3 times removed
Elizabeth Helena van Heerden [Voster] is related [14 steps]
Elizabeth Jacomina van Heerden [Venter] is related [14 steps]
Elizabeth Johanna Geldenhuys is a 3rd cousin 4 times removed
Elizabeth Johanna Geldenhuys is a 4th cousin 3 times removed
Elizabeth Johanna Magdalena Geldenhuys is a 3rd cousin 4 times removed
Elizabeth Johanna Wesselina Geldenhuys is a 4th cousin 3 times removed
Elizabeth Johanna Wessels [Geldenhuys] is a 2nd cousin 5 times removed
Elizabeth Luytjie Geldenhuys [Swart] is the wife of a 2nd cousin 5 times removed
Elizabeth Magdalena Geldenhuys [Ungerer] is the wife of a 3rd cousin 4 times removed
Elizabeth Magdalena Malan [Moller] is a great-great-grandmother of the wife
Elizabeth Magdalena Maude Preller is a great-granddaughter of a great-great-grandfather

Elizabeth Margaretha van Heerden is related [16 steps]
Elizabeth Maria Eksteen [Geldenhuys] is a sister of a great-grandfather
Elizabeth Maria Geldenhuys [Muller] is the wife of a 4th cousin 3 times removed
Elizabeth Maria Geldenhuys is a 1st cousin 4 times removed
Elizabeth Maria Geldenhuys is a 2nd cousin 4 times removed
Elizabeth Maria Geldenhuys is a 3rd cousin 4 times removed
Elizabeth Maria Geldenhuys is a 5th cousin twice removed
Elizabeth Maria Helena Geldenhuys is a 3rd cousin 5 times removed
Elizabeth Maria Susanna Geldenhuys is a 4th cousin 4 times removed
Elizabeth Moodie [Dunbar] is a direct ancestor of a son-in-law
Elizabeth Rachel Geldenhuys [de Villiers] is the wife of a 3rd cousin 5 times removed
Elizabeth Rachel Geldenhuys is a 4th cousin 4 times removed
Elizabeth Sophia Moodie [Pigot] is related [10 steps]
Elizabeth Susanna Johanna Geldenhuys is a 4th cousin twice removed
Elizabeth Susarah 'Elize' Venter [van Zyl] is related [8 steps]
Elize van der Westhuizen [Venter] is a niece of the wife of a cousin of the wife
Elizna Marelise Bexter [J. van Noordwyk] is related [8 steps]
Eloise Geldenhuys [Howard] is a daughter-in-law (the wife of his son)
Eloise Preller [Harper] is the wife of a 3rd cousin twice removed
Elsa Johanna Geldenhuys is a 3rd cousin 3 times removed
Elsa Malan [Jordaan] is the wife of a nephew of the wife
Elsabe Barendina Francina Swart [Geldenhuys] is a 4th cousin twice removed
Elsabe Cornelia Geertruy Anna Geldenhuys is a 2nd cousin 4 times removed
Elsabe Cornelia Geldenhuys [Matthee] is the wife of a 1st cousin 5 times removed
Elsabe Cornelia Geldenhuys is a 3rd cousin 4 times removed
Elsabe Dina Geldenhuys [Lourens - b3c5d2e?] is the wife of a 2nd cousin 4 times removed
Elsabe Dina Geldenhuys [Lourens] is related [11 steps]
Elsabe Eksteen [Geldenhuys] is a 2nd cousin 6 times removed
Elsabe Geldenhuys [Meyer] is a sister-in-law of a direct ancestor
Elsabe Geldenhuys [Swart] is the wife of a 1st cousin 6 times removed
Elsabe Geldenhuys [Swart] is the wife of a 4th cousin 3 times removed
Elsabe Johanna Jacomina Geldenhuys is a 5th cousin twice removed
Elsabe Johanna Wesselina Geldenhuys is a 4th cousin 3 times removed
Elsabe Luitje Geldenhuys is a 4th cousin 3 times removed
Elsabe Luytje Ebersohn [Geldenhuys] is a 4th cousin 3 times removed
Elsabe Malan [Wium] is related [11 steps]
Elsa-Lou Cornelia Nel [Malan] is a niece of the wife
Elsebe Geldenhuys [Swart] is the wife of a 2nd cousin 5 times removed
Elsie Cornelia Preller [Voster] is the wife of a grandson of a great-great-grandfather
Elsie Elizabeth van Heerden [Myburgh] is related [14 steps]
Elsie 'Ellie' Kotzé [Venter] is a sister-in-law of a cousin of the wife
Elsie Johanna Geldenhuys is a 1st cousin 5 times removed
Elsie Johanna van der Merwe [van Heerden] is related [11 steps]
Elsie Maria Aletta Schoeman [van Heerden] is the mother-in-law of a brother of a great-grandfather
Elsie Maria Marais [van Heerden] is an aunt of the wife of a cousin of the wife
Elsie Susanna van Heerden [du Preez] is related [14 steps]
Elsie van der Heever [van der Westhuizen] is related [9 steps]
Elsie van der Heever [van Heerden] is a sister of a grandfather of the wife of a cousin of the wife
Elsie van der Merwe [van Heerden] is related [13 steps]
Elsie van Wyk [Geldenhuys] is a sister of a direct ancestor
Elsie Wilhelmina van Heerden is related [15 steps]
Elsje Geldenhuys is a 1st cousin 7 times removed
Elsje Gildenhuisz van der Heiden [Geldenhuys] is a sister of a direct ancestor
Elsje Jacoba van Heerden is related [10 steps]
Elsje van Heerden is related [12 steps]
Elsken Geldenhuys [von Coesfeld] is a direct ancestor (10 generations; great-great-great-great-great-great-great-great-grandmother)

Elste van Heerden [van der Westhuizen] is related [8 steps]
Elysabeth Dircx Tol [van der Piet] is a direct ancestor (9 generations; great-great-great-great-great-great-great-grandmother)
Emma Moodie [Haddon] is related [8 steps]
Eran Waldeck is a 1st cousin twice removed
Erens Lodewyk Johannes Venter is a brother-in-law of a cousin of the wife
Eric van Rooyen is an uncle of the husband of a niece
Erica Preller [de Vos] is the wife of a 3rd cousin once removed
Erna Lotter is a first cousin
Erna? Lotter [NN?] is an aunt by marriage
Ernestine Marlene Geldenhuys [Steinbach] is the wife of a 2nd cousin once removed
Erwin Uhlmann is the husband of a 2nd cousin
Ettienne First Husband is a nephew of the wife of a nephew
Eugene Constante Geldenhuys is an ex-husband of a 4th cousin once removed
Eve Elisabeth McColl [Boxall] is an ex-wife of the ex-husband of a sister
Eveline Frances Roberts [Coleman] is a sister of a great-grandmother of a son-in-law
Evert Grobbelaar is the father-in-law of a 4th cousin 4 times removed
Evert Johannes Geldenhuys is a 6th cousin twice removed
Felix Festus Malan is an uncle of the wife
First Husband is a brother-in-law of the wife of a nephew
Flora Agnes Strickland Moodie is a 2nd cousin 4 times removed of a son-in-law
Florence Nellie Isabella Preller is a great-granddaughter of a great-great-grandfather
Florence Preller is a first cousin twice removed (first cousin of grandmother)
Floris Petrus Jacobus de Meyer is the husband of a sister of a great-grandfather
Francina Frederika Geldenhuys [Prinsloo] is the wife of a 3rd cousin 3 times removed
Francina Geldenhuys is a 7th cousin once removed
Francina Jacoba Geldenhuys [Latsky] is the wife of a 4th cousin 3 times removed
Francina Johanna Geldenhuys is a 2nd cousin 3 times removed
Francina Tesner [Cordier] is the mother-in-law of a 1st cousin 6 times removed
Francis Vincent Holstock Roberts is a 2nd cousin once removed of a son-in-law
Francis Winnifred (Winnie) Deacon [Preller] is a first cousin once removed (cousin of father)
Francois Bezuidenhout is a nephew of the wife
Francois Daniel Malan is a brother-in-law (brother of his wife)
Francois Daniel Malan is a nephew of the wife
Francois Daniel Malan is the father-in-law
Francois Gustav Mulder is a 4th cousin twice removed
Francois Johannes Preller is a grandson of a great-great-grandfather
Francois Lodewyk Johannes Geldenhuys is a 5th cousin 3 times removed
Francois Retief is a direct ancestor of the wife
Francois van der Walt is a brother of a daughter-in-law of a sister-in-law
Frank Geldenhuys is a 2nd cousin twice removed
Frank Victor Preller is a great-grandson of a great-great-grandfather
Frans Hendrik Badenhorst is the husband of a 2nd cousin 5 times removed
Frans Jacobus Anthonie Geldenhuys is a 4th cousin 3 times removed
Frans Lodewyk Geldenhuys is a 4th cousin 3 times removed
Frans Lodewyk Gresse is the father-in-law of a 3rd cousin 4 times removed
Fred Robert Moor is related [12 steps]
Frederick Brink is a brother of a grandfather of the husband of a niece
Frederick Jacobus Malan is an uncle of the wife
Frederik Geldenhuys is a 5th cousin twice removed
Frederik Johannes Jacobus Geldenhuys is a direct descendant of a direct ancestor
Frederik Johannes van Heerden is related[16 steps]
Frederika Johanna Catharina Maria van Heerden [Botha] is related [16 steps]
Fritz Lippert is a 2nd cousin once removed
G A van Niekerk is the husband of a 4th cousin 3 times removed
G Preller is related [9 steps]
Gabriel Petrus Stephanus Geldenhuys is a 3rd cousin 4 times removed
Gabriel Stephanus le Roux Geldenhuys is a 3rd cousin 4 times removed
Garth Patrick Geldenhuys is a 4th cousin once removed

Geertruida Johanna Geldenhuys is a 1st cousin 3 times removed
Geertruy Anna Elizabeth Geldenhuys is a 3rd cousin 3 times removed
Geertruy Anna Geldenhuys is a 2nd cousin 4 times removed
Geertruy Anna Geldenhuys is a sister of a great-grandfather of the father
Geertruy Anna Johanna Geldenhuys is a sister of a great-grandfather
Geertruy Anna NN [Geldenhuys] is a sister of a direct ancestor
Geertruy Geldenhuys is a sister of a direct ancestor
Geertruy Johanna Fourie [Geldenhuys] is a 3rd cousin 4 times removed
Geertruy Johanna Geldenhuys is a 1st cousin 5 times removed
Geertruy Siek [Helms] is a direct ancestor (9 generations; great-great-great-great-great-great-great-grandmother)
Geertruyda Anna Johanna Geldenhuys is a 1st cousin 4 times removed
Geertruyda Elizabeth Geldenhuys is a 2nd cousin 5 times removed
Geertruyda Geldenhuys [Grobbelaar] is a sister-in-law of a direct ancestor
Geertruyda Geldenhuys [Swart] is the wife of a 2nd cousin 5 times removed
Geertruyda Jacoba Geldenhuys is a 4th cousin 3 times removed
Geertruyda Johanna Elizabeth Coetzee [Geldenhuys] is a 1st cousin 3 times removed
Geertruyda Johanna Geldenhuys is a 1st cousin 3 times removed
Geertruyda Johanna Geldenhuys is a 1st cousin 3 times removed
Geertruyda Johanna Geldenhuys is a sister of a great-grandfather of the father
Geertruyda Johanna Kuhn [Geldenhuys] is a 3rd cousin 4 times removed
Geertruyda Maria Geldenhuys is a 2nd cousin 5 times removed
Geertruyda Petronella Dippenaar [van Niekerk] is related [9 steps]
Geertruyda Petronella Dippenaar is a 2nd cousin twice removed of an ex-wife of the brother
Geertruyda Susanna Geldenhuys [Wessels] is the wife of a 1st cousin 6 times removed
Geertruyda Susanna Geldenhuys is a 3rd cousin 4 times removed
Geertruyda Wilhelmina Geldenhuys is a 4th cousin 3 times removed
Geertruyda Wouttrina Geldenhuys [Kriel] is the wife of a 5th cousin 3 times removed
Gem Brink is a granddaughter of a sister
George Benjamin Dunbar Moodie is a 2nd cousin 4 times removed of a son-in-law
George Benjamin Dunbar Moodie is a 3rd cousin 3 times removed of a son-in-law
George Benjamin Dunbar Moodie is related [9 steps]
George David Cornelis Beyers is the husband of a 4th cousin 3 times removed
George Diederick Prinsloo is the husband of a 1st cousin 3 times removed
George Peter Lt General Walls is related [14 steps]
George Pigot Moodie is a 1st cousin 5 times removed of a son-in-law
Gerald Habig is a nephew of the ex-wife of a brother
Gerald Habig is the husband of a sister of the ex-wife of the brother
Gerhard - j1 Geldenhuys is a 6th cousin
Gerhardus Bernardus - g7 Geldenhuys is a 3rd cousin 3 times removed
Gerhardus Bernardus - h4 Geldenhuys is a 4th cousin twice removed
Gerhardus Bernardus - i1 Geldenhuys is a 5th cousin once removed
Gerrit Geldenhuys is a 1st cousin 7 times removed
Gerrit van Deventer is the husband of a 3rd cousin 4 times removed
Gerry Burns is the father-in-law of a 3rd cousin
Gert Johannes van den Hever is the husband of a 2nd cousin 4 times removed
Gert Nel is the father-in-law of a 3rd cousin once removed
Gert Stephan van der Westhuizen is related [21 steps]
Gert Stephanus van der Westhuizen is related [21 steps]
Gertruida Adriana 'Ada' Venter [van Zyl] is related [8 steps]
Gertruida Johanna Bezuidenhout [Malan] is a sister-in-law (sister of his wife)
Gertruida Johanna Malan [van Eeden] is a grandmother of the wife
Gertruida Margaretha Preller is a first cousin twice removed (first cousin of grandmother)
Gesina Catharina Geldenhuys [de Jager] is the wife of a 4th cousin 3 times removed
Gesina Catharina Geldenhuys is a 5th cousin twice removed
Gesina Geldenhuys is a 4th cousin 4 times removed
Gideon Theodorus Geldenhuys is a 4th cousin 4 times removed
Gideon van Dyk is the husband of a 4th cousin 4 times removed
Gideon van Eeden Malan is an uncle of the wife

Gillian Preller [Scotson] is related [9 steps]
Gillian Sinton [Macaulay] is a great-grandmother of a grandson
Girl NN [Lotter] is an aunt (a sister of his mother)
Glenn Cameron Culhane is a nephew of the husband of a niece
Godfrey Jelley is a great-grandfather of a son-in-law
Grace Dunckers [NN] is the mother of an ex-husband of the cousin
Grace Rimer is a 3rd cousin 3 times removed of a son-in-law
Grahame David Jelley is a son-in-law (the husband of his daughter)
Gretha le Roux is a daughter of a sister-in-law of the wife
Grieselde Henriette Thorne [Venter] is a niece of the wife of a cousin of the wife
Grietje Hoefnagels [Cornelis] is a direct ancestor   (10 generations; great-great-great-great-great-great-great-great-grandmother)
Guilliam (or Gideon) Theodorus Geldenhuys is a 3rd cousin 5 times removed
Guilliam Hendrik Geldenhuys is a 2nd cousin 6 times removed
Guilliam Hendrik Geldenhuys is a 3rd cousin 5 times removed
Guilliam Hendrik Geldenhuys is a 4th cousin 4 times removed
Guilliam Hendrik Heems is the husband of a 1st cousin 7 times removed
Guilliam Jacob Geldenhuys is a 4th cousin 4 times removed
Guilliam Petrus Geldenhuys is a 4th cousin 4 times removed
Gunter van der Westhuizen is related [8 steps]
Gustav Preller is a 2nd cousin once removed
Gustav Preller is a 3rd cousin
Gustav Schoeman Preller is a first cousin twice removed (first cousin of grandmother)
Gustav Thomas Venter is a nephew of the wife of a cousin of the wife
Guy Rimer is a 3rd cousin 3 times removed of a son-in-law
Gwen van Rooyen [NN] is a grandmother of the husband of a niece
H J Lourens is the husband of a granddaughter of a direct ancestor
Hannelie Geldenhuys [Booysen] is the wife of a 3rd cousin
Hans Jacob Blom Geldenhuys is a 5th cousin twice removed
Hans Jacob Brits is a direct ancestor   (8 generations; great-great-great-great-great-great-grandfather)
Hans Jacob Geldenhuys is a 2nd cousin 3 times removed
Hans Jacob Geldenhuys is a 4th cousin 3 times removed
Hans Jacob Stanford Geldenhuys is a 3rd cousin twice removed
Hans Jacob Swart is the father-in-law of a 1st cousin 4 times removed
"Hansie" Johannes Jurgens Bezuidenhout is a brother-in-law of the wife
Harriet Susan Moodie is a sister of a great-grandmother of an in-law
Harry Moodie is a 2nd cousin 4 times removed of a son-in-law
Haydn Venter is a 3rd cousin 3 times removed
Hazel Nel [Blume] is the mother-in-law of a 3rd cousin once removed
Hazel Schlemer [Brink] is an aunt of the husband of a niece
Heila Magdalena Malan is an aunt of the wife
Heinrich (Hendrik) Venter is related [12 steps]
Heinrich du Plooy is a brother-in-law of a direct ancestor
Heinrich Oswald Eksteen is the father-in-law of a 2nd cousin 6 times removed
Heinrich Schmidt is the father of a sister-in-law of a direct ancestor
Heinrich Tesner is the father-in-law of a 1st cousin 6 times removed
Helena Alberta Malan [Lock] is a sister-in-law of the wife
Helena Catharina van Dyk [Siewers] is a direct ancestor   (8 generations; great-great-great-great-great-great-grandmother)
Helena Catherina van Heerden [Geldenhuys] is related [16 steps]
Helena Gerharda Geldenhuys [Keulder] is the wife of a 3rd cousin 5 times removed
Helena Johanna Geldenhuys [van Schalkwyk] is the wife of a 4th cousin 4 times removed
Helena Johanna Geldenhuys is a 4th cousin 4 times removed
Helena Maria Geldenhuys [Walters] is the wife of a 2nd cousin 6 times removed
Helena Steenkamp [van Heerden] is related [13 steps]
Helena Templeton Preller [Walker] is the wife of a first cousin once removed
Helina de Waal [Meyer] is related [10 steps]

Helletta Lephina Geldenhuys is an aunt (a sister of his father)
Helletta Lephina Preller [Botha] is a great-grandmother
Helletta Levina Preller is a sister of a grandmother
Hendricus Petrus Beneke is the husband of a 3rd cousin 4 times removed
Hendrik (b8) Geldenhuys is a brother of a direct ancestor
Hendrik (c3) Geldenhuys is a direct ancestor (7 generations; great-great-great-great-great-grandfather)
Hendrik Abraham Johannes Geldenhuys is a 4th cousin 4 times removed
Hendrik Abraham Johannes Geldenhuys is a 5th cousin 3 times removed
Hendrik Abraham Johannes Geldenhuys is a 6th cousin twice removed
Hendrik Albertus Geldenhuys is a 1st cousin 7 times removed
Hendrik Albertus Geldenhuys is a 3rd cousin 5 times removed
Hendrik Albertus Geldenhuys is a 4th cousin 4 times removed
Hendrik Albertus Geldenhuys is a 5th cousin 3 times removed
Hendrik Albertus Swart is the husband of a 4th cousin twice removed
Hendrik Andries Geldenhuys is a 1st cousin 6 times removed
Hendrik Andries Geldenhuys is a 2nd cousin 5 times removed
Hendrik Andries Geldenhuys is a 3rd cousin 4 times removed
Hendrik Andries Geldenhuys is a 4th cousin 3 times removed
Hendrik Daniel Geldenhuys is a 2nd cousin 3 times removed
Hendrik de Waal is related [11 steps]
Hendrik Francois Malan is a brother-in-law (brother of his wife)
Hendrik Francois Malan is a grandfather of the wife
Hendrik Francois Malan is a great-grandfather of the wife
Hendrik Francois Malan is an uncle of the wife
Hendrik Gabriel Johannes Stephanus Geldenhuys is a 4th cousin 3 times removed
Hendrik Geldenhuys is a 2nd cousin 4 times removed
Hendrik Geldenhuys is a 2nd cousin 6 times removed
Hendrik Geldenhuys is a 4th cousin 4 times removed
Hendrik Geldenhuys is a 7th cousin once removed
Hendrik Geldenhuys is a brother of a direct ancestor
Hendrik Jacobus (Hennie) Geldenhuys is a first cousin once removed (son of first cousin)
Hendrik Jacobus Geldenhuys is a 1st cousin 3 times removed
Hendrik Jacobus Geldenhuys is a 1st cousin 5 times removed
Hendrik Jacobus Geldenhuys is a 2nd cousin 3 times removed
Hendrik Jacobus Geldenhuys is a 2nd cousin 4 times removed
Hendrik Jacobus Geldenhuys is a 3rd cousin 3 times removed
Hendrik Jacobus Geldenhuys is a 3rd cousin twice removed
Hendrik Jacobus Geldenhuys is a brother of a great-grandfather
Hendrik Jacobus Geldenhuys is a brother of a great-grandfather of the father
Hendrik Jacobus Geldenhuys is a great-grandfather
Hendrik Jacobus Geldenhuys is an uncle (a brother of his father)
Hendrik Jacobus van Aardt is a nephew of the wife
Hendrik Johannes (Gildenhuizen) Geldenhuys is the husband of a 4th cousin 4 times removed
Hendrik Johannes Fourie is the husband of a 3rd cousin 4 times removed
Hendrik Johannes Geldenhuys is a 1st cousin 4 times removed
Hendrik Johannes Geldenhuys is a 2nd cousin 4 times removed
Hendrik Johannes Geldenhuys is a 3rd cousin 5 times removed
Hendrik Johannes Geldenhuys is a 4th cousin 4 times removed
Hendrik Johannes Lacock is the husband of a 5th cousin twice removed
Hendrik Marthinus Geldenhuys is a 4th cousin 4 times removed
Hendrik Marthinus Geldenhuys is a 6th cousin twice removed
Hendrik Oostwald Loubser Geldenhuys is a 4th cousin 4 times removed
Hendrik Otto is the father-in-law of a 3rd cousin 4 times removed
Hendrik Petrus Dippenaar is a 1st cousin 3 times removed of an ex-wife of the brother
Hendrik Petrus Geldenhuys is a 5th cousin twice removed
Hendrik Petrus Geldenhuys is a grandson of a direct ancestor
Hendrik Phillipus 'Phillip' Liebenberg is a nephew of the ex-wife of a brother
Hendrik van Heerden is related [12 steps]

Hendrina Jacoba Geldenhuys is a 1st cousin 3 times removed
Henricus Geldenhuisz ab1c3 Geldenhuys is a 1st cousin 7 times removed
Henrietta Heddle [Moodie] is related [9 steps]
Henrika Francina Geldenhuys [Cloete] is the wife of a 5th cousin once removed
Henritta Moodie is related [9 steps]
Henry Glen Brink is a brother of a grandfather of the husband of a niece
Henry Nourse is the husband of a first cousin twice removed
Hercules Venter is related [10 steps]
Herman Otto Preller is a great-grandson of a great-great-grandfather
Hermann Erwin Rudibert 'Rudi' Geldenhuys is a 3rd cousin
Hermanus Johannes 'Herman' Venter is a nephew of the wife of a cousin of the wife
Hermanus Johannes Smartenryk Venter is the father-in-law of a cousin of the wife
Hermanus Johannes Willem Malan is a 4th cousin 3 times removed of the wife
Hermanus Kriel is related [10 steps]
Hermanus Malan is a first cousin once removed of the wife
Hermanus Stephanus (Sterk Bosman is the father-in-law of a brother of a great-grandfather
Hermanus van der Westhuizen is related [9 steps]
Hermanus van Heerden is a brother of a grandfather of the wife of a cousin of the wife
Hester Elizabeth Johanna van der Westhuizen [Voster] is related [9 steps]
Hester Elizabeth Johanna van Heerden [Voster] is related [9 steps]
Hester Elizabeth van Heerden is related [10 steps]
Hester Helena Moodie [Meyer] is related [12 steps]
Hester Helena Moodie is a 3rd cousin 3 times removed of a son-in-law
Hester Johanna Fouche [Geldenhuys] is a 1st cousin 5 times removed
Hester Johanna Geldenhuys is a 5th cousin twice removed
Hester Magaretha Dippenaar is related [9 steps]
Hester Magdalena Deale [Moodie] is a 1st cousin 3 times removed of a son-in-law
Hester Magdalena Moodie is a 2nd cousin twice removed of a son-in-law
Hester Margaretha Johanna van Heerden [Botha] is related [17 steps]
Hester Pelser [van der Westhuizen] is related [9 steps]
Hester Pelser [van Heerden] is a sister of a grandfather of the wife of a cousin of the wife
Hester Sophia Dippenaar is a sister of a great-grandfather of the father of the ex-wife of the brother
Hester van der Heiden [Kyper] is the mother of a brother-in-law of a direct ancestor
Hester Venter [Nel] is related [11 steps]
Hilda Mildred Moodie is a 3rd cousin 3 times removed of a son-in-law
Hilletje Aletta Geldenhuys [Smit] is the wife of a 3rd cousin 5 times removed
Hilletje Aletta Hendrina Smit [Geldenhuys] is a 5th cousin 3 times removed
Hilletje Aletta Johanna Brand [Geldenhuys] is a 4th cousin 4 times removed
Hilletje van Heerden [van der Westhuizen] is related [16 steps]
Hilletjie de Beer [Smit] is a direct ancestor   (7 generations; great-great-great-great-great-grandmother)
Hugo Lock is a brother of a sister-in-law of the wife
Ian Jannie Geldenhuys is a grandson of a brother
Ingrid Stella Howard [Estment] is an in-law
Iris Anne van der Walt [Heywood] is an in-law of a sister-in-law
Iris Brink is a sister of a grandfather of the husband of a niece
Isaac Jacobus van Heerden is related [10 steps]
Isaac Jacobus van Heerden is related [15 steps]
isaac Jacobus van Heerden is related [17 steps]
Isaac Lodewicus van Heerden is related [14 steps]
Isaac Petrus van Heerden is related [14 steps]
Isaac van Heerden is related [12 steps]
Isabeau Elisabeth Malan [le Long] is a direct ancestor of the wife
Isle Gaupner [Preller] is a 2nd cousin
Isobel Anderson [Barclay] is a direct ancestor of a grandson
Ivan Preller is a 2nd cousin once removed
Izak Francois Mulder is the husband of a 4th cousin once removed
Izak Geldenhuys is a 3rd cousin

Izak George Geldenhuys is a 3rd cousin
Izak George Geldenhuys is a first cousin twice removed (first cousin of grandfather)
Izak George 'Sakkie' Geldenhuys is a 2nd cousin once removed
J F Beeslaar is the father-in-law of a 4th cousin 3 times removed
J J Taljaard is the husband of a granddaughter of a direct ancestor
J P H Vermeulen is the husband of a 3rd cousin twice removed
Jaco Danie van der Westhuizen is related [21 steps]
Jaco Drotskie is a nephew of the wife of a nephew
Jaco Olivier is a grandson of a sister of the wife
Jacob Alewijnsz Tol is a direct ancestor (9 generations; great-great-great-great-great-great-great-grandfather)
Jacob du Toit is the husband of a 3rd cousin twice removed
Jacob Jacobus 'Jaco' Venter is a nephew of the wife of a cousin of the wife
Jacob Jacobus van Heerden is an uncle of the wife of a cousin of the wife
Jacob van Heerden is related [13 steps]
Jacoba Aletta Dippenaar is a 2nd cousin twice removed of an ex-wife of the brother
Jacoba Catharina Geldenhuys is a 5th cousin twice removed
Jacoba Cornelia 'Corli' Geldenhuys [Opperman] is the wife of a 4th cousin once removed
Jacoba Elizabeth van Heerden [Potgieter] is related [19 steps]
Jacoba 'Jabje' van der Merwe [van Heerden] is related [13 steps]
Jacoba Margaretha Geldenhuys [Swart] is the wife of a 2nd cousin 4 times removed
Jacoba Margaretha Geldenhuys is a 1st cousin 3 times removed
Jacoba Margaretha Prinsloo [Geldenhuys] is a 1st cousin 3 times removed
Jacoba Maria Geldenhuys is a 1st cousin 3 times removed
Jacoba Petronella Magdalena Preller is a granddaughter of a great-great-grandfather
Jacoba Petronella Nourse [Preller] is a first cousin twice removed (first cousin of grandmother)
Jacoba Petronella Preller [Heyneman] is the wife of a great-great-grandfather
Jacoba Petronella Preller is a first cousin twice removed (first cousin of grandmother)
Jacobus ' Kosie' Geldenhuys is a 3rd cousin
Jacobus (Willem Schalk) van Heerden is related [11 steps]
Jacobus Adriaan 'Kotie Jr' Geldenhuys is a 3rd cousin
Jacobus Albertus van Zyl is a brother-in-law of a direct ancestor
Jacobus Arnoldus Louw is the husband of a 4th cousin 4 times removed
Jacobus Bernandus Malan is an uncle of the wife
Jacobus Carel Geldenhuys is a 3rd cousin 5 times removed
Jacobus Geldenhuys is a 1st cousin 6 times removed
Jacobus Geldenhuys is a 1st cousin 7 times removed
Jacobus Geldenhuys is a 2nd cousin 5 times removed
Jacobus Geldenhuys is a 4th cousin 3 times removed
Jacobus Hendrik Geldenhuys is a 4th cousin 3 times removed
Jacobus Hendrik Odendaal is the husband of a 4th cousin 3 times removed
Jacobus Hermanus Malan is a 1st cousin 6 times removed of the wife
Jacobus Jacob Hendrik Geldenhuys is a 3rd cousin 4 times removed
Jacobus Johannes Geldenhuys is a 3rd cousin 4 times removed
Jacobus Johannes Malan is a direct ancestor of the wife
Jacobus Johannes Opperman is a brother-in-law of a 4th cousin once removed
Jacobus Johannes van Heerden is related [14 steps]
Jacobus Johannes van Heerden is related [16 steps]
Jacobus Lodewyk van Heerden is related [16 steps]
Jacobus Louw is related [11 steps]
Jacobus Malan is related [9 steps]
Jacobus Nicolaas Matthee is the husband of a 1st cousin 3 times removed
Jacobus Petrus Cornelis Geldenhuys is a 5th cousin twice removed
Jacobus Strydom 'Kotie Sr' Geldenhuys is a 2nd cousin once removed
Jacobus van der Heiden is a 1st cousin 7 times removed
Jacobus van der Heiden is a brother-in-law of a direct ancestor
Jacobus van Heerden is related [12 steps]
Jacomina Geertruyda Cooper [Geldenhuys] is a 3rd cousin 4 times removed
Jacqueline Joan Lock is a granddaughter of a brother of a sister-in-law of the wife

Jacques de Villiers is a great-grandson of a sister-in-law
Jacques Malan is a direct ancestor of the wife
Jacques Smith is a 3rd cousin once removed
Jake Geldenhuys is a grandson
Jakobus Muller Geldenhuys is a 5th cousin twice removed
James Alexander (Johnny) Howard is a grandfather of the wife of a son
James Benjamin Donald Moodie is a direct ancestor of a son-in-law
James Benjamin Donald Moodie is related [9 steps]
James Henry Lane Flint is related [9 steps]
James Major Moodie is a direct ancestor of a son-in-law
James Michael (Jakobus Michiel) Preller is a brother of a great-grandfather
James Moodie is a 1st cousin 3 times removed of a son-in-law
James Scott Sinton is a great-great-grandfather of a grandson
Jan Abraham Willem van Heerden is related [18 steps]
Jan Adriaan Geldenhuys is a 6th cousin twice removed
Jan Bastiaan Rabie is a brother-in-law of a direct ancestor
Jan Bezuidenhout is related [9 steps]
Jan Cornelis Swart is the husband of a 1st cousin 5 times removed
Jan Gerhardus (John) de Waal is a great-great-grandfather of the wife of a nephew
Jan Gerhardus de Waal is a brother of a daughter-in-law of a brother
Jan Gerhardus de Waal is a grandfather of the wife of a nephew
Jan Gerhardus de Waal is an in-law of a brother
Jan Gerhardus 'JG' de Waal is a nephew of the wife of a nephew
Jan Hendrik Badenhorst is the husband of a granddaughter of a direct ancestor
Jan Hendrik Coetzee is the husband of a 1st cousin 3 times removed
Jan Hendrik Geldenhuys is a 2nd cousin 6 times removed
Jan Hendrik Geldenhuys is a 3rd cousin 4 times removed
Jan Hendrik Geldenhuys is a 3rd cousin 5 times removed
Jan Jurgen Hamman is a brother-in-law of a direct ancestor
Jan Lotter is a first cousin
Jan Lotter is an uncle (a brother of his mother)
Jan Lotter is the maternal grandfather
Jan Louw is the husband of a 1st cousin 7 times removed
Jan NN Lotter is a great-grandfather
Jan Pieter Furstenburg 'Jack' Furstenberg Preller is a grandson of a great-great-grandfather
Jan Pieterz van Dijk van Dyk is a direct ancestor (9 generations; great-great-great-great-great-great-great-grandfather)
Jan Smit is a direct ancestor (8 generations; great-great-great-great-great-great-grandfather)
Jan Valentyn Venter is a brother-in-law of the wife of a nephew
Jan Willemse Alexander Geldenhuys is a 3rd cousin twice removed
Jane Elizabeth Brink is a sister of a grandfather of the husband of a niece
Jane Rachel Elizabeth Brink is a sister of a grandfather of the husband of a niece
Jane Sarah Brink [Glenn] is a great-grandmother of the husband of a niece
Janel Groenewald [van Stryp] is related [8 steps]
Janet Dunbar is a direct ancestor of a son-in-law
Janet Jesse Nicholson [Moodie] is related [9 steps]
Janine Dippenaar is a niece of the ex-wife of a brother
Jannie Jordaan is a first cousin
'Japie' Jacob Jacobus Venter is a brother-in-law of a cousin of the wife
Jared Bezuidenhoudt is a grandson of a sister of the wife
Jason Froneman is a grandson of a brother
Jason Neil Krahner is the husband of a 4th cousin once removed
Jaunita Carr [Dippenaar] is a sister of the ex-wife of the brother
Jaydene Bezuidenhout is a grandson of a sister of the wife
Jean Costeux is a brother-in-law of a direct ancestor
Jean Jelley is the wife of a brother of a son-in-law
Jean Preller is a 2nd cousin once removed
Jenny Culhane [Brink] is a sister of a son-in-law of a sister
Jerry Bouwer is a brother of a sister-in-law of the wife

Jesse Wigston is an in-law of a sister-in-law
Jessie Venus Preller is a great-granddaughter of a great-great-grandfather
JJ Drotskie is a nephew of the wife of a nephew
Joan Geldenhuys [Collett] is the wife of a 4th cousin
Jo-ann 'Jo' Pearson [J. van Noordwyk] is related [8 steps]
Joey Geldenhuys is a sister of a grandfather
Johan Annandale is a brother-in-law of the wife of a nephew
Johan Bezuidenhout is a nephew of the wife
Johan Carel Friedrich Johann Preller is a brother of a great-grandfather
Johan Christian Lambrecht Coetzee is the husband of a 1st cousin 3 times removed
Johan Diederik Ungerer Geldenhuys is a 4th cousin 3 times removed
Johan Drotskie is a brother-in-law of the wife of a nephew
Johan Frederik Johann Friedrich Preller is a direct ancestor   (5 generations; great-great-great-grandfather)
Johan Frederik Preller is a first cousin twice removed   (first cousin of grandmother)
Johan Frederik Preller is a grandson of a great-great-grandfather
Johan Friedrich Johann Preller is a brother of a great-grandfather of the father
Johan J van Rensen is the father of an uncle by marriage
Johan Kruger is the husband of a 2nd cousin
Johan Siek is a direct ancestor   (9 generations; great-great-great-great-great-great-great-grandfather)
Johan van Rensen is a first cousin
Johan van Rooyen is an uncle of the husband of a niece
Johann Casper Schlee is related [10 steps]
Johann Friedrich Carel Johan Preller is a brother of a great-grandfather
Johann Friedrich Frederick Preller is a son of a great-great-grandfather
Johann Friedrich Preller is a direct ancestor   (6 generations; great-great-great-great-grandfather)
Johanna Adriana Geldenhuys [Mullholland] is the wife of a 4th cousin 4 times removed
Johanna Adriana van Heerden [Voster] is related [10 steps]
Johanna Albertus Wessels is the husband of a 1st cousin 4 times removed
Johanna Aletta Geldenhuys is a 1st cousin 4 times removed
Johanna Aletta van Heerden is related [15 steps]
Johanna Carolina Preller is a granddaughter of a great-great-grandfather
Johanna Catharina Geldenhuys [Grobbelaar] is the wife of a 4th cousin 4 times removed
Johanna Catharina Maria Venter [Olivier] is related [9 steps]
Johanna Cecilia van Heerden is related [10 steps]
Johanna Christina Amelia Geldenhuys is a 5th cousin 3 times removed
Johanna Christina Geldenhuys [Germishuizen] is the wife of a 3rd cousin 4 times removed
Johanna Christina Geldenhuys is a 1st cousin 3 times removed
Johanna Christina Magdalena Geldenhuys is a 5th cousin twice removed
Johanna Christina Moodie [van Zyl] is related [9 steps]
Johanna Christina Preller [Pretorius] is the wife of a first cousin twice removed
Johanna Christina Vermeulen [Geldenhuys] is a 3rd cousin twice removed
Johanna Cornelia Geldenhuys is a 2nd cousin 4 times removed
Johanna Cornelia Geldenhuys is a 4th cousin twice removed
Johanna Cornelia Geldenhuys is a sister of a great-grandfather of the father
Johanna de Waal is related [11 steps]
Johanna Dorothea Lourens [Geldenhuys] is a granddaughter of a direct ancestor
Johanna Dorothea Preller [Philemann] is a direct ancestor   (6 generations; great-great-great-great-grandmother)
Johanna du Rand [Geldenhuys] is a 1st cousin 7 times removed
Johanna Elizabeth (Linette) Geldenhuys [Kotzé] is the wife of a first cousin once removed
Johanna Elizabeth 'Baby' Venter [Robbertze] is a sister-in-law of the wife of a cousin of the wife
Johanna Elizabeth Catharina Lacock [Geldenhuys] is a 5th cousin twice removed
Johanna Elizabeth 'Joey' de Waal [Cloete] is an in-law of a brother
Johanna Elsabe Streicher [Geldenhuys] is a sister of a great-grandfather of the father
Johanna Fronica Magdalena (Joey) Luyt [Preller] is a daughter of a great-grandfather
Johanna Geertruyda Cornelia Susanna Geldenhuys is a 4th cousin 3 times removed

Johanna Geertruyda Geldenhuys [Gildenhuizen] is a direct ancestor (5 generations; great-great-great-grandmother)
Johanna Geldenhuys [le Roux] is a direct ancestor (6 generations; great-great-great-great-grandmother)
Johanna Geldenhuys [Matthee] is a sister-in-law of a direct ancestor
Johanna Geldenhuys [Vermaak] is the wife of a 6th cousin twice removed
Johanna Hendrika Maria van Dyk [Geldenhuys] is a 4th cousin 4 times removed
Johanna Hendrina Prins [Geldenhuys] is a 3rd cousin 5 times removed
Johanna Hendrina van Heerden [du Preez] is a grandmother of the wife of a brother of a great-grandfather
Johanna Jacoba Geldenhuys is a 4th cousin 4 times removed
Johanna Jacomina Maria Geldenhuys is a 6th cousin twice removed
Johanna Jochemina van Rensburg [Geldenhuys] is a 4th cousin 3 times removed
Johanna Magdalena (Madeleine Brink is a granddaughter of a great-grandfather
Johanna Magdalena Beyers [Lourens] is the mother-in-law of a 4th cousin 3 times removed
Johanna Magdalena Geldenhuys [Bruynzwart] is the wife of a 3rd cousin 5 times removed
Johanna Magdalena Geldenhuys is a 2nd cousin 3 times removed
Johanna Magdalena Geldenhuys is a 4th cousin 3 times removed
Johanna Magdalena Geldenhuys is a 5th cousin 3 times removed
Johanna Magdalena Louw [Baard] is the mother-in-law of a 4th cousin 4 times removed
Johanna Magdalena Susanna Geldenhuys is a 2nd cousin 3 times removed
Johanna Margaretha Charlotte (Onnie) Preller [Wessels] is a sister-in-law of a grandmother (aunt by marriage of the father)
Johanna Margaretha Geertruyda Geldenhuys [Rossouw] is a sister-in-law of a great-great-grandfather
Johanna Margaretha Geldenhuys is a 1st cousin 4 times removed
Johanna Margaretha Hamman [Geldenhuys] is a sister of a direct ancestor
Johanna Margaretha Preller [Wessels] is the wife of a great-grandfather
Johanna Margaretha van Heerden [Pretorius] is related [15 steps]
Johanna Maria (or Adriana) Geldenhuys is a 5th cousin 3 times removed
Johanna Maria Dreyer [Malan] is a direct ancestor (5 generations; great-great-great-grandmother)
Johanna Maria Geldenhuys is a 4th cousin 4 times removed
Johanna Nicolaas Geldenhuys is a 6th cousin twice removed
Johanna Susanna Elizabeth (father - Juli van die Kaap) [Geldenhuys] is a 1st cousin 4 times removed
Johanna Susanna Geldenhuys [Bester] is the wife of a 1st cousin 4 times removed
Johanna Susanna Heyne [Geldenhuys] is a 1st cousin 4 times removed
Johanna Susanna Keyter [Preller] is a daughter of a great-great-grandfather
Johanna Susanna Maria de Meyer [Geldenhuys] is a sister of a great-grandfather
Johanna Susanna Preller is a sister of a great-grandfather
Johanna van Heerden [Theron] is related [13 steps]
Johanna Wessels Preller is a first cousin once removed (cousin of father)
Johannes (Dons) le Roux is a son of a sister-in-law of the wife
Johannes (Jan) Albertus Geldenhuys is the paternal grandfather
Johannes (Jannie) Albertus Geldenhuys is a 1st cousin twice removed
Johannes Albertus (Gildenhuizen) Geldenhuys is the husband of a 2nd cousin 4 times removed
Johannes Albertus (Jannie) Geldenhuys is a first cousin
Johannes Albertus Bernardus Geldenhuys is a brother of a great-grandfather
Johannes Albertus Geldenhuys is a 1st cousin 3 times removed
Johannes Albertus Geldenhuys is a 1st cousin 4 times removed
Johannes Albertus Geldenhuys is a 2nd cousin 3 times removed
Johannes Albertus Geldenhuys is a 3rd cousin 4 times removed
Johannes Albertus Geldenhuys is a 3rd cousin 5 times removed
Johannes Albertus Geldenhuys is a 5th cousin 3 times removed
Johannes Albertus Geldenhuys is a brother of a direct ancestor
Johannes Albertus Geldenhuys is a brother
Johannes Albertus Geldenhuys is a direct ancestor (6 generations; great-great-great-great-

grandfather)
Johannes Albertus Geldenhuys is a first cousin twice removed (first cousin of grandfather)
Johannes Albertus Geldenhuys is a great-great-grandfather
Johannes Albertus Jochemus Geldenhuys is a 2nd cousin 3 times removed
Johannes Bernardus Venter is related [8 steps]
Johannes Christjan Beukes is the husband of a cousin
Johannes Cornelis Beukes is related [10 steps]
Johannes David Beyers is the father-in-law of a 4th cousin 3 times removed
Johannes de Waal is a direct ancestor of the wife of a nephew
Johannes de Waal is related [11 steps]
Johannes Frederik Uys is the husband of a 4th cousin 3 times removed
Johannes Gerhardus Dreyer is a direct ancestor (5 generations; great-great-great-grandfather)
Johannes Grobbelaar (or Grobler) is related [10 steps]
Johannes Hendrik Jacobus van Heerden is related [15 steps]
Johannes Hermanus Geldenhuys is a 3rd cousin 4 times removed
Johannes Jacobus Brink is a brother of a grandfather of the husband of a niece
Johannes Jacobus Carel Geldenhuys is a 4th cousin 4 times removed
Johannes Jacobus Francois Bouwer is an ex-husband of the sister
Johannes Jacobus Gerber is a brother-in-law of a great-great-grandfather
Johannes Jacobus Malan is a 3rd cousin 4 times removed of the wife
Johannes Jacobus Reynierse Malan is a 3rd cousin 4 times removed of the wife
Johannes Jacobus Rudolf le Roux is an ex-husband of a sister-in-law of the wife
Johannes Joachemus Geldenhuys is a 4th cousin 3 times removed
Johannes Joachimus Geldenhuys is a 3rd cousin 4 times removed
Johannes Jurie Cooper is the husband of a 3rd cousin 4 times removed
Johannes Lodewicus van Heerden is related [13 & 15 steps]
Johannes Marthinus Depner Dippenaar is a direct ancestor of an ex-wife of the brother
Johannes Marthinus Dippenaar is a 1st cousin 5 times removed of an ex-wife of the brother
Johannes Marthinus Dippenaar is related [8 & 9 steps]
Johannes Marthinus Opperman is a brother-in-law of a 4th cousin once removed
Johannes Matthys Ebersohn is the husband of a 4th cousin 3 times removed
Johannes Nicolas Colyn Cloete is the father-in-law of a 3rd cousin once removed
Johannes Nicolas Colyn Vos is the father-in-law of a 3rd cousin
Johannes Petrus Dippenaar is the father of the ex-wife of the brother
Johannes Urbanus Geldenhuys is a 3rd cousin 3 times removed
Johannus Petrus Dippenaar is a grandfather of the ex-wife of a brother
John Bell Moodie is a 1st cousin 5 times removed of a son-in-law
John Benjamin Moodie is a brother of a great-grandmother of an in-law
John Estment is a great-grandfather of a daughter-in-law
John Maurice Preller is a great-grandson of a great-great-grandfather
John Peter Dippenaar is a nephew of the ex-wife of a brother
John Peter Habig is a nephew of the ex-wife of a brother
John Preller is a direct descendant of a great-great-grandfather
John Robert Brink is a brother of a son-in-law of a sister
John Scott Sinton is a brother of a great-grandfather of a grandson
John Wedderburn Dunbar Moodie is related [9 steps]
John William "Jackie" Carr is the husband of a sister of the ex-wife of the brother
Johnny van Biljon is a first cousin
Joleen van Aardt [Geldenhuys] is the wife sisters daughter in law
Jolise van der Westhuizen is related [8 steps]
Joost Pietersz van Dijk van Dyk is a direct ancestor (8 generations; great-great-great-great-great-grandfather)
Jordyn Dylan Howard is a nephew of the wife of a son
Joseph P Kok is the husband of a 1st cousin 3 times removed
Josua Adriaan Groenewald is a nephew of the wife of a cousin of the wife
Josua Adriaan 'Groenie' Groenewald is a brother-in-law of the wife of a cousin of the wife
Joy Geldenhuys [Goldsworthy] is the wife of a nephew
Joyce Edith McColl [Matchett] is the mother of ex-husband of the sister
Joyce Heywood [NN] is a grandmother of the wife of a nephew of the wife

Joyce Pamela Jelley [Deeves] is the step-mother of an in-law
Joyce Rimer is a 3rd cousin 3 times removed of a son-in-law
Judith Christina Elizabeth Geldenhuys is a 4th cousin 3 times removed
Judith Cornelia Margaretha Geldenhuys is a sister of a great-grandfather
Judith Geldenhuys [Smit (Schmidt)] is a sister-in-law of a direct ancestor
Judith Margaretha Elsabe Geldenhuys is a 3rd cousin 3 times removed
Judith Margaretha Geldenhuys [Gildenhuizen] is a great-great-grandmother
Judith Margaretha Geldenhuys is a 1st cousin 3 times removed
Judith Margaretha Geldenhuys is a 2nd cousin 4 times removed
Judith Margaretha Geldenhuys is a first cousin twice removed (first cousin of grandfather)
Judith Wilhelmina Geldenhuys is a 4th cousin 3 times removed
Julia Lillian Geldenhuys [Dippenaar] is the wife of the brother
June E Mussell [Estment] is an aunt of the wife of a son
June Hazel Preller [Torlage] is the wife of a 2nd cousin
June Mussell [Howard] is an aunt of the wife of a son
Jurgen Johannes Geldenhuys is a 2nd cousin 5 times removed
Jurgen Johannes Geldenhuys is a 3rd cousin 4 times removed
Jurie Geldenhuys is a 3rd cousin
Jurie Johannes Geldenhuys is a 1st cousin 6 times removed
Jurie Johannes Geldenhuys is a 3rd cousin 4 times removed
Jurie Johannes Geldenhuys is a 4th cousin 3 times removed
Jurie Johannes Geldenhuys is a 5th cousin twice removed
Jurie Petrus Wessel Geldenhuys is a 3rd cousin 4 times removed
Justin Reginald Burger is a nephew of the wife of a nephew
Karel Frederik Preller is a first cousin twice removed (first cousin of grandmother)
Karel Frederik Preller is a grandson of a great-great-grandfather
Karel Frederik Preller is a son of a great-great-grandfather
Karen Dunckers [Botha] is the partner of a first cousin once removed
Karen Geldenhuys [de Waal] is the wife of a nephew
Karen Lippert [Preller] is a 2nd cousin
Katherine Mary Whiteley [Foster] is a sister-in-law of a grandfather of an in-law
Kathleen Nora Roberts [Baskerville] is related [8 steps]
Kayla Venter is a 3rd cousin 3 times removed
Keanu Brandon Mulder is a 4th cousin twice removed
Keith Brian Jelley is a brother of a son-in-law
Kelley Anne Trichardt [Brown] is the wife of a 4th cousin once removed
Kenneth Steve Howard is an in-law
Kevin Ferreira is related [9 steps]
Kim Chanelle Muirhead is a niece of the husband of a niece
Koeks NN Geldenhuys [Koeks] is the wife of a 2nd cousin once removed
L Preller is related [9 steps]
Lance Froneman is a first cousin once removed (son of first cousin)
Laura Els [Preller] is a direct descendant of a great-great-grandfather
Lauretta Smith [Geldenhuys] is a 3rd cousin
Laurie 'Lorrie' Geldenhuys is a 2nd cousin twice removed
Lavinia Liebenberg is a granddaughter of a sister of an ex-wife of the brother
Leah Ann Krahner is a 4th cousin twice removed
Leander Star Jameson Moodie is a 3rd cousin 3 times removed of a son-in-law
Leizel Geldenhuys is a 3rd cousin once removed
Lena Geldenhuys is a 3rd cousin once removed
Leonard Cresswell Roberts is a first cousin twice removed of a son-in-law
Leonard Farewell Holstock Roberts is a brother-in-law of a grandmother of an in-law
Leonore Moor is a 3rd cousin 3 times removed of a son-in-law
Les Rolink is the husband of a sister of the ex-wife of the brother
Lesley Ann Malan [Reeve] is the wife of a nephew of the wife
Lesley Ann Venter [Thomas] is a sister-in-law of the wife of a cousin of the wife
Letitia Gooding [Bezuidenhout] is a niece of the wife
Letitia Hermina Preller is a first cousin twice removed (first cousin of grandmother)
Letizia Clelia Ester Geldenhuys [Boggio Bozzo] is the mother of the ex-husband of a 4th cousin

once removed
Liam Connor Culhane is a nephew of the husband of a niece
Liesl Adriana de Villiers [Oosthuisen] is a granddaughter of a sister of the wife
Lilla Moodie [Turton] is related [12 steps]
Linda de Waal is a sister of a daughter-in-law of a brother
Linda Magdalene Geldenhuys [Geere] is the wife of a 4th cousin
Linda Uhlmann [Preller] is a 2nd cousin
Lisa Gaupner is a 2nd cousin once removed
Lisa Joubert [Geldenhuys] is a 6th cousin once removed
Lizelle Ferreira [Thorne] is related [8 steps]
Llewellin Quintin Heywood is a grandfather of the wife of a nephew of the wife
Lorraine Geldenhuys is a 4th cousin
Lotter is a great-grandmother
Louis Hosia Dippenaar is a brother of the ex-wife of the brother
Louis Liebenberg xx van Wyk xxx Rolink is a nephew of the ex-wife of a brother
Louis Preller is a great-granddaughter of a great-great-grandfather
Louis Trichardt is related [14 steps]
Louisa Catharina Jacobs [van Heerden] is related [10 steps]
Louisa Jacoba van Heerden is related [9 steps]
Louisa Maria Meintjies [van Heerden] is related [11 steps]
Louisa van Heerden [van der Merwe] is related [11 steps]
Louise Geldenhuys is a granddaughter of a brother
Lourens Geldenhuys is a 1st cousin 3 times removed
Lourens Geldenhuys is a brother of a great-grandfather of the father
Lourens Geldenhuys is a direct ancestor (5 generations; great-great-great-grandfather)
Lourens Johannes Albertus Geldenhuys is a 1st cousin 3 times removed
Lourens Johannes Prinsloo is the husband of a 3rd cousin 3 times removed
Lourens Pieter Arnoldus Geldenhuys is a brother of a great-grandfather
Lourens Pieter Geldenhuys is a first cousin twice removed (first cousin of grandfather)
Louzya Christina Dippenaar [de Bruyn] is the mother of the ex-wife of the brother
Louzya Christina Liebenberg xx van Wyk xxx Rolink [Dippenaar] is a sister of the wife of the brother
Lucas Marthinus Geldenhuys is a 3rd cousin 4 times removed
Lucielle Carr is a niece of the wife of a brother
Lucretia Maria Arnott [Coleman] is a great-grandmother of a son-in-law
Lucy Hope Geldenhuys is a granddaughter
Lukas Liebenberg xx van Wyk xxx Rolink is the husband of a sister of the ex-wife of the brother
Lynette Moira McQueen [Hardy] is related [12 steps]
Lynn Muirhead [Brink] is a sister of a son-in-law of a sister
M. Preller is a direct descendant of a great-great-grandfather
Maatjie Catharina Jacoba Geldenhuys [Steenkamp] is the wife of a 2nd cousin twice removed
Madelein Whiteley [Cooper] is a sister-in-law of a grandfather of a son-in-law
Magda le Roux is a daughter of a sister-in-law of the wife
Magdalena Adriana Dippenaar is related [9 steps]
Magdalena Catharina Geldenhuys is a 4th cousin 4 times removed
Magdalena Catharina Susanna Geldenhuys is a 5th cousin 3 times removed
Magdalena Francina Geldenhuys is a 4th cousin 4 times removed
Magdalena Haumann [Moller] is a grandmother of the wife of a brother of a great-grandfather
Magdalena Jacoba Geldenhuys is a 3rd cousin 4 times removed
Magdalena Johanna Geldenhuys [Louw] is the wife of a 3rd cousin 4 times removed
Magdalena Malan [Odendaal] is related [12 steps]
Magdalena Maria Nel is an in-law of a brother-in-law
Magdalena Petronella Gerber is the mother of a sister-in-law of the wife
Magdalena van Heerden [Theron] is related [13 steps]
Magdalena Wilhelmina Kok [Geldenhuys] is a 1st cousin 3 times removed
Magtilt van Heerden [van der Merwe] is related [13 steps]
Majorie Moor is a 3rd cousin 3 times removed of a son-in-law
Malcolm (Major) Nicholson is related [10 steps]
Malcolm James Dunbar Moodie is a 2nd cousin 4 times removed of a son-in-law

Mandy Howard [Pienaar] is the partner of a brother of a daughter-in-law
Mannetjie NN is a first cousin
Mardel Froneman [van Biljon] is a first cousin
Margaret Mary Elaine 'Marjel' Jelley [Whiteley] is an in-law
Margaret Moodie [Malcolmsen] is a direct ancestor of a son-in-law
Margareth Helene 'Marita' Brodie [Geldenhuys] is a 4th cousin
Margaretha Agatha Johanna Geldenhuys is a 3rd cousin 4 times removed
Margaretha Christina Maria Geldenhuys is a 3rd cousin 4 times removed
Margaretha de Waal [Lategan] is related [10 steps]
Margaretha du Plooy [Geldenhuys] is a sister of a direct ancestor
Margaretha Fredrika Geldenhuys is a 5th cousin 3 times removed
Margaretha Geldenhuys [Hoefnagels] is a direct ancestor (9 generations; great-great-great-great-great-great-great-grandmother)
Margaretha Geldenhuys is a sister of a direct ancestor
Margaretha Georgina Fredrika Geldenhuys [Rorich] is the wife of a 4th cousin 4 times removed
Margaretha Johanna Elizabeth (Gildenhuizen) Geldenhuys is a 4th cousin 4 times removed
Margaretha Johanna Elizabeth Eybers [Geldenhuys] is a 6th cousin twice removed
Margaretha Johanna Elizabeth Geldenhuys [(Gildenhuizen) Geldenhuys] is the wife of a 4th cousin 4 times removed
Margaretha Johanna Elizabeth Geldenhuys is a 5th cousin 3 times removed
Margaretha Johanna Geldenhuys [van Aarde] is the wife of a 2nd cousin 6 times removed
Margaretha Johanna Martha Jordaan [Geldenhuys] is a 4th cousin 4 times removed
Margaretha Judik Maria Geldenhuys is a 4th cousin 3 times removed
Margaretha Louisa Elizabeth Geldenhuys is a 3rd cousin 5 times removed
Margaretha Louw [Geldenhuys] is a 1st cousin 7 times removed
Margaretha Maria Geldenhuys [Maree] is the wife of a 3rd cousin 4 times removed
Margaretha Maria Geldenhuys [Scheepers] is the wife of a 2nd cousin 5 times removed
Margaretha Maria Geldenhuys [Wessels] is a sister-in-law of a direct ancestor
Margaretha Maria Geldenhuys is a 2nd cousin 4 times removed
Margaretha Maria Geldenhuys is a 5th cousin twice removed
Margaretha Maria Momsen [Geldenhuys] is a 5th cousin 3 times removed
Margarita Elizabeth Malan [Retief] is a direct ancestor of the wife
Margery Hester Coleman [Moodie] is a great-great-grandmother of a son-in-law
Margrijet Gildehuijsen Geldenhuys is a 1st cousin 7 times removed
Maria (Mimi) Aletta Preller [Kruger] is the wife of a 3rd cousin once removed
Maria Adriana Moodie is related [11 steps]
Maria Aletta van Deventer [Geldenhuys] is a 3rd cousin 4 times removed
Maria Catharina (Gildenhuizen) Geldenhuys [Reyneke] is the mother-in-law of a 4th cousin 4 times removed
Maria Catharina Dippenaar is related [9 steps]
Maria Catharina Ebersohn [Geldenhuys] is a 4th cousin 3 times removed
Maria Catharina Geldenhuys [Reyneke] is the wife of a 3rd cousin 5 times removed
Maria Catharina Geldenhuys is a 2nd cousin 3 times removed
Maria Catharina Geldenhuys is a direct descendant of a direct ancestor
Maria Catharina Magdalena Geldenhuys is a 4th cousin 3 times removed
Maria Catharina Taljaard [Geldenhuys] is a granddaughter of a direct ancestor
Maria Chistina Beneke [Geldenhuys] is a 3rd cousin 4 times removed
Maria Chistina Catharina Geldenhuys is a 3rd cousin 4 times removed
Maria Chistina Geldenhuys [Tesner] is the wife of a 1st cousin 6 times removed
Maria Chistina Geldenhuys is a 3rd cousin 4 times removed
Maria Dorothea Catharina Petronella Geldenhuys is a 3rd cousin 4 times removed
Maria Dorothea Elizabeth Geldenhuys is a 3rd cousin 4 times removed
Maria Dorothea Geldenhuys [Radyn] is the wife of a 1st cousin 6 times removed
Maria Dorothea Rabe [Preller] is a sister of a great-grandfather of the father
Maria Elizabeth Geldenhuys [Diederiks] is a sister-in-law of a direct ancestor
Maria Elizabeth Geldenhuys [Matthee] is a sister-in-law of a direct ancestor
Maria Elizabeth Geldenhuys is a 1st cousin 4 times removed
Maria Elizabeth Geldenhuys is a 2nd cousin 6 times removed
Maria Elizabeth Geldenhuys is a 4th cousin 4 times removed

Maria Elizabeth Johanna Geldenhuys [Gunter] is a sister-in-law of a great-great-grandfather
Maria Elizabeth Magdalena Johanna Coetzee [Geldenhuys] is a 1st cousin 3 times removed
Maria Elizabeth Preller [Pretorius] is the wife of a great-grandfather
Maria Elizabeth Susanna Geldenhuys [Luwes] is the wife of a 4th cousin 3 times removed
Maria Elizabeth Susanna Geldenhuys is a 5th cousin twice removed
Maria Elizabeth van Eeden [Geldenhuys] is a 1st cousin 5 times removed
Maria Elizabeth van Wyk [Geldenhuys] is a 1st cousin 3 times removed
Maria Elizabeth Venter [Keynhans] is related[8 steps]
Maria Francina Geldenhuys [van Dyk] is the wife of a 3rd cousin 4 times removed
Maria Geldenhuys is a sister of a grandfather
Maria Johanna Geldenhuys [Cooper] is the wife of a 3rd cousin 4 times removed
Maria Johanna Geldenhuys is a 2nd cousin 5 times removed
Maria Johanna Petronella Geldenhuys is a 4th cousin 4 times removed
Maria Louw [Malan] is related [9 steps]
Maria Louw [van Braken] is related [11 steps]
Maria Magdalena (Maraai) Preller is a daughter of a great-grandfather
Maria Magdalena Basson [Dippenaar] is a 1st cousin 5 times removed of an ex-wife of the brother
Maria Magdalena Dippenaar [Schmidt] is a direct ancestor of an ex-wife of the brother
Maria Magdalena Geldenhuys [Swart] is the wife of a 1st cousin 4 times removed
Maria Magdalena Geldenhuys is a 1st cousin 4 times removed
Maria Magdalena Isabella Liversage [Martens] is a great-great-grandmother of the husband of a niece
Maria Malan [Verdeau] is related [10 steps]
Maria Margaretha Geldenhuys is a 3rd cousin 5 times removed
Maria Margaretha Otto [Geldenhuys] is a 1st cousin 6 times removed
Maria Margaretha Preller [Naude (Botma)] is a great-great-grandmother
Maria Margaretha Preller is a sister of a grandmother
Maria Nienaber [van der Westhuizen] is related [9 steps]
Maria Nienaber [van Heerden] is a sister of a grandfather of the wife of a cousin of the wife
Maria Petronella de Waal [Greyling] is a direct ancestor of the wife of a nephew
Maria Retief [Mouit] is a direct ancestor of the wife
Maria Sophia Geldenhuys is a 5th cousin 3 times removed
Maria Susanna Wilhelmina Geldenhuys [Schickerling] is the wife of a brother of a great-grandfather
Maria Susanna Wilhelmina van Rensen [Geldenhuys] is an aunt (a sister of his father)
Maria van Heerden [van der Merwe] is related [13 steps]
Maria Venter [Preller] is a 3rd cousin twice removed
Marianne Geldenhuys is a 3rd cousin once removed
Marie Bouwer is the mother of ex-husband of the sister
Marie-Jeanne Kruger [Preller] is a 2nd cousin
Marion Geldenhuys [Muller] is an ex-wife of the son
Marion Walters [Moor] is a 3rd cousin 3 times removed of a son-in-law
Maritsa Lourens [le Roux] is a daughter of a sister-in-law of the wife
Marjorie Muirhead [Hockaday] is the mother of a brother-in-law of the husband of a niece
Mark Anthony Preller is a 3rd cousin twice removed
Marlene de Waal [Taljaart] is a sister-in-law of the wife of a nephew
Marriët Geldenhuys [Kloppers] is the wife of a 3rd cousin
Martha Aletta van Heerden is related [10 steps]
Martha Colyn [Geldenhuys] is a 1st cousin 5 times removed
Martha Jacoba Aletta Dippenaar is a sister of a great-grandfather of an ex-wife of the brother
Martha Jacoba Aletta Geldenhuys is a direct descendant of a direct ancestor
Martha Jacoba van der Merwe [Geldenhuys] is a 3rd cousin 5 times removed
Martha Johanna Geldenhuys [Gresse] is the wife of a 3rd cousin 4 times removed
Martha Johanna Geldenhuys is a 4th cousin 3 times removed
Martha Johanna Jacoba Geldenhuys is a 5th cousin 3 times removed
Martha Johanna van Heerden [Geldenhuys] is related [16 steps]
Martha Johanna van Heerden [Voster] is related [16 steps]
Martha Louisa Barnard [Geldenhuys] is a 5th cousin 3 times removed

Martha Louisa Geldenhuys [le Roux] is the wife of a 3rd cousin 5 times removed
Martha Louisa Geldenhuys is a 4th cousin 4 times removed
Martha Magdalena Magdelena Preller [Strydom] is the wife of a great-great-grandfather
Martha Margaretha van Heerden [Schoeman] is related [16 steps]
Martha Maria Geldenhuys [du Toit] is the wife of a 3rd cousin 5 times removed
Martha Maria Geldenhuys is a 5th cousin 3 times removed
Martha Maria van Heerden [Ronge] is related [18 steps]
Martha Petronelle (Floss) Estment [Coetzer] is a grandmother of the wife of a son
Martha Sophia Burger - then Smit [van Heerden] is related [11 steps]
Martha Sophia van Heerden [van der Merwe] is related [15 steps]
Martha Susanna Geldenhuys [van Biljon] is related [13 steps]
Martha van Heerden [van der Merwe] is related [12 steps]
Martha van Heerden is related [14 steps]
Marthinus Cornelis (Martin) Brink is a grandson of a great-grandfather
Martina Jacoba Geldenhuys is a 4th cousin twice removed
Martina Stoffeli Johanna van der Westhuizen is related [9 steps]
Martina Stoffelina Johanna du Toit [van Heerden] is a sister of a grandfather of the wife of a cousin of the wife
Martinus Christoffel Johannes van Heerden is related [8 steps]
Martinus Johannes van Heerden is an uncle of the wife of a cousin of the wife
Martinus Petrus Johannes van der Westhuizen is related [9 steps]
Martinus Petrus Johannes van Heerden is a grandfather of the wife of a cousin of the wife
Martinus Petrus Johannes Venter is a brother-in-law of a cousin of the wife
Martinus Rudolph 'Martin' J. van Noordwyk is related [8 steps]
Mary Armstrong [Walls] is related [14 steps]
Mary Kate Whiteley [Parkinson] is a great-grandmother of a son-in-law
Mary Brown Whiteley [Broadbent] is a sister-in-law of a grandfather of a son-in-law
Mary Jelley [McKenzie] is a great-grandmother of a son-in-law
Mary Margaret "Molly" Jelley is a sister-in-law of a grandfather of a son-in-law
Mary McRobert Jelley [Paterson] is a grandmother of the husband of a daughter
Mary Victoria Howard [Milton] is a grandmother of the wife of a son
Mathew Carl Trichardt is a 4th cousin twice removed
Mathilda Marietta du Toit [Geldenhuys] is a 3rd cousin twice removed
Mathilda Marietta Geldenhuys [Behr] is the wife of a 2nd cousin 3 times removed
Matilda 'Mathy' Preller is a first cousin twice removed (first cousin of grandmother)
Matilda Moodie [Hunt] is related [11 steps]
Mattheuwina Gerhardina Wessels (Matt) Brink [Preller] is a daughter of a great-grandfather
Matthew Dylan (Howard) Geldenhuys is a grandson
Matthew van Biljon is a first cousin
Matthys Johannes (Gildenhuizen) Geldenhuys is a 2nd cousin 3 times removed
Matthys Johannes Heyne is a 2nd cousin 3 times removed
Matthys Johannes Lourens Geldenhuys is a direct descendant of a direct ancestor
Matthys Micheelse Basson is related [11 steps]
Matthys Petrus Lourens Geldenhuys is a 6th cousin twice removed
Matthys Wilhelm Beyers is the husband of a 4th cousin 3 times removed
Mattia Martha Geldenhuys [Lotter] is the mother
Mattys Johannes Lourens Geldenhuys is a 3rd cousin 3 times removed
Maud Nellie Brink [Liversage] is a grandmother of the husband of a niece
Maureen Louisa Grobler is related [21 steps]
Maureen Louisa van Heerden [Liebenberg] is related [20 steps]
Mauritz Herman Otto Preller is a grandson of a great-great-grandfather
Mauritz Herman Otto Preller is a son of a great-great-grandfather
Melanie Stephanie Human is a niece of the wife of a nephew
Mercia Phillus Louw [Geldenhuys] is a 3rd cousin once removed
Micayla Angelique Geldenhuys is a 4th cousin twice removed
Michael Casparus Geldenhuys is a first cousin twice removed (first cousin of grandfather)
Michael Christoffel Dippenaar is a 1st cousin 3 times removed of the wife of the brother
Michael Christoffel Dippenaar is a brother of a great-grandfather of the father of the wife of the brother

Michael Christoffel Dippenaar is a direct ancestor of the wife of the brother
Michael de Oliveira is a 1st cousin twice removed of the wife
Michael Geldenhuys is a brother of a grandfather
Michelle de Oliveira is a 1st cousin twice removed of the wife
Michelle Geldenhuys [Rodriques] is the wife of a 4th cousin once removed
Michelle Geldenhuys [Trichardt] is a 4th cousin once removed
Michiel de Waal is a direct ancestor of the wife of a nephew
Mien Beljohn [Lotter] is related [5 steps]
Mien van Biljon [Lotter] is an aunt (a sister of his mother)
Mikhail Preller is a direct descendant of a great-great-grandfather
Mona Daphne Brink [van Rooyen] is an in-law of a sister
Moodie is related [12 steps]
Morgan Thomson is a great-grandson of a sister-in-law
Mr Simpkins is the father-in-law of an ex-husband of the sister
Myrl Maureen Smith / Trichardt [Geldenhuys] is a 4th cousin
Myrna Roberts [McQueen] is related [9 steps]
Nan Ngaire Brodie is the mother-in-law of a 4th cousin
Nea D Brink is a granddaughter of a sister
Neil Wynn Muirhead is a brother-in-law of the husband of a niece
Nellie Preller [von Solms] is the wife of a 3rd cousin twice removed
Nicholaas Hendrik van Aardt is a brother-in-law of the wife
Nicholas Frazer Fraser Preller is a 3rd cousin once removed
Nicolaas Johannes Geldenhuys is a 3rd cousin 4 times removed
Nicolaas Johannes Geldenhuys is a 4th cousin 3 times removed
Nicolene van Aardt is a niece of the wife
NN (father - Juli van die Kaap) is the husband of a 1st cousin 4 times removed
NN Boxall is the father of the ex-wife of an ex-husband of the sister
NN Broadbent [Brown?] is the mother of an aunt by marriage of an in-law
NN Buys is the husband of a 7th cousin once removed
NN Cilliers is the husband of a first cousin twice removed
NN Coleman is a direct ancestor of a son-in-law
NN de Waal [Minnaar] is a great-grandmother of the wife of a nephew
NN de Waal [van der Westhuizen] is a grandmother of the wife of a nephew
NN Geldenhuys [NN] is the wife of a 1st cousin 3 times removed
NN Geldenhuys [Wessels] is the wife of a 2nd cousin once removed
NN Jacobs is an uncle by marriage of the wife of a cousin of the wife
NN Lance Snr Froneman is the husband of a cousin
NN Lotter [NN] is the maternal grandmother
NN Lourens is a son-in-law of a sister-in-law of the wife
NN Matchett is a grandfather of the ex-husband of a sister
NN McColl is a grandfather of the husband of a sister
NN Nienaber is related [10 steps]
NN Paterson is a great-grandfather of a son-in-law
NN Pelser is related [10 steps]
NN Roos is an uncle by marriage
NN Simpson is the husband of a first cousin twice removed
NN Smit is a direct ancestor (9 generations; great-great-great-great-great-great-great-grandfather)
NN van Biljon is an uncle by marriage
NN van der Heever is related [10 steps]
NN Voster is related [10 steps]
Norman Robert Dunbar Moodie is a 2nd cousin 4 times removed of a son-in-law
Ockert Lotter is an uncle (a brother of his mother)
Olof Abram Jacobus de Meyer is a first cousin twice removed (first cousin of grandfather)
Oonagh Lorraine Mahnke [Geldenhuys] is a 4th cousin once removed
Oscar Abraham Preller is a first cousin once removed (cousin of father)
Oubaas Geldenhuys is a brother of a grandfather
Owen Walters is related [13 steps]
P N Geldenhuyzen Geldenhuys [NN] is the wife of a 5th cousin twice removed

P Willemse is the husband of a 3rd cousin twice removed
Pa Bouwer is the father of a sister-in-law of the wife
Pat Armstrong is related [15 steps]
Patricia Jean Hardy [Walls] is related [13 steps]
Patricia 'Patsi' Geldenhuys is a 3rd cousin once removed
Patrick Preller is a 3rd cousin
Paul Henricus Eksteen is the husband of a 2nd cousin 6 times removed
Paul Jordaan is a first cousin
Paul Lodewyk Kuhn is the husband of a 3rd cousin 4 times removed
Paul Preller Geldenhuys is a nephew
Paul Preller is a 3rd cousin twice removed
Percival Whiteley is a brother of a great-grandfather of a son-in-law
Percy Whiteley is a brother of a grandfather of the husband of a daughter
Peter John McColl is the father of the husband of the sister
Peter van der Walt is an in-law of a sister-in-law
Petronella Daniellina Johanna Geldenhuys is a 5th cousin 3 times removed
Petronella Marthina 'Nellie' Venter [Vermeulen] is a sister-in-law of the wife of a cousin of the wife
Petronella Marthina 'Zenelle' Venter is related [8 steps]
Petronella Moller [van Heerden] is related [13 steps]
Petronella Sophia Moodie [Pretorius] is related [9 steps]
Petronella Wilhelmina Geldenhuys [Prinsloo] is related [12 steps] is a direct descendant of a direct ancestor
Petrus Arnoldus - d10 Geldenhuys is a brother of a direct ancestor
Petrus Arnoldus - e5 Geldenhuys is a 1st cousin 5 times removed
Petrus Arnoldus Geldenhuys is a 1st cousin 4 times removed
Petrus Arnoldus Geldenhuys is a 1st cousin 6 times removed
Petrus Arnoldus Geldenhuys is a 2nd cousin 3 times removed
Petrus Arnoldus Geldenhuys is a 2nd cousin 4 times removed
Petrus Arnoldus Geldenhuys is a 3rd cousin 3 times removed
Petrus Arnoldus Geldenhuys is a 3rd cousin twice removed
Petrus Arnoldus Geldenhuys is a brother of a direct ancestor
Petrus Arnoldus Geldenhuys is a direct descendant of a direct ancestor
Petrus Arnoldus Geldenhuys is a grandson of a direct ancestor
Petrus Arnoldus Geldenhuys is a great-grandson of a direct ancestor
Petrus Arnoldus Jacobus Geldenhuys is a 2nd cousin 3 times removed
Petrus Cornelis Bouwer is the husband of a 1st cousin 3 times removed
Petrus Geldenhuys is a 2nd cousin 6 times removed
Petrus Gideon Geldenhuys is a 5th cousin 3 times removed
Petrus Guilaume Geldenhuys is a 3rd cousin 5 times removed
Petrus Guillaume (Gildenhuizen) Geldenhuys is the father-in-law of a 4th cousin 4 times removed
Petrus Guillaume Geldenhuys is a 4th cousin 4 times removed
Petrus Guilliam Geldenhuys is a 4th cousin 4 times removed
Petrus Jacobus Geldenhuys is a 2nd cousin 3 times removed
Petrus Johannes Badenhorst is the husband of a 2nd cousin 4 times removed
Petrus Johannes Beneke is the husband of a 3rd cousin 4 times removed
Petrus Johannes Dippenaar is a great-grandfather of an ex-wife of the brother
Petrus Johannes Geldenhuys is a 4th cousin 4 times removed
Petrus Johannes Germishuysen is the husband of a 1st cousin 4 times removed
Petrus Johannes 'Pieter' Maass is related [8 steps]
Petrus Johannes Preller is a brother of a great-grandfather
Petrus Johannes van Heerden is related [12 & 13 steps]
Petrus Jurie Hendrik Geldenhuys is a 3rd cousin 4 times removed
Petrus Lafras Daniel Geldenhuys is a 4th cousin 3 times removed
Petrus Lafras Geldenhuys is a 3rd cousin 4 times removed
Pey Malan Geldenhuys is a son
Philip Malan is a nephew of the wife
Philip Rudolph Geldenhuys is a 3rd cousin 4 times removed
Philippus Johannes Malan is a brother-in-law (brother of his wife)
Philippus Richter is a brother-in-law of a direct ancestor

Philipus Johannes Malan is a cousin of the wife
Phillipus Albertus Opperman is a brother-in-law of a 4th cousin once removed
Philomena Bernadette Mary Walls [Lawler] is related [14 steps]
Piere Lotter is a first cousin
Piere Lotter is an uncle (a brother of his mother)
Piet Daniel de Villiers is the father-in-law of a 3rd cousin 5 times removed
Piet Liebenberg is a nephew of the ex-wife of a brother
Pieter Albertus Cornelis Geldenhuys is a 4th cousin 4 times removed
Pieter Arnoldus Geldenhuys is a 1st cousin 5 times removed
Pieter Arnoldus Geldenhuys is a brother of a great-grandfather of the father
Pieter Burger Geldenhuys is a 5th cousin twice removed
Pieter C Luyt is a son-in-law of a great-grandfather
Pieter Daniel Geldenhuys is a 4th cousin 4 times removed
Pieter Daniel Geldenhuys is a 5th cousin 3 times removed
Pieter Daniel Malan is a 4th cousin 3 times removed of the wife
Pieter David Geldenhuys is a 4th cousin 4 times removed
Pieter du Toit is the father-in-law of a 3rd cousin 5 times removed
Pieter Eduard Edward Haumann is a grandfather of the wife of a brother of a great-grandfather
Pieter Geldenhuys is a brother of a grandfather
Pieter Gerhardus Human is the husband of a 1st cousin 5 times removed
Pieter Johannes Geldenhuys is a 3rd cousin 5 times removed
Pieter Johannes Geldenhuys is a 4th cousin 4 times removed
Pieter Lucas Jacobus Geldenhuys is a 4th cousin 3 times removed
Pieter Malan is a 2nd cousin 5 times removed of the wife
Pieter Schalk van Heerden is related [13 and 14 steps]
Pieter Venter is related [11 steps]
Pieter Willem van Heerden is related [12, 13 and 14 steps]
Pietus Taillefer Geldenhuys is a 4th cousin 4 times removed
Portia Preller [Cloete] is the wife of a 3rd cousin once removed
Quintus Deacon is the husband of a first cousin once removed
Rachael Elizabeth Brink is a sister of a grandfather of the husband of a niece
Rachel Maria (Gildenhuizen) Geldenhuys is a 4th cousin 4 times removed
Rachel Maria Burger [Dippenaar] is related [8 steps]
Rachel Maria Gildenhuisen Geldenhuys is the wife of a 4th cousin 4 times removed
Rachel Marie Geldenhuys [Jordaan] is the wife of a 3rd cousin 5 times removed
Ralph Arnold Dunckers is an ex-husband of the cousin
Raymond Geldenhuys is a 4th cousin
Regina Elizabeth Brink is a sister of a grandfather of the husband of a niece
Renee Edith Heath [Preller] is a 2nd cousin
Renene Delene Jelley [Geldenhuys] is a daughter
Rensha Bouwer is a niece
Rev J Francis MacCreath is the husband of a first cousin once removed
Rhett Preller is a 3rd cousin twice removed
'Ria' Maria Magdalena Malan [Venter] is the wife of a cousin of the wife
Riaan Geldenhuys Strydom is a 4th cousin once removed
Richard Brink is a brother of a son-in-law of a sister
Richard Rimer is related [12 steps]
Rina Malan [Gerber] is a sister-in-law of the wife
Robert Anderson is a direct ancestor of a grandson
Robert Clunie Logie is a brother-in-law of a great-great-grandfather
Robert Clunie Logie Preller is a brother of a great-grandfather
Robert Heddle is related [10 steps]
Robert James Preller is a 2nd cousin
Robert Llewellin Llewelyn Preller is a great-grandson of a great-great-grandfather
Robert Logie Preller is a grandson of a great-great-grandfather
Robert Mervyn Preller is a 2nd cousin once removed
Rocco NN is a first cousin
Roelof Gabriel Thomas Geldenhuys is a 4th cousin 4 times removed
Roelof van Heerden is related [12 steps]

Roland Andrew Allan Preller is a 2nd cousin once removed
Roland John Preller is a 3rd cousin once removed
Roland-Jon Preller is a 3rd cousin twice removed
Rolene Preller is a 3rd cousin
Ronald Carr is a nephew of the ex-wife of a brother
Ronald Mark Gooding is the husband of a niece of the wife
Ronel van Heerden [Geldenhuys] is related [19 steps]
Ronnie van Rooyen is an uncle of the husband of a niece
Rory Jon-Jon Preller is a 3rd cousin twice removed
Rory Terence Culhane is a brother-in-law of the husband of a niece
Roux Malan is a nephew of the wife
Ruben Benjamin Geldenhuys is a 3rd cousin once removed
Ruben Neville Geldenhuys is a 4th cousin
Russell Allan Geldenhuys is a 4th cousin once removed
Ryck Rudolph de Waal is a direct ancestor of the wife of a nephew
Rykie Hester de Waal [van Brakel] is a direct ancestor of the wife of a nephew
Sachararya Magdalena Geldenhuys [van Deventer] is the wife of a 2nd cousin 5 times removed
Salomina Adriana 'Adri' Maass [Venter] is a niece of the wife of a cousin of the wife
Salomina Adriana de Oliveira [Malan] is a first cousin once removed of the wife
Salomina Adriana Venter [van Heerden] is the mother-in-law of a cousin of the wife
Salomon Ignatius Gerber is the father of a sister-in-law of the wife
Samantha-Renay Preller [Ysell] is the wife of a 3rd cousin twice removed
Samuel Jacobus de Beer is a direct ancestor (7 generations; great-great-great-great-great-grandf
Samuel Liversage is a direct ancestor of the husband of a niece
Sandra La Bella [Simpkins] is a sister-in-law of an ex-husband of the sister
Sannie Geldenhuys [Bloemmenstein] is the wife of a first cousin twice removed
Sara Johanna (Gildenhuyzen) Odendaal [Geldenhuys] is the mother-in-law of a 1st cousin 5
    times removed
Sara Johanna Geldenhuys [Eksteen] is the wife of a brother of a great-grandfather
Sara Johanna Geldenhuys [Kleynsmit] is the wife of a 3rd cousin 4 times removed
Sara Johanna Geldenhuys [Odendaal] is the wife of a 1st cousin 5 times removed
Sara Johanna Geldenhuys [Swart] is the wife of a direct ancestor
Sara Johanna Geldenhuys is a 1st cousin 4 times removed
Sara Johanna Geldenhuys is a 2nd cousin 4 times removed
Sara Johanna Geldenhuys is a 3rd cousin 3 times removed
Sara Johanna Geldenhuys is a first cousin twice removed (first cousin of grandfather)
Sara Johanna Odendaal [Geldenhuys] is a daughter of a direct ancestor
Sara Johanna Uys [Geldenhuys] is a granddaughter of a direct ancestor
Sara Magdalena Wolfaard [Geldenhuys] is a 1st cousin 5 times removed
Sara Maria Johanna Moodie [van Zyl] is a direct ancestor of a son-in-law
Sara Maria Moodie is related [12 steps]
Sara Susanna Cilliers [Preller] is a first cousin twice removed (first cousin of grandmother)
Sara Susanna Susara Bosman [Haumann] is the mother-in-law of a brother of a great-grandfather
Sarah Johanna Louw 'Sally' Geldenhuys [Groenewald] is the wife of a 3rd cousin once removed
Sarah Maria Moodie is a 1st cousin 3 times removed of a son-in-law
Sarel Francois Kotzé is a brother-in-law of the wife of a cousin of the wife
Sarel Johannes Geldenhuys is the father of the ex-husband of a 4th cousin once removed
Sarie Lotte Magdalena Opperman is a sister-in-law of a 4th cousin once removed
Schalk Reginald Brink is an in-law of a sister
Schalk Richard Brink is a grandfather of the husband of a niece
Schalk Richard Brink is a great-grandfather of the husband of a niece
Schalk van der Westhuizen is related [8 steps]
Schalk Willem Dippenaar is a brother of the ex-wife of the brother
Schalk Willem Dippenaar is a great-great-grandfather of an ex-wife of the brother
Schalk Willem van Heerden is related [10 and 11 steps]
Sebastiaan 'Basie' Geldenhuys is a 3rd cousin
Servaas Malan is a 4th cousin 3 times removed of the wife
Seuntjie Preller is a brother of a great-grandfather
Shaun Burger is a brother-in-law of the wife of a nephew

Shaydon Bezuidenhout is a great-grandson of a sister-in-law
Shayne Ross Brodie is a 4th cousin once removed
Shelley Lock is a niece of the wife of a brother-in-law
Shireen le Roux [Thorne] is related [8 steps]
Shirley Moor is a 3rd cousin 3 times removed of a son-in-law
Shirley van Biljon is a first cousin
Sibella Jacoba Geldenhuys [Jordaan] is the wife of a 3rd cousin 5 times removed
Sidney Carr is a nephew of the ex-wife of a brother
Siebert Frederik Geldenhuys is a 6th cousin twice removed
Simon David Geldenhuys is a 4th cousin once removed
Simon Frederik Streicher is a brother-in-law of a great-great-grandfather
Skya-Rayne Thomson is a great-granddaughter of a sister-in-law
Snowy is an uncle by marriage
Sonja Preller [Nel] is the wife of a 3rd cousin once removed
Sophia Barendina Jacoba Geldenhuys is a 1st cousin 3 times removed
Sophia Catharina Elizabeth Geldenhuys is a 4th cousin 4 times removed
Sophia Catharina Geldenhuys [Loubser] is the wife of a 2nd cousin 6 times removed
Sophia Jordaan [van Heerden] is related [13 steps]
Sophia Margaretha Geldenhuys is a 1st cousin 4 times removed
Sophia Margaretha Geldenhuys is a 2nd cousin 4 times removed
Sophia Margaretha Malan [van Brakel] is related [13 steps]
Sophia Sibella Helina Geldenhuys is a 4th cousin 4 times removed
Spouse Dippenaar is a grandmother of the wife of a brother
Spouse Dippenaar is a great-grandmother of the wife of the brother
Spouse Dippenaar is the wife of a brother of the wife of the brother
Stella Nesta Whiteley [Arnott] is a grandmother of the husband of a daughter
Stephanus Jacobus Botha is the husband of a 2nd cousin 5 times removed
Stephanus Jacobus Johannes Geldenhuys is a 3rd cousin 4 times removed
Stephanus Johannes Lourens Geldenhuys is a 6th cousin twice removed
Stephanus Jordaan is the husband of a 4th cousin 4 times removed
Stephanus Kuun is a brother-in-law of a direct ancestor
Stephanus Nicolaas Geldenhuys is a 4th cousin 4 times removed
Stephanus Schoeman is the father-in-law of a brother of a great-grandfather
Stephen Theron Moodie is a 3rd cousin once removed of a son-in-law
Stevina Maria Aletta 'Poppie' Preller [Schoeman] is the wife of a brother of a great-grandfather
Stuart John McColl is the husband of the sister
Stuart William Geldenhuys is a nephew
Sue Simpkins is the mother-in-law of an ex-husband of the sister
Sulindie Preller is a 2nd cousin once removed
Susan de Waal is a sister of a daughter-in-law of a brother
Susanna Catharina Geldenhuys [Malan] is the wife
Susanna Catharina Malan [le Roux] is an aunt by marriage of the wife
Susanna Catharina Margaretha Trichardt [de Villiers] is the mother-in-law of a 4th cousin
Susanna Dorothea Geldenhuys is a 1st cousin 3 times removed
Susanna Dorothea Swart [Geldenhuys] is a 1st cousin 5 times removed
Susanna Elizabeth (Gildenhuizen) Geldenhuys [le Roux] is the mother-in-law of a 4th cousin 4 times removed
Susanna Elizabeth Cecilia Dippenaar [Markgraaff] is related [8 steps]
Susanna Elizabeth Geldenhuys [le Roux] is the wife of a 3rd cousin 5 times removed
Susanna Elizabeth Swart [Geldenhuys] is a 1st cousin 6 times removed
Susanna Geertruyda Smit [Geldenhuys] is a 1st cousin 5 times removed
Susanna Hermina Geldenhuys is a granddaughter of a direct ancestor
Susanna Hermina Uys [Geldenhuys] is a 4th cousin 3 times removed
Susanna Jacoba Geldenhuys is a 2nd cousin 6 times removed
Susanna Jacoba Heems [Geldenhuys] is a 1st cousin 7 times removed
Susanna Jacoba Louw [Geldenhuys] is a 4th cousin 4 times removed
Susanna Johanna Geldenhuys [Cooper] is the wife of a 4th cousin 3 times removed
Susanna Johanna Geldenhuys is a 1st cousin 3 times removed
Susanna Johanna Louw [NN] is the mother-in-law of a 3rd cousin 4 times removed

Susanna Johanna Maria Geldenhuys is a 4th cousin twice removed
Susanna Lodewyka J. van Noordwyk [Venter] is a niece of the wife of a cousin of the wife
Susanna Magrieta van Heerden [le Roux] is an aunt by marriage of the wife of a cousin of the wife
Susanna Margaretha Badenhorst [Geldenhuys] is a 2nd cousin 5 times removed
Susanna Margaretha Geldenhuys [Nigrini] is the wife of a 4th cousin 4 times removed
Susanna Margaretha Geldenhuys is a 1st cousin 7 times removed
Susanna Margaretha Geldenhuys is a 3rd cousin 3 times removed
Susanna Maria Elizabeth Geldenhuys [Bester] is the wife of a 4th cousin twice removed
Susanna Maria Geldenhuys [Moolman] is a daughter-in-law of a direct ancestor
Susanna Maria Geldenhuys is a 1st cousin 5 times removed
Susanna Maria Geldenhuys is a 2nd cousin 4 times removed
Susanna Maria Geldenhuys is a first cousin twice removed (first cousin of grandfather)
Susanna Maria Margaretha Geldenhuys is a 3rd cousin 3 times removed
Susanna Maria Preller is a first cousin twice removed (first cousin of grandmother)
Susanna Maria Salomina Preller [Otto] is the wife of a brother of a great-grandfather
Susanna Maria 'Sannie' Elizabeth Preller [Bosman] is the wife of a brother of a great-grandfather
Susanna Moodie [Strickland] is related [10 steps]
Susanna Petronella Geldenhuys is a 4th cousin 4 times removed
Susanna Petronella Reyneke [Geldenhuys] is a 3rd cousin 5 times removed
Susanna van Heerden [Geldenhuys] is related [18 steps]
Susanna Voster [van der Westhuizen] is related [9 steps]
Susanna Voster [van Heerden] is a sister of a grandfather of the wife of a cousin of the wife
Susanna Wessels [Odendaal] is the mother-in-law of a 1st cousin 6 times removed
Susara Johanna Elizabeth Elsabe Geldenhuys is a sister of a great-grandfather
Susara Johanna Geldenhuys [van Vuuren] is the wife of a 5th cousin 3 times removed
Suzanne Geldenhuys is a 3rd cousin once removed
Sybrand van Dyk is a direct ancestor (7 generations; great-great-great-great-great-grandfather)
Sydney Nathaniel Arnott is a great-grandfather of a son-in-law
Tal J Brink is a grandson of a sister
Talei Lisi 'Torika' Brodie [Bjorn] is the wife of a 4th cousin once removed
Tane Jurgens Bezuidenhout is a grandson of a sister of the wife
Tara Patricia Liebenberg is a granddaughter of a sister of an ex-wife of the brother
Tasmin Preller is a 3rd cousin twice removed
Teda Magdalena Geldenhuys is a 4th cousin 3 times removed
Tersius Maass is related [8 steps]
Thea Marie First Husband is a niece of the wife of a nephew
Theodore Johan van Rensen is an uncle by marriage
Theodorus Louis Geldenhuys is a 4th cousin 4 times removed
Theodorus Louis Hermanus Geldenhuys is a 3rd cousin 5 times removed
Theodorus Louis Kriel is the husband of a 3rd cousin 5 times removed
Theresa (Tessa) le Roux is a daughter of a sister-in-law of the wife
Thersia Grobbelaar [J. van Noordwyk] is related [8 steps]
Theunis Gerhardus Geldenhuys is a 5th cousin 3 times removed
Theunis Louis Preller is a brother of a grandmother
Thomas Moodie is a 1st cousin 3 times removed of a son-in-law
Thomas Moodie is a 3rd cousin once removed of a son-in-law
Thomas Moodie is a brother of a great-grandmother of an in-law
Tiaan Quinton van der Westhuizen is related [21 steps]
Tilley Roos is a first cousin
Tjaard Venter is a 3rd cousin 3 times removed
Tjaart (Kiwiet) Venter is the husband of a 3rd cousin twice removed
Tony van Rooyen is an uncle of the husband of a niece
Tracy-Leigh Preller is a 2nd cousin once removed
Trish Sinton [NN] is the paternal grandmother of a grandson
Tristan Roland Clark Preller is a 3rd cousin 3 times removed
Val Bouwer is a sister of the ex-husband of the sister
Valerie Linda Bezuidenhout [Wigston] is the wife of a nephew of the wife
Van Zyl Venter is related [8 steps]
Venables Wessels Preller is a great-grandson of a great-great-grandfather

Veronica Geldenhuys [Engelbrecht] is the wife of a 3rd cousin
Veronica Joan Geldenhuys is a 4th cousin once removed
Vicky Bezuidenhout [NN] is the wife of a grandson of a sister-in-law
Victor Septimus Preller is a grandson of a great-great-grandfather
Vinny La Bella is a brother-in-law of the wife of an ex-husband of the sister
Violet Preller [Muggleton] is a sister-in-law of a grandmother (aunt by marriage of the father)
Vista Emma Ina Moodie is a 3rd cousin 3 times removed of a son-in-law
Vivian Balfour-Cunningham [Carr] is a niece of the ex-wife of a brother
W L Ebersohn is the husband of a 4th cousin 3 times removed
Walter Whiteley is a brother of a grandfather of the husband of a daughter
Wanda Strydom [Geldenhuys] is a 4th cousin
Wendy Liebenberg [Welsh] is the wife of a grandson of a sister of the ex-wife of the brother
Wernher Els is related [10 steps]
Wessel Johannes Geldenhuys is a 2nd cousin 5 times removed
Wessel Johannes Gildenhuizen (Geldenhuys) is the husband of a 2nd cousin 5 times removed
Wessel Johannes Willem Geldenhuys is a 4th cousin 3 times removed
Wessel Wessels is the father-in-law of a 1st cousin 6 times removed
Wessel Wessels is the husband of a 2nd cousin 5 times removed
Wilbur Dunckers is the father of an ex-husband of the cousin
Wilhelmina Barendina Venter [Keynhans] is a grandmother of the wife of a cousin of the wife
Wilhelmina Johanna Hendrina Geldenhuys is a 4th cousin 3 times removed
Willem Adrian van der Walt is a grandfather of the wife of a nephew of the wife
Willem Bouwer is the father of ex-husband of the sister
Willem Francois Petrus van der Westhuizen is related [9 steps]
Willem Francois Petrus van Heerden is a brother of a grandfather of the wife of a cousin of the wife
Willem Francois Petrus van Heerden is related [9 steps]
Willem Geldenhuys is a 3rd cousin once removed
Willem Geldenhuys Trichardt is a 4th cousin once removed
Willem Hendrik Cloete is a grandfather of the wife of a 3rd cousin once removed
Willem Hendrik Vos is a grandfather of the wife of a 3rd cousin
Willem Johannes Geldenhuys is a 2nd cousin 3 times removed
Willem Lodewicus van Heerden is related [13 and 15 steps]
Willem Oosthuisen is the husband of a niece of the wife
Willem Petrus (WP) Nel is the husband of a niece of the wife and an in-law of a brother-in-law
Willem Schalk van Heerden is related [10 steps]
Willem Steenkamp Geldenhuys is a 4th cousin
Willem Steenkamp is the father-in-law of a 2nd cousin twice removed
Willem Stefanus Malan is an uncle of the wife
Willem van der Merwe is related [14 steps]
Willem van der Westhuizen is related [9 steps]
Willem van Heerden is a brother of a grandfather of the wife of a cousin of the wife
Willem van Heerden is related [12 steps]
Willem 'Willie' Geldenhuys is a 4th cousin twice removed
William Alexander Dunbar Moodie is a 2nd cousin 4 times removed of a son-in-law
William Anderson is a direct ancestor of a grandson
William Henry Estment is a grandfather of the wife of a son
William James Dunbar Moodie is a 1st cousin 5 times removed of a son-in-law
William Patterson Jelley is an in-law
William Peter van der Walt is a nephew of the wife of a nephew of the wife
William Whiteley is a great-great-grandfather of a son-in-law
Wilna Geldenhuys [Bester] is the wife of a 3rd cousin
Winifred van der Walt [NN] is a grandmother of the wife of a nephew of the wife
Wybrand Hebershausen Geldenhuys is a 5th cousin twice removed
Wynand Hendrik Geldenhuys is a 1st cousin 5 times removed
Wynand Hendrik Johannes Geldenhuys is a 2nd cousin 4 times removed
Wynne Muirhead is the father of a brother-in-law of the husband of a niece
Y-anka Venter is a 3rd cousin 3 times removed
Yolande de Waal is a niece of the wife of a nephew

Yuonne Julie Venter is a niece of the wife of a cousin of the wife
Yvette Marie Oosthuisen is a granddaughter of a sister of the wife
Yvonne Liebenberg [Webb] is a daughter-in-law of a sister of the ex-wife of the brother
Zacharia Christina Carolina Preller is a sister of a great-grandfather
Zacharia Christina Preller [de Beer] is a direct ancestor (5 generations; great-great-great-grandmother)
Zacharia Christina Preller is a daughter of a great-great-grandfather
Zacharias de Beer is a direct ancestor (6 generations; great-great-great-great-grandfather)
Zacharya Geertruy (Gildenhuizen) Rabie, then van Zyl [Geldenhuys] is a sister of a direct ancestor
Zacharyas Johannes Wessel Geldenhuys is a 3rd cousin twice removed
Zandalee Geldenhuys is a 4th cousin twice removed
Zane Preller is a 3rd cousin twice removed
Zoe Irene Marie Sinton [Anderson] is a great-great-grandmother of a grandson

GELDENHUYS INTERMARRIAGES

The following is a list of family names that Geldenhuys is related to by marriage.

Appel x 3	ve Villiers x 3	Hurter	Nel x 2	Smit x 4
Axelson	de Vries	Jansen	Niemand x 2	Snyman
Bacon	de Waal x 3	Jelley	Niemann	Steyn x 3
Badenhorst x 6	de Wege	Jonker x 3	(Niemand)	Streicher x 2
Bam	de Wet	Jordaan x 6	Nigrini x 2	Swanepoel x 2
Barnard	de Wit x 2	Kannemeyer	Nortier	Steyn
Barry	Delport x 2	Kasselman	Norval	Swart x 19
Basson	Diederiks	Kemp	O'Connell	Taillefer x 2
Beeslaar	Diederksen	Keulder x 2	Odendaal x 6	Taljaard x 8
Behr	Dippenaar	Kleynsmit x 6	Olivier x 3	Terblanche
Bekker	Dixie	Klopper x 2	Olwage	Tesner
Beneke x 2	Dreyer x 2	Klynsmit x 4	Oostendorp	Tesselaar
Berntzen	du Buis	Koekemoer	Oosthuizen x 4	Theron x 3
Bester x 4	du Plessis x 5	Koen	Otto x 3	Thiele
Beukes	du Plooy x 2	Kok	Painter	Truter
Beukman	du Preez x 2	Kriel	Pas	Ungerer
Beyers x 2	du Rand	Kuhn	Pauw	Uys x 12
Beyleveld	du Toit x 4	Kuun x 3	Perdijk	van Aarde
Bloem	Duminy x 2	Lacock	Peters	van As
Blom x 5	Ebersohn	Lamprecht	(Pieterse)	van Blerk
Blomerus	Eksteen x 5	Latsky	Pieterse x 3	van Biljon
Botha x 4	Engelbrecht	le Roux x 6	Pienaar x 3	van Coller
Bosman	Erwee	Linde	Plooy	van Dalen
Bouwer x 2	Eybers	(Linden)	Pogenpoel	van Deventer x 3
Brand x 2	Fabricius	Lombard	Preller	van Dyk x 5
Bredell	Falck	Lotter	Pretorius x 2	van den Hever
Breedt	Ferreira	Lotz	Price	van der Heiden
Brink	Fouché	Loubser x 2	Prins x 3	van der Merwe
Brits x 3	Fourie x 4	Loulo	Prinsloo x 6	van Eck
Brönn	Fraser	Lourens x 13	Rabbets	van Eeden x 2
Bruynzwart	Freysen	Louw x 3	Rabie	van Greunen
Burger x 2	Gadney x 6	Lubbe	Radyn x 2	van Jaarsveld x 2
Bury	Geldenhuys x 9	Lucas	Rall	van Niekerk
Buys	Gerber	Luwes	Raubenheimer	van Noordwyk x 2
Celliers	Germishuysen	Malan	Reynders	van Rensen
Coerie	Germishuizen	Marais	Reyneke x 3	van Rensburg x 4
Coetzee x 5	Gresse	Maree x 8	Richter x 2	van Schalkwyk
Colyn	Grobbelaar x 2	Mars	Robertson	van Vuuren x 2
Combrink	Groenewald x 5	Matthee x 8	Rörich	van Wyngaard (den)
Cooper x 4	Groenewaldt	Meiring	Rossouw x 3	van Wyk x 8
Cordier	Gunter x 3	Merts	Roux	van Zyl
Costeux	Hall	Meyer x 4	Ryke x 2	Vermaak
Crause	Hamman	Meyhuyzen	Sadler	Vermeulen
Cronje x 3	Hansen	Minnaar	Schickerling	Viljoen
Crous x 3	Havenga x 7	Michealides	Schimper x 2	Visser
Dannhauser	Heems	Minnie x 3	Schoeman	Vosloo
de Beer	Heyne	Momsen	Serdyn	Wagenaar x 2
de Bruyn	Hilliard	Moolman x 6	Siebert	Walters
de Jager x 4	Hoefnagels	Muhsfeldt	Siek	Wessels x 14
de Kock x 3	Hoffmann	Mulder	Scheepers	Wiese
de Lange	Honiball	Muller x 3	Schimper x 2	Willemse
de le Rey	Hopkins	Mullholland	Schmidt	Wittman
de Meyer	Howard	Müszler	Schumann	Wolfaard
	Human x 4	Mynhardt	Slabbert x 2	Wolmarans

INDEX
Ziegelmeier

Props update = 2009-11-24

Take Note: Surnames that are in **UPPERCASE** are 'Indexed' from the Gedcom (Gimp / MyHeritage website insert), as per the Genealogy Section, and are thus duplicated in the Index listing below. Readers will need to look up both the **UPPERCASE** as well as the **Lowercase** when looking for specific persons.

a - Albert Barends Geldenhuys (stamvader), 403
ab6 - Barend Geldenhuys, 403
ab6c3 - Hendrik Geldenhuys, 397, 404
ab6c3d5e10f6 - Wynand Hendrik Johannes Geldenhuys - 1836, 406
ab6c3d7 - Johannes Albertus Geldenhuys, 397, 406
ab6c3d7e1f5 - Elias Jacobus Geldenhuys, 406
ab6c3d7e1f5g4 - Johannes Albertus Geldenhuys - 1841, 406
ab6c3d7e1f8 - Hendrik Johannes Geldenhuys, 406
ab6c3d7e2 - Cornelia Geertruy Geldenhuys, 406
ab6c3d7e3 - Hendrik Geldenhuys - 1775, 406
ab6c3d7e3f1 - Johannes Albertus Geldenhuys - 1815, 406
ab6c3d7e3f10 - Johannes Albertus Geldenhuys - 1829, 407
ab6c3d7e3f11 - Louw Hermanus Geldenhuys - 1831, 407
ab6c3d7e3f13 - Barend Johannes Geldenhuys - 1835, 407
ab6c3d7e3f3 - Hendrik Johannes Geldenhuys 1817, 406
ab6c3d7e3f6 - Elias Wynand Geldenhuys, 406
ab6c3d7e4 - Lourens Geldenhuys, 407
ab6c3d7e4f3 - Johannes Albertus Geldenhuys, 407
ab6c3d7e4f3g4 - Lourens Pieter Arnoldus Geldenhuys, 407
ab6c3d7e4f3g4h1 - Johannes Albertus Geldenhuys - 1860, 407
ab6c3d7e4f3g4h3 - Michiel Casparus Geldenhuys, 407
ab6c3d7e4f3g4h6 - Lourens Pieter Geldenhuys, 407
ab6c3d7e4f3g5 - Hendrik Jacobus Geldenhuys, 408
ab6c3d7e4f3g5h1 - Johannes Albertus Geldenhuys, 408
ab6c3d7e4f3g5h1i6 - Abram Carl Frederik Preller Geldenhuys, 409
ab6c3d7e4f3g5h1i6j1 - Johannes Albertus Geldenhuys, 409
ab6c3d7e4f3g5h1i6j2 - Preller Matt Geldenhuys, 409
ab6c3d7e4f3g5h1i6j2k2 - Pey Malan Geldenhuys, 199, 398, 403, 409, 451, 455
ab6c3d7e4f3g7h1 - Izak George Geldenhuys, 407
ab6c3d7e8 = Lourens Gildenhuys / Geldenhuys, 397
ab6c3d7e8f7 = Johannes Albertus Geldenhuys, 397
ab6c3d7e8f7g9 = Hendrik Johannes Geldenhuys, 397
ab6c3d7e8f7g9h1 = Johannes Albertus Geldenhuys, 397
ab6c3d7e8f7g9h1i6 = Abram Carl Federik Preller Geldenhuys, 397
ab6c3d7e8f7g9h1i6j1 = Johannes Albertus Geldenhuys, 397
ab6c3d7e8f7g9h1i6j1k3 - Paul Preller Geldenhuys, 198, 397, 409
ab6c3d7e8f7g9h1i6j1k3l2 - Craig Jannie Geldenhuys, 151, 397, 409
Abel Software, 85
abolition of slavery, 32, 34
Abraamskraal, 52
Ackerman KF - great-granddaughter of Hendrik Potgieter, 294
Ackermann, Cpl, 299
Adele van der Walt, 103, 105
Adriaanse, Ronel Christene, 431
Afmadu, 298, 299
Afrikaanse Taalgenoodskap, 290, 292
Afrikaans-Hollandse Toneelvereniging, 291, 292
Albany, 33, 34, 459
Albany settlers, 34
Albert Barend - Gildenhuizen, Geldenhuys Stamvader, 216
Albert Falls, 74
Alberton, 245, 310, 454
Aldrin, Edwin Buzz, 77
Aletta Magdalena Susanna le Roux, 246
Alexandra High School, 73
Algoa Bay, 33
Alps, 77
Amersfoort, 24, 32
Amsterdam, 9, 24, 100, 121, 216
Ancona, 64, 192
Anderson, Zoe, 305, 465

Anglo-Boer War, 21, 23, 33, 41, 42, 44, 45, 47, 51, 52, 55, 56, 58, 60, 85, 108, 128, 132, 134, 136, 156, 160, 164, 170, 172, 173, 174, 183, 189, 190, 196, 200, 201, 202, 207, 242, 258, 281, 283, 284, 288, 291, 292, 297, 298, 300, 380, 407, 410, 417, 419, 457, 462, 463
Anglo-Rhodesian War, 68
Anglo-Saxon, 16
Angola, 24, 172
Angwa River, 69, 232
Animal Kingdom, 76
Anker farm, 68, 258
Annotech, 70, 199
Anthonis, Catharina - first freed slave, 24, 32, 100
Apollo, 77
Appel, Ferdinandus, 16, 26, 27, 30
Argentina, 289
Arkles Bay, 112
Armstrong, Neil, 77
Armstrong, Patrick, 101
Arnott, Stella Nesta, 65, 402, 459
Arnott, Sydney Nathaniel, 402
Atlanta, 75, 76
Atlantis, 77
Atlas road, 22
Atlasville, 75
Auckland, 70, 78, 79, 109, 112, 113, 154, 199, 205, 227, 398, 401, 440, 441, 451, 463
Augsburg, 9, 31, 241, 242
Australia, 79, 122, 124, 210, 223, 232, 445, 454
Avignon, 9, 259, 452
Ayr, 9, 234, 449
BAARD
   Johanna Magdalena, 360
BADENHORST
   Christina Geertruyda (GELDENHUYS) (1769-), 346
   Christina Magdalena (GELDENHUYS) (1773-1839), 345
   Cornelia Margaretha (GELDENHUYS) (1814-1858), 352
   Frans Hendrik, 346
   Jan Hendrik (1771-), 345
   Petrus Johannes, 346, 352
   Susanna Margaretha (GELDENHUYS) (1771-), 346
Badenhorst, Geertruyda Johanna, 404
Badenhorst, Jacomina Margaretha, 408
Badenhorst, Marile, 102
Badenhorst, Petrus Johannes, 405, 420
Badenhorst, Wessel Johannes, 406
Baden-Powell, General Robert SS, 52
Bainsfather-Cloete, Shirley and son Peter, 30
Bam, Jan Andreas, 32

Bam, Johanna Dorothea, 32
Bam, Sue, 158, 408
Banfield, Lauren, 198
Bangwela, 181
Barlow, Cynthia, 29
BARNARD
   Adam, 373
   Martha Louisa (GELDENHUYS) (1841-1874), 373
Barnett, Susan, 266, 402
Barnett, William, 30
Basoetuland war, 33, 36, 38
BASSON
   Catharina Jacoba, 357
Basson, Leandi, 139
Basutoland, 36, 39, 42
Batavia, 100
Battle of Armoedskoppie, 174
Battle of Belmont, 45, 46, 47, 174, 200
Battle of Blood River, 35
Battle of Boomplaats, 35
Battle of Enslin, 47
Battle of eThaleni, 34
Battle of Graspan, 47
Battle of Inyantue, 68
Battle of Langeberg, 50
Battle of Magersfontein, 23
Battle of Modder River, 48
Battle of Tweeriviere, 48
Bauden, Tracy, 218
Bay of Plenty, 78, 112, 205, 224, 231
Beatrice, 20, 21, 248, 255, 460
Beauford West, 34
Beaver, Richard, 75, 92
Bee Line, 77
BEESLAAR
   Anna Sophia Aletta, 369, 378
   J F, 378
Bega farm, 20
BEHR
   Mathilda Marietta (1836-), 365, 376
Beit Bridge, 163
Belfour-Cunningham, Bianca, 102, 117, 278, 308
Belgium, 9, 18, 121
BELJOHN
   Mardel, 392
Bellevue, 59, 122
Belmont farm, 19
BENEKE
   Christina Geertruyda Maria (GELDENHUYS) (1813-), 355
   Hendricus Petrus, 355
   Maria Chistina (GELDENHUYS) (1817-), 355
   Petrus Johannes, 355
Bengal, 24, 100
Bengasi, 64, 191
Bengu, 122, 124, 198

Benoni, 198, 226, 418
Berg China, 25, 259
Berg River Valley, 25
Berry, Mary Ann Dorothy, 105
BESTER
   Johanna Susanna, 350, 364
   Susanna Maria Elizabeth (1886-1978), 377, 382
   Wilna, 384, 388
Bester crest, 102
Bester, Helletje Levina, 108
Bester, Johanna Susanna, 364, 406
Bester, Wilna, 102, 146, 168, 193, 211, 407, 408
Besterkraal farm, 19
Besterskraal, 20
Besuidenhout, Elisabeth Susanna 'Elise', 104
Bethlehem, 39, 77, 145, 172, 175, 268, 269, 402, 432, 447, 458
Bethulie, 59, 122
Beukes
   Elizabeth (Libby) Adriana (van Rensen) (1941-), 383
   Johannes Christjan (1947-), 383, 387
BEUKES
   Barend Hendrik, 347
   Christina Magdalena (GELDENHUYS) (1781-), 347
   Christopher (1983-), 388
   Elizabeth (Libby) Adriana (van Rensen) (1941-), 387
Beukes crest, 102
Beukes, Christopher, 103, 409
Beukes, Cornelius and Martinus, 282
Beukes, Libby, 66, 92, 94, 157, 317
Beukes, Petrus Jacobus, 404
BEYERS
   Aletta Catharina Elizabeth (GELDENHUYS) (1837-), 369
   Cornelia Johanna Alberta (GELDENHUYS) (1837-), 370
   George David Cornelis (1831-1895), 370
   Johanna Magdalena (LOURENS) (1808-1861), 370
   Johannes David (1809-1885), 370
   Matthys Wilhelm (1830-1883), 369
Beyers, Christina, 122
Bezuidenhoud, CW, 160
Bezuidenhout crest, 103
Bezuidenhout, 'Gerta' Gertruida Johanna, 105
Bezuidenhout, Adele, 103, 105
Bezuidenhout, Aiden Kyle, 103, 312
Bezuidenhout, Benjamin James, 104
Bezuidenhout, Brent, 103
Bezuidenhout, Bronwyn, 104, 105
Bezuidenhout, Elizabeth 'Betty' Susanna, 104

Bezuidenhout, Francois, 104, 106, 319, 481
Bezuidenhout, Fred, 105
Bezuidenhout, Gerda, 105, 171, *See* Gerda Geldenhuys
Bezuidenhout, Gerta, 94
Bezuidenhout, Jared, 94, 106, 312
Bezuidenhout, Jaydene, 104, 106
Bezuidenhout, Johan, 68, 81, 103, 104, 105, 106, 257, 312, 488
Bezuidenhout, Johannes Jurgens 'Hansie', 68, 81, 85, 94, 104, 105, 106, 107, 235, 236, 254, 255, 256, 258, 454, 483
Bezuidenhout, Johannes Wilhelmus, 105
Bezuidenhout, Letitia, 106, 219, 274
Bezuidenhout, Petrus, 41
Bezuidenhout, Tane Jurgens, 104, 107, 501
Bezuidenhout, Wynand, 105, 107, 235
Bhengu, 182
Birchenough Bridge, 66
BJORN
   Talei Lisi 'Torika' (1978-), 389
Blaaupan, 22
Blaauwkrantz River, 34
Blackwood farm, 20
Blesbokfontein farm, 19
BLOEM
   Elizabeth Catharina, 354, 370
BLOEMMENSTEIN
   Sannie, 375
Blommenstein, Sannie, 407
Blood River, 35, 37, 144
Boere Oorlog, 248, *See* Anglo-Boer War
BOGGIO BOZZO
   Letizia Clelia Ester (1941-), 393
BOHM
   Angela Adriana de Jager (GELDENHUYS) (1908-), 381, 384
   Oscar, 381, 384
Bonaero Park, 22
Books published, 333
BOOYSEN
   Hannelie, 384, 388
Booysen, Hannelie, 168, 193, 211, 407
Borghetto, 64, 192
Borman, Martha Magdalena, 125
Borruso, Charmaine, 107, *See* Geldenhuys, Charmaine
Borruso, Peter, 107, 124, 148, 210, 409
Borruso, Stuart. *See* Geldenhuys, Stuart
Bosman, Aletta, 259, 399
Bosman, Hermanus, 259
Bosman, Martha Elizabeth, 122
Botes, Louisa Frederick, 171, 187
Botha
   Karen, 393
BOTHA

Christina Maria (GELDENHUYS) (1794-1837), 347
Elizabeth Debora, 347, 355
Helletta Lephina (-1889), 380
Karen, 388
Stephanus Jacobus, 347
Botha crest, 108
Botha, Anneen, 129
Botha, General Louis, 21, 55, 190
Botha, Heiltjie Levina, 41
Botha, Helletta Lephina, 42, 136, 281, 282, 283, 400, 462
Botha, Hendrik, 136
Botha, Johanna Maria, 297
Botha, Karen, 127
Botha, Lourens (Louw) Rasmus, 108
Botha, Renier, 136
Botha, Theunis Louis - Gladdedrift and founder of Bothaville, 19, 21, 23, 40, 41, 108, 125, 281
Botha, Theuns, 282
Botha, Theuns Louw, 39
Botharania, 282
Botharnia farm, 19, 21, 41, 108, 125
Bothaville, 14, 19, 20, 21, 22, 23, 36, 40, 41, 54, 55, 58, 60, 64, 65, 66, 108, 125, 136, 158, 164, 165, 172, 175, 176, 178, 179, 180, 181, 182, 192, 202, 281, 282, 283, 284, 285, 286, 397, 401, 408, 409, 451, 455, 462, 463
Bothma, CP, 400
Bothma, Rita, 109, 211
Bourbon street, 76
BOUWER
   Barendina Petronella (GELDENHUYS) (1852-), 363
   Chanli (1970-), 387, 392
   Delene Elizabeth (GELDENHUYS) (1945-), 383, 387
   Johannes Jacobus Francois (1943-), 383, 387
   Marie, 387
   Petrus Cornelis, 363
   Rensha (1972-), 387
   Willem, 387
Bouwer - meaning of Surname, 18
Bouwer crest, 109
Bouwer, Chanli G, 64, 66, 78, 109, 110, 112, 113, 114, 115, 154, 190, 195, 205, 227, 272, 398, 401, 410, 440, 441, 451, 463
Bouwer, Debra, 109, 304
Bouwer, Elcora, 81, 94, 110, 236, 247, 262, 455, 479
Bouwer, Jeremias, 110
Bouwer, Johann Ludwig - Stamvader, 9, 110
Bouwer, Johannes Jacobus Francois, 64, 66, 109, 110, 111, 154, 235, 304, 305, 383, 387, 398, 401, 410, 440, 441
Bouwer, Petrus Frederik, 110
Bouwer, Rensha, 64, 66, 110, 111, 154, 205, 398, 401, 410, 440, 451, 463, 498
Bouwer, Willem Christiaan, 110
Bovlei, 20, 257, 456
Boxall, Eve Elizabeth, 264
Braamfontein, 20, 21, 23, 44, 43, 55, 56, 155, 159, 160, 189
Braamfontein farm, 19
Brand, President Jan, 39
Brazil, 199
Bredasdorp, 20, 245, 310, 405, 406, 408, 413, 414, 420, 421, 437, 454
Bremen, 11, 303, 403
Brewis, Frank, 56, 177, 178
Brewis, Frikkie, 56
Briers, Daniel Francois, 241
BRINK
   Chanli (BOUWER) (1970-), 387, 392
   Charles Roy (1961-), 387, 392
   Deu G (1999-), 392
   Gem (2001-), 392
   Mona Daphne (VAN ROOYEN) (1934-1987), 392
   Nea D (1998-), 392
   Schalk Reginald (1933-1988), 392
   Tal J (1995-), 392
Brink - meaning of Surname, 18
Brink crest, 111
Brink, Andries - Stamvader, 9, 111, 440
Brink, Anje, 112, 113, 132
Brink, Carol, 112
Brink, Chanli, 229, 475
Brink, Charles Roy, 64, 66, 78, 109, 111, 112, 113, 114, 115, 154, 190, 195, 272, 392, 398, 401, 410, 440, 441, 451, 463, 476
Brink, Charlie and Chanli, 78
Brink, Christie, 114
Brink, Cornelis, 23, 111
Brink, Daniel, 111
Brink, Deu, 9, 109, 110, 112, 227, 398, 401, 410, 440, 441, 451, 463, 478
Brink, Dirk J, 463
Brink, Gem, 9, 78, 109, 110, 112, 113, 227, 271, 398, 401, 410, 440, 441, 451, 463, 482
Brink, Jana, 113, 133
Brink, Jenny, 113
Brink, Johannes, 111
Brink, John Robert, 113, 301, 490
Brink, Joshua Dean, 113, 301
Brink, Kellie Marie, 114
Brink, Lynn, 272, 492
Brink, Melt, 290

Brink, Nea, 9, 109, 110, 112, 114, 227, 398, 401, 410, 440, 441, 451, 463, 496
Brink, Richard, 114
Brink, Schalk Reginald, 114, 313, 440
Brink, Schalk Richard, 114, 440
Brink, Tal, 9, 109, 110, 112, 114, 115, 227, 228, 398, 401, 410, 440, 441, 451, 463, 501
Britain, 14, 24, 36, 39, 59, 122, 173, 204, 244, 258, 263
British South Africa Company, 42
BRODIE
   Donald 'Ross' (1947-), 385, 389
   Margareth Helene 'Marita' (GELDENHUYS) (1946-), 385, 389
   Shayne Ross (1973-), 389
   Talei Lisi 'Torika' (BJORN) (1978-), 389
Brodie crest, 115
Brodie, Donald 'Ross', 115, 192
Brodie, Shyane and Tonja, 193
Brodie, Tonja, 193
Brooks, Heidi, 208
BROWN
   Craig, 387
   Kelley Anne, 389, 394
   Rensha (BOUWER) (1972-), 387
Brown, Craig, 64, 66, 111, 154, 398, 440
Bruwer, Eduard, 140
BRUYNZWART
   Bartholomeus, 360
   Johanna Magdalena, 349, 360
Buckle, Catherine, 147
Buffelshoek farm, 20
Bukes, Jacomina Margaretha, 165
Bulawayo, 52, 63, 68, 69, 105, 210, 232, 233, 241, 409
Buller, Redvers, 41
Bulwer, 74
Burger Street, 74
Burger, Cornelia, 110
Burger, Schalk Johannes, 170
Burger, SP, 248
Burgsteinfurt, 9, 24, 25, 100, 396, 403
BURNS
   Gerry, 388
Burns crest, 116
Burns, Deirdre, 116, 153, 167, 408
Busby, James, 228
Bush Babies Lodge, 122, 124, 182, 198
Butler, John, 228
BUYS
   Anna (GELDENHUYS), 382
   NN, 382
Cairo, 77, 183
Calitz, Tremayne, 145
Camphor trees, 23, 29, 30
Canada, 14, 205, 232, 233, 234, 319, 460
Canberra, 68, 70, 75, 78, 202, 232, 233
Cape Governor, 16, 30, 35, 143

Cape of Good Hope, 28, 100
Cape Town, 18, 19, 20, 24, 25, 31, 33, 44, 55, 75, 100, 117, 122, 123, 143, 164, 183, 184, 185, 187, 188, 198, 199, 213, 214, 216, 231, 232, 257, 258, 259, 289, 291, 292, 294, 396, 397, 403, 404, 405, 407, 409, 413, 414, 419, 420, 422, 430, 432, 433, 434, 435, 436, 443, 444, 447, 448, 452, 453, 456, 457, 460
Carelse, Antonia, 142
Carnwath, 234, 449
Carr, Vivian, 117, 278, 308
Castigani, Emilio, 284
Castignani, Renaldo and Cicero, 284
Cellier, Sarel, 34, 39
Celliers, Charles, 39
Cetshwayo, Zulu King, 42
Ceylon, 55, 56, 58, 59, 132, 166, 170, 190, 407, 436
Chanetza, Peter - Zanu-PF, 147
Chegwyn - KIA, 65
Chegwyn, Lt RL, 183
Chelmsford, General, 41
Chinditu farm, 20
Chinese, 16
Chingola, 63, 64, 66, 153, 180, 242, 398, 410, 451
Chipinga, 21, 42, 248, 255, 257, 268, 269
Chipinge, 64, 70, 205, 223, 227, 231, 398, 401, 450, 451, 455, 459, 463, 468
Chiredzi, 199, 204, 231, 248, 254, 255, 263, 455
Chirundu, 163
Chiyangwa - Zanu-PF, 147
Chombo - Zanu-PF, 147
Christian Church, 16
Christie, 74
Christie Road, 73
Christon Bank, 69, 234
Cilliers, Willem Adriaan, 404
Claas, Coenelis, 100
Claasen, Herman, 281
Clanwilliam, 33
Clark, Vanessa, 161, 418, 461
Cleveland, 22
CLOETE
   Henrika Francina (1908-), 382, 385
   Johanna Elizabeth 'Joey' (1929-2008), 392
Cloete crest, 117
Cloete, Catharina, 28
Cloete, Christina Catharina, 24, 117
Cloete, Coenraad, 24, 117
Cloete, Dirk, 118
Cloete, Gerhard or Gerrit, 24, 117
Cloete, Hendrik, 24, 25, 100
Cloete, Hendrik - largest land owner, 117
Cloete, Jacob, 24, 25, 33, 100, 117, 118

Cloete, Johanna Catharina, 33
Cloete, Johanna Elizabeth, 118, 122
Cloete, Portia, 299
Coetser, Jacob Kutzer - stamvader, 441
COETZEE
    Dirkie Susanna Elizabeth, 349, 362
    Dirkie Susanna Elizabeth (-1899), 349, 362
    Geertruyda Johanna Elizabeth (GELDENHUYS) (1846-), 363
    Jan Hendrik, 363
    Johan Christian Lambrecht, 363
    Maria Elizabeth Magdalena Johanna (GELDENHUYS) (1843-), 363
Coetzee, Karel, 174, 281
Coetzer, Martha Petronelle (Floss), 128
Cole, Barbara, 68
Cole, Peter, 68
Coleman, Edmund Francis, 402, 459
Coleman, Lucretia Maria, 225, 402, 459
Coleman, Margery Hester, 42
Colenso, 53, 198, 289
Colesberg, 32, 52, 53, 56, 242, 288, 298, 405, 436, 437, 445
Colleton, Colonel, 55, 177
COLLETT
    Joan (1943-), 385, 390
Collins, Michael, 77
Colombo, 58, 166, 190
Coloureds, 32
Colyn, Johannes Lamberus, 404
Common names, 18
Congo, 68, 279
Conradie, Rita, 144, 152, 207, 208, 209
Constantia, 24, 25, 100, 117, 122
Cooke, Anne, 69, 234
Cooke, Peter, 68, 69, 232, 233
COOPER
    Jacomina Geertruyda (GELDENHUYS) (1834-), 355
    Johannes Jurie, 355
    Maria Johanna, 356, 372
    Susanna Johanna, 373
Cooper, Susanna Maria Margaretha, 169
Copperbelt, 63, 64, 66, 180, 181, 242
CORDIER
    Francina, 347
Cordier, Chris, 255
CORNELIS
    Grietje, 339
Cornelis, Grietje, 25, 100
Cornelisse, Helena, 241
COSTEUX
    Anna (GELDENHUYS) (1689-), 340
    Jean, 340
Courtney - meaning of Name, 18
Craddock, 33, 34, 459
Craig - meaning of Name, 18
Craig Jannie Geldenhuys, 99

Crammond, 74
Creetown, 9, 449
Creighton, 74
Crest
    Bester, 102
    Beukes, 102
    Bezuidenhout, 103
    Botha, 108
    Bouwer, 109, 439
    Brink, 111, 440
    Brodie, 115
    Burns, 116
    Cloete, 117
    Coetzer, 441
    Culhane, 118
    de Waal, 121, 444
    Delport, 120
    Dreyer, 125
    Dunckers, 126
    Engelbrecht, 127
    Estment, 127, 446
    Geldenhuys, 135, 136, 403
    Howard, 221, 447
    Jelley, 223, 449
    le Roux, 236, 450
    Liebenberg, 238
    Lock, 239
    Lotter, 450
    Lötter, 241
    Malan, 243, 244, 452
    McColl, 264
    Moodie, 266, 458
    Mueller, 270
    Muirhead, 270
    Mussell, 273
    Nel, 274
    Odendaal, 460
    Olivier, 275
    Page, 276
    Preller, 279, 461
    Pretorius, 301
    Simpkins, 304
    Sinton, 305, 465
    Steenkamp, 306
    Stoltz, 306
    Stopforth, 307
    Thomas, 308
    van Wyk, 314
    Venter, 314
    Whiteley, 318
Cronje, Andries, 51
Cronje, Piet, 51
Cross, Captain, 24
Cruikens, 234, 449
Culhane crest, 118
Culhane, Caitlin Sinead, 118
Culhane, Glenn Cameron, 113
Culhane, James Joseph Michael, 118
Culhane, James Michael Sheenan, 119

Culhane, Joseph Aloysius, 119
Culhane, Liam Connor, 113
Culhane, Michael William, 119
Culhane, Rory Terence, 113, 119
Culhane, Sean Kevin, 118
Culhane, William Joseph Michael, 119
Curren, Kevin, 204
Currin, Graham, 82
Currin, Ian, 82, 240
Currin, Ian, Taylor and Sarah Kate, 82
Currin, Margie, 82
Cydonia, 22
da Gama, Vasco, 24
Dalgleish, J, 65, 183
Dan Pienaarville, 22
Dansfontein farm, 19
Danskraal, 34
David, David, 20
Day of the Vow, 35
De Bank farm, 19, 41, 57, 108, 283, 285, 408, 463
de Beer, Albert, 82
de Beer, Zacharia Christina, 11, 33, 294, 400, 461
de Bertodano - chief provost, 176
DE BRUYN
   Louzya Christina (1898-1970), 386
de Bruyn, Louzya Christina, 124, 125
de Bryn, Louzya Christina, 124
de Hoop op Constantia farm, 20
DE JAGER
   Anna Christina, 352, 367
   Annie, 381
   Carel Pieter (-1896), 378
   Gesina Catharina, 371, 378
de Jager, Annie, 306
de Jager, Carel Pieter, 163, 428
de Jager, Gesina Catharina, 163
de Jager, LJ, 65, 183
de Kock, Emmarentia, 122
de Kock, WJ - Professor, 100, 294
de la Rey, General Koos, 47, 48, 50, 51, 298
de Landsheer, dr, 55
de Leeuw, Cornelis, 121
DE MEYER
   Floris Petrus Jacobus, 362, 376
   Johanna Susanna Maria (GELDENHUYS) (1847-1881), 362, 376
   Olof Abram Jacobus (1880-), 376
de Meyer, Floris Petrus Jacobus, 376, 408
de Oliveira, Carlos Alberto Lopes, 119
de Oliveira, Michael, 120
de Oliveira, Michelle, 120
de Raedt, Frans - discovered coal, 284
DE VILLIERS
   Elizabeth Rachel, 348, 359
   Piet Daniel, 359

   Susanna Catharina Margaretha (1906-1986), 389
de Vos, Erica, 300
DE WAAL
   Jan Gerhardus (1921-1972), 392
   Johanna Elizabeth 'Joey' (CLOETE) (1929-2008), 392
   Karen (1966-), 386, 392
de Waal crest, 121
de Waal, Alida, 111, 440
de Waal, Arend, 151
de Waal, Arthur, 121
de Waal, Attie, 422
de Waal, Daniel Malherbe, 123
de Waal, David Christiaan, 122
de Waal, Gideon Daniel, 123
de Waal, Hermanus Lambertus, 123
de Waal, Jan, 21, 151, 444
de Waal, Jan - Stamvader, 9, 121
de Waal, Jan Christoffel, 59, 122, 151
de Waal, Jan Gerhardus, 118, 151
de Waal, Jan Gerhardus – (1), 122
de Waal, Jan Gerhardus – (2), 122
de Waal, Jan Gerhardus – (3), 122
de Waal, Jan Hendrik Hofmeyr (Jannie), 122
de Waal, Karen, 63, 118, 122, 146, 151, 198, 263, 397, 400, 409, 446, 451, 463
de Waal, Pieter, 151, 424
de Waal, Sir Nicolaas Frederic, 123
de Wachter, Jan, 283
de Wet, Elmé, 201
de Wet, General Christiaan, 22, 51, 52, 53, 54, 55, 59, 128, 175, 176, 242
de Wet, Johannes Francois, 437
de Wet, NJ, 290
Dead Sea, 77
Dean, FJ, 65
Dean, Lt Cdr FJ, 183
Deelkraal farm, 19
Deeves, Joyce Pamela, 223, 227
Delagoa Bay, 34
Delport crest, 120
Delport, Danita, 120
Delport, Hennie, 120, 152, 210
Dias, Bartolomeu, 24
Dick, David B, 65, 162
Dictionary of Biographies, 15, 16
Die Oorlogsherinneringe van Lizzie Geldenhuys, 281
DIEDERIKS
   Maria Elizabeth, 342, 344
Diederiks, Maria Elizabeth, 344, 404
Dingaan, Zulu King, 291, 302
Dingane, 34, 35
Dipner, 9, 15
DIPPENAAR
   Johannes Petrus (1898-1968), 386
   Julia Lillian (1936-), 383, 386

Louzya Christina (DE BRUYN) (1898-1970), 386
Dippenaar - meaning of Surname, 18
Dippenaar, Alwyn Jacobus, 123, 151
Dippenaar, Alwyn Johannes, 151
Dippenaar, Anna Johanna Sophia, 123
Dippenaar, Johan Martinus Depner - stamvader, 9
Dippenaar, Johanna Maria Barendina, 123
Dippenaar, Johannes Marthinus, 21, 31, 124
Dippenaar, Johannes Petrus, 123, 124, 125, 151, 490
Dippenaar, Jouanita, 124
Dippenaar, Julia Lillian, 63, 107, 122, 123, 124, 148, 151, 180, 181, 198, 210, 238, 263, 312, 397, 400, 409, 445, 451, 462
Dippenaar, Louis Hosea, 125
Dippenaar, Lousya Christina, 125
Dippenaar, Louzya, 239
Dippenaar, Schalk Willem, 125
Discovery, 77
Disney World, 75, 76
Diyatalawa, POW Camp, 55, 58, 59, 132
Doble - KIA, 65
Doble, Lt IJ, 183
Donges, Pastor, 283
Doopregister, 15, 16
Doorn Kop farm, 21
Doornbult, 33, 40, 156, 173, 349, 362, 407
Doornbult farm, 19, 156
Doorndraai farm, 19
Doornhoek farm, 20
Doornkop-Wes farm, 19
Doornspruit farm, 19
Dordogne, 14
Douwes, H, 67
Dovey, John, 45, 338
Downtown Disney, 76
Drake, Sir Frances, 24
Drakensberg, 34, 35, 37, 64, 69, 144, 204, 231, 398, 399, 401, 409, 450, 451, 455, 459, 463, 468
Drakenstein, 15, 20, 247, 259, 399, 452, 453, 457
Dresden, 11
Dreyer crest, 125
Dreyer, "Kil", 41
Dreyer, Anna, 282
Dreyer, Anna Elizabeth, 108, 125, 281
Dreyer, Christiaan Lourens, 125, 476
Dreyer, Christiaan Lourens "Kil", 125
Dreyer, Elizabeth, 41
Dreyer, Herculaas Philip, 125
Dreyer, Johannes Gerhardus, 39, 125, 490
Dreyer, Kil, 166, 180, 192
Dreyer, Lukas Ignatius, 41
Driehoek, 22
Driekoppies, 20

du Plessis, Adele, 126
du Plessis, Jan, 126, 158, 208
DU PLOOY
   Heinrich, 339
   Margaretha (GELDENHUYS) (1684-), 339
du Plooy, Heinrich, 11, 31, 216, 483
du Plooy, Hendrik Willem, 11
du Plooy, Margaretha, 11
du Preez, Carol-Ann, 118
du T. Malherbe, Professor, 15
DU TOIT
   Jacob, 377
   Martha Maria, 348, 358
   Mathilda Marietta (GELDENHUYS), 377
   Pieter, 358
du Toit, André le Roux - 'Koos Kombuis', 187
du Toit, Anna Margarita, 399
du Toit, Dr JD, 290
du Toit, Gen SP, 183
Dunbar, Elizabeth, 266
Dunckers
   Brandon Arne (1965-), 388, 393
   Caryn Sandra (1963-), 388
   Elizabeth (Libby) Adriana (van Rensen) (1941-), 383, 387
   Karen (Botha), 393
   Ralph Arnold (1943-), 383, 387
   Wilbur, 387
DUNCKERS
   Arne (1986-), 393
   Caryn Sandra (1963-), 392
   Grace (NN), 387
   Karen (BOTHA), 388
Dunckers crest, 126
Dunckers, Arné, 127
Dunckers, Brandon, 127
Dunckers, Brandon Arne, 409
Dunckers, Caryn Sandra, 409
Dunn, Jerry, 233
Dunn, John Robert, 42
Durban, 19, 34, 35, 64, 70, 75, 78, 79, 111, 122, 128, 136, 146, 151, 171, 178, 181, 182, 191, 198, 199, 202, 218, 221, 222, 226, 232, 267, 268, 270, 286, 397, 398, 399, 400, 401, 409, 410, 446, 451, 455, 463, 468
Dutch, 16, 18, 24, 25, 26, 30, 31, 32, 34, 41, 55, 100, 117, 178, 217, 289, 290, 291
Dutch East India Company, 26, 33, 100, 117
Dylan, Bob - singer, 128
Eagle, 77
East Prussia., 9
EBERSOHN
   Elsabe Luytje (GELDENHUYS) (1830-), 370
   Johannes Matthys, 370

Maria Catharina (GELDENHUYS) (1827-), 370
W L, 370
Edenvale, 63, 122, 124, 397, 409, 451, 463
Egypt, 199, 279
Eikelboom farm, 20
Eilat, 77
EKSTEEN
  Elsabe (GELDENHUYS) (1738-), 343
  Heinrich Oswald (1678-1741), 343
  Paul Henricus (1737-), 343
  Sara Johanna, 362, 375
Eksteen, Michiel Casparus, 407
Eksteen, Sara Johanna, 375, 407
Elandsfontein, 19, 22, 44, 159, 189
Elandsfontein farm, 19
Elandslaagte, 21, 55
Elbers, Geertruyt, 15, 16
Ellis, WE, 65
Ellis, William E, 162
Elmira, 75
Emmarentia, 21, 22, 33, 43, 56, 122, 189, 190, 411, 412, 427
Emmerich, 9, 121
Endeavour, 77, 229
Engela, JG, 290
ENGELBRECHT
  Veronica, 384
Engelbrecht crest, 127
Engelbrecht, Adriaan and Suzanne, 127
Engelbrecht, André, 127, 185
Engelbrecht, Veronica, 168, 209, 408
Engelse Oorlog, 45
England, 18, 24, 34, 179, 183, 237, 245, 260, 315, 468
English, 16, 18, 24, 52, 54, 55, 174, 175, 176, 177, 178, 179, 183, 282, 285, 286, 289, 291, 292, 417
Epcot, 76
Erasmus, Elizabeth Johanna, 108
Erinvale farm, 21
Erisha, Corporal - killed, 69, 233
Ermelo, 53, 115, 156, 192, 193, 195, 289, 410
ERWEE
  Cornelia Susanna (1833-), 355
Estcourt, 22, 73, 75, 171, 198, 199, 202, 204, 221, 398, 401, 410, 449, 451, 463
ESTMENT
  Ingrid Stella (1950-), 391
Estment crest, 127
Estment, Ingrid Stella, 128, 221, 222, 449, 485
Estment, June, 128
Estment, Norman Bruce, 128
Estment, William Henry, 128
Eston, 74
Europe, 60, 64, 160, 244, 279
Falconer, Lt Col Keith, 46

Family tree - 12 generations, 329, 395
Featherstonhaugh, General, 46
Feltcott, Captain, 76
Fer Schekhoven, Hermann, 100
Ferreira, 158
Ferreira, Estie, 213
Ferreira, Louis, 21, 248, 269
Ferry and Bay, 122, 181
Fincham, Victor, 140, 191
Finchams' Farm, 46
Fire Patrol, 74
Fischer, Abraham, 284
Fish Bay, 24
Fish River, 33, 44
Fisher, Luke Ian, 193
Fisher, Scarlett and Stevie, 193
Fitzherbert, sea captain, 24
Flemish, 25
Florence, 64, 192, 462
Florida, 14, 22, 75, 76, 77
Forestry, 73, 74, 75, 160, 202
Forestry Office, 73, 74
Fort Frederick, 33
Fort Lauderdale, 75
Fort Victoria, 20, 35, 64, 66, 154, 202, 242, 255, 262, 263, 268, 269, 397, 399, 401, 409, 451, 455, 459, 463
Fouche, Johannes Hendrik, 404
Fouche, Philippus Johannes, 404
FOURIE
  Anna (1752-1840), 343, 346
  Barend Petrus, 353
  Elizabeth Dorothea Magdalena (GELDENHUYS) (1819-), 353
  Geertruy Johanna (GELDENHUYS) (1806-), 353
  Hendrik Johannes (1802-), 353
Fourie, Freda Johanna, 185
Fourie, PJ, 56, 170
Fox Glacier, 77
France, 9, 11, 14, 25, 65, 237, 244, 259, 448, 452
Francois Daniel Malan, 126, 256, 315, 338, 481
Franklin Roosevelt suburb, 22
Frans Geldenhuys Park, 21
Frans Josef glacier, 77
Franschhoek, 20, 25, 259
Franschoek, 9, 434, 436
French, 16, 18, 25, 51, 237, 291
French Huguenots, 25
Frieze, Othon, 280
Fritz, Henrietta, 144
Fritz, Henrietta Wilhelmina Cornelia, 144
FRONEMAN
  Charmaine (GELDENHUYS) (1960-), 386, 391
  Jason (1996-), 392
  Lance, 386, 392

Froneman, Jason, 63, 99, 128, 148, 409, 446, 487
Froneman, Lance, 128, 148, 172, 181, 198, 409, 446, 491
Galilee, 77
Garissa, 298, 299
GEERE
  Linda Magdalene (1954-), 385, 390
Geldebhuys, Lourens, 151
Geldehuys, Corné, 185
Geldenhuijs, J.F. See Geldenhuys, Jacobus Francois
Geldenhuijs, Jacobus Francois, 56, 58
Geldenhuis - meaning of Surname, 18
Geldenhuis Deep Bowling Club, 22
Geldenhuis railway siding, 22
Geldenhuis Road, 22
Geldenhuis Street, 22
Geldenhuis, Albertus Hendrik, 128, 129
Geldenhuis, Albertus Hendrik 'Bert', 131
Geldenhuis, Arina, 129
Geldenhuis, Chrisna, 301
Geldenhuis, Chrisna and Jaun-Pierre, 131
Geldenhuis, Christo, 129, 130
Geldenhuis, Cleopatra and Joanna, 130
Geldenhuis, Daniel, 129
Geldenhuis, Dawie, 129, 130
Geldenhuis, Eban, 130
Geldenhuis, Eben, 130, 133, 220
Geldenhuis, Eddie,, 131
Geldenhuis, Elsie, 131
Geldenhuis, Faith Dabin, 133
Geldenhuis, Gideon Theodorus, 434, 482
Geldenhuis, Gilbert Jacobus, 129, 131, 301
Geldenhuis, Hendru, Johaaeke, and Marli, 129
Geldenhuis, Jacobus Viljoen, 132
Geldenhuis, Jana, 112
Geldenhuis, Jaun-Pierre, 301
Geldenhuis, Ken, 132
Geldenhuis, Koos, 131
Geldenhuis, Martinus, 128
Geldenhuis, Maureen, 133
Geldenhuis, Melchoir J, 133
Geldenhuis, Melchoir Jacobus, 434
Geldenhuis, Melda, 133, 274, 434
Geldenhuis, Mellie, 113, 133
Geldenhuis, Monja, 133, 220
Geldenhuis, Pieter, 130, 133
Geldenhuis, Pieter Jacobus, 134
Geldenhuis, PJ, 58
Geldenhuis, Rhodean, 134
Geldenhuis, Tionette Kritzinger, 134
Geldenhuis, Trevor, 131, 133, 134, 220
Geldenhuis, Tyger, 135
GeldenhuisFaith Dabin, 220
Geldenhuys
  Adriaan Izak 'Attie', 381, 384
  Debora (Viljoen) (1901-), 381
  Elsie (1746-), 342
  Geertruyda (Grobbelaar) (1753-1837), 342
  Hendrik (1744-), 342
  Izak George, 381
  Jacobus ' Kosie', 384
  Johanna (le Roux) (1748-), 342
  Johannes Albertus (1743-), 342
  Johannes Albertus (1750-), 342
  Koeks NN (NN Koeks), 384
  Margaretha Maria (Wessels) (-1801), 342
  Sara Johanna (1751-1836), 342
  Susanna Catharina (Malan) (1945-), 338
GELDENHUYS
  Abraham Jacobus, 348, 358
  Abraham Jacobus (1835-1907), 373, 379
  Abraham Jacobus Josua (1872-), 379
  Abraham Johannes (1845-), 352
  Abraham Josua (1808-), 358, 373
  Abram Carl Frederik Preller (1916-1972), 381, 383
  Ada (PRINGLE), 376, 381
  Adriaan (1817-), 360
  Adriaan (1993-), 389
  Adriaan 'Attie', 384
  Adriaan Hendrik, 379
  Adriaan Hendrik (1830-), 371
  Adriaan Izaak (1823-), 352
  Adriaan Izak 'Aap' (1843-1904), 362, 376
  Adriaan Johannes, 382
  Adriaan Johannes (1810-1867), 352, 367
  Adriaan Johannes (1843-), 366, 368, 377
  Adriaan Johannes (1867-1898), 377, 382
  Adriaan Johannes (1877-), 378
  Adrian Johannes - f2 (1810-1867), 351, 366
  Adriana Alberta, 379
  Adrianna Marta Maria (Max) (KEYZER), 380, 382
  Albert Barend (1712-), 340
  Albert Barend (1748-), 343, 348
  Albert Barend (1784-), 348, 360
  Albert Barend (1788-), 348, 358
  Albert Barend (1802-), 359, 374
  Albert Barend (1819-), 358
  Albert Barend (1828-), 361
  Albert Barend (1829-), 374
  Albert Barends Gildenhuisz (1630-1693), 339
  Albert Barentse (1709-), 341
  Albert Hendrik (1746-), 343, 347
  Albert Hendrik (1797-), 347
  Albert Hendrik (1816-), 354, 371
  Albert Hendrik (1891-), 347
  Albert Hendrik Stephanus (1822-), 355
  Albertus Barend (1811-), 359
  Albertus Bernardus (1846-), 367
  Aletta Catharina Elizabeth (1837-), 369

Aletta Johanna (MARAIS) (1787-), 344, 350
Aletta Petronella (1815-), 350
Alida Johanna (1813-), 360
Allan (1989-), 393
Allan Derek (1949-), 385, 390
Andrew Mark (1967-), 390
Andries Johannes (1875-), 379
Andries Lodewicus Stephanus, 379
Angela Adriana de Jager (1908-), 381, 384
Anna, 382
Anna (1689-), 340
Anna (FOURIE) (1752-1840), 343, 346
Anna Catharina (1840-), 367
Anna Catharina (MULDER), 347, 356
Anna Catharina Cornelia Susanna (1854-), 372
Anna Catharina Hendrina (1816-), 360
Anna Catharina Hendrina (VAN DYK), 348, 360
Anna Catharina Louisa Jacoba (1872-), 379
Anna Catharina Margaretha (VAN VUUREN) (1848-1879), 373, 379
Anna Christina, 376
Anna Christina (DE JAGER), 352, 367
Anna Christina (GROENEWALD), 347, 356
Anna Christina Elizabeth (1801-), 353
Anna Christina Elizabeth (SWART), 350, 365
Anna Christina Elizabeth Cornelia (1827-), 369
Anna Christina Geertruyda (1827-), 356
Anna Christina Geertruyda (1860-), 373
Anna Dorothea (1777-), 345
Anna Dorothea (1780-), 347
Anna Elisabeth (Lizzie) (PRELLER) (1879-1976), 375, 380
Anna Elizabeth (1904-), 381
Anna Francina Elizabeth (GRESSE), 355, 371
Anna Geertruyda Elizabeth (1836-), 368
Anna Geertruyda Fredrika (OTTO) (1818-), 354, 371
Anna Geertruyda Gildenhuizen, 346, 353
Anna Geertryda Gildenhuizen, 346, 352
Anna Jacoba Susanna (1843-), 367
Anna Judith Geertruyda (KUUN), 353, 368
Anna Magdalena, 380
Anna Magdalena (1807-), 358
Anna Magdalena Elizabeth (LOULO), 375, 380
Anna Margaretha (1739-), 342
Anna Margaretha (1752-), 343
Anna Margaretha (1840-), 371

Anna Margaretha (SIEK) (1685-), 339, 340
Anna Margaretha Magdalena, 379
Anna Maria (1798-), 345
Anna Maria (1992-), 390
Anna Maria (HOGEWIND) (-1932), 379
Anna Maria (LE ROUX), 347, 354
Anna Maria (SMIT), 347, 356
Anna Maria Margaretha Alberta (1830-), 354
Anna Sophia Aletta (BEESLAAR), 369, 378
Anna Susanna (1819-1878), 351
Anna Susanna Wilhelmina (SERDYN), 359
Annaline (ODENDAAL) (1940-), 386, 390
Annelie (STRYDOM) (1971-), 384, 388
Arend Gildenhuisz (1673-), 339, 340
Barbara Ann (1975-), 390, 394
Barend (1682-1721), 339, 340
Barend (1719-1771), 340, 343
Barend (1742-), 342, 343, 344, 346
Barend (1772-1819), 346, 353
Barend (1774-), 346
Barend (1775-1841), 345
Barend (1779-), 344, 350
Barend Hendrik (1798-), 348
Barend Hendrik (1809-1878), 347, 356
Barend Hermanus (1815-1840), 354, 369
Barend Hermanus (1878-1916), 378
Barend Hermanus Nicolaas (1840-), 369, 378
Barend Johannes Hermanus (1837-1940), 369, 378
Barend Petrus, 364
Barend Petrus (1792-), 347, 354
Barend Petrus (1797-), 347, 356
Barend Petrus (1815-1868), 349, 363
Barend Petrus (1822-), 355
Barend Petrus (1833-), 356, 373
Barend Petrus (1864-), 363
Barend Petrus Albertus (1840-), 371
Barend Petrus Johannes (1812-), 353, 368
Barend Petrus Johannes (1832-), 354
Barendina Petronella (1852-), 363
Beatrix Geertruyda (GERBER), 356, 373
Bernd Gildenhausen (1610-), 339
Burgent Christiaan (1838-1895), 369
Burgert Wynand (1846-), 370
Cabous (1998-), 388
Carel Pieter, 379
Casparus Abraham (1814-), 357
Catharina Elizabeth (1775-), 345
Catharina Elizabeth (1813-), 354
Catharina Elizabeth (1837-), 365
Catharina Helena (OOSTHUIZEN), 349, 363
Catharina Helena Johanna (LUCAS), 374

Catharina Jacoba (BASSON), 357
Catharina Maria Christina (1824-), 356
Catharina Maria Johanna (1824-), 355
Catharina Susanna (Carien) (1931-), 382
Chanel (1990-), 392
Charles Jacobus (1822-), 357
Charmaine (1960-), 386, 391
Cheryl (1955-), 385
Christiaan Cornelis, 356
Christina Aletta, 374
Christina Berlina Geertruyda (1838-), 368
Christina Elizabeth (1838-), 366, 368
Christina Elizabeth Cornelia (1872-), 378
Christina Francina Johanna (1831-), 356
Christina Geertruyda (1769-), 346
Christina Geertruyda Maria (1813-), 355
Christina Johanna (1833-), 367
Christina Magdalena (1773-1839), 345
Christina Magdalena (1781-), 347
Christina Magdalena (1783-), 347
Christina Magdalena (RADYN), 340, 343
Christina Margaretha (1762-), 343
Christina Maria (1794-1837), 347
Christina Maria Geertruy (1817-), 353
Christoffel Christiaan (1814-), 359
Christoffel Christiaan (1831-), 374
Coenraad Johannes (1835-), 356
Cornelia (1768-), 345
Cornelia (SWART) (1720-1750), 340, 342
Cornelia Christina Johanna (1833-), 368
Cornelia Geertruida Anna (1847-), 365
Cornelia Geertruy (1773-), 344
Cornelia Geertruy (1808-), 350
Cornelia Geertruy (1809-), 351
Cornelia Geertruyda Dina (HUMAN), 352, 366
Cornelia Geertruyda Gildenhuizen, 353, 369
Cornelia Geertruyda Margaretha (1849-), 367
Cornelia Johanna, 366
Cornelia Johanna (1834-), 367
Cornelia Johanna (KLEYNSMIT), 346, 352
Cornelia Johanna (KLEYNSMIT) (1785-), 344, 351
Cornelia Johanna Alberta (1837-), 370
Cornelia Margaretha (1753-), 343
Cornelia Margaretha (1775-1839), 345
Cornelia Margaretha (1814-1858), 352
Cornelia Margaretha (SWART), 349, 364
Cornelia Margaretha Susanna (1823-), 350
Cornelia Susanna (1792-), 346
Cornelia Susanna (ERWEE) (1833-), 355
Cornelis Janse, 366
Cornelis Janse (1855-), 363
Cornelis Johannes, 356
Cornelis Michael, 380

Craig Jannie (1994-), 392
Danie, 376
Daniel Johannes, 374
Daniel Johannes (1852-), 370
David Jacobus (1815-), 358
David Jacobus Abraham (1820-), 359
Dawn (Dawnie) (1949-1954), 383
Debora (VILJOEN) (1901-), 376
Debora 'Debbie', 384
Deirdre (TAPSON - ADOPTED BURNS) (1967-), 384, 388
Delene Elizabeth (1945-), 383, 387
Dina Maria (1790-), 346
Dina Maria (1838-), 371
Dina Maria (UYS), 343, 345
Dina Maria (UYS) (-1839), 342, 344
Dina Maria Elizabeth (1842-), 370
Dina Maria Kleynsmit, 354, 370
Dirk Cornelis (1801-), 346
Dirk Cornelis (1858-1929), 362, 363, 376
Dirk Cornelis (-1965), 376, 381
Dirk Jacobus (1880-), 380
Dirk Johannes (1829-), 374
Dirkie Susanna Elizabeth (COETZEE), 349, 362
Dirkie Susanna Elizabeth (COETZEE) (-1899), 349, 362
Dorothy (HURST) (1919-2002), 381, 385
Eenst Hendrik Schalk, 382
Elena Catharina (1844-), 369
Elias Caledon (1824-), 351
Elias Jacobus, 377
Elias Jacobus (1809-), 350, 365
Elias Jacobus (1832-), 352
Elias Jacobus (1834-), 364
Elisabeth Catharina (1783-), 345
Elizabeth (Bess) (1904-), 380, 383
Elizabeth (SCHIKKERLING) (1858-), 362, 375
Elizabeth (TAILLEFER), 341, 343
Elizabeth Catharina (BLOEM), 354, 370
Elizabeth Catharina Christina, 379
Elizabeth Christina (VAN WYK), 344, 350
Elizabeth Debora (BOTHA), 347, 355
Elizabeth Dorothea Magdalena (1819-), 353
Elizabeth Elsabe (1774-), 348
Elizabeth Elsabe (1828-), 358
Elizabeth Elsabe Hendrina (1816-), 357
Elizabeth Helena, 363
Elizabeth Helena (1839-), 365
Elizabeth Helena (SWART), 350, 365
Elizabeth Johanna (1774-), 347
Elizabeth Johanna (1808-), 353
Elizabeth Johanna (1844-), 371
Elizabeth Johanna Magdalena (1825-), 356
Elizabeth Johanna Wesselina (1823-), 368

Elizabeth Luytjie (SWART), 347, 354
Elizabeth Magdalena (UNGERER), 356, 372
Elizabeth Maria, 362
Elizabeth Maria (1804-), 350
Elizabeth Maria (1817-), 354
Elizabeth Maria (1826-), 352
Elizabeth Maria (1869-1895), 378
Elizabeth Maria (MULLER) (1846-1895), 369, 378
Elizabeth Maria Helena (1788-), 349
Elizabeth Maria Susanna (1824-), 360
Elizabeth Rachel (1823-), 359
Elizabeth Rachel (DE VILLIERS), 348, 359
Elizabeth Susanna Johanna (1865-), 377
Eloise (HOWARD) (1972-), 386, 391
Elsa Johanna (1837-), 367
Elsabe (1738-), 343
Elsabe (MEYER) (1697-1721), 340, 341
Elsabe (SWART), 370
Elsabe (SWART) (1777-), 343, 347
Elsabe Barendina Francina (1867-1940), 377
Elsabe Cornelia (1810-), 353
Elsabe Cornelia (MATTHEE), 345, 352
Elsabe Cornelia Geertruy Anna (1835-), 352
Elsabe Dina (LOURENS - B3C5D2E?), 351, 366
Elsabe Dina (LOURENS), 352, 367
Elsabe Johanna Jacomina, 379
Elsabe Johanna Wesselina (1823-), 368
Elsabe Luitje (1836-), 371
Elsabe Luytje (1830-), 370
Elsebe (SWART), 346, 353
Elsie Johanna (1792-1857), 345
Elsje (1708-), 341
Elsje Gildenhuisz (1674-), 339, 341
Elsken (VON COESFELD) (-1680), 339
Ernestine Marlene (STEINBACH) (1934-2002), 381, 384
Eugene Constante (1965-), 389, 393
Evert Johannes (1876-), 380
Francina, 382
Francina Frederika (PRINSLOO), 366, 377
Francina Jacoba (LATSKY), 372
Francina Johanna (1831-), 364
Francois Lodewyk Johannes, 374
Frank, 376
Frans Jacobus Anthonie (1862-), 373
Frans Lodewyk (1847-), 372
Frans Lodewyk (1849-), 372
Frederik (1879-1895), 378
Frederik Johannes Jacobus (1837-), 367
Gabriel Petrus Stephanus (1823-), 354
Gabriel Stephanus le Roux (1818-), 354
Garth Patrick (1966-1995), 390

Geertruida Johanna (1841-), 363
Geertruy (1712-), 340
Geertruy Anna (1785-), 344, 351
Geertruy Anna (1805-), 349
Geertruy Anna (1809-), 352
Geertruy Anna Elizabeth (1853-), 367
Geertruy Anna Johanna (1833-), 362
Geertruy Johanna (1787-1888), 345
Geertruy Johanna (1806-), 353
Geertruyda (GROBBELAAR) (1753-1837), 345
Geertruyda (SWART) (1793-), 347, 355
Geertruyda Anna Johanna (1811-), 351
Geertruyda Elizabeth (1778-), 346
Geertruyda Jacoba (1844-), 371
Geertruyda Johanna, 364
Geertruyda Johanna (1813-1888), 349
Geertruyda Johanna (1829-), 355
Geertruyda Johanna Elizabeth (1846-), 363
Geertruyda Maria (1785-), 346
Geertruyda Susanna (1810-), 353
Geertruyda Susanna (WESSELS) (1746-), 343, 346
Geertruyda Wilhelmina (1852-), 372
Geertruyda Wouttrina (KRIEL), 374, 380
Gerhard - j1 (1937-), 386, 390
Gerhardus Bernardus - g7 (1850-1936), 366, 377
Gerhardus Bernardus - h4 (1878-1964), 377, 382
Gerhardus Bernardus - i1 (1910-1976), 382, 385
Gerrit (1718-), 341
Gesina (1804-), 357
Gesina Catharina, 379
Gesina Catharina (DE JAGER), 371, 378
Gideon Theodorus (1826-), 359
Guilliam (or Gideon) Theodorus (1793-), 348, 358
Guilliam Hendrik (1750-), 343, 349
Guilliam Hendrik (1795-), 349
Guilliam Hendrik (1815-), 360
Guilliam Jacob (1820-), 360
Guilliam Petrus (1809-), 360
Hannelie (BOOYSEN), 384, 388
Hans Jacob (1841-), 366
Hans Jacob (1842-1899), 371, 378
Hans Jacob (1855-), 370
Hans Jacob Blom, 379
Hans Jacob Stanford, 377
Helena Gerharda (KEULDER), 343, 348, 357
Helena Johanna (1825-), 360
Helena Johanna (VAN SCHALKWYK), 359, 374
Helena Maria (WALTERS), 343, 349
Helletta Lephina (1900-1901), 380
Hendrik, 382

Hendrik (1742-), 343, 348
Hendrik (1744-), 345
Hendrik (1775-), 344
Hendrik (1825-), 359
Hendrik (1827-), 352
Hendrik (b8) (1687-), 340, 341
Hendrik (c3) (1717-1770), 340, 342
Hendrik Abraham Johannes (1815-), 358, 374
Hendrik Abraham Johannes (1848-1881), 374, 380
Hendrik Abraham Johannes (1871-), 380
Hendrik Albertus (1717-), 341, 343
Hendrik Albertus (1778-), 348, 357
Hendrik Albertus (1779-), 349, 360
Hendrik Albertus (1781-1836), 348, 359
Hendrik Albertus (1801-), 357
Hendrik Albertus (1825-), 374
Hendrik Albertus (1853-1897), 375, 380
Hendrik Andries (1771-), 343, 347
Hendrik Andries (1794-), 347, 355
HendriK Andries (1827-), 356, 372
Hendrik Andries (1829-), 356, 372
Hendrik Andries (1831-), 355
Hendrik Andries (1860-), 373
HendriK Andries (1863-), 372
Hendrik Daniel (1844-), 365
Hendrik Gabriel Johannes Stephanus (1842-), 371
Hendrik Jacobus, 364, 377
Hendrik Jacobus (1785-1861), 345, 351
Hendrik Jacobus (1816-1857), 352, 366
Hendrik Jacobus (1816-1879), 349, 364
Hendrik Jacobus (1837-1924), 362, 375
Hendrik Jacobus (1841-), 364
Hendrik Jacobus (1844-), 367
Hendrik Jacobus (1849-), 362
Hendrik Jacobus (1902-1967), 380, 382
Hendrik Jacobus (Hennie) (1964-), 387, 392
Hendrik Johannes (1803-), 348, 357
Hendrik Johannes (1804-), 358
Hendrik Johannes (1806-), 357
Hendrik Johannes (1810-), 358
Hendrik Johannes (1825-), 351
Hendrik Johannes (1840-), 352
Hendrik Marthinus, 380
Hendrik Marthinus (1818-1897), 360, 375
Hendrik Oostwald Loubser (1831-), 360
Hendrik Petrus, 379
Hendrik Petrus (1782-1869), 346
Hendrina Jacoba, 364
Henricus Geldenhuisz ab1c3 (1705-), 340
Henrika Francina (CLOETE) (1908-), 382, 385
Hermann Erwin Rudibert 'Rudi' (1964-), 384, 388
Hester Johanna, 379

Hester Johanna (1781-), 345
Hilletje Aletta (SMIT), 348, 359
Hilletje Aletta Hendrina (1823-), 374
Hilletje Aletta Johanna (1813-), 360
Ian Jannie (1985-), 391
Izak, 384
Izak George, 376
Izak George (1958-), 384, 388
Izak George 'Sakkie', 381, 384
Jacoba Catharina, 379
Jacoba Cornelia 'Corli' (OPPERMAN) (1963-), 389, 393
Jacoba Margaretha (1839-), 363
Jacoba Margaretha (1849-), 363
Jacoba Margaretha (SWART), 352, 366
Jacoba Maria, 364
Jacobus, 347, 355
Jacobus (1712-), 341
Jacobus (1759-), 343, 347
Jacobus (1777-), 346
Jacobus (1839-), 371
Jacobus (1845-), 372
Jacobus Adriaan 'Kotie Jr' (1973-), 384
Jacobus Carel (1780-), 348
Jacobus Hendrik (1849-), 372
Jacobus Jacob Hendrik (1815-), 355, 371
Jacobus Johannes (1822-), 356
Jacobus Petrus Cornelis, 379
Jacobus Strydom 'Kotie Sr' (1929-2008), 381, 384
Jacomina Geertruyda (1834-), 355
Jake (2007-2007), 391
Jakobus Muller (1873-1895), 378
Jan Adriaan, 380
Jan Hendrik (1777-), 343, 348, 357
Jan Hendrik (1852-1867), 357
Jan Willemse Alexander, 377
Joan (COLLETT) (1943-), 385, 390
Joey (1883-), 375
Johan Diederik Ungerer (1865-), 372
Johanna (1720-), 341
Johanna (LE ROUX) (1748-), 344
Johanna (MATTHEE), 344, 350
Johanna (VERMAAK), 380, 382
Johanna Adriana (MULLHOLLAND), 357, 373
Johanna Aletta (1806-), 350
Johanna Catharina (GROBBELAAR) (1818-), 358, 374
Johanna Christina, 364, 377
Johanna Christina (GERMISHUIZEN), 353, 368
Johanna Christina Amelia (1861-), 374
Johanna Christina Magdalena (1864-), 378
Johanna Cornelia (1806-), 349
Johanna Cornelia (1843-), 352
Johanna Cornelia (1878-), 378
Johanna Dorothea (1798-), 346

Johanna Elizabeth (Linette) (KOTZÉ), 387, 392
Johanna Elizabeth Catharina, 379
Johanna Elsabe (1821-), 349
Johanna Geertruyda (GILDENHUIZEN) (1787-1888), 344, 349
Johanna Geertruyda Cornelia Susanna (1825-), 369
Johanna Hendrika Maria (1805-), 359
Johanna Hendrina (1790-), 349
Johanna Jacoba (1819-), 359
Johanna Jacomina Maria (1869-), 379
Johanna Jochemina (1845-), 370
Johanna Magdalena (1829-), 369
Johanna Magdalena (1836-), 365
Johanna Magdalena (1849-), 375
Johanna Magdalena (BRUYNZWART), 349, 360
Johanna Magdalena Susanna (1836-), 364
Johanna Margaretha (1720-), 340
Johanna Margaretha (1807-), 350
Johanna Margaretha Geertruyda (ROSSOUW), 349, 364
Johanna Maria (1813-), 360
Johanna Maria (or Adriana) (1850-), 373
Johanna Nicolaas (1873-), 380
Johanna Susanna (1808-), 350, 365
Johanna Susanna (BESTER), 350, 364
Johanna Susanna Elizabeth (1799-), 351, 366
Johanna Susanna Maria (1847-1881), 362, 376
Johannes (Jan) Albertus (1877-1944), 375, 380
Johannes (Jannie) Albertus (1989-), 392
Johannes Albertus, 364, 374
Johannes Albertus (1750-), 344
Johannes Albertus (1772-), 344, 350
Johannes Albertus (1786-), 349
Johannes Albertus (1803-), 350, 364
Johannes Albertus (1806-), 350, 365
Johannes Albertus (1807-1894), 349, 362
Johannes Albertus (1819-), 354
Johannes Albertus (1829-), 364
Johannes Albertus (1841-), 365
Johannes Albertus (1860-), 375
Johannes Albertus (1867-), 363
Johannes Albertus (1940-), 383, 386
Johannes Albertus (Gildenhuizen) (-1890), 352
Johannes Albertus (Jannie) (1937-1985), 383, 387
Johannes Albertus Bernardus (1840-), 362
Johannes Albertus Jochemus (1843-), 366
Johannes Hermanus (1839-), 356
Johannes Jacobus Carel (1819-), 357, 373
Johannes Joachemus (1834-), 371
Johannes Joachemus (1849-), 370
Johannes Joachimus (1802-1874), 354, 369
Johannes Urbanus, 367
Joy (GOLDSWORTHY), 386, 391
Judith (SMIT (SCHMIDT)) (1672-1713), 339, 340
Judith Christina Elizabeth (1857-), 372
Judith Cornelia Margaretha (1844-), 362
Judith Margaretha, 364, 376
Judith Margaretha (1812-1890), 352
Judith Margaretha (GILDENHUIZEN) (1812-1890), 349, 362
Judith Margaretha Elsabe (1855-), 367
Judith Wilhelmina (1857-), 372
Julia Lillian (DIPPENAAR) (1936-), 383, 386
Jurgen Johannes (1776-), 347, 354
Jurgen Johannes (1783-), 346
Jurgen Johannes (1798-), 347, 355
Jurgen Johannes (1802-), 354
Jurgen Johannes (1806-), 354, 370
Jurie, 384
Jurie Johannes, 379
Jurie Johannes (1744-1777), 343, 346
Jurie Johannes (1804-), 353, 369
Jurie Johannes (1827-), 371
Jurie Johannes (1833-), 370
Jurie Petrus Wessel (1838-), 354
Karen (DE WAAL) (1966-), 386, 392
Koeks NN (NN KOEKS), 381
Lauretta (1960-), 384, 388
Laurie 'Lorrie', 376, 381
Leizel, 388
Lena, 388
Letizia Clelia Ester (BOGGIO BOZZO) (1941-), 393
Linda Magdalene (GEERE) (1954-), 385, 390
Lisa (1964-), 390
Lorraine (1942-), 385
Louise (1987-), 391
Lourens (1777-1843), 344, 349
Lourens (1811-), 349, 362
Lourens (1837-), 364
Lourens (1864-), 362, 363
Lourens Johannes Albertus (1858-1864), 363
Lourens Pieter, 376
Lourens Pieter Arnoldus (1835-1902), 362, 375
Lucas Marthinus (1827-), 355
Lucy Hope (2009-), 391
Maatjie Catharina Jacoba (STEENKAMP) (1887-1918), 376, 381
Magdalena Catharina (1804-), 357

Magdalena Catharina Susanna (1847-), 373
Magdalena Francina (1823-), 358
Magdalena Jacoba (1829-), 356
Magdalena Johanna (LOUW) (1815-1899), 354, 370
Magdalena Wilhelmina (1871-), 363
Margareth Helene 'Marita' (1946-), 385, 389
Margaretha (1680-1684), 339
Margaretha (1684-), 339
Margaretha (1702-1770), 340
Margaretha (HOEFNAGELS) (1649-), 339
Margaretha Agatha Johanna (1821-), 354
Margaretha Christina Maria (1835-), 355
Margaretha Fredrika (1851-), 375
Margaretha Fredrika (1855-), 375
Margaretha Georgina Fredrika (RORICH), 360, 375
Margaretha Johanna (VAN AARDE), 343, 348
Margaretha Johanna Elizabeth ((GILDENHUIZEN) GELDENHUYS) (1809-), 358, 373
Margaretha Johanna Elizabeth (1809-), 357
Margaretha Johanna Elizabeth (1854-), 373
Margaretha Johanna Elizabeth (1870-), 379
Margaretha Johanna Martha (1806-), 357
Margaretha Judik Maria (1842-), 369
Margaretha Louisa Elizabeth (1791-), 348
Margaretha Maria, 374
Margaretha Maria (1829-), 352
Margaretha Maria (1877-1895), 378
Margaretha Maria (MAREE), 354, 369
Margaretha Maria (SCHEEPERS), 347, 356
Margaretha Maria (WESSELS) (-1801), 345
Margrijet Gildehuijsen (1700-), 340
Maria (1880-1901), 375
Maria Aletta (1808-), 353
Maria Catharina (1795-), 346
Maria Catharina (1827-), 370
Maria Catharina (1833-), 365
Maria Catharina (1843-), 367
Maria Catharina (REYNEKE), 348, 357
Maria Catharina Magdalena (1852-), 371
Maria Chistina (1817-), 355
Maria Chistina (1825-), 356
Maria Chistina (TESNER) (1757-), 343, 347
Maria Chistina Catharina (1822-), 356
Maria Dorothea (RADYN), 343, 347
Maria Dorothea Catharina Petronella (1828-), 354

Maria Dorothea Elizabeth (1826-), 355
Maria Elizabeth (1744-), 343
Maria Elizabeth (1770-), 345
Maria Elizabeth (1804-), 350
Maria Elizabeth (1807-), 360
Maria Elizabeth (1813-), 350
Maria Elizabeth (1860-), 362, 363
Maria Elizabeth (DIEDERIKS), 342, 344
Maria Elizabeth (MATTHEE), 344, 350
Maria Elizabeth Johanna (GUNTER) (-1862), 349, 363
Maria Elizabeth Magdalena Johanna (1843-), 363
Maria Elizabeth Susanna, 379
Maria Elizabeth Susanna (LUWES) (1851-1920), 371, 378
Maria Francina (VAN DYK) (-1849), 354, 370
Maria Johanna (1780-), 346
Maria Johanna (1790-), 346
Maria Johanna (COOPER), 356, 372
Maria Johanna Petronella (1810-), 358
Maria Magdalena (1821-), 351
Maria Magdalena (SWART), 351, 365
Maria Margaretha (1759-), 343
Maria Margaretha (1780-), 349
Maria Sophia (1859-), 374
Maria Susanna Wilhelmina (1911-1995), 381, 383
Maria Susanna Wilhelmina (SCHICKERLING) (1855-1890), 362, 376
Marianne (1986-), 388
Marion (MULLER), 386, 391
Marriët (KLOPPERS) (1979-), 384
Martha (1767-), 344
Martha Jacoba (1786-), 348
Martha Jacoba Aletta, 382
Martha Johanna (1842-), 371
Martha Johanna (1847-), 372
Martha Johanna (GRESSE), 355, 372
Martha Johanna Jacoba (1865-), 373
Martha Louisa (1812-), 358
Martha Louisa (1841-1874), 373
Martha Louisa (LE ROUX), 348, 358
Martha Maria (1856-), 373
Martha Maria (DU TOIT), 348, 358
Martha Susanna (VAN BILJON), 377, 382
Martina Jacoba (1875-), 378
Mathilda Marietta, 377
Mathilda Marietta (BEHR) (1836-), 365, 376
Matthew Dylan (Howard) (2001-), 391
Matthys Johannes Lourens (1841-), 368
Matthys Petrus Lourens (1878-), 379
Mattia Martha (LOTTER) (1916-1987), 381, 383

Mattys Johannes Lourens (1841-), 366, 377
Mercia Phillus (1911-), 381
Micayla Angelique (1994-), 394
Michael (1882-), 375
Michael Casparus, 375
Michelle (RODRIQUES) (1971-), 390
Michelle (TRICHARDT) (1968-), 389, 393
Myrl Maureen (1938-), 385, 389
Nicolaas Johannes (1820-), 355, 372
Nicolaas Johannes (1851-), 372
Nicolaas Johannes (1854-), 372
NN (NN), 362, 363, 376
NN (WESSELS), 381, 384
Oonagh Lorraine (1984-), 390
Oubaas (1885-), 375
P N Geldenhuyzen (NN), 378
Patricia 'Patsi', 381
Paul Preller (1966-), 386, 392
Petronella Daniellina Johanna, 374
Petronella Wilhelmina, 382
Petronella Wilhelmina (PRINSLOO), 366, 368, 377
Petrus (1740-), 343
Petrus Arnoldus, 366, 377
Petrus Arnoldus - d10 (1755-1836), 342, 344
Petrus Arnoldus - e5 (1785-), 344, 351
Petrus Arnoldus (1750-), 343
Petrus Arnoldus (1781-1846), 344, 350
Petrus Arnoldus (1785-), 346, 352
Petrus Arnoldus (1808-), 351, 352, 367
Petrus Arnoldus (1815-1846), 351, 365
Petrus Arnoldus (1831-1887), 365, 376
Petrus Arnoldus (1836-), 367
Petrus Arnoldus Jacobus (1838-), 366
Petrus Gideon (1862-), 373
Petrus Guilaume (1781-), 348, 357
Petrus Guillaume (1817-), 358
Petrus Guilliam (1812-), 357
Petrus Jacobus (1842-), 364
Petrus Johannes (1810-), 357
Petrus Jurie Hendrik (1835-), 354
Petrus Lafras (1803-), 353, 368
Petrus Lafras Daniel (1832-), 369
PetrusD Arnoldus - duplicated branch (1755-1839), 343, 345
Pey Malan (1970-), 386, 391
Philip R(udolph?), 356
Philip Rudolph (1825-), 355
Pieter (1879-), 375
Pieter Albertus Cornelis (1817-), 358
Pieter Arnoldus (1795-1852), 345
Pieter Arnoldus (1818-1838), 349
Pieter Burger (1884-1910), 378
Pieter Daniel, 374
Pieter Daniel (1828-1889), 359, 374
Pieter David (1822-), 359
Pieter Johannes (1782-), 348, 359

Pieter Johannes (1814-), 360
Pieter Johannes (1826-), 360
Pieter Lucas Jacobus (1840-), 369
Pietus Taillefer (1823-), 360
Preller Matt Wg Cdr (Rtd) (1943-), 338, 383, 386
Rachel Maria (1813-), 357
Rachel Maria Gildenhuisen, 358
Rachel Marie (JORDAAN), 348, 357
Raymond (1952-), 385
Renene Delene (1968-), 386, 391
Roelof Gabriel Thomas (1825-), 358
Ruben Benjamin (1916-1987), 381, 385
Ruben Neville (1940-), 385, 390
Russell Allan (1960-), 389, 393
Sachararya Magdalena (VAN DEVENTER), 347, 355
Sannie (BLOEMMENSTEIN), 375
Sara Johanna, 367, 375
Sara Johanna (1788-), 346
Sara Johanna (1807-), 351
Sara Johanna (1813-), 351
Sara Johanna (1835-), 370
Sara Johanna (EKSTEEN), 362, 375
Sara Johanna (Gildenhuyzen) (1751-1836), 351
Sara Johanna (KLEYNSMIT) (-1845), 354, 370
Sara Johanna (ODENDAAL) (1783-), 345, 351
Sara Johanna (SWART), 340, 342
Sara Magdalena (1785-), 345
Sarah Johanna Louw 'Sally' (GROENEWALD) (1914-1989), 381, 385
Sarel Johannes (1941-2008), 393
Sebastiaan 'Basie', 384
Sibella Jacoba (JORDAAN), 348, 359
Siebert Frederik, 380, 382
Simon David (1987-), 390
Sophia Barendina Jacoba, 364
Sophia Catharina (1808-), 359
Sophia Catharina (LOUBSER) (1756-1836), 343, 348
Sophia Catharina Elizabeth (1815-), 360
Sophia Catharina Elizabeth (1816-), 360
Sophia Margaretha (1817-), 351
Sophia Margaretha (1838-), 352
Sophia Sibella Helina (1811-), 359
Stephanus Jacobus Johannes (1830-), 355
Stephanus Johannes Lourens (1877-), 379
Stephanus Nicolaas (1829-), 360
Stuart William (1957-), 386, 391
Susanna Catharina (MALAN) (1945-), 383, 386
Susanna Dorothea (1790-1863), 345
Susanna Dorothea (1848-), 364

Susanna Elizabeth (1764-), 343
Susanna Elizabeth (LE ROUX), 348, 358
Susanna Geertruyda (1779-), 345
Susanna Hermina (1780-), 346
Susanna Hermina (1840-), 370
Susanna Jacoba (1721-), 341
Susanna Jacoba (1746-), 343
Susanna Jacoba (1811-1852), 360
Susanna Johanna, 364
Susanna Johanna (COOPER), 373
Susanna Johanna Maria (1870-), 378
Susanna Margaretha (1715-), 341
Susanna Margaretha (1771-), 346
Susanna Margaretha (1851-), 367
Susanna Margaretha (NIGRINI) (-1863), 359, 374
Susanna Maria, 375
Susanna Maria (1790-), 345
Susanna Maria (1821-), 352
Susanna Maria (MOOLMAN) (1754-), 343, 345
Susanna Maria Elizabeth (BESTER) (1886-1978), 377, 382
Susanna Maria Margaretha (1857-), 367
Susanna Petronella (1785-), 348
Susanna Petronella (1826-), 357
Susanna Petronella (1827-), 359
Susara Johanna (VAN VUUREN), 373, 379
Susara Johanna Elizabeth Elsabe, 362
Suzanne, 388
Teda Magdalena (1829-), 369
Theodorus Louis (1820-), 358
Theodorus Louis Hermanus (1796-), 348, 359
Theunis Gerhardus (1827-), 374
Veronica (ENGELBRECHT), 384
Veronica Joan (1970-), 390
Wanda (1949-), 385, 389
Wessel Johannes (1775-), 346, 352, 353
Wessel Johannes Willem (1832-), 368
Wilhelmina Johanna Hendrina (1835-), 369
Willem (1913-1988), 381, 385
Willem Johannes (1833-), 364
Willem Steenkamp (1943-), 385
Willem 'Willie' (1986-), 393
Wilna (BESTER), 384, 388
Wybrand Hebershausen, 379
Wynand Hendrik (1801-), 345, 352
Wynand Hendrik Johannes (1836-), 352
Zacharya Geertruy (Gildenhuizen) (1741-), 342
Zacharyas Johannes Wessel, 377
Zandalee (1992-), 394
Geldenhuys - places of birth, 19
Geldenhuys Bowling Club, 21
Geldenhuys crest, 135, 136
Geldenhuys Deep mine, 21, 22, 43, 55, 155

Geldenhuys Deep Mine, 21
Geldenhuys Estate, 33, 189
Geldenhuys genealogy, 396
Geldenhuys House, 21
Geldenhuys Interchange, 22, 33, 189
Geldenhuys Inter-change, 21
Geldenhuys intermarriages, 504
Geldenhuys International Registry, 14
Geldenhuys Louise, 188
Geldenhuys railway siding, 21, 22
Geldenhuys Road, 21, 22
Geldenhuys Station, 21
Geldenhuys Straat, 22
Geldenhuys street, 22
Geldenhuys Street, 22
Geldenhuys, Aap, 136
Geldenhuys, Aap and Meraai - Uncle to Jan, 174, 285
Geldenhuys, Abraham Jacubus, 19
Geldenhuys, Abraham Johannes, 406
Geldenhuys, Abram Carl Frederik Preller, 8, 9, 18, 20, 23, 31, 34, 60, 63, 66, 136, 137, 151, 153, 154, 162, 163, 180, 192, 200, 202, 225, 242, 281, 327, 400, 409, 451, 455, 462, 470
Geldenhuys, Adéle, 137, 200
Geldenhuys, Adiaan Izak (Attie), 407
Geldenhuys, Adraan Izak, 405
Geldenhuys, Adri, 137, 213
Geldenhuys, Adri and Alta, 148, 149, 150
Geldenhuys, Adriaan, 138, 153, 185, 408
Geldenhuys, Adriaan 'Attie', 408
Geldenhuys, Adriaan Hendrik, 163
Geldenhuys, Adriaan Izaac, 19
Geldenhuys, Adriaan Izak, 407
Geldenhuys, Adriaan Izak 'Aap', 170
Geldenhuys, Adriaan Johannes, 138
Geldenhuys, Adriaan Willem, 158
Geldenhuys, Adriaan Willem Steyn, 408
Geldenhuys, Adriana Alberta, 163
Geldenhuys, Albert Barend, 20, 28, 170, 216, 403
Geldenhuys, Albert Barends, 164
Geldenhuys, Albert Barends, Stamvader - also spelt Gildenhuisz or Gildenhuizen, 100
Geldenhuys, Albie, 138
Geldenhuys, Aletta, 138, 139, 404
Geldenhuys, Alfred, 139
Geldenhuys, Alicia, 149
Geldenhuys, Allan, 139
Geldenhuys, Almaré, 139
Geldenhuys, Alta, 137, 183
Geldenhuys, Alta and Adri, 209
Geldenhuys, Alwyn, 140
Geldenhuys, Amanda, 211
Geldenhuys, Amor, 140
Geldenhuys, Andre, 140, 191
Geldenhuys, André, 140, 147, 212

Geldenhuys, Andrea, 141, 206
Geldenhuys, Andrea 'Annie', 408
Geldenhuys, Andries, 141, 187, 206, 484
Geldenhuys, Andries Johannes, 163
Geldenhuys, Andries Lodewikus Stephanus, 163
Geldenhuys, Anel, 141
Geldenhuys, Angelique, 141
Geldenhuys, Anna Dorothea, 404
Geldenhuys, Anna Elizabeth, 8, 60, 327, 400, 409
Geldenhuys, Anna Francina, 404
Geldenhuys, Anna Jacoba Susanna, 405
Geldenhuys, Anna Margaretha, 404
Geldenhuys, Anna Margaretha Magdalena, 163
Geldenhuys, Anna Maria, 406
Geldenhuys, Anna Susanna, 406, 407
Geldenhuys, Annette, 11
Geldenhuys, Annette Galianos, 142
Geldenhuys, Anthonina, 142
Geldenhuys, Anthony, 142
Geldenhuys, Antonie Michael, 144
Geldenhuys, Anzelle, 142
Geldenhuys, Arend, 25
Geldenhuys, Barend, 11, 20, 25, 28, 30, 143, 216, 259, 303, 397, 403, 404
Geldenhuys, Barend - 2nd Generation, 143
Geldenhuys, Barend Hermanus, 143, 196, 437
Geldenhuys, Barend Johannes, 407
Geldenhuys, Barend Johannes Hermanus, 143
Geldenhuys, Barend Leendert, 404
Geldenhuys, Barend Nicolas Daniel, 143
Geldenhuys, Barend Petrus, 19, 37, 306, 412
Geldenhuys, Barend Petrus (Ben, 143, 144
Geldenhuys, Barend Petrus (Ben), 172
Geldenhuys, Barend Petrus 'Ben', 432
Geldenhuys, Barend Petrus Lodewyk, 120, 144, 152
Geldenhuys, Bernadette, 141
Geldenhuys, Beukes, 144
Geldenhuys, Bianca, 167
Geldenhuys, Bruce le Roux, 145
Geldenhuys, Bruwer, 145, 172
Geldenhuys, Burger - Springbok, 145
Geldenhuys, Byron, 145
Geldenhuys, Cabous, 102, 146, 168, 193, 211, 408
Geldenhuys, Carel Pieter, 163
Geldenhuys, Carienie, 146, 165, 243, 408, 475
Geldenhuys, Carin, 146
Geldenhuys, Caroli, 162
Geldenhuys, Casper Hendrik Jurie Johannes, 404
Geldenhuys, Catharina Magdalena, 405
Geldenhuys, Catharina Susanna (Carienie), 408, 475
Geldenhuys, Cathy, 159, 184
Geldenhuys, Cecelia, 161
Geldenhuys, Chanel, 5, 9, 18, 64, 118, 122, 123, 124, 146, 147, 198, 203, 242, 397, 400, 409, 446, 451, 463, 475
Geldenhuys, Chanté, 274
Geldenhuys, Charl, 147
Geldenhuys, Charles, 147
Geldenhuys, Charmaine, 63, 107, 124, 128, 148, 172, 397, 409, 446, 476
Geldenhuys, Charne, 148
Geldenhuys, Charné, 140, 147, 212
Geldenhuys, Chris, 148, 149, 206
Geldenhuys, Christelle, 149, 150
Geldenhuys, Christiaan, 149
Geldenhuys, Christina, 150
Geldenhuys, Christina Johanna, 404
Geldenhuys, Christina Johanna van Zyl, 404
Geldenhuys, Christina Magdalena, 404
Geldenhuys, Christo, 149
Geldenhuys, Christoffel, 149, 150
Geldenhuys, Cleopatra and Joanna, 220
Geldenhuys, Coenraad, 150
Geldenhuys, Cornelia, 404
Geldenhuys, Cornelia Dorothea van Eeden, 404
Geldenhuys, Cornelia Geertruida Anna, 406
Geldenhuys, Cornelia Geertruy, 406
Geldenhuys, Cornelia Geertruyda, 407
Geldenhuys, Cornelia Geertruyda Margaretha, 405
Geldenhuys, Cornelia Gertruida Dina, 407, 464
Geldenhuys, Cornelia Hendrina van Eeden, 404
Geldenhuys, Cornelia Margaretha, 404, 405
Geldenhuys, Cornelis Janse, 346, 370, 412, 415, 417, 420, 421, 436, 477
Geldenhuys, Cornelius, 150
Geldenhuys, Craig Jannie, 5, 9, 18, 64, 99, 107, 118, 122, 123, 124, 151, 198, 203, 242, 397, 400, 403, 409, 446, 451, 463, 477
Geldenhuys, Dane, 152
Geldenhuys, Danie, 120, 144, 152, 208, 209, 477
Geldenhuys, Daniel, 152, 157, 207, 404
Geldenhuys, Daniel Johannes Albertus, 437
Geldenhuys, Danuelle, 431
Geldenhuys, Darryn, 153
Geldenhuys, Dawn, 18, 64, 66, 137, 153, 242, 398, 410, 451, 478
Geldenhuys, Deirdre, 138, 153

Geldenhuys, Delene Elizabeth, 18, 46, 64, 66, 108, 109, 110, 111, 112, 115, 137, 153, 154, 174, 190, 195, 202, 205, 227, 242, 262, 265, 398, 401, 410, 440, 441, 451, 458, 463, 478
Geldenhuys, Delene, Elizabeth, 263
Geldenhuys, Deon, 154
Geldenhuys, Derek, 155
Geldenhuys, Dik Willem, 174, 285
Geldenhuys, Dina and Dirk, 155
Geldenhuys, Dirk, 156, 406
Geldenhuys, Dirk Christoffel, 412
Geldenhuys, Dirk Cornelis, 21, 22, 23, 44, 43, 55, 155, 160, 189, 410
Geldenhuys, Dirk Cornelius, 156, 160, 193, 195, 306, 411
Geldenhuys, Dorothea, 156
Geldenhuys, Dorothea M, 58
Geldenhuys, Douw, 157
Geldenhuys, Elandré, 431
Geldenhuys, Elias Jacobus, 406, 413
Geldenhuys, Elias Wynand, 406
Geldenhuys, Elisabeth 'Bess', 158
Geldenhuys, Elizabeth, 8, 297, 327, 400
Geldenhuys, Elizabeth (Bess), 383, 408, 479
Geldenhuys, Elizabeth 'Bess', 479
Geldenhuys, Elizabeth Catharina, 404
Geldenhuys, Elizabeth Catharina Christina, 163
Geldenhuys, Elizabeth Helena, 406
Geldenhuys, Elizabeth Maria, 406, 407
Geldenhuys, Ellen, 140
Geldenhuys, Elnarette, 152, 157
Geldenhuys, Eloise, 86, 198, 199, 273
Geldenhuys, Elsabe, 157
Geldenhuys, Elsabe Johanna Jacomina, 163
Geldenhuys, Elsie, 406
Geldenhuys, Elsie Johanna, 405
Geldenhuys, Elsje, 25, 26, 158
Geldenhuys, Elsje Johanna, 405
Geldenhuys, Ernastina Helena (Esté), 158
Geldenhuys, Esabe Cornelia Geertruy Anna, 406
Geldenhuys, Estie, 149
Geldenhuys, Eugene, 126, 158, 159, 184, 208
Geldenhuys, Evelyn, 170
Geldenhuys, Finette, 159
Geldenhuys, Flip, 195, 200
Geldenhuys, Francina Johanna, 406
Geldenhuys, Francois, 159
Geldenhuys, Frans, 159, 160, 184
Geldenhuys, Frans and Lou, 19
Geldenhuys, Frans D, 159
Geldenhuys, Frans Eduard, 21, 43, 155, 160, 189, 410
Geldenhuys, Frans Edward, 160

Geldenhuys, Fred, 431
Geldenhuys, Frederick Jacobus van Eeden, 404
Geldenhuys, Frederick Jacobus van Zyl, 404
Geldenhuys, Frederik Gerhardus, 217
Geldenhuys, Geertruy, 28, 404
Geldenhuys, Geertruy Anna, 405, 407
Geldenhuys, Geertruy Anna Johanna, 407
Geldenhuys, Geertruy Johanna, 405
Geldenhuys, Geertruy van Zyl, 404
Geldenhuys, Geertruyda Anna, 406
Geldenhuys, Geertruyda Johanna, 404, 405
Geldenhuys, General Jannie, 145, 171
  brother to Ouboet Johan, 172
  eldest son Harper Martin, 163
  father owned Dansfontein farm, 19
  father to Ben, 143
  father to Bruwer, 145
  visit to Heliopolous cemetry, 183
Geldenhuys, George, 144, 431
Geldenhuys, Gerda, 161
Geldenhuys, Gerhard, 23, 138, 161, 164, 187, 418, 421
Geldenhuys, Gerhard Robyn, 161
Geldenhuys, Gertuida Johanna, 162
Geldenhuys, Geruan, 162
Geldenhuys, Gesina Catharina, 163
Geldenhuys, Gideon Johannes van Eeden, 404
Geldenhuys, GJ, 65
Geldenhuys, Glen Llewellyn, 162
Geldenhuys, Gysbert J, 162
Geldenhuys, Gysbert Jacobus, 162
Geldenhuys, Gysbrant Jacobus, 65
Geldenhuys, Hanna, 163
Geldenhuys, Hans Jacob, 23, 163, 186, 428, 483
Geldenhuys, Hans Jacob Blom, 163
Geldenhuys, Hans Jacob Stanford, 413
Geldenhuys, Harper Martin, 163, 172
Geldenhuys, Heinrich, 164, 211
Geldenhuys, Helletje Levina, 8, 327, 408
Geldenhuys, Helletta Levina, 164, 400
Geldenhuys, Hendriëtte, 164
Geldenhuys, Hendrik, 31, 207, 397, 404, 406
Geldenhuys, Hendrik - 1687, 164
Geldenhuys, Hendrik - 1717, 164, 200
Geldenhuys, Hendrik - 1775, 164, 406
Geldenhuys, Hendrik 'Hennie', 166
Geldenhuys, Hendrik Albertus, 19
Geldenhuys, Hendrik and Nelie - Uncle to Jan, 174, 285
Geldenhuys, Hendrik Andreas, 144
Geldenhuys, Hendrik Barend, 28
Geldenhuys, Hendrik Daniel, 406

Geldenhuys, Hendrik 'Hennie' Jacobus, 172
Geldenhuys, Hendrik Jacobus, 8, 19, 20, 36, 40, 56, 60, 65, 146, 180, 182, 243, 297, 327, 397, 400, 405, 407, 413, 462, 484
Geldenhuys, Hendrik Jacobus - 1816, 164, 405
Geldenhuys, Hendrik Jacobus - 1837, 184, 192, 407
Geldenhuys, Hendrik Jacobus - 1841, 406
Geldenhuys, Hendrik Jacobus - 1844, 405
Geldenhuys, Hendrik Jacobus - 1849, 8, 200, 225, 327, 408
Geldenhuys, Hendrik Jacobus - 1902, 8, 327, 408
Geldenhuys, Hendrik Jacobus (Hennie), 408
Geldenhuys, Hendrik Jacobus (Hennie) 1964, 165
Geldenhuys, Hendrik Jacobus 1837-1924, 164
Geldenhuys, Hendrik Jacobus 1849-1930, 164
Geldenhuys, Hendrik Jacobus 1902-1967, 165
Geldenhuys, Hendrik Johannes, 406
Geldenhuys, Hendrik P., 166
Geldenhuys, Hendrik Petrus, 163, 405
Geldenhuys, Hendrik Willem van Eeden, 172, 421
Geldenhuys, Henricus, 403
Geldenhuys, Henriëtte, 158
Geldenhuys, Herman, 166, 167
Geldenhuys, Hermann Erwin Rudibert 'Rudi', 138, 167, 170
Geldenhuys, Hermann Erwin Rudibert 'Rudi', 408
Geldenhuys, Hester Johanna, 163, 404
Geldenhuys, Hilda, 167
Geldenhuys, Hope Lucy, 86
Geldenhuys, HP, 58
Geldenhuys, Ian, 9
Geldenhuys, Ian Jannie, 63, 168, 218, 409
Geldenhuys, Izak, 408
Geldenhuys, Izak George, 102, 146, 168, 170, 193, 211, 407
Geldenhuys, Izak George (Sakkie), 408
Geldenhuys, Izak George 'Sakkie', 209
Geldenhuys, Izak George "Sakkie", 168
Geldenhuys, Izak Jacobus, 144, 169, 306
Geldenhuys, J. C. M. - Petty Officer SA Navy, 183
Geldenhuys, J. N. - died 1945, 183
Geldenhuys, J.N. - died Boer War, Paardeberg, 183
Geldenhuys, J.N.E. – died 1942, 183
Geldenhuys, Jaco, 169
Geldenhuys, Jaco – 1986, 169
Geldenhuys, Jacoba Catharina,, 163
Geldenhuys, Jacoba Johanna Hendrina, 196
Geldenhuys, Jacobus, 403
Geldenhuys, Jacobus - 1908, 169
Geldenhuys, Jacobus - 1971, 169
Geldenhuys, Jacobus 'Jaco', 169, 191
Geldenhuys, Jacobus 'Kotie' Strydom, 168
Geldenhuys, Jacobus Adriaan 'Kotie', 170, 408
Geldenhuys, Jacobus Albertus van Eeden, 404
Geldenhuys, Jacobus Francois, 56, 93, 128, 170
Geldenhuys, Jacobus Jacob 'Kobus', 170
Geldenhuys, Jacobus Petrus Cornelis, 163
Geldenhuys, Jacobus Strydom (Kotie Sr), 170, 407
Geldenhuys, Jacobus Viljoen, 58, 170
Geldenhuys, Jacques, 171
Geldenhuys, Jaden, 431
Geldenhuys, Jake, 5, 18, 64, 70, 78, 88, 171, 199, 221, 222, 224, 398, 399, 401, 410, 449, 451, 455, 463, 487
Geldenhuys, James Henry, 144, 171, 187, 431
Geldenhuys, Jan, 78
Geldenhuys, Jan Hendrik, 404
Geldenhuys, Jan Petrus, 93
Geldenhuys, Jan Stael, 285
Geldenhuys, Jan Willemse Alexander, 413
Geldenhuys, Jana, 132
Geldenhuys, Janine and Marna, 150
Geldenhuys, Jannie - General SADF, 174
Geldenhuys, Jason, 172
Geldenhuys, JCM, 65
Geldenhuys, Jeanne, 159, 184
Geldenhuys, Jimmy, 431
Geldenhuys, JN, 65
Geldenhuys, JN - KIA, 65
Geldenhuys, Joan, 142
Geldenhuys, Joané, 166
Geldenhuys, Joelene, 245, 310, 466
Geldenhuys, Joey, 184
Geldenhuys, Johan, 211
Geldenhuys, Johan (Ouboet), 172
Geldenhuys, Johanna, 403
Geldenhuys, Johanna Christina, 405
Geldenhuys, Johanna Cornelia, 406, 407
Geldenhuys, Johanna Elizabeth (Joané), 165, 172, 408
Geldenhuys, Johanna Elizabeth Catharina, 163
Geldenhuys, Johanna Helena, 196, 437
Geldenhuys, Johanna Magdalena, 406
Geldenhuys, Johanna Magdalena Susanna, 406
Geldenhuys, Johanna Margaretha, 28

Geldenhuys, Johanna Petronella Elizabeth, 404
Geldenhuys, Johanna Susanna, 406
Geldenhuys, Johanna Susanna Elizabeth, 414
Geldenhuys, Johanna Susanna Maria, 408
Geldenhuys, Johannes (Jan) Albertus - 1877, 8, 327
Geldenhuys, Johannes (Jan) Albertus - 1940, 63, 66, 124, 137, 148, 151, 180, 182, 198, 210, 242, 312, 397, 400, 409, 445, 451, 462
Geldenhuys, Johannes (Jannie) Albertus - 1937, 180
Geldenhuys, Johannes (Ou Dad) Albertus - 1877, 19, 23, 33, 42, 45, 46, 53, 54, 56, 59, 60, 63, 65, 125, 136, 137, 151, 164, 173, 174, 175, 176, 178, 179, 180, 196, 200, 225, 281, 282, 285, 293, 297, 397, 400, 408, 462
Geldenhuys, Johannes (OuDad) Albertus - 1877, 8, 327
Geldenhuys, Johannes 'Hannes', 183
Geldenhuys, Johannes Albertus, 39, 40, 45, 56, 60, 125, 164, 192, 405, 421, 434, 450, 489
Geldenhuys, Johannes Albertus - 1722, 173
Geldenhuys, Johannes Albertus - 1743, 172, 173, 404
Geldenhuys, Johannes Albertus - 1750, 8, 18, 31, 33, 151, 172, 173, 188, 200, 225, 327, 397, 406
Geldenhuys, Johannes Albertus - 1772, 173, 406
Geldenhuys, Johannes Albertus - 1786, 435
Geldenhuys, Johannes Albertus - 1803, 173, 406
Geldenhuys, Johannes Albertus - 1806, 413
Geldenhuys, Johannes Albertus - 1807, 8, 33, 36, 151, 173, 200, 225, 327, 397, 407
Geldenhuys, Johannes Albertus - 1815, 406
Geldenhuys, Johannes Albertus - 1819, 421
Geldenhuys, Johannes Albertus - 1828, 406
Geldenhuys, Johannes Albertus - 1829, 407
Geldenhuys, Johannes Albertus - 1841, 406
Geldenhuys, Johannes Albertus - 1849, 412
Geldenhuys, Johannes Albertus - 1860, 407
Geldenhuys, Johannes Albertus - 1867, 412
Geldenhuys, Johannes Albertus - 1877, 192
Geldenhuys, Johannes Albertus - 1890, 405
Geldenhuys, Johannes Albertus - 1937, 146, 165, 408
Geldenhuys, Johannes Albertus - 1940, 66, 75, 90, 263, 267
Geldenhuys, Johannes Albertus - 1989, 182, 408
Geldenhuys, Johannes Albertus Bernardus, 18, 407
Geldenhuys, Johannes Albertus Jochemus, 414
Geldenhuys, Johannes Hendrik, 20
Geldenhuys, Johannes Joachim, 142
Geldenhuys, Johannes Norval - 1918, 183
Geldenhuys, Johannes Urbanus, 405
Geldenhuys, Johannes Wilhelmus, 143
Geldenhuys, Joleen, 93, 147, 172, 198, 245, 275, 309, 310, 311, 421, 437, 454, 490
Geldenhuys, Joseph, 144
Geldenhuys, Jovan, 212
Geldenhuys, Joy, 308
Geldenhuys, Joyce, 184
Geldenhuys, Jozua, 201
Geldenhuys, Judith, 43
Geldenhuys, Judith Cornelia Margaretha, 408
Geldenhuys, Judith Margaretha, 164, 405, 407, 464
Geldenhuys, Judith Margaretha Elsabe, 405
Geldenhuys, Julanda, 127, 185
Geldenhuys, Julia Lilian, 148
Geldenhuys, Julia Lillian, 491
Geldenhuys, Jurie, 146, 168, 185, 186, 285, 408
Geldenhuys, Jurie Johannes, 142, 163, 185, 186
Geldenhuys, Karli-Mari, 137, 195
Geldenhuys, Kayla, 186
Geldenhuys, Lauretta, 408
Geldenhuys, Leane, 172
Geldenhuys, Lena, 102, 134, 146, 168, 211, 408
Geldenhuys, Lianca and Chante, 197
Geldenhuys, Liane Muir, 186
Geldenhuys, Lianke, 431
Geldenhuys, Lida, 186
Geldenhuys, Liesel, 168
Geldenhuys, Liezel, 211, 407
Geldenhuys, Linette, 187
Geldenhuys, Lisa, 161
Geldenhuys, Liza, 187
Geldenhuys, Lize, 210
Geldenhuys, Logan, 431
Geldenhuys, Loretta, 190

Geldenhuys, Lou-Ann, 187
Geldenhuys, Louis, 166, 188, 431
Geldenhuys, Louis Botes, 187, 431
Geldenhuys, Louis Frederick Botes, 171, 187, 235, 431
Geldenhuys, Louise, 9, 63, 187, 188, 218, 409, 431
Geldenhuys, Lou-Mare, 141
Geldenhuys, Lounette, 139
Geldenhuys, Lourene, 412
Geldenhuys, Lourens, 8, 19, 20, 21, 22, 33, 43, 56, 155, 159, 162, 188, 190, 327, 407, 410, 411, 412
Geldenhuys, Lourens - 1777, 200, 225, 405
Geldenhuys, Lourens (Louw) - 1864, 189, 190
Geldenhuys, Lourens Dirk Cornelis, 189, 410
Geldenhuys, Lourens Johannes Albertus, 412
Geldenhuys, Lourens Pieter, 60, 407
Geldenhuys, Lourens Pieter Arnoldus, 56, 58, 190, 407, 492
Geldenhuys, Louw, 190
Geldenhuys, Louw Hermanus, 407
Geldenhuys, Luan, 431
Geldenhuys, Lucas Marthinus, 191
Geldenhuys, Lucas Martinus, 404
Geldenhuys, Lucille, 140, 191
Geldenhuys, Lucy, 191
Geldenhuys, Lucy Hope, 5, 9, 19, 64, 70, 85, 199, 203, 221, 222, 398, 400, 401, 410, 441, 442, 449, 451, 455, 463, 492
Geldenhuys, Lue-Ann, 141
Geldenhuys, Luka, 208
Geldenhuys, Lukas Marthinus, 169
Geldenhuys, M, 64, 191
Geldenhuys, Madelene, 217
Geldenhuys, Madiah, 170
Geldenhuys, Magda, 137
Geldenhuys, Marelie, 183
Geldenhuys, Margaretha, 25, 162, 403
Geldenhuys, Margaretha Helene 'Marita', 115, 192
Geldenhuys, Margaretha Maria, 406, 407
Geldenhuys, Maria, 192
Geldenhuys, Maria Catharina, 406
Geldenhuys, Maria Elizabeth, 404
Geldenhuys, Maria Elizabeth Gildenhuijze, 404
Geldenhuys, Maria Elizabeth Susanna, 163
Geldenhuys, Maria Magdalena, 404
Geldenhuys, Maria Susanna Wilhelmina, 8, 60, 157, 192, 327, 400, 409, 462
Geldenhuys, Mariaane, 168
Geldenhuys, Mariana, 20, 192
Geldenhuys, Marianne, 193, 211, 407
Geldenhuys, Marile, 192, 210
Geldenhuys, Mario, 187, 431

Geldenhuys, Mariza, 193, 212
Geldenhuys, Martelize, 139
Geldenhuys, Martha, 93, 404
Geldenhuys, Martin, 193
Geldenhuys, Martin Lourens, 183, 194, 243
Geldenhuys, Matthew, 86
Geldenhuys, Matthew Dylan, 5, 70, 128, 199, 205, 221, 222, 305, 398, 399, 401, 410, 441, 442, 449, 451, 455, 463, 465, 495
Geldenhuys, Matthys Johannes, 100, 406
Geldenhuys, Mauritz Herman Otto, 143, 194
Geldenhuys, Meryerene, 195
Geldenhuys, Michael, 410
Geldenhuys, Michael Conrad, 137, 195
Geldenhuys, Michael Francis, 159, 195
Geldenhuys, Michael Petrus, 137
Geldenhuys, Michael Pieter, 195, 200
Geldenhuys, Michiel Casparus, 407
Geldenhuys, Mike, 196
Geldenhuys, Mila Cecilia, 161
Geldenhuys, Monica, 194, 196
Geldenhuys, Mynhardt, 320
Geldenhuys, Mynhart, 197
Geldenhuys, Myrl Maureen, 156, 192, 195, 208, 385, 389, 393, 411, 496
Geldenhuys, Nicolaas, 123, 144, 172, 196, 245, 310, 311, 355, 363, 372, 378, 405, 412, 420, 421, 430, 431, 432, 433, 435, 437, 454, 465, 466, 473, 486, 489, 496, 500
Geldenhuys, Nicolaas Daniel, 172
Geldenhuys, Nicolaas Daniël, 196
Geldenhuys, Nicoleen, 197
Geldenhuys, Nicolette, 197
Geldenhuys, Okkie, 147, 198
Geldenhuys, Oubaas and Bessie - parents of Jan, 164, 173, 174, 200, 285
Geldenhuys, P A., 201
Geldenhuys, Paul Preller, 9, 63, 122, 124, 146, 151, 182, 198, 263, 397, 400, 409, 446, 451, 463, 497
Geldenhuys, Peter, 198, 199
Geldenhuys, Petrus Arnoldus, 19, 20, 413, 414
Geldenhuys, Petrus Jacobus, 406
Geldenhuys, Petrus Johannes, 166, 405
Geldenhuys, Pey Malan, 9, 18, 33, 35, 36, 64, 66, 70, 73, 74, 76, 77, 78, 79, 85, 86, 99, 113, 128, 162, 165, 171, 191, 198, 199, 200, 202, 205, 218, 221, 222, 227, 255, 256, 257, 263, 270, 277, 305, 398, 399, 401, 403, 409, 442, 449, 451, 455, 463
descendant of Albert Barend Gildenhuizen, 9
descendant of Jacques Malan, 9
Geldenhuys genealogy, 409

Geldenhuys genealogy, abreviated, 398
genealogy lettering, 403
genealogy listing, 455
Lotter gegealogy, 451
Malan genealogy, 455
Malan genealogy,abbreviated, 399
Preller genealogy, 463
Geldenhuys, Philip, 137, 200
Geldenhuys, Pieter, 18, 46, 56, 59, 164, 174, 197, 200, 201, 320, 410, 475, 492, 498
Geldenhuys, Pieter Arnoldus, 405
Geldenhuys, Pieter Daniel, 421
Geldenhuys, Pieter David, 201
Geldenhuys, Pieter Gabriël Jacobus, 201
Geldenhuys, Pieter Jacobus, 201
Geldenhuys, Pieter Theunis Blomerus, 196
Geldenhuys, Preller Matt, 2, 9, 18, 60, 63, 64, 66, 68, 69, 70, 74, 85, 86, 93, 98, 128, 154, 182, 199, 200, 202, 204, 219, 223, 225, 227, 232, 233, 236, 242, 244, 245, 257, 258, 259, 260, 262, 266, 267, 281, 309, 312, 315, 316, 341, 409, 450, 451, 455, 463, 469
 COIN Course, 202
 Geldenhuys genealogy - abbreviated, 397
 married Rina Malan, 399
 Preller genealogy, 401
Geldenhuys, Quintin, 203
Geldenhuys, R, 204
Geldenhuys, Regardt, 102, 204
Geldenhuys, Renene Delene, 19, 44, 64, 66, 68, 69, 74, 77, 78, 98, 154, 204, 205, 223, 225, 227, 231, 234, 263, 319, 398, 399, 401, 402, 409, 450, 451, 455, 459, 463, 468
 Amazing Grace, 204
 befriended Stott's, 74
 Chipinga home, 44
 daughter-in-law to Bill Jelley, 68
 emigrated to New Zealand, 77, 78
 Estcourt school, 204
 female names, 19
 genealogy listing, 398, 399, 402, 409, 450, 451, 455, 459, 463, 468
 Gentle Annie, 205
 Gentle Annie re-union, 78
 nursing at Grey's, 74
 Russell school, 73
 sponsorship, 85
Geldenhuys, Renier, 141, 148, 206
Geldenhuys, Resje, 206, 211
Geldenhuys, Riaan, 152, 157, 207, 208
Geldenhuys, Rian, 207
Geldenhuys, Riandi, 152, 207
Geldenhuys, Rina, 73, 75, 77, 78, 81, 86, 90, 246, 437

Geldenhuys, Rina (Susanna Catharina nee Malan - Oumie), 203, 205, 227, 228, 229
Geldenhuys, Rina -1986, 207
Geldenhuys, Robyn, 161
Geldenhuys, Ronald Olwen Rhodesian - KIA, 207
Geldenhuys, Ruben, 208
Geldenhuys, Ruben Benjamin, 411
Geldenhuys, Ruben Neville, 411
Geldenhuys, Russell, 208
Geldenhuys, Ryno, 208
Geldenhuys, Sara Johanna, 405, 406, 407
Geldenhuys, Sara Magdalena, 404
Geldenhuys, Schikkie, 192, 209
Geldenhuys, Sebastiaan 'Basie', 209, 408
Geldenhuys, Sharika, 212
Geldenhuys, Shawn, 209, 274
Geldenhuys, Simeon, 137, 148, 209
Geldenhuys, sisters - Suzanne, Marianne and Liezel, 146
Geldenhuys, Sonja, 152, 209
Geldenhuys, Sophia Margaretha, 406
Geldenhuys, Sorina Nefdt, 193, 212
Geldenhuys, Stephan, 192, 210
Geldenhuys, Stephanie, 431
Geldenhuys, Stephen Lee, 211
Geldenhuys, Steve, 210
Geldenhuys, Stuart William, 63, 107, 124, 168, 188, 210, 218, 397, 409, 446, 500
Geldenhuys, Susan, 159
Geldenhuys, Susanna Christina, 404
Geldenhuys, Susanna Dorothea, 405
Geldenhuys, Susanna Geertruyda, 404
Geldenhuys, Susanna Maria, 404, 405, 407
Geldenhuys, Susanna Maria Margaretha, 405
Geldenhuys, Susanne, 168
Geldenhuys, Susara Johanna Elizabeth Elsabe, 407
Geldenhuys, Suzanne, 185, 211, 407
Geldenhuys, Teresa, 211
Geldenhuys, Tersia, 207, 211
Geldenhuys, Tertia, 147
Geldenhuys, Timotheus 'Timo', 412
Geldenhuys, Tol, 285
Geldenhuys, Ulrich, 109, 211
Geldenhuys, Vanessa, 140, 147, 212
Geldenhuys, Victor, 212
Geldenhuys, Wb, 212
Geldenhuys, Wedré, 193, 197, 212
Geldenhuys, Wessel, 139
Geldenhuys, Willem, 195, 208, 411
Geldenhuys, Willem Johannes, 406
Geldenhuys, Wimpie, 150
Geldenhuys, Wybrand Hebershausen, 163
Geldenhuys, Wynand Hendrik, 406
Geldenhuys, Wynand Hendrik Johannes, 406
Geldenhuys, Zach, 208

Geldenhuys, Zacharia Geertruida van Eeden, 404
Geldenhuys, Zacharya Geertruy, 404
Geldenhuys, Zacharyas Johannes Wessel, 413
Geldenhuys, Zane, 137, 149, 213
Geldenhuys,Pey Malan, 314
Gemini, 77
Genealogy
  Geldenhuys, 396
  Malan, 398
  Moodie, 401
General Jannie
  attended Lourens Geldenhuys funeral, 190
Gentle Annie, 78, 205, 231
George Pigot, 266
Georgetown, 22
GERBER
  Beatrix Geertruyda, 356, 373
Gerber, Rina, 81, 85, 213, 243, 247, 262, 454
German, 9, 11, 16, 18, 24, 25, 28, 121, 213, 216, 237, 238, 241, 244
Germany, 9, 11, 24, 31, 32, 33, 60, 64, 100, 110, 117, 121, 124, 199, 222, 241, 242, 288, 298, 303, 403, 439, 452
GERMISHUIZEN
  Johanna Christina, 353, 368
GERMISHUYSEN
  Cornelia Geertruy (GELDENHUYS) (1808-), 350
  Petrus Johannes, 350
Germishuysen, Petrus Johannes, 406
Germiston, 21, 22, 189, 218
Gilbert and Sullivan - school plays, 202
Gildehaus - town in Germany, 170
Gildenhaus, Casper Heinrich, 32, 213
Gildenhuijsen, Margareta - associated with van den Heyden, 15
Gildenhuis, Elizbe, 213, 214
Gildenhuis, Irma, 214
Gildenhuis, John, 214
Gildenhuis, Louise, 214
Gildenhuis, Tiaan, 214
Gildenhuisz, Albert Barends, 196, 339, 470
Gildenhuisz, Barend, 214
Gildenhuisz, Lourens, 397
GILDENHUIZEN
  Johanna Geertruyda (1787-1888), 344, 349
  Judith Margaretha (1812-1890), 349, 362
GILDENHUIZEN (GELDENHUYS)
  Anna Dorothea (GELDENHUYS) (1780-), 347
  Wessel Johannes, 347
Gildenhuizen, Albert Barend - Geldenhuys Stamvader, 9, 15, 23, 24, 25, 26, 31, 32, 100, 117, 118, 143, 151, 158, 200, 213, 214, 216, 225, 396, 403, See Geldenhuys Stamvader Albert Barend
Gildenhuizen, Christina Francina, 217
Gildenhuizen, Elsje, 11, 15, 26, 158, 216, 403
Gildenhuizen, Geertruy Johanna, 8, 33, 327
Gildenhuizen, Hendrik, 8, 327
Gildenhuizen, Hendrik Jacobus, 188
Gildenhuizen, Johanna Geertruyda, 407
Gildenhuizen, Johanna Geertryda, 188
Gildenhuizen, Johanna Gertruyda, 397
Gildenhuizen, Johanna Susanna Elizabeth, 32, 216
Gildenhuizen, Judith Margaretha, 8, 33, 36, 327, 397, 407
Gildenhuizen, Lourens - 1777, 405
Gildenhuizen, Margaretha, 11, 173
Gildenhuys, Albertus Barend, 214
Gildenhuys, Anna, 28
Gildenhuys, Bart, 215
Gildenhuys, Bernard, 215
Gildenhuys, Celia, 215
Gildenhuys, Chris, 215
Gildenhuys, Christiaan, 215, 216
Gildenhuys, Clive Peter, 216
Gildenhuys, David, 215, 216
Gildenhuys, Eric, 213
Gildenhuys, Johannes 'Jannie', 216
Gildenhuys, Tanya, 214
Gildenhuysen, Hendrik Willem, 216
Gildenhuysen, Johanna Margaretha, 11
Gildenhuysen, Margaretha, 216
Gildenhuyzen, Elsje, 216
  married van der Heiden, 216
Gildenhuyzen, Sara Johanna, 405
Gildenhuyzen, Geertruy Anna, 32
Gildenhuyzs, Matthys Johannes, 15, 32, 100, 216
  grandfather was Juli van der Kaap, 217
Gildenhuyzs, Matthys Johannes - uncertain parentage, 23
Gill, Elsa, 217
GILLESPIE
  Angela Adriana de Jager (GELDENHUYS) (1908-), 381, 384
  George, 381, 384
  Ian, 385
Gilson, Dennis Michael, 218
Gilson, Marcelle, 64, 70, 77, 199, 218
Gimpe, Hans Jurgen, 30
Gladdedrif, 281, 282, 283
Gladdedrift, 20, 40, 41, 108, 125, 282
Gladdedrift farm, 19, 21, 108
Glastonbury, Alison, 119
Glenn, Jane Sarah, 440
Goblet, 198
Godlieb, Jan, 111
Gold Mines, Simmer & Jack, 22

GOLDSWORTHY
  Joy, 386, 391
Goldsworthy, Joy, 63, 168, 188, 210, 218, 267, 391, 409, 490
Gooding, Adam, 218
Gooding, Adam Daniel, 106
Gooding, Benjaman Luke, 106, 219
Gooding, Braydon, 218
Gooding, Braydon Lee, 106, 219
Gooding, Cherie Jane, 106, 219
Gooding, Dean Mark, 106, 219
Gooding, Katelyn, 218
Gooding, Marissa, 218
Gooding, Ronald Mark, 106, 219, 274, 499
Goosen, Anthonie, 282
Gough, Colonel, 46
Gouritz River, 24
Gous, Martinus, 404
Government Chambers, 284
Graaff-Reinet, 9, 20, 32, 33, 34, 56, 57, 58, 128, 170, 294, 432, 439, 441, 442, 443, 460
Graham, Colonel John, 33, 117
Grand Prior Award - to Courtney Jelley, 85
Great Boer War, 45
Great North Road, 22
Great Trek, 34, 291, 292, 293
GRESSE
  Anna Francina Elizabeth, 355, 371
  Frans Lodewyk, 372
  Martha Johanna, 355, 372
Greyling, Barend, 281
Greyling, Lourens Petrus, 41
Greymouth, 78, 205
Greys Hospital, 74, 204
Greytown, 74, 315
Griffiths, Cherie, 219, 305, 465
GROBBELAAR
  Evert, 374
  Geertruyda (1753-1837), 342, 345
  Johanna Catharina (1818-), 358, 374
Grobbelaar, Christiaan, 174
Grobbelaar, Geertruida, 188
Grobbelaar, Geertruyda, 31, 33, 349
Grobbelaar, Geertuida, 8, 327
Grobbelaar, Ilse, 162
Grobbelaar, Judine, 247
Grobler, Judith Fredrika Salomina, 217
Groene Valley, 9, 31, 124
Groene Valley farm, 21
GROENEWALD
  Anna Christina, 347, 356
  Sarah Johanna Louw 'Sally' (1914-1989), 381, 385
Groenewald, Coen, 55, 59, 170
Groenewald, Maria Magdalena, 185
Groenewald, Sarah Johanna Louw 'Sally', 195
Groenfontein farm, 20

Groenpunt POW camp, 59, 156, 190
Grootdraai farm, 41, 108
Grootrivier, 122, 250
Grootvaders Bosch, 266
Grootvaders Bosch farm, 44
Grove, Sophia, 111
Gulih, Helena, 16
Gun Hill, 46
GUNTER
  Maria Elizabeth Johanna (-1862), 349, 363
Gurney, Nerissa, 130
Gurney, Nerissa Geldenhuys, 220
Guy, Richard, 74
Gwelo, 19, 64, 66, 69, 70, 154, 199, 202, 204, 231, 232, 233, 254, 255, 257, 260, 262, 263, 316, 398, 399, 401, 402, 409, 449, 451, 455, 459, 463, 468
Haarlem, 9, 11, 26, 216, 403
Haenertsburg, 246
Hakuna Matata, 181, 198
Halle, 9, 11, 31, 33, 124, 288, 294, 298
Hameln, 315
HAMMAN
  Jan Jurgen (1705-1788), 340
  Johanna Margaretha (GELDENHUYS) (1720-), 340
Hamman, Elizabeth Susanna, 105
Hamman, Jan Jurgen, 143
Hamman, Johann Jürgen, 11
Hamman, Johannes Jurgens, 106
Hamman, Wynand Allen, 105
Happy Vale farm, 20
Harding, 74
Harding, Monja, 133, 220
Harrison, George, 155
Harrison, Wilfred, 57
Hartley, 282
Hattiesburg, 76
Hawkins, Leonard, 30
Haynes, Desirée, 220, 264
Hayward, Maria Elizabeth 'Elbe', 129
HEEMS
  Guilliam Hendrik, 341
  Susanna Jacoba (GELDENHUYS) (1721-), 341
Heidelberg, 21
Helm, Geertruyd, 11, 303
Helm, Johann, 11
HELMS
  Geertruy (1664-1715), 340
Helms, Geertruy, 25, 143, 403
Hendriksz, Alida, 30
Hendriksz, Hendrik, 30
Henry, Sir John - OFS President, 38
Herberg Oranje, 46
Herder, Getrude Augusta Maria, 217
Hermann Erwin Rudibert 'Rudi', 116
Hertog, Jan, 143

Herts, 14
Herwerden's widow, 24
HEYNE
  Christoffel Christiaan, 350, 365
  Johanna Susanna (GELDENHUYS) (1808-), 350, 365
  Matthys Johannes (1822-), 365
Heyne, Christoffel Christiaan, 406
Heyneman, Jacoba Petronella, 400
Highflats, 74
Hippo Valley, 205, 231
Hirohito, Emperor, 64
Hitler, Adolf, 64
Hobolochitty, 76
HOEFNAGELS
  Arend, 339
  Grietje (CORNELIS), 339
  Margaretha (1649-), 339
Hoefnagels, Arend, 25, 100
Hoefnagels, Margaretha, 8, 9, 25, 32, 100, 143, 158, 164, 196, 214, 216, 327, 339, 396, 403
Hoffman, 30
Hofmeyr, Hester Sophia, 122
Hofmeyr, Jan Hendrik, 122
Hofmeyr, Onze Jan JH, 30
HOGEWIND
  Anna Maria (-1932), 379
Hogge, WS, 36
Holfontein farm, 19
Holland, 9, 18, 20, 25, 26, 27, 30, 34, 100, 121, 143, 292, 396, 452, 457
Hollywood, 77
Holy Land, 77
Hoogenhout, Dr NM, 290
Hoogenhout, Imker, 160
Hoppe, Catharina Maria, 121
Hot Springs, 66
Hotnots, 32
Hottentot Coloured, 34
Hottentots Holland, 9, 26
HOWARD
  Eloise (1972-), 386, 391
  Ingrid Stella (ESTMENT) (1950-), 391
  Kenneth Steve (1947-), 391
Howard crest, 221
Howard, Dylan, 221, 449, 479
Howard, Eileen, 222
Howard, Eloise, 64, 70, 85, 113, 128, 171, 191, 199, 200, 205, 221, 222, 273, 305, 314, 398, 399, 401, 409, 442, 451, 455, 463, 465
  married Pey, 221
Howard, Eloise Eloise, 449
Howard, James Alexander 'Johnny', 222, 487
Howard, June, 222, 273, 314
Howard, Kenneth Steve, 222, 449, 491

Howard, Matthew Dylan, 5, 70, 128, 199, 205, 221, 222, 305, 398, 399, 401, 410, 441, 442, 449, 451, 455, 463
Howard, Steve Kenneth, 221
Howick, 74
Hubble, Jack, 74
Hugo, Andrew, 240
Hugo, Magdalena, 52
HUMAN
  Cornelia Geertruyda Dina, 352, 366
  Cornelia Margaretha (GELDENHUYS) (1775-1839), 345
  Dirk, 345
  Elisabeth Catharina (GELDENHUYS) (1783-), 345
  Pieter Gerhardus, 345
Human, Cornelia Geertruyda Dina, 367, 405
Human, Joan, 149
Human, Pieter Gelhardus, 404
Hunt, Lauren, 149
HURST
  Dorothy (1919-2002), 381, 385
Husing, Henning, 16, 26, 27, 30
ijacop. See Jacobus van der Heiden or Heyden
Illovo Beach, 124, 267
India, 24, 26, 28, 53, 55, 56, 59, 100, 117, 136, 164, 174, 178, 179, 180, 200, 217, 289, 298
International Registry, 14
Israel, 77, 199
Italy, 16, 60, 64, 160, 192, 279, 284, 298
Ixopo, 74
Jacobs, Jakkie, 82
Jacobs, Susanna Sophie, 241
Jan Lotter, 136, 180, 451
Jan Smuts Airport., 22
Jansen, Ernest George, 294
Jason Froneman, 99
Jehle, Walter, 222
Jelle, Thomas, 9, 234, 449
JELLEY
  Brendan Vaughan (1996-), 391
  Courtney Sacha (1993-), 391
  Grahame David (1959-), 386, 391
  Margaret Mary Elaine (WHITELEY) (1935-), 391
  Renene Delene (GELDENHUYS) (1968-), 386, 391
  William Patterson (1935-2009), 391
Jelley crest, 223
Jelley, Basil Owen, 223
Jelley, Brenda, 223
Jelley, Brenda Merle, 223
Jelley, Brendan Vaughan, 5, 9, 30, 42, 64, 65, 70, 77, 78, 85, 86, 90, 91, 99, 203, 204, 205, 222, 223, 224, 225, 226, 227, 228, 229, 230, 232, 234, 242, 258,

266, 319, 398, 399, 401, 402, 409, 450, 451, 455, 459, 463, 468, 474
  genealogy listing, 398, 399, 401, 402, 450, 451, 459, 463, 468
Jelley, Brian Godfrey, 226
Jelley, Cecil William Gordon, 223, 225, 226, 232, 234, 449, 475
Jelley, Courtney, 77
Jelley, Courtney Sacha, 5, 9, 18, 30, 42, 64, 65, 69, 85, 86, 90, 91, 202, 203, 204, 205, 223, 224, 226, 227, 230, 232, 234, 242, 258, 266, 276, 319, 398, 401, 402, 409, 450, 451, 455, 459, 463, 468, 477
Jelley, Godfrey, 9
Jelley, Grahame David, 44, 64, 69, 77, 86, 91, 98, 204, 205, 223, 225, 227, 231, 232, 234, 319, 398, 399, 401, 402, 409, 450, 451, 455, 459, 463, 468, 483
Jelley, Jean, 79
Jelley, Keith Brian, 79, 232, 314, 319, 450, 468
Jelley, Leonard William, 232
Jelley, Mary Margaret 'Molly', 223, 232
Jelley, Renene Delene, 86, 91
Jelley, Valentine Godfrey, 226, 234
Jelley, William Paterson, 9, 68, 69, 71, 79, 81, 225, 231, 232, 233, 319, 402, 459, 468
Jelley, William Patterson, 223
Jellie, Andrew, 225, 234, 449
Jellie, William of Carnwath, 225, 234, 449
Jelly, William, 9, 16, 225, 449
Jely, Thomas, 9, 16, 225, 234, 449
Jerusalem, 77
Jewel of Africa, 66
Johannesburg, 19, 21, 22, 43, 54, 55, 63, 64, 75, 128, 136, 155, 160, 168, 172, 180, 188, 189, 190, 198, 218, 226, 242, 245, 253, 258, 265, 279, 284, 291, 292, 310, 397, 400, 409, 410, 411, 419, 445, 451, 454, 455, 462
Johnson-Worboys, Heather, 234, 319, 468
Joleen Geldenhuys, 437
Joleen van Aardt, 490
Jonson, John Watson, 11
JORDAAN
  Jannie, 383
  Margaretha Johanna Martha (GELDENHUYS) (1806-), 357
  Paul, 383
  Rachel Marie, 348, 357
  Sibella Jacoba, 348, 359
  Stephanus, 357
Jordaan, Elzet, 408
Jordaan, Eunice Elizabeth, 160
Jordaan, Johannes 'Jannie' Albertus, 158
Jordaan, Johannes Albertus, 408
Jordaan, Juan, 408
Jordaan, Lulu, 158, 408
Jordaan, Marie Louise, 408
Jordaan, Paul, 158, 408
Jordaan, Paul Christiaan Gideon Steyn, 8, 60, 158, 327, 400, 408, 462
Jordaan, Pieter Christian Gideon Steyn, 297
Joubert, General Piet, 52, 189, 456
Joubert, Hendrina, 52
Joubert, Susanna Magdalena, 162
Jourdan, Jean, 11, 25, 259
Jourdan, Pierre, 25, 259
Jules road, 22
Juli v.d. K. = Juli van die Kaap, 32, 217
Jury, Marilyn Rosemary, 119
Kala, Anton J, 234
Kaltwasser, SJ, 41, 204
Kariba, 68, 105, 199, 202, 204, 258, 263
Karoi, 68, 105, 106, 258
Kassel, 9, 110, 439
Kata, Anton J, 319
Katbos View, 57, 286
Katbos View farm, 19
Kellar, Coral Evelyn, 465
Kemp, Catharina Magdalena, 405
Kemp, Ernest, 228
Kempton Park, 22, 455
Kenilworth farm, 21
Kennedy, President John F, 77
Kenya, 241, 298, 299, 448, 465
Kerkenberg, 37, 144
KEULDER
  Carel Hendrik Francois, 358
  Elizabeth Elsabe (GELDENHUYS) (1828-), 358
  Helena Gerharda, 343, 348, 357
Keulen, 24, 117
Keurskrif vir Kroonstad, 303
Keyser, Adriana Martha Maria (Max), 8, 165, 327
Keyser, Adrianna Martha Maria, 400, 462
KEYZER
  Adrianna Marta Maria (Max), 380, 382
Khoikhoi, 24, 32
Kimberley, 48, 50, 51, 55, 136, 165, 174, 245, 282, 284, 419, 431, 437, 453
King, Dick, 35
Kismayu, 298, 299
Kitchener, Lord, 21, 55, 58
Klaas, Zusanna, 16
Klerksdorp, 52, 179, 180, 192, 242, 256, 282, 284, 408, 455
KLEYNSMIT
  Adriaan Johannes, 350
  Cornelia Johanna, 346, 352
  Cornelia Johanna (1785-), 344, 351
  Cornelia Margaretha Susanna (GELDENHUYS) (1823-), 350
  Sara Johanna (-1845), 354, 370
Klipdrift farm, 19

Kliprivier farm, 19
Kloeten, Fijtie, 16
Kloof, 31, 38, 78
Kloofendal, 22
KLOPPERS
   Marriët (1979-), 384
Kloppers, Marriët, 170, 235, 408
Kluyts, Annalise, 11
Kluyts, Curly, 11
Kluyts, Theo, 11
Knierim, Delmarie, 211
Knoetze, Willem, 283
Knoop, Louisa Regina, 171, 187, 235, 431
Knorhoek farm, 20
Knox, General Charles, 54
Knutsford farm, 21
Kock, Judge, 21, 55
Koekemoer, Anna Catharina, 403
KOK
   Joseph P, 363
   Magdalena Wilhelmina (GELDENHUYS) (1871-), 363
Kok, Adam, 143
Kokstad, 74
Kombisa farm, 20
Koos Kombuis, 187, 390
KOTZÉ
   Johanna Elizabeth (Linette), 387, 392
Kotze, Chritiaan Petrus, 196
Kotzé, Johanna Elizabeth (Linette), 158, 165, 408
Kotzé, Linette, 166, 172, 182
KRAHNER
   Barbara Ann (GELDENHUYS) (1975-), 390, 394
   Campbell Fred (2007-), 394
   Jason Neil (1972-), 390, 394
   Leah Ann (2004-), 394
Kranskop, 74
Krause, Dr. F.E.T., 21, 55
Krause, Judge, 21
Krause, Roxanne, 153
KRIEL
   Elizabeth Elsabe (GELDENHUYS) (1774-), 348
   Geertruyda Wouttrina, 374, 380
   Theodorus Louis, 348
Kromkuil farm, 19
Kromspruit, 165, 166, 180, 408
Kromspruit farm, 19
Kroonstad, 14, 19, 20, 22, 23, 33, 35, 36, 38, 39, 40, 41, 50, 53, 54, 58, 60, 65, 108, 125, 136, 143, 156, 172, 174, 176, 178, 179, 180, 181, 190, 192, 200, 254, 282, 283, 284, 285, 286, 397, 403, 407, 408, 409, 412, 413, 417, 461, 462, 463
Kruger, Bellinda Geraldine, 186
Kruger, Dorothea 'Dot' Johanna, 107, 235
Kruger, Paul, 52, 155, 291

Kruger, Ronel, 211
Krugersdorp, 22, 41, 144, 169, 189, 306, 432
Kuala Lumpur, 78
KUHN
   Geertruyda Johanna (GELDENHUYS) (1829-), 355
   Paul Lodewyk, 355
Kuhn, Carlé, 216
Kuilsrivier, 122
Kuiperskraal farm, 20
Kunn, Stephanus, 404
KUUN
   Anna Judith Geertruyda, 353, 368
   Anna Margaretha (GELDENHUYS) (1739-), 342
   Stephanus, 342
Kwaggasdrift farm, 19
Kyle Dam, 66, 242
KYPER
   Hester, 341
La Bella, Vinny, 235, 304
La Motte, 9, 25, 259, 452
la Motte farm, 20
Lace Mine, 283, 284
LACOCK
   Hendrik Johannes (1868-1952), 379
   Johanna Elizabeth Catharina (GELDENHUYS), 379
Ladismith, 245, 289, 310, 454, 461
Lake Bangwelo, 66
Lake Mrewa, 66
Lake Nyasa (now Malawi), 66
Lampula, 181
Lanark, CR, 234, 449
Land-en-Zeesicht, 20, 28, 30
Langdeel farm, 19
Langebaan, 181, 198
Langlaagte, 44, 155, 189, 190
LATSKY
   Francina Jacoba, 372
Laurel, 75, 76
ldenhuys, Lourens - 1777, 407
le Long, Elizabeth, 11, 25
le Long, Isabeau, 399
le Long, Isabeau Elisabeth, 452
le Roux
   Aletta Magdalena Susanna (1913-1997), 338
LE ROUX
   Abraham, 358
   Aletta Magdalena Susanna (1913-1997), 386
   Anna Maria, 347, 354
   Johanna (1748-), 342, 344
   Martha Louisa, 348, 358
   Susanna Elizabeth, 348, 357, 358
le Roux - meaning of Surname, 18
le Roux crest, 236

le Roux,, 236
le Roux, "Lettie" Aletta Magdalena Susanna, 248, 256, 269
le Roux, Aletta Magdalena Susanna, 238, 248, 259, 260, 262, 399
le Roux, Daan, 66
le Roux, Johanna, 8, 31, 33, 173, 188, 327, 397, 405, 406
le Roux, Johannes, 237, 238
le Roux, Pieter Hugo, 210
le Roux, Susanna Catharina, 246
le Roux, Susanna Catharina 'Suster', 238
Lean, Major, 54
Leeuenjacht farm, 20
Leeuwenvallei farm, 20
Legden, 9, 25, 100, 216, 396, 403
Lekkerlewe, 165, 180
Lekkerlewe farm, 19
Lesotho, 36, 39
Libertas farm, 20
Lichtenburg, 20, 51, 61, 236, 248, 250, 251, 252, 253, 254, 255, 257, 258, 260, 262, 399, 451, 453, 454, 455, 456
Liebenberg crest, 238
Liebenberg, Meisie, 238, 239, 263
Liebenberg, Philip, 239
Liebenberg, Piet, 238
Liebenberg, Tara, 239
Liesbeeck Valley, 25
Liesbeek River, 24, 117
Linden, 22, 190, 504
Liversage, Maud Nellie, 114, 440
Livingstone, 163, 226
Lobengula, Zulu Chief, 42, 292
Lock crest, 239
Lock, Aletta, 236
Lock, Anna, 239
Lock, Helena, 240
Lock, Helena Alberta, 81, 85, 455
Lock, Hugo, 82, 240, 241, 485
Lock, Ina, 82, 240
Lock, Jacqueline Joan, 240
Lock, Shelley Jacqueline, 240
Lock, Willem, Tom and Shelley, 82
Lombard, Piet S, 55
Longmarket Street, 74
Lorenco Marques, 34
LOTTER
   Jan, 383
   Mattia Martha (1916-1987), 381, 383
   NN (NN), 383
Lotter - meaning of Surname, 18
Lötter crest, 241
Lotter, Carel David
   married Catharina van Echten, 242
Lotter, Christoffel, 241
Lotter, Johannes Casparus, 241
Lotter, Johannes George, 241
Lotter, Lourens Johannes, 242

Lotter, Mathia Martha, 455
Lotter, Matt, 31, 128
Lotter, Matthia Martha, 9, 63, 153, 154, 180, 202, 242, 400, 409
Lotter, Matthias, 9, 31, 241, 242
Lotter, Matthias - stamvader, 451
Lotter, Matthias Johannes, 241
Lotter, Mattia Martha, 136, 397, 495
Lotter, Salomon, 242
Lotter, Willem Godfried, 241, 242
Loubcher, Nicolette, 242
Loubscher, Nicolette, 185
LOUBSER
   Sophia Catharina (1756-1836), 343, 348
Loubser, Nicholas, 197, 413
Louis Geldenhuys., 188
Louise Geldenhuys, 492
Louisiana, 76
LOULO
   Anna Magdalena Elizabeth, 375, 380
LOURENS
   C P, 346
   Cornelia Susanna (GELDENHUYS) (1792-), 346
   D C, 346
   Dina Maria (GELDENHUYS) (1790-), 346
   Elsabe Dina, 352, 367
   H J, 346
   Johanna Dorothea (GELDENHUYS) (1798-), 346
   Johanna Magdalena (1808-1861), 370
LOURENS - B3C5D2E?
   Elsabe Dina, 351, 366
Lourens, Anelia, 243
Lourens, Elsabe Dina, 138
Lourens, Hendrik, 281
Lourens, Hester Anna, 24, 117
Lourens, Maritza, 81, 243, 455
Lourensford farm, 21
LOUW
   Albertus Wynand (1769-), 360
   Daniel Johannes, 370
   Jacobus Arnoldus (1802-1856), 360
   Jan (1674-1770), 340
   Johanna Magdalena (BAARD), 360
   Magdalena Johanna (1815-1899), 354, 370
   Margaretha (GELDENHUYS) (1702-1770), 340
   Susanna Jacoba (GELDENHUYS) (1811-1852), 360
   Susanna Johanna (NN), 370
Louw Geldenhuys Primary School, 22, 190
Louw Geldenhuys View, 21
Louw, Anna Elizabeth, 30
Louw, Elisabeth Judith, 121
Louw, Jan, 25
Louw, Jannis, 193
Louw, Susanna Gertruida, 122

Luanshya, 66, 124, 153, 180, 181, 398, 409, 410, 445, 451, 462
LUCAS
  Catharina Helena Johanna, 374
Lunar Buggies, 77
Lupani Detachment, 68
LUWES
  Maria Elizabeth Susanna (1851-1920), 371, 378
Luwes, Maria Elizabeth Susanna, 163
Lydenberg, 36
Maasdorp, Arnoldus, 28
Macaulay, Gillian, 305, 465
Macrae, Alphonso, 408
MacRae, Alphonso, 243
Macrae, Alphonso 'Phonnie', 146
Magersfontein, 23, 48, 50, 174, 200
Magic Kingdom, 76
Magoebaskloof, 246
MAHNKE
  Chris, 390
  Oonagh Lorraine (GELDENHUYS) (1984-), 390
Mahon, Colonel Bryan T, 52
Main Reef Road, 22
Malan
  Aletta Magdalena Susanna (le Roux) (1913-1997), 338
  Francois Daniel (1907-1988), 338
  Susanna Catharina (1945-), 338
MALAN
  Aletta Magdalena Susanna (LE ROUX) (1913-1997), 386
  Francois Daniel (1907-1988), 386
  Susanna Catharina (1945-), 383, 386
Malan - meaning of Surname, 18
Malan crest, 243, 244
Malan genealogy, 398
Malan, "Lettie" Aletta Magdalena Susanna, 75, 81, 82, 236, 245, 251, 252, 253, 254, 255, 256, 309, 310, 454
Malan, Adolf, 244
Malan, Aletta Magdalena, 465
Malan, Aletta Magdalena Susanna, 81
Malan, Amanda, 81, 90, 246, 257, 262, 307, 455
Malan, Carel Wynand, 52
Malan, Catharina, 30
Malan, Damien and Cloe, 81
Malan, Daniel, 20, 30, 246
Malan, Daniel Francois., 246
Malan, Daniel Gerhardus, 20, 257
Malan, Daniel Johannes, 20
Malan, Daniel Josias, 20
Malan, Daniel Stefanus, 61, 256, 260
Malan, Daniel Stephanus, 20, 258
Malan, Daniel Stephanus - 1801, 200, 225, 399, 453
Malan, Daniel Stephanus - 1842, 456

Malan, Daniel Wouter, 20
Malan, David, 23, 29, 30, 34, 200, 225, 247, 320
Malan, David - 1708, 247, 399, 452
Malan, David - 1765, 20, 399, 453
Malan, David Daniel, 20, 39
Malan, David Jacobus, 20, 258
Malan, David Jakob, 61, 256
Malan, DF, 22, 290
Malan, Eddie Deon, 213, 247, 455
Malan, Elizabeth, 258
Malan, Elsa-Lou Cornelia, 110, 247, 274, 455, 480
Malan, Felix Festus, 62, 256
Malan, Francois, 81, 90, 236, 484
Malan, Francois Daniel, 213, 236, 246, 481
Malan, Francois Daniel - 1844, 20, 456
Malan, Francois Daniel - 1907, 20, 23, 200, 225, 248, 256, 258, 259, 260, 262, 399, 454
  1907 - 88, 61
  Chipinga - Knutsford farm, 21
  farmed Rusthof in 1941, 20, 21
  Levensverhaal - Life story, 248
Malan, Francois Daniel - 1949, 81, 82, 236, 240, 246, 257, 455
Malan, Francois Daniel - 1976, 257, 455
Malan, Francois Daniel Johannes - 1794, 453
Malan, Francois Stephanus, 257, 259
Malan, Frans, 81, 236, 257
Malan, Franscois Daniel, 315
Malan, Frederik Jakobus, 20, 61, 256
Malan, General Wynand Charl, 52
Malan, Gert Johannes, 62, 256
Malan, Gertruida "Gerta" Johanna, 68, 81, 82, 85, 105, 106, 236, 251, 253, 254, 258, 454
Malan, Gertruida Johanna, 61, 482
Malan, Gideon van Eeden, 62
Malan, Gideon Van Eeden, 256
Malan, Heila Magdalena, 62, 256, 258, 454, 456
Malan, Hendrik, 248
Malan, Hendrik Francois, 20, 92, 96, 262
Malan, Hendrik Francois - 1833, 200, 225, 258, 399, 453
Malan, Hendrik Francois - 1878, 61, 200, 225, 258
Malan, Hendrik Francois - 1879, 399, 454
Malan, Hendrik Francois - 1904, 61, 256
Malan, Hendrik Francois - 1943, 68, 81, 82, 85, 213, 243, 253, 259, 454, 484
Malan, Hendrik Philippus, 19, 20
Malan, Hercules, 259
Malan, Hercules Philip, 34, 41, 52, 58
Malan, Hermanus Johannes, 20
Malan, Jacob, 20
Malan, Jacobus, 20, 29, 41, 247, 320

Malan, Jacobus Bernandus, 256
Malan, Jacobus Bernardus, 62
Malan, Jacobus Francois, 20
Malan, Jacobus Hermanus, 20, 30
Malan, Jacobus Johannes - 1739, 20, 259, 399, 453
Malan, Jacques, 11, 30, 200, 225, 259
Malan, Jacques - stamvader, 9, 11, 20, 25, 28, 257, 399, 452
Malan, Johanna Maria, 125
Malan, Johannes Augustinus, 34, 41
Malan, Johannes Jacobus, 20
Malan, Komdt Abram Hugo, 52
Malan, Lian Jandra, 247
Malan, Monique and Dillan, 81
Malan, Phil, 81, 94, 257
Malan, Philip, 90, 262, 455
Malan, Philip - son of Hendrik, 81, 243, 455
Malan, Philip Johannes, 119, 120, 260, 262, 316
Malan, Philippus Johannes, 247, 497
Malan, Philippus Johannes - 1945, 23, 68, 82, 236, 253, 254, 255, 260, 261, 262, 455
Malan, Philipus Johannes, 315, 316
Malan, Phillip, 81
Malan, Phillipus Johannes, 467
Malan, Riaan, 29, 247, 320
Malan, Roux, 81, 262
Malan, Roux Daniel, 110, 301, 455
Malan, Salome, 119, 260
Malan, Stephanus, 20, 258, 294
Malan, Susanna Catharina, 9, 27, 64, 66, 68, 81, 85, 94, 96, 157, 199, 200, 204, 223, 225, 227, 236, 246, 258, 259, 262, 266, 269, 315, 316, 397, 399, 401, 409, 450, 451, 455, 463
Malan, Willem Stefanus, 61, 256
Malan,Francois Daniel, 68, 81, 248, 259
Malanskraal, 22
Malanspruit, 22
Malaya, 199
Malcolmsen, Margaret, 266, 402
Malgasrivier, 19, 33, 173, 397, 405, 407
Malgasrivier farm, 19
Malherbe, DF, 290
Malherbe, Dion, 60, 409
Malherbe, Dr DF du T, 217
Malherbe, Dr WMR, 290
Malherbe, Gideon, 60, 400, 409, 462
Malherbe, Jan, 60, 409
Malherbe, Willem, 60, 409
Malvern East, 21, 22
Manzini, 63, 210, 409
Maputo, 34
MARAIS
  Aletta Johanna (1787-), 344, 350
Marais, Anna, 259
Marais, Elisabeth, 247, 399

Marais, Eugene N., 289
Marais, W, 30
Mardi Gras, 76
MAREE
  Margaretha Maria, 354, 369
Maree, Maria Magdalena, 404
Maree, Wessel, 208
Marias, Eugene, 289
Marias, Maria, 259
Maritz, Gerrit - Voortrekker, 34
Maritz, Louise, 109
Martins, Marié, 172
Masonite, 73, 74, 75, 76, 78, 202
MATCHETT
  Joyce Edith, 387
Matchett, Joyce Edith, 265, 458, 490, 496
Matebeleland, 34
Mathee, Johanna, 173
Mathee, Sophia Margaretha, 173
Matheson, Brenda Joan, 114
MATTHEE
  Elizabeth Helena (GELDENHUYS), 363
  Elsabe Cornelia, 345, 352
  Jacobus Nicolaas, 363
  Johanna, 344, 350
  Maria Elizabeth, 344, 350
Matthee, Esabe Cornelia, 406
Matthee, Johanna Magdalena, 173
Matthews, Wayne, 238, 263
Mbeya, 181
MCCOLL
  Delene Elizabeth (GELDENHUYS) (1945-), 383, 387
  Joyce Edith (MATCHETT), 387
  Peter John, 387
  Stuart John (1949-), 383, 387
McColl crest, 264
McColl, Davyd, 220
McColl, Davyd John Charles, 264, 265
McColl, Delene, 59, 78, 86, 114
McColl, Isis, 264
McColl, Joyce Edith, 265
McColl, Peter John, 265, 497
McColl, Stuart John, 35, 42, 46, 78, 86, 154, 205, 220, 264, 265, 387, 398, 401, 410, 451, 458, 500
McKenna, Jock, 233
McLaren, Mick, 68, 232
McQueen, Brian, 317
McRoberts, Mary, 265
Meaning of Surname, 18
Mears Shuttle, 76
Meerland, Jan, 16, 26
Melbourne, 232
Melius, Eleonora, 399
Melkhoutboom farm, 44
Melville Kopies, 22
Melville Koppies, 43, 35, 412
Menzel, OF, 28

Mercury, 77
Meredith, Martin, 147
Merindol, 9, 25, 259, 452
Methuen, General, 46, 47, 48
Methuen, Lord, 46
MEYER
  Elsabe (1697-1721), 340, 341
Meyer, Adriaana Wilhelmina Petronella, 407
Meyer, Field Cornet, 189
MGM Studios, 76
Mica Point, 68, 105, 258
Middelburg, 100, 412
Milton, Mary Victoria, 222
Mini-All Black - Brendan Jelley, 99
Miracle Memorial, 78
Mississippi, 75, 76
Moddergat, 122
Modderrivier farm, 19
Modderspruit, 53, 289
Moerdijk, Gerard, 294
Mokihunui, 78
Moller, Elisabeth Magdalena, 399
Momsen, meneer, 249
Moodie - Meaning of Surname, 18
Moodie crest, 266
Moodie genealogy, 401
Moodie Trek, 266, 269, 459
Moodie, Benjamin, 21, 33, 42, 44, 225, 231, 232, 266, 402, 458, 474, 490
Moodie, Benjamin - Stamvader, 266
Moodie, Donald, 21, 33, 44, 266, 267
Moodie, Dunbar, 21, 33, 44, 188, 267, 268, 269
Moodie, George Benjamin Dunbar, 266, 267
Moodie, James, 44, 225, 266, 269, 319, 458, 487
Moodie, James Benjamin Donald, 402
Moodie, Margery Hester, 42, 225, 402, 459
Moodie, Thomas, 23, 42, 266, 268, 269
Moodie, Thomas - Groot Tom, 269
Moodie, William James Dunbar, 267
Moodies Rest farm, 21
Mooi River, 22
MOOLMAN
  Catharina Elizabeth, 365
  Susanna Maria (1754-), 343, 345
Moordspruit, 34
Morgenster, 25, 28, 29, 30, 247, 259, 320
Morgenster farm, 20
Morkel, Catharina, 30
Morkel, Daniel, 30
Morkel, Philip, 30
Morkels, Catharina, 29
Morris, Donald R., 35, 42
Moshoeshoe, Basotho Chief, 38, 39
Mostert, Hilletje, 121
Motke, Pieter, 269, 311

Mould, Sgt, 244
Mount Kilamanjaro, 110, 304
Mozambique, 68, 69, 78, 226, 232
Mueller crest, 270
Mueller, Marion, 70
Mueller, Marion Janine, 270
Muir-Geldenhuys, Liane, 270
Muirhead crest, 270
Muirhead, Bevan Glyn, 113, 271, 474
Muirhead, Byron, 271, 474
Muirhead, Kim Chanelle, 271, 491
Muirhead, Lynn, 272, 492
Muirhead, Neil Wynn, 272, 496
MULDER
  Anna Catharina, 347, 356
  Francois Gustav (2001-), 394
  Izak Francois (1966-), 389, 393
  Keanu Brandon (2003-), 394
  Michelle (TRICHARDT) (1968-), 389, 393
Mulder, Zena, 154
MULLER
  Elizabeth Maria (1846-1895), 369, 378
  Marion, 386, 391
Muller JC - granddaughter of Andries Pretorius, 294
Muller, Cornelius, 405
Muller, Marion, 64, 199, 398, 399, 401, 409, 451, 455, 463
MULLHOLLAND
  Johanna Adriana, 357, 373
Murray, Jordan Elizabeth, 112, 272, 441
Murray, Stephen James, 112, 272
Murrayfield, 74
Musenga Plots, 64, 66, 153, 410, 451
Mussell crest, 272
Mussell, Maurice, 273, 314
Mussell, Pierre, 273, 314
Mutadi, Harold, Norse Earl of Orkney. See Mwera, 181
Myburgh, Chantelle, 209, 274
Mycroft, Jurita, 185, 197
Mzilikazi, 34
Naboomspruit, 183, 190
Nairobi, 298
Name Changes, 15
Natal, 19, 22, 24, 34, 35, 38, 41, 42, 53, 54, 73, 74, 78, 124, 181, 189, 199, 260, 266, 267, 289, 315, 399, 459
National Warplane Museum, 75
Naude, Maria Catherine Susana 'Modi', 128
Naude, Maria Margaretha, 400, 461
Navarre farm, 20
Nazareth, 77
Nchanga Copper Mine, 66
Ncome River, 35
Ndebele, 34, 42
Ndola, 63, 198, 397, 400, 409, 446, 451, 463

Neethling, Miss, 248
Nefdt, Sorina, 193, 212
Nefdt-Geldenhuys, Sorina, 197
Neilson, Nancy, 219, 274
Nel crest, 274
Nel, Aletta Catharina, 110
Nel, Ignatius, 56, 170
Nel, Magdalena Christina, 309
Nel, Willem Petrus, 110, 274, 455
Nel, Willem Petrus (Snr), 274
Nel, Willem Petrus (WP), 247
Nel, Willem Petrus 'WP', 274
Netherland, 444
Netherlands, 9, 11, 26, 123, 160, 216, 403, 436
New Holland, 34
New Orleans, 75, 76
New Zealand, 44, 70, 75, 77, 78, 85, 109, 112, 114, 154, 191, 199, 205, 224, 227, 228, 229, 231, 232, 234, 265, 398, 401, 440, 441, 451, 463
New Zealanders, 9, 52, 58
Nickel Cross, 68, 78, 137, 182, 202, 207, 244, 281
Nicolaas Daniel van Aardt, 437
Niemand, Jacobus Magiel, 169
Niemand, Maria Magdalena Susanna, 169
NIGRINI
  Susanna Margaretha (-1863), 359, 374
NN
  Geertruy Anna (GELDENHUYS) (1785-), 344, 351
  Grace, 387
  NN, 344, 351, 362, 363, 376, 383
  P N Geldenhuyzen, 378
  Susanna Johanna, 370
NN Koeks
  Koeks NN, 384
NN KOEKS
  Koeks NN, 381
Nobel, Aletta, 26, 216
Noetje, Renaldo, 274
Nordic, 16
Normandy, 20, 60, 165, 245, 408
Normandy farm, 19
North Island, 78, 205, 224, 231
Nortje, Renaldo, 133
Norval, Mabel Aletta Louw, 183
Oats, Jessie, 118
Obbes, Alta, 169, 191
ODENDAAL
  Adriaan Izaak (1732-), 351
  Annaline (1940-), 386, 390
  Jacobus Hendrik, 370
  Sara Johanna (1783-), 345, 351
  Sara Johanna (GELDENHUYS) (1835-), 370
  Sara Johanna (Gildenhuyzen) (GELDENHUYS) (1751-1836), 351
  Susanna (1716-), 346
Odendaal, Adriaan Izaak, 405, 470
Odendaal, Annaline, 161, 164, 187, 461
Odendaal, Maria, 26
Odendaal, Sara Johanna, 8, 33, 36, 327, 351, 405, 499
Ohope, 79, 205, 224, 227, 229, 231, 232, 234
Ohrigstad, 35, 36, 214
Old Oak Tree, 21
Olewagen, Daniel, 56, 170
Olifantsrivier, 9, 21, 31, 124
Olivier crest, 275
Olivier, A Charles, 275
Olivier, Anna Josephene, 147, 172, 421
Olivier, Anneke, 275, 310, 311, 454
Olivier, Corné, 185, 197
Olivier, Jaco, 82, 275, 310, 311, 454
Olivier, Nicolene, 82
Olivier, Reinier, 245, 310, 454
Olivier, Reneir, 275
Olivier, Renier, 275, 311
onomastics - the study of names, 16
Ontario, 14
Oosthuisen, GC, 155
Oosthuisen, Liesl Adriaana, 276, 310
Oosthuisen, Liesl Adriana, 310
Oosthuisen, Schalk Johannes, 310
Oosthuisen, Sckalk Johannes, 276, 310
Oosthuisen, Willem, 465
Oosthuisen, Willem Adriaan Jacobus, 245, 276, 310, 454
Oosthuisen, Yvette Marie, 276
OOSTHUIZEN
  Alida Jacoba Cornelia (1935-), 393
  Catharina Helena, 349, 363
Oosthuizen, Elizma, 152
Oosthuizen, Liesl Adriana, 465
Oosthuizen, Willem, 310
Operation
  Miracle, 78
Operation Cauldron, 69, 232, 233
Operation Griffin, 69
Operation Knuckle, 69, 233
Operation Mansion, 69, 233
Operation Miracle memorial, 89
Oppenheimer, Harry, 245
OPPERMAN
  Alida Jacoba Cornelia (OOSTHUIZEN) (1935-), 393
  Jacoba Cornelia 'Corli' (1963-), 389, 393
  Phillipus Albertus (1924-1987), 393
Opperman, "Corli"Jacoba Cornelia, 208
ORAFs, 81
Orange Free State, 34, 36, 39, 40, 46, 54, 122, 245, 268
Orange Grove, 226
Orange River Station, 46, 58
Oranje, 36, 46, 172, 397

Oranje river, 34
Oribi, 74
Orlando, 75, 76, 77
Osnabruck, 32, 213
OTTO
  Anna Geertruyda Fredrika (1818-), 354, 371
  Hendrik, 371
Otto, Dorothea, 28
Otto, Maria, 222
Otto, Michael, 11, 28, 32, 303
Oudshoorn, 19, 137
Oudtshoorn, 64, 66, 154, 398, 401, 410, 419, 440, 451, 463
Oumam. See Preller, Anna "Lizzie" Elizabeth
Owen, CM, 36
Owen, Francis, 302
Paardeberg, 51, 58, 183, 459
Paardekop, 288
Paarl, 20, 122, 247, 257, 259, 399, 432, 433, 434, 435, 444, 452, 453, 456, 457
Page crest, 276
Page, Mark, 276
Palmer, Brandon and Nicky, 82
Palmer, Shaun, 82
Palmiet Valleij farm, 20
Palmietfontein farm, 19
Pamula Park, 22
Pasea, Doug, 78
Paterson, Mary McRobert, 226, 232
PATU, 68, 258
PATU – BSA Police Anti-Terrorist Unit, 68, 258
Pelotonia, 22
Pennsylvania, 75
Peter Petter-Bowyer, 36
Petterson, Cpl, 299
Pey Malan Geldenhuys, 99, 222, 497
Peysoft, 70, 199
Pfeiffer, LFS, 56, 170
Philemann, Johanna Dorothea, 11, 33
Philemon, Johanna Dorothea, 294
Philippolis, 53, 298
Phillips - KIA, 65
Phillips, AC, 183
Phillips, Lady Florence, 29
Phillips, Sir Lionel, 29
Pienaar, Eddie, 166
Pienaar, Mandy, 277, 493
Pienaar, SW, 290
Pienaar, Tammy, 278
Pietermaritzburg, 35, 73, 74, 75, 199, 202, 204, 231, 267, 294, 400, 459, 460, 461, 465
Pietersburg, 81, 213, 259, 289, 308, 455
Pigot, Elizabeth Sophia, 266, 267
Piper Cub, 75
Pittsburgh, 75, 76

Places of birth - Geldenhuys, 19
Planet Hollywood, 76
Platrand, 53, 289
Pleasure Island, 76
Plumer, Lt-Col HCO, 52
Polokwane, 81, 246, 307
Pondoland, 24, 42, 459
Poplar Grove, 52
Port Natal, 34, 35
Port Shepstone, 74, 453
Porter, Cayden, 278
Porter, Chad, 102, 117, 278, 475
Postma, Rev W, 290
Potchefstroom, 22, 35, 134, 165, 412, 462
Potgieter, Andries - Voortrekker, 34
Potgieter, Cathleen Elizabeth, 218
PRELLER
  Abraham Christofel Naude Christoffel (1853-1907), 380
  Anna Elisabeth (Lizzie) (1879-1976), 375, 380
  Helletta Lephina (BOTHA) (-1889), 380
Preller - meaning of Surname, 18
Preller crest, 278, 279
Preller Drive, 22
Preller Genealogy, 400
Preller Place, 22
Preller Sentrum shopping centre, 22
Preller Street, 21, 22
Preller, Abraham - 1987, 279
Preller, Abraham Christoffel Naudé, 19, 22, 34, 40, 41, 42, 58, 108, 136, 174, 179, 281, 282, 283, 285, 400, 462
Preller, Abram, 19, 21
Preller, Abram Christoffel Naude, 56
Preller, Abri, 279, 294
Preller, Alesta, 295
Preller, Alexis, 279
Preller, Anna "Lizzie" Elizabeth, 8, 19, 23, 33, 40, 41, 42, 45, 54, 56, 57, 59, 60, 108, 125, 136, 137, 164, 165, 170, 173, 174, 176, 177, 180, 281, 282, 283, 284, 285, 286, 293, 297, 327, 397, 400, 408, 462
Preller, Anna Elisabeth, 192
Preller, Anna Elizabeth, 60, 173, 297
Preller, Annette, wife of Bob, 287
Preller, Bertus, 286, 295
Preller, Beverly Anthony, 299
Preller, Bob, 286
Preller, Braam, 46, 60
Preller, Carel (Charlie) Friedrich, 297
Preller, Carel Friedrich, 19, 34, 279, 294, 400, 461
Preller, Carl, 295
Preller, Carl Frederik, 128, 162, 200, 282, 383, 464, 470
Preller, Carl,, 287
Preller, Charles Walker, 300

Preller, Commandant Robert, 56
Preller, Dain, 288, 295
Preller, Douglas Bruce, 300
Preller, Friedrich, 288
Preller, Gustav Schoeman, 22, 23, 30, 53, 55, 56, 57, 59, 60, 170, 202, 281, 288, 289, 290, 291, 292, 293
Preller, Herman, 295
Preller, Isaac Andrew, 464
Preller, Ivan, 279, 294, 300
Preller, J.C, 293
Preller, James, 294
Preller, Jeane, 286
Preller, Johan Carel, 34
Preller, Johan Frederik, 11, 33, 34, 279, 294, 400, 461
Preller, Johan Friedrich, 288, 298
Preller, Johann Fredrick, 258
Preller, Johann Friedrich, 9, 11, 33, 294, 461
Preller, Johann Friedrich 1764-1825, 294
Preller, John, 303
Preller, Jon-Jon, 295
Preller, Kaai, 287, 295
Preller, Karen, 295
Preller, Karin, 296
Preller, Kirsten, 295, 296
Preller, Lara Nieuwoudt, 296
Preller, Mark Anthony, 296
Preller, Maryna, 286, 287
Preller, Mauritz Herman Otto, 464
Preller, Nicholas Fraser, 296
Preller, Paul, 296
Preller, Paul T, 297
Preller, Petrus Johannes, 297
Preller, Preller, 280
Preller, Rhett, 295, 297
Preller, Rita, 297
Preller, Robert Clunie, 298
Preller, Robert Clunie Logie, 39, 52, 56, 288
Preller, Robert H, 298, 299
Preller, Roland, 295, 297, 299
Preller, Ryno, 295
Preller, Tasmin, 300
Preller, Tessa, 300
Preller, Tina, 279, 300
Preller, Tracy-Leigh, 300
Preller, William Abraham, 464
Preller, Winston, 464
Pretoria, 19, 36, 52, 53, 54, 56, 60, 64, 66, 110, 136, 143, 154, 160, 165, 179, 183, 189, 192, 253, 254, 259, 279, 282, 285, 286, 288, 289, 291, 292, 293, 294, 298, 397, 398, 409, 410, 451, 455, 462, 463
Pretorius crest, 301
Pretorius, Andries, 34, 35, 291
Pretorius, Angelique, 212
Pretorius, Christina, 288
Pretorius, Debbie-Ann, 301
Pretorius, Debbie-Anne, 131
Pretorius, Gen. AWJ, 288
Pretorius, General AM, 35
Pretorius, H, 38
Pretorius, Henning PN, 288
Pretorius, Jacomine, 144
Pretorius, Jacomine Geldenhuys, 301
Pretorius, Maria Elizabeth, 400, 462
Pretorius, MW, 36
Pretorius, Piet, 288
Pretorius, Professor Fransjohan, 53, 298
Pretorius, Ria, 186
Pretorius, Stoffelina, 431, 495
Pretotius, Andries, 38
Prince, Nils, 233
Princesse Royale, 9, 24, 100, 151
Princeton USA, 183
PRINGLE
   Ada, 376, 381
Prins, Elsie Sophia, 189, 410
PRINSLOO
   Christina Elizabeth (GELDENHUYS) (1838-), 366, 368
   Francina Frederika, 366, 377
   George Diederick, 363
   Jacoba Margaretha (GELDENHUYS) (1849-), 363
   Lourens Johannes, 366, 368
   Petronella Wilhelmina, 366, 368, 377
Prinsloo, General, 46
Prinsloo, Martinus, 175
Prinsloo, Yolande, 113, 301
Protea North, 22
Provence, 9, 259, 452
Provost, 68, 202, 232, 233, 260, 315
Putfontein, 22
Qantas, 78
Qumbo, 226, 234
Raadsaal - Government Chambers, 284
RABIE
   Jan Bastiaan Rabie, 342
   Zacharya Geertruy (Gildenhuizen) (GELDENHUYS) (1741-), 342
Rabie, Jan Bastiaan, 404
Rabie, JSM, 289, 290
Raderotjes, Fytje (Sophia), 24, 117
RADYN
   Christina Magdalena, 340, 343
   Maria Dorothea, 343, 347
Radyn - meaning of Surname, 18
Radyn, Christina Magdalena, 143
Radyn, Jurgen, 28, 29, 247, 320
Rainforest Café, 77
Ramdam, 46
Randburg, 22
Randpark, 22
Rautenbach, Esme, 82
Rautenbach, Johan, 20, 166, 180, 192, 408

Reeve, Lesley Ann, 110, 301
Reid-Daly, Ron, 68
Reinier, Anneke, 245
Reinier, Jaco, 245
Reitgat farm, 20
Reitz, Joubert, 290
Relationship with distant relatives, 14, 469
Renene, Jelley, 85
Renoster River, 285
Retief, Anna Aletta, 259, 399, 453
Retief, Francois, 259
Retief, Margarita Elizabeth, 399
Retief, Piet, 34, 37, 41, 143, 288, 291, 292, 293, 302
Retief, Piet - Voortrekker, 37, 144, 293, 294, 302
REYNEKE
   Adam Johannes, 348
   Maria Catharina, 348, 357, 373
   Susanna Petronella (GELDENHUYS) (1785-), 348
Reynolds, Mike, 233
Rhodes, Cecil John, 42, 51, 189, 199, 268
Rhodesia, 19, 20, 42, 64, 65, 66, 68, 69, 71, 79, 104, 105, 124, 136, 154, 180, 199, 204, 210, 223, 226, 231, 232, 246, 248, 254, 261, 262, 266, 267, 268, 269, 397, 398, 399, 401, 402, 409, 417, 440, 449, 451, 459, 463, 465
Rhodesian Air Force, 68, 70, 78, 81, 118, 232, 233, 299
Rhodesian Air Force Operations with Air Strike Log, 78
Rhodesian Memorials, 85
Rhodesian War, 68, 72, 85, 105, 207, 226, 232, 257, 260
Rhodesian War Casualties and Air Force Memorials, 85
Rhone farm, 20
Richards Bay, 198
RICHTER
   Margaretha (GELDENHUYS) (1684-), 339
   Philippus, 339
Richter, Jan, 282
Richter, Philippus, 31, 216
Richter, Philipus, 11
Ridge, Trooper E - killed, 69, 233
Riebeekskasteel, 315
Rietgat farm, 19, 164, 248, 251, 362, 375, 408
Rietondale, 60, 192
Roan Antelope Copper Mine, 66, 153
Robben Island, 24, 100
Robbertse - KIA, 65
Robbertse, J, 183
Roberts, Lord, 21, 51, 52, 55
Robertse, Hendrina, 302
Robertse, Tersia, 303

Robertson, JB, 43
Robin, Roberts, 139
Robinson, Brian, 68
Rockvale, 74
RODRIQUES
   Michelle (1971-), 390
Roge, Susanna, 31, 241
Romans, 16
Rommel, Erwin, 238
Rondebossie, 284
Roodepoort farm, 20
Roodeport, 22
RORICH
   Margaretha Georgina Fredrika, 360, 375
Rosenthal, Eric, 18
ROSSOUW
   Johanna Margaretha Geertruyda, 349, 364
Rossouw, Daniel, 142
Rossouw, Johanna Margaretha Geertruyda, 164
Roux, Johannes Hermanus, 56, 170
Royal Flying Corps, 65
Royal Rhodesian Air Force, 64, 66, 202
Rozenburg, 9, 121
Rudd, C., 189
Russell school, 73, 204
Russell, Monique, 169
Rust, A, 160
Rustfontein farm, 19
Rusthof farm, 20
Rustpan, 19, 20, 23, 57, 58, 60, 64, 66, 136, 164, 165, 174, 180, 192, 281, 286, 297, 397, 401, 408, 409, 451, 462, 463
Rustverstooring farm, 19
SAAF Staff College, 233
Saale, 9, 11, 33, 288, 294, 298
SAFA juice, 181
Saldanha Bay, 33
Salisbury, 63, 65, 104, 111, 136, 223, 226, 233, 245, 255, 257, 263, 268, 269, 276, 310, 311, 398, 401, 402, 409, 440, 451, 454, 455, 463, 465, 468
Salt, Beryl, 65
Sand River Convention, 35, 36, 58
Sandvelders, 284, 285
Saturn, 77
Savoia, 64, 191
Scandinavians, 25
Schakelmann, Hendrik, 25, 100
SCHEEPERS
   Margaretha Maria, 347, 356
Scheepers, Gideon, 93, 242
Scheepers, Gideon Komdt, 56, 57, 170, 176
SCHICKERLING
   Maria Susanna Wilhelmina (1855-1890), 362, 376
Schickerling, Elizabeth, 407, 408, 464

Schickerling, Jan Pieter, 407
Schickerling, Maria Susanna Wilhelmina, 376, 407
Schikerling, John Peter, 407
SCHIKKERLING
  Elizabeth (1858-), 362, 375
Schikkerling - meaning of Surname, 18
Schikkerling, Elizabeth, 8, 24, 34, 164, 173, 200, 303, 327, 397, 410
Schikkerling, Hendrik, 33, 56
Schikkerling, Hendrik Jacobus, 34
Schikkerling, Hennie, 136
Schikspruit, 33
SCHMIDT
  Heinrich, 340
Schmidt, Christian, 31, 124
Schmidt, Maria Magdalena, 31, 124
Schoeman, Hendrik, 288
Schoeman, Stephanie Maria Aletta, 52
Schoeman, Stephanus, 53, 288, 298, 462
Schoeman, Stephina, 288, 298
Schulze, Annie Alida, 119
Schweitzer, Albert, 72
Schwerin - Germany, 32, 213
Scotland, 9, 44, 117, 234, 266, 269, 402, 449, 458, 459
Scotson, 303
Scotson, Gillian, 303
Scott, Leonie, 166
Sea World, 76
Seegers, Johan, 150
Sekhukhune, 39
Sekonyela, Chief, 302
SERDYN
  Anna Susanna Wilhelmina, 359
Serfontein, Dot, 174, 281, 303
Serfontein, Dot - Author of "Keurskrif van Kroonstad, 23, 40, 156, 180, 190, 192, 200, 283, 285, 286
Serfontein, Dot - Author of "Keurskrif vir Kroonstad, 136
Shillinge, sea captain, 24
Shuttleworth, Laurie, 65, 162
Sidestep farm, 20
SIEK
  Anna Margaretha (1685-), 339, 340
  Geertruy (HELMS) (1664-1715), 340
  Johan (1664-1715), 340
Siek, Anna Margaretha, 8, 11, 25, 143, 303, 327, 340, 397, 403
Siek, Johan, 143
Siek, Johann, 25, 303, 403
Simons Bay, 25
Simons Berg, 25
Simonstown, 25, 59
Simpkins crest, 304
Simpkins, Debra, 109, 110, 304
Simpkins, Sandra, 235, 304
Simpkins, Sue, 305

Sinton crest, 305, 465
Sinton, Alasdair, 305
Sinton, Alisdair, 465
Sinton, David James, 305, 449, 465, 478
Sinton, David Murray, 305, 465, 478
Sinton, David Scott, 305, 465
Sinton, James Scott, 305, 465
Sinton, John Scott, 305, 465
Sinton, Mark, 219, 305, 465
Sinton, Neil, 305, 465
Sinton, Sinton, 305, 465
Sinton, Trish, 305, 465, 501
Skalkwyk, Meneer, 248
Skoorsteenberg, 59, 122
Skoorsteenberg farm, 21
Slabber, Francois, 196, 197
Slabber, sisters Joalien, Francis and Petra, 196
Slater, Mike, 75
Slaughter, Sgt, 65, 162
Small Bez. *See* Johan Bezuidenhout
SMIT
  Anna Maria, 347, 356
  Christaan Samuel Frederik, 374
  Hilletje Aletta, 348, 359
  Hilletje Aletta Hendrina (GELDENHUYS) (1823-), 374
Smit - murdered, 38
SMIT (SCHMIDT)
  Judith (1672-1713), 339, 340
Smit, Alewyn Johannes, 404
Smit, Anneli, 186
SMITH
  Antony, 384, 388
  Charles Lauton, 388
  Duncan Allan, 385, 389
  Jacques, 388
  Lauretta (GELDENHUYS) (1960-), 384, 388
  Myrl Maureen (GELDENHUYS) (1938-), 385, 389
Smith, Antony, 408
Smith, Captain Thomas, 35
Smith, Charles Lauton, 408
Smith, Ian Douglas, 36, 59
Smith, Jacques, 408
Smith, Sir Harry, 35
Smith, Sir Sydney, 267
Smithfield, 21, 38, 59, 122, 459
Smuts, General Jannie, 190
Smythe, Sir Thomas, 24
Sneeuberg farm, 20
Snyman, Rev PC, 290
Soest, 11, 31, 216, 432
Somaliland, 298, 299
Somerset East, 34
Somerset West, 9, 11, 26, 28, 122
Sotho, 38, 39

South African, 9, 18, 24, 31, 35, 36, 45, 58, 60, 64, 65, 66, 100, 136, 137, 143, 160, 172, 183, 185, 191, 198, 199, 202, 216, 226, 232, 237, 238, 242, 244, 258, 259, 288, 294, 298
South African Air Force, 66, 162
South Africans, 9, 237
South Island, 77, 78, 205, 231
Soutpansberg, 34
Soweto, 22
Space Centre, 75, 77
Space shuttle Challenger, 77
Space Shuttle Explorer, 77
Special Air Service, 68
St Martini D'Aigues, 259, 399
St. Valentine, 56, 170
Stael, Jan, 24, 100
Standerton, 288, 419, 459
Stanford farm, 20
Stanmore farm, 20, 66
STEENKAMP
  Annie (DE JAGER), 381
  Maatjie Catharina Jacoba (1887-1918), 376, 381
  Willem, 381
Steenkamp crest, 306
Steenkamp, de Jager and Smit, 155
Steenkamp, Maatje Catharina Jacoba, 156, 306
Steenkamp, Willem, 306
STEINBACH
  Ernestine Marlene (1934-2002), 381, 384
Steinbach, Enrnestine Marlene, 170
Steinbach, Ernestine Marlene, 384, 407
Stellenbosch, 19, 20, 25, 30, 31, 32, 33, 60, 100, 122, 143, 160, 161, 173, 184, 185, 187, 188, 216, 257, 259, 289, 291, 292, 315, 399, 406, 407, 409, 414, 418, 420, 422, 426, 429, 430, 432, 433, 435, 436, 444, 452, 454, 456, 461
Stevens, Thomas, 24
Stevenson, Pilot Officer, 244
Steyn, Christina, 125
Steyn, Helena Frederika, 180, 192, 408
Steyn, Jan, 283, 284
Steyn, Johanna Wilhelmina, 404
Steyn, Marthinus, 36, 39
Steyn, Martinus Johannes, 405
Steyn, Martinus Theunis, 175
Steyn, President, 48, 50, 55
Steyn, President Martinus, 52
Steyn, Riaan, 20, 158
Stoltz crest, 306
Stoltz, Anneke, 144, 169, 306, 432
Stopforth crest, 307
Stopforth, Andrew, 246, 307
Stopforth, Charles, 81, 90, 246, 307, 308, 455, 476
Stopforth, Charles Joseph, 307
Stopforth, Dominique, 246, 307
Stopforth, Dominique, Michael and Andrew, 81
Stopforth, Martie, 81
Stopforth, Michael, 246, 307
Stopforth, Pieter, 81, 308
Stopforth, Rochelle, 81
Stott, Jo, 74
STREICHER
  Johanna Elsabe (GELDENHUYS) (1821-), 349
  Simon Frederik (1819-1882), 350
Strubensvallei, 22
Strydfontein farm, 20
STRYDOM
  Adriaan Johannes (1947-), 385, 389
  Annelie (1971-), 384, 388
  Riaan Geldenhuys (1981-2010), 390
  Wanda (GELDENHUYS) (1949-), 385, 389
Strydom, Alecia, 279
Strydom, MM, 400
Strydom, Rene, 78
Stuben, Frederick, 189
Suid-Afrikaanse Akademie vir Wetenskap en Kuns, 290
Swahili, 64, 66, 153, 181, 242
SWART
  Anna Christina Elizabeth, 350, 365
  Catharina Elizabeth (MOOLMAN), 365
  Cornelia (1720-1750), 340, 342
  Cornelia Margaretha, 349, 364
  Elizabeth Helena, 350, 365
  Elizabeth Luytjie, 347, 354
  Elsabe, 370
  Elsabe (1777-), 343, 347
  Elsabe Barendina Francina (GELDENHUYS) (1867-1940), 377
  Elsebe, 346, 353
  Geertruyda (1793-), 347, 355
  Hans Jacob, 365
  Hendrik Albertus (1865-1940), 377
  Jacoba Margaretha, 352, 366
  Jan Cornelis, 345
  Maria Magdalena, 351, 365
  Sara Johanna, 340, 342
  Susanna Dorothea (GELDENHUYS) (1790-1863), 345
Swart - meaning of Surname, 18
Swart, Barend, 405
Swart, Cornelia, 8, 30, 31, 143, 164, 173, 327, 342, 397, 404, 450
Swart, Cornelia Margaretha, 164
Swart, Elizabeth Helena, 406
Swart, Flip, 253
Swart, Jacoba Margaretha, 366, 405
Swart, Jan Cornelis, 405
Swart, Johannes, 8, 31, 33, 173, 188, 327, 397, 406

Swart, Sara Johanna, 8, 30, 143, 164, 327, 342, 397, 404
Swazi, 35
Swellendam, 19, 21, 31, 32, 33, 34, 44, 58, 163, 173, 189, 190, 216, 269, 397, 405, 406, 407, 410, 412, 413, 414, 415, 416, 417, 418, 420, 421, 422, 423, 424, 428, 437, 459
Swiss, 25
Table Bay, 24, 33
TAILLEFER
  Elizabeth, 341, 343
TALJAARD
  J J, 346
  Maria Catharina (GELDENHUYS) (1795-), 346
Tallahassee, 76
Tanganyika, 52, 153, 181, 456
Tanzania, 181, 279
TAPSON - ADOPTED BURNS
  Deirdre (1967-), 384, 388
Tarka, 34
Tas, Adam, 16, 26, 30, 150, 259
Tauranga, 78, 109, 112, 114, 398, 401, 440, 451
Taurico Gardens, 124
Taylor, Major, 54
Technikon Natal, 74
Tel-Aviv, 77
Tengwe, 68, 105, 106, 258
TESNER
  Francina (CORDIER), 347
  Heinrich, 347
  Maria Chistina (1757-), 343, 347
Thailand, 123, 147, 199
The Anglo-Boer War Diaries of Jan Geldenhuys, 47, 85
The Vow, 36
Theron, Danie, 51
Theron, Jacoba Johanna Hendrina, 196, 437
Theron, Theresa, 158
Theunissen, Martinus Wilhelmus, 29
Thomas crest, 308
Thomas, Lesley Ann, 308, 315
Thompson, Dan, 308
Thompson, Rhayla-Rayne, 308
Thornhill High School, 66, 202, 315, 316
Timmins, Howard, 18
Tol Janeke, 69, 233
Torlage, June Hazel, 300
Towanda, 75, 76
Transvaal, 19, 34, 35, 41, 42, 45, 52, 134, 136, 145, 160, 176, 181, 189, 242, 260, 262, 279, 282, 288, 289, 291, 292, 293, 397, 411
Trekboers, 37
Triangle, 64, 69, 205, 227, 398, 401, 402, 450, 451, 455, 459, 463, 468

TRICHARDT
  Albertus Marthinus "Bertie" (1967-), 389, 393
  Albertus Marthinus (1887-1953), 389
  Albertus Marthinus (1940-), 385, 389
  Cameron Michael (2000-), 393
  Carolyn (WOODLEY) (1967-), 389, 393
  Connor William, 394
  Kelley Anne (BROWN), 389, 394
  Mathew Carl (1997-), 393
  Michelle (1968-), 389, 393
  Myrl Maureen (GELDENHUYS) (1938-), 385, 389
  Susanna Catharina Margaretha (DE VILLIERS) (1906-1986), 389
  Willem Geldenhuys (1971-), 389, 394
Trichardt, Albertus Martinus, 195, 411
Trichardt, Carolus Johannes, 195, 475
Trichardt, Louis, 34
Trickling Waters farm, 20
Tshipise, 66
Tsirindanis, Joy, 308
Tulbagh, 20, 32, 258, 399, 413, 434, 435, 444, 446, 453, 454, 456
Tweefontein, 176
Tweelingspruit farm, 20
Tylden-Wright - KIA, 65
Tylden-Wright, Lt PM, 183
Uitenhage, 32, 34, 437
Uiterwyk, 122
Uitkyk, 81, 166, 180, 192, 246, 307
Umballa - POW camp in India, 55, 56, 59, 136, 164, 174, 178, 179, 200
Umbilo POW Camp, 60
Umdloti, 199
Umtali, 66, 240, 268
UNGERER
  Elizabeth Magdalena, 356, 372
Utrecht, 36, 292
UYS
  Cornelis Janse, 346, 370
  Dina Maria, 343, 345
  Dina Maria (-1839), 342, 344
  Johannes Frederik, 370
  Sara Johanna (GELDENHUYS) (1788-), 346
  Susanna Hermina (GELDENHUYS) (1840-), 370
Uys, Dirk, 41
Uys, Piet, 34, 41, 82
Vaal River, 34, 35, 36, 55, 175, 176, 177, 285
Valkier, Wouter - Commissioner, 26
Vals River, 41, 282, 283, 285
Vals Rivier, 65
Vampire, 68, 69, 202, 232, 233
VAN AARDE
  Margaretha Johanna, 343, 348
van Aardt, Aletta Magdalena Susanna, 309

van Aardt, Alta, 310
van Aardt, Gerrit Jansz, 309
van Aardt, Hendrik, 172, 198, 311
van Aardt, Hendrik Jacobus, 245, 309, 310, 311, 421, 437, 454, 466, 484
van Aardt, Joleen, 490
van Aardt, Leane, 309, 311, 421, 437, 454
van Aardt, Lettie, 81
van Aardt, Lianie, 269, 311
van Aardt, Nic, 81, 93, 236, 257
van Aardt, Nicolaas, 465
van Aardt, Nicolaas Daniel, 311, 421, 454, 466
Van Aardt, Nicolaas Hendrik, 309, 310, 320
van Aardt, Nicolas Daniel, 310
van Aardt, Nicolene, 245, 275, 310, 311, 454, 496
van Aert, Gerritsz, 309
van Bengalen, Maria - married Jan Stael, 100
van Bengalen, Maria – slave married Jan Stael, 32
van Bengalen, Maria - slave married to Jan Stael, 24
VAN BILJON
  Martha Susanna, 377, 382
van Biljon, Aubry, Ivor, Mara and Millicent, 56
van Biljon, Cornelia, 308
van Biljon, Ernst, 60, 177, 179
van Biljon, Kitty, 56, 177, 179
van Biljon, Lettie, 56
van Biljon, Martiens, 56, 174, 177
van Blommenstein, Jan, 282
van Brakel, Elisabeth, 16
van Braken, Elisabeth, 30
van Breda, Maria, 121
van Coller, Piet and Stoffel, 156, 190
van Dam, Jaco, 170
van den Berg, Anna Dorothea, 241
VAN DEN HEVER
  Cornelia Margaretha (GELDENHUYS) (1814-1858), 352
  Gert Johannes, 352
van den Hever, Gert Johannes, 405
van der Bank, Regina Dorothea, 110
van der Bijl, Alexander, 30
van der Bijl, Pieter, 15, 16, 26, 27, 30
VAN DER HEIDEN
  Andries, 341
  Anna (1694-), 341
  Elsje Gildenhuisz (GELDENHUYS) (1674-), 339, 341
  Hester (KYPER), 341
  Jacobus (1670-1726), 339, 341
  Jacobus (1695-), 341
van der Heiden, Andries, 26
van der Heiden, Jacobus, 11, 15, 16, 21, 25, 26, 27, 28, 29, 30, 143, 158, 216

van der Heijde, Jacobis, 15, 16, See van der Heiden or Heyden
van der Linde, Boet, 136
van der Lingen, Dominee, 282
van der Merwe, 145
VAN DER MERWE
  Carel Lodewyk, 348
  Martha Jacoba (GELDENHUYS) (1786-), 348
van der Merwe, Kommandant, 46
van der Stel, Francois, 16
van der Stel, Frans - son of Simon, 27
van der Stel, Katryna, 16
van der Stel, Simon - Cape Governor, 25, 31
van der Stel, Simon – Cape Governor, 16
van der Stel, Willem Adriaan, 158, 404
van der Stel, Willem Adriaan - Cape Governor - son of Simon, 9, 11, 23, 25, 26, 27, 28, 29, 30, 143, 216, 259
van der Walt, Adele, 81, 106, 312
van der Westhuizen, Gerhard, 186
VAN DEVENTER
  Gerrit, 353
  Maria Aletta (GELDENHUYS) (1808-), 353
  Sachararya Magdalena, 347, 355
van Deventer, Hennie, 208
van die Kaap, Ragel, 32, 213
VAN DYK
  Anna Catharina Hendrina, 348, 360
  Gideon (1802-), 359
  Johanna Hendrika Maria (GELDENHUYS) (1805-), 359
  Maria Francina (-1849), 354, 370
van Dyk, Maria Francina, 406
van Dyk, Michiel Burgert, 406
van Echten, Catharina Dorothea, 242
van Eck, Elisabeth, 121
van Eeden, Frederik Jacobus, 404, 454
van Eeden, Getruida Johanna, 248, 399
van Eeden, Jacob, 404
van Groen, Rijkloff, 24
van Heerden, Izak, 290
van Heerden, Martha, 93, 495
van Heerden, Pieter Willem - Stamvader, 466
van Heerden, Salomina Adriana, 315
van Kerken, Johanna Catharina, 241
van Malabar, Paulus, 100
van Malsen, Rick, 101
VAN NIEKERK
  Dina Maria Elizabeth (GELDENHUYS) (1842-), 370
  G A, 370
van Niekerk, Cheyenne, 214, 215
van Niekerk, Johann, 74
van Niekerk, NJ, 207
van Reenen, Frederik, 33, 294

VAN RENSBURG
　Albertus Bernardus, 370
　Johanna Jochemina (GELDENHUYS) (1845-), 370
van Rensburg, J, 56, 170
van Rensburg, Japie, 281
van Rensburg, Johannes, 34
van Rensen
　Adrian Henry (1949-), 383
　Adrianna, 383
　Elizabeth (Libby) Adriana (1941-), 387
　Johan (1944-), 383
　Johan J, 383
　Maria Susanna Wilhelmina (Geldenhuys) (1911-1995), 381, 383
　Theodore Johan (1913-1983), 381, 383
van Rensen, Adrian, 94, 302, 303, 312
van Rensen, Adrian Henry, 60, 192, 409
van Rensen, Elizabeth, 66, 103, 127, 157
van Rensen, Elizabeth 'Libby', 60, 127, 192, 312, 313, 317, 383, 388, 409
van Rensen, Johan, 60, 192, 312, 313, 409
van Rensen, Louise, 313
van Rensen, Theodore, 313
van Rensen, Theodorus, 60, 192, 312, 400, 462
van Riebeeck Society, 258
van Riebeeck, Jan - Cape Founder, 9, 24, 32, 100, 117, 213, 217, 315
VAN ROOYEN
　Mona Daphne (1934-1987), 392
van Rooyen, Mona Daphne, 114, 313, 440
VAN SCHALKWYK
　Helena Johanna, 359, 374
van Staden, Etienne, 141
van Tonder, Magdelena Johanna, 201
VAN VUUREN
　Anna Catharina Margaretha (1848-1879), 373, 379
　Susara Johanna, 373, 379
VAN WYK
　Elizabeth Christina, 344, 350
van Wyk crest, 314
van Wyk, Christiaan Johannes, 41
van Wyk, Dolf, 281
van Wyk, Jacob Pieter, 41
van Wyk, Jean, 314, 468
van Wyk, Long Piet, 281
van Wyk, Piet, 41
van Wyk, Wynand, 406
VAN ZYL
　Jacobus Albertus, 342
　Zacharya Geertruy (Gildenhuizen) (GELDENHUYS) (1741-), 342
van Zyl, Gideon and Winnie, 82
van Zyl, Jacobus Albertus, 404
van Zyl, Johannes Willem, 405
van Zyl, Sara Maria Johanna, 402
van, Aardt, Leane, 466

Varikas, Angela, 273, 314
Venetian, 16
Venter - KIA, 65
Venter crest, 314
Venter, Benjamin Louis, 315, 467, 474
Venter, Erens Lodewyk Johannes, 308, 315, 467
Venter, Gustaf Thomas, 315, 467
Venter, Heinrich (Hendrik), 315
Venter, Japie, 316
Venter, Johannes Smartenryk Venter, 315
Venter, Ria, 119, 120, 260, 315, 316, 454
Venter, WAJ, 183
Venter, Yuonne Julie, 315, 316
Verdruk-my-Niet farm, 20
Vereeniging, 56, 109, 236, 248, 257, 398, 399, 401, 440, 454
Vergelegen, 20, 164
Vergelegen, Wine Estate, just east of Somerset West, 9, 11, 16, 20, 23, 25, 26, 27, 28, 29, 30, 32, 143, 216, 247, 259, 320
Verlaatspruit, 281
VERMAAK
　Johanna, 380, 382
Vermaak, Hester, 66
Vermaak, Susanna, 110
VERMEULEN
　J P H, 377
　Johanna Christina (GELDENHUYS), 377
Vermeulen, Maryna, 140
Vernier Hill, 46
Verrekijker farm, 20
Verwoed, HF, 217
Vierfontein, 284
Viljoen
　Debora (1901-), 381
VILJOEN
　Debora (1901-), 376
Viljoen, Debra, 168
Viljoen, General Ben, 189
Viljoen, Johannes, 315
Visscher, H, 290
Vleeschbank farm, 315
VOC, 24, 32, 33, 100, 117
Vogelvallei farm, 20
VON COESFELD
　Elsken (-1680), 339
von Jehle, Julius, 222
Voortrekker, 32, 39, 40, 41, 55, 233, 291, 457
Voortrekkerhoogte, 66, 172
Voortrekkers, 34, 35, 37, 144
Vorster, Louis, 289
Vos, Alice Francis, 299
Vosloo, Susan, 212
Vroom, Abigail, 15, 16
Vrugbaar farm, 20
Vryburger, 24, 100

Vrye Lieden, 100
Waarden, 9, 111
Wagenaar, Frederick Jacobus, 162
Wagendrift, 199, 221
Wagner, Zacharias - became Wagenaar, 24
Waihu, 90
Waitakere, 78, 109, 112, 114, 398, 401, 440, 451
Waldeck
  Alwyn, 388, 393
  Caryn Sandra (Dunckers) (1963-), 388
  Eran (1997-), 393
WALDECK
  Caryn Sandra (DUNCKERS) (1963-), 392
Waldeck, Alwyn, 316
Waldeck, Caryn, 317
Waldeck, Erin, 317
Waldek, Caryn, 317
Wale, 9, 121
Walker, George, 155
Walls, General Peter, 101
Walls, Mary, 101, 317, 498
Walls, Peter, 317, 318
WALTERS
  Helena Maria, 343, 349
Warmbaths, 66
Warrington - KIA, 65
Warrington, R, 183
Washing of the Spears, 35, 42
Waterfall farm (Moodies Rest), 21
Waterkloof farm, 20
Wauchope, Major General Andy, 48, 50
Wave Dancer, 182, 198
Wave Master, 124, 182, 198
Webdynamix, 70, 199
Weenen, 34
Wegelegen farm, 20
Wehlau, 9, 31, 124, 444
Welgelegen farm, 20
Welkom, 401
Wellington, 20, 59, 150, 205, 247, 257, 399, 432, 453, 456
Wentzel, Jacobus Johannes, 163, 428
Wentzel, Wilhelmina, 241
Wessel, Johannes, 170
Wessels
  Margaretha Maria (-1801), 342
WESSELS
  Anna Susanna (GELDENHUYS) (1819-1878), 351
  Elizabeth Johanna (GELDENHUYS) (1774-), 347
  Geertruyda Susanna (1746-), 343, 346
  Johanna Albertus, 351
  Margaretha Maria (-1801), 345
  NN, 381, 384
  Susanna (ODENDAAL) (1716-), 346
  Wessel, 347

Wessel (1716-1787), 346
Wessels, Coen, 166, 180, 408
Wessels, Cornelis, 284
Wessels, Johanna, 16, 283, 463
Wessels, Johanna Magdalena, 400, 462
Wessels, Johannes Albertus, 414
Wessels, Margaretha Maria, 31, 345, 404
West Park Cemetery, 21, 22, 189
West, Maria Magdalena Susanna, 169
Westfale, 11, 24, 31, 216, 396, 403
Westport, 77, 78, 205, 224, 227, 231
Whangaparoa, 78, 112, 227
WHITELEY
  Margaret Mary Elaine (1935-), 391
Whiteley crest, 318
Whiteley, Alan, 65, 225, 402, 470
Whiteley, Alan Raymond Malcolm, 234, *468*
Whiteley, Leonard, 318
Whiteley, Margaret Mary Elaine, 42, 69, 223, 225, 231, 232, 234, 265, 266, 317, 319, 402, 449, 459, 468, 493
Whiteley, Percival, 225
Whiteley, William - stamvader, 468
Whitely, Alan Raymond Malcolm, 319
Wigston, Doug and Jessie, 104
Wigston, Jessie, 319
Wigston, Valerie, 106, 107, 319
Wigston, Valerie Linda, 104
Wiid, Rina, 46, 156
Wikowmore, 11
Wilgespruit farm, 20
WILLEMSE
  Anna Christina (GELDENHUYS), 376
  P, 376
Willowgrange, 22
Willows, Humph, 233
Wilson, Alan, 75
Wilson, Grahame, 68
Witwatersrand, 44, 155, 189, 293
Wodehouse, Sir Philip, 39
Wolfaardt, Ester, 320
Wonderboom, 282
Wonderheuvel farm, 20
Wood, Evelyn, 41
Wood, Lt - fataly wounded, 46
Wood, William Samuel - Basuto war casualty, 39
WOODLEY
  Carolyn (1967-), 389, 393
Worthington, Sanette, 320
Woutersz, Jan - married first freed slave, 24, 100
Yeats, Captain R, 191
Yeats, R, 64
Zambia, 63, 68, 69, 198, 232, 397, 400, 409, 445, 446, 463
Zambian Copperbelt, 210
Zamoyski, Graaf, 30

Zara (Slave), 23, 29, 247, 320
Zeeland, 9, 111
Zimbabwe, 20, 42, 66, 68, 69, 77, 104, 147, 202, 223, 226, 227, 231, 234, 241, 258, 398, 401, 402, 419, 459, 463
Zimbabweans, 9

Zoutekloof farm, 20
Zuid Afrikaansche Republic, 282
Zuid-Afrikaanse Akademie voor Taal, Letterkunde, 290
Zulus, 34, 35, 42
Zwagershoek farm, 20

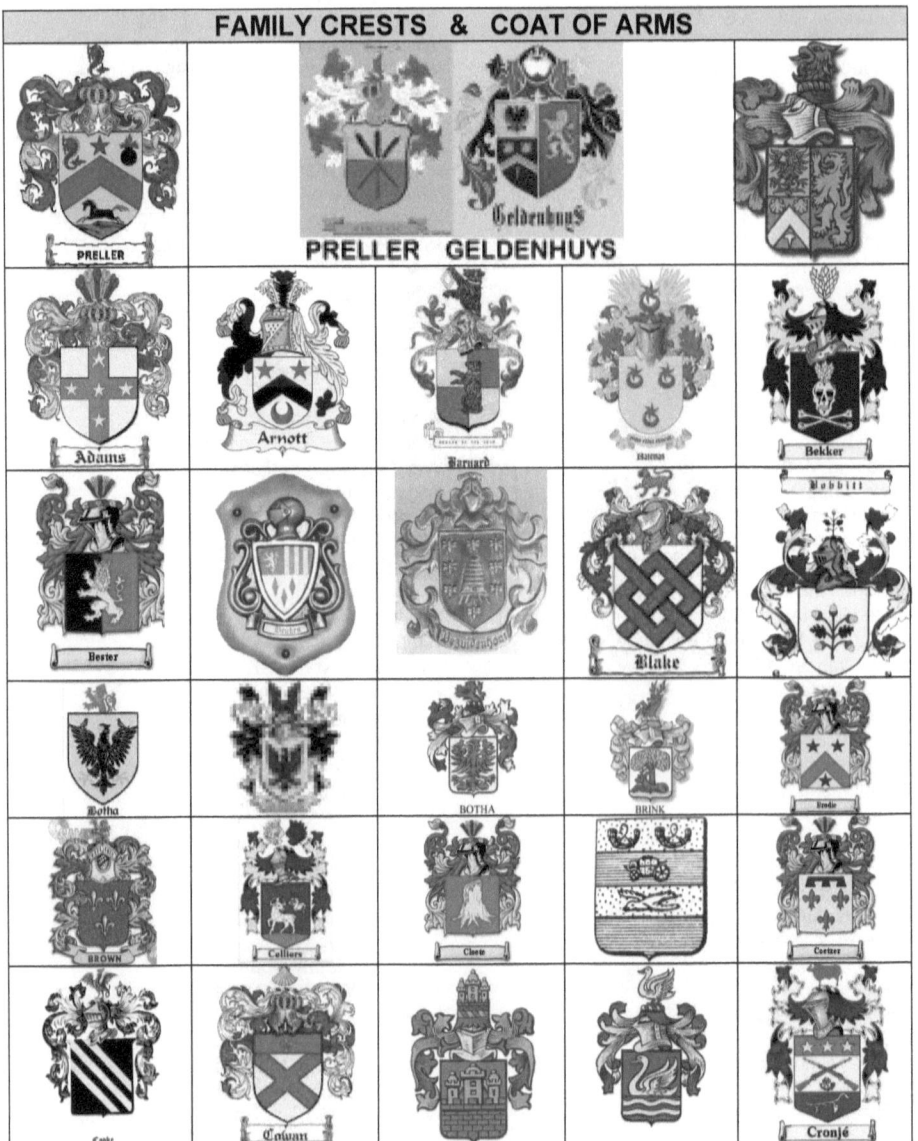

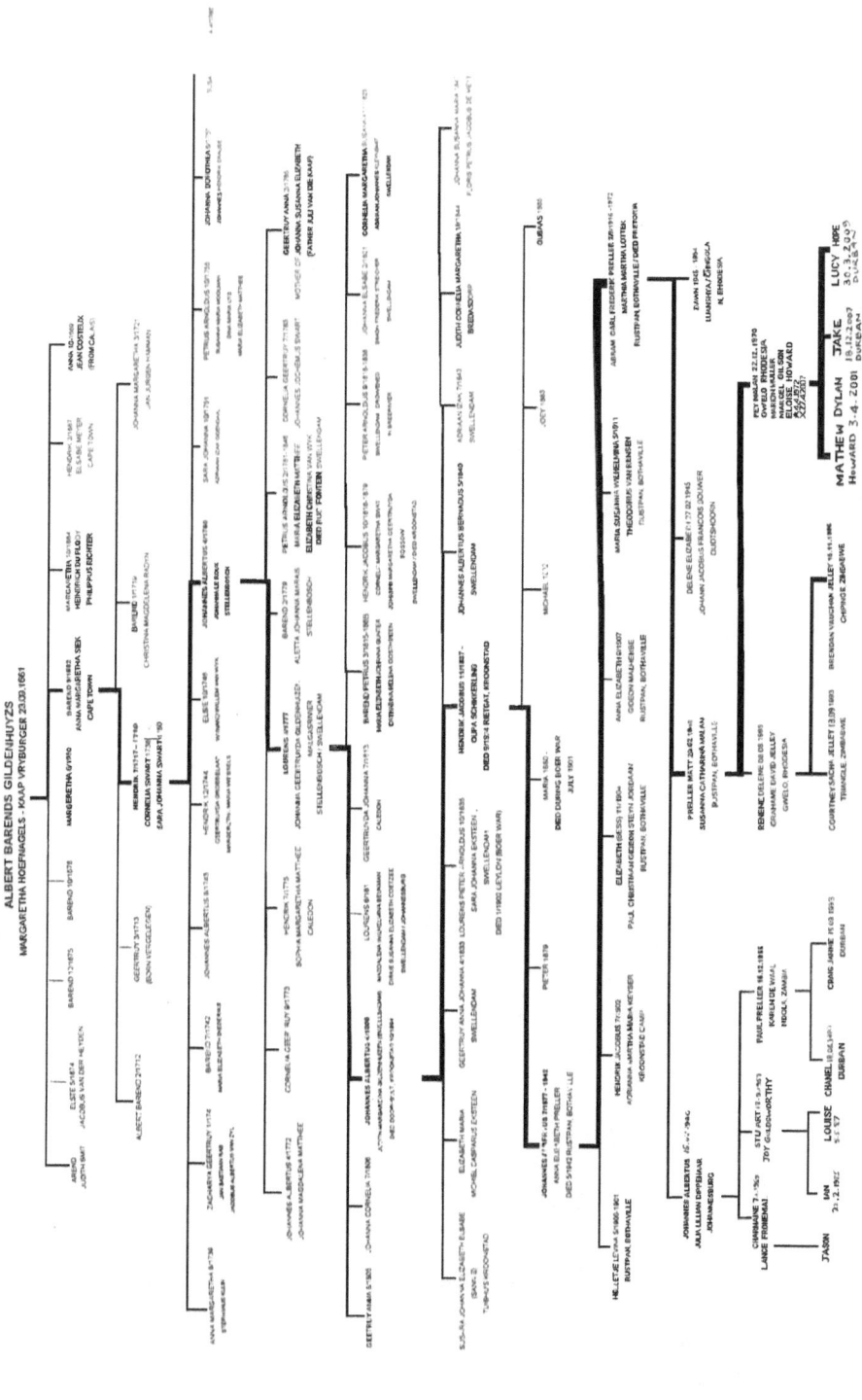

www.ingramcontent.com/pod-product-compliance
Lightning Source LLC
Chambersburg PA
CBHW020632300426
44112CB00007B/94